# FUNDAMENTALS OF MANAGEMENT

### Seventh Canadian Edition

## Stephen P. Robbins
San Diego State University

## David A. DeCenzo
Coastal Carolina University

## Mary Coulter
Missouri State University

## Ian Anderson
Algonquin College

## PEARSON

Toronto

**Vice-President, Editorial Director:** Gary Bennett
**Editor-in-Chief:** Nicole Lukach
**Acquisitions Editor:** Nick Durie
**Sponsoring Editor:** Kathleen McGill
**Marketing Manager:** Leigh-Anne Graham
**Supervising Developmental Editor:** Darryl Kamo
**Developmental Editor:** Alexandra Dyer and Jill Renaud
**Project Manager:** Marissa Lok
**Production Editor:** Rashmi Tickyani, Aptara®, Inc.
**Copy Editor:** Carolyn Zapf
**Proofreader:** Julie Fletcher
**Compositor:** Aptara®, Inc.
**Photo and Permissions Researcher:** Tara Smith
**Art Director:** Julia Hall
**Cover and Interior Designer:** Anthony Leung
**Cover Image:** Andy Baker/GettyImages

10 9 8 7 6 5 4 3 2 CKV

**Library and Archives Canada Cataloguing in Publication**

Fundamentals of management / Stephen P. Robbins . . . [et al.].
—7th Cdn. ed.

Includes bibliographical references and index.
ISBN 978-0-13-260692-9

1. Management—Textbooks.   I. Robbins, Stephen P., 1943–

HD31.R5643 2013        658.4        C2012-905692-8

ISBN 978-0-13-260692-9

# Brief Contents

Preface  ix

About the Authors  xvi

## Part One  Defining the Manager's Terrain  2

Chapter 1:  Introduction to Management and Organizations  2

Supplement 1:  Small and Medium-Sized Enterprises and Organizations  22

Chapter 2:  Environmental Constraints on Managers  26

**Video Case Incidents**  54

## Part Two  Planning  56

Chapter 3:  Planning and Strategic Management  56

Chapter 4:  Decision Making  88

**Video Case Incidents**  122

## Part Three  Organizing  124

Chapter 5:  Organizational Structure and Design  124

Chapter 6:  Communication and Information Technology  154

Chapter 7:  Human Resource Management  184

**Video Case Incidents**  213

## Part Four  Leading  214

Chapter 8:  Leadership  214

Chapter 9:  Motivating Employees  242

Chapter 10:  Understanding Groups and Teams  274

**Video Case Incidents**  298

## Part Five  Controlling  300

Chapter 11:  Foundations of Control  300

Chapter 12:  Managing Change  334

**Video Case Incidents**  360

Endnotes  362

Glossary  396

Subject Index  403

Name/Organization Index  417

List of Canadian Companies, by Province  425

List of International Companies, by Country  428

Photo Credits  431

# Contents

Preface ix

About the Authors xvi

## Part 1 Defining the Manager's Terrain 2

### Chapter 1 Introduction to Management and Organizations 2

**Who Are Managers? 4**
Types of Managers 5

**What Is Management and What Do Managers Do? 6**
Efficiency and Effectiveness 6
Management Functions 6
Management Roles 8
Management Skills 10

**What Is an Organization? 11**
The Size of Organizations 12
The Types of Organizations 12

**Why Study Management? 13**
The Universality of Management 14
The Reality of Work 14
Self-Employment 15

**Review and Apply**
Summary of Learning Objectives 16 • Snapshot Summary 16 • MyManagementLab Learning Resources 17 • Interpret What You Have Read 18 • Analyze What You Have Read 18 • Assess Your Skills 18 • Practise What You Have Learned 19 • Team Exercises 20 • Business Cases 21

### Supplement 1: Small and Medium-Sized Enterprises and Organizations 22

**What Is a Small and Medium-Sized Enterprise? 22**

**What Is a Small and Medium-Sized Organization? 22**

**SMEs and SMOs in Canada—Key Characteristics 23**

### Chapter 2 Environmental Constraints on Managers 26

**The Manager: How Much Control? 28**

**The External Environment 29**
The Specific Environment 29
The General Environment 32

**Understanding the Global Environment 34**
Global Trade 35
PESTEL–Global Environment 36

**Doing Business Globally 38**
Different Types of International Organizations 39
How Organizations Go Global 40

**How the Environment Affects Managers 42**
Assessing Environmental Uncertainty 42
The Pros and Cons of Globalization 44

**Review and Apply**
Summary of Learning Objectives 46 • Snapshot Summary 46 • MyManagementLab Learning Resources 47 • Interpret What You Have Read 48 • Analyze What You Have Read 48 • Assess Your Skills 48 • Practise What You Have Learned 49 • Team Exercises 51 • Business Cases 52

**Video Case Incidents**

Greenlite 54

Mountain Equipment Co-op 55

## Part 2 Planning 56

### Chapter 3 Planning and Strategic Management 56

**What Is Planning? 58**
Purposes of Planning 58
Planning and Performance 59
Criticisms of Planning 59

**How Do Managers Plan? 60**
Approaches to Establishing Goals 61
Steps in Goal Setting 62
Developing Plans 63

**Organizational Strategy: Choosing a Niche 65**
Step 1: Identify the Organization's Current Vision, Mission, Goals, and Strategies 66
Step 2: Do an Internal Analysis 68
Step 3: Do an External Analysis 68
Step 4: Formulate Strategies 71
Step 5: Implement Strategies 72
Step 6: Evaluate Results 72

**Types of Organizational Strategies 72**

    Corporate Strategy 72

    Business Strategy 76

    Functional Strategy 79

**Review and Apply**

Summary of Learning Objectives 80 • Snapshot Summary 80 • MyManagementLab Learning Resources 81 • Interpret What You Have Read 82 • Analyze What You Have Read 82 • Assess Your Skills 82 • Practise What You Have Learned 83 • Team Exercises 83 • Business Cases 86

**Chapter 4  Decision Making 88**

**The Decision-Making Process 90**

    Step 1: Identify a Problem 90

    Step 2: Identify Decision Criteria 90

    Step 3: Allocate Weights to Criteria 92

    Step 4: Develop Alternatives 93

    Step 5: Analyze Alternatives 93

    Step 6: Select an Alternative 93

    Step 7: Implement the Alternative 94

    Step 8: Evaluate Decision Effectiveness 94

**The Manager as Decision Maker 95**

    Making Decisions: Rationality, Bounded Rationality, and Intuition 95

    Types of Problems and Decisions 98

    Decision-Making Conditions 100

    Decision-Making Styles 101

    Group Decision Making 102

    Individual vs. Group Decision Making 104

    Decision-Making Biases and Errors 104

**Ethics, Corporate Social Responsibility, and Decision Making 106**

    Four Views of Ethics 107

    Improving Ethical Behaviour 108

    Corporate Social Responsibility 109

**Review and Apply**

Summary of Learning Objectives 114 • Snapshot Summary 114 • MyManagementLab Learning Resources 115 • Interpret What You Have Read 116 • Analyze What You Have Read 116 • Assess Your Skills 116 • Practise What You Have Learned 117 • Team Exercises 119 • Business Cases 121

**Video Case Incidents**

Bulldog Interactive Fitness 122

Ben & Jerry's Ice Cream Dream 123

# Part 3  Organizing 124

**Chapter 5  Organizational Structure and Design 124**

**Defining Organizational Structure 126**

    Work Specialization 127

    Departmentalization 127

    Chain of Command 130

    Span of Control 131

    Centralization and Decentralization 132

    Formalization 133

**Organizational Design Decisions 134**

    Mechanistic and Organic Organizations 134

    Contingency Factors 135

**Common Organizational Designs 137**

    Traditional Organizational Designs 138

    Contemporary Organizational Designs 138

    Organizational Design Challenges 144

    A Final Thought 145

**Review and Apply**

Summary of Learning Objectives 146 • Snapshot Summary 146 • MyManagementLab Learning Resources 147 • Interpret What You Have Read 148 • Analyze What You Have Read 148 • Assess Your Skills 148 • Practise What You Have Learned 149 • Team Exercises 151 • Business Cases 153

**Chapter 6  Communication and Information Technology 154**

**Understanding Communication 156**

    What Is Communication? 156

    Functions of Communication 157

**Interpersonal Communication 158**

    How Distortions Can Happen in Interpersonal Communication 159

    Channels for Communicating Interpersonally 160

    Barriers to Effective Interpersonal Communication 161

    Overcoming the Barriers 164

**Organizational Communication 166**

    Formal vs. Informal Communication 166

    Direction of Communication Flow 166

    Organizational Communication Networks 168

**Understanding Information Technology 169**

    How Information Technology Affects Organizational Communication 170

    How Information Technology Affects Organizations 172

    How Businesses Can Use Social Media 172

**Review and Apply**

Summary of Learning Objectives 174 • Snapshot Summary 174 • MyManagementLab Learning Resources 175 • Interpret What You Have Read 176 • Analyze What You Have Read 176 • Assess Your Skills 176 • Practise What You Have Learned 178 • Team Exercises 180 • Business Cases 182–183

**Chapter 7  Human Resource Management 184**

**The Human Resource Management Process 186**

    Environmental Factors Affecting HRM 186

**Human Resource Requirements 189**
Job Analysis and Design 189
Human Resource Planning 190
Meeting Future Needs 190

**Staffing the Organization 190**
Recruitment 191
Selection 192

**Orientation and Training 195**
Orientation 195
Training 196

**Performance Management 197**
Performance Management System 197
What Happens When Performance
Falls Short? 199

**Total Rewards 200**
Strategic Compensation 200
Benefits 201
Work–Life Balance 201
Performance and Recognition 202
Career Development 202

**Employee Relations 203**
Occupational Health and Safety 204
Employee Engagement 204

Review and Apply
Summary of Learning Objectives 205 • Snapshot
Summary 206 • MyManagementLab
Learning Resources 207 • Interpret What You
Have Read 208 • Analyze What You Have
Read 208 • Assess Your Skills 208 • Practise
What You Have Learned 209 • Team
Exercises 210 • Business Cases 211

**Video Case Incidents**
Tamarack Lake Electric Boat
Company 213

# Part 4  Leading 214

Chapter 8   Leadership 214
**Managers vs. Leaders 216**
**Early Leadership Theories 217**
Trait Theories 217
Behavioural Theories 219

**Contingency Theories of Leadership 220**
Hersey and Blanchard's Situational
Leadership® 220
Path-Goal Theory 221

**Leading Change 223**
Charismatic–Visionary Leadership 223
Transformational Leadership 225

**Current Issues in Leadership 226**
Managing Power 226
Developing Trust 227
Providing Ethical Leadership 228
Providing Online Leadership 228
Team Leadership 230
Understanding Gender Differences and
Leadership 231

Review and Apply
Summary of Learning Objectives 234 • Snapshot
Summary 234 • MyManagementLab
Learning Resources 235 • Interpret What You
Have Read 236 • Analyze What You Have
Read 236 • Assess Your Skills 236 • Practise
What You Have Learned 238 • Team
Exercises 239 • Business Cases 241

Chapter 9   Motivating Employees 242
**What Is Motivation? 244**
**Early Theories of Motivation 245**
Maslow's Hierarchy of Needs Theory 246
McGregor's Theory X and Theory Y 247
Herzberg's Motivation-Hygiene Theory 248
McClelland's Theory of Needs 250

**Contemporary Theories of Motivation 250**
Four-Drive Theory 250
Reinforcement Theory 252
Equity Theory 253
Expectancy Theory 255
Integrating Contemporary Theories of
Motivation 256

**Current Issues in Motivation 256**
Motivating a Diverse Workforce 257
Designing Effective Rewards Programs 260
Improving Work–Life Balance 262

**From Theory to Practice: Suggestions for
Motivating Employees 264**
Review and Apply
Summary of Learning Objectives 266 • Snapshot
Summary 266 • MyManagementLab
Learning Resources 267 • Interpret What You
Have Read 268 • Analyze What You Have
Read 268 • Assess Your Skills 268 • Practise
What You Have Learned 269 • Team
Exercises 270 • Business Cases 273

Chapter 10   Understanding Groups and
Teams 274
**Understanding Groups and Teams 276**
What Is a Team? 276
Informal Groups 276
Stages of Team Development 277

**Turning Individuals into Team Players 279**
The Challenges of Creating Team Players 279
What Roles Do Team Members Play? 280
Shaping Team Behaviour 280

**Turning Groups into Effective Teams 281**
Characteristics of Effective Teams 282
Building Group Cohesiveness 283
Managing Group Conflict 284
Preventing Social Loafing 286

**Current Challenges in Managing Teams 287**

Managing Global Teams 287

Beware! Teams Are Not Always the Answer 288

Review and Apply

Summary of Learning Objectives 290 • Snapshot Summary 290 • MyManagementLab Learning Resources 291 • Interpret What You Have Read 292 • Analyze What You Have Read 292 • Assess Your Skills 292 • Practise What You Have Learned 293 • Team Exercises 295 • Business Cases 297

**Video Case Incidents**

Leading with Integrity: Quova's Marie Alexander 298

Work–Life Balance: Canadian Voices and the British Experiment 299

# Part 5 Controlling 300

**Chapter 11 Foundations of Control 300**

**What Is Control? 302**

Performance Standards 302

Measures of Organizational Performance 302

Why Is Control Important? 303

**The Control Process 304**

Measuring Performance 304

Comparing Performance Against Standard 306

Taking Managerial Action 308

Summary of Managerial Decisions 309

**When to Introduce Control 310**

Feedforward Control 310

Concurrent Control 310

Feedback Control 311

**Methods of Control 311**

Market Control 312

Bureaucratic Control 312

Clan Control 312

**Financial and Information Controls 316**

Traditional Financial Control Measures 316

Other Financial Control Measures 317

Information Controls 318

**Current Issues in Control 320**

Balanced Scorecard 320

Corporate Governance 321

Cross-Cultural Differences 322

Workplace Concerns 323

Customer Interactions 325

Review and Apply

Summary of Learning Objectives 327 • Snapshot Summary 328 • MyManagementLab Learning Resources 329 • Interpret What You Have Read 330 • Analyze What You Have Read 330 • Assess Your Skills 330 • Practise What You Have Learned 331 • Team Exercises 332 • Business Cases 333

**Chapter 12 Managing Change 334**

**Forces for Change 336**

External Forces 336

Internal Forces 337

**Two Views of the Change Process 337**

The Calm Waters Metaphor 338

The White-Water Rapids Metaphor 339

Putting the Two Views in Perspective 339

**Managing Change 340**

What Is Organizational Change? 340

Types of Change 340

Making Change Happen Successfully 342

Managing Resistance to Change 344

**Common Approaches to Organizational Change 346**

Action Research 346

Appreciative Inquiry 346

**Current Issues in Managing Change 347**

Changing Organizational Culture 347

Handling Employee Stress 349

Review and Apply

Summary of Learning Objectives 352 • Snapshot Summary 352 • MyManagementLab Learning Resources 353 • Interpret What You Have Read 354 • Analyze What You Have Read 354 • Assess Your Skills 354 • Practise What You Have Learned 356 • Team Exercises 357 • Business Cases 358

**Video Case Incidents**

Eco-Preneurs: Easywash, the World's Most Eco-friendly Carwash Company 360

NB Power and Protest 361

Endnotes 362
Glossary 396
Subject Index 403
Name/Organization Index 417
List of Canadian Companies, by Province 425
List of International Companies, by Country 428
Photo Credits 431

# Preface

Welcome to the seventh Canadian edition of *Fundamentals of Management*, by Stephen P. Robbins, David A. DeCenzo, Mary Coulter, and Ian Anderson. This edition continues the fresh approach to management coverage through

- current and relevant examples
- updated theory
- a new pedagogically sound design

The philosophy behind this revision was to put additional emphasis on the idea that "management is for everyone." Students who are not managers, or who do not envision themselves as managers, may not always see why studying management is important. We use examples from a variety of settings to help students understand the relevance of studying management to their day-to-day lives.

## CHAPTER PEDAGOGICAL FEATURES

We have enhanced the seventh Canadian edition through a rich variety of pedagogical features, including the following:

- Learning objectives to guide student learning begin each chapter. These questions are repeated at the start of each major chapter section to reinforce the learning objective.
- An opening case starts the body of the chapter and is threaded throughout the chapter to help students apply a story to the concepts they are learning.
- *Think About It* questions follow the opening case to give students a chance to put themselves in the shoes of managers in various situations.
- Integrated questions (in the form of yellow notes) throughout the chapters help students relate management to their everyday lives.

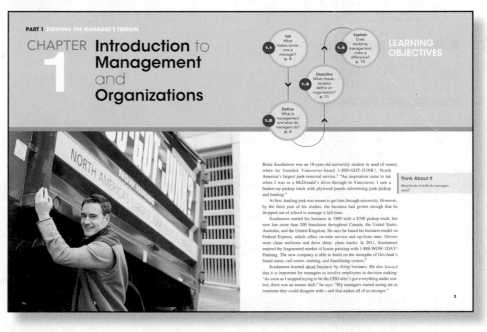

- *Tips for Managers* boxes provide "take-aways" from the chapter—things that managers and would-be managers can start to put into action right now, based on what they have learned in the chapter.

## END-OF-CHAPTER APPLICATIONS

The entire end-of-chapter section, *Review and Apply*, provides a wealth of exercises and applications.

- The *Summary of Learning Objectives* provides responses to the outcome-based questions identified at the beginning of each chapter. Accompanying this feature is a *Snapshot Summary* box that provides a quick look at the organization of the chapter topics.

- The *MyManagementLab Learning Resources* table provides a synopsis of key study tools found on the MyLab.

- *Interpret What You Have Read* allows students to review their understanding of the chapter content.
- *Analyze What You Have Read* helps students see the application of theory to management situations.
- *Assess Your Skills* gives students an opportunity to discover things about themselves, their attitudes, and their personal strengths and weaknesses. Each chapter includes one self-assessment exercise that students can fill out and refers students to the MyManagementLab website where they can access additional interactive self-assessment exercises.

- *Practise What You Have Learned* lets students apply material to their daily lives as well as to real business situations related to the chapter material, helping them see that planning, leading, organizing, and controlling are useful in one's day-to-day life too. This feature includes several exercises, such as the ones described below:
  - *Dilemma* presents an everyday scenario for students to resolve using management tools.
  - *Becoming a Manager* provides suggestions for students on activities and actions they can do right now to help them prepare to become a manager.
  - *Developing Your Diagnostic and Analytical Skills* asks students to apply chapter material to analyze a case.
  - *Developing Your Interpersonal Skills* emphasizes the importance of communication and interaction skills.

- *Team Exercises* give students a chance to work together in groups to solve a management challenge and include two new exercises: *3BL: The Triple Bottom Line* and *Be the Consultant*. Both of these exercises were added to the seventh Canadian edition in order to increase the sustainability component of the text and to give students more of a hands-on perspective into consulting.

- The *Business Cases* are decision-focused cases that ask students to determine what they would do if they were in the situation described.

# MyManagementLab®

An access code to MyManagementLab is included with the textbook *Fundamentals of Management*. MyManagementLab is an online study tool for students and an online homework and assessment tool for faculty. For the seventh Canadian edition, MyManagementLab resources and features have been specifically tailored by two innovative and experienced Canadian contributors. This new author team has ensured that key chapter concepts are supported by specific and easy-to-navigate online and instructor activities highlighted with icons in the textbook, MyManagementLab, and the Instructor's Manual.

The new MyManagementLab resources and features are built on an instructor-driven philosophy of presenting activities that challenge students on many different levels of learning. Key MyManagementLab activities have been highlighted in the text using carefully placed icons that link key concepts and examples to corresponding online study tools. This new framework and set of activities support the established and popular features of MyManagementLab, such as the Personalized Study Plan, Auto-Graded Tests and Assignments, Pearson eText, Glossary Flashcards, Robbins *OnLine Learning System (R.O.L.L.S.)*, the Self-Assessment Library, and much more! Learn more about MyManagementLab at **www.mymanagementlab.com**.

For more details about the philosophy and vision for the new textbook, MyManagementLab, and supplement integration strategy, see the MyManagementLab authors' message below.

## A Message from our MyManagementLab Author Team

As instructors who have used *Fundamentals of Management* over the past several years in our management courses, we are delighted to be involved in the development of the seventh Canadian edition. The world of business affects our lives every day, and "management" will affect the lives of all of us who work for a living. Our goal, therefore, has been to help deliver a text, supplemental materials, and online learning package that will engage students in a positive and direct manner as they build their fundamental knowledge of business in general and management in particular. In addition to viewing the material from the student perspective, we also strove to facilitate the instructor's use and application of the rich subject material and resources to provide a dynamic, interactive, and enjoyable classroom experience.

As a preamble, we thought it would be helpful to outline the basic assumptions and philosophy underlying our contributions to the *Fundamentals of Management* text, MyManagementLab, and supplemental materials. First, we know that for most students this course is their introduction to business and to management. For this reason, we approach the subject material with a view to building the student's knowledge one block at a time. Second, we believe that once students learn the material, they should have an opportunity to "play" with it as they think about it. The interactive nature of MyManagementLab offers the perfect environment within which students may play and learn. Finally, we want to encourage students, as they master the material, to reach into their new "tool kit" to problem solve, and in doing so, understand the relevance of the concepts to both their personal, and eventually, working lives. Again, we are ever mindful of providing the instructor with his or her own tool box for delivering the material in an interesting and engaging manner.

To reinforce our building-block approach, our directives to Interpret, Analyze, and Practise, in alignment with the learning objectives, have been based upon the following pedagogy:

- Comprehension—Interpret What You Have Read
- Application—Analyze What You Have Read
- Synthesis/Evaluation—Practise What You Have Learned

To these ends we have

- Used the learning objectives as our guide in linking chapter content with the MyManagementLab activities and in the preparation of related exercises and activities;
- Prepared activities to complement the in-text cases and exercises, and to encourage students to interpret, analyze, and practise the subject material;
- Indicated which MyManagementLab content is best linked to the textbook by explicitly referencing this material as part of our exercises and activities;
- Identified where and with what material we believe the content icons directing students to Interpret, Analyze, and Practise should be associated in the chapter;

We sincerely hope that both student and instructor will find this text and the accompanying supplemental materials to be a practical and enjoyable route to learning and using the fundamental tools of business management.

*Amanda Bickell (Kwantlen Polytechnic University) and Floyd Simpkins (St. Clair College)*

## Study on the Go

Featured at the end of each chapter, you will find a unique barcode providing access to Study on the Go, an unprecedented mobile integration between text and online content. Students link to Pearson's unique Study on the Go content directly from their smartphones, allowing them to study whenever and wherever they wish! Go to one of the sites below to see how you can download an app to your smartphone for free. Once the app is installed, your phone will scan the code and link to a website containing Pearson's Study on the Go content, including the popular study tools Glossary Flashcards, Audio Summaries, and Quizzes, which can be accessed anytime.

**ScanLife**
http://getscanlife.com

**NeoReader**
http://get.neoreader.com/

**QuickMark**
http://www.quickmark.com.tw/

# NEW TO THE SEVENTH CANADIAN EDITION

In addition to the new pedagogical features highlighted on previous pages, we have introduced or revised other learning aids and made significant changes to content.

## Case Program

This edition offers a variety of cases that can be used in or out of the classroom.

- End of Chapter Cases

At the end of each chapter we offer brief, chapter-specific cases in the *Practise What You Have Learned* and *Business Cases* sections. These cases include a variety of open-ended questions for classroom discussion or small-group assignment.

- End of Part Cases

For more dynamic case presentation, we have provided video cases at the end of each part. The cases are based on high quality videos that range in length from 3 to 18 minutes. They focus on several management issues within a part and include a set of all new objectives-based questions. Sandra Wellman (Seneca College) carefully selected the videos and wrote the cases and questions to provide instructors with engaging material for their students. The videos are available on the MyManagementLab and in DVD format (ISBN 978-0-13-266832-7).

- Management Mini-Cases (MyManagementLab)

Hosted within MyManagementLab and tied to each chapter are a set of 12 Management Mini-Cases with associated multiple-choice questions. These mini-cases are perfect for assignments, as the students' results feed directly into the MyManagementLab Gradebook.

- NEW Multi-Chapter Cases (MyManagementLab)

Hosted within MyManagementLab and prepared by the textbook author, Ian Anderson, are three NEW, multi-chapter cases: "Canada Still Loves A&W" for Part 2 (Planning), "Transformation at Air Canada" for Part 3 (Organizing), and "The Canadian Call Centre Industry" for Part 4 (Leading). Assessments for these multi-chapter cases include online multiple-choice and short-answer questions.

# CHAPTER-BY-CHAPTER HIGHLIGHTS

Below, we highlight the new material that has been added to this edition.

## Chapter 1

- Updated opening case on 1-800-GOT-JUNK?
- New end-of-chapter (EOC) material (*Be the Consultant, 3BL, Business Cases,* heavily revised *Dilemma/Becoming a Manager,* etc.)

## Supplement 1

- Brand new supplement on Small and Medium-Sized Enterprises and Organizations

## Chapter 2

- New opening case on TransCanada and the Keystone Pipeline Project
- Heavily revised *The General Environment,* with all subsections updated plus new material added on environmental conditions
- New EOC material (*Be the Consultant, 3BL, Business Cases,* etc.)

## Chapter 3

- New opening case on Maple Leaf Foods
- *Criticisms of Planning* moved to early in the chapter
- New material on forecasting, contingency planning, scenario planning, and benchmarking
- New exhibit on SWOT Analysis and new material on PESTEL Analysis
- Learning Objective #5 from the sixth Canadian edition (How can quality be a competitive advantage?) and its corresponding chapter material on quality management, ISO 9000, and Six Sigma deleted
- New EOC material (*Developing Your Interpersonal Skills, 3BL, Business Cases,* revised *Dilemma/Becoming a Manager,* etc.)

## Chapter 4

- New opening case on Nurse Next Door
- New material on bounded decision making
- New material on employee involvement in decision making
- New EOC material (*Be the Consultant, 3BL, Business Cases,* etc.)

## Chapter 5

- Updated opening case on Maple Leaf Sports and Entertainment
- New EOC material (*Be the Consultant, 3BL, Business Cases,* etc.)

## Chapter 6

- Updated opening case on Facebook and social networking
- New material on mental models
- New *Tips for Mangers* box on Communication with Diverse Individuals

- New tips on Receiving Feedback added to *Tips for Managers* box on Giving Feedback
- Enhanced information on email and instant messaging, and new material on wikis and blogs
- New *Tips for Managers* box on Getting Started with Social Media
- New material on social media strategies
- New EOC material (*Be the Consultant, 3BL, Business Cases,* etc.)

## Chapter 7

- New opening case on the Calgary Chamber of Voluntary Organizations
- Material on organizational change (moved from Chapter 11), demographic trends, and technology added to *Human Resource Management Process*
- New Exhibit 7-1 on the Human Resource Management Process
- New material on job design added to *Human Resource Requirements*
- Reduced sub-section on *Types of Selection Devices* in *Staffing the Organization* (reviewers found that Exhibit 7-5 sufficiently explained these devices)
- Updated *Tips for Managers* box, which now covers Behavioural and Situational Questions
- Updated and reorganized *Compensation and Rewards*— Learning Objective #6 now focuses on how "Total Rewards" motivate employees (this change was well received by reviewers)
- New Learning Objective #7 (What can organizations do to maximize employee relations?)—corresponding chapter sections incorporate some material from the sixth edition section *Current Issues in HRM* as well as new and updated topics on occupational health and safety, corporate wellness initiatives, sexual harassment, and employee engagement
- New EOC material (*Networking, 3BL, Business Cases,* revised *Becoming a Manager,* etc.)
- Note: a primary goal for this chapter was to make it more concise and more relevant to students taking an introductory overview of management (versus an introductory HR course)

## Chapter 8

- New material on the difference between managers and leaders
- New material on female leaders
- New *Tips for Future Leaders* material
- New EOC material (*3BL, Business Cases,* revised *Becoming a Manager,* etc.)

## Chapter 9

- New opening case on Yellow House Events
- New material on four-drive theory (replaces *Job Characteristics Model*)
- New EOC material (*3BL, Business Cases,* revised *Becoming a Manager,* etc.)

### Chapter 10

- New opening case on Great Little Box Company
- New material on what makes up a team and teamwork
- New material on turning groups into teams
- New EOC material (*3BL*, *Business Cases*, revised *Becoming a Manager*, etc.)

### Chapter 11

- New opening case on Canadian Curling Association
- New EOC material (*3BL*, *Business Cases*, revised *Becoming a Manager*, etc.)

### Chapter 12

- New opening case on BP
- New Learning Objective #4 and corresponding section on *Common Approaches to Organizational Change*
- New EOC material (*Be the Consultant*, *3BL*, revised *Becoming a Manager*, etc.)

## SUPPLEMENTS

For instructors, we have created an outstanding supplements package, conveniently available online through MyManagementLab in the special instructor area and downloadable from our product catalogue at **www.pearsoncanada.ca**.

- Instructor's Manual (includes video teaching notes, detailed lecture outlines, and suggestions on how to integrate the MyManagementLab material into your course), prepared by Floyd Simpkins of St. Clair College and Amanda Bickell of Kwantlen Polytechnic University
- PowerPoint Slides, prepared by Floyd Simpkins of St. Clair College and Amanda Bickell of Kwantlen Polytechnic University
- MyTest, prepared by Floyd Simpkins of St. Clair College and Amanda Bickell of Kwantlen Polytechnic University
- Video cases (available in DVD format [ISBN 978-0-13-266832-7] and on the MyManagementLab), prepared by Sandra Wellman of Seneca College

## ACKNOWLEDGMENTS

A number of people have worked hard to update and enliven this seventh Canadian edition of *Fundamentals of Management*. Alexandra Dyer was developmental editor on this project. Her understanding, patience, helpfulness, support, and organizational skills made working on this textbook enjoyable and enriching. She also played a key role in handling many aspects of the editorial work needed during the production process. Nick Durie, acquisitions editor, was very supportive of finding new directions for the textbook. Kathleen McGill, sponsoring editor, continues to be easy to work with on various projects and is always in the author's corner.

I'd also like to thank project manager Marissa Lok, project editor Rashmi Tickyani, and copy editor Carolyn Zapf, as well as the many others—proofreaders, designers, permissions researchers, marketing and sales representatives—who have all contributed to the transformation of my manuscript into this textbook and seen it delivered into your hands. The Pearson Canada sales team is an exceptional group, and I know they will do everything possible to make the book successful. I continue to appreciate and value their support and interaction, particularly that of Molly Armstrong, my local sales representative.

Thank you to Floyd Simpkins and Amanda Bickell for developing new features and resources in MyManagementLab and making it more integrated with the textbook in this edition, and to Sandra Wellman for selecting and writing the new video cases. Finally, I would like to thank the reviewers of this textbook for their detailed and helpful comments:

J. J. Collins, St. Clair College
Ronald Gallagher, New Brunswick Community College
Cheryl Dowell, Algonquin College
Michael Khan, University of Toronto–Mississauga
Tim Richardson, Seneca College
Allan MacKenzie, Wilfrid Laurier University
Yan Yabar, Red Deer College
Larry Chung, Camosun College
Halinka Szwender, Camosun College
Al Morrison, Camosun College
Karen Stephens, Camosun College
Troy Dunning, Camosun College
Tim Kemp, Camosun College
Nancy Nowlan, Capilano University
Hana Carbert, CMA-BC
Robert Willis, Vancouver Island University
Michael Pearl, Seneca College
Foster Stewart, SAIT
Horatio Morgan, Ryerson University
Michael Hobeck, Nova Scotia Community College

I dedicate this book to my two sons, Shaun and Isaac.

Ian Anderson
August 2012

# About the Authors

**STEPHEN P. ROBBINS** received his Ph.D. from the University of Arizona. He previously worked for the Shell Oil Company and Reynolds Metals Company and has taught at the University of Nebraska at Omaha, Concordia University in Montreal, the University of Baltimore, Southern Illinois University at Edwardsville, and San Diego State University. He is currently professor emeritus in management at San Diego State.

Dr. Robbins's research interests have focused on conflict, power, and politics in organizations, behavioural decision making, and the development of effective interpersonal skills. His articles on these and other topics have appeared in such journals as *Business Horizons*, the *California Management Review*, *Business and Economic Perspectives*, *International Management*, *Management Review*, *Canadian Personnel*, and *Industrial Relations*, and *The Journal of Management Education.*

Dr. Robbins is the world's best-selling textbook author in the areas of management and organizational behavior. His books have sold more than 5 million copies and have been translated into 20 languages. His books are currently used at more than 1,500 US colleges and universities, as well as hundreds of schools throughout Canada, Latin America, Australia, New Zealand, Asia, and Europe.

Dr. Robbins also participates in masters track competition. Since turning 50 in 1993, he's won 23 national championships and 14 world titles. He was inducted into the US Masters Track & Field Hall of Fame in 2005 and is currently the world record holder at 100m and 200m for men 65 and over.

**DAVID A. DECENZO** (Ph.D., West Virginia University) is president of Coastal Carolina University in Conway, South Carolina. In his capacity as president, Dr. DeCenzo is responsible for the overall vision and leadership of the university. He has been at Coastal since 2002 when he took over leadership of the E. Craig Wall Sr. College of Business. Since then, the college established an economics major and developed an MBA program. During that period, student enrollment and faculty positions nearly doubled. The college also established significant internship opportunities locally, nationally, and internationally in major *Fortune* 100 companies. As provost, Dr. DeCenzo worked with faculty leadership to pass a revised general education core curriculum as well as institute a minimum salary level for the university's faculty members. Before joining the Coastal faculty in 2002, he served as director of partnership development in the College of Business and Economics at Towson University in Maryland. He is an experienced industry consultant, corporate trainer, and public speaker. Dr. DeCenzo is the author of numerous textbooks that are used widely at colleges and universities throughout the United States and the world.

Dr. DeCenzo and his wife, Terri, have four children and reside in Pawleys Island, South Carolina.

**MARY COULTER** (Ph.D., University of Arkansas) held different jobs including high school teacher, legal assistant, and city government program planner before completing her graduate work. She has taught at Drury University, the University of Arkansas, Trinity University, and Missouri State University. She is currently professor emeritus of management at Missouri State University. Dr. Coulter's research interests were focused on competitive strategies for not-for-profit arts organizations and the use of new media in the educational process. Her research on these and other topics has appeared in such journals as *International Journal of Business Disciplines*, *Journal of Business Strategies*, *Journal of Business Research*, *Journal of Nonprofit and Public Sector Marketing*, and *Case Research Journal*. In additional to *Fundamentals of Management*, Dr. Coulter has published other books with Prentice Hall including *Management* (with Stephen P. Robbins), *Strategic Management in Action*, and *Entrepreneurship in Action*.

When she's not busy writing, Dr. Coulter enjoys puttering around in her flower gardens, trying new recipes, reading all different types of books, and enjoying many different activities with Ron, Sarah and James, Katie and Matt, and especially with her new granddaughter, Brooklynn. Love ya' my sweet baby girl!

**IAN ANDERSON** received his Bachelor of Business Administration from the University of Regina, including studies at the University of Ottawa. Before commencing his college teaching career, he was the Director of HR for a large Ottawa-based IT company. Ian is also an HR and Management consultant with Association Management, Consulting & Educational Services (AMCES) and has been actively consulting for more than 25 years. At Algonquin College, Ian is a Professor and Coordinator in Marketing and Management Studies, and coaches students in business case and college marketing competitions.

In Ian's "other life," he is a sommelier and works regularly with Groovy Grapes providing tutored tastings and wine and scotch education. Ian's parents, Bob and Katharine, are from the Niagara area, and Ian has visited wine regions in Australia, New Zealand, Canada, the United States, Austria, and Germany. Ian has coached hockey and soccer for more than 20 years.

# CHAPTER 1 Introduction to Management and Organizations

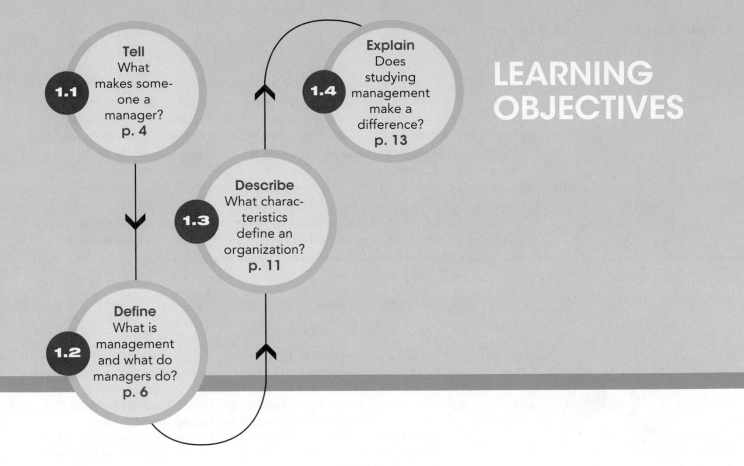

## LEARNING OBJECTIVES

**1.1 Tell** What makes someone a manager? p. 4

**1.2 Define** What is management and what do managers do? p. 6

**1.3 Describe** What characteristics define an organization? p. 11

**1.4 Explain** Does studying management make a difference? p. 13

Brian Scudamore was an 18-year-old university student in need of money when he founded Vancouver-based 1-800-GOT-JUNK?, North America's largest junk-removal service.[1] "An inspiration came to me when I was in a McDonald's drive-through in Vancouver. I saw a beaten-up pickup truck with plywood panels advertising junk pickup and hauling."

At first, hauling junk was meant to get him through university. However, by the third year of his studies, the business had grown enough that he dropped out of school to manage it full time.

Scudamore started his business in 1989 with a $700 pickup truck, but now has more than 200 franchises throughout Canada, the United States, Australia, and the United Kingdom. He says he based his business model on Federal Express, which offers on-time service and up-front rates. Drivers wear clean uniforms and drive shiny, clean trucks. In 2011, Scudamore entered the fragmented market of house painting with 1-888-WOW-1DAY! Painting. The new company is able to build on the strengths of Got-Junk's brand name, call centre, training, and franchising system.[2]

Scudamore learned about business by doing business. He also learned that it is important for managers to involve employees in decision making: "As soon as I stopped trying to be the CEO who's got everything under control, there was an instant shift," he says. "My managers started seeing me as someone they could disagree with—and that makes all of us stronger."

**Think About It**

What kinds of skills do managers need?

Brian Scudamore is a good example of what today's successful managers are like and what skills they must have to deal with the problems and challenges of managing in the twenty-first century. This textbook is about the important managerial work that Brian Scudamore and the millions of other managers like him do. It recognizes the reality today's managers face: new technologies and new ways of organizing work are altering old approaches. Today's successful managers must be able to blend tried-and-true management styles with new ideas. In many chapters throughout the text, you will find the feature *Tips for Managers*, which presents actions managers can take in specific situations in the workplace.

In this chapter, we introduce you to managers and management by looking at who managers are, what management is, what managers do, and what an organization is. We will wrap up the chapter by discussing the challenges managers face and why it is important to study management.

## WHO ARE MANAGERS?

**Tell**
What makes someone a manager?

**1.1**

As founder of 1-800-GOT-JUNK?, Brian Scudamore manages the largest junk removal service in North America.[3] He attended Dawson College in Montreal, and then spent one year each at Concordia and the University of British Columbia studying business before dropping out to run his business full-time. Part of his job is making sure that those who run the 1-800-GOT-JUNK? franchises around the world are successful in carrying out his business model. "By relying on franchise owners to come in and share some of the risk, I realized I could expand the firm without having to turn to outside investors or other funding sources," Scudamore said. "To me, this was a solid plan for growth." In March 2012, Scudamore was featured on *Undercover Boss Canada*. His TV appearance has rapidly increased the number of interested franchisees for 1-888-WOW-1DAY! Painting. The company had 12 signed franchises by May 2012 and expect that number to double by the end of the year.[4]

### Think About It

What makes Brian Scudamore a manager?

Managers may not be who or what you might expect. They could be under age 18 or even over age 80. They run large corporations as well as entrepreneurial start-ups. They are found in government departments, hospitals, small businesses, not-for-profit agencies, museums, schools, and even nontraditional organizations such as political campaigns and consumer cooperatives. They can be found doing managerial work in every country around the globe and operate at many levels, from top-level managers to first-line managers.

No matter where managers are found or what gender they are, managers have exciting and challenging jobs. And organizations need managers more than ever in these uncertain, complex, and chaotic times. *Managers do matter!* How do we know that? The Gallup Organization, which has polled millions of employees and tens of thousands of managers, has found that the single most important variable in employee productivity and loyalty is neither pay nor benefits nor workplace environment; it is the quality of the relationship between employees and their direct supervisors.[5] A KPMG/Ipsos-Reid study found that many Canadian companies with high scores for effective human resource practices also scored high on financial performance and best long-term investment value.[6] In addition, global consulting firm Watson Wyatt Worldwide found that the way a company manages its people can significantly affect its financial performance.[7] We can conclude from such reports that managers *do* matter!

Defining who managers were used to be fairly simple: Managers were the organizational members who told others what to do and how to do it. It was easy to differentiate *managers* from *nonmanagerial employees*. But life is not quite as simple anymore. In many organizations, the changing nature of work has blurred the distinction between managers and nonmanagerial employees. Many nonmanagerial jobs now include managerial activities.[8] For example, at General Cable Corporation's facility in Moose Jaw, Saskatchewan, managerial responsibilities are shared by managers and team members. Most of the employees at Moose Jaw are cross-trained and multiskilled. Within a single shift, an employee may be a team leader, an equipment operator, a maintenance technician, a quality inspector, and an improvement planner.[9]

How do we define who managers are? A **manager** is someone who works with and through other people by coordinating their work activities in order to accomplish organizational goals. A manager's job is not about *personal* achievement—it is about helping *others* do their work and achieve results.

## Types of Managers

Is there some way to classify managers in organizations? In traditionally structured organizations, identifying exactly who the managers are is not difficult, although they may have a variety of titles. **Lower-level managers** are at the lowest level of management and manage the work of nonmanagerial employees who are directly or indirectly involved with the production or creation of the organization's products. They are often called *supervisors*, but may also be called *shift managers*, *district managers*, *department managers*, or *office managers*. **Middle-level managers** include all levels of management between the first-line level and the top level of the organization. These managers manage the work of first-line managers and may have titles such as *regional manager*, *project leader*, *plant manager*, or *division manager*. At or near the top of the organization are the **top-level managers**, who are responsible for making organization-wide decisions and establishing the plans and goals that affect the entire organization. These individuals typically have titles such as *executive vice-president*, *president*, *managing director*, *chief operating officer*, *chief executive officer*, or *chair of the board*. In the chapter-opening case, Brian Scudamore is a top-level manager for 1-800-GOT-JUNK? He is involved in creating and implementing broad and comprehensive changes that affect the entire organization.

Not all organizations get work done using a traditional pyramidal form, with the three levels of managers on the top of the pyramid. Some organizations, for example, are more flexible and loosely structured with work being done by ever-changing teams of employees who move from one project to another as work demands arise. Although it is not as easy to tell who the managers are in these organizations, we do know that someone must fulfill that role—there must be someone who works with and through other people by coordinating their work to accomplish organizational goals.

Allyson Koteski loves her job as the manager of the Toys "R" Us store in Annapolis, Maryland. She loves the chaos created by lots of kids, toys, and noise. She even loves the long and variable hours during hectic holiday seasons. Because employee turnover is a huge issue in the retail world, Allyson enjoys the challenge of keeping her employees motivated and engaged so they will not quit. The occasional disgruntled customers do not faze her either. She patiently listens to their problems and tries to resolve them satisfactorily. This is what Allyson's life as a manager is like.

**manager**
Someone who works with and through other people by coordinating their work activities in order to accomplish organizational goals.

**lower-level managers**
Managers at the lowest level of the organization who manage the work of nonmanagerial employees

directly or indirectly involved with the production or creation of the organization's products.

**middle-level managers**
Managers between the first-line level and the top level of the organization who manage the work of first-line managers.

**top-level managers**
Managers at or near the top level of the organization who are responsible for making organization-wide decisions and establishing the plans and goals that affect the entire organization.

**1.2** Define
What is management and what do managers do?

# WHAT IS MANAGEMENT AND WHAT DO MANAGERS DO?

Managers plan, lead, organize, and control, and Brian Scudamore certainly carries out all of these tasks. He has to coordinate the work activities of his entire company efficiently and effectively. With franchises located in four countries, he has to make sure that work is carried out consistently to protect his brand. He also has to support his managers. He provides support for them by having a call centre operation in Vancouver that makes all the booking arrangements, no matter where the caller is from. This set-up allows managers at other locations to focus on the business of picking up junk. Scudamore works on his plans to expand the business. "One of our goals at 1-800-GOT-JUNK?," he says, "has been to become a globally admired company with a presence in 10 different countries." He adds, "It's important to stay focused when entering new markets. No matter how well you do your research, there will always be unexpected details that have to be managed differently."

## Think About It

As a manager, Brian Scudamore needs to plan, lead, organize, and control, and he needs to be efficient and effective. How might Scudamore balance the needs of efficiency and effectiveness in his role as founder and CEO of 1-800-GOT-JUNK? What skills are needed for him to plan, lead, organize, and control effectively? What challenges does he face performing these functions while running an international business?

Simply speaking, management is what managers do. But that simple statement does not tell us much, does it? Here is a more thorough explanation: **Management** is coordinating work activities so that they are completed *efficiently* and *effectively* with and through other people. Management researchers have developed three specific categories to describe what managers do: functions, roles, and skills. In this section, we'll consider the challenges of balancing efficiency and effectiveness, and then examine the approaches that look at what managers do. In reviewing these categories, it might be helpful to understand that management is something that is a learned talent, rather than something that comes "naturally." Many people do not know how to be a manager when they first are appointed to that role.

## Efficiency and Effectiveness

**Efficiency** refers to getting the most output from the least amount of inputs, or as management expert Peter Drucker explained, "doing things right."[10] Because managers deal with scarce inputs—including resources such as people, money, and equipment—they are concerned with the efficient use of those resources by getting things done at the least cost.

Just being efficient is not enough, however. Management is also responsible for being effective—completing activities so that organizational goals are achieved. **Effectiveness** is often described as "doing the right things"—that is, those work activities that will help the organization reach its goals. Hospitals might try to be efficient by reducing the number of days that patients stay in hospital. However, they may not be effective if patients get sick at home shortly after being released.

While efficiency is about ways to get things done, effectiveness deals with the ends, or attaining organizational goals (see Exhibit 1-1). Management is concerned, then, not only with completing activities to meet organizational goals (effectiveness), but also with doing so as efficiently as possible. In successful organizations, high efficiency and high effectiveness typically go hand in hand. Poor management is most often due to both inefficiency and ineffectiveness or to effectiveness achieved through inefficiency.

*Think about a manager you have had and identify the extent to which he or she engaged in planning, organizing, leading, and controlling.*

## Management Functions

According to the functions approach, managers perform certain activities or duties as they efficiently and effectively coordinate the work of others. What are

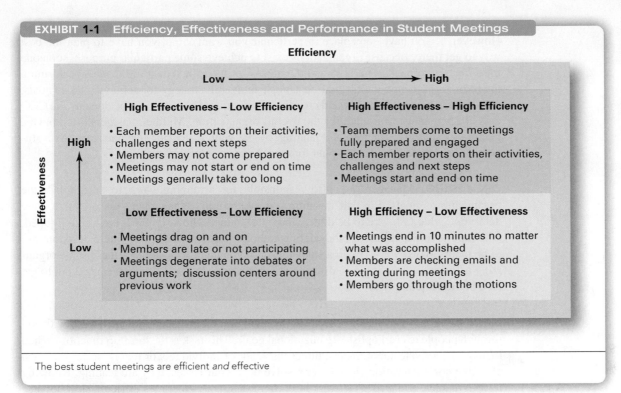

**EXHIBIT 1-1** Efficiency, Effectiveness and Performance in Student Meetings

Efficiency

Low ────────────────────→ High

**High Effectiveness – Low Efficiency**

High

- Each member reports on their activities, challenges and next steps
- Members may not come prepared
- Meetings may not start or end on time
- Meetings generally take too long

**High Effectiveness – High Efficiency**

- Team members come to meetings fully prepared and engaged
- Each member reports on their activities, challenges and next steps
- Meetings start and end on time

Effectiveness

**Low Effectiveness – Low Efficiency**

Low

- Meetings drag on and on
- Members are late or not participating
- Meetings degenerate into debates or arguments; discussion centers around previous work

**High Efficiency – Low Effectiveness**

- Meetings end in 10 minutes no matter what was accomplished
- Members are checking emails and texting during meetings
- Members go through the motions

The best student meetings are efficient *and* effective

these activities, or functions? In the early part of the twentieth century, French industrialist Henri Fayol first proposed that all managers perform five functions: planning, organizing, commanding, coordinating, and controlling.[11] Today, most management textbooks (including this one) are organized around four **management functions**: planning, organizing, leading, and controlling (see Exhibit 1-2). But you do not have to be a manager in order to have a need to plan, organize, lead, and control, so understanding these processes is important for everyone. Let us briefly define what each of these functions encompasses.

**EXHIBIT 1-2** Management Functions

| Planning | Organizing | Leading | Controlling | Lead to |
|---|---|---|---|---|
| Defining goals, establishing strategy, and developing subplans to coordinate activities | Determining what needs to be done, how it will be done, and who is to do it | Directing and motivating all involved parties and resolving conflicts | Monitoring activities to ensure that they are accomplished as planned | Achieving the organization's stated purpose |

**management**
Coordinating work activities so that they are completed efficiently and effectively with and through other people.

**efficiency**
Getting the most output from the least amount of inputs; referred to as "doing things right."

**effectiveness**
Completing activities so that organizational goals are achieved; referred to as "doing the right things."

**management functions**
Planning, organizing, leading, and controlling.

**PLANNING**   If you have no particular destination in mind, then you can take any road. However, if you have someplace in particular you want to go, you have to plan the best way to get there. Because organizations exist to achieve some particular purpose, someone must clearly define that purpose and the means for its achievement. Managers performing the **planning** function define goals, establish an overall strategy for achieving those goals, and develop plans to integrate and coordinate activities. This work can be done by the CEO and senior management team for the overall organization. Middle managers often have a planning role within their units. Planning, by the way, is not just for managers. As a student, for example, you need to plan for exams and for your financial needs.

**ORGANIZING**   Managers are also responsible for arranging work to accomplish the organization's goals. We call this function **organizing**. When managers organize, they determine what tasks are to be done, who is to do them, how the tasks are to be grouped, who reports to whom (that is, they define authority relationships), and where decisions are to be made. When you work in a student group, you engage in some of these same organizing activities—deciding on a division of labour, and what tasks will be carried out to get an assignment completed.

**LEADING**   Every organization contains people. Part of a manager's job is to work with and through people to accomplish organizational goals. This task is the **leading** function. When managers motivate subordinates, direct the work of individuals or teams, select the most effective communication channel, or resolve behaviour issues, they are leading. Knowing how to manage and lead effectively is an important, and sometimes difficult, skill because it requires the ability to successfully communicate. Leading is not just for managers, however. As a student, you might want to practise leadership skills when working in groups or club activities. You might also want to evaluate whether you need to improve your leadership skills in anticipation of the needs of future jobs. Brian Scudamore believes that leadership is about listening, transparency, and honesty. Transparency and being open about where the business is going are the keys to building trust.[12]

**CONTROLLING**   The final management function is **controlling**. After the goals are set (planning), the plans formulated (planning), the structural arrangements determined (organizing), and the people hired, trained, and motivated (leading), there has to be some evaluation of whether things are going as planned (controlling). To ensure that work is proceeding as it should, managers need to monitor and evaluate employees' performance. Actual performance must be compared with previously set goals. If the performance of individuals or units does not match the goals set, the manager's job is to get performance back on track. This process of monitoring, comparing, and correcting is what we mean by the controlling function. Individuals, whether working in groups or alone, also face the responsibility of controlling; that is, they must make sure the goals and actions are achieved and take corrective action when necessary.

Just how well does the functions approach describe what managers do? Do managers always plan, organize, lead, and then control? In practice, what a manager does may not always happen in this logical and sequential order. But that reality does not negate the importance of the basic functions managers perform. Regardless of the order in which the functions are carried out, managers do plan, organize, lead, and control as they manage.

The continued popularity of the functions approach is a tribute to its clarity and simplicity. But some have argued that this approach is not appropriate or relevant.[13] So let us look at another perspective.

Interpret

## Management Roles

Henry Mintzberg, a prominent management researcher at McGill University, has studied actual managers at work. He says that what managers do can best be understood by looking at the roles they play at work. His studies allowed him to conclude that managers perform 10 different but highly interrelated management roles.[14] The term **management roles**

**EXHIBIT 1-3** Mintzberg's Management Roles

| Role | Description | Examples of Identifiable Activities |
|------|-------------|-------------------------------------|
| **Interpersonal** | | |
| Figurehead | Symbolic head; obliged to perform a number of routine duties of a legal or social nature | Greeting visitors; signing legal documents |
| Leader | Responsible for the motivation of subordinates; responsible for staffing, training, and associated duties | Performing virtually all activities that involve subordinates |
| Liaison | Maintains self-developed network of outside contacts and informers who provide favours and information | Acknowledging mail; doing external board work; performing other activities that involve outsiders |
| **Informational** | | |
| Monitor | Seeks and receives a wide variety of internal and external information to develop a thorough understanding of organization and environment | Reading periodicals and reports; maintaining personal contacts |
| Disseminator | Transmits information received from outsiders or from subordinates to members of the organization | Holding informational meetings; making phone calls to relay information |
| Spokesperson | Transmits information to outsiders on organization's plans, policies, actions, results, etc. | Holding board meetings; giving information to the media |
| **Decisional** | | |
| Entrepreneur | Searches organization and its environment for opportunities and initiates "improvement projects" to bring about changes | Organizing strategy and review sessions to develop new programs |
| Disturbance handler | Responsible for corrective action when organization faces important, unexpected disturbances | Organizing strategy and review sessions that involve disturbances and crises |
| Resource allocator | Responsible for the allocation of organizational resources of all kinds—making or approving all significant organizational decisions | Scheduling; requesting authorization; performing any activity that involves budgeting and the programming of subordinates' work |
| Negotiator | Responsible for representing the organization at major negotiations | Participating in union contract negotiations |

*Source:* H. Mintzberg, *The Nature of Managerial Work* (New York: Harper and Row, 1973), pp. 93–94. Copyright © 1973 by Henry Mintzberg. Reprinted by permission of Harper & Row, Publishers, Inc.

refers to specific categories of managerial behaviour. (Think of the different roles you play and the different behaviours you are expected to perform in the roles of student, sibling, employee, volunteer, and so forth.) As shown in Exhibit 1-3, Mintzberg's 10 management roles are grouped around interpersonal relationships, the transfer of information, and decision making.

The **interpersonal roles** involve working with people (subordinates and persons outside the organization) or performing duties that are ceremonial and symbolic in nature. The three interpersonal roles include figurehead, leader, and liaison. The **informational roles**

**planning**
A management function that involves defining goals, establishing a strategy for achieving those goals, and developing plans to integrate and coordinate activities.

**organizing**
A management function that involves determining what tasks are to be done, who is to do them, how the tasks are to be grouped, who reports to whom, and where decisions are to be made.

**leading**
A management function that involves motivating subordinates, directing the work of individuals or teams, selecting the most effective communication channels, and resolving employee behaviour issues.

**controlling**
A management function that involves monitoring actual performance, comparing actual performance to a standard, and taking corrective action when necessary.

**management roles**
Specific categories of managerial behaviour.

**interpersonal roles**
Management roles that involve working with people or performing duties that are ceremonial and symbolic in nature.

**informational roles**
Management roles that involve receiving, collecting, and disseminating information.

involve receiving, collecting, and disseminating information. The three informational roles include monitor, disseminator, and spokesperson. Finally, the **decisional roles** involve making significant choices that affect the organization. The four decisional roles include entrepreneur, disturbance handler, resource allocator, and negotiator.

**FUNCTIONS VS. ROLES** So which approach to describing what managers do is correct—functions or roles? Each has merit. However, the functions approach still represents the most useful way of conceptualizing the manager's job. Managers carry out so many diverse activities and utilize such varying techniques that functions are needed to provide clarity and a means for categorizing ways to achieve organizational goals.[15] Many of Mintzberg's roles align well with one or more of the functions. For example, resource allocation is part of planning, as is the entrepreneurial role, and all three of the interpersonal roles are part of the leading function. Although most of the other roles fit into one or more of the four functions, not all of them do. The discrepancy occurs because all managers do some work that is not purely managerial.[16]

## Management Skills

Dell Inc. is one company that understands the importance of management skills.[17] It started an intensive five-day off-site skills training program for first-line managers as a way to improve its operations. One of Dell's directors of learning and development thought this initiative was the best way to develop "leaders who can build that strong relationship with their front-line employees." What have the supervisors learned from the skills training? Some things they have mentioned were how to communicate more effectively and how to refrain from jumping to conclusions when discussing a problem with an employee.

What types of skills does a manager need? Research by management scholar Robert L. Katz found that managers needed three essential skills: technical skills, human skills, and conceptual skills.[18]

**Technical skills** include knowledge of and expertise in a certain specialized field, such as engineering, computers, accounting, or manufacturing. These skills are more important at lower levels of management since these managers are dealing directly with employees doing the organization's work.

**Human skills** involve the ability to work well with other people both individually and in a group. Because managers deal directly with people, this skill is crucial! Managers with good human skills are able to get the best from their people. They know how to communicate, motivate, lead, and inspire enthusiasm and trust. These skills are equally important at all levels of management. According to management professor Jin Nam Choi of McGill University, 40 percent of managers either leave or stop performing within 18 months of joining an organization "because they have failed to develop relationships with bosses, colleagues or subordinates."[19] Choi's comment underscores the importance of developing human skills.

Finally, **conceptual skills** refer to the mental ability to analyze and generate ideas about abstract and complex situations. These skills help managers see the organization as a whole, understand the relationships among various subunits, and visualize how the organization fits into its broader environment. These skills are most important at the top managerial level. Exhibit 1-4 shows the relationship of the three skills to each level of management. Note that the three skills are important to more than one level. In very flat organizations with little hierarchy, human, technical, and conceptual skills would be needed throughout the organization. The employees that Brian Scudamore looks for are able to see possibilities, ask "What if?," and figure out a way to make it happen.[20]

As you study management functions in more depth, the exercises in *Team Exercises*, found at the end of each chapter, will give you the opportunity to practise some of the key skills that are part of doing what a manager does. Skill-building exercises cannot make you an instant managerial expert, but they can provide you with a basic understanding of some of the skills you will need to master to become an effective manager.

Analyze

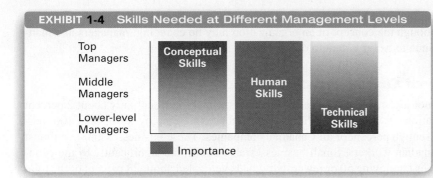

EXHIBIT 1-4  Skills Needed at Different Management Levels

## WHAT IS AN ORGANIZATION?

Brian Scudamore is the founder of 1-800-GOT-JUNK? Though he has a board of advisors, he is the sole shareholder of the company. Therefore he gets to set his own plans and goals. The company has over 200 franchises in four countries, which means his management skills have to include awareness of the challenges of managing in other countries.

### Think About It

Do managers act differently when they work for large organizations rather than smaller ones?

**Describe**
1.3 What characteristics define an organization?

Managers work in organizations. But what is an organization? An **organization** is a deliberate arrangement of people who act together to accomplish some specific purpose. Your college or university is an organization; so are government departments, churches, Amazon.ca, your neighbourhood video store, the United Way, the Toronto Raptors basketball team, and the Hudson's Bay Company. These examples are all organizations because they have three common characteristics:

- *Distinct purpose.* This purpose is typically expressed in terms of a goal or a set of goals that the organization hopes to accomplish.
- *People.* One person working alone is not an organization. An organization requires people to perform the work necessary to achieve its goals.
- *Deliberate structure.* Whether that structure is open and flexible or traditional and clearly defined, the structure defines members' work relationships.

In summary, the term *organization* refers to an entity that has a distinct purpose, includes people or members, and has some type of deliberate structure.

Although these three characteristics are important to our definition of *what* an organization is, the concept of an organization is changing. It is no longer appropriate to assume that all organizations are going to be structured like Air Canada, Petro-Canada, or General Motors, with clearly identifiable divisions, departments, and work units. Just how is the concept of an organization changing? Today's organizations are becoming more open, flexible, and responsive to change.[21]

Why are organizations changing? Because the world around them has changed and continues to change. Societal, economic, political, global, and technological changes have created an environment in which successful organizations (those that

*Does your college or university or an organization in which you have worked represent a "new organization"? Why or why not?*

---

**decisional roles**
Management roles that involve making significant choices that affect the organization.

**technical skills**
Knowledge of and expertise in a specialized field.

**human skills**
The ability to work well with other people both individually and in a group.

**conceptual skills**
The mental ability to analyze and generate ideas about abstract and complex situations.

**organization**
A deliberate arrangement of people who act together to accomplish some specific purpose.

consistently attain their goals) must embrace new ways of getting work done. As we stated earlier, even though the concept of an organization may be changing, managers and management continue to be important to organizations.

## The Size of Organizations

Managers do not just manage in large organizations, which represent only about 2 percent of all organizations in Canada. Small businesses (those that employ fewer than 100 individuals) represent 98 percent of all Canadian companies. These businesses employ almost half of all Canadian workers. Small businesses also contribute significantly to the economy. Businesses employing 50 or fewer individuals generated about 28 percent of the total gross domestic product (GDP) in 2009.[22] Organizations of every size need managers. Moreover, in 2012, about 15 percent of the labour force was self-employed, meaning that these people were managing themselves.[23]

Managers are also not confined to manufacturing work, as only 10 percent of Canadians work in manufacturing organizations. Most Canadians (around 78 percent) work in the service sector of the economy, with 21 percent working in public sector jobs (those in the local, provincial, or federal government).[24] Industry Canada defines small and medium-sized enterprises (SMEs) as businesses with fewer than 500 employees. SMEs currently make up 48 percent of Canadian businesses.[25] Supplement 1 following this chapter looks at SMEs in more detail.

## The Types of Organizations

Managers work in a variety of situations, and therefore the people to whom they are held accountable vary considerably. Large organizations in the **private sector** are often

Canada Post is a Crown corporation that has been in operation for more than 150 years serving more than 15 million Canadian addresses. Its 69 000+ full- and part-time employees run the country's most extensive distribution network, which includes 6500 postal outlets, 20 sorting plants, 500 letter carrier depots, and about 6800 vehicles.[26]

**publicly held**, which means that their shares are available on the stock exchange for public trading. Managers of publicly held companies report to a board of directors that is responsible to shareholders (also known as stockholders). There are also numerous **privately held organizations** (whose shares are not available on the stock exchange), both large and small. Privately held organizations can be individually owned, family-owned, or owned by some other group of individuals. A number of managers work in the **nonprofit sector**, where the emphasis is on providing charity or services rather than on making a profit. Examples of such organizations include the SPCA (Society for the Prevention of Cruelty to Animals), Toronto's Royal Ontario Museum, and Vancouver's Bard on the Beach Festival. Other organizational forms, such as **nongovernmental organizations (NGOs)**, partnerships, and cooperatives, also require managers. Many of these nonprofit organizations are referred to as SMOs (small and medium-sized organizations). Supplement 1 will compare SMOs and SMEs in Canada.

Many managers work in the **public sector** as **civil servants** for the local, provincial, or federal government. The challenges of managing within government departments can be quite different from the challenges of managing in publicly held organizations. Critics argue that working for governments is less demanding because there are few measurable performance objectives, allowing employees to feel less accountable for their actions.

Some managers and employees work for **Crown corporations**, such as Canada Post, the CBC, and the Business Development Bank of Canada. Crown corporations are structured like private sector corporations and have boards of directors, chief executive officers (CEOs), and so on, but are owned by governments rather than shareholders. Employees in Crown corporations are not civil servants, and managers in Crown corporations are more independent than the senior bureaucrats who manage government departments.

Many of Canada's larger organizations are actually subsidiaries of American parent organizations (e.g., Sears, Safeway, General Motors, and Ford Motor Company). Their managers often report to American top managers and are not always free to set their own goals and targets. Conflicts can arise when Canadian managers and the American managers to whom they report do not agree on how things should be done.

## WHY STUDY MANAGEMENT?

You may be wondering why you need to study management. If you are an accounting major, a marketing major, or any major other than management, you may not understand how studying management will help you in your career. We can explain the value of studying management by looking at the universality of management, the reality of work, and how management applies to anyone wanting to be self-employed.

**1.4** Explain Does studying management make a difference?

---

**private sector**
The part of the economy run by organizations that are free from direct government control; enterprises in this sector operate to make a profit.

**publicly held organization**
A company whose shares are available on the stock exchange for public trading by brokers/dealers.

**privately held organizations**
Companies whose shares are not available on the stock exchange but are privately held.

**nonprofit sector**
The part of the economy run by organizations that operate for purposes other than making a profit (that is, providing charity or services).

**nongovernmental organization (NGO)**
A nongovernmental organization that emphasizes humanitarian issues, development, and sustainability.

**public sector**
The part of the economy directly controlled by government.

**civil servants**
People who work in a local, provincial, or federal government department.

**Crown corporations**
Commercial companies owned by the government but independently managed.

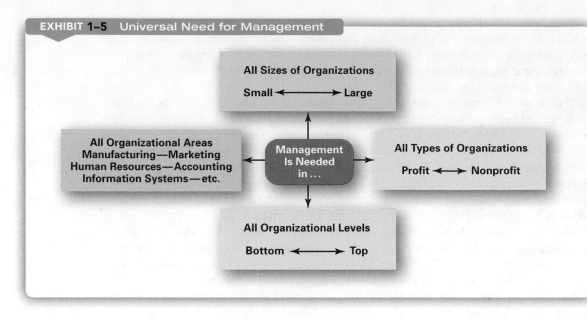

**EXHIBIT 1–5** Universal Need for Management

## The Universality of Management

Just how universal is the need for management in organizations? We can say with absolute certainty that management is needed in all types and sizes of organizations, at all organizational levels, in all organizational work areas, and in all organizations, no matter what countries they are located in. This reality is known as the **universality of management** (see Exhibit 1-5). Managers in all these settings will plan, organize, lead, and control. However, management is not done the same way in all settings. The differences between what a supervisor in a software applications–testing facility at Microsoft does and what the CEO of Microsoft does are a matter of degree and emphasis, not of function. Because both are managers, both will plan, organize, lead, and control, but how they do so will differ.

Since management is universally needed in all organizations, we have a vested interest in improving the way organizations are managed. Why? We interact with organizations every single day of our lives. Are you irritated when none of the salespeople in a department store seems interested in helping you? Do you get annoyed when you call your computer's technical help desk because your CD-ROM drive is no longer working, go through seven voice menus, and then get put on hold for 15 minutes? These situations are examples of problems created by poor management. Organizations that are well managed—and we will share many examples of these—develop a loyal customer base, grow, and prosper. Those that are poorly managed find themselves with a declining customer base and reduced revenues. By studying management, you will be able to recognize poor management and work to get it corrected. In addition, you will be able to recognize good management and encourage it, whether it is in an organization with which you are simply interacting or an organization in which you are employed.

## The Reality of Work

Most of you, once you graduate and begin your careers, will either manage or be managed. This reality is another reason why you should study management. For those who plan on management careers, an understanding of the management process forms the foundation on which to build management skills. For those of you who do not see yourselves in management positions, this same understanding will help you work more effectively with your future managers. Also, assuming that you will have to work for a living and recognizing that you are very likely to work in an organization, you will probably have some managerial responsibilities, even if you are not managers. Our experience tells us that you can gain a great deal of insight into the way your manager behaves and the internal workings of organizations by studying management. You do not have to aspire to be a manager to gain something valuable from a course in management.

## Self-Employment

Practise

You may decide that you want to run your own business rather than work for someone else. This type of employment will require that you manage yourself, and may involve managing other people as well. Thus, an understanding of management is equally important, whether you are a manager in someone else's business or running your own business.

**universality of management**
The reality that management is needed in all types and sizes of organizations, at all organizational levels, in all organizational work areas, and in organizations in all countries around the globe.

## Summary of Learning Objectives

 **What makes someone a manager?** Managers work with and through other people by coordinating employee work activity in order to accomplish organizational goals. Managers may have personal goals, but management is not about *personal* achievement—it is about helping *others* achieve for the benefit of the organization as a whole.

As we saw with Brian Scudamore, he sees his role as a cheerleader to help everyone in the organization do a better job.

**1.2 What is management and what do managers do?** Management is coordinating work activities of people so that they are done efficiently and effectively. Efficiency means "doing things right" and getting things done at the least cost. Effectiveness means "doing the right things" and completing activities that will help achieve the organization's goals. To do their jobs, managers plan, organize, lead, and control. In other words, they set goals and plan how to achieve those goals; they figure out what tasks need to be done and who should do them; they motivate individuals to achieve goals and communicate effectively with others; and they put accountability measures into place to make sure that goals are achieved efficiently and effectively.

In Brian Scudamore's role as CEO of 1-800-GOT-JUNK?, he sets the goals for the overall organization, working with the various franchise partners. One of the challenges he faces is determining how rapidly his company can expand without diluting its brand.

**1.3 What characteristics define an organization?** There is no single type of organization. Managers work in a variety of organizations, both large and small. They also work in a variety of industries, including manufacturing and the service sector. The organizations they work for can be publicly held (meaning shares are traded on the stock exchange and managers are responsible to shareholders), privately held (meaning shares are not available to the public), public sector

(where the government is the employer), or nonprofit (where the emphasis is on providing charity or services rather than on making a profit).

Brian Scudamore owns his company and thus is ultimately responsible to himself. Most managers report to someone else.

**1.4 Does studying management make a difference?** There are many reasons why students end up in management courses. Some of you are already managers and are hoping to learn more about the subject. Some of you hope to be managers someday. Some of you may never have thought about being managers. Career aspirations are only one reason to study management, however. Any organization you encounter will have managers, and it is often useful to understand their responsibilities, challenges, and experiences. Understanding management also helps us improve organizations.

### SNAPSHOT SUMMARY

 **Who Are Managers?**
Types of Managers

 **What Is Management and What Do Managers Do?**
Efficiency and Effectiveness
Management Functions
Management Roles
Management Skills

 **What Is an Organization?**
The Size of Organizations
The Types of Organizations

 **Why Study Management?**
The Universality of Management
The Reality of Work
Self-Employment

# MyManagementLab® Learning Resources

## Resources

Explore and enhance your understanding of key
chapter topics through the following online resources:

- Student PowerPoints
- Audio Summary of Chapter
- ROLLS
- CBC Videos for Part 1
- MySearchLab

Visit the **Study Plan** area to test your progress with **Pre-Tests** and **Post-Tests**.

Build on your knowledge and practise real-world applications
using the following online activities:

## Interpret

- Opening Case Activity:
  The Management
  Functions
- Review and Apply:
  Solutions to Interpret
  section questions and
  activities
- Glossary Flashcards

## Analyze

- Opening Case Activity:
  Focus on Management
  Skills
- Review and Apply:
  Solutions to Analyze
  section questions and
  activities
- Self-Assessment Library

## Practise

- Opening Case Activity:
  Pearson Simulation—
  What is Management?
- Review and Apply:
  Solutions to Practice
  section questions and
  activities
- Decision Making
  Simulation:
  What is Management?

# Interpret What You Have Read

1. How does a manager's job change with his or her level in the organization?

2. What four common activities compose the functions approach to management? Briefly describe each of them.

3. What are the three categories of management roles proposed by Mintzberg? Provide an example of each.

4. What are the three skills that affect managerial effectiveness?

5. How is management universal?

# Analyze What You Have Read

1. Are effective organizations always efficient? Discuss. If you had to choose between being effective or being efficient, which would you say is more important? Why?

2. In today's economic environment, which is more important to organizations—efficiency or effectiveness? Explain your choice.

3. Contrast planning, organizing, leading, and controlling with Mintzberg's 10 management roles.

4. Is your instructor a manager? Discuss in terms of planning, organizing, leading, and controlling, and of Mintzberg's managerial roles.

5. In what ways would the job activities of an owner of an automotive repair shop that employs two people and the Executive Director of the Canadian Cancer Society be similar?

6. Some individuals today have the title of project leader. They manage projects of various sizes and durations and must coordinate the talents of many people to accomplish their goals, but none of the employees on their projects reports directly to them. Can these project leaders really be considered managers if they have no employees over whom they have direct authority? Discuss.

# Assess Your Skills

## HOW MOTIVATED AM I TO MANAGE?

For each of the following statements, circle the level of agreement or disagreement that you personally feel:[27]

> 1 = Strongly Disagree   2 = Moderately Disagree   3 = Slightly Disagree   4 = Neither Agree nor Disagree
> 5 = Slightly Agree   6 = Moderately Agree   7 = Strongly Agree

| | |
|---|---|
| **1.** I have a generally positive attitude toward those holding positions of authority over me. | 1 2 3 4 5 6 7 |
| **2.** I enjoy competition and striving to win for myself and my work group. | 1 2 3 4 5 6 7 |
| **3.** I like to tell others what to do and have no problem with imposing sanctions to enforce my directives. | 1 2 3 4 5 6 7 |
| **4.** I like being active, assertive, and protecting the members of my work group. | 1 2 3 4 5 6 7 |
| **5.** I enjoy the idea of standing out from the group, behaving in a unique manner, and being highly visible. | 1 2 3 4 5 6 7 |
| **6.** I am willing to perform routine, day-to-day administrative tasks and duties. | 1 2 3 4 5 6 7 |

**SCORING KEY**   Add up your responses to the six items.

**ANALYSIS AND INTERPRETATION**

Not everyone is motivated to perform managerial functions. This instrument taps six components that have been found to be related to managerial success, especially in larger organizations. These are a favourable attitude toward authority; a desire to compete; a desire to exercise power; assertiveness; a desire for a distinctive position; and a willingness to engage in repetitive tasks.

Scores on this instrument will range from 6 to 42. Arbitrary cut-offs suggest that scores of 6 to 18 indicate low motivation to manage; 19 to 29 is moderate motivation; and 30 and above is high motivation.

What meaning can you draw from your score? It gives you an idea of how comfortable you would be doing managerial activities. Note, however, that this instrument emphasizes tasks associated with managing in larger and more bureaucratic organizations. A low or moderate score may indicate that you are more suited to managing in a small firm, in an organic organization, or in entrepreneurial situations.

**More Self-Assessments**

To learn more about your skills, abilities, and interests, take the following self-assessments on the MyManagementLab®:

- I.A.4.—How Well Do I Handle Ambiguity?
- I.E.1.—What's My Emotional Intelligence Score?
- I.E.4.—Am I Likely to Become an Entrepreneur?
- III.C.1.—How Well Do I Respond to Turbulent Change? (This exercise also appears in Chapter 12 on pages 354–355.)

# Practise What You Have Learned

## DILEMMA

Management is about achieving the highest possible return given the investment of money, people, time, and other resources. It is also about achieving results in the most efficient manner. Think about where you hope to be in your life five years from now (that is, your major goal). What is your competitive advantage for achieving your goal? Your education is a way of managing yourself and developing your career, which helps you achieve that goal. Here are some other things you can do to get the most out of yourself:

## BECOMING A MANAGER

- What is a better way of completing this task?
- What is my 80/20 rule—what 20 percent of my efforts are resulting in 80 percent of my outputs?

- What is the best use of my time today?
- How can I make better use of the abilities and time of my colleagues, subordinates, and superiors?
- Am I thinking for myself as much as I could?

## DEVELOPING YOUR INTERPERSONAL SKILLS

Earlier you had a chance to assess your skills in terms of Mintzberg's 10 Management Roles. You can learn to be more effective at managing people by using the following tips to enhance those management roles:

| Mintzberg's 10 Roles | How to Enhance Your Management Skills |
|---|---|
| Figurehead | Lead by example, improve your reputation, and be a good role model. |
| Leader | Improve your emotional intelligence and earn respect from your team. |
| Liaison | Work on your professional networking skills; use tools such as LinkedIn. |
| Monitor | Keep up to date with industry news by learning how to gather and process information more effectively. |
| Disseminator | Develop your communication skills and learn how best to share information through written communication and informal briefings. |
| Spokesperson | Work on your presentation skills; attend conferences and workshops. |
| Entrepreneur | Develop your creativity and problem-solving skills; learn more about change management. |
| Disturbance handler | Learn about mediation and conflict resolution. |
| Resource allocator | Practise managing budgets and prioritizing your time effectively. |
| Negotiator | Practise with role playing to learn about win-win negotiations. |

## YOUR ESSENTIAL MANAGEMENT READING LIST

Learning from key management experts can help us understand today's management theory and practice. Here is a list of some of the more influential management books:

- *Theory Z* (William Ouchi)
- *Competitive Advantage* (Michael Porter)

- *In Search of Excellence* (Tom Peters and Robert Waterman)
- *Total Quality Management* (W. Edward Deming)
- *The Essential Drucker* and *The Daily Drucker* (Peter Drucker)

# Team Exercises

## 3BL: THE TRIPLE BOTTOM LINE

### WHAT ARE THE BUSINESS CASE BENEFITS OF 3BL?

The components of the Triple Bottom Line are *people*, *profit*, and *planet*. The focus on *people* deals with internal employee aspects such as diversity, empowerment, and health and safety. It also expands to charitable contributions and corporate relations. Organizations that focus on more than the financial bottom line typically generate *profit* through ethical behaviour as well as cost savings through sustainable practices. The *planet* element looks beyond environmentalism and finds eco-efficiency in operations, manufacturing, and product development.[28] Over the next eleven chapters, we will examine 3BL in practical circumstances.

### THINKING STRATEGICALLY ABOUT 3BL

The business case benefits of 3BL are illustrated in the table below:

| Business Case Benefits | Business Case Components |
|---|---|
| Reduced recruiting costs | A stronger reputation means stronger employer branding |
| Reduced turnover costs | Higher employee morale decreases attrition |
| Increased productivity | Higher employee moral leads to higher productivity, increased sustainability awareness, and more innovation |
| Reduced manufacturing expenses | Cost savings, continual improvement |
| Reduced resource consumption | Reduced water, energy, and consumables expenses |
| Increased revenue and market share | Access to markets and customers, higher customer loyalty, improved relationships with regulators |
| Reduced risk/easier financing | Reduced risks of non-sustainable practices, improved stakeholder relations, better reputation in financial industry |

Adapted from B. Willard, *The Next Sustainability Wave* (Canada: New Society Publishers, 2005), p. 130.

## MANAGERIAL SKILLS

Exhibit 1-1 on page 7 lists the three essential managerial skills (conceptual, human, and technical) and the three main levels of manager (lower-level, middle-level, and top-level). Form small groups of four to five students and identify the skills required in each of the three levels. Estimate the level of complexity of tasks performed by these managers. As a group, be prepared to explain the skills that good managers at each level are most likely to utilize.

| | Lower-level manager | Middle-level manager | Top-level manager |
|---|---|---|---|
| Conceptual skills | | | |
| Human skills | | | |
| Technical skills | | | |

## BE THE CONSULTANT

In teams of four to five people, discuss the following scenario. One person will report back to the class on your recommendations.

Your student association has decided to open a new campus comedy club. They have strong financial backing with a bank loan of $750 000. They have little experience in the hospitality industry or with managing small businesses and have asked your team for advice and support. A student employment program from Human Resources and Skills Development Canada has provided each of you with a six-month contract to help get the club up and running.

How will you split up the key management functions of planning, organizing, leading, and controlling? What are three key decisions that you will have to make in each of the four functions that will help the comedy club become successful? What metrics will you use to evaluate the effectiveness of your managerial roles at the end of six months?

# Business Cases

## SHOPIFY

It may surprise you that two snowboard enthusiasts who simply wanted a better way to sell their snowboards online have created an e-commerce platform that now has over $275 million in sales and hosts more than 20 000 online retailers, including Pixar, Angry Birds, and the Foo Fighters.[29]

Tobias Lütke, CEO and founder, has created a business that allows companies of all sizes to set up their own online store, taking a task that used to take months and trimming it down to as little as half an hour. Shopify takes care of everything behind the scenes in return for a subscription fee and transaction fees.

The accolades have poured in. In 2011, for the second consecutive year, the *Ottawa Business Journal* named Shopify Ottawa's fastest growing company.[30] It was also named one of Fast Company's 50 Most Innovative Companies.[31]

Shopify focuses on developing entrepreneurs, both within its own company and externally. It launched a Build-A-Business contest, inviting online entrepreneurs to dream up something to sell using Shopify and compete to bring in the most revenue within two months for the chance to win more than $500 000 in prizes. "Our first two competitions were extremely successful. In total 4438 new businesses were created, selling over $15 million worth of products," said Tobias Lütke, founder and CEO of Shopify.[32] Harley Finkelstein, Shopify's chief platform officer, is a judge for the Future Entrepreneurial Leaders (FuEL) Awards.[33]

Shopify's commitment to its people is evident even in the little details. It has moved for the second time in a year to accommodate the recently doubled workforce of 70. Its new office is in Ottawa's trendy Market area, so staff members have a great variety of fun places to eat and play after work. The office itself is a mix of glass and exposed brick, with open concept workspaces.

"We want you to be able to produce your best work here at Shopify. You can wear whatever clothing you like, start work late in the morning, and play video games whenever you need a break."[34] Shopify has many benefits and perks, including very popular company video game tournaments, share options for all employees, daily catered lunches, and even the chance to go to any conference of their choice at the company's expense.

The company has expanded through acquisitions and partnerships to extend its capabilities on mobile devices and through cloud computing. The company financed its initial growth through angel investors like John Phillips. In 2010, it took on $7 million from three venture capitalists.[35]

"Our mission continues to be to make it as easy as possible for retailers of all sizes to start and run a business online," said Tobias Lütke.[36] That mission also extends to its employees—hard-working, talented individuals who get things done and always push themselves to improve.

# Small and Medium-Sized Enterprises and Organizations

## WHAT IS A SMALL AND MEDIUM-SIZED ENTERPRISE?

Small and medium-sized enterprises (SMEs) refers to all businesses with fewer than 500 employees, whereas firms with 500 or more employees are classified as "large" businesses.

Canada has more than 1.5 million SMEs, which generate close to half of Canada's private-sector gross domestic product (GDP). SMEs account for the vast majority of businesses in Canada, represent over 60 percent of private-sector employment, and generate more than 80 percent of new job creation.[1] They are active in all sectors of the Canadian economy, with two-thirds in the service sector (64 percent), one-fifth in the goods-producing sector (21 percent), and a significant number (15 percent) in the resource-based sector.[2]

The majority of SMEs are self-managed enterprises, offering entrepreneurs the pride of personal achievement, the ability to help their customers and clients, the benefits of being their own boss, and the opportunity to make more money.[3] Their biggest challenges for SMEs are finding new markets and customers, dealing with finances, and handling government regulations and paperwork. Entrepreneurs also work longer hours, logging an average of 48.7 hours per week. Thirty-five percent of entrepreneurs work more than 50 hours per week, compared with five percent of employees.[4]

While about 75 percent of SMEs in Canada have been in business for five years or more, failure rates are relatively high in the first few years after start-up, with two out of five firms not surviving beyond their second year of operation.[5] Debt financing is the primary source of financing for SMEs, with debt accounting for 75 percent of their long-term financing structure. SMEs use more informal financing sources, including owner savings and retained earnings. Use of government financing is less important for SMEs than other types of financing.[6]

### Key Findings[7]

- Canada's 1.5 million SMEs generate 43 percent of private sector GDP.
- Eighty-six percent of Canadian exporters are SMEs, generating $80 billion in exports.
- Ninety-eight percent of SMEs have less than 100 employees, and 80 percent are either self-employed businesses or micro organizations (1–4 employees).
- Between 1985 and 1999, SMEs created 661,000 jobs, while large businesses shed 348,000.
- Forty-one percent of Canada's entrepreneurs have previously owned a business.
- Forty-six percent of SMEs had some degree of female ownership.

## WHAT IS A SMALL AND MEDIUM-SIZED ORGANIZATION?

Small and medium-sized organizations (SMOs) are community organizations that, like SMEs, have fewer than 500 paid staff. SMOs comprise nearly 99 percent of nonprofits in Canada. The term "community organization" is used broadly to include a wide variety of nonprofit organizations in Canada: charitable and voluntary organizations; parapublic organizations such as hospitals and post-secondary education institutions; and social economy organizations, community economic development organizations, and cooperatives.[8]

Imagine Canada, working with a consortium of organizations, conducted the largest survey of nonprofit enterprises in Canada. According to the 2003 survey, Canada has approximately 161 000 nonprofit and voluntary organizations, which generate revenues greater than $100 billion and employ over 2 million people.[9] The organizations are spread throughout Canada, with more than 900 in Prince Edward Island and more than 20 000 in Toronto alone. One-third of all organizations are hospitals, universities, and colleges, while sport and recreation organizations comprise another 21 percent.[10] This sector also reports close to 20 million volunteers contributing more than 2 billion volunteer hours per year—the same as 1 million full-time jobs![11] The Capital City Condors have a membership base of 60, whereas the entire Canadian nonprofit sector features 139 million memberships.[12] Exhibit S1-1 shows the economic impact of the nonprofit sector in Canada, compared to other industries.

### Key Findings[13]

- Canada's nonprofit and voluntary sector is the second largest in the world; the Netherlands is the largest, while the United States is fifth.
- Fifty-four percent of the estimated 161 000 nonprofits and charities in Canada are run entirely by volunteers.
- Two million people are employed by these organizations, representing 11.1 percent of the economically active population.
- The nonprofit and voluntary sector represents $79.1 billion or 7.8 percent of the GDP (larger than the automotive or manufacturing industries).
- Forty-nine percent of revenues are from government, although this figure drops to 36 percent when

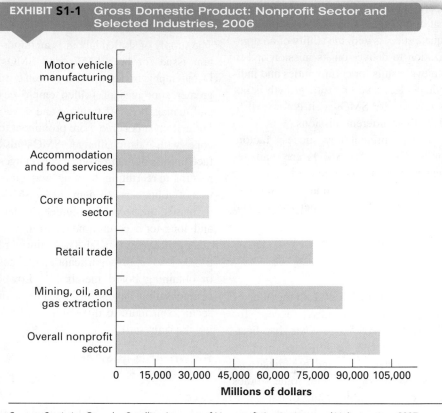

**EXHIBIT S1-1    Gross Domestic Product: Nonprofit Sector and Selected Industries, 2006**

Motor vehicle manufacturing
Agriculture
Accommodation and food services
Core nonprofit sector
Retail trade
Mining, oil, and gas extraction
Overall nonprofit sector

0   15,000   30,000   45,000   60,000   75,000   90,000   105,000
**Millions of dollars**

*Source:* Statistics Canada, *Satellite Account of Non-profit Institutions and Volunteering, 2007,* Catalogue no. 13-015-X (Ottawa: Statistics Canada, 2009), p. 11, http://www.statcan.gc.ca/pub/13-015-x/13-015-x2009000-eng.pdf.

hospitals, universities, and colleges are excluded.
- Canadians contribute more than 2 billion hours annually through SMOs.

Looking at the Canadian nonprofit sector can help us understand that management is very similar in all organizations. SMOs participate fully in social, economic, community, and civic life. They run food banks and homeless shelters, provide child care, build bike paths, and welcome new Canadians to the country. Increasingly, governments at all levels rely on community organizations to delivery essential public services.

SMOs face significant challenges, including increasing service demands, diminishing financial resources, and staff burn-out. They receive most of their revenue from earned income and government sources. Large community organizations represent less than 1 percent of the market, but receive almost one-third of revenues.

## SMEs AND SMOs IN CANADA—KEY CHARACTERISTICS

SMEs and SMOs in Canada have many important similarities as well as significant differences. The key distinction between SMEs and SMOs is whether they seek to generate a profit or are nonprofit. At the same time, successful SMOs are run with a profit mentality to ensure that they remain financially viable. With the rise of social entrepreneurship, the boundaries between SMEs and SMOs may become somewhat blurred.[14]

Another major difference between SMEs and SMOs is their use of volunteers. While some SMEs may have unpaid family members or others who work in the enterprise, volunteers are the life-blood of SMOs. Most SMOs rely heavily on volunteers to deliver their mission.

For SMEs, success is usually defined in terms of growth—in sales, profits, firm size, and market share. SMOs, even those that provide goods and services, typically equate success with the ability of an organization to deliver on its mission and to achieve results for communities and individuals. Revenue or profit growth is not as relevant for SMOs as it is for SMES, given their different missions.

The prominent key success factors for SMEs and for SMOs are management skills and competencies, human resources, access to financing, innovation capacity, and networks and partnerships.

## Management in SMEs and SMOs

Management skills and competencies are integral to business success for SMEs. Research has shown that business failures can be attributed in large part to management and organizational weaknesses. For example, some studies have found that almost half of bankruptcies result from these internal factors rather than external ones.[15]

SMEs require a wide variety of management skills, including leadership, strategic planning, financial and human resources management, communications and marketing, organizational development, entrepreneurial skills, and networking and partnership skills. In the start-up phase, management focuses more on vision, marketing, and communications skills. As a firm expands, financial and human resources management and expertise become more prominent.

Many of these same management skills and competencies are also important for SMOs. SMOs often lack middle management levels, featuring only an executive director and perhaps a few project managers, resulting in a lack of time for planning. The management of issues around the recruitment, training, support, recognition, and retention of volunteers, as well as volunteer burnout, is critically important for community organizations, given that they rely heavily on volunteers to deliver their missions. The ability to work effectively with boards of directors is also a unique management competency.[16]

## Human Resources in SMEs and SMOs

The supply of skilled labour is an important issue for both SMEs and SMOs. Demographic trends will likely mean even greater shortages of skilled employees and managers. Staff training and development must become more prominent to cope with this challenge. SMOs also face unique human resources challenges relating to recruiting, training, and retention of volunteers. As demand for SMOs increases, the need for volunteer leaders and long-term commitments from volunteers becomes crucial. The majority of SMOs also report significant challenges in obtaining board members.[17] Lower compensation levels in the nonprofit sector contribute to difficulties in finding the right staff.

## Financing in SMEs and SMOs

Access to financing is equally critical for both SMEs and SMOs; however, the financing challenges they face are very different. Smaller and start-up organizations have difficulty accessing external financing due to a lack of assets and collateral, smaller profits, and uncertain return-on-investment. A lack of investment capital is a further problem for SMEs in Canada.[18]

SMOs face significant challenges with regard to both *financing* (access to private and commercial revenue sources) and *funding* (grants and contributions from government/public sources for goods and services provided). Typically funding is tied to projects and does not cover the operational, administrative, and overhead costs. SMOs must absorb or finance these costs from other sources, which limits their financial capability and flexibility.

## Innovation in SMEs and SMOs

Innovation applies to both SMEs and SMOs in terms of new and improved products, services, and processes. For SMEs, innovation is seen as the single most important factor for growth and success, and is usually measured in research and development (R&D). SMEs in Canada

spend much less on R&D than larger firms, but as a percentage of revenue R&D spending by SMEs is much greater.[19] Since SMEs have fewer resources, they may select innovation opportunities missed by larger firms. Their organizational flexibility can be a big advantage, but the ability to bring these innovations to market and make money on them is more challenging than for larger firms.

For SMOs, innovation is their lifeblood. Through their strong local networks, hands-on experience, and community interaction, they are able to find innovative solutions to community and individual needs. The bigger challenge is how to apply these community-based innovations to other areas of activity and to other communities and regions.

The Peter Drucker Canadian Foundation has studied hundreds of examples of innovation by Canadian nonprofit organizations and has identified six key criteria for successful innovation, shown in Exhibit S1-2.

## Networks and Partnerships in SMEs and SMOs

Networks and partnerships are critical for organizations to access information, knowledge, expertise, and technology. Firms can use these partnerships to help predict and take advantage of strategic opportunities, and to mobilize available resources. They are also important factors for fostering innovation.[20]

SMEs in Canada benefit from organizations such as local and national Chambers of Commerce, boards of trade, and the Canadian Federation of Independent Businesses (CFIB). This infrastructure fosters the exchange of knowledge and expertise, as well as the development of collaboration among firms for common purposes. SMOs have much less access to infrastructure networks. Networks such as the Calgary Chamber of Charities or the British Columbia Voluntary Organizations Coalition are deliberately cross-sector and provide opportunities for collaboration and collective action, but the majority of SMOs continue to operate alone.

**EXHIBIT S1-2**   Criteria for Successful Innovation in SMOs

| | |
|---|---|
| Adaptability | The extent to which an organization has had to adapt innovative practices to deliver programs and services |
| Criticality | How mission-critical the activity is for the association |
| Sustainability | The viability of the program/service |
| Replicability | The ability to duplicate the program/service in another organization |
| Impact | How the programs/services help to improve the organization's work |
| Partnerships | Building partnerships between organizations in the sector or across sectors |

# CHAPTER 2 Environmental Constraints on Managers

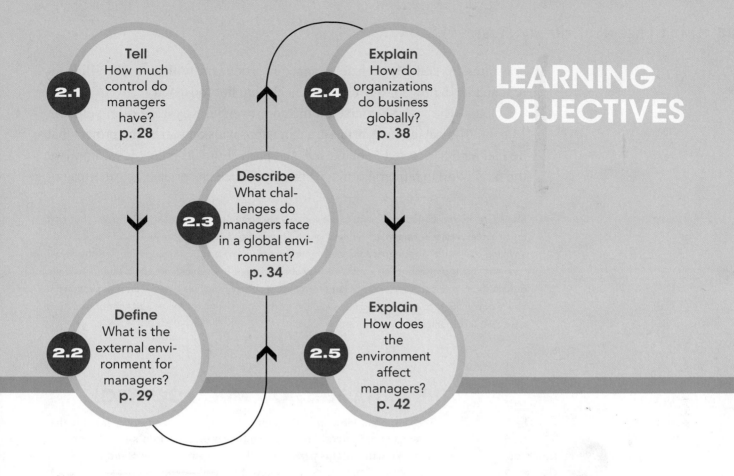

**2.1 Tell** How much control do managers have? p. 28

**2.4 Explain** How do organizations do business globally? p. 38

**2.3 Describe** What challenges do managers face in a global environment? p. 34

**2.2 Define** What is the external environment for managers? p. 29

**2.5 Explain** How does the environment affect managers? p. 42

Social media was a major force in putting pressure on President Barack Obama and the US government in January 2012 to scrap the multi-billion dollar Keystone pipeline project designed to carry oil from Alberta to the Gulf of Mexico. Environmental groups took to Facebook and Twitter to lobby against the deal, despite approval for the project from Canada's National Energy Board and the US Environmental Protection Agency.[1] The pipeline project quickly became a hot topic in the US election. In 2011, Canada supplied the United States with 2.1 million barrels of oil and 8.9 billion cubic feet of gas a day, making Canada the largest supplier of imported US oil and gas.

TransCanada managers were forced to re-evaluate their markets for oil.[2] This reality caused a shift in focus to the Asian market generally and to China specifically. As Obama backtracked, the pace of Asian investment in the Canadian energy sector quickened. Sinopec acquired Daylight Energy for $2.1 billion. Mitsubishi invested $2.9 billion in a joint venture with Encana on its BC gas assets. Both companies are looking at the potential to ship gas to BC for the Asian liquefied natural gas market. PetroChina expanded its oil sands investments by acquiring oil sands assets from Athabasca Oil Sands Corporation and a 20 percent interest in Shell's Groundbirch operations.[3]

As companies like TransCanada and Enbridge diversify away from the United States to Asia, Canada will receive two additional benefits: better oil prices and access to cheap Asian capital. According to a report by oil

**Think About It**

Should large corporations have to report the details of all negotiations concerning Canadian natural resources? Put yourself in the shoes of TransCanada's CEO. What responsibilities do organizations have when negotiating international contracts for natural resources?

consultant Wood Mackenzie, Canadian producers will lose $8 billion in revenue a year by 2020 if US bottlenecks are not loosened.

Obama did reverse course on the controversial Keystone oil pipeline in March 2012, saying he was fast-tracking approvals on part of the project that he had earlier rejected. Obama said the project would create jobs, improve the flow of oil to refineries, and eventually reduce gas prices for Americans.[4]

Managers at TransCanada are responsible for overseeing the production and sales of oil. But how much actual impact does a manager have on an organization's success or failure? Can managers do anything they want? These questions raise more general questions: Do managers control their environment, or are they controlled by it? Are they affected more by circumstances outside or inside the organization? In this chapter, we consider the impact of an organization's external environment on the ability of managers to act. We begin our exploration by considering the degree of control managers have over an organization's performance.

# THE MANAGER: HOW MUCH CONTROL?

**Tell**
**2.1** How much control do managers have?

The dominant view in management theory and society in general is that managers are directly responsible for an organization's success or failure. We will call this perspective the **omnipotent view of management**. The view of managers as omnipotent is consistent with the stereotypical picture of the take-charge business executive who can overcome any obstacle in carrying out the organization's goals. In the omnipotent view, when organizations perform poorly, someone has to be held accountable regardless of the reasons, and in our society that "someone" is the manager. Of course, when things go well, we need someone to praise. So managers also get the credit—even if they had little to do with achieving positive outcomes.

In contrast, some observers have argued that much of an organization's success or failure is due to external forces outside managers' control. For example, when tunnelling for the Canada Line transit system began tearing up Vancouver's Cambie Street, the street became noisy, there was no parking, and the area was a traffic nightmare. Once a busy shopping area, customers stopped coming to the stores and restaurants. The **symbolic view of management** would suggest that the loss of sales was not the managers' fault. The symbolic view says that a manager's ability to affect outcomes is influenced and constrained by external factors.[5] In this view, expecting managers to significantly affect an organization's performance is unreasonable. Instead, an organization's results are strongly influenced by factors outside the control of managers. These factors include, for example, the economy, customers, government policies, competitors' actions, industry conditions, control over proprietary technology, and decisions made by previous managers.

In reality, managers are neither helpless nor all powerful. Internal and external constraints that restrict a manager's decision-making options exist within every organization. Internal constraints arise from the organization's culture (which we discuss in Chapter 11) and external constraints come from the organization's environment, as shown in Exhibit 2-1.

**EXHIBIT 2–1  Parameters of Managerial Discretion**

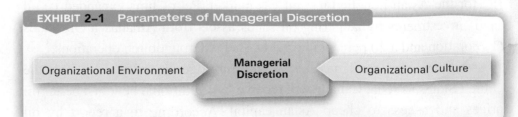

Organizational Environment → **Managerial Discretion** ← Organizational Culture

In our chapter-opening vignette we saw how the external environment can place constraints on managers' ability to control the success of an organization. In the remainder of this chapter, we will explore the idea of how an organization's internal and external environment imposes constraints on managers. In other chapters, however, we will learn that these constraints do not mean that a manager's hands are tied; managers can and do influence their culture and environment.

## THE EXTERNAL ENVIRONMENT

After the United States initially blocked the Keystone XL pipeline project, Canada changed gears, and Prime Minister Stephen Harper visited China to encourage Chinese investment in the oil sector. Harper supports regulatory approval for Northern Gateway and other proposed oil sands pipelines.[6]

**2.2** **Define** What is the external environment for managers?

### Think About It

What forces and institutions outside of TransCanada will the company need to work with as they develop the oil pipeline project?

Some viewed Canada's overtures to China as leverage in negotiations with the United States. However, David Goldwyn, a former energy official in the Obama administration, does not view China's investment in the Canadian oil sands as a threat. "In the short term it provides additional investment to increase Canadian supply; that's a good thing. Longer-term, if Canadian oil goes to China, that means China's demand is being met by a non-OPEC country, and that's a good thing for global oil supply."[7]

As we discussed in Chapter 1, management is no longer constrained by national borders. Managers in all sizes and types of organizations are faced with the opportunities and challenges of managing in a global environment. For example, global sourcing of ingredients can provide a competitive advantage for food processors, but can also come with risks if the foreign country's food inspection standards are lower than those in North America.

The term **external environment** refers to forces and institutions outside the organization that potentially can affect its performance. The external environment is made up of three components, as shown in Exhibit 2-2 on page 31: the specific environment, the general environment, and the global environment.

In 2008, the impact of defaults on subprime mortgages in the United States started to have a ripple effect throughout the world. The impact on employment and earnings in Canada was huge, even though Canadian bankers had been far more conservative in their mortgage products. This example illustrates some of the forces in the environment that play a major role in shaping managers' actions. In this section, we identify some of the critical environmental forces that affect managers and show how they constrain managerial discretion.

### The Specific Environment

The **specific environment** represents the micro level and includes those external forces that have a direct and immediate impact on managers' decisions and actions and are directly relevant to the achievement of the organization's goals. Each organization's specific environment is unique and changes with conditions. For example, Timex and Rolex both make

---

**omnipotent view of management**
The view that managers are directly responsible for an organization's success or failure.

**symbolic view of management**
The view that managers have only a limited effect on substantive organizational outcomes because

of the large number of factors outside their control.

**external environment**
Outside forces and institutions that can potentially affect the organization's performance.

**specific environment**
The part of the external environment that is directly relevant to the achievement of an organization's goals.

Canadians spent $2.2 billion on bottled water in 2011,[8] but complaints by environmentalist David Suzuki and others that bottled water is not good for the environment have slowly started to change individuals' views about drinking bottled water.[9] The City of Toronto passed a comprehensive ban on bottled water in 2008, which led to many other municipalities in Canada following suit. The result has had a major impact on the big three bottled water manufacturers: Nestlé, Coca Cola, and Pepsi.[10]

watches, but their specific environments differ because they operate in distinctly different market niches. Managers are affected by the nature of the relationships they have with external stakeholders. The more obvious and secure these relationships become, the more influence managers will have over organizational outcomes.

Who are **stakeholders**? We define them as groups in the organization's external environment that are affected by and/or have an effect on the organization's decisions and actions. These groups have a stake in or are significantly influenced by what the organization does. In turn, these groups can influence the organization. For example, think of the groups that might be affected by the decisions and actions of Starbucks' managers—coffee bean farmers, employees, specialty-coffee competitors, local communities, and so forth. Some of these stakeholders may also affect the decisions and actions of Starbucks' managers. Starbucks recently changed the way it purchased coffee beans after activists pressured the company to stop buying from plantations that treated their workers poorly. *Stakeholders* should not be confused with *shareholders*, although shareholders are also stakeholders in an organization. **Shareholders** (also known as stockholders) own one or more shares of stock in a company.

What types of stakeholders might an organization have to deal with? The inner circle of Exhibit 2-2 identifies some of the most common. Note that these stakeholders include internal and external groups. Why? Because both can affect what an organization does and how it operates. In this chapter, however, we are primarily interested in the external groups and their impact on managers' discretion in planning, organizing, leading, and controlling. We will address the equally important issue of internal stakeholders, primarily employees, throughout the rest of the textbook.

Why is stakeholder-relationship management important? Why should managers care about stakeholders?[11] Taking stakeholders' interests into account in management decisions can lead to organizational outcomes such as improved predictability of environmental changes, more successful innovations, a greater degree of trust among stakeholders, and greater organizational flexibility to reduce the impact of change. But does this management style affect organizational performance? The answer is yes! Management researchers who have looked at this issue are finding that managers of high-performing companies tend to consider the interests of all major stakeholder groups as they make decisions.[12]

Another reason given for managing external stakeholder relationships is that it is the "right" thing to do. What does this mean? It means that an organization depends on these external groups as sources of inputs (resources) and as outlets for outputs (goods and services), and managers should consider these external groups' interests as they make decisions and take actions.

The more critical the stakeholder and the more uncertain the environment, the more managers need to rely on establishing explicit stakeholder partnerships rather than just acknowledging their existence.

What are the key forces that make up the specific environment? The main ones are customers, suppliers, and competitors.

**CUSTOMERS** An organization exists to meet the needs of customers who use its output. Customers represent potential uncertainty to an organization. Their tastes can change, or they can become dissatisfied with the organization's products or service. They may also have an interest in a more direct relationship with the organization. Samsung Electronics Canada is following the model of Apple and Sony to open retail outlets throughout the country to provide customers with more access to the brand and the products.

**SUPPLIERS** Managers seek to ensure a steady flow of needed inputs (supplies) at the lowest price possible. A limit on an organization's supplies or a delay in delivery can constrain

**EXHIBIT 2–2** The External Environment

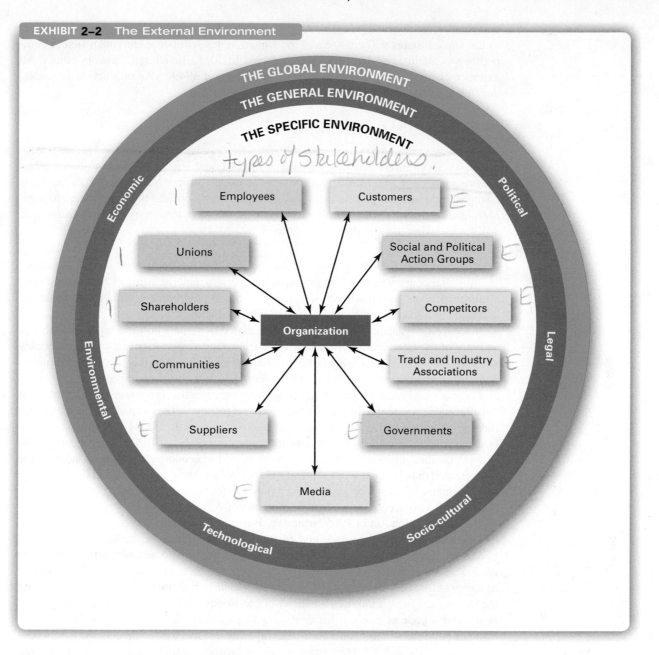

managers' decisions and actions. Walt Disney World, for example, must make sure it has supplies of soft drinks, computers, food, flowers and other nursery stock, concrete, paper products, and so forth. Suppliers also provide financial and labour inputs. A lack of qualified nurses continues to be a serious problem plaguing health care providers, affecting their ability to meet demand and keep service levels high. Virtually all of Alberta's oil and natural gas exports go to the United States, making Alberta a key supplier for the US government.

**COMPETITORS** All organizations—profit and nonprofit—have one or more competitors. The major television broadcast networks used to control what you watched on television. Now they face competition from digital cable, satellite, and the Internet, all of which offer

**stakeholders**
Any constituencies in the organization's external environment that are affected by the organization's decisions and actions.

**shareholders**
Individuals or companies that own stocks in a business.

customers a much broader choice. As US oil production grows, Alberta's role as supplier to the United States will change and the United States will become a much fiercer competitor to Canadian oil and natural gas exports. In 2011, the United States became a net exporter of petroleum products for the first time since 1949.[13] As production increases, dependence on Alberta petroleum will decrease.

## The General Environment

The **general environment** represents the macro level and includes the broad political, economic, socio-cultural, technological, environmental, and legal conditions that *may* affect the organization. Changes in any of these areas usually do not have as large an impact as changes in the specific environment, but managers must consider them as they plan, organize, lead, and control. PESTEL is an acronym for the six macro environmental factors and will be discussed in more detail in Chapter 3.

**POLITICAL CONDITIONS**  Political conditions include the political climate, the general stability of a country in which an organization operates, and the attitudes that elected government officials hold toward business. The political environment influences businesses and also has a major impact on consumer confidence and spending.

In Canada, organizations have generally operated in a stable political environment. The stability of the Canadian political landscape allows businesses to invest in and enter new markets. One challenging aspect of the Canadian marketplace is the government policies concerning taxation and regulation, which may vary from province to province.

Organizations spend a great deal of time and money meeting government regulations, but the effects of these regulations go beyond time and money.[14] They can also reduce managerial discretion by limiting the choices available to managers. In a 2004 COMPAS survey of business leaders, most respondents cited interprovincial trade barriers as a significant hurdle to doing business in this country, calling the barriers "bad economics." One respondent to the survey noted that the federal government fails "to realize that in today's global economy, our real 'competitors' are no longer in the next province (or the next city), not even in the United States or Mexico but are the emerging economies of Asia and Europe."[15]

The Competition Act of 1985 created the Bureau of Competition Policy (now called the Competition Bureau) to oversee and encourage competition in Canada. For example, if two major competing companies consider merging, they will come under scrutiny from the bureau. Heather Reisman and Gerry Schwartz's purchase of Chapters in 2001 needed approval before they could merge Chapters with their Indigo bookstores. Before approving the merger, the bureau imposed a number of conditions, including the sale or closing of 20 stores and a code of conduct for dealing with publishers. The code of conduct was the result of publishers' complaints about the way Chapters had treated them in the past. These rules affected the way Chapters Indigo could do business until 2006. Beyond that time, the bookseller was allowed to operate without restraint by the Competition Bureau.[16]

To protect farmers, the Canadian government has created marketing boards that regulate the pricing and production of such items as milk and eggs. Those who decide they want to manufacture small amounts of cheese would have great difficulty doing so, because the Canadian government does not open production quotas to new producers very often. Marketing boards restrict imports of some products, but the unintended result is that foreign governments oppose exports from Canada.

**ECONOMIC CONDITIONS**  Interest rates, inflation, changes in disposable income, stock market fluctuations, and the stage of the general business cycle are some of the economic factors that can affect management practices in Canada. For example, many specialty retailers such as IKEA, Roots, Birks, and Williams-Sonoma are acutely aware of the impact consumer disposable income has on their sales. When consumers' incomes fall or confidence about job security declines, such as happened in 2009, consumers will postpone purchasing anything that is not a necessity. Even charitable organizations such as the United Way and the Heart and Stroke Foundation feel the impact of economic factors. During economic downturns, not only does the demand for their services increase, but also their contributions typically decrease.

**SOCIO-CULTURAL CONDITIONS**  In 2004, Cambridge, Ontario–based Frito Lay Canada announced that it was eliminating trans fatty acids (TFAs) from Doritos, Tostitos, and SunChips (it had already done so for its Lay's, Ruffles, and Miss Vickie's chips). Marc Guay, president of Frito Lay Canada, explained his decision at the time: "Eliminating trans fat is a major step in Frito Lay Canada's on-going commitment to offer consumers a wide variety of great-tasting snacks made with more healthful oils."[17] Burlington, Ontario–based Voortman Cookies was the first Canadian cookie maker to drop TFAs from its products. President and co-founder Harry Voortman said he dropped the TFAs after his daughter, Lynn, a naturopathic doctor, became concerned enough that she stopped eating her father's cookies altogether.[18]

Why did Frito Lay Canada and Voortman Cookies change their products? Because health officials and consumers became increasingly anxious about the link between TFAs and heart disease.[19] Managers must adapt their practices to the changing expectations of the societies in which they operate. As societal values, customs, and tastes change, managers also must change. For example, as employees have begun seeking more balance in their lives, organizations have had to adjust by offering family leave policies, more flexible work hours, and even on-site child care facilities. These trends may pose a constraint on managers' decisions and actions. If an organization does business in other countries, managers need to be familiar with those countries' values and cultures, and manage in ways that recognize and embrace those specific socio-cultural aspects.

Demographics are part of social-cultural conditions and encompass trends in the physical characteristics of a population such as gender, age, level of education, geographic location, income, family composition, and so forth. Changes in these characteristics may constrain how managers plan, organize, lead, and control.

A population group you will be very familiar with is the Baby Boomers, made up of individuals born between 1947 and 1966—approximately 33 percent of the Canadian population.[20] As that very large group ages, Canada's workforce faces major skill shortages. Alberta alone faces a shortage of more than 75 000 workers within the next 10 years.[21]

**TECHNOLOGICAL CONDITIONS**  In terms of the general environment, the most rapid changes have occurred in technology. We live in a time of continuous technological change. For example, the human genetic code has been cracked. Just think of the implications of such an incredible breakthrough! Information gadgets are getting smaller and more powerful. We have automated offices, electronic meetings, robotic manufacturing, lasers, integrated circuits, faster and more powerful microprocessors, synthetic fuels, and entirely new models of doing business in an electronic age. Companies that capitalize on technology, such as Apple, eBay, and Google, prosper. In addition, many successful retailers such as Walmart use sophisticated information systems to keep on top of current sales trends. Similarly, hospitals, universities, airports, police departments, and even military organizations that adapt to major technological advances have a competitive edge over those that do not. The whole area of technology is radically changing the fundamental ways that organizations are structured and the way that managers manage.

**ENVIRONMENTAL CONDITIONS**  The environment has become a bigger issue in terms of sustainability of raw materials. The triple bottom line approach discussed throughout the text indicates the importance of the environmental bottom-line for companies. Reducing the carbon footprint has become a focus for many organizations as they attempt to reduce waste; protect air, water, and land quality; and increase biodegradable and recyclable packaging. The Canadian Association of Petroleum Producers (CAPP) developed a Responsible Canadian Energy program to track greenhouse gas (GHG) emissions, fresh water usage, and land cleared

**general environment**
Broad external conditions that may affect the organization.

and reclaimed for mining operations.[22] For the oil industry, going green is as much about financial and marketing conditions as it is about the environment. Cleaner extraction methods make oil more marketable in markets with low carbon-fuel standards such as California.[23]

**LEGAL CONDITIONS**  The legal environment is often closely related to the political environment, because laws and regulations are enacted by politicians. Laws related to employment, health and safety, and product safety can have a major impact on how businesses operate.

Federal, provincial, and local governments influence what organizations can and cannot do. Some federal legislation has significant implications. The Canadian Human Rights Act makes it illegal for any employer or service provider falling within federal jurisdiction to discriminate on the following grounds: race, national or ethnic origin, colour, religion, age, sex (including pregnancy and childbirth), marital status, family status, mental or physical disability (including previous or current drug or alcohol dependence), pardoned conviction, or sexual orientation. The Act covers federal departments and agencies, Crown corporations, chartered banks, national airlines, interprovincial communications and telephone companies, interprovincial transportation companies, and other federally regulated industries, including certain mining operations.

Interpret

Canada's Employment Equity Act of 1995 protects several categories of employees from employment barriers: Aboriginal peoples (whether First Nation, Inuit, or Metis); persons with disabilities; members of visible minorities (nonCaucasian in race or nonwhite in colour); and women. This legislation aims to ensure that members of these four groups are treated equitably. Employers covered by the Canadian Human Rights Act are also covered by the Employment Equity Act.

# UNDERSTANDING THE GLOBAL ENVIRONMENT

Menu Foods was founded in 1971 and bought its first US factory in New Jersey in 1977, hoping to use that factory to launch an expansion into the US market.[24] Today the global company has four pet food processing plants: one in Canada (Mississauga, Ontario) and three in the United States (Emporia, Kansas; Pennsauken, New Jersey; and North Sioux City, South Dakota). The company's Canadian and American plants operate close to the areas they serve, which reduces shipping expenses. According to the company's website, "Menu's ability to serve [retailers] from four locations provides it with service and freight cost advantages compared to other single or two plant private-label competitors."

Menu Foods buys the ingredients for its pet food products from a variety of companies, and those companies in turn may buy ingredients for their products from other companies around the world. As the tainted pet food investigation found, an ingredient that originated in China was responsible for the deaths caused by Menu Foods' various pet foods. Menu Foods gets some of its ingredients from suppliers, who may themselves rely on external suppliers. As a result, Menu Foods may not always be aware of the original source of every ingredient it uses.

Historically, Canada has been slow to face the global challenge, although the relatively small size of many Canadian firms may be a contributing factor in this pattern.[25] The *Fortune* list of the Top 100 Global Companies of 2011 does not include any Canadian firms (although there are 11 in the Top 500).[26] The majority of firms listed are American, but the number of Chinese firms on the list has grown from only 11 in 2001 to over 60 companies.[27]

The global environment presents both opportunities and challenges for managers. With the entire world as a market and national borders becoming increasingly irrelevant, the

**Describe**
What challenges do managers face in a global environment?

**2.3**

## Think About It

How is Menu Foods structured to do business globally? Would it be better for Menu Foods to operate out of only one location in North America?

potential for organizations to grow is expanding dramatically. To evaluate your fit for an international position, see *Assess Your Skills—Am I Well Suited for a Career as a Global Manager?* on pages 48–49 at the end of the chapter.

However, even large successful organizations with talented managers face challenges in managing in the global environment. Managers must deal with cultural, economic, and political differences. Meanwhile, new competitors can suddenly appear at any time from any place on the globe. Managers who make no attempt to learn and adapt to changes in the global environment end up reacting rather than innovating. As a result, their organizations often become uncompetitive and fail.[28] Below, we discuss the issues managers have to face in managing in a global environment.

## Global Trade

What is the global environment like? An important feature is global trade. Global trade is not new. Countries and organizations have been trading with each other for centuries. According to the World Trade Organization (WTO), "Trade is central to human health, prosperity, and social welfare."[29] When trade is allowed to flow freely, countries benefit from economic growth and productivity gains because they produce the goods they are best at producing and import goods that are more efficiently produced elsewhere. Global trade is being shaped by two forces: regional trading alliances and the agreements negotiated through the WTO.

**REGIONAL TRADING ALLIANCES**   The major regional trading alliances are as follows:

- The **European Union (EU)**: The signing of the Maastricht Treaty (named for the Dutch town where the treaty was signed) in February 1992 created the European Union (EU), a unified economic and trade entity with 12 member countries— Belgium, Denmark, France, Greece, Ireland, Italy, Luxembourg, the Netherlands, Portugal, Spain, the United Kingdom, and Germany. By 2007, the EU comprised 27 countries. Three other countries (Croatia, the former Yugoslav Republic of Macedonia, and Turkey) have submitted applications to join the EU. The EU's economic power has diminished somewhat with the European economic crisis, but the current EU membership encompasses more than 490 million people.[30]

- The **North American Free Trade Agreement (NAFTA)**: When agreements in key issues covered by the North American Free Trade Agreement (NAFTA) were reached by the Canadian, US, and Mexican governments in August 1992, a vast economic bloc was created in which barriers to free trade were reduced. In 2011, Canadian exports to the United States were $331 billion, which accounted for 72 percent of our total exports.[31] Canada's exports to Mexico have quadrupled since the NAFTA agreement was signed, and its foreign investments in Mexico increased by a factor of five.[32] Westcoast Energy, Scotiabank, and BCE are just a few Canadian companies that have expanded their operations to Mexico. Many economists argue that reducing the barriers to trade (tariffs, import licensing requirements, customs user fees) has resulted in a strengthening of the economic power of all three countries. Free trade did not eliminate all trade problems between Canada and the United States, however, as the ongoing softwood lumber negotiations show.

- The **Association of Southeast Asian Nations (ASEAN)**: A trading alliance of 10 Southeast Asian countries, ASEAN encompasses a region with a population of about 500 million and a combined gross domestic product of $1496 billion.[33] During the years ahead, the Southeast Asian region promises to be one of the fastest-growing

---

**European Union (EU)**
A union of 27 European countries that forms an economic and political entity.

**North American Free Trade Agreement (NAFTA)**
An agreement among the Canadian, American, and Mexican governments in which barriers to free trade are reduced.

**Association of Southeast Asian Nations (ASEAN)**
A trading alliance of 10 Southeast Asian countries.

economic regions of the world. It will be an increasingly important regional economic and political alliance whose impact eventually could rival that of both NAFTA and the EU.

- **Trans-Pacific Partnership (TPP)**: The TPP is a group of nine countries comprising the United States, Australia, New Zealand, Singapore, Peru, Vietnam, Malaysia, Brunei, and Chile, which is intending to revolutionize Asian trade relations. Canada asked for a seat at the TPP table in late 2011.[34]
- **Brazil, Russia, India, China, and South Africa (BRICS)**: BRICS is not a political alliance or a trading association, but it is a unique grouping with shared opportunities and common challenges. South Africa joined in 2011, and the group currently meets to create mechanisms for consultation and cooperation.[35]

**THE WORLD TRADE ORGANIZATION**  The **World Trade Organization (WTO)** is a global organization that sets rules for international trade and helps countries negotiate trade problems and settle trade disputes.[36]

The WTO was formed in 1995 and evolved from the General Agreement on Tariffs and Trade (GATT), an agreement in effect since the end of World War II. Today, the WTO is the only *global* organization dealing with the rules of trade among nations. Its membership consists of 153 member countries and 31 observer governments (which have a specific time frame within which they must apply to become members). At its core are various trade agreements negotiated and ratified by the vast majority of the world's trading nations. The goal of the WTO is to help businesses conduct trade between countries (importing and exporting) without undesired side effects. Although a number of vocal critics have staged highly visible protests and criticized the WTO, claiming that it destroys jobs and the natural environment, the WTO appears to play an important role in monitoring and promoting global trade.

## PESTEL–Global Environment

Canadian managers are accustomed to stable legal and political systems. Changes are slow, and legal and political procedures are well established. The stability of laws governing the actions of individuals and institutions allows for accurate predictions. The same cannot be said for all countries. Managers in a global organization must stay informed of the specific laws in countries where they do business.

Some countries have a history of unstable governments. Managers of businesses in these countries face dramatically greater uncertainty as a result of political instability or interference. The Chinese government controls what organizations do and how they do it within China's borders. Google has struggled with determining how to manage its website in China. "Figuring out how to deal with China has been a difficult exercise for Google," said Elliot Schrage, former vice-president of global communications and public affairs at Google. "The requirements of doing business in China include self-censorship—something that runs counter to Google's most basic values and commitments as a company."[37]

The legal and political environments do not have to be unstable or revolutionary to be a concern to managers. Just the fact that a country's laws and political system differ from those of Canada is important. Managers must recognize these differences to understand the constraints under which they operate and the opportunities that exist.

The global manager must also be aware of economic issues when doing business in other countries. Understanding the type of economic system under which the country operates is crucial. The two major types are a market economy and a planned economy. A **market economy** is one in which resources are primarily owned and controlled by the private sector. A **planned economy** is one in which all economic decisions are planned by a central government. In actuality, no economy is purely market or planned. Canada and the United States are two countries at the market end of the spectrum, but they do have some governmental control. The economies of Vietnam and North Korea, however, are more planning based. Then there is China, a country that has utilized a planned economy for decades but is moving toward becoming more market based. Why would managers need to know about a country's economic system? Because it has the potential to constrain decisions and actions. Other economic issues a manager would need to understand include currency exchange rates, inflation rates, and diverse tax policies.

Which is more important to a manager—national culture or organizational culture? Research by Geert Hofstede, a professor at Maastricht University in the Netherlands, indicates that national culture has a greater effect on employees than does their organization's culture.[38] For example, German employees at an IBM facility in Munich will be influenced more by German culture than by IBM's culture. In other words, as influential as organizational culture may be on managerial practice, **national culture** is even more influential.

*In what ways do you think culture affects doing business in other countries?*

Hofstede developed one of the most widely referenced approaches to helping managers better understand differences between national cultures. His research found that managers and employees vary on five dimensions of national culture, which are as follows:

- *Individualism vs. collectivism.* Individualism is the degree to which people in a country prefer to act as individuals rather than as members of groups. In an individualistic society, people are supposed to look after their own interests and those of their immediate family. They are able to do so because of the large amount of freedom an individualistic society allows its citizens. The opposite is collectivism, which is characterized by a social framework in which people prefer to act as members of groups and expect others in groups of which they are a part (such as a family or an organization) to look after them and to protect them.

- *Power distance.* Hofstede used the term *power distance* as a measure of the extent to which a society accepts the fact that power in institutions and organizations is distributed unequally. A high power distance society accepts wide differences in power in organizations. Employees show a great deal of respect for those in authority. Titles, rank, and status carry a lot of weight. In contrast, a low power distance society plays down inequalities as much as possible. Superiors still have authority, but employees are not afraid of or in awe of the boss.

- *Uncertainty avoidance.* Uncertainty avoidance describes the degree to which people tolerate risk and prefer structured over unstructured situations. People in low uncertainty avoidance societies are relatively comfortable with risks. They are also relatively tolerant of behaviour and opinions that differ from their own because they do not feel threatened by them. On the other hand, people in a society that is high in uncertainty avoidance feel threatened by uncertainty and ambiguity and experience high levels of anxiety, which manifests itself in nervousness, high stress, and aggressiveness.

- *Achievement vs. nurturing.* The fourth cultural dimension, like individualism/collectivism, is a dichotomy. Achievement is the degree to which values such as assertiveness, the acquisition of money and material goods, and competition prevail. Nurturing is a national cultural attribute that emphasizes relationships and concern for others.[39]

- *Long-term and short-term orientation.* This cultural attribute looks at a country's orientation toward life and work. People in cultures with long-term orientation look to the future and value thrift and persistence. In these cultures, leisure time is not so important, and it is believed that the most important events in life will occur in the future. A short-term orientation values the past and present, and emphasizes respect for tradition and fulfilling social obligations. Leisure time is important, and it is believed that the most important events in life happened in the past or occur in the present.

The five dimensions are described in Exhibit 2-3, which also shows some of the countries characterized by these dimensions.

---

**EXHIBIT 2–3**   Hofstede's Five Dimensions of National Culture

(1) *Individualistic*—People look after their own and family interests
*Collectivistic*—People expect group to look after and protect them

| *Individualistic*<br>United States, Canada, Australia | ←——— Japan ———→ | *Collectivistic*<br>Mexico, Thailand |
|---|---|---|

(2) *High power distance*—Accepts wide differences in power, great deal of respect for those in authority
*Low power distance*—Plays down inequalities: employees are not afraid to approach, nor are they in awe of the boss

| *High power distance*<br>Mexico, Singapore, France | ←——— Italy, Japan ———→ | *Low power distance*<br>United States, Sweden |
|---|---|---|

(3) *High uncertainty avoidance*—Threatened by ambiguity and experience high levels of anxiety
*Low uncertainty avoidance*—Comfortable with risks; tolerant of different behaviour and opinions

| *High uncertainty avoidance*<br>Italy, Mexico, France | ←——— United Kingdom ———→ | *Low uncertainty avoidance*<br>Canada, United States, Singapore |
|---|---|---|

(4) *Achievement*—Values such as assertiveness, acquiring money and goods, and competition prevail
*Nurturing*—Values such as relationships and concern for others prevail

| *Achievement*<br>United States, Japan, Mexico | ←——— Canada, Greece ———→ | *Nurturing*<br>France, Sweden |
|---|---|---|

(5) *Long-term orientation*—People look to the future and value thrift and persistence
*Short-term orientation*—People value tradition and the past

| *Short-term thinking*<br>Germany, Australia, United States, Canada | ←——— ———→ | *Long-term thinking*<br>China, Taiwan, Japan |
|---|---|---|

---

Hofstede's findings are based on research that is nearly three decades old and has been subject to some criticism, which he refutes.[40] He has recently updated his research and included studies from a variety of disciplines that support his findings.[41] *Developing Your Interpersonal Skills—Becoming More Culturally Aware* on pages 50–51 encourages you to think about how to become more comfortable when interacting with people from different cultures.

# DOING BUSINESS GLOBALLY

**Explain**
**2.4** How do organizations do business globally?

**Analyze**

Menu Foods was forced to remove 60 million packages of its wet pet foods off grocery and pet food store shelves in March 2007.[42] The pet food had been contaminated with melamine, a nonfood product. Investigators found that the melamine had been mixed with wheat gluten (an ingredient in pet food) at Xuzhou Anying factory in China. Employees apparently deliberately mixed the melamine into the wheat gluten because melamine mimics protein when mixed with gluten. The resulting product would then appear to have a higher nutrient value than it actually did.

China's animal feed producer had been supplementing the feed with melamine for a number of years. "Many companies buy melamine scrap to make animal feed, such as fish feed," says Ji Denghui, general manager of the Fujian Sanming Dinghui Chemical Company, which sells melamine. The additive is inexpensive, thus it reduces product costs. Ji also explains, "I don't know if there's a regulation on it. Probably not. No law or regulation says 'don't do it,' so everyone's doing it. The laws in China are like that, aren't they? If there's no accident, there won't be any regulation."

Organizations in different industries and from different countries are pursuing global opportunities. In this section, we look at different types of global organizations and how they do business in the global marketplace.

**Think About It**

How have the global legal–political and economic environments affected Menu Foods' ability to produce its pet food?

## Different Types of International Organizations

Although doing business internationally is widespread, the terms used to describe the different types of international companies are not standardized—different authors use different terminology. In this text, we use the terms *multinational*, *multidomestic*, *global*, and *transnational* to describe the various types of international organizations.[43]

**MULTINATIONAL CORPORATIONS** Organizations doing business globally are not anything new. DuPont started doing business in China in 1863. H. J. Heinz Company was manufacturing food products in the United Kingdom in 1905. Ford Motor Company set up its first overseas sales branch in France in 1908. But it was not until the mid-1960s that international companies became commonplace. A **multinational corporation (MNC)** is a broad term normally used to refer to any and all types of companies that maintain operations in multiple countries but manage them from a base in the home country. Today, most companies have some type of international dealings.

**MULTIDOMESTIC CORPORATIONS** A **multidomestic corporation** is an MNC that maintains significant operations in more than one country but decentralizes management to the local country. This type of organization does not attempt to manage foreign operations from its home country. Instead, local employees typically are hired to manage the business, and marketing strategies are tailored to that country's unique characteristics. Switzerland-based Nestlé can be described as a multidomestic corporation. With operations in almost every country on the globe, its managers match the company's products to its consumers. In parts of Europe, Nestlé sells products that are not available in North America or Latin America. Another example of a multidomestic corporation is Frito-Lay, a division of PepsiCo, which markets a Doritos chip in the British market that differs in both taste and texture from the Canadian and US versions. Many consumer companies manage their global businesses using this approach because they must adapt their products and services to meet the needs of the local markets.

**GLOBAL COMPANIES** A **global company** is international in scope but centralizes its management and other decisions in the home country. These companies treat the world market as an integrated whole and focus on the need for global efficiency. Although these companies may have considerable global holdings, management decisions with company-wide implications are made from headquarters in the home country. Some examples of companies that can be considered global companies include Montreal-based transport manufacturer Bombardier, Montreal-based aluminum producer Rio Tinto Alcan, Tokyo-based consumer electronics firm Sony, Frankfurt-based Deutsche Bank AG, and New York City–based financial services provider Merrill Lynch.

**TRANSNATIONAL OR BORDERLESS ORGANIZATIONS** Many companies are going global by eliminating structural divisions that impose artificial geographical barriers. This type of global organization is called a **transnational corporation (TNC) or borderless organization**. For example, IBM dropped its organizational structure based on country and reorganized into industry groups such as business solutions, software, IT services, and financing. Borderless management is an attempt by organizations to increase efficiency and effectiveness in a competitive global marketplace.[44]

---

**multinational corporation (MNC)**
A broad term referring to any and all types of international companies that maintain operations in multiple countries.

**multidomestic corporation**
An international company that decentralizes management and other decisions to the local country.

**global company**
An international company that centralizes management and other decisions in the home country.

**transnational corporation (TNC) or borderless organization**
A type of international company in which artificial geographical barriers are eliminated.

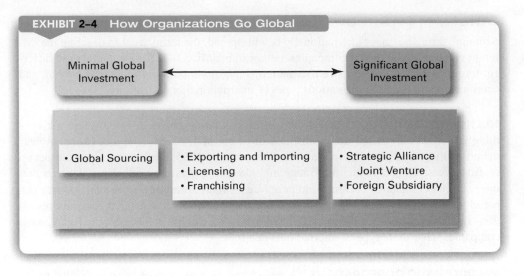

**EXHIBIT 2–4** How Organizations Go Global

**BORN GLOBALS** Our classification of different types of international organizations tends to describe large international businesses. However, an increasing number of businesses, called **born globals**, choose to go global from inception.[45] These companies (also known as *international new ventures* or *INVs*) commit resources upfront (material, people, financing) to doing business in more than one country and are likely to continue to play an increasingly important role in international business.

## How Organizations Go Global

When organizations do go global, they often use different approaches depending on whether they are just starting or whether they have been doing business internationally for a while (see Exhibit 2-4). During the initial stages of going global, managers look at ways to get into a global market without having to invest a lot of capital. At this stage, companies may start with **global sourcing** (also called *global outsourcing*), which refers to the purchasing of materials or labour from around the world, wherever it is cheapest. The goal is to take advantage of lower costs in order to be more competitive. In 2006, for example, Montreal-based Bell Canada contracted with Sitel India and two other Indian companies to provide technical support and customer care to Canadian customers. Some of that business was pulled back in 2009 due to Canadian customer complaints, but outsourcing call centres globally continues to rise. Recently, the Philippines overtook India as the hub of call centres.[46] Although global sourcing is often the first step in going global, many organizations continue to use this approach, even as they become more international, because of the competitive advantages it offers. Beyond global sourcing, however, each successive stage of becoming more international requires more investment and thus entails more risk for the organization.

**IMPORTING AND EXPORTING** An organization can go global by **exporting** its products to other countries—that is, by making products at home and selling them overseas. In addition, an organization can go global by **importing** products—that is, by selling products at home that are made abroad. Both exporting and importing are small steps toward becoming a global business and usually involve minimal investment and minimal risk. Many organizations start doing business globally this way. Many, especially small businesses, continue with exporting or importing as the way they do business globally. For example, Haribhai's Spice Emporium, a small business in Durban, South Africa, exports spices and rice to customers all over Africa, Europe, and the United States. Montreal-based Mega Brands (formerly Mega Bloks), with sales in over 100 countries, focuses on exporting. The company holds the number-one position in Canada and Spain, and has a 43 percent share of the UK market.[47] The company operates in eight countries, with more than 1000 employees. Mega

*If a company wants to do business in other countries, what choices does it have?*

Brands is only one example of Canada's increasing reliance on export business. The value of merchandise exported from Canada totalled $399.4 billion in 2010, recovering to 2001 levels after massive losses in 2008 and 2009.[48] Transportation equipment manufacturing, primary metal manufacturing, and paper manufacturing account for the largest volume of Canadian exports.

**LICENSING AND FRANCHISING**   Some managers use licensing or franchising in the early stages of doing business internationally. Licensing and franchising are similar in that they both involve one organization giving another the right to use its brand name, technology, or product specifications in return for a lump-sum payment or a fee that is usually based on sales. The only difference is that **licensing** is primarily used by manufacturing organizations that make or sell another company's products and **franchising** is primarily used by service organizations that want to use another company's name and operating methods. For example, Russian consumers can enjoy McDonald's hamburgers because McDonald's Canada opened the first Russian franchise in Moscow. Franchises have also made it possible for Mexicans to dine on Richmond, BC–based Boston Pizza and Koreans to consume frozen yogourt from Markham, Ontario–based Coolbrands' Yogen Früz. Currently, US franchisors are making Canada a priority for growth. Puroclean, a US property disaster restoration firm, is aggressively expanding into the Canadian market, and franchises have been performing twice as well as those in the United States.[49] Licensing and franchising involve more investment and risk than exporting and importing because the company's brand is more at stake.

Fast-food giant KFC, like many big franchise firms, is opening more new outlets overseas. Along the way, the company is making appropriate changes in its menu offerings, such as substituting juice and fruit for Coke and fries. This Shanghai promotion features egg tarts.

**born globals**
International companies that choose to go global from inception.

**global sourcing**
Purchasing materials or labour from around the world, wherever they are cheapest.

**exporting**
An approach to going global that involves making products at home and selling them abroad.

**importing**
An approach to going global that involves acquiring products made abroad and selling them at home.

**licensing**
An approach to going global in which a manufacturer gives another organization the right to use its brand name, technology, or product specifications.

**franchising**
An approach to going global in which a service organization gives a person or group the right to sell a product, using specific business methods and practices that are standardized.

**STRATEGIC ALLIANCE**  Typically, once an organization has been doing business internationally for some time and has gained experience in international markets, managers may decide to make a more direct investment. One way they can do this is through a **strategic alliance**—a partnership between a domestic and a foreign company in which both share resources and knowledge in developing new products or building production facilities. The partners also share the risks and rewards of this alliance. Finding a partner, however, is not always easy. When Starbucks decided to open coffee shops in France, four major French food companies it approached as possible joint venture partners turned the proposal down. Jean-Paul Brayer, former head of one of the food companies Starbucks approached, commented, "Their contract was way too expensive. It was a win-win situation—but only for Starbucks."[50] Starbucks ended up partnering with a Spanish firm, Grupo VIPS, and together they opened the first Parisian Starbucks in January 2004.

A specific type of strategic alliance in which the partners agree to form a separate, independent organization for some business purpose is called a **joint venture**. Hewlett-Packard (HP) has had numerous joint ventures with various suppliers around the globe to develop different components for its computer equipment, such as Tokyo-based Hitachi, which supplies hard drives for HP. These partnerships provide a faster and more inexpensive way for companies to compete globally than doing it on their own.

**FOREIGN SUBSIDIARY**  Managers can make a direct investment in a foreign country by setting up a **foreign subsidiary**, a separate and independent production facility or office. This subsidiary can be managed as an MNC (domestic control) or a TNC or borderless organization (foreign or global control). As you can probably guess, this arrangement involves the greatest commitment of resources and poses the greatest amount of risk. Many of the larger companies operating in Canada are actually subsidiaries of US corporations, including GM Canada, Procter & Gamble Canada, and McDonald's Canada. Canadian subsidiaries manage their operations and set their own targets and goals, but they also report to head office in the United States.

# HOW THE ENVIRONMENT AFFECTS MANAGERS

**2.5** **Explain** How does the environment affect managers?

Knowing *what* the various components of the environment are is important to managers. However, understanding *how* the environment affects managers is equally important. The environment affects managers through the degree of environmental uncertainty that is present, through the various stakeholder relationships that exist between the organization and its external constituencies, and through the challenges of managing in a global environment.

## Assessing Environmental Uncertainty

Not all environments are the same. They differ by what we call their degree of **environmental uncertainty**, which can be defined as the degree of change and complexity in an organization's environment (see Exhibit 2-5).

The first dimension is the degree of change. If components in an organization's environment change frequently, we call it a *dynamic* environment. If change is minimal, we call it a *stable* one. A stable environment might be one in which there are no new competitors, few technological breakthroughs by current competitors, little activity by pressure groups to influence the organization, and so forth. Zippo Canada, best known for its Zippo lighters, enjoys a relatively stable environment, with few competitors and little technological change. The main environmental concern for the company is the declining trend in tobacco smokers, although the company's lighters have other uses and global markets remain attractive.

In contrast, the recorded music industry faces a highly uncertain and unpredictable environment. Digital formats such as MP3, music-streaming Internet services like VEVO, online piracy, and the ability to buy individual songs from companies such as iTunes have

**EXHIBIT 2–5**  Environmental Uncertainty Matrix

| | | Degree of Change | |
|---|---|---|---|
| | | **Stable** | **Dynamic** |
| **Degree of Complexity** | **Simple** | **Stable and predictable environment**<br><br>Few components in environment<br><br>Components are somewhat similar and remain basically the same<br><br>Minimal need for sophisticated knowledge of components | **Dynamic and unpredictable environment**<br><br>Few components in environment<br><br>Components are somewhat similar but are in continual process of change<br><br>Minimal need for sophisticated knowledge of components |
| | **Complex** | **Stable and predictable environment**<br><br>Many components in environment<br><br>Components are not similar to one another and remain basically the same<br><br>High need for sophisticated knowledge of components | **Dynamic and unpredictable environment**<br><br>Many components in environment<br><br>Components are not similar to one another and are in continual process of change<br><br>High need for sophisticated knowledge of components |

turned the industry upside down. The global music market has declined a staggering 30 percent from 2004 to 2009, despite a total increase in digital sales of 940 percent.[51] Although music companies traditionally earned revenues by selling physical products such as LP records, cassettes, and CDs, the digital future represents chaos and uncertainty. Companies are trying to harness the mobile music environment and to stem the illegal downloading of music.[52] This environment can definitely be described as dynamic.

What about predictable rapid change? Is this type of change considered a dynamic environment? Bricks-and-mortar retail department stores provide a good example. They typically make one-quarter to one-third of their sales in December. The drop-off from December to January is significant. However, because the change is predictable, we do not consider the environment to be dynamic. When we talk about degree of change, we mean unpredictable change. If change can be accurately anticipated, it does not represent uncertainty that managers must confront.

The second dimension of uncertainty describes the degree of **environmental complexity**. Degree of complexity refers to the number of components in an organization's environment and the extent of the knowledge the organization has about those components. For example, Hasbro, the world's second-largest toy manufacturer (behind Mattel), has simplified its environment by acquiring many of its competitors such as Tiger Electronics, Wizards of the Coast, Kenner Toys, Parker Brothers, and Tonka Toys. The fewer competitors, customers, suppliers, government agencies, and so forth that an organization must deal with, the less complexity and, therefore, the less uncertainty there is in its environment.

Complexity is also measured in terms of the knowledge an organization needs to have about its environment. For example, managers at the online brokerage E*TRADE must know a great deal about their Internet service provider's operations if they want to ensure that their website is available, reliable, and secure for their stock-trading customers. On the other hand, managers of grocery stores have a minimal need for sophisticated knowledge about their suppliers.

**strategic alliance**
An approach to going global that involves a partnership between a domestic and a foreign company in which both share resources and knowledge in developing new products or building production facilities.

**joint venture**
An approach to going global in which the partners agree to form a separate, independent organization for some business purpose; it is a type of strategic alliance.

**foreign subsidiary**
An approach to going global that involves a direct investment in a foreign country by setting up a separate and independent production facility or office.

**environmental uncertainty**
The degree of change and the degree of complexity in an organization's environment.

**environmental complexity**
The number of components in an organization's environment and the extent of the organization's knowledge about those components.

How does the concept of environmental uncertainty influence managers? Looking again at Exhibit 2-5, each of the four cells represents different combinations of degree of complexity and degree of change. Cell 1 (an environment that is stable and simple) represents the lowest level of environmental uncertainty. Cell 4 (an environment that is dynamic and complex) represents the highest. Not surprisingly, managers' influence on organizational outcomes is greatest in cell 1 and least in cell 4.

Because uncertainty is a threat to an organization's effectiveness, managers try to minimize it. Given a choice, managers would prefer to operate in environments such as those in cell 1. However, they rarely have full control over that choice. Most industries today are facing greater dynamic change, making their environments more uncertain. Thus, managers, as planners, need to consider the environment they currently face, as well as thinking ahead about possible changes in the environment, and act accordingly. In a simple, stable environment, a manager may decide to continue doing things in the usual way. In a dynamic, complex environment, a manager may want to establish plans to keep the organization ahead of competitors or develop new niches in which to operate.

## The Pros and Cons of Globalization

*What is your attitude toward globalization? Is it favourable or unfavourable?*

Doing business globally today isn't easy! Advocates praise the economic and social benefits that come from globalization. Yet that very globalization has created challenges and controversy because of the potential negative impact it can have on the world's poor. Instances of the use of child labour to produce North American goods have come to light. Also, globalization has led to the economic interdependence of trading countries. If one country's economy falters, it could potentially have a domino effect on other countries with which it does business.

Some have predicted that globalization is dead, including Canadian philosopher John Ralston Saul. However, Joel Bakan, a University of British Columbia law professor who wrote *The Corporation* and co-produced the documentary of the same name, claims, "It's overly optimistic to say globalization is dead."[53]

Although supporters of globalization praise it for its economic benefits, others think globalization is simply a euphemism for "Americanization"—that is, the spread of US cultural values and business philosophy throughout the world.[54] Critics claim that this attitude of the "almighty American dollar wanting to spread the American way to every single country" has created many problems.[55] Exhibit 2-6 outlines the major pro- and anti-globalization arguments. Some of the dominant opponents of globalization include the

---

**EXHIBIT 2–6** Sample Positions of Anti- and Pro-Globalization Groups

| Anti-Globalization Positions | Pro-Globalization Positions |
|---|---|
| • Globalization is a synonym for Western imperialism. | • Globalization promotes economic prosperity; it offers access to foreign capital, export markets, and advanced technology. |
| • Trade liberalization may hinder economic development for poorer countries. | • Globalization encourages the efficient use of natural resources and raises environmental awareness and, thus, helps protect the environment. |
| • There are environmental, social, and economic costs to globalization. | |
| • Globalization erodes the power of local organizations and local decision-making methods. | • Globalization minimizes government intervention, which can hinder development in business and in people's lives. |
| • Globalization can lead to the exploitation of workers' rights and human rights. | • Globalization is a positive force that has encouraged the development of markets, which can bring about prosperity. |
| • Globalization usually benefits wealthy countries at the expense of poor countries. | |
| • Lessening or removing trade regulations hurts the poor by pushing up the price of necessities, such as seeds for planting crops, and medicine. | |

The Occupy movement, which started in New York in 2011, aims to redress economic and social disparity, including the impact of globalization on local economies.[56]

International Institute for Sustainable Development; the International Forum on Globalization; Greenpeace; the Canadian-based Centre for Research on Globalization; and Canadian author, journalist, and activist Naomi Klein, who is well known for her book *No Logo: Taking Aim at the Brand Bullies*. Some of the main supporters of globalization include London-based International Policy Network, Washington-based Competitive Enterprise Institute, and the Cato Institute.

Because Canada is not seen as a country that wants to spread Canadian values and culture, Canadian managers may have some advantages over their American counterparts in doing business internationally. Managers will need to be aware of how their decisions and actions will be viewed, not only by those who may agree, but, more importantly, by those who may disagree. They will need to adjust their leadership styles and management approaches to accommodate these diverse views. Yet, as always, they will need to do this while still being as efficient and effective as possible in reaching the organization's goals.

Practise

## Summary of Learning Objectives

**2.1** **How much control do managers have?** The omnipotent view of management suggests that managers are directly responsible for an organization's success or failure. While this is the dominant view of managers, there is another perspective. The symbolic view of management argues that much of an organization's success or failure is due to external forces outside managers' control. The reality is probably somewhere in between these two views, with managers often able to exert control, but also facing situations over which they have no control.

TransCanada and its managers were well prepared for Keystone XL to go ahead, but the US decision to shut down the pipeline project was beyond the control of TransCanada managers. So the company had to work with Stephen Harper and the Canadian government to make plans to develop China as a major customer.

**2.2** **What is the external environment for managers?** The external environment plays a major role in shaping managers' actions. In the specific environment, managers have to be responsive to customers and suppliers while being aware of competitors and public pressure groups. As well, political, economic, socio-cultural, technological, environmental, and legal conditions in the general environment affect the issues managers face in doing their job.

TransCanada and other Canadian energy exporters provided more than 80 percent of their exports to the US market. When political decision making was pressured by environmental interest groups, the Canadian companies needed to look at other markets such as China for their exports.

**2.3** **What challenges do managers face in a global environment?** When managers do business in other countries, they will be affected by the global legal, political, and economic environments of those countries. Differing laws and political systems can create constraints as well as opportunities for managers. The type of economic system in some countries can place restrictions on how foreign companies are able to conduct business there. In addition, managers must be aware of the culture of the countries in which they do business to understand *how* business is done and what customers expect.

Conducting business in China is different than in the United States. The United States imposes far stricter rules on the environmental impact of the oil sands than does China. Social media pressure by Chinese citizens is almost a non-issue, whereas in the United States it was the major factor in Obama's initial decision to shut down the Keystone project.

**2.4** **How do organizations do business globally?** Organizations can take on a variety of structures when they go global, including multinational corporations, multidomestic corporations, global companies, and tran-

snational or borderless organizations. An organization can opt for lower-risk and lower-investment strategies for going global through importing or exporting, hiring foreign representation, or contracting with foreign manufacturers. It can also increase its presence in another country by joining with another business to form a strategic alliance or joint venture. Or it can set up a foreign subsidiary in order to have a full presence in the foreign country.

TransCanada is a global energy company that focuses on pipelines, power generation, and oil and gas storage. Its headquarters are in Canada, and it has customers around the world. It uses pipelines such as Keystone XL to safely and efficiently transport oil crude and natural gas.

**2.5** **How does the environment affect managers?** Because environments can change, sometimes even unexpectedly, managers have to be aware of the degree of environmental uncertainty they face. They also have to be aware of the complexity of their environment. Managers need to manage relationships with their stakeholders—individuals who are influenced by and have an influence on the organization's decisions and actions. Successfully managing in today's global environment requires incredible sensitivity and understanding. Canadian managers may have some advantages over their American counterparts in doing business internationally, because American companies are sometimes viewed as trying to impose American culture on foreign countries.

### SNAPSHOT SUMMARY

**2.1** The Manager: How Much Control?

**2.2** The External Environment
The Specific Environment
The General Environment

**2.3** Understanding the Global Environment
Global Trade
PESTEL–Global Environment

**2.4** Doing Business Globally
Different Types of International Organizations
How Organizations Go Global

**2.5** How the Environment Affects Managers
Assessing Environmental Uncertainty
The Pros and Cons of Globalization

# MyManagementLab® Learning Resources

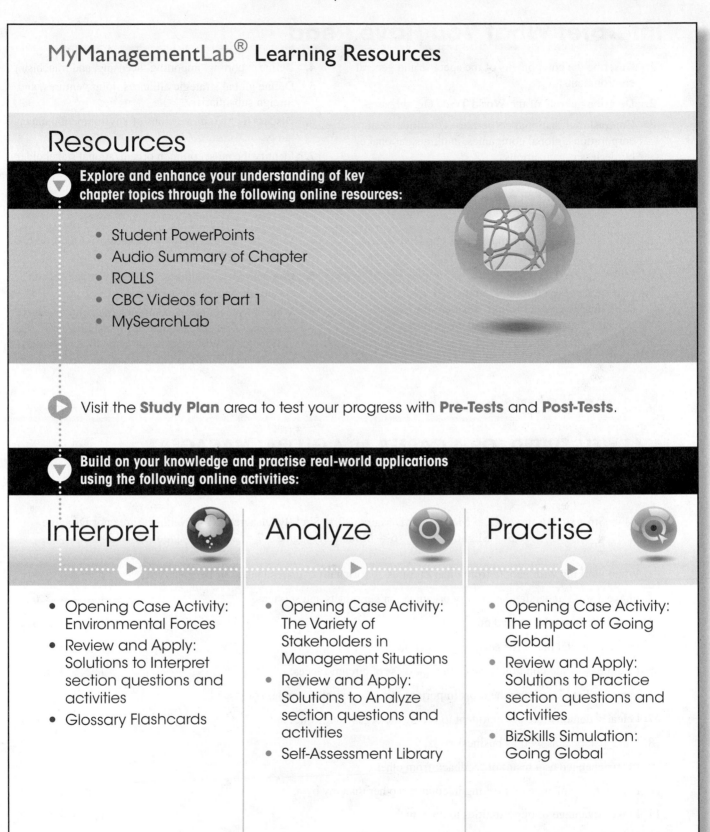

## Resources

**Explore and enhance your understanding of key chapter topics through the following online resources:**

- Student PowerPoints
- Audio Summary of Chapter
- ROLLS
- CBC Videos for Part 1
- MySearchLab

Visit the **Study Plan** area to test your progress with **Pre-Tests** and **Post-Tests**.

**Build on your knowledge and practise real-world applications using the following online activities:**

### Interpret

- Opening Case Activity: Environmental Forces
- Review and Apply: Solutions to Interpret section questions and activities
- Glossary Flashcards

### Analyze

- Opening Case Activity: The Variety of Stakeholders in Management Situations
- Review and Apply: Solutions to Analyze section questions and activities
- Self-Assessment Library

### Practise

- Opening Case Activity: The Impact of Going Global
- Review and Apply: Solutions to Practice section questions and activities
- BizSkills Simulation: Going Global

# Interpret What You Have Read

1. Describe the components of the specific and general environments.

2. Describe the role of the World Trade Organization.

3. Contrast multinational corporations, multidomestic corporations, global companies, and transnational or borderless organizations.

4. Define exporting, importing, licensing, and franchising.

5. Define global strategic alliances, joint ventures, and foreign subsidiaries.

6. Discuss the two dimensions of environmental uncertainty.

7. Identify the most common organizational stakeholders.

# Analyze What You Have Read

1. Why is it important for managers to understand the external forces that act on them and their organizations?

2. "Businesses are built on relationships." What do you think this statement means? What are the implications for managing the external environment?

3. What would be the drawbacks in not managing stakeholder relationships?

4. What are the managerial implications of a borderless organization?

5. Compare the advantages and disadvantages of the various approaches to going global.

6. What challenges might confront a Mexican manager transferred to Canada to manage a manufacturing plant in Winnipeg? Will these be the same for a Canadian manager transferred to Guadalajara, Mexico? Explain.

# Assess Your Skills

## AM I WELL SUITED FOR A CAREER AS A GLOBAL MANAGER?

For each of the following statements, circle the level of agreement or disagreement according to how well the statement describes you:[57]

> 1 = Strongly Disagree   2 = Moderately Disagree   3 = Slightly Disagree   4 = Neither Agree nor Disagree
> 5 = Slightly Agree   6 = Moderately Agree   7 = Strongly Agree

| | |
|---|---|
| 1. When working with people from other cultures, I work hard to understand their perspectives. | 1 2 3 4 5 6 7 |
| 2. I have a solid understanding of my organization's products and services. | 1 2 3 4 5 6 7 |
| 3. I am willing to take a stand on issues. | 1 2 3 4 5 6 7 |
| 4. I have a special talent for dealing with people. | 1 2 3 4 5 6 7 |
| 5. I can be depended on to tell the truth regardless of circumstances. | 1 2 3 4 5 6 7 |
| 6. I am good at identifying the most important part of a complex problem or issue. | 1 2 3 4 5 6 7 |
| 7. I clearly demonstrate commitment to seeing the organization succeed. | 1 2 3 4 5 6 7 |
| 8. I take personal as well as business risks. | 1 2 3 4 5 6 7 |
| 9. I have changed as a result of feedback from others. | 1 2 3 4 5 6 7 |
| 10. I enjoy the challenge of working in countries other than my own. | 1 2 3 4 5 6 7 |
| 11. I take advantage of opportunities to do new things. | 1 2 3 4 5 6 7 |
| 12. I find criticism hard to take. | 1 2 3 4 5 6 7 |
| 13. I seek feedback even when others are reluctant to give it. | 1 2 3 4 5 6 7 |
| 14. I don't get so invested in things that I cannot change when something does not work. | 1 2 3 4 5 6 7 |

**SCORING KEY**   Reverse your scoring for item 12 (that is, 1 = 7, 2 = 6, 3 = 5, etc.), and then add up your total score.

## ANALYSIS AND INTERPRETATION

Your total score will range from 14 to 98. The higher your score, the greater your potential for success as an international manager.

In today's global economy, being a manager often means being a global manager. But unfortunately, not all managers are able to transfer their skills smoothly from domestic environments to global ones. Your results here can help you assess whether your skills align with those needed to succeed as an international manager.

> **More Self-Assessments**
>
> To learn more about your skills, abilities, and interests, take the following self-assessment on the MyManagementLab®:
>
> • III.B.3.—Am I Experiencing Work/Family Conflict?

# Practise What You Have Learned

## DILEMMA

You are considering organizing an event to raise funds for a special cause (children living in poverty, breast cancer research, illiteracy, or another cause of your choice). Think about who you might invite to this event (that is, your "customers"—those who will buy tickets to the event). What type of event might appeal to them? What suppliers might you approach for help in organizing the event? What legal issues might you face in setting up this event? After considering all these specific environmental forces, describe the challenges you could face in holding this event.

## BECOMING A MANAGER

- Familiarize yourself with current global political, economic, and cultural issues.
- If given the opportunity, try to have your class projects or reports (in this class and other classes) cover global issues or global companies.
- Talk to instructors or students who may be from other countries and ask them what the business world is like in their countries.
- When you evaluate companies for class assignments (for this class and others you may be enrolled in), make a habit of looking at the stakeholders that might be affected by these companies' decisions and actions.

## DEVELOPING YOUR DIAGNOSTIC AND ANALYTICAL SKILLS: WHEN YES DOES NOT ALWAYS MEAN YES, AND NO DOES NOT ALWAYS MEAN NO

When a major chip-manufacturing project ran more than a month late, David Sommers, vice-president for engineering at Adaptec, felt that perhaps the company's Indian engineers "didn't understand the sense of urgency" in getting the project completed.[58] In the Scottish Highlands, Bill Matthews, the general manager of McTavish's Kitchens, is quite satisfied with his non-Scottish employees—cooks who are German, Swedish, and Slovak and waitresses who are mostly Polish. Other Highland hotels and restaurants also have a large number of Eastern European staff. Despite the obvious language barriers, these Scottish employers are finding ways to help their foreign employees adapt and be successful. When Lee Epting, the US-born vice-president of Forum Nokia, gave a presentation to a Finnish audience and asked for feedback, she was told, "That was good." Based on his interpretation of that phrase, he assumed that it must have been just an okay presentation—nothing spectacular. However, because Finns tend to be generally much quieter and more reserved than North Americans, that response actually meant, "That was great, off the scale."

Being a successful global manager is not easy, especially when it comes to dealing with cultural differences. Research by Wilson Learning Worldwide says there is an "iceberg of culture, of which we can only see the top 15 percent—food, appearance, and language." Although these elements themselves can be complicated, it is the other 85 percent of the "iceberg," which is not initially apparent, that managers need to be especially concerned about. What does that include? Workplace issues such as communication styles, prioritizing, role expectations, work tempo, negotiation styles, nonverbal communication, attitudes toward planning, and so forth. Understanding these issues requires developing a global mindset and skill set. Many organizations are relying on cultural awareness training to help them do just that.

Having outsourced some engineering jobs to India, Axcelis Technologies had its North American–based employees go through a training program in which they role-played scenarios with one person pretending to be Indian and the other his or her North American co-worker. One of the company's human resources directors said, "At first I was skeptical and wondered what I'd get out of the class, but it was enlightening for me. Not everyone operates like we do in North America." In our global world, successful managers must learn to recognize and appreciate cultural differences and to understand how to work effectively and efficiently with employees, no matter what their nationality.

### Questions

1. What global attitude do you think would most support, promote, and encourage cultural awareness? Explain.

2. Would legal, political, and economic differences play a role as companies design appropriate cultural awareness training for employees? Explain.

3. Pick one of the countries mentioned in the case and do some cultural research on it. What did you find out about the culture of that country? How might this information affect the way a manager in that country plans, organizes, leads, and controls?

4. UK-based company Kwintessential has several cultural awareness "quizzes" on its website (www.kwintessential. co.uk/resources/culture-tests.html). Go to the company's website and try two or three of these quizzes. Were you surprised at your score? What does your score tell you about your cultural awareness?

5. What advice might you give to a manager who has little experience working with people in other countries?

# DEVELOPING YOUR INTERPERSONAL SKILLS: BECOMING MORE CULTURALLY AWARE

## ABOUT THE SKILL

"Understanding and managing people who are similar to us are challenges—but understanding and managing those who are dissimilar from us and from each other can be even tougher." Workplaces around the world are becoming increasingly diverse. Thus, managers need to recognize that not all employees want the same thing, act in the same manner, and can be managed in the same way. What is a diverse workforce? It is one that is heterogeneous in terms of gender, race, ethnicity, age, and other characteristics that reflect differences. Valuing diversity and helping a diverse workforce achieve its maximum potential are becoming indispensable skills for more and more managers.

## STEPS IN DEVELOPING THE SKILL

The diversity issues an individual manager might face are many. They could include communicating with employees whose familiarity with the language might be limited; creating career development programs that fit the skills, needs, and values of a variety of employees; helping a diverse team cope with a conflict over goals or work assignments; or learning which rewards are valued by different groups of employees. You can improve your handling of diversity issues by following these eight behaviours:[59]

1. FULLY ACCEPT DIVERSITY. Successfully valuing diversity starts with each individual accepting the principle of multiculturalism. Accept the value of diversity for its own sake—not simply because you have to. Accepting and valuing diversity is important because it is the right thing to do. And it is important that you reflect your acceptance in all you say and do.

2. RECRUIT BROADLY. When you have job openings, work to get a diverse applicant pool. Although referrals from current employees can be a good source of applicants, they tend to produce candidates similar to the current workforce.

3. SELECT FAIRLY. Make sure that the selection process does not discriminate. One suggestion is to use job-specific tests rather than general aptitude or knowledge tests. Such tests measure specific skills, not subjective characteristics.

4. PROVIDE ORIENTATION AND TRAINING FOR MINORITIES. Making the transition from outsider to insider can be particularly difficult for an employee who belongs to a minority group. Provide support either through a group or through a mentoring arrangement.

5. SENSITIZE NONMINORITIES. Not only do you personally need to accept and value diversity, but as a manager you need to encourage all your employees to do so. Many organizations do this through diversity training programs, in which employees examine the cultural norms of different groups. The most important thing a manager can do is show by his or her actions that diversity is valued.

6. STRIVE TO BE FLEXIBLE. Part of valuing diversity is recognizing that different groups have different needs and values. Be flexible in accommodating employees' requests.

7. SEEK TO MOTIVATE INDIVIDUALLY. Motivating employees is an important skill for any manager; motivating a diverse workforce has its own special challenges. Managers must be more in tune with the background, cultures, and values of employees. What motivates a single mother with two young children and who is working full time to support her family is likely to be different from the needs of a young, single, part-time employee or an older employee who is working to supplement his or her retirement income.

8. REINFORCE EMPLOYEE DIFFERENCES. Encourage individuals to embrace and value diverse views. Create traditions and ceremonies that promote diversity. Celebrate diversity by accentuating its positive aspects. However, be prepared to deal with the challenges of diversity such as mistrust, miscommunication, lack of cohesiveness, attitudinal differences, and stress.

## PRACTISING THE SKILL

Read the descriptions of the following employees who work for the same organization. After reading each description, write a short paragraph describing what you think the goals and priorities of each employee might be. With what types of employee issues might the manager of each employee have to deal? How could these managers exhibit the value of diversity?

**Lester** is 57 years old, a college graduate, and a vice-president of the firm. His two children are married, and he is a grandparent of three grandchildren. He lives in a condo with his wife who does volunteer work and is active in their church.

Lester is healthy and likes to stay active, both physically and mentally.

**Sanjyot** is a 30-year-old clerical worker who came to Canada from Indonesia 10 years ago. She completed high school after moving to Canada and has begun to attend evening classes at a local college. Sanjyot is a single parent with two children under the age of eight. Although her health is excellent, one of her children suffers from a severe learning disability.

**Yuri** is a recent immigrant from one of the former Soviet republics. He is 42 years old and his English communication skills are quite limited. He has an engineering degree from his country, but since he is not licensed to practise in Canada, he works as a parts clerk. He is unmarried and has no children but feels an obligation to his relatives back in his home country. He sends much of his paycheque to them.

# Team Exercises

## 3BL: THE TRIPLE BOTTOM LINE

### WHAT SHOULD KINDER MORGAN CANADA DO WHEN IT ANTICIPATES OPPOSITION TO EXPANSION OF ITS OIL PIPELINE IN B.C.?

Kinder Morgan Canada has been running the Trans Mountain pipeline for more than 60 years. In 2008, with little fanfare, the company spent $750 million and added 13 new pump stations to increase capacity by 75 000 barrels for the Edmonton-to-Vancouver pipeline. With oil and gas pipeline projects very much under the public eye in 2013, company President Ian Anderson expects significant opposition to a $5 billion pipeline expansion. The issue is no longer a simple matter of profit—people are concerned about oil sands growth and its impact on communities and workers.

The profit bottom line is straightforward—expanding pipeline capacity is good business for oil sands producers, refiners, and overseas customers. The expansion will provide a building block for the development of the Asian market.

People are concerned because Kinder Morgan Energy Partners is a Houston-based infrastructure giant, so Kinder Morgan Canada may have to increase its presence in Vancouver. A Vancouver presence would mean more jobs for local workers and higher tax revenues for governments and First Nations groups.

The main concern stems from the potential environmental impact of the oil sands generally, and the Trans Mountain pipeline specifically. Increasing capacity means more tankers in the Vancouver harbour, which increases the chance of an oil spill. An oil spill would hurt both Vancouver's tourism industry and its image as a "green" city. In fact, Kinder Morgan has been using tankers for more than 60 years without any incidents, but the perception of that reality is distorted by incidents such as the BP oil spill in the Gulf of Mexico.

Opposition is expected from Vancouver and Burnaby municipal politicians, First Nations peoples, including the Tsleil-Waututh Nation near Burrard Inlet, and the broader environmental movement. Kinder Morgan has split the environmental stakeholders into three groups. The first group includes organizations like the Pembina Institute, a Canadian think-tank concerned about sustainable energy solutions. Anderson feels that meaningful dialogue about environmental impact is possible with this group. The second group encompasses environmental activists who use lobbying, campaigns, and protest to make their viewpoint heard. Anderson acknowledges that discussions and progress will be harder to make with these stakeholders. The third group is what Kinder Morgan calls the larger group in the middle, who are interested in the specifics of why the pipeline should be expanded and how to minimize the environmental risks of the project.

### THINKING STRATEGICALLY ABOUT 3BL

Anderson's game plan involves building alliances among business groups like the BC Chamber of Commerce, with First Nations and environmental organizations across BC, and with municipal politicians. He plans to meet with various stakeholders for a full two years before entering the regulatory process. How should he approach each of the three environmental factions? What are the differing environmental stakeholder perspectives on the pipeline expansion?

*Source:* Claudia Cattaneo, "Trans Mountain: Same Pipeline, New Realities," *Financial Post*, April 27, 2012.

## ASSESSING EMPLOYEES' GLOBAL APTITUDES

Moving to a foreign country is not easy, no matter how many times you have done it or how receptive you are to new experiences. Successful global organizations are able to identify the best candidates for global assignments, and one of the ways they do this is through individual assessments prior to assigning people to global facilities. Form groups of three to five individuals. Your newly formed team, the Global Assignment Task Force, has been given the responsibility for developing a global aptitude assessment form for Zara, the successful European clothing retailer.[60] Although the company is not well known in North America, Zara's managers have positioned the company for continued global success. Their success is based on a simple principle—in fashion, nothing is as important as time to market.

Zara's store managers (more than 600 worldwide) offer suggestions every day on cuts, fabrics, and even new lines. After reviewing the ideas, a team at headquarters in La Coruna, Spain, decides what to make. Designers draw up the ideas and send them over the company's intranet to nearby factories. Within days, the cutting, dyeing, sewing, and assembling start. In three weeks, the clothes will be in stores from Barcelona to Berlin to Buenos Aires. That is 12 times faster than its competitors. Zara has a twice-a-week delivery schedule that restocks old styles and brings in new designs. Competitors tend to get new designs once or twice a season.

Because Zara is expanding its global operations significantly, management wants to make sure they are sending the best possible people to the various global locations. Your team's assignment is to come up with a rough draft of a form to assess people's global aptitudes. Think about the characteristics, skills, attitudes, and so on, that you think a successful global employee would need. Your team's draft should be at least a half page but not longer than one page. Be prepared to present your ideas to your classmates and instructor.

## BE THE CONSULTANT: ETHICAL DECISION MAKING

In teams of five or six people, discuss each of the following scenarios and come to an agreement on the most ethical courses of action in each situation.

**Scenario 1:** You work for a large Canadian nonprofit organization that holds a big annual conference. The conference rotates throughout Canada on a yearly basis. A resort and conference company in Hawaii invites you and one other person down for a one-week paid vacation so that you can check out their conference facilities. Should you:

(a) Accept the vacation?
(b) Turn down the vacation?
(c) Accept the vacation if your boss poses no objection?
(d) Accept the vacation if the majority of the conference attendees are in favour of holding the conference in Hawaii?

**Scenario 2:** You work for a large manufacturer of farm equipment in Saskatchewan. You are anticipating that a bid you submitted for a big project is going to be successful. The final decision is being delayed by bureaucracy with the international combine manufacturer. It is likely that you are to be awarded the contract and the tight timelines mean that you need to get started right away. You begin negotiations with a supplier and decide to tell them:

(a) "Approval is done. We can skip the technical details and start production immediately."

(b) "Start producing the product and we'll cover your costs when we sign the contract."
(c) "We are anticipating that the proposal will be approved. We can sign an interim contract to cover the first phase of the project, which we will initiate on a tentative basis."
(d) "The deal is almost done. It is going to be a big deal for both of us, but we need you to shoulder the start-up costs until the contract is signed. Then we can work out a contract between the two of us."

**Scenario 3:** You work for a medium-sized IT consulting firm in Quebec. You submit the lowest bid for a government contract. You do not have the staffing in place to meet the contract at the moment and you anticipate that it will take you three months longer than your main competitor to build the IT infrastructure awarded in the contract. Your government client asks for details on your schedule before awarding the contract to you or your main competitor. What do you do?

(a) Indicate that your schedule is "basically the same" as what you believe your competitor's is to build the infrastructure.
(b) Commit to completing the job in the same timeframe as your competitor and tell your internal team that they must shorten their timeframe by three months or else.
(c) Ignore the scheduling question and focus on the quality of your firm's work and the lowest cost component of your bid.
(d) Admit that your schedule is longer than your competitor's, but reconfirm the quality of your work and hope that you don't lose too many points in the evaluation process.

**Scenario 4:** Your newest hire is a friend of yours. Her performance is lacking and her relationships with her co-workers are poor. What do you do?

(a) Call her in to discuss her poor performance.
(b) Meet with her co-workers and tell them to give her some slack.
(c) Ask HR to meet with her and develop a performance management plan.
(d) Do nothing because she is new on the job and will perform better.

# Business Cases

## EARTH RATED POOPBAGS

Fashionable. Affordable. Earth-friendly. Poop bags. Abby Gnanendran, president and co-founder of Montreal-based Earth Rated PoopBags, started his business when grocery stores began charging for plastic bags. Pet owners now had to pay for bags, and Gnanendran realized that an

affordable and eco-friendly bag would be a big hit in the marketplace.[61]

The pet supply market is very strong, with more than 12.5 millions pets in Canada alone.[62] Market growth continues to be strong, and as the economy improves, consumers are more likely to increase spending on pets. From the outset, Gnanendran sold his product exclusively online through his company's website, poopbags.ca. The company relied on Google AdWords and Facebook to generate interest and sales. Increasing fan numbers have opened up avenues to share stories and keep fans up to date on environmental issues as well as animal care, rescue, and shelter programs.

Going retail was not part of the original plan, but repeated calls from pet supply stores convinced Earth Rated PoopBags to move from online to retail. They used a long-term strategy that sacrificed short-term profits as they distributed more than 5 million free bags to retail stores, dog walkers, and bloggers. The move paid off: The conversion rate was higher than 70 percent, with retailers placing orders within a month of receiv-

ing the samples. The poop bags are now carried in more than 900 stores in North America and parts of Europe. Company sales were ten times higher in their second year of operation, and sales were on pace to triple in 2012. The company moved away from online sales and instead uses their web presence to communicate via social media with customers, retailers, and the charities that they support. They have built high awareness and now need to turn that into higher sales and engagement.

What strategies can Gnanendran use to maintain social media momentum? How can Earth Rated continue to expand into the US and European markets? What world market should they target next?

# CBC

# Greenlite

With growing concern over climate change, governments around the world are looking for ways to reduce greenhouse gases and consumption of fossil fuels. One simple solution that has garnered government support is phasing out energy-inefficient light bulbs and replacing them with energy-efficient ones. The most popular and affordable commercially available bulbs are compact fluorescent light bulbs (CFLs). CFLs use approximately 75 percent less energy than regular incandescent light bulbs. CFLs also have a long lifespan, typically 6000 to 15 000 hours, as compared to the 750- to 1000-hour lifespan of a normal incandescent bulb.

Beginning in 2006, the Government of Canada began replacing light bulbs in all federal government buildings with CFLs. In April 2007, the Government of Canada announced it would legislate a complete ban on the sale of inefficient light bulbs by 2012. According to the Minister of Natural Resources, Gary Lunn, the ban will reduce greenhouse gas emissions by over 6 million tonnes a year.

Canada was not the only country to phase out energy-inefficient light bulbs. In 2007, the United States government signed the Clean Energy Act into law. This legislation effectively phases out the sale of incandescent bulbs in the United States by January 2014.

Canadian Nina Gupta viewed these developments as a business opportunity. Her father owned a factory in India that made halogen bulbs for cars. She founded Greenlite Lighting Corporation, managed the transition in her father's factory from halogen bulbs to the production of CFLs, and began selling CFLs in India, Canada, and the United States. "We recognized that the green movement was the wave of the future," she says, "so we found a product that was ecologically and environmentally friendly and focused on that."

Greenlite is now one of the leading producers of CFLs in the world, selling over 30 million CFLs a year.

## QUESTIONS

### Interpret

1. What is the external environment? Differentiate between the general and specific environments.

### Analyze

2. How did the general environment influence Nina Gupta's decision to sell energy efficient light bulbs in North America?

3. Explain how the specific environment for Greenlite will change if it decides to sell solar power to customers in China.

### Practise

4. Greenlite plans to expand its business by building a solar power factory in India and managing the employees in this factory. The company may decide to sell the factory's product to consumers in China. What challenges do you anticipate the corporation could face in carrying out these plans for globalization?

5. Some university researchers have noted a number of health risks associated with CFLs. Most bulbs contain a high amount of mercury, which can be dangerous for children if the bulbs are broken and the mercury is released into the air. Furthermore, some research has shown that emission of UV radiation is associated with skin rashes and migraines in adults. These problems should not be of concern to the management of Greenlite, as their only responsibility is to maximize the profits of the business. Do you agree?

*Sources:* "My First Million: Greenlite," *Fortune Hunters*, Season 2, Canadian Broadcasting Corporation, February 28, 2009; Greenlite Lighting Corporation website, www.greenlite.ca; Petition filed with the Office of the Auditor General of Canada, www.oag-bvg.gc.ca/internet/English/pet_254_e_31427.html; "Lights Go Out On Inefficient Bulbs by 2012," CBC News, April 25, 2007, www.cbc.ca/canada/story/2007/04/25/lunn-bulbs.html; "Health Canada Testing Compact Fluorescent Bulbs For Harmful Radiation," *CBC News*, January 21, 2009, www.cbc.ca/health/story/2009/01/21/bulbs.html.

# CBC

# Mountain Equipment Co-op

In 1971, Mountain Equipment Co-op (MEC) was founded in Vancouver by a group of Canadian rock climbers who needed a store to buy gear that other, more conventional, retailers did not carry, including gear for mountaineering, rock climbing, and hiking. MEC is a cooperative in which members employ their shared purchasing power to obtain goods and services for outdoor activities. Anyone can become a member at MEC by buying a $5 membership share. In 2010, MEC ranked 14th in the government's list of the top 50 nonfinancial retail cooperatives in Canada, with revenues of $264 billion. In terms of membership, MEC ranks number one, with 3.4 billion members. MEC is notable for its commitment to the environment and now operates in fifteen cities across Canada.

In its first 30 years, MEC focused on the sale of clothing made only in Canada. MEC billed its "made in Canada" strategy as an initiative promoting corporate social responsibility that supported the local economy and created jobs for Canadians. In recent years, however, the cooperative's commitment to this strategy has lagged. In 2002, 70 percent of the clothing it sold was made in Canada, while in 2007 only 50 percent of the clothing in its stores was made locally.

The stated reason for this change in strategy is that locally made clothing is too costly. MEC's major foreign suppliers are now located in India and China, and these suppliers sell their products at lower prices due to the lower cost of labour in these countries. Some foreign-made products can be sold to members for nearly half the cost of the same products made in Canada. Former MEC CEO Steve Robinson reported that to sell more Canadian-produced goods the organization would have to "eat the profit margin" in order to make these goods affordable for its members. The company's latest research shows that, in general, most members will pay only slightly more for clothing made in Canada. Beyond a certain point, MEC is likely to lose the sale.

This change in strategy is bad news for Canadian outdoor clothing manufacturers.

## QUESTIONS

### Interpret

1. Identify the stakeholders affected by MEC's decision to carry more products manufactured in offshore facilities?

### Analyze

2. Explain how each stakeholder is affected by MEC's decision to buy less expensive foreign-made clothing. Which stakeholders benefit from this decision? Who suffers?

3. Explain how MEC is "going global," and describe what degree of risk and investment is involved in this endeavour.

### Practise

4. As a company created in Canada, managed in Canada, and selling goods exclusively in Canada, MEC has a social responsibility to sell primarily Canadian manufactured goods. Do you agree?

5. Go to the Canadian Co-operative Association's website and read about MEC's sustainability policy (see the URL listed below). What are the four key pillars of its sustainability strategy? What are MEC's three long-term goals moving forward?

http://www.coopscanada.coop/public_html/assets/firefly/files/files/environmental_sustainability/MEC-_web_style.pdf

*Sources:* "MEC," *The National*, CBC News, May 30, 2007; Mountain Equipment Co-op website, www.mec.ca; Government of Canada, Co-operatives Secretariat, "Top 50 Non-financial Co-operatives in Canada in 2010," January 1, 2012, http://www.coop.gc.ca/COOP/display-afficher.do?id=1325270945531&lang=eng; Karen Bains, "Mountain Equipment Co-op—Demonstrating the Best of What a Business Can Be," Canadian Co-operative Association, September 2009, http://www.coopscanada.coop/public_html/assets/firefly/files/files/environmental_sustainability/MEC-_web_style.pdf.

# CHAPTER 3

# Planning and Strategic Management

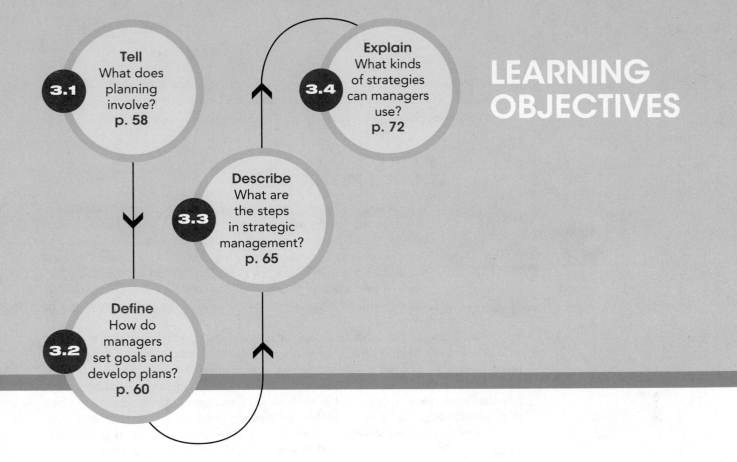

**Tell**
What does planning involve?
p. 58

**3.1**

**Explain**
What kinds of strategies can managers use?
p. 72

**3.4**

**Describe**
What are the steps in strategic management?
p. 65

**3.3**

**Define**
How do managers set goals and develop plans?
p. 60

**3.2**

# LEARNING OBJECTIVES

Planning provides companies an opportunity to focus their resources on their key priorities. In 2011, Maple Leaf Foods Inc. announced the third and final phase of a multiyear restructuring plan, spending $560 million on a new plant in Hamilton and on upgrades to three other plants. They also closed five plants, which eliminated 1500 net jobs.

The parity of the Canadian dollar with the US greenback has exposed manufacturing inefficiencies at many Canadian firms, making it hard for them to compete against larger, more productive US food companies. Maple Leaf, one of the country's largest food manufacturers, is an example of why companies need to change to become more competitive.

Maple Leaf will close most of its aging meat-processing factories in Canada in a bid to slash costs, including the Kitchener meat-processing and distribution centre, which dates back to 1890. Approximately 2500 jobs are being cut overall, while the new Hamilton plant will create 1000 new jobs.

"The final phase of this plan will establish Maple Leaf Foods as a more streamlined and profitable company, well positioned to deliver significant and sustainable value to its shareholders," said Michael McCain, President and CEO. "We are creating, through one of the largest single investments in the Canadian food industry, a highly efficient, world-class prepared meats production and distribution network that will markedly increase our competitiveness and close the cost gap with our US peers."[1]

## Think About It

Maple Leaf Foods has faced many challenges in its business environment that have necessitated a review and change of its strategy. As you learn more about this company, its business, and the challenges it has faced in recent years, think about all the different aspects of the business that the company's managers and Board of Directors have to consider when they are making their plans for the future. In the example above, what factors did the Board of Directors take into account when they analyzed the strategic, financial, and operational elements of their plan?

Managers everywhere need to plan. In this chapter, we present the basics of planning: what it is, why managers plan, and how they plan. We will also discuss the importance of strategic management and choosing effective strategies to develop a competitive advantage.

## WHAT IS PLANNING?

**Tell**
3.1 What does planning involve?

As we stated in Chapter 1, **planning** involves defining goals, establishing an overall strategy for achieving those goals, and developing a comprehensive set of plans to integrate and coordinate the work needed to achieve the goals. It is concerned both with ends (what is to be done) and means (how it is to be done). For example, you and your classmates may want to organize a large graduation dinner dance. To do so, you would set goals, establish a strategy, develop plans, and assign committees to get the work done.

Planning can either be formal or informal. In informal planning, nothing is written down, and there is little or no sharing of goals with others. Informal planning is general and lacks continuity. Although more common in smaller organizations where the owner-manager has a vision of where he or she wants the business to go and how to get there, informal planning does exist in some large organizations. At the same time, some small businesses may have very sophisticated planning processes and formal plans.

When we use the term *planning* in this book, we mean *formal* planning. In formal planning, specific goals covering a period of years are defined. These goals are written and shared with organization members. Then a specific action program for the achievement of these goals is developed: managers clearly define the path they want to take to get the organization and the various work units from where they are to where they want them to be.

Setting goals, establishing a strategy to achieve those goals, and developing a set of plans to integrate and coordinate activities seem pretty complicated. So why would managers want to plan? Does planning affect performance? We address these issues next.

### Purposes of Planning

We can identify at least four reasons for planning:

*Are you a planner or a doer? Do you prefer to make plans or just act?*

- *Planning provides direction to managers and nonmanagers alike.* When employees know where the organization or work unit is going and what they must contribute to reach goals, they can coordinate their activities, cooperate with each other, and do what it takes to accomplish those goals. Without planning, departments and individuals might work at cross purposes, preventing the organization from moving efficiently toward its goals. This would also be true if you and your friends were planning your grad party— if you did not coordinate and cooperate, you might not actually get the party organized in time.

- *Planning reduces uncertainty by forcing managers to look ahead, anticipate change, consider the impact of change, and develop appropriate responses.* Even though planning cannot eliminate change or uncertainty, managers plan in order to anticipate change and develop the most effective response to it. This increased preparation for change helps develop managers' skills and provides flexibility to the organization.

- *Planning reduces overlapping and wasteful activities.* When work activities are coordinated around established plans, redundancy can be minimized and time management is enhanced. Furthermore, when means and ends are made clear through planning, inefficiencies become obvious and can be corrected or eliminated. For a look at your personal planning skills, see *Assess Your Skills—How Good Am I at Personal Planning?* on pages 82–83 at the end of the chapter.

- *Planning establishes the goals or standards that are used in controlling.* If we are unsure of what we are trying to accomplish, how can we determine whether we have actually achieved it? In planning, we develop the goals and the plans. Then, through controlling, we compare actual performance against the goals, identify any significant deviations, and take any necessary corrective action. Without planning, there would be no way to control outcomes.

Renato Zambonini, board member of Ottawa-based Cognos, notes that planning went out of fashion during the dot-com years. He found that in both California and Ottawa, entrepreneurs worked "90 hours a week, but the whole goal [was] not to build a business or a company. [All they really wanted was] someone to buy them out."[2] Unfortunately, many of those companies were not bought out, but folded. Planning might have helped them be more successful.

## Planning and Performance

Is planning worthwhile? Do managers and organizations that plan outperform those that do not? Intuitively, you would expect the answer to be a resounding yes. While results from studies examining performance in organizations that plan are generally positive, we cannot say organizations that formally plan *always* outperform those that do not plan.

Numerous studies have looked at the relationship between planning and performance.[3] We can draw the following four conclusions from these studies. First, formal planning is generally associated with higher profits, higher return on assets, and other positive financial results. Second, the quality of the planning process and the appropriate implementation of the plans probably contribute more to high performance than does the extent of planning. Third, in those studies in which formal planning did not lead to higher performance, the external environment was often the culprit. Government regulations, powerful labour unions, and other critical environmental forces constrain managers' options and reduce the impact of planning on an organization's performance. Fourth, the planning/performance relationship is influenced by the planning time frame. Organizations need at least four years of systematic formal planning before performance is affected.

Planning is definitely not just for managers. When families in the *Vancouver Sun's* distribution area were asked to take the newspaper's "car free challenge" for a month, they learned that planning became a much greater part of their lives. The three families pictured above took the challenge and found that figuring out how long a journey took and the best way to get there required being more aware of their schedules than when they could just grab their car keys and drive off. Planning provided the families with a better understanding of scheduling, which allowed them to make improvements.

*Are you skeptical of planning? Do you wonder whether planning really pays off?*

*What if you really don't like to make plans?*

## Criticisms of Planning

Formal organizational planning became popular in the 1960s and, for the most part, is still popular today. It makes sense for an organization to establish its direction. But critics have challenged some of the basic assumptions underlying planning. What are the primary criticisms directed at formal planning?

- *Planning may create rigidity.*[4] Formal planning efforts can lock an organization into specific goals to be achieved within specific timetables. When these goals are set, the assumption may be that the environment will not change during the time period the goals cover. If that assumption is faulty, managers who follow a plan may face trouble. Rather than remaining flexible—and possibly throwing out the plan—managers who continue to do the things required to achieve the original goals may not be able to cope with the changed environment. Forcing a course of action when the environment is fluid can be a recipe for disaster.

**planning**
A management function that involves defining goals, establishing a strategy for achieving those goals, and developing plans to integrate and coordinate activities.

- *Plans cannot be developed for a dynamic environment.*[5] Most organizations today face dynamic environments. If a basic assumption of making plans—that the environment will not change—is faulty, then how can you make plans at all? Today's business environment is often chaotic at best. By definition, that means random and unpredictable. Managing under those conditions requires flexibility, which may mean not being tied to formal plans.

- *Formal plans cannot replace intuition and creativity.*[6] Successful organizations are typically the result of someone's innovative vision. But visions have a tendency to become formalized as they evolve. Formal planning efforts typically involve a thorough investigation of the organization's capabilities and opportunities, and a mechanical analysis that reduces the vision to some type of programmed routine. That approach can spell disaster for an organization. Apple Computer learned this the hard way. In the late 1970s and throughout the 1980s, Apple's success was attributed, in part, to the innovative and creative approaches of co-founder Steve Jobs. Steve Jobs left Apple in 1985 due to a power struggle with Apple's Board of Directors. With his departure came increased organizational formality, including detailed planning—the same things that Jobs despised so much because he felt that they hampered creativity. During the 1990s, the situation at Apple became so bad that Jobs returned as permanent CEO in 2000 and spearheaded the iPod and iTunes, the iPhone, and eventually the iPad—changes that led Apple to become one of the world's dominant players.

- *Planning focuses managers' attention on today's competition, not on tomorrow's survival.*[7] Formal planning has a tendency to focus on how to capitalize on existing business opportunities within an industry. It often does not allow managers to consider creating or reinventing an industry. Consequently, formal plans with long timeframes may result in lost market share and high catch-up costs when other competitors take the lead. In contrast, companies such as Intel, General Electric, Nokia, and Sony have found success by forging into uncharted waters, spawning new industries as they go.

- *Formal planning reinforces success, which may lead to failure.*[8] Changing or discarding previously successful plans is hard. It means leaving the comfort of what works for the anxiety of the unknown. Successful plans, however, may provide a false sense of security, generating more confidence in the formal plans than is warranted. Many managers will not face the unknown until they are forced to do so by environmental changes. By then, it may be too late!

Interpret

How valid are these criticisms? Should managers forget about planning? No! Although the criticisms have merit when directed at rigid, inflexible planning, today's managers can be effective planners if they understand the need to be flexible in responding to environmental change.

## HOW DO MANAGERS PLAN?

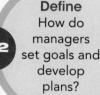

**Define**
How do managers set goals and develop plans?

3.2

Planning is often called the primary management function because it establishes the basis for all the other functions that managers perform. Without planning, managers would not know what to organize, lead, or control. In fact, without plans, there would not be anything to organize, lead, or control! So how do managers plan?

Planning involves two important elements: goals and plans. **Goals (objectives)** are the desired outcomes for individuals, groups, or entire organizations.[9] Goals are objectives, and we use the two terms interchangeably. Goals provide the direction for all management decisions and form the criteria against which actual work accomplishments can be measured. That is why they are often called the foundation of planning. You have to know the desired target or outcome before you can establish plans for reaching it. **Plans** are documents that outline how goals are going to be met and that typically describe resource allocations, schedules, and other necessary actions to accomplish the goals. As managers plan, they are developing both goals and plans.

In the next section, we consider how to establish goals.

## Approaches to Establishing Goals

Goals provide the direction for all management decisions and actions, and form the criteria against which actual accomplishments are measured. Everything organizational members do should be oriented toward helping both their work units and the organization achieve the goals that have been set. Goals can be established through a process of traditional goal setting or management by objectives.

**TRADITIONAL GOAL SETTING**  In **traditional goal setting**, goals are set at the top of the organization and then broken into subgoals for each organizational level. This process works reasonably well when an organization is hierarchically structured. This traditional perspective assumes that top managers know what is best because they see "the big picture." Thus, the goals that are established and passed down to each succeeding level serve to direct and guide, and in some ways constrain, individual employees' work behaviours. Employees work to meet the goals that have been assigned in their areas of responsibility.

In traditional goal setting, if top management wants to increase sales by 10 percent for the year, the marketing and sales departments need to develop action plans that will yield these results. The manufacturing department needs to develop plans for how to produce more product. An individual salesperson may need to make more calls to new clients or convince current clients that they need more product. Thus, each of the lower levels (individual employee, sales, marketing, production) becomes a means to achieving the corporate end of increasing sales.

**MANAGEMENT BY OBJECTIVES**  Instead of traditional goal setting, many organizations use **management by objectives (MBO)**, an approach in which specific performance goals are jointly determined by employees and their managers, progress toward accomplishing these goals is periodically reviewed, and rewards are allocated on the basis of this progress. Rather than using goals only as controls, MBO uses them to motivate employees as well. Employees will be more committed to goals that they help set.

Management by objectives consists of four elements: goal specificity, participative decision making, an explicit time period, and performance feedback.[10] Its appeal lies in its focus on the accomplishment of participatively set objectives as the reason for and motivation behind individuals' work efforts. Exhibit 3-1 lists the steps in a typical MBO program.

Do MBO programs work? Studies of actual MBO programs confirm that MBO increases employee performance and organizational productivity. A review of 70 programs, for example, found organizational productivity gains in 68 of them.[11] This same review also identified top management commitment and involvement as important conditions for MBO to succeed.

*Have you occasionally failed at your goals? How can you develop more achievable goals?*

**CHARACTERISTICS OF WELL-DESIGNED GOALS**  Goals are not all created equal. Some goals are better than others. How can you tell the difference? What makes a "well-designed" goal?[12] Exhibit 3-2 outlines the characteristics of well-designed goals.

---

**goals (objectives)**
Desired outcomes for individuals, groups, or entire organizations.

**plans**
Documents that outline how goals are going to be met and describe resource allocations, schedules, and other necessary actions to accomplish the goals.

**traditional goal setting**
An approach to setting goals in which goals are set at the top of the organization and then broken into subgoals for each organizational level.

**management by objectives (MBO)**
An approach to goal setting in which specific measurable goals are jointly set by employees and their managers, progress toward accomplishing those goals is periodically reviewed, and rewards are allocated on the basis of this progress.

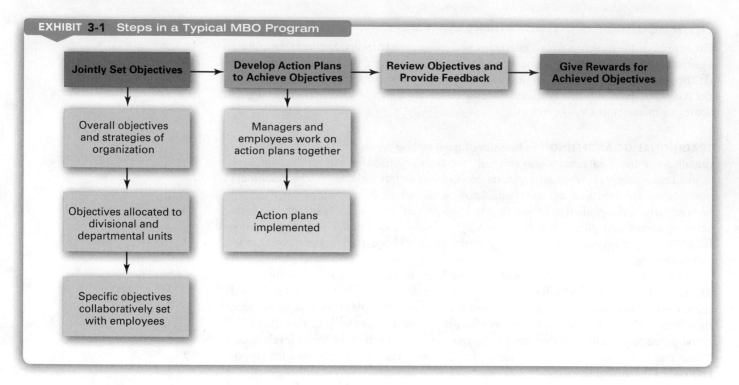

**EXHIBIT 3-1** Steps in a Typical MBO Program

Jointly Set Objectives → Develop Action Plans to Achieve Objectives → Review Objectives and Provide Feedback → Give Rewards for Achieved Objectives

Jointly Set Objectives:
- Overall objectives and strategies of organization
- Objectives allocated to divisional and departmental units
- Specific objectives collaboratively set with employees

Develop Action Plans to Achieve Objectives:
- Managers and employees work on action plans together
- Action plans implemented

## Steps in Goal Setting

What steps should managers follow in setting goals? The goal-setting process consists of five steps.

1. *Review the organization's vision and mission.* The **vision and mission** reflect the purpose of an organization as statements of what the organization hopes to accomplish. Reviewing these statements before writing goals is important, because the goals need to reflect what is contained in the vision and mission statements.

2. *Evaluate available resources.* You do not want to set goals that are impossible to achieve given your available resources. Even though goals should be challenging, they must be realistic. After all, if the resources you have to work with will not allow you to achieve a goal no matter how hard you try or how much effort is exerted, that goal should not be set. That would be like the person with a $50 000 annual income and no other financial resources setting a goal of building an investment portfolio worth $1 million in three years. No matter how hard he or she works at it, it will not happen.

3. *Determine the goals individually or with input from others.* The goals reflect desired outcomes and should be consistent with the organization's mission and goals in other organizational areas. These goals should be measurable, specific, and include a time frame for accomplishment.

4. *Write down the goals and communicate them to all who need to know.* We have already explained the benefit of writing down and communicating goals.

5. *Review results and whether goals are being met.* Make changes as needed. For any plan to be effective, reviews need to be done.

**EXHIBIT 3-2** Characteristics of Well-Designed Goals

- Written in terms of outcomes rather than actions
- Measurable and quantifiable
- Clear time frame

- Challenging yet attainable
- Feature participation and feedback from all necessary organizational members

## Developing Plans

Once goals have been established, written down, and communicated, a manager is ready to develop plans for pursuing the goals.

What are the advantages of specifying the plans to achieve goals? Jean-Marc Eustache, president and CEO of Montreal-based Transat A.T., knows he cannot relax just because he has one of the largest international travel and tourism companies in the world. He recently told shareholders that he plans "to double [Transat's] revenues during the next three-and-a-half years."[13] To accomplish this goal, he plans to do the following: increase the company's share of the leisure travel business into and out of Ontario; increase the company's share of the leisure travel business in France; increase flights between Canada and the United Kingdom; move into the United States and offer flights to Mexico and the Caribbean; and increase the company's ownership and management of hotels in the Caribbean and Mexico. By specifying the plans to achieve his goal to double revenues, Eustache let Transat employees know where to focus attention when helping people make their travel plans.

**TYPES OF PLANS**  The most popular ways to describe an organization's plans are by their breadth (strategic vs. operational), time frame (short term vs. long term), specificity (directional vs. specific), and frequency of use (single use vs. standing). These planning classifications are not independent. As Exhibit 3-3 illustrates, strategic plans are long-term, directional, and single-use. Operational plans are short-term, specific, and standing. Let's examine each of these types of plans.

**Strategic plans** are plans that apply to the entire organization, establish the organization's overall goals, and seek to position the organization in terms of its environment. Plans that specify the details of how the overall goals are to be achieved are called **operational plans**. How do the two types of plans differ? Strategic plans tend to cover a longer time frame and a broader view of the organization. Strategic plans also include the formulation of goals, whereas operational plans define ways to achieve the goals. Also, operational plans tend to cover short time periods—monthly, weekly, and day-to-day.

The difference in years between short term and long term has shortened considerably. It used to be that long term meant anything more than seven years. Try to imagine what you would like to be doing in seven years, and you can begin to appreciate how difficult it was for managers to establish plans that far into the future. As organizational environments have become more uncertain, the definition of *long term* has changed. We define **long-term plans** as those with a time frame beyond three years.[14] For example, an organization may develop a five-year plan for increasing its sales in Asia. We define **short-term plans** as those with a time frame of one year or less. For example, a company may decide that it will increase sales by 10 percent over the next year. The *intermediate term* is any time period in between. Although these time classifications are fairly common, an organization can designate any time frame it wants for planning purposes.

Intuitively, it would seem that specific plans would be preferable to directional, or loosely guided, plans. **Specific plans** are plans that are clearly defined and leave no room for interpretation. They have clearly defined objectives. There is no ambiguity and no problem with misunderstanding. For example, a manager who seeks to increase his or her unit's work output by 8 percent over a given 12-month period might establish specific procedures,

---

**vision and mission**
The purpose of an organization.

**strategic plans**
Plans that apply to the entire organization, establish the organization's overall goals, and seek to position the organization in terms of its environment.

**operational plans**
Plans that specify the details of how the overall goals are to be achieved.

**long-term plans**
Plans with a time frame beyond three years.

**short-term plans**
Plans with a time frame of one year or less.

**specific plans**
Plans that are clearly defined and leave no room for interpretation.

**EXHIBIT 3-3** Types of Plans

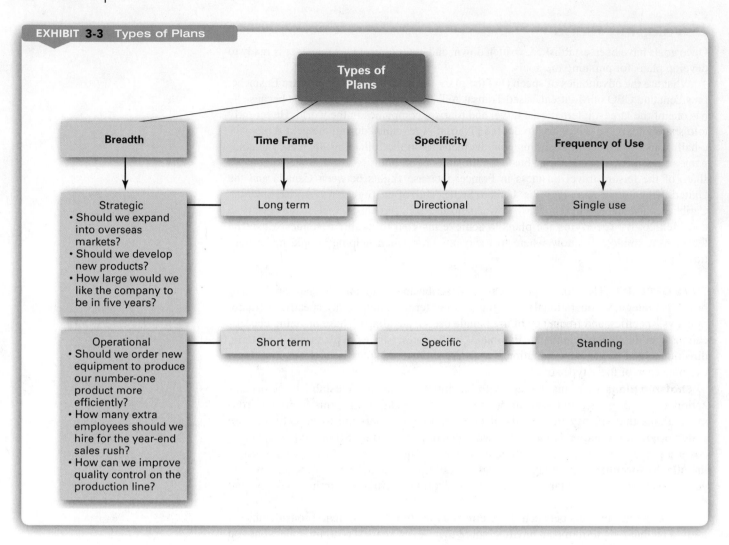

budget allocations, and schedules of activities to reach that goal. The drawbacks of specific plans are that they require clarity and a sense of predictability that often do not exist.

When uncertainty is high and managers must be flexible in order to respond to unexpected changes, directional plans are preferable. **Directional plans** are flexible plans that set out general guidelines. They provide focus but don't lock managers into specific goals or courses of action. Instead of detailing a specific plan to cut costs by 4 percent and increase revenues by 6 percent in the next six months, managers might formulate a directional plan for improving profits by 5 to 10 percent over the next six months. The flexibility inherent in directional plans must be weighed against the loss of clarity provided by specific plans.

Some plans that managers develop are ongoing, while others are used only once. A **single-use plan** is a one-time plan specifically designed to meet the needs of a unique situation. Budgets and projects are examples of single-use plans. For example, when Charles Schwab introduced its online discount stock-brokerage service, top-level executives used a single-use plan to guide the creation and implementation of the new service. In contrast, standing plans are ongoing and provide guidance for activities performed repeatedly. **Standing plans** include policies, rules, and procedures, which we define in Chapter 4. An example of a standing plan would be the discrimination and harassment policy developed by the University of British Columbia. The policy provides guidance to university administrators, faculty, and staff as they perform their job duties.

**PLANNING TOOLS AND TECHNIQUES** Managers use various tools and techniques to maximize the benefits of planning.[15]

| Forecasting | Attempting to predict the future and developing plans accordingly |
|---|---|
| Contingency planning | Identifying alternative plans for outcomes that are different than expected |
| Scenario planning | Predicting various future outcomes and making plans for each |
| Benchmarking | Developing plans based on the practices of competitors |

**Forecasting**   Forecasting involves predicting future events and developing plans to deal with those events. Expert opinions and statistical analysis are two types of forecasting techniques.[16] Canadian financial analysts regularly predict what will happen with the Canadian and world economies, and businesses use that information to help plan their strategy.

**Contingency Planning**   Adjusting plans for various future situations is called contingency planning. The process of developing these plans is influenced by changing circumstances in the environment.[17] When environmental uncertainty is high, plans should be specific, but flexible. Managers must be prepared to amend plans as they are implemented. At times, managers may even have to abandon their plans.[18]

**Scenario Planning**   Scenario planning is a type of contingency planning that involves a longer time frame. Royal Dutch Shell has used scenarios since the early 1970s as part of a process for generating and evaluating its strategic options. Shell used these scenarios to develop better oil forecasts than its competitors and to predict the overcapacity issue in the tanker business earlier.[19]

**Benchmarking**   Benchmarking involves the search for the best practices among competitors or noncompetitors that lead to their superior performance.[20] The basic idea underlying benchmarking is that management can improve quality by analyzing and then copying the methods of leaders in various fields. A local charity organization can benefit from the experience and successful practices of other Canadian charities.

## ORGANIZATIONAL STRATEGY: CHOOSING A NICHE

### Think About It

Think about the different aspects of the business that Maple Leaf Food's managers and Board of Directors have to consider when they are making their plans for the future. For example, Maple Leaf Foods has successfully used acquisitions, such as the purchase of Schneider Corporation in 2004, to diversify their product mix. How would some acquisitions be more effective than others?

Maple Leaf Foods combines strategy and innovation to stay abreast of the trends in consumer purchasing. Each year, it introduces up to 100 new products. In 2009, Maple Leaf opened the ThinkFOOD! Centre, created to provide customers with an opportunity to collaborate with the product development team and culinary experts. By involving customers in the design of food products, Maple Leaf hopes to increase sales for its global baker and protein businesses.[21]

To begin to understand why organizational strategy matters, you need look no further than at what has happened in the discount retail industry in

**3.3**

**Describe**
What are the steps in strategic management?

---

**directional plans**
Plans that are flexible and that set out general guidelines.

**single-use plan**
A one-time plan specifically designed to meet the needs of a unique situation.

**standing plans**
Ongoing plans that provide guidance for activities performed repeatedly.

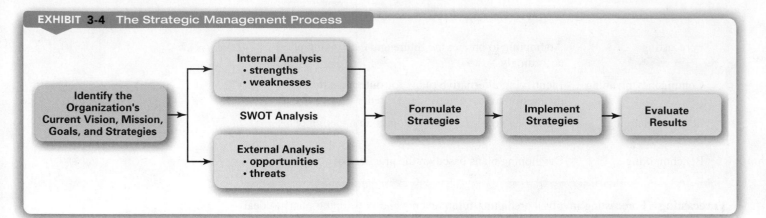

**EXHIBIT 3-4** The Strategic Management Process

Canada. The industry's two largest competitors—Walmart and Zellers—have battled for market dominance since Walmart entered Canada in 1992. The two chains have some striking similarities: store atmosphere, markets served, and organizational purpose. Yet Walmart's performance (financial and otherwise) has taken market share from Zellers every single year. Walmart is the world's largest and most successful retailer, and Zellers is the second-largest discount retailer in Canada. Why the difference in performance? Organizations vary in how well they perform because of differences in their strategies and differences in competitive abilities.[22] Walmart excels at strategic management, while Zellers' struggle to find the right niche ultimately led to US retailer Target purchasing 220 of its stores.[23] Walmart now has to adapt their strategic planning to the entry of a formidable competitor in the Canadian market.

**Strategic management** is what managers do to develop the organization's strategies. What are an organization's **strategies**? They are the plans for how the organization will do whatever it is in business to do, how it will compete successfully, and how it will attract and satisfy its customers in order to achieve its goals.[24]

One term that is often used in conjunction with strategic management and strategies is **business model**, which is a strategic design for how a company intends to profit from its strategies, work processes, and work activities. A company's business model focuses on two things: (1) whether customers will value what the company is providing and (2) whether the company can make any money doing that.[25] Dell pioneered a new business model for selling computers to consumers directly on the Internet instead of selling its computers, like all the other computer manufacturers, through computer retailers. Did customers "value" that? Absolutely! Did Dell make money doing it that way? Absolutely! As managers think about strategies for their businesses, they need to give some thought to the economic viability of their business model.

The **strategic management process**, as illustrated in Exhibit 3-4, is a six-step process that encompasses strategic planning, implementation, and evaluation. Although the first four steps describe the planning that must take place, implementation and evaluation are just as important. Even the best strategies can fail if management does not implement or evaluate them properly. Let's examine the six steps in detail.

*How would you develop a strategic plan for the next five or ten years of your life? What would be your vision, mission, goals, and strategies?*

## Step 1: Identify the Organization's Current Vision, Mission, Goals, and Strategies

Together the vision and mission provide an organization's statement of purpose. The vision answers the question, What will this business be in the future?[26] The mission answers the question, What is our reason for being in business? Defining the organization's mission forces managers to carefully identify the scope of their products or services. These statements provide clues to what organizations see as their reason for being in business. Exhibit 3-5 on page 67 describes the typical components of a mission statement.

It is important for managers to identify goals and strategies consistent with the vision and mission being pursued. For example, the Workers' Compensation Board of BC, now known as Work Safe BC, has the following vision, mission, and goals:[27]

| EXHIBIT **3-5** Components of a Mission Statement | |
|---|---|
| Customers: | **Who are the organization's customers?** |
| | We believe our first responsibility is to the doctors, nurses and patients, to mothers, fathers and all others who use our products and services. (Johnson & Johnson) |
| Markets: | **Where does the organization compete geographically?** |
| | To invoke the senses, evoke the imagination and provoke the emotions of people around the world! (Cirque du Soleil) |
| Concern for survival, growth, and profitability: | **Is the organization committed to growth and financial stability?** |
| | We expand our thinking and grow faster than the industry average, and we enjoy being seen as a young aggressive company. We believe that we do not have to compromise our integrity to be profit driven. (G.A.P Adventures) |
| Philosophy: | **What are the organization's basic beliefs, values, and ethical priorities?** |
| | Ducks Unlimited Canada (DUC) envisions Canada as a nation that can sustain use by people and wildlife without endangering the amount or functions of natural lands. DUC leads wetland conservation for waterfowl, other wildlife and people in North America. (Ducks Unlimited Canada) |
| Concern for public image: | **How responsive is the organization to societal and environmental concerns?** |
| | As a vital measure of integrity, we will ensure the health and safety of our communities, and protect the environment in all we do. (Dow Chemical) |
| Products or services: | **What are the organization's major products or services?** |
| | To enrich the lives of everyone in WestJet's world by providing safe, friendly and affordable air travel. (WestJet Airlines) |
| Technology: | **Is the organization's technology current?** |
| | **Pushing the limits of what technology can accomplish:** Pushing the limits means focusing more of our resources and attention on what we do not know rather than on controlling what we already know. The fact that something has not worked in the past does not mean that it cannot be made to work in the future; and the fact that something did work in the past doesn't mean that it can't be improved upon. (Syncrude Canada) |
| Self-concept: | **What are the organization's major competitive advantage and core competencies?** |
| | CBC Television, as Canada's national public television broadcaster, has a cultural mandate to tell compelling, original, audacious and entertaining Canadian stories in a way that Canadians want to watch, and in large numbers. (CBC Television) |
| Concern for employees: | **Are employees a valuable asset of the organization?** |
| | We recognize contributions and celebrate accomplishments. (Tourism BC) |

**Our vision**

Workers and workplaces safe and secure from injury, illness, and disease.

**Our mission**

To add value for workers and employers by:

- Assisting them to create a culture of health and safety in the workplace
- Delivering quality decisions and advice
- Providing compassionate and supportive service
- Ensuring solid financial stewardship now and in the future

**strategic management**
What managers do to develop the organization's strategies.

**strategies**
The decisions and actions that determine the long-run performance of an organization.

**business model**
A strategic design for how a company intends to profit from its strategies, work processes, and work activities.

**strategic management process**
A six-step process that encompasses strategic planning, implementation, and evaluation.

## Step 2: Do an Internal Analysis

Now we move from looking outside the organization to looking inside. The internal analysis provides important information about an organization's specific resources and capabilities. An organization's **resources** are its assets—financial, physical, human, intangible—that are used by the organization to develop, manufacture, and deliver products or services to its customers. Its **capabilities** are its skills and abilities in doing the work activities needed in its business. The major value-creating capabilities and skills of the organization are known as its **core competencies**.[28] Both resources and core competencies can determine the organization's competitive weapons. Procter & Gamble's core competencies were historically based on innovation and brand-building.[29] P&G has focused on supply chain management by increasing forecasting accuracy. Supply chain management has become a core competence as the company has earned very high rankings annually, including #2 in AMR Research's 2010 Supply Chain Top 25.[30] Companies like P&G or Maple Leaf that are committed to continually improving the quality of their products and services are attempting to use **quality management**. Kerry Shapansky, president of Toronto-based Pareto, a marketing services company, emphasizes the value of quality as a competitive advantage. "You can do 984 things right and just one thing wrong for it all to come apart," he says. "Nobody remembers the 984 things you did right; all focus is on that one thing you did wrong."

After doing the internal analysis, managers should be able to identify organizational strengths and weaknesses. **Strengths** are any activities the organization does well or any unique resources that it has. **Weaknesses** are activities the organization does not do well or resources it needs but does not possess. This step forces managers to recognize that their organizations, no matter how large or successful, are constrained by the resources and capabilities they have.

*What are your strengths and weaknesses for developing a successful career?*

Doing an internal analysis of an organization's financial and physical assets is fairly easy because information on those areas is readily available. However, evaluating an organization's intangible assets—things such as employees' skills, talents, and knowledge; databases and other IT assets; organizational culture; and so forth—is a bit more challenging. Organizational culture, specifically, is one crucial part of the internal analysis that is often overlooked.[31] Assessing the company's culture is critical because strong and weak cultures have different effects on strategy, and the content of a culture has a major effect on strategies pursued. What is a strategically appropriate culture? It is one that supports the firm's chosen strategy. For a number of years, Avis, the number-two US car rental company, has stood at the top of its category in an annual survey of brand loyalty. By creating a culture in which employees obsess over every step of the rental car experience, Avis has built an unmatched record for customer loyalty.[32]

Another intangible asset that is important, but difficult to assess during an internal analysis, is corporate reputation. Does the fact that Montreal-based aluminum producer Rio Tinto Alcan is ranked as one of Canada's "most admired corporations" make a difference? Does the fact that Calgary-based WestJet Airlines often makes the list of "Canada's 10 Most Admired Corporate Cultures™" mean anything? Does the fact that Coca-Cola has the world's most powerful global brand give it any edge? Studies of reputation on corporate performance show that it can have a positive impact.[33] As one researcher stated, "[A] strong, well-managed reputation can and should be an asset for any organization."[34]

## Step 3: Do an External Analysis

*What changes in the world are happening that could affect how your career might unfold over time? How would this affect your strategic plan?*

In Chapter 2, we described the external environment as an important constraint on a manager's actions. Analyzing that environment is a critical step in the strategic management process. Managers in every organization need to do an external analysis. They need to know, for example, what the competition is doing, what pending legislation might affect the organization, or what the labour supply is like in locations where it operates. In analyzing the external environment, managers should examine both the specific and general environments to see what trends and changes are occurring.

After analyzing the environment, managers need to assess what they have learned in terms of opportunities the organization can exploit, and threats it must counteract. **Opportunities** are positive trends in external environmental factors; **threats** are negative trends. For Indigo Books & Music managers, one opportunity is the increased use of the Internet, and managers have looked for ways to get more revenue from this medium. Threats to Indigo include a decreasing number of people who read books and greater competition from alternative sources of entertainment, including movies, radio, and television programs. As a result, Indigo is betting on home décor and gifts as book sales are expected to drop from 75 percent to 50 percent of Indigo's business.[35]

One last thing to understand about external analysis is that the same environment can present opportunities to one organization and pose threats to another in the same industry because of their different resources and capabilities. For example, WestJet Airlines has prospered in a turbulent industry, while Air Canada has struggled.

The combined external and internal analyses are called the **SWOT analysis**—an analysis of the organization's *s*trengths, *w*eaknesses, *o*pportunities, and *t*hreats. Based on the SWOT analysis, managers can identify a strategic niche that the organization might exploit (see Exhibit 3-6). For example, owner Leonard Lee started Ottawa-based Lee Valley Tools in 1982 to help individual woodworkers, and later gardeners, find just the right tools for their tasks. This niche strategy enabled Lee to grow Lee Valley into one of North America's leading garden and woodworking catalogue companies.

Paul Holland, CEO of Vancouver-based A&W, celebrates with employee Fatemeh Divsaler Mohajer. Despite the downturn in the economic environment, A&W's sales increased 10 percent in 2008, due to Holland's strategy of focusing on Baby Boomers' taste for nostalgia.

SWOT analysis is effective when the analysis helps companies make specific observations and draw conclusions, and allows them to develop plans to act upon this information. Exhibit 3-7 shows some common areas to investigate when performing SWOT analysis.

**EXHIBIT 3-6** Identifying the Organization's Opportunities

Organization's Resources/Capabilities — Organization's Opportunities — Opportunities in the Environment

---

**resources**
An organization's assets—financial, physical, human, intangible—that are used to develop, manufacture, and deliver products or services to customers.

**capabilities**
An organization's skills and abilities that enable it to do the work activities needed in its business.

**core competencies**
An organization's major value-creating skills, capabilities, and resources that determine its competitive weapons.

**quality management**
A philosophy of management driven by continual improvement and responding to customer needs and expectations.

**strengths**
Any activities the organization does well or any unique resources that it has.

**weaknesses**
Activities the organization does not do well or resources it needs but does not possess.

**opportunities**
Positive trends in external environmental factors.

**threats**
Negative trends in external environmental factors.

**SWOT analysis**
An analysis of the organization's strengths, weaknesses, opportunities, and threats.

**EXHIBIT 3-7 SWOT Analysis**

| Strengths | Weaknesses |
|---|---|
| • Financial condition: adequate resources, returns, revenues, profit | • Financial condition: inadequate resources, debt, declining revenues, subpar profitability |
| • Operations: cost advantages, economies of scale, location/geographic coverage, good supply chain management | • Operations: obsolete facilities, weak R&D, internal operating problems, underutilized capacity, weak dealer network |
| • Product: product innovation, price/value/quality, PL breadth | • Product: too narrow a product line, cannibalization, saturation, limited features |
| • Management: proven management team, history of success, succession planning | • Management: lack of depth and talent, key executive departures |
| • Competition: insulated from competitive pressures, market leader | • Competition: losing market share, inferior intellectual capital |
| • Technology: proprietary technology, patents | • Technology: lack of presence in e-commerce |
| • Marketing: brand awareness and recognition, brand equity, distribution, strong advertising | • Marketing: weak brand image or reputation, no unique sales proposition, lack of reach |
| • Customers: attractive customer base, well thought of by buyers | • Customers: declining customer base, poorly regarded by buyers |
| • Strategies: powerful strategy, key functional area strategies | • Strategies: lacking clear strategic direction, poor track record in strategy implementation |
| • Organization: culture, climate | • Organization: culture, climate |
| • History: track record of success, experience, knowledge, data | • History: still overcoming negative trends, poor triple bottom line reputation |
| • People: accreditations, qualifications, training, low turnover, high customer service, intellectual capital | • People: high turnover, poor training, low morale, poor customer service, missing key skills or competencies |
| • Competencies/capabilities suited to industry | • Lack of developed or proven competencies |
| • IT: processes, systems, infrastructure, communications | • IT: processes, systems, infrastructure, communications |
| • Alliances/joint ventures with key industry partners | • Alliances/joint ventures with key industry partners |
| • Innovation: proven and unique | • Innovation: weak or unproven |

| Opportunities | Threats |
|---|---|
| • Markets: new markets or segments, vertical/horizontal integration, niche markets | • Competition: likely entry of new competitors, existing competition, substitute products |
| • Customers: serve additional customer groups, lifestyle or demand trends | • Buyers: changing needs and preferences, growing purchasing power |
| • Product: PL expansion (broader range of customer needs), add complementary products, diversification | • Demographics: adverse changes, skills shortages |
| • Competition: complacency among rivals, rival vulnerabilities, winning market share | • Supply: limited supply, growing bargaining power of suppliers |
| • Market developments: faster market or industry growth | • Economy: home and abroad, vulnerability to recession and business cycle |
| • Technology: development/adaptation innovation, online sales/e-commerce | • Political/legislative: effects from changes, restrictive trade policies, costly new regulatory requirements |
| • Operational: using existing skills/know-how to enter new product lines or new businesses, production economies, supply chain integration | • Market: slower growth, decreasing demand |
| • Integration: forward/backward | • Environmental: seasonality, weather effects |
| • Global: new influences, export /import, lowering trade barriers | • Technology: new services, technologies, ideas |
| • Tactics: surprise element, major contracts, alliances/joint ventures/partnerships, acquisition of rivals | • Organization: loss of key staff, insurmountable weaknesses, vital contracts and partners |
| • Seasonal: weather, fashion influences, trends | |
| • Marketing: New USPs?, research, product development | |

**EXHIBIT 3-8  PESTEL Analysis**

**Political**

- How stable is the political environment?
- What are local taxation policies and how do these affect your business?
- Is the government involved in trading agreements such as EU, NAFTA, ASEAN, or others?
- What are the foreign-trade regulations?
- What are the social-welfare policies?

**Economic**

- What are current and projected interest rates?
- What is the level of inflation, what is it projected to be, and how does this projection reflect the growth of your market?
- What are local employment levels per capita and how are they changing?
- What are the long-term prospects for gross domestic product (GDP) per capita and so on?
- What are exchange rates between critical markets and how will they affect production and distribution of your goods?

**Socio-cultural**

- What are local lifestyle trends?
- What are the current demographics and how are they changing?
- What is the level and distribution of education and income?
- What are the dominant local religions and what influence do they have on consumer attitudes and opinions?
- What is the level of consumerism and what are popular attitudes toward it?
- What pending legislation affects corporate social policies (e.g., domestic-partner benefits, maternity/paternity leave)?
- What are the attitudes toward work and leisure?

**Technological**

- What is the level of research funding in government and industry and are those levels changing?
- What is the government and industry's level of interest and focus on technology?
- How mature is the technology?
- What is the status of intellectual-property issues in the local environment?
- Are potentially disruptive technologies in adjacent industries creeping in at the edges of the focal industry?

**Environmental**

- What are local environmental issues?
- Are there any pending ecological or environmental issues relevant to your industry?
- How do the activities of international pressure groups (e.g., Greenpeace, Earth First, PETA) affect your business?
- Are there environmental protection laws?
- What are the regulations regarding waste disposal and energy consumption?

**Legal**

- What are the regulations regarding monopolies and private property?
- Does intellectual property have legal protections?
- Are there relevant consumer laws?
- What is the status of employment, health and safety, and product safety laws?

*Source:* Strategic Management, Carpenter Sanders © 2011, p. 75; "Reprinted with permission by Pearson Canada Inc."

**PESTEL ANALYSIS**  PESTEL is an acronym for six contextual factors that shape a company's external environment: *p*olitical, *e*conomic, *s*ocio-cultural, *t*echnological, *e*nvironmental, and *l*egal. The questions in Exhibit 3-8 help determine the nature of opportunities and threats facing a company in the future. **PESTEL analysis** is a way for a company to align its strategy with the external environment.[36]

## Step 4: Formulate Strategies

Once the SWOT analysis is complete, managers need to develop and evaluate strategic alternatives and then select strategies that either capitalize on the organization's strengths and exploit environmental opportunities or correct the organization's weaknesses and buffer it against threats. Strategies need to be established for the corporate, business, and functional levels of the organization, which we will describe shortly. This step is complete

**PESTEL analysis**
A way for a company to align its strategy with the external environment by analyzing six contextual

factors that shape the external environment: political, economic, socio-cultural, technological, environmental, and legal.

when managers have developed a set of strategies that gives the organization a relative advantage over its rivals. Professor Henry Mintzberg of McGill Business School notes that strategies often emerge from actions that organizations take rather than simply reflect the original strategic intent of the organization.[37]

### Step 5: Implement Strategies

After strategies are formulated, they must be implemented. No matter how effectively an organization has planned its strategies, it cannot succeed if the strategies are not implemented properly. Involving all members of the organization in strategic planning is also important.

### Step 6: Evaluate Results

Analyze

The final step in the strategic management process is evaluating results. How effective have the strategies been? A winning strategy is one that provides competitive advantage, leads to improved performance, and fits the industry and competitive situation.[38] What adjustments, if any, are necessary? Revisions become necessary for several reasons: specific company performance, changing environmental conditions, and new opportunities.[39] We discuss this step in our coverage of the control process in Chapter 11.

# TYPES OF ORGANIZATIONAL STRATEGIES

**Explain**
**3.4** What kinds of strategies can managers use?

There are three types of organizational strategy: corporate, business, and functional (see Exhibit 3-9). They relate to the particular level of the organization that introduces the strategy. Managers at the top level of the organization typically are responsible for corporate strategies; for example, Michael McCain plans Maple Leaf Foods' restructuring strategy. Maple Leaf has three separate business-level divisions and directors reporting to McCain: Meat Products group, Agribusiness group, and Bakery Products group. Managers within each division are responsible for functional strategies such as accounting and marketing. Let's look at each type of organizational strategy.

## Corporate Strategy

*If you were to develop your own company, what business would it be in? Why?*

**Corporate strategy** is a strategy that evaluates what businesses a company is in, should be in, or wants to be in, and what it wants to do with those businesses. The corporate strategy is based on the mission and goals of the organization and the roles that each business unit of the organization will play. Take PepsiCo, for example. Its mission is to be a successful producer and marketer of beverage and packaged food products, and its strategy for pursuing that mission and various goals is through its different businesses including North American Soft Drinks, Frito-Lay, Gatorade, Tropicana Products, and PepsiCo International. At one time, PepsiCo had a restaurant division that included Taco Bell, Pizza Hut, and KFC, but because

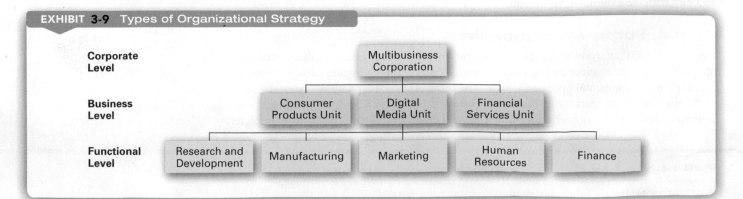

**EXHIBIT 3-9** Types of Organizational Strategy

of intense competitive pressures in the restaurant industry and the division's inability to contribute to corporate growth, PepsiCo made a strategic decision to spin off that division as a separate and independent business entity, now known as YUM! Brands Inc. What types of corporate strategies do organizations such as PepsiCo use?

In choosing what businesses to be in, senior management can choose among three main types of corporate strategies: growth, stability, and renewal. To illustrate, Walmart, Cadbury Schweppes, and General Motors (GM) are companies that seem to be going in different directions. Walmart is rapidly expanding its operations and developing new business and retailing concepts. Cadbury's managers, on the other hand, are content to maintain the status quo and focus on the candy industry. Meanwhile, sluggish sales and an uncertain outlook in the automobile industry have prompted GM to take drastic measures in dealing with its problems. Each of these organizations is using a different type of corporate strategy. Let's look closer at each type.

**GROWTH**  Even though Walmart is the world's number-one retailer, it continues to grow, and over the next five years will concentrate its growth efforts internationally. Walmart Canada opened 40 new supercentres in 2012, which increased its number of supercentres by 33 percent![40] Walmart's international operations included more than 3400 stores in 2009, and these stores account for about 25 percent of the company's revenue.[41] A **growth strategy** is used when an organization wants to grow and does so by expanding the number of products offered or markets served, either through its current business(es) or through new business(es). As a result of its growth strategy, the organization may increase sales revenues, number of employees, market share, or other quantitative measures. How can organizations grow? Through concentration, vertical integration, horizontal integration, or diversification.

**Concentration**  Growth through *concentration* is achieved when an organization concentrates on its primary line of business and increases the number of products offered or markets served in this primary business. No other firms are acquired or merged with; instead the company chooses to grow by increasing its own business operations. For example, Oakville, Ontario–based Tim Hortons opens about 200 new stores a year and is currently focusing most of its new openings on small-town western Canada, Quebec, and the United States, where it had 184 stores in 2004.[42]

**Vertical Integration**  A company also might choose to grow by *vertical integration*, which is an attempt to gain control of inputs (backward vertical integration), outputs (forward vertical integration), or both. In backward vertical integration, the organization attempts to gain control of its inputs by becoming its own supplier. For example, French hospitality giant Accor, which owns Motel 6, Red Roof Inns, and numerous other lodging properties, also owns a majority of Carlson Wagonlit Travel, one of the world's largest travel

Maple Leaf Foods follows a strategy of vertical integration with its AgriBusiness group, where it controls hog production.

**corporate strategy**
An organizational strategy that evaluates what businesses a company is in, should be in, or wants to be in, and what it wants to do with those businesses.

**growth strategy**
A corporate strategy used when an organization wants to grow and does so by expanding the number of products offered or markets served,

either through its current business(es) or through new business(es).

agencies. In forward vertical integration, the organization gains control of its outputs (products or services) by becoming its own distributor. For example, several manufacturers with strong brands—including Coach, Apple, LaCoste, and Lego—have opened select stores where customers can buy products. In other words, they have become their own distributors.

**Horizontal Integration**    In *horizontal integration*, a company grows by combining with other organizations in the same industry—that is, combining operations with competitors. Anheuser-Busch InBev of Belgium, which owns Alexander Keith's and Labatt, is the leading brewer in the world; it is a dominant player in North America, South America, Europe, Australia, and parts of Asia and Africa because of its acquisition of local breweries. In recent years, horizontal integration has been frequently considered in the Canadian banking industry as well.

Because combining with competitors might decrease the amount of competition in an industry, Competition Bureau Canada assesses the impact of proposed horizontal integration strategies and must approve such plans before they are allowed to go forward in this country. Other countries have similar bodies to protect fair competition. For example, in the United States the Federal Trade Commission examines proposals for horizontal integration. In early 2007, Sirius Satellite Radio and XM Satellite Radio announced plans to merge and create a single satellite radio network in the United States and Canada. The companies face significant hurdles in the United States to finalize their agreement because the merger would create a monopoly in satellite radio. The merger was also difficult to achieve in Canada, as approval was needed from both the Competition Bureau Canada and the Canadian Radio-television and Telecommunications Commission (CRTC), leading to a delay of almost four years.[43]

**Diversification**    Finally, an organization can grow through *diversification*, either related or unrelated. In **related diversification** a company grows by merging with or acquiring firms in different, but related, industries. For example, Toronto-based Weston Foods is involved in the baking and dairy industries, while its ownership of Loblaw Companies Limited (Loblaw) provides for the distribution of Weston's food products. In **unrelated diversification** a company grows by merging with or acquiring firms in different and unrelated industries. Toronto-based Brookfield Asset Management (formerly Brascan) is one of the few Canadian conglomerates that pursues a diversified strategy. Under CEO Bruce Flatt, Brascan has focused its development in three areas: real estate (Brookfield Properties), financial services (Brookfield Asset Management), and power generation (Brookfield Power). The company also owns 49 percent of Fraser Papers, a leading manufacturer of specialized printing, publishing, and converting papers; 38 percent of Norbord, a paperboard company; and 23 percent of Stelco, a steel producer.[44] However, unrelated diversification has fallen out of favour in recent years. Too much diversification can cause managers to lose control of their organizations' core business, which can reduce value rather than create it.[45] Unrelated diversification also suffers from a lack of strategic fit. Related diversification allows companies to benefit from economies of scale and knowledge transfer.[46]

Many companies use a combination of these approaches to grow. McDonald's has grown using the concentration strategy by opening more than 32 000 outlets in more than 100 countries, of which about 30 percent are company-owned. In addition, it has used horizontal integration by purchasing Boston Market and Chipotle Mexican Grill (which it spun off as a separate entity in 2006). McDonald's newest twist on its growth strategy is a move into the premium coffee market with its McCafé coffee shops.

**STABILITY**    A **stability strategy** is a corporate strategy characterized by an absence of significant change in what the organization is currently doing. Examples of this strategy include continuing to serve the same clients by offering the same product or service, maintaining market share, and sustaining the organization's business operations. The organization does not grow, but it does not fall behind either.

Although it may seem strange that an organization might not want to grow, there are times when its resources, capabilities, and core competencies are stretched to their limits, and expanding operations further might jeopardize its future success. When might managers decide that a stability strategy is the most appropriate choice? One situation might be that the industry is in a period of rapid upheaval with external forces drastically changing and making the future uncertain. At times like these, managers might decide that the prudent course of action is to sit tight and wait to see what happens.

Another situation where a stability strategy might be appropriate is if the industry is facing slow- or no-growth opportunities. In such situations, managers might decide to keep the organization operating at its current levels before making any strategic moves. This period of stability would allow them time to analyze their strategic options. The grocery industry is growing very slowly. This fact, plus the all-out push of Walmart into grocery retailing, for example, led managers at Montreal, Quebec–based grocery chain Metro to use a stability strategy.

Finally, owners and managers of small businesses, such as small neighbourhood grocers, often purposefully choose to follow a stability strategy. Why? They may feel that their business is successful enough as it is, that it adequately meets their personal goals, and that they don't want the hassles of a growing business.

**RENEWAL** Popular business periodicals frequently print stories about organizations that are not meeting their goals or whose performance is declining. When an organization is in trouble, something needs to be done. Managers need to develop strategies that address organizational weaknesses that are leading to performance declines. These strategies are called **renewal strategies**. There are two main types of renewal strategies: retrenchment and turnaround.

A **retrenchment strategy** reduces the organization's activities or operations. Retrenchment strategies include cost reductions, layoffs, closure of underperforming units, or closure of entire product lines or services.[47] There is no shortage of companies that have pursued a retrenchment strategy. A partial list includes some big corporate names: Procter & Gamble, Sears Canada, Corel, and Nortel Networks. When an organization is facing minor performance setbacks, a retrenchment strategy helps it stabilize operations, revitalize organizational resources and capabilities, and prepare to compete once again.

What happens if an organization's problems are more serious? What if the organization's profits are not just declining, but instead there are no profits, just losses? The **turnaround strategy** is a renewal strategy for times when the organization's performance problems are more critical.

Ecotrust Canada successfully engineered a turnaround strategy to improve the triple-bottom line performance of Iisaak Forest Resources, a 100 percent First Nations forest operator on the BC coast. Iisaak has outperformed its competitors while developing strong community relationships, financial stability, and sustainable business systems. It has also achieved Forest Stewardship Council (FSC) certification while meeting strict environmental recommendations.

---

**related diversification**
When a company grows by combining with firms in different, but related, industries.

**unrelated diversification**
When a company grows by combining with firms in different and unrelated industries.

**stability strategy**
A corporate strategy characterized by an absence of significant change in what the organization is currently doing.

**renewal strategies**
Corporate strategies designed to address organizational weaknesses that are leading to performance declines.

**retrenchment strategy**
A short-term renewal strategy that reduces the organization's activities or operations.

**turnaround strategy**
A renewal strategy for situations in which the organization's performance problems are more serious.

## Business Strategy

*What might be the competitive advantage of a business you would like to create?*

The selection of a corporate strategy sets the direction for the entire organization. Subsequently, each unit within the organization has to translate this corporate strategy into a set of business strategies that will give the organization a competitive advantage. **Competitive advantage** is what sets an organization apart: that is, its distinct edge. That distinct edge comes from the organization's core competencies—what the organization does that others cannot do or what it does better than others can do.

**COMPETITIVE STRATEGIES** Many important ideas in strategic management have come from the work of Michael Porter, Professor at Harvard Business School.[48] His competitive strategies framework identifies three generic strategies from which managers can choose. Success depends on selecting the right strategy—one that fits the competitive strengths (resources and capabilities) of the organization and the industry it is in. Porter's major contribution has been to explain how managers can create and sustain a competitive advantage that will give a company above-average profitability. An important element in doing this is an industry analysis.

Porter proposes that some industries are inherently more profitable (and, therefore, more attractive to enter and remain in) than others. For example, the pharmaceutical industry is one with historically high profit margins, and the airline industry is one with notoriously low ones. But a company can still make a lot of money in a "dull" industry and lose money in a "glamorous" industry. The key is to exploit a competitive advantage.

In any industry, six competitive forces dictate the rules of competition. Together, these six forces (see Exhibit 3-10 on page 77) determine industry attractiveness and profitability. Managers assess an industry's attractiveness using these forces:

- *Threat of new entrants.* Factors such as economies of scale, brand loyalty, and capital requirements determine how easy or hard it is for new competitors to enter an industry.
- *Threat of substitutes.* Factors such as switching costs and buyer loyalty determine the degree to which customers are likely to buy a substitute product.
- *Bargaining power of buyers.* Factors such as number of customers in the market, customer information, and the availability of substitutes determine the amount of influence that buyers have in an industry.
- *Bargaining power of suppliers.* Factors such as the degree of supplier concentration and availability of substitute inputs determine the amount of power that suppliers have over firms in the industry.
- *Current-competitor rivalry.* Factors such as industry growth rate, increasing or falling demand, and product differences determine how intense the competitive rivalry will be among firms currently in the industry.
- *Power of complementors.* A complementor is another industry whose product tends to increase the sales of a product in another industry.[49] Companies in the computer and electronics industries sell products that must be used together.[50]

Other stakeholders such as special interest groups, trade associations, and local communities can also wield powerful influence and therefore impact the competitive landscape of an industry.

Once managers have assessed the five forces and determined what threats and opportunities exist, they are ready to select an appropriate competitive strategy. According to Porter, no firm can be successful by trying to be all things to all people. He proposes that managers select a strategy that will give the organization a competitive advantage, which he says arises out of either having lower costs than all other industry competitors or by being significantly different from competitors. On that basis, managers can choose one of three strategies: cost leadership, differentiation, or focus. Which strategy managers select depends on the organization's strengths and core competencies and its competitors' weaknesses (see Exhibit 3-11).

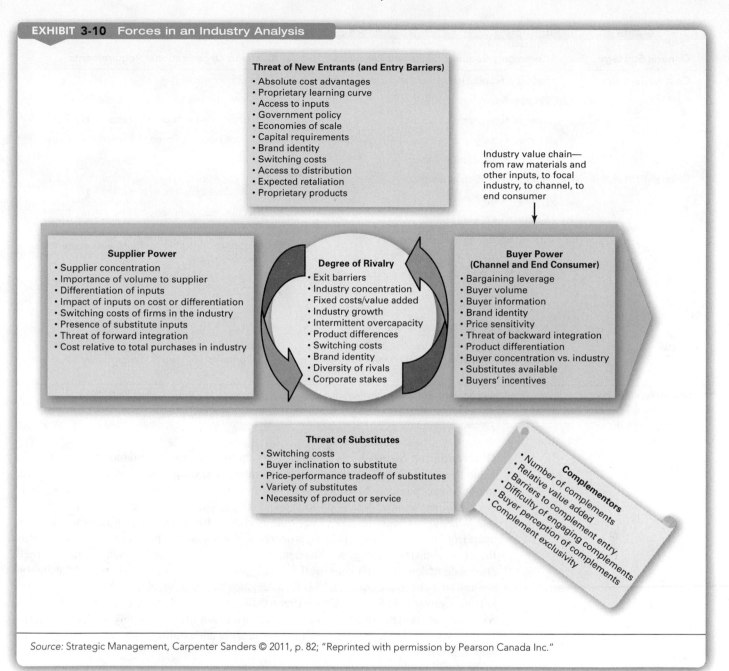

**EXHIBIT 3-10** Forces in an Industry Analysis

**Threat of New Entrants (and Entry Barriers)**
- Absolute cost advantages
- Proprietary learning curve
- Access to inputs
- Government policy
- Economies of scale
- Capital requirements
- Brand identity
- Switching costs
- Access to distribution
- Expected retaliation
- Proprietary products

Industry value chain—from raw materials and other inputs, to focal industry, to channel, to end consumer

**Supplier Power**
- Supplier concentration
- Importance of volume to supplier
- Differentiation of inputs
- Impact of inputs on cost or differentiation
- Switching costs of firms in the industry
- Presence of substitute inputs
- Threat of forward integration
- Cost relative to total purchases in industry

**Degree of Rivalry**
- Exit barriers
- Industry concentration
- Fixed costs/value added
- Industry growth
- Intermittent overcapacity
- Product differences
- Switching costs
- Brand identity
- Diversity of rivals
- Corporate stakes

**Buyer Power (Channel and End Consumer)**
- Bargaining leverage
- Buyer volume
- Buyer information
- Brand identity
- Price sensitivity
- Threat of backward integration
- Product differentiation
- Buyer concentration vs. industry
- Substitutes available
- Buyers' incentives

**Threat of Substitutes**
- Switching costs
- Buyer inclination to substitute
- Price-performance tradeoff of substitutes
- Variety of substitutes
- Necessity of product or service

**Complementors**
- Number of complements
- Relative value added
- Barriers to complement entry
- Difficulty of engaging complements
- Buyer perception of complements
- Complement exclusivity

*Source:* Strategic Management, Carpenter Sanders © 2011, p. 82; "Reprinted with permission by Pearson Canada Inc."

**Cost Leadership Strategy**   When an organization sets out to be the lowest-cost producer in its industry, it is following a **cost leadership strategy**. A low-cost leader aggressively searches out efficiencies in production, marketing, and other areas of operation. Overhead is kept to a minimum, and the firm does everything it can to cut costs. You will not find expensive art or interior décor at offices of low-cost leaders. For example, at Walmart's headquarters in Bentonville, Arkansas, office furnishings are sparse and drab but functional.

Although low-cost leaders do not place a lot of emphasis on "frills," the product or service being sold must be perceived as comparable in quality to that offered by rivals or at least be acceptable to buyers. Examples of companies that have used a low-cost leadership strategy include Target, Hyundai, and WestJet Airlines.

**competitive advantage**
What sets an organization apart; its distinct edge.

**cost leadership strategy**
A business strategy in which the organization sets out to be the lowest-cost producer in its industry.

**EXHIBIT 3-11** Requirements for Successfully Pursuing Porter's Competitive Strategies

| Generic Strategy | Commonly Required Skills and Resources | Common Organizational Requirements |
|---|---|---|
| Cost leadership | Sustained capital investment and access to capital | Tight cost control |
| | Process engineering skills | Frequent, detailed control reports |
| | Intense supervision of labour | Structured organization and responsibilities |
| | Products designed for ease in manufacture | Incentives based on meeting strict quantitative targets |
| | Low-cost distribution system | |
| Differentiation | Strong marketing abilities | Strong coordination among functions in R & D, product development, and marketing |
| | Product engineering | |
| | Creative flair | Subjective measurement and incentives instead of quantitative measures |
| | Strong capability in basic research | |
| | Corporate reputation for quality or technological leadership | Amenities to attract highly skilled labour, scientists, or creative people |
| | Long tradition in the industry or unique combination of skills drawn from other businesses | |
| | Strong cooperation from channels | |
| Focus | Combination of the foregoing skills and resources directed at the particular strategic target | Combination of the foregoing organizational requirements directed at the particular strategic target |

Source: Reprinted from M. E. Porter, *Competitive Strategy: Techniques for Analyzing Industries and Competitors* (New York: Free Press, 1980).

**Differentiation Strategy** A company seeking to offer unique products that are widely valued by customers is following a **differentiation strategy**. Sources of differentiation might be exceptionally high quality, extraordinary service, innovative design, technological capability, or an unusually positive brand image. The key to this competitive strategy is that whatever product or service attribute is chosen for differentiating must set the firm apart from its competitors and be significant enough to justify a price premium that exceeds the cost of differentiating. St. Stephen, New Brunswick–based Ganong Bros., a small chocolate maker, differentiates itself from bigger boxed-chocolate makers by focusing on the assorted chocolates market. This focus enables it to rank second in Canada in that market. Vancouver City Savings Credit Union differentiates itself from competitors through a focus on the community and the customer. Profit is not the bank's only goal, and in 2010 Vancity returned a record $23.5 million to members and communities, up from $15.2 million in 2009.[51]

By looking at successful consumer products or services, a company's differentiation strategy is often clear: Calgary-based WestJet Airlines—customer service; Ontario Power Authority–sponsored Team North—energy-efficient and innovative solar product design; Vancouver-based Martha Sturdy—sleek furniture design and brand image; and Ottawa-based Lee Valley Tools—quality product design.

**Focus Strategy** The first two of Michael Porter's competitive strategies seek a competitive advantage in the broad marketplace. However, the **focus strategy** involves a cost advantage (cost leadership focus) or a differentiation advantage (differentiation focus) in a narrow industry segment. That is, managers select a market segment in an industry and tailor their strategy to serve it rather than the broad market. Segments can be based on product variety, type of end buyer, distribution channel, or geographical location of buyers. For example, at Compania Chilena de Fosforos SA, a large Chilean wood products manufacturer, Vice-Chair Gustavo Romero Zapata devised a focus strategy to sell chopsticks in Japan. Competitors, and even other company managers, thought he was crazy. However, by focusing on this segment, Romero's strategy managed to create more demand for his company's chopsticks than it had mature trees with which to make the products. Whether a focus strategy is feasible depends on the size of the segment and whether the organization can support the additional cost of focusing. Research suggests that the focus strategy may be the most effective choice for small businesses because they typically do not have the economies of scale or internal resources to successfully pursue one of the other two strategies.[52]

**Stuck in the Middle**   What happens if an organization is unable to develop a competitive advantage through either cost or differentiation? Porter uses the term **stuck in the middle** to describe those organizations that find it very difficult to achieve long-term success. He goes on to note that successful organizations frequently get into trouble by reaching beyond their competitive advantage and ending up stuck in the middle. The Hudson's Bay Company department store in recent years seems to have had this strategy, avoiding the low-cost strategy of Walmart, but also avoiding the strategies of higher-end fashion boutiques such as Holt Renfrew.

We now realize organizations *can* achieve competitive advantage by pursuing a cost-leadership and a differentiation strategy at the same time. Studies have shown that such a dual emphasis can result in high performance.[53] However, an organization must be strongly committed to quality products or services, and consumers of those products or services must value quality. By providing high-quality products or services, an organization differentiates itself from its rivals. Consumers who value high quality will purchase more of the organization's products, and the increased demand will lead to economies of scale and lower per-unit costs. For example, companies such as Molson, Toyota, Intel, and Coca-Cola differentiate their products while at the same time maintaining low-cost operations.

## Functional Strategy

**Functional strategies** are the strategies used by an organization's various functional departments to support the business strategy. For organizations with traditional functional departments such as manufacturing, marketing, human resources, research and development, and finance, these strategies must support the business strategy. Problems arise when employees and customers do not understand a company's strategy. Air Canada attempted to compete as a low-cost competitor to WestJet through Zip. This low-cost division ceased operations due to poor marketing (lack of branding) and human resource strategies (Zip employees were paid less than Air Canada employees).[54] By contrast, WestJet Airlines communicates a very clear strategy to its employees: enjoyable flights and an affordable experience for travellers. Employees are asked to implement this strategy by working to keep costs down and improve turnaround time. Aware of the strategy, all WestJet employees know what is expected of them in a crisis, and all employees help in whatever ways are necessary to meet this strategy.

Practise

---

**differentiation strategy**
A business strategy in which a company seeks to offer unique products that are widely valued by customers.

**focus strategy**
A business strategy in which a company pursues a cost or differentiation advantage in a narrow industry segment.

**stuck in the middle**
A situation in which an organization is unable to develop a competitive advantage through cost or differentiation.

**functional strategy**
A strategy used by a functional department to support the business strategy of the organization.

# 3 Review and Apply

## Summary of Learning Objectives

**3.1 What does planning involve?** Planning is the process of defining goals and assessing how those goals can best be achieved. The goals are written and shared with organizational members. Once the goals are agreed on, specific action plans are created to achieve the goals. The purpose of planning is to provide direction, reduce uncertainty, reduce overlapping and wasteful activities, and establish the goals or standards used in controlling. Without planning, managers would not know what to organize, lead, or control.

**3.2 How do managers set goals and develop plans?** Planning involves two important elements: goals and plans. Goals are the desired outcomes for individuals, groups, or entire organizations. They provide the direction for all management decisions and form the criteria against which actual work accomplishments can be measured. Goals can be set at the top of the organization or through management by objectives (MBO), in which employees and managers jointly develop goals. Once goals have been established, managers develop plans to achieve them, either on their own or with the help of employees. Plans outline how goals are going to be met. They typically describe resource allocations, schedules, and other necessary actions to accomplish the goals. Planning can lock people into a particular way of behaving, which might not be appropriate at a later point. Therefore, plans need to be somewhat flexible so that managers can respond to environmental changes.

**3.3 What are the steps in strategic management?** The strategic management process is a six-step process that encompasses strategic planning, implementation, and evaluation. The first four steps involve planning: identifying the organization's current mission, goals, and strategies; analyzing the internal environment; analyzing the external environment; and formulating strategies. The fifth step is implementing strategies, and the sixth step is evaluating the results. Even the best strategies can fail if management does not implement or evaluate them properly.

Maple Leaf Foods is reinventing itself as a more streamlined and profitable company, making one of the largest single investments in the Canadian food industry to create a highly efficient, world-class prepared meats production and distribution network. If this does not close the cost gap with its US rivals, Maple Leaf will need to investigate other strategies that will do so.

**3.4 What kinds of strategies can managers use?** There are three types of organizational strategies: corporate, business, and functional. They relate to the particular level of the organization that introduces the strategy. At the corporate level, organizations can engage in growth, stability, and renewal strategies. At the business level, strategies look at how an organization should compete in each of its businesses: through cost leadership, differentiation, or focus. At the functional level, strategies of the various functional departments support the business strategy.

## SNAPSHOT SUMMARY

**3.1 What Is Planning?**
Purposes of Planning
Planning and Performance
Criticisms of Planning

**3.2 How Do Managers Plan?**
Approaches to Establishing Goals
Steps in Goal Setting
Developing Plans

**3.3 Organizational Strategy: Choosing a Niche**
Step 1. Identify the Organization's Current Vision, Mission, Goals, and Strategies
Step 2. Do an Internal Analysis
Step 3. Do an External Analysis
Step 4. Formulate Strategies
Step 5. Implement Strategies
Step 6. Evaluate Results

**3.4 Types of Organizational Strategies**
Corporate Strategy
Business Strategy
Functional Strategy

## MyManagementLab® Learning Resources

# Resources

▼ **Explore and enhance your understanding of key chapter topics through the following online resources:**

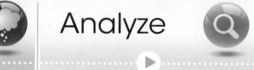

- Student PowerPoints
- Audio Summary of Chapter
- ROLLS
- CBC Videos for Part 2
- MySearchLab

▶ Visit the **Study Plan** area to test your progress with **Pre-Tests** and **Post-Tests**.

▼ **Build on your knowledge and practise real-world applications using the following online activities:**

# Interpret

- Opening Case Activity: The Purposes of Planning
- Review and Apply: Solutions to Interpret section questions and activities
- Glossary Flashcards

# Analyze

- Opening Case Activity: The Strategic Management Process
- Review and Apply: Solutions to Analyze section questions and activities
- Self-Assessment Library

# Practise

- Opening Case Activity: Planning for Action
- Review and Apply: Solutions to Practice section questions and activities
- BizSkills Simulations:
  –Plan for Success
  –Conducting a SWOT Analysis
- Decision Making Simulation: Strategic Management

# Interpret What You Have Read

1. Contrast formal and informal planning.
2. Under what circumstances are short-term plans preferred? Under what circumstances are specific plans preferred?
3. Describe the differences and explain the relationships between (a) strategic and operational plans, (b) short- and long-term plans, and (c) specific and directional plans.
4. If planning is so crucial, why do some managers choose not to do it? What are the consequences of not planning?
5. Will planning become more or less important to managers in the future? Why?
6. Compare an organization's vision and mission with its goals.
7. Describe the six-step strategic management process.
8. What is a SWOT analysis?
9. What is PESTEL analysis?

# Analyze What You Have Read

1. "Organizations that fail to plan are planning to fail." Do you agree or disagree with this statement? Explain your position.
2. Under what circumstances do you believe management by objectives and traditional goal setting would be most useful? Discuss.
3. Using Michael Porter's generic strategies (cost leadership, differentiation, and focus), describe the strategy used by each of the following companies in the automotive industry: Kia, Toyota, and Ferrari.
4. How does planning differ for small versus large organizations? How is it different for a nonprofit organization versus a for-profit organization?
5. "The primary means of sustaining a competitive advantage is to adjust faster to the environment than your competitors do." Do you agree or disagree with this statement? Explain your position.

# Assess Your Skills

## HOW GOOD AM I AT PERSONAL PLANNING?

Indicate how much you agree or disagree with each of the six statements as they relate to your school and personal life. Use the following scale to record your answers:

1 = Strongly Disagree   2 = Disagree   3 = Neither Agree nor Disagree
4 = Agree   5 = Strongly Agree

| | |
|---|---|
| 1. I am proactive rather than reactive. | 1 2 3 4 5 |
| 2. I set aside enough time and resources to study and complete projects. | 1 2 3 4 5 |
| 3. I am able to budget money to buy the things I really want without going broke. | 1 2 3 4 5 |
| 4. I have thought through what I want to do in school. | 1 2 3 4 5 |
| 5. I have a plan for completing my major. | 1 2 3 4 5 |
| 6. My goals for the future are realistic. | 1 2 3 4 5 |

**SCORING KEY** A score of 5 on any item means that you are doing well in planning and goal setting in that area. The authors of this instrument suggest that scores of 3 or less on any item indicate you need to gain a better understanding of the importance of goal setting and what is involved in the process.

## ANALYSIS AND INTERPRETATION

Successful people have goals and establish plans to help them achieve those goals. This exercise is designed to get you to think about goal setting as it relates to your school and personal life.

If your performance on this instrument was less than you desire, consider practising skills related to goal setting and time management. Toward that end, you might want to read one or more of the following books: D. K. Smith, *Make Success Measurable! A Mindbook-Workbook for Setting Goals and Taking Action* (New York: Wiley, 1999); G. R. Blair, *Goal Setting 101: How to Set and Achieve a Goal!* (Syracuse, NY: GoalsGuy Learning, 2000); and M. Leboeuf, *Working Smart: How to Accomplish More in Half the Time* (New York: Warner Books, 1993).

# Practise What You Have Learned

## DILEMMA

Think ahead to five years from now, to consider what it is that you might like to be doing with your life. Develop your own vision and mission statements. Conduct a personal SWOT analysis. Establish a set of goals that will help you achieve your vision and mission. Develop a five-year plan that maps out the steps you need to take in order to get to where you want to be with your life at that time. Use this plan as a basis for prioritizing tasks with your time management techniques.

## BECOMING A MANAGER

- Write a personal mission statement in under 200 words
- What are your strengths and weaknesses as a student? What opportunities and threats exist in your college or university environment?
- Develop some specific and challenging goals for various aspects of your life, such as academic studies, career preparation, family, and so forth.
- Set some deadlines and milestones for your goals. Monitor and evaluate your performance every six to twelve months.
- For goals that you have developed, write out plans for achieving those goals.

- Think of a job that you would like to have five years from now. See if your goals and plans will help you to obtain this job.

## DEVELOPING YOUR INTERPERSONAL SKILLS: GOAL SETTING FOR YOUR PROFESSOR

### ABOUT THE SKILL

Management by objectives was described earlier in the chapter. Setting objectives jointly provides for greater commitment and motivation.

### PRACTISING THE SKILL

Have a discussion with your professor. Provide responses to the following three questions as they relate to your classroom:

1. What should the professor stop doing?

2. What should the professor start doing?

3. What should the professor continue doing?

Now develop a list of three goals that would be critical to your professor's performance. Ensure that these goals meet the characteristics of well-designed goals (Exhibit 3-2). Now develop an action plan for your professor to achieve the goals.

# Team Exercises

## 3BL: THE TRIPLE BOTTOM LINE

### ETHICAL COMPETITIVE INTELLIGENCE

Some companies use competitive intelligence to get a sense of a competitor's possible strategic options, to find out information on their cost structure, or even to get an early read on

a new product. If a firm does so unethically, the profit bottom line may create a negative tradeoff on the people bottom line in the organization. Acting unethically, even if it generates more profit, can lead employees to believe that their interests and those of the broader community are no longer being served.

In 2004, Air Canada filed a $5 million lawsuit against rival WestJet, alleging that WestJet executives used a former Air Canada employee's password to gain access to confidential information on flight load schedules. WestJet used this information to increase service out of Toronto and adjust US routes to the detriment of Air Canada. The case was settled in 2006, when WestJet paid $5.5 million to Air Canada in damages and agreed to donate $10 million to children's charities in the names of both airlines.

### THINKING CRITICALLY ABOUT ETHICAL COMPETITIVE INTELLIGENCE

Which of the following situations would be examples of ethical competitive intelligence? Why or why not?

- Attending a trade show with a name badge and gathering information at the competitor's booth
- Accessing annual reports and industry market surveys
- Obtaining information from the competitor's public website
- Interviewing competitors' employees to access confidential information
- Hiring professional investigators to get some specific details about the competitor
- Secretly monitoring statements made by competitors' employees

## YOUR COLLEGE OR UNIVERSITY'S VISION, MISSION, AND STRATEGIES

You might not pay much attention to the goals and objectives of your college or university because you are focusing on your studies. But your college or university had to carve out its niche in an effort to provide something of value to its students, and it must continue to monitor its performance.

For this exercise, break up into small groups. The task of each small group is to prepare responses to the following questions and present findings to the class.

1. What is your college or university's vision and mission? What resources does your college or university have that support its vision and mission?

2. How would you describe your college or university's environment in terms of PESTEL?

3. What do you believe are the strengths and weaknesses of your college or university? What are its opportunities and threats?

4. Obtain the strategic plan for your college or university. Which corporate strategy is your college or university following? How does this relate to its strengths, weaknesses, opportunities, and threats?

5. Which of Porter's generic strategies is evident at your college or university?

6. What do you believe is your college or university's competitive advantage? What do you think your college or university should do to sustain its competitive advantage?

7. Is strategic planning as important in education as it is in business?

A two-hour meeting with four people leads to a potential productivity loss of eight hours.

# BE THE CONSULTANT: MAKING MEETINGS MORE EFFECTIVE

Try these tips at your next group meeting and discuss the impact they made on your meeting.

| | | |
|---|---|---|
| Objectify yourself | The meeting needs to have a clear outcome: "At the end of the meeting, we will . . ." | Make a decision? Generate ideas? Update status? |
| The basket case | Collect everyone's PDA, tablet, or cell phone at the start of the meeting and return them at the end of the meeting | Collecting electronic devices will reduce distractions and keep people on task |
| Share and share again | Distribute the agenda in advance<br><br>Get the minutes out quickly | Attendees can prepare more effectively in advance<br><br>Having an agenda allows you to keep the meeting on track and on time<br><br>Momentum will not be lost if you can get the action items in the hands of the participants |
| Take a stand | Motivational speaker and author Jon Petz suggests having the meeting in a space with no chairs, tables, or laptops—only a whiteboard | People will work more quickly and will not extend the time of the meeting unnecessarily |
| Two-minute warning | Petz suggests that each participant gets two minutes uninterrupted to state their case or provide information | Participants must stay focused<br><br>Cut people off if they go over and reward them if they finish sooner |

# Business Cases

## SILVERBIRCH HOTELS & RESORTS

The name SilverBirch Hotels & Resorts may be unfamiliar, but you have likely heard of brands such as Radisson, Hilton, Best Western, and Ramada. SilverBirch is one of Canada's leading hotel management companies and manages over 20 hotels and resorts across Canada. The Vancouver-based company manages independent hotels and hotels operating under major franchise brands listed previously.

Over the past decade, SilverBirch Hotels & Resorts has experienced success due in large part to a strong regional infrastructure, sales growth, marketing programs and support, excellent franchise relations, and an unusual approach to branding. For consumer marketing purposes, the name GreatCanadianHotels is used instead of SilverBirch, to address the lack of a franchise brand.

SilverBirch entered a partnership with Marriott International Inc. to open the first branded extended-stay hotel in the summer of 2012. The partnership gives Marriott a partner very familiar with the Canadian market, while aligning with a strong international brand is helping SilverBirch with its strategy of acquiring and building new branded properties across the country.

SilverBirch has also shown a strong environmental ethic since it was established in 1997. Its vision, mission, and values include "safety and respect for the environment" as one of its key values. The Hotel Association of Canada (HAC) administers a Green Key Eco-rating program, and SilverBirch was the first hotel management company in Canada to have all of its properties certified by HAC.

Determine whether the following SilverBirch decisions are strategic (S) or operational (O):

_____ Partnering with Marriott International
_____ Planting 1800 trees at one of its hotels to offset the greenhouse gas emissions produced by meetings and events at its property
_____ Creating educational internship programs for students at culinary and hospitality training schools
_____ Installing a computerized reservation system
_____ Developing a new vision statement: "We excite our markets with the liveliest hotels in Canada, each with its own rich, Canadian sense of place."
_____ Holding a wine and food pairing fall promotion in its Saskatoon hotel

*Sources:*
http://www.silverbirchhotels.com/about/environment.html
http://www.silverbirchhotels.com/about/vision.html
http://www.silverbirchhotels.com/about/history.html
http://www.silverbirchhotels.com/press/
http://www.hotelassociation.ca/site/programs/green_key.htm

## CANADIAN WINE INDUSTRY

The Canada-US Free Trade Agreement was expected to destroy the Canadian wine industry. Initially, market share and vineyard hectarage both were reduced. The increase of competition forced the remaining Canadian wineries to increase product quality and find new markets. The Canadian wine industry overcame a very sluggish period in the 1990s with growth of more than 7 percent annually due to a shift in higher quality grape species (*vitis vinifera*), the establishment of the Vintners Quality Alliance (VQA), and new markets for cool climate wines. The industry is fragmented, with only two major players: Vincor and Andrés Wines. This fragmentation provides major challenges through the lack of economies of scale and brand recognition. The industry is concentrated in Ontario and BC, with small operations in Quebec and other provinces. Canadian provincial distribution monopolies (except for Alberta and Quebec) lead to heavy mark-ups and high sales taxes, which hurt domestic wine sales.

Imports once made up only 25 percent of domestic consumption, but now total two-thirds of domestic market share. Canadian wine consumption is growing at a faster rate than that of beer and spirits, but import growth has been spurred by the reduction of non-tariff barriers, the strength of the Canadian dollar, and geographic limitations on red wine production in Canada. Climate conditions hamper Canadian wine production both in scale and competitiveness. Poor weather leads to a short season and major fluctuations in quality from year to year for all wines except for Icewine, in which Canada has become a world leader. Canada has successfully exploited the cool climate wine niche, and exports in this area reached $11.7 billion in 2007.

Other domestic challenges include the absence of external credibility due to poor export market penetration and persisting perceptions of low-quality wines, which date back to the lower-quality grape species used in the 70s and 80s. Exporting challenges for Canadian wines include lack of capacity, lack of marketing expertise, and insufficient financial resources.

Ontario, which accounts for 80 percent of domestic production, developed a strategic plan in the early 2000s to optimize land use planning, increase wine quality through VQA, and increase wine tourism. The strategic dilemma facing Canadian winemakers is whether to focus on domestic or international markets. While exports are likely to remain small in the short term, it is possible to target smaller, fast-growth markets.

### Questions

1. How is the planning process in the wine industry similar to that in other manufacturing industries?

2. What kinds of contingency plans are required in the Canadian wine industry?

3. What elements would be required in a Canadian national or provincial exporting strategy?

4. What growth strategies are most suitable for the Canadian wine industry?

*Sources:* Kenrick Jordan, *The Canadian Wine Industry: A Summary View* (Special Report for BMO Capital Markets), July 6, 2011.

Agriculture and Agri-Food Canada, "The Canadian Wine Industry (NAICS 31213)," http://www4.agr.gc.ca/AAFC-AAC/display-afficher.do?id=1172244915663&lang=eng

# CHAPTER 4

# Decision Making

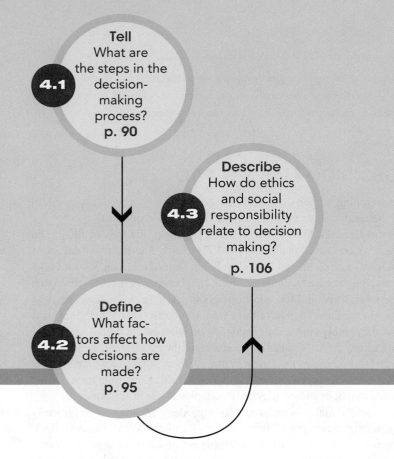

**Tell**
What are the steps in the decision-making process?
p. 90
**4.1**

**Describe**
How do ethics and social responsibility relate to decision making?
p. 106
**4.3**

**Define**
What factors affect how decisions are made?
p. 95
**4.2**

Lucie Shaw saw first-hand a market niche not being well served as she struggled to find home health care services for her in-laws. Because North Americans are living longer, elder care is putting a stress on baby boomers, who try to keep their parents living on their own as long as possible, and on the already squeezed health care system. Shaw left her job as an operations manager at Air Canada and purchased a Nurse Next Door franchise.

More and more women are making the decision to become entrepreneurs. At Nurse Next Door, 68 percent of franchisees are women. According to TD economists Beata Caranci and Leslie Preston, "[P]rospects are looking brighter for women entrepreneurs." Female franchise owners have a higher percentage of post-secondary education than their male counterparts and are more likely to expand their businesses, but face slightly lower revenue growth.[1] The Canadian franchise industry is the second largest in the world, with more than $100 billion in sales annually. At present, the highest franchise growth is in home-based businesses such as Nurse Next Door.[2]

Nurse Next Door founders John DeHart and Ken Sim acknowledge that running a home care business can be very challenging due to all the administrative demands such as employee and client scheduling, which happens on a 24/7 basis. So they decided to offer 24/7 scheduling for their franchise partners, allowing the franchise managers to focus on the more important decisions regarding how to develop the business.[3]

## Think About It

Put yourself in Lucie Shaw's shoes. What steps would you have taken to determine whether Shaw should leave a corporate job and purchase a Nurse Next Door franchise? How could Shaw evaluate the risk and return parameters of the decision to purchase the franchise? What decision criteria might she use?

Making good decisions is something that every manager strives to do, since the overall quality of managerial decisions has a major influence on organizational success or failure. In this chapter, we examine the concept of decision making and how managers can make ethical decisions.

# THE DECISION-MAKING PROCESS

**Tell**
What are the steps in the decision-making process?

**4.1**

While watching a sports competition, have you ever felt that you could make better decisions than the coaches on the field or court?

In the Helsinki, Finland, suburb of Pukinmaki, the fans of PK-35, an amateur soccer team, get that chance![4] The coach does not make decisions about what to do on the field by himself, but instead relies on 300 fans who text message their instructions via their cellphones. Each week, the coach posts between three and ten questions about training, team selection, and game tactics to the fans. They have three minutes to respond via cellphone text messaging, and they receive immediate feedback on what others think.

Does shared decision making work? During the first season of the experiment, the team won first place in its division and was promoted to the next higher division. Although we are unlikely to see this type of wireless interactive decision making in organizations any time soon, it does illustrate that decisions, and maybe even how they are made, play a role in performance.

Individuals must continually make **decisions**. Although decision making is typically described as "choosing among alternatives," that view is simplistic. Why? Because decision making is a comprehensive process, not just a simple act of choosing among alternatives.[5] Even for something as straightforward as deciding where to go for lunch, you do more than just choose burgers or pizza. You may consider various restaurants, how you will get there, who might go with you. Granted, you may not spend a lot of time contemplating a lunch decision, but you still go through a process when making that decision. What *does* the decision-making process involve?

Exhibit 4-1 illustrates the **decision-making process**, a set of eight steps that begins with identifying a problem, the decision criteria, and the weights for those criteria; moves to developing, analyzing, and selecting an alternative that can resolve the problem; then moves to implementing the alternative; and concludes with evaluating the decision's effectiveness. Many individuals use most or all of the steps implicitly, if not explicitly. Often, when a poor decision is made, it is because one of the steps was not carefully considered.

This process is as relevant to your personal decision about what movie to see on a Friday night as it is to a corporate action such as a decision to use technology in managing client relationships. The process can also be used to describe both individual and group decisions. Let us take a closer look at the process in order to understand what each step involves. We will use an example—a manager deciding what tablet is best to purchase—to illustrate these steps.

## Step 1: Identify a Problem

The decision-making process begins with the existence of a **problem** or, more specifically, a discrepancy between an existing and a desired state of affairs.[6] Take Amanda, a sales manager whose sales representatives need new tablets because their old laptops are inadequate to do their jobs efficiently and effectively. For simplicity's sake, assume that Amanda has determined that it is not economical to simply add memory to the old computers and that the organization's policy prefers managers to purchase new computers rather than lease them. Now we have a problem. There is a disparity between the capabilities of the sales reps' current computers and the capabilities that the sales reps require of their new tablets in order to do their jobs properly. Amanda has a decision to make.

## Step 2: Identify Decision Criteria

Once a manager has identified a problem, the **decision criteria** important to resolving the problem must be identified. Managers must determine what is relevant in making a

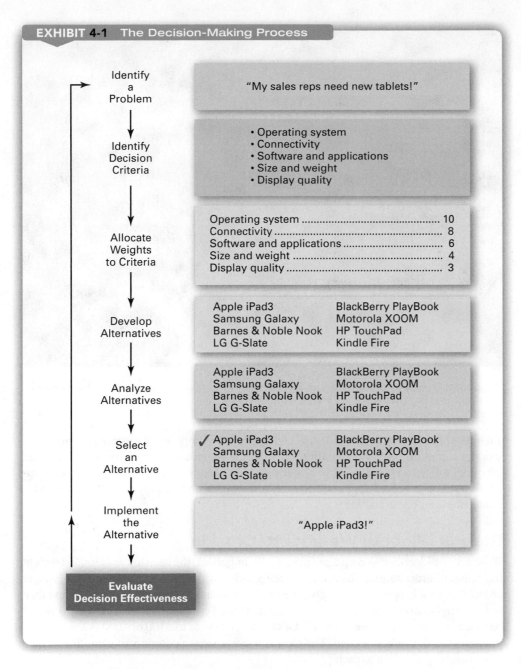

**EXHIBIT 4-1** The Decision-Making Process

Identify a Problem
"My sales reps need new tablets!"

Identify Decision Criteria
- Operating system
- Connectivity
- Software and applications
- Size and weight
- Display quality

Allocate Weights to Criteria
Operating system ............................................... 10
Connectivity ......................................................... 8
Software and applications ................................ 6
Size and weight ................................................... 4
Display quality ..................................................... 3

Develop Alternatives
Apple iPad3     BlackBerry PlayBook
Samsung Galaxy     Motorola XOOM
Barnes & Noble Nook     HP TouchPad
LG G-Slate     Kindle Fire

Analyze Alternatives
Apple iPad3     BlackBerry PlayBook
Samsung Galaxy     Motorola XOOM
Barnes & Noble Nook     HP TouchPad
LG G-Slate     Kindle Fire

Select an Alternative
✓ Apple iPad3     BlackBerry PlayBook
Samsung Galaxy     Motorola XOOM
Barnes & Noble Nook     HP TouchPad
LG G-Slate     Kindle Fire

Implement the Alternative
"Apple iPad3!"

Evaluate Decision Effectiveness

decision. Whether explicitly stated or not, every decision maker has criteria that guide his or her decisions. These criteria are generally determined by one's objectives. For example, when you buy a car, your objective might be to have a car that shouts "status symbol." Or you might want a car that is low maintenance. With your objective in mind, you might consider speed, fuel efficiency, colour, manufacturer, size, and so on as criteria on which to evaluate which car to buy. In our tablet purchase example, Amanda has to assess what factors are relevant to her decision. These factors might include criteria

**decision**
A choice from two or more alternatives.

**decision-making process**
A set of eight steps that includes identifying a problem, selecting an alternative, and evaluating the decision's effectiveness.

**problem**
A discrepancy between an existing and a desired state of affairs.

**decision criteria**
Criteria that define what is relevant in making a decision.

The choice of a new tablet relies on specific decision criteria such as price, reputation, operating system, software and applications, display quality, battery life, and size and weight.

such as price, connectivity, software and applications, operating system, memory and storage capabilities, display quality, battery life, expansion capability, warranty, and carrying weight. After careful consideration, she decides that operating system, connectivity, software and applications, size and weight, and display quality are the relevant criteria in her decision.

## Step 3: Allocate Weights to Criteria

If the criteria identified in Step 2 are not equally important, the decision maker must weight the items in order to give them the correct priority in the decision. How do you weight criteria? A simple approach is to give the most important criterion a weight of 10 and then assign weights to the rest against that standard. Thus, a criterion with a weight of 10 would be twice as important as one given a 5. Of course, you could use 100 or 1000 or any number you select as the highest weight. The idea is to prioritize the criteria you identified in Step 2 by assigning a weight to each.

Exhibit 4-2 lists the criteria and weights that Amanda developed for her computer replacement decision. As you can see, operating system is the most important criterion in her decision, and display quality is the least important. Amanda chose operating system because it was a major aspect in evaluating other factors. She had to choose between the

| EXHIBIT 4-2 Criteria and Weights for Tablet Replacement Decision | |
|---|---|
| **Criterion** | **Weight** |
| Operating system | 10 |
| Connectivity | 8 |
| Software and applications | 6 |
| Size and weight | 4 |
| Display quality | 3 |

Android system (Google), BlackBerry (RIM), iOS (Apple), webOS (HP), and Windows (Microsoft).

## Step 4: Develop Alternatives

The fourth step requires the decision maker to list viable alternatives that could resolve the problem. No attempt is made to evaluate the alternatives, only to list them. Our sales manager, Amanda, identified eight tablets as possible choices, including Apple iPad3, Samsung Galaxy, Barnes & Noble Nook, LG G-Slate, BlackBerry PlayBook, Motorola XOOM, HP TouchPad, and Kindle Fire.

## Step 5: Analyze Alternatives

Once the alternatives have been identified, a decision maker must analyze each one. How? By appraising each against the criteria established in steps 2 and 3. From this comparison, the strengths and weaknesses of each alternative become evident. Exhibit 4-3 shows the assessed values that Amanda gave each of her eight alternatives after she had talked to some tablet experts and read the latest information from computer magazines, blogs, and user reviews.

Keep in mind that size and weight is easy to determine by looking at descriptions online or in computer magazines. However, the assessment of display quality is more of a personal judgment. The point is that most decisions by managers involve judgments—the criteria chosen in Step 2, the weights given to the criteria in Step 3, and the analysis of alternatives in Step 5. This fact explains why two tablet buyers with the same amount of money may look at two totally different sets of alternatives or even rate the same alternatives differently.

Exhibit 4-3 represents only an assessment of the eight alternatives against the decision criteria. It does not reflect the weighting done in Step 3. If you multiply each alternative's assessed value (Exhibit 4-3) by its weight (Exhibit 4-2), you get the scores presented in Exhibit 4-4 on page 94. The sum of these scores represents an evaluation of each alternative against both the established criteria and weights. At times a decision maker might not have to take this step. If one choice had scored 10 on every criterion, you would not need to consider the weights. Similarly, if the weights were all equal, you could evaluate each alternative merely by summing up the appropriate lines in Exhibit 4-3.

## Step 6: Select an Alternative

Step 6 is choosing the best alternative from among those considered. Once all the pertinent criteria in the decision have been weighted and viable alternatives analyzed, we simply choose the alternative that generated the highest total in Step 5. In our example (Exhibit 4-4), Amanda would choose the Apple iPad3 because it scored highest (284 total) on the basis of the criteria identified, the weights given to the criteria, and her assessment of each tablet's ranking on the criteria.

*What does it mean if the "best" alternative does not feel right to you after going through the decision-making steps?*

### EXHIBIT 4-3 Assessed Values of Tablets Using Decision Criteria

|  | Operating system | Connectivity | Software and applications | Size and weight | Display quality |
|---|---|---|---|---|---|
| Apple iPad3 | 10 | 9 | 9 | 7 | 10 |
| Samsung Galaxy | 9 | 10 | 8 | 9 | 7 |
| Barnes & Noble Nook | 6 | 6 | 7 | 7 | 8 |
| LG G-Slate | 7 | 7 | 8 | 6 | 8 |
| BlackBerry PlayBook | 8 | 8 | 6 | 8 | 7 |
| Motorola XOOM | 7 | 7 | 8 | 5 | 8 |
| HP TouchPad | 7 | 7 | 8 | 5 | 7 |
| Kindle Fire | 9 | 10 | 6 | 8 | 6 |

**EXHIBIT 4-4** Evaluation of Tablet Alternatives Against Weighted Criteria

| | Operating system | Connectivity | Software and applications | Size and weight | Display quality | Total |
|---|---|---|---|---|---|---|
| **Weight** | **10** | **8** | **6** | **4** | **3** | |
| Apple iPad3 | 100 | 72 | 54 | 28 | 30 | 284 |
| Samsung Galaxy | 90 | 80 | 48 | 36 | 21 | 275 |
| Barnes & Noble Nook | 60 | 48 | 42 | 28 | 24 | 202 |
| LG G-Slate | 70 | 56 | 48 | 24 | 24 | 222 |
| BlackBerry PlayBook | 80 | 64 | 36 | 32 | 21 | 233 |
| Motorola XOOM | 70 | 56 | 48 | 20 | 24 | 218 |
| HP TouchPad | 70 | 56 | 48 | 20 | 21 | 215 |

That said, occasionally when one gets to this step, the alternative that looks best according to the numbers may not feel like the best solution (e.g., your intuition might suggest some other alternative). Often the reason is that the individual did not give the correct weight to one or more criteria (perhaps because one criterion was actually much more important than the individual realized initially, when assigning weights). Thus, if the individual finds that the "best alternative" does not seem like the right alternative, the decision maker needs to decide before implementing the alternative if a review of the criteria is necessary.

## Step 7: Implement the Alternative

Step 7 is concerned with putting the decision into action. This step involves conveying the decision to those affected by it and getting their commitment to it. Managers often fail to get buy-in from those around them before making a decision, even though successful implementation requires participation. One study found that managers used participation in only 20 percent of decisions, even though broad participation in decisions led to successful implementation 80 percent of the time. The same study found that managers most commonly tried to implement decisions through power or persuasion (used in 60 percent of decisions). These tactics were successful in only one of three decisions, however.[7] If the people who must carry out a decision participate in the process, they are more likely to enthusiastically support the outcome than if they are just told what to do. Parts 3, 4, and 5 of this book discuss how decisions are implemented by effective organizing, leading, and controlling.

## Step 8: Evaluate Decision Effectiveness

The last step in the decision-making process involves evaluating the outcome of the decision to see if the problem has been resolved. Did the alternative chosen in Step 6 and implemented in Step 7 accomplish the desired result? In Part 5 of this book, in which we look at the controlling function, we will see how to evaluate the results of decisions.

What if the evaluation shows the problem still exists? The manager would need to assess what went wrong. Was the problem incorrectly defined? Were errors made in the evaluation of the various alternatives? Was the right alternative selected but poorly implemented? Answers to questions such as these might send the manager back to one of the earlier steps. It might even require re-doing the whole decision process. To learn more about creativity and decision making, see *Be the Consultant—Solving Problems Creatively* on page 118 at the end of the chapter.

Interpret

# THE MANAGER AS DECISION MAKER

Potential entrepreneurs looking at franchise opportunities need to make a decision based on which sectors provide the greatest opportunity for growth. The Canadian Franchise Association identifies the five hottest franchise opportunities: meal preparation, child-based services, senior care, pets, and computers.[8] This analysis supports the decision made by Lucie Shaw to invest $40 000 in a franchise fee and another $85 000 in marketing and first-year working capital.[9]

Did Shaw need a nursing background to be successful? Would she be able to build a nest egg for her retirement while doing something she loved? She did her research and due diligence, and jumped in with something she felt passionate about—a business where she could give back to the community.

Everyone in an organization makes decisions, but decision making is particularly important in a manager's job. As Exhibit 4-5 shows, decision making is part of all four managerial functions. That's why managers—when they plan, organize, lead, and control—are frequently called *decision makers*.

The decision-making process described in Exhibit 4-1 on page 91 suggests that individuals make rational, carefully scripted decisions. But, is *rational* the best word to describe the decision-making process and the person who actually makes the decisions? We look at these issues in this section. We start by looking at three perspectives on how decisions are made.

## Think About It

What biases might enter into a franchisee like Shaw's decision making, and how might she overcome these? How can Shaw improve her decision making, given that she is dealing with a high amount of uncertainty and risk in choosing entrepreneurship as her source of income?

> **4.2** Define
> What factors affect how decisions are made?

## Making Decisions: Rationality, Bounded Rationality, and Intuition

Our model of the decision-making process implies that individuals engage in **rational decision making**. By that we mean people make consistent, value-maximizing choices within

---

**EXHIBIT 4-5   Decisions in the Management Functions**

| Planning | Leading |
|---|---|
| • What are the organization's long-term objectives? | • How do I handle employees who appear to be low in motivation? |
| • What strategies will best achieve those objectives? | • What is the most effective leadership style in a given situation? |
| • What should the organization's short-term objectives be? | • How will a specific change affect worker productivity? |
| • How difficult should individual goals be? | • When is the right time to stimulate conflict? |

| Organizing | Controlling |
|---|---|
| • How many employees should I have report directly to me? | • What activities in the organization need to be controlled? |
| • How much centralization should there be in the organization? | • How should those activities be controlled? |
| • How should jobs be designed? | • When is a performance deviation significant? |
| • When should the organization implement a different structure? | • What type of management information system should the organization have? |

---

**rational decision making**
Making decisions that are consistent and value-maximizing within specified constraints.

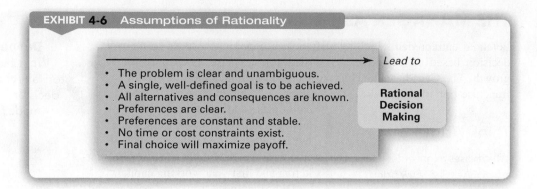

**EXHIBIT 4-6** Assumptions of Rationality

- The problem is clear and unambiguous.
- A single, well-defined goal is to be achieved.
- All alternatives and consequences are known.
- Preferences are clear.
- Preferences are constant and stable.
- No time or cost constraints exist.
- Final choice will maximize payoff.

Lead to → **Rational Decision Making**

specified constraints.[10] What are the underlying assumptions of rationality, and how valid are those assumptions?

*Would you say you make decisions rationally or do you rely on gut instinct?*

**ASSUMPTIONS OF RATIONALITY** A decision maker who was perfectly rational would be fully objective and logical. He or she would carefully define a problem and would have a clear and specific goal. Moreover, making decisions using rationality would consistently lead to selecting the alternative that maximizes the likelihood of achieving that goal. Exhibit 4-6 summarizes the assumptions of rationality.

The assumptions of rationality apply to any decision—personal or managerial. However, because we are concerned with managerial decision making, we need to add one further assumption. Rational managerial decision making assumes that decisions are made in the best interests of the organization. That is, the decision maker is assumed to be maximizing the organization's interests, not his or her own interests.

How realistic are these assumptions? Not all problems are simple, with clear goals and limited alternatives. Often, time pressures are involved in decision making. There can be high costs in seeking out and evaluating alternatives. For these reasons, most decisions that managers face in the real world do not meet the assumptions of rationality.[11] So how are most decisions in organizations usually made? The concept of bounded rationality can help answer that question.

**BOUNDED RATIONALITY** Managers tend to operate under assumptions of **bounded rationality**. They make decisions rationally but are limited (bounded) by their ability to interpret, process, and act on information.[12] There are bounds on other aspects of decision making as well, as seen in Exhibit 4-7. Bounded awareness and ethicality are limits that people have on observing information, while bounded willpower and self-interest are limits on weighting priorities.[13]

Because they cannot possibly analyze all information about all alternatives, managers **satisfice** rather than maximize. They accept a solution that is both satisfactory and sufficient. When managers satisfice, they limit their review of alternatives to some of the more conspicuous ones. Rather than carefully evaluate each alternative in great detail, managers settle on an alternative that is "good enough"—one that meets an acceptable level of performance. The first alternative that meets the "good enough" criterion ends the search. Another problem is that the decision maker may evaluate alternatives against one that is his or her preferred alternative. In choosing a tablet for her sales team, Amanda may have a personal favourite that she compares all the other tablets to, rather than evaluating all tablets at the same time.

Let us look at an example. Suppose you are a finance major and upon graduation you want a job, preferably as a personal financial planner, with a minimum annual salary of $50 000 and a location within 100 kilometres of your hometown. You are in a hurry to get a job, so you accept a job offer as a business credit analyst—not exactly a personal financial planner but still in the finance field—at a bank 50 kilometres from your hometown at a starting salary of $55 000. A more comprehensive job search would have revealed a job in personal financial planning at a trust company only 25 kilometres from your hometown

**EXHIBIT 4-7** Bounded Decision Making

| | Definition | Example |
|---|---|---|
| Bounded Awareness | People overlooking important information during the decision making process | The music industry's failure to see the threat of Napster and file sharing |
| Bounded Ethicality | Personal ethical preferences may not be in sync with our actual behaviour | A hiring manager who views himself/herself as egalitarian but has different eye contact and body language with one group of people versus another |
| Bounded Rationality | We employ shortcuts (heuristics) to help make sense of things | Limited time to perform or a lack of understanding of financial ratios might lead to decisions made with improper financial support |
| Bounded Willpower | We give too much focus to the present and not enough to the future | A person not saving enough for retirement early in their career |
| Bounded Self-Interest | Attaching a priority to the outcomes of others rather than simply trying to maximize our own payoffs | Employing principles of fairness rather than trying to crush your competitors |

*Source: Rotman Magazine*, Winter 2009, Dolly Chu interview with Karen Christensen.

with a starting salary of $57 000. Because the first job offer was satisfactory (or "good enough"), you behaved in a boundedly rational manner by accepting it, although according to the assumptions of perfect rationality you did not maximize your decision by searching all possible alternatives and then choosing the best.

**INTUITION** When managers at stapler-maker Swingline saw the company's market share declining, they decided to use a logical scientific approach to help them address the issue. For three years, they exhaustively researched stapler users before deciding what new products to develop. However, at newcomer Accentra, Inc., founder Todd Moses used a more intuitive decision approach to come up with his line of unique PaperPro staplers. His stapler sold 1 million units in 6 months in a market that sells only 25 million units annually in total—a pretty good result for a new product.[14]

Like Todd Moses, managers regularly use their intuition, which may actually help improve their decision making.[15] What is **intuitive decision making**? It is making decisions on the basis of experience, feelings, and accumulated judgment. Researchers studying managers' use of intuitive decision making identified five different aspects of intuition, which are described in Exhibit 4-8.

Making a decision on intuition or "gut feeling" does not necessarily happen independently of rational analysis; rather, the two complement each other. A manager who has had experience with a particular, or even similar, type of problem or situation often can act quickly with what appears to be limited information. Such a manager does not rely on a systematic and thorough analysis of the problem or identification and evaluation of alternatives but instead uses his or her experience and judgment to make a decision.

How accurate is intuitive decision making? A recent study suggests that complex decisions may be better if made "in the absence of attentive deliberation."[16] To discover your own intuitive abilities, see *Assess Your Skills—How Intuitive Am I?* on pages 116–117 at the end of the chapter.

*Do you prefer to make decisions intuitively? Are these good decisions?*

Analyze

---

**bounded rationality**
Limitations on a person's ability to interpret, process, and act on information.

**intuitive decision making**
Making decisions on the basis of experience, feelings, and accumulated judgment.

**satisfice**
To accept solutions that are "good enough."

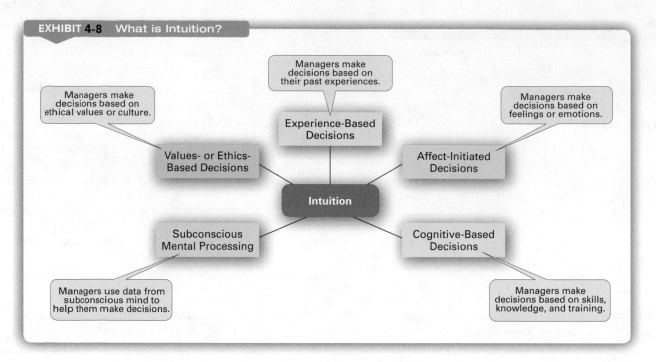

**EXHIBIT 4-8** What is Intuition?

Managers make decisions based on their past experiences.
— Experience-Based Decisions

Managers make decisions based on ethical values or culture.
— Values- or Ethics-Based Decisions

Managers make decisions based on feelings or emotions.
— Affect-Initiated Decisions

Intuition

Managers use data from subconscious mind to help them make decisions.
— Subconscious Mental Processing

Managers make decisions based on skills, knowledge, and training.
— Cognitive-Based Decisions

## Types of Problems and Decisions

Managers at eating establishments in Whitehorse, Yukon, make decisions weekly about purchasing food supplies and scheduling employee work shifts. It is something they have done countless times. But in 2007, they faced a decision they had never encountered—how to adapt to a newly enacted no-smoking bylaw in public places, which included restaurants and bars. This situation is not all that unusual. Managers in all kinds of organizations will face different types of problems and decisions as they do their jobs. Depending on the nature of the problem, a manager can use different types of decisions.

**STRUCTURED PROBLEMS AND PROGRAMMED DECISIONS**   Some problems are straightforward. The goal of the decision maker is clear, the problem is familiar, and information about the problem is easily defined and complete. Examples of these types of problems could include what to do when a customer returns a purchase to a store, a supplier delivers an important product late, a news team wants to respond to a fast-breaking event, or a student wants to drop a class. Such situations are called **structured problems** because they are straightforward, familiar, and easily defined. When situations are structured, there is probably some standardized routine for handling problems that may arise. For example, when a restaurant server spills a drink on a customer's coat, the manager offers to have the coat cleaned at the restaurant's expense. This action is what we call a **programmed decision**—a repetitive decision that can be handled by a routine approach. Because the problem is structured, the manager does not have to go to the trouble and expense of following an involved decision process.

Programmed decisions can have negative consequences, however, particularly when decision makers deal with diverse populations/clients/customers. For example, it may be difficult to have one's coat cleaned immediately if one is away from home on a business trip in the middle of winter. Employees of Ottawa-based JDS Uniphase were not happy with the programmed decision they received from the Canada Revenue Agency about hefty taxes they were asked to pay on their company stock options. When JDS stock was trading at $300 per share, employees were saddled with tax bills of several hundred thousand dollars for their stock options, even though they had not cashed them in. When employees asked the Canada Revenue Agency how they could be expected to pay such big tax bills when they earned only $50 000 per year, the agency responded unsympathetically that they had to pay up.[17]

Managers make programmed decisions by falling back on procedures, rules, and policies.

A **procedure** is a series of interrelated sequential steps that a decision maker can use to respond to a structured problem. The only real difficulty is in identifying the problem. Once it is clear, so is the procedure. When bad weather grounds airplanes, airlines have procedures for helping customers who miss their flights. Customers may request that they be put up in a hotel for the night. The customer service agent knows how to make this decision—follow the established airline procedure for dealing with customers when flights are grounded.

A **rule** is an explicit statement that tells a decision maker what he or she can or cannot do. Rules are frequently used because they are simple to follow and ensure consistency. For example, rules about lateness and absenteeism permit supervisors to make disciplinary decisions rapidly and fairly.

A **policy** is a guideline for making a decision. In contrast to a rule, a policy establishes general parameters for the decision maker rather than specifically stating what should or should not be done. Policies typically contain an ambiguous term that leaves interpretation up to the decision maker. "The customer always comes first and should always be *satisfied*" is an example of a policy statement. While ambiguity of policies is often intended to allow more flexibility in action, not all employees and customers are comfortable with flexibly determined policies.

**UNSTRUCTURED PROBLEMS AND NONPROGRAMMED DECISIONS** Many organizational situations involve **unstructured problems**, new or unusual problems for which information is ambiguous or incomplete. Whether to build a new manufacturing facility in Beijing is an example of an unstructured problem.

**Nonprogrammed decisions** are unique and nonrecurring, and require custom-made solutions. For example, if an office building were to be flooded because sprinklers went off accidentally, CEOs with businesses in the buildings would have to decide when and how to start operating again, and what to do for employees whose offices were completely ruined. When a manager confronts an unstructured problem, there is no cut-and-dried solution. The problem requires a custom-made response through nonprogrammed decision making.

Few managerial decisions in the real world are either fully programmed or nonprogrammed. These are extremes, and most decisions fall somewhere in between. Few programmed decisions are designed to eliminate individual judgment completely. At the other extreme, even a unique situation requiring a nonprogrammed decision can be helped by programmed routines. It is best to think of decisions as *mainly* programmed or *mainly* nonprogrammed, rather than as completely one or the other.

The problems confronting managers usually become more unstructured as they move up the organizational hierarchy. Why? Because lower-level managers handle the routine decisions themselves and let upper-level managers deal with the decisions they find unusual or difficult. Similarly, higher-level managers delegate routine decisions to their subordinates so they, the managers, can deal with more difficult issues.[18]

One of the more challenging tasks facing managers as they make decisions is analyzing decision alternatives (Step 5 in the decision-making process). In the next section, we look at analyzing alternatives under different conditions.

---

**structured problems**
Problems that are straightforward, familiar, and easily defined.

**programmed decision**
A repetitive decision that can be handled by a routine approach.

**procedure**
A series of interrelated sequential steps that a decision maker can use to respond to a structured problem.

**rule**
An explicit statement that tells a decision maker what he or she can or cannot do.

**policy**
A guideline for making a decision.

**unstructured problems**
Problems that are new or unusual and for which information is ambiguous or incomplete.

**nonprogrammed decisions**
Decisions that are unique and nonrecurring, and require custom-made solutions.

Many people believe that China will become the next big market for powerful brand-name products, and Zong Qinghou, founder of China's Wahaha beverage group, is ready. But brand names are a new concept in Chinese markets, and Zong prefers his own first-hand information to market research. He will face many nonprogrammed decisions as he tries to make his brand strong at home and abroad.

## Decision-Making Conditions

When managers make decisions, they face three conditions: certainty, risk, and uncertainty. What are the characteristics of each?

**CERTAINTY**   The ideal condition for making decisions is one of **certainty**, that is, a condition in which a decision maker can make accurate decisions because the outcome of every alternative is known. For example, when Alberta's finance minister is deciding in which bank to deposit excess provincial funds, he knows the exact interest rate being offered by each bank and the amount that will be earned on the funds. He is certain about the outcomes of each alternative. As you might expect, most managerial decisions are not like this.

*How much do uncertainty and risk affect your decisions?*

**RISK**   A far more common condition is one of **risk**, a condition in which a decision maker is able to estimate the likelihood of certain outcomes. The ability to assign probabilities to outcomes may be the result of personal experiences or secondary information. With risk, managers have historical data that let them assign probabilities to different alternatives. Let us work through an example.

Suppose that you manage a ski resort in Whistler, BC. You are thinking about adding another lift to your current facility. Obviously, your decision will be influenced by the additional revenue that the new lift would generate, and additional revenue will depend on snowfall. The decision is made somewhat clearer because you have fairly reliable weather data from the past ten years on snowfall levels in your area—three years of heavy snowfall, five years of normal snowfall, and two years of light snowfall. Can you use this information to help you make your decision about adding the new lift? If you have good information on the amount of revenues generated during each level of snowfall, the answer is yes.

You can calculate expected value—the expected return from each possible outcome—by multiplying expected revenues by snowfall probabilities. The result is the average revenue you can expect over time if the given probabilities hold. As Exhibit 4-9 shows, the expected revenue from adding a new ski lift is $687 500. Of course, whether that justifies a decision to build or not depends on the costs involved in generating the revenue, such as the cost to build the lift, the additional annual operating expenses for the lift, the interest rate for borrowing money, and so forth.

| **EXHIBIT 4-9** Expected Value for Revenues from the Addition of One Ski Lift | | | | | | |
|---|---|---|---|---|---|---|
| Event | Expected Revenues | × | Probability | = | Expected Value of Each Alternative | |
| Heavy snowfall | $850 000 | | 0.3 | | $255 000 | |
| Normal snowfall | 725 000 | | 0.5 | | 362 500 | |
| Light snowfall | 350 000 | | 0.2 | | 70 000 | |
| | | | | | $687 500 | |

**UNCERTAINTY**   What happens if you have a decision where you are not certain about the outcomes and cannot even make reasonable probability estimates? We call such a condition **uncertainty**. Managers do face decision-making situations of uncertainty. Under these conditions, the choice of alternative is influenced by the limited amount of information available to the decision maker and by the psychological orientation of the decision maker. The optimistic manager will follow a *maximax* choice (maximizing the maximum possible payoff) in order to get the largest possible gain. The pessimist will follow a *maximin* choice (maximizing the minimum possible payoff) to make the best of a situation should the worst possible outcome occur. The manager who desires to minimize his maximum "regret" will opt for a *minimax* choice, to avoid having big regrets after decisions play out.

## Decision-Making Styles

Suppose that you are a new manager at Sony or at the local YMCA. How would you make decisions? Decision-making styles differ along two dimensions.[19] The first dimension is an individual's *way of thinking*. Some of us are more rational and logical in the way we process information. A rational type processes information in order and makes sure that it is logical and consistent before making a decision. Others tend to be creative and intuitive. An intuitive type does not have to process information in a certain order and is comfortable looking at it as a whole.

The other dimension is an individual's *tolerance for ambiguity*. Some of us have a low tolerance for ambiguity. These types need consistency and order in the way they structure information so that ambiguity is minimized. On the other hand, some of us can tolerate high levels of ambiguity and are able to process many thoughts at the same time. When we diagram these two dimensions, four decision-making styles are evident: directive, analytic, conceptual, and behavioural (see Exhibit 4-10). Let us look more closely at each style.

- *Directive style.* Individuals with a **directive style** have low tolerance for ambiguity and are rational in their way of thinking. They are efficient and logical. Directive types make fast decisions and focus on the short run. Their efficiency and speed in making decisions often result in decisions that are made with minimal information and assessment of few alternatives.
- *Analytic style.* Individuals with an **analytic style** have much greater tolerance for ambiguity than do directive types. They want more information before making a decision and consider

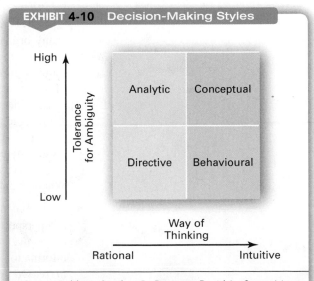

**EXHIBIT 4-10   Decision-Making Styles**

*Source:* Robbins, Stephen P.; Decenzo, David A., *Supervision Today*, 2nd Ed., © 1998. Reprinted and Electronically reproduced by permission of Pearson Education, Inc., Upper Saddle River, New Jersey.

**certainty**
A condition in which a decision maker can make accurate decisions because the outcome of every alternative is known.

**risk**
A condition in which a decision maker is able to estimate the likelihood of certain outcomes.

**uncertainty**
A condition in which a decision maker is not certain about the outcomes and cannot even make reasonable probability estimates.

**directive style**
A decision-making style characterized by a low tolerance for ambiguity and a rational way of thinking.

**analytic style**
A decision-making style characterized by a high tolerance for ambiguity and a rational way of thinking.

more alternatives than directive-style decision makers do. Analytic-style decision makers are characterized as careful decision makers with the ability to adapt to or cope with unique situations.

- *Conceptual style.* Individuals with a **conceptual style** tend to be very broad in their outlook and consider many alternatives. They are intuitive, focus on the long run, and are very good at finding creative solutions to problems. They are also adaptive and flexible.

- *Behavioural style.* Individuals with a **behavioural style** have a low tolerance for ambiguity and an intuitive way of thinking. They are sociable, friendly, and supportive. They work well with others, are concerned about the achievements of those around them, and are receptive to suggestions from others. They often use meetings to communicate, although they try to avoid conflict. Acceptance by others is important in this decision-making style.

Although these four decision-making styles are distinct, most managers have characteristics of more than one style. It is probably more realistic to think of a manager's dominant style and his or her alternative styles. Although some managers will rely almost exclusively on their dominant style, others are more flexible and can shift their style depending on the situation.

Managers should also recognize that their employees may use different decision-making styles. Some employees may take their time, carefully weighing alternatives and considering riskier options (analytic style), while other employees may be more concerned about getting suggestions from others before making decisions (behavioural style). These differences do not make one approach better than the other. The decision-making styles are just different. For a look at the issues associated with diversity and making decisions, see *Managing Workforce Diversity—The Value of Diversity in Decision Making* on page 118 at the end of the chapter.

## Group Decision Making

*Do you think individuals or groups make better decisions?*

Many organizational decisions are made by groups. It is a rare organization that does not at some time use committees, task forces, review panels, study teams, or similar groups to make decisions. Studies show that managers may spend up to 30 hours a week in group meetings.[20] Undoubtedly, a large portion of that time is spent identifying problems, developing solutions, and determining how to implement the solutions. It is possible, in fact, for groups to be assigned any of the eight steps in the decision-making process. In this section, we look at the advantages and disadvantages of group decision making, discuss when groups would be preferred, and review some techniques for improving group decision making. What advantages do group decisions have over individual decisions?

- *More complete information and knowledge.* A group brings a diversity of experience and perspectives to the decision process that an individual cannot.
- *More diverse alternatives.* Because groups have a greater amount and diversity of information, they can identify more diverse alternatives than an individual.
- *Increased acceptance of a solution.* Group members are reluctant to fight or undermine a decision they have helped develop.
- *Increased legitimacy.* Decisions made by groups may be perceived as more legitimate than decisions made unilaterally by one person.

If groups are so good at making decisions, how did the phrase "A camel is a horse put together by a committee" become so popular? The answer, of course, is that group decisions also have disadvantages:

- *Increased time to reach a solution.* Groups almost always take more time to reach a solution than it would take an individual.
- *Opportunity for minority domination.* The inequality of group members creates the opportunity for one or more members to dominate others. A dominant and vocal minority frequently can have an excessive influence on the final decision.

- *Ambiguous responsibility.* Group members share responsibility, but the responsibility of any single member is diluted.
- *Pressures to conform.* There can be pressures to conform in groups. This pressure undermines critical thinking in the group and eventually harms the quality of the final decision.[21]

**GROUPTHINK**   The pressure to conform is what social psychologist Irving Janis called the "groupthink" phenomenon. Have you ever been in a situation in which several people were sitting around discussing a particular item and you had something to say that ran contrary to the consensus views of the group, but you remained silent? Were you surprised to learn later that others shared your views and had also remained silent? What you experienced is what Janis termed **groupthink**.[22] This behaviour is a form of conformity in which group members withhold deviant, minority, or unpopular views in order to give the appearance of agreement. As a result, groupthink undermines critical thinking in the group and eventually harms the quality of the final decision.

Groupthink applies to a situation in which a group's ability to appraise alternatives objectively and arrive at a quality decision is jeopardized. Because of pressures for conformity, groups often deter individuals from critically appraising unusual, minority, or unpopular views. Consequently, an individual's mental efficiency, reality testing, and moral judgment deteriorate.

How does groupthink occur? The following are examples of situations in which groupthink is evident:

- Group members rationalize any resistance to the assumptions they have made.
- Members apply direct pressure on those who momentarily express doubts about any of the group's shared views or who question the validity of arguments favoured by the majority.
- Those members who have doubts or hold differing points of view seek to avoid going against what appears to be group consensus.
- There is an illusion of unanimity. If someone does not speak, it is assumed that he or she is in full agreement.

In 2003, Richard Branson, founder of the Virgin Group of companies, wanted to compete with Apple's entry in the MP3 music player industry—the iPod. Virgin's management team was strongly opposed to Virgin producing its own MP3 player. Branson insisted they launch the Virgin Pulse, at a design cost of $20 million. However, it bombed and they had to write off the investment. Had Branson listened more to his management employees, the huge investment failure could have been avoided.[23]

---

**conceptual style**
A decision-making style characterized by a high tolerance for ambiguity and an intuitive way of thinking.

**behavioural style**
A decision-making style characterized by a low tolerance for ambiguity and an intuitive way of thinking.

**groupthink**
The withholding by group members of different views in order to appear to be in agreement.

Does groupthink really hinder decision making? Yes. Several research studies have found that groupthink symptoms were associated with poorer-quality decision outcomes. But groupthink can be minimized if the group is cohesive, fosters open discussion, and has an impartial leader who seeks input from all members.[24]

## Individual vs. Group Decision Making

Determining whether a group or an individual will be more effective in making a particular decision depends on the criteria you use to assess effectiveness.[25] Group decisions are preferable when accuracy, creativity, and degree of acceptance are required, while individual decision making offers greater speed and efficiency.

Keep in mind, however, that the effectiveness of group decision making is also influenced by the size of the group. Although a larger group provides greater opportunity for diverse representation, it also requires more coordination and more time for members to contribute their ideas. So groups should not be too large. Evidence indicates, in fact, that groups of five, and to a lesser extent, seven, are the most effective.[26] Having an odd number in the group helps avoid decision deadlocks. These groups are large enough for members to shift roles and withdraw from unfavourable positions, but still small enough for quieter members to participate actively in discussions.

Employee involvement, present in every organization to some extent, leads to higher commitment from the employees for the decisions. A recent study found that employee involvement also increases skill variety and feelings of autonomy, which results in higher job enrichment and motivation.[27] What is the right amount of employee involvement? Exhibit 4-11 looks at the situational factors that have an impact on the effectiveness of employee involvement outcomes.[28] The four contingencies are:

- *Decision structure*. Programmed decisions require less employee involvement.
- *Source of decision knowledge*. Employees may have more relevant and timely information than managers, increasing the need for involvement.
- *Decision commitment*. If participants might be against a decision without their input, then involvement is more necessary.
- *Risk of conflict*. If there are conflicting employee and organizational goals, involvement is useful in minimizing conflict.

## Decision-Making Biases and Errors

When managers make decisions, not only do they use their own particular style, but many use "rules of thumb," or **heuristics**, to simplify their decision making. Rules of thumb can

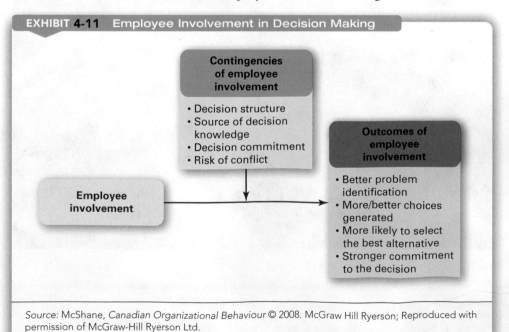

**EXHIBIT 4-11  Employee Involvement in Decision Making**

**Contingencies of employee involvement**
- Decision structure
- Source of decision knowledge
- Decision commitment
- Risk of conflict

**Employee involvement**

**Outcomes of employee involvement**
- Better problem identification
- More/better choices generated
- More likely to select the best alternative
- Stronger commitment to the decision

*Source:* McShane, *Canadian Organizational Behaviour* © 2008. McGraw Hill Ryerson; Reproduced with permission of McGraw-Hill Ryerson Ltd.

be useful to decision makers because they help make sense of complex, uncertain, and ambiguous information.[29] Even though managers may use rules of thumb, that does not mean those rules are reliable. Why? Because they may lead to errors and biases in processing and evaluating information. Exhibit 4-12 identifies seven common decision-making biases and errors. Let us take a quick look at each of them.[30]

- *Overconfidence bias.* Decision makers tend to think they know more than they do or hold unrealistically positive views of themselves and their performance. For example, a sales manager brags that his presentation was so good that there is no doubt the sale will be his. Later he learns that he lost the sale because the client found him obnoxious.
- *Selective perception bias.* Decision makers selectively organize and interpret events based on their biased perceptions. This bias influences the information they pay attention to, the problems they identify, and the alternatives they develop. For example, before John meets with two job candidates, he learns that one went to his alma mater. He does not seriously consider the other job candidate because he believes that graduating from the same university as he did makes the first candidate superior.
- *Confirmation bias.* Decision makers seek out information that reaffirms their past choices and discount information that contradicts past judgments. These people tend to accept at face value information that confirms their preconceived views and are critical and skeptical of information that challenges these views. For example, Pierre continues to give business to the same supplier, even though the supplier has been late on several deliveries. Pierre thinks the supplier is a nice person, and the supplier keeps promising to deliver on time.
- *Sunk-costs error.* Decision makers forget that current choices cannot correct the past. They incorrectly fixate on past expenditures of time, money, or effort in assessing choices rather than on future consequences. For example, Hakan has spent thousands of dollars and several months introducing new procedures for handling customer complaints. Both customers and employees are complaining about the new procedures. Hakan does not want to consider the possibility that the procedures are needlessly complicated because of the investment in time and money he has already made.

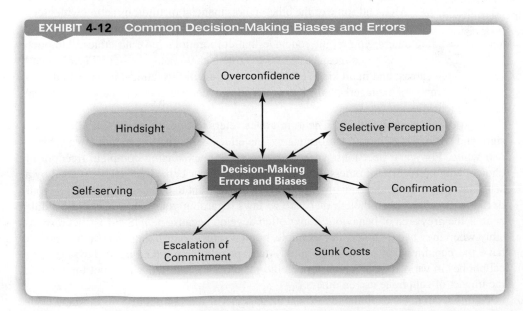

**EXHIBIT 4-12** Common Decision-Making Biases and Errors

**heuristics**
Rules of thumb that managers use to simplify decision making.

- *Escalation-of-commitment error.* Decisions can also be influenced by a phenomenon called **escalation of commitment**, which is an increased commitment to a previous decision despite evidence that it might have been wrong.[31] For example, studies of the events leading up to the space shuttle *Columbia* disaster in 2003 point to an escalation of commitment by decision makers to ignore the possible damage that foam striking the shuttle at takeoff might have had, even though the decision was questioned by some individuals. Why would decision makers want to escalate commitment to a bad decision? Because they don't want to admit that their initial decision might have been flawed. Rather than search for new alternatives, they simply increase their commitment to the original solution.
- *Self-serving bias.* Decision makers take credit for their successes and blame failure on outside factors. For example, Jesse dismisses his team's efforts when he wins a contract, although he blames them for the small error that was in the final report.
- *Hindsight bias.* Decision makers falsely believe that they would have accurately predicted the outcome of an event once that outcome is actually known. For example, after a client cancelled a contract that had been drawn up, Cindy tells her manager she knew ahead of time that was going to happen, even though she'd had no such thoughts before the contract was cancelled. After the fact, some outcomes seem more obvious than they did beforehand.

Practise

How can managers avoid the negative effects of these decision errors and biases? The main strategy is to be aware of them and then try not to exhibit them. Beyond that, managers should also pay attention to "how" they make decisions: They should try to identify the heuristics they typically use and critically evaluate how appropriate those are. Finally, managers might want to ask people around them to help identify weaknesses in their decision-making style and try to improve.

# ETHICS, CORPORATE SOCIAL RESPONSIBILITY, AND DECISION MAKING

**Describe**
How do ethics and social responsibility relate to decision making?

**4.3**

When you see top managers such as those formerly at Merrill-Lynch, AIG, and some of the other major financial institutions acting with greed and using financial manipulations, lying, and group pressure to deceive others, you might conclude that corporations have no ethics. Although that is by no means true, what *is* true is that managers—at all levels, in all areas, and in all kinds of organizations—will face ethical issues and dilemmas. As managers plan, organize, lead, and control, they must consider ethical dimensions.

What do we mean by ethics? The term **ethics** refers to rules and principles that define right and wrong behaviour.[32] Unfortunately, the ethics of a situation are not always black and white. For some decisions, you can make choices exercising complete freedom of choice, with no regard for others. For other decisions, your behaviour will be guided by a set of laws. In between are situations where you might want to consider the impact of your decision on others, even though there are no laws regarding your behaviour. This middle zone is the grey area of behaviour. Laws often develop because people did not act responsibly when they had a choice. For example, not too long ago drinking and driving did not have the penalties that are in place now. Many people have talked about laws banning cellphones in various situations for much the same reason: Individuals do not think about the impact of cellphone use on others.

In this section, we examine the ethical dimensions of managerial decisions. Many decisions that managers make require them to consider who may be affected—in terms of the result as well as the process.[33] To better understand the complicated issues involved in managerial ethics, we will look at four different views of ethics and the factors that influence a person's ethics, and offer some suggestions for what organizations can do to improve the ethical behaviour of employees.

## Four Views of Ethics

There are four views of ethics: the utilitarian view, the rights view, the theory of justice view, and the integrative social contracts theory.[34]

**THE UTILITARIAN VIEW OF ETHICS**  The **utilitarian view of ethics** maintains that ethical decisions are made solely on the basis of their outcomes or consequences. Utilitarian theory uses a quantitative method for making ethical decisions by looking at how to provide the greatest good for the greatest number. Following the utilitarian view, a manager might conclude that laying off 20 percent of the workforce in the plant is justified because it will increase the plant's profitability, improve job security for the remaining 80 percent, and be in the best interest of stockholders. Utilitarianism encourages efficiency and productivity, and is consistent with the goal of profit maximization. However, it can result in biased allocations of resources, especially when some of those affected by the decision lack representation or a voice in the decision. Utilitarianism can also result in the rights of some stakeholders being ignored.

**THE RIGHTS VIEW OF ETHICS**  The **rights view of ethics** is concerned with respecting and protecting individual liberties and privileges such as the rights to privacy, freedom of conscience, free speech, life and safety, and due process. This view would include, for example, protecting the free speech rights of employees who report legal violations by their employers. The positive side of the rights perspective is that it protects individuals' basic rights. The drawback, however, is that it can hinder productivity and efficiency by creating a work climate more concerned with protecting individuals' rights than with getting the job done. For example, an individual's right to privacy might make it difficult to make special arrangements for an employee whose illness is preventing her or him from carrying out job responsibilities.

**THE THEORY OF JUSTICE VIEW OF ETHICS**  According to the **theory of justice view of ethics**, managers impose and enforce rules fairly and impartially, and do so by following all legal rules and regulations. A manager following this view would decide to provide the same rate of pay to individuals who are similar in their levels of skills, performance, or responsibility, and not base that decision on arbitrary differences such as gender, personality, race, or personal favourites. Using standards of justice also has pluses and minuses. It protects the interests of those stakeholders who may be underrepresented or lack power, but it can encourage a sense of entitlement that might make employees reduce risk-taking, innovation, and productivity.

**THE INTEGRATIVE SOCIAL CONTRACTS THEORY**  The **integrative social contracts theory** proposes that ethical decisions be based on existing ethical norms in industries and communities in order to determine what constitutes right and wrong. This view of ethics is based on the integration of two "contracts": the general social contract that allows businesses to operate and defines the acceptable ground rules, and a more specific contract among members of a community that addresses acceptable ways of behaving. In deciding

---

**escalation of commitment**
An increased commitment to a previous decision despite evidence that the decision might have been wrong.

**ethics**
Rules and principles that define right and wrong behaviour.

**utilitarian view of ethics**
A view of ethics maintaining that ethical decisions are made solely on the basis of their outcomes or consequences.

**rights view of ethics**
A view of ethics concerned with respecting and protecting individual liberties and privileges.

**theory of justice view of ethics**
A view of ethics in which managers impose and enforce rules fairly and impartially, and do so by following all legal rules and regulations.

**integrative social contracts theory**
A view of ethics proposing that ethical decisions be based on existing ethical norms in industries and communities in order to determine what constitutes right and wrong.

what wage to pay employees in a new factory in Ciudad Juarez, Mexico, Canadian managers following the integrative social contracts theory would base the decision on existing wage levels in the community, rather than paying what Canadians might consider a "fair wage" in that context. Although this theory focuses on looking at existing practices, the problem is that some of these practices may be unethical.[35]

Which approach to ethics do most businesspeople follow? Not surprisingly, most follow the utilitarian approach. Why? It's consistent with such business goals as efficiency, productivity, and profits. However, that perspective needs to change because of the changing world facing managers. Trends toward individual rights, social justice, and community standards mean that managers need ethical standards based on nonutilitarian criteria. This new demand is an obvious challenge for managers, because making decisions based on such criteria involves far more ambiguities than using utilitarian criteria such as efficiency and profits. The result, of course, is that managers increasingly find themselves struggling with the question of the right thing to do.

## Improving Ethical Behaviour

Managers can do a number of things if they are serious about reducing unethical behaviour in their organizations. They can seek to hire individuals with high ethical standards, establish codes of ethics and decision rules, lead by example, delineate job goals and performance appraisal mechanisms, provide ethics training, conduct independent social audits, and provide support to individuals facing ethical dilemmas. Taken individually, these actions will probably not have much impact. But when all or most of them are implemented as part of a comprehensive ethics program, they have the potential to significantly improve an organization's ethical climate. The key term here, however, is *potential*. There are no guarantees that a well-designed ethics program will lead to the desired outcome.

Sometimes corporate ethics programs can be little more than public relations gestures, having minimal influence on managers and employees. Retailer Sears has a long history of encouraging ethical business practices and, in fact, has a corporate Office of Compliance and Ethics. However, the company's ethics programs did not stop managers from illegally trying to collect payments from bankrupt charge-account holders or from routinely deceiving automotive service centre customers in California into thinking they needed unnecessary repairs.

**CODES OF ETHICS AND DECISION RULES** Toronto-based Royal Bank of Canada has had a corporate code of conduct for more than 25 years. Christina Donely, the bank's senior adviser on employee relations and policy governance, says that the code "focuses on outlining behaviours that support honesty and integrity . . . and covers environmental [and] social issues."[36] However, that is not the way it is in all organizations. The US government passed the Sarbanes–Oxley Act in 2002 to crack down on business wrongdoing in publicly traded companies. Following the American example, the Canadian Securities Administrators put best corporate governance practices into effect in March 2004, although these are not as tough as the American rules.[37] As well, the securities regulators in all ten provinces and three territories have proposed that all public companies adopt written codes of ethics and conduct, or explain why they do not have them.[38] But these proposals carry no enforcement requirements or mechanisms.

Ambiguity about what is and is not ethical can be a problem for employees. A **code of ethics**—a formal statement of an organization's primary values and the ethical rules it expects its employees to follow—is a popular choice for reducing that ambiguity. About 60 percent of Canada's 650 largest corporations have some sort of ethics code.[39] Codes of ethics are also becoming more popular globally. A survey of business organizations in 80 countries found that 80 percent have formally stated ethics standards and codes of ethics.[40]

What should a code of ethics look like? It has been suggested that codes should be specific enough to show employees the spirit in which they are supposed to do things yet loose enough to allow for freedom of judgment.[41] A survey of companies' codes of ethics found their content tended to fall into three categories: (1) be a dependable organizational citizen; (2) don't do anything unlawful or improper that will harm the organization; and (3) be good to customers.[42]

How well do codes of ethics work? In reality, they are not always effective in encouraging ethical behaviour in organizations. While no comparable Canadian data are available, a survey of employees in US businesses with ethics codes found that 75 percent of those surveyed had observed ethical or legal violations in the previous 12 months, including such things as deceptive sales practices, unsafe working conditions, sexual harassment, conflicts of interest, and environmental violations.[43] Companies with codes of ethics may not do enough monitoring. For example, David Nitkin, president of Toronto-based EthicScan Canada, an ethics consultancy, notes that "only about 15 percent of [larger Canadian corporations with codes of ethics] have designated an ethics officer or ombudsman" or provide an ethics hotline, and that less than 10 percent offer whistle-blower protection.[44] Vancouver public employees were concerned enough about whistle-blower protection that the issue was one of the major stumbling blocks in reaching an agreement for a new collective agreement in summer 2007, leading to a 12-week strike.

Does this mean that codes of ethics should not be developed? No. But there are some suggestions managers can follow. First, an organization's code of ethics should be developed and then communicated clearly to employees. Second, all levels of management should continually reaffirm the importance of the ethics code and the organization's commitment to it, and consistently discipline those who break it. When managers consider the code of ethics important, regularly affirm its content, and publicly reprimand rule breakers, ethics codes can supply a strong foundation for an effective corporate ethics program.[45] Finally, an organization's code of ethics might be designed around the 12 questions listed in Exhibit 4-13, which can be used as decision rules to guide managers when they handle ethical dilemmas in decision making.[46]

## Corporate Social Responsibility

We define **corporate social responsibility** as a business's obligation, beyond that required by law and economics, to do the right things and act in ways that are good for society.[47]

---

**EXHIBIT 4-13**   12 Questions for Examining the Ethics of a Business Decision

1. Have you defined the problem accurately?

2. How would you define the problem if you stood on the other side of the fence?

3. How did this situation occur in the first place?

4. To whom and to what do you give your loyalty as a person and as a member of the corporation?

5. What is your intention in making this decision?

6. How does this intention compare with the probable results?

7. Whom could your decision or action injure?

8. Can you discuss the problem with the affected parties before you make the decision?

9. Are you confident that your position will be as valid over a long period of time as it seems now?

10. Could you disclose without qualm your decision or action to your boss, your chief executive officer, the board of directors, your family, society as a whole?

11. What is the symbolic potential of your action if understood? If misunderstood?

12. Under what conditions would you allow exceptions to your stand?

*Source:* Reprinted with permission from "Ethics Without the Sermon" by Laura L. Nash. Harvard Business Review, Nov. 1981 Copyright © 1981 by Harvard Business Publishing; all rights reserved.

---

**code of ethics**
A formal statement of an organization's primary values and the ethical rules it expects its employees to follow.

**corporate social responsibility**
A business's obligation, beyond that required by law and economics, to do the right things and act in ways that are good for society.

Note that this definition assumes that a business obeys laws and pursues economic interests. But also note that this definition views business as a moral agent—that is, in its effort to do good for society, a business must differentiate between right and wrong. A great deal of attention has been focused on the extent to which organizations and management should act in socially responsible ways. On one side, there is the classical—or purely economic—view, and on the other side is the socio-economic view.

**THE CLASSICAL VIEW** The **classical view** holds that management's only social responsibility is to maximize profits. The most outspoken advocate of this approach is the late economist and Nobel laureate Milton Friedman.[48] He argues that managers' primary responsibility is to operate the business in the best interests of the stockholders (the owners of a corporation). What are those interests? Friedman contends that stockholders have a single concern: financial return. He also argues that any time managers decide to spend the organization's resources for "social good," they are adding to the costs of doing business. These costs have to be passed on to consumers either through higher prices or absorbed by stockholders through a smaller profit returned as dividends. We must be clear that Friedman is not saying that organizations should *not* be socially responsible; he thinks they should. But the extent of that responsibility is to maximize organizational profits for stockholders.

Joel Bakan, professor of law at the University of British Columbia, author of *The Corporation*, and co-director of the documentary of the same name, is more critical of organizations than Friedman, although he finds that current laws support corporate behaviour some might find troubling. Bakan suggests that today's corporations have many of the same characteristics as a psychopathic personality (that is, self-interested, lacking empathy, manipulative, and reckless in one's disregard of others). Bakan notes that even though companies have a tendency to act psychopathically, this behaviour is not why they are fixated on profits. Rather, though they may have social responsibilities, the only *legal* responsibility corporations have is to maximize organizational profits for stockholders.[49] He suggests that more laws and more restraints need to be put in place if corporations are to behave more socially responsibly, because current laws direct corporations to be responsible to their shareholders and make little mention of responsibility toward other stakeholders.

**THE SOCIO-ECONOMIC VIEW** The **socio-economic view** maintains that management's social responsibility goes beyond making profits to include protecting and improving society's welfare. This position is based on the belief that corporations are *not* independent entities responsible only to stockholders. They also have a responsibility to the larger society that endorses their creation through various laws and regulations and that supports them by purchasing their products and services.

In addition, proponents of this view believe that business organizations are not mere economic institutions. Society expects and even encourages businesses to become involved in social, political, and legal issues. Proponents of the socio-economic view would say that Avon Products was being socially responsible when it initiated its Breast Cancer Crusade to provide women with breast cancer education and early detection screening services, and which, after 14 years, has raised more than $400 million worldwide.[50]

Educational programs implemented by Brazilian cosmetics manufacturer Natura Cosméticos SA in public primary schools in São Paulo to improve children's literacy and decision-making skills are also viewed as socially responsible.[51] Why? Through these programs, the managers are protecting and improving society's welfare. More and more organizations around the world are taking their social responsibilities seriously, especially in Europe, where the view that businesses need to focus on more than just profits has a stronger tradition than in North America.[52] Some even try to measure their "triple bottom line," which takes into account not only financial responsibilities, but social and environmental

*Is it wrong for Canadian companies to employ children to work in factories in countries where child labour is legal?*

ones as well.[53] Throughout the textbook are examples of Triple Bottom Line (3BL) issues at the end of each chapter.

**COMPARING THE TWO VIEWS**　The key differences between the two views of corporate social responsibility are easier to understand if we think in terms of the people to whom organizations are responsible. Classicists would say that shareholders, or owners, are the only legitimate concern. Those supporting the socioeconomic view would respond that managers should be responsible to any group affected by the organization's decisions and actions—that is, the stakeholders (such as employees and community members).[54] Exhibit 4-14 shows four different approaches an organization can take toward corporate social responsibility.[55] The defensive approach is consistent with the classical view, while the accommodative and proactive approaches are consistent with the socio-economic view.

Those who avoid corporate social responsibility altogether take an **obstructionist approach**. Obstructionist managers engage in unethical and illegal behaviour, and try to hide their behaviour from organizational stakeholders and society at large.

Those taking the minimal position toward corporate social responsibility use a **defensive approach**. These organizations have a commitment to ethical behaviour, making sure that employees behave legally and no harm is done to others. The claims and interests of shareholders come first with this approach, and little attention is paid to other stakeholders. Managers taking a defensive perspective rely only on legally established rules to guide their behaviour. They do not believe they should make socially responsible choices that are not spelled out in laws and regulations. For example, a company that meets pollution control standards established by the federal government or that does not discriminate against employees over the age of 40 in promotion decisions is meeting its social obligation and nothing more because there are laws mandating these actions.

Some managers go beyond legal requirements, choosing to support corporate social responsibility in a balanced fashion. These managers take an **accommodative approach**

> *Would you be willing to stop eating your favourite snack if you found out the company did not use environmentally friendly packaging for its products?*

**EXHIBIT 4-14**　Approaches to Corporate Social Responsibility

| Obstructionist Approach | Defensive Approach | Accommodative Approach | Proactive Approach |
|---|---|---|---|
| Disregard for social responsibility | Minimal commitment to social responsibility | Moderate commitment to social responsibility | Strong commitment to social responsibility |

No Social Responsibility　　　　　　　　　　　　　　　　　High Social Responsibility

**classical view**
The view that management's only social responsibility is to maximize profits.

**socio-economic view**
The view that management's social responsibility goes beyond making profits to include protecting and improving society's welfare.

**obstructionist approach**
The avoidance of corporate social responsibility; managers engage in unethical and illegal behaviour that they try to hide from organizational stakeholders and society.

**defensive approach**
Managers relying only on legally established rules to take the minimal position toward corporate social responsibility.

**accommodative approach**
Managers make choices that try to balance the interests of shareholders with those of other stakeholders.

Richard Kouwenhoven, manager of digital services of Burnaby, BC–based Hemlock Printers, founded by his father, has been one of the leaders of his generation's push to have the company, already known for its green practices, become a leader in sustainable paper use.

to corporate social responsibility. Accommodative managers make choices that try to balance the interests of shareholders with those of other stakeholders. Corporate social responsibility goals for suppliers and customers might include fair prices, high-quality products and services, safe products, good supplier relations, and similar actions. Their philosophy is that they can meet their responsibilities to stockholders only by meeting the needs of these other stakeholders.

Finally, some managers take an active interest in corporate social responsibility. These managers take a **proactive approach** to find out about and meet the needs of different stakeholder groups. They promote the interests of shareholders *and* stakeholders, using organizational resources to do so. These managers feel a responsibility to society as a whole. They view their business as a public entity and feel a responsibility to advance the public good, even if such actions may decrease profits. The acceptance of such responsibility means that managers actively promote social justice, preserve the environment, and support social and cultural activities. For example, Vancouver-based Weyerhaeuser Canada is committed to sustainable forestry practices and has a formal policy for building relationships with Canada's Aboriginal peoples.

**CORPORATE SOCIAL RESPONSIBILITY AND ECONOMIC PERFORMANCE** How do socially responsible activities affect a company's economic performance? Findings from a number of research studies can help us answer this question.[56] The majority of these studies show a positive relationship between social involvement and economic performance. One study found that firms' corporate social performance was positively associated with both *prior* and *future* financial performance.[57] But we should be cautious about making any compelling assumptions from these findings because of methodological questions associated with trying to measure "corporate social responsibility" and "economic performance."[58] Most of these studies determined a company's social performance by analyzing the content of annual reports, citations of social actions in news articles on the company, or "reputation" indexes based on public perception. Such criteria certainly have drawbacks as reliable measures of corporate social responsibility.

We can also look at what consumers say about corporate social responsibility. A recent survey conducted by GlobeScan, which specializes in corporate issues, found that "83 percent of Canadians believe that corporations should go beyond their traditional economic role; 51 percent say they have punished a socially irresponsible company in the past year."[59] As for naming a socially responsible company, 43 percent of Canadians said they could not do so.

What conclusion can we draw from all of this? Corporate social responsibility is generally good for the bottom line. It matters to consumers and there is little evidence to say that a company's social actions hurt its long-term economic performance. Given political and societal pressures on business to be socially involved, managers would be wise to take social goals into consideration as they plan, organize, lead, and control.

Practise

**proactive approach**
When managers actively promote the interests of stockholders and stakeholders, using organizational resources to do so.

## Summary of Learning Objectives

**4.1** **What are the steps in the decision-making process?** The steps include identifying a problem and the decision criteria; allocating weights to those criteria; developing, analyzing, and selecting an alternative that can resolve the problem; implementing the alternative; and evaluating the decision's effectiveness.

Lucie Shaw realized there was a strong market for providing health care to seniors and recognized that a Nurse Next Door franchise was a good way to exploit that opportunity and quench her thirst for entrepreneurship. However, Shaw did have a well paying operations manager job at Air Canada and starting a franchise could be risky. Which would be the best alternative?

**4.2** **What factors affect how decisions are made?** It is often assumed that managers make decisions that follow the steps of the rational decision-making process. However, not all decisions follow that process for a variety of reasons. Often managers work with bounded rationality, because they are not able to collect and process all the information on all possible alternatives. Or they might make a satisficing decision—one that is "good enough" rather than the "best." Managers sometimes use intuition to enhance their decision-making process. Managers also need to decide whether they should make decisions themselves or encourage a team to help make the decision. Teams can make better decisions in many cases, but the time to make the decision generally increases. Managers are affected by a variety of biases and errors: overconfidence bias, selective perception bias, confirmation bias, sunk-costs error, escalation of commitment error, self-serving bias, and hindsight bias.

Lucie Shaw was aware of a variety of positives and negatives in the decision to start her own Nurse Next Door franchise. It was important for her to recognize that her preference for work that inspired her passion and the desire to see her in-laws and other seniors taken care of might affect how she made her decision.

**4.3** **How do ethics and social responsibility relate to decision making?** Ethics refers to rules and principles that define right and wrong conduct. There are four views of ethics: the utilitarian view, the rights view, the theory of justice view, and the integrative social contracts theory. The utilitarian view of ethics maintains that ethical decisions are made solely on the basis of their outcomes or consequences. The rights view of ethics is concerned with respecting and pro-

tecting individual liberties and privileges. According to the theory of justice view of ethics, managers impose and enforce rules fairly and impartially, following all legal rules and regulations. The integrative social contracts theory proposes that ethical decisions be based on existing ethical norms in industries and communities.

To improve ethical behaviour, managers can hire individuals with high ethical standards, design and implement a code of ethics, lead by example, undertake performance appraisals, provide ethics training, conduct independent social audits, and provide formal protective mechanisms for employees who face ethical dilemmas.

Beyond ethics, managers are increasingly asked to be more socially responsible in the decisions they make. In doing so, some organizations are likely to simply give lip service to social responsibility, while others are much more committed to actually being socially responsible.

### SNAPSHOT SUMMARY

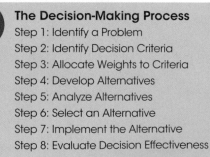

**4.1** **The Decision-Making Process**
Step 1: Identify a Problem
Step 2: Identify Decision Criteria
Step 3: Allocate Weights to Criteria
Step 4: Develop Alternatives
Step 5: Analyze Alternatives
Step 6: Select an Alternative
Step 7: Implement the Alternative
Step 8: Evaluate Decision Effectiveness

**4.2** **The Manager as Decision Maker**
Making Decisions: Rationality, Bounded Rationality, and Intuition
Types of Problems and Decisions
Decision-Making Conditions
Decision-Making Styles
Group Decision Making
Individual vs. Group Decision Making
Decision-Making Biases and Errors

**4.3** **Ethics, Corporate Social Responsibility, and Decision Making**
Four Views of Ethics
Improving Ethical Behaviour
Corporate Social Responsibility

# MyManagementLab® Learning Resources

## Resources

▼ **Explore and enhance your understanding of key chapter topics through the following online resources:**

- Student PowerPoints
- Audio Summary of Chapter
- ROLLS
- CBC Videos for Part 2
- MySearchLab

▶ Visit the **Study Plan** area to test your progress with **Pre-Tests** and **Post-Tests**.

▼ **Build on your knowledge and practise real-world applications using the following online activities:**

## Interpret

- Opening Case Activity: Steps of the Decision Making Process
- Review and Apply: Solutions to Interpret section questions and activities
- Glossary Flashcards

## Analyze

- Opening Case Activity: Using the Rational Decision Making Process
- Review and Apply: Solutions to Analyze section questions and activities
- Self-Assessment Library

## Practise

- Opening Case Activity: Ethics in the Workplace
- Review and Apply: Solutions to Practice section questions and activities
- BizSkills Simulations:
  –Ethics and Social Responsibility
  –Navigating Murky Ethical Waters

# Interpret What You Have Read

1. Why is decision making often described as the essence of a manager's job?

2. How is implementation important to the decision-making process?

3. What is a satisficing decision? How does it differ from a maximizing decision?

4. How do certainty, risk, and uncertainty affect decision making?

5. What is groupthink? How does it affect decision making?

6. Describe the decision-making biases and errors managers may exhibit.

7. How does escalation of commitment affect decision making? Have you had an example of this in your decision making?

8. Define the four views of ethics.

9. Contrast the classical and socio-economic views of corporate social responsibility.

10. Discuss the role that stakeholders play in the four approaches to corporate social responsibility.

# Analyze What You Have Read

1. Describe a decision you have made that closely aligns with the assumptions of perfect rationality. Compare this with the process you used to select your major. Did you depart from the rational model in your choice of major? Explain.

2. Is the order in which alternatives are considered more critical under assumptions of perfect rationality or bounded rationality? Why?

3. Explain how a manager might deal with making decisions under conditions of uncertainty.

4. Give an example drawn from your personal decision making that illustrates satisficing. What steps would be necessary to make a better decision in that situation?

5. Why do you think organizations have increased the use of groups for making decisions during the past 20 years? When would you recommend using groups to make decisions?

6. Do you think it is difficult to make ethical decisions when a company focuses primarily on the bottom line?

7. What does corporate social responsibility mean to you personally? Do you think business organizations should be socially responsible? Explain.

8. How does your college or university apply the triple bottom line in its practices? What evidence is there for concern for employees and the environment?

# Assess Your Skills

## HOW INTUITIVE AM I?

For each of the following questions, select the response that first appeals to you:

1. When working on a project, I prefer to
   (a) be told what the problem is, but left free to decide how to solve it.
   (b) get very clear instructions about how to go about solving the problem before I start.

2. When working on a project, I prefer to work with colleagues who are
   (a) realistic.
   (b) imaginative.

3. I most admire people who are
   (a) creative.
   (b) careful.

4. The friends I choose tend to be
   (a) serious and hard-working.
   (b) exciting and often emotional.

5. When I ask a colleague for advice on a problem I have, I
   (a) seldom or never get upset if he/she questions my basic assumptions.
   (b) often get upset if he/she questions my basic assumptions.

**6.** When I start my day, I
   (a) seldom make or follow a specific plan.
   (b) usually make a plan first to follow.

**7.** When working with numbers, I find that I
   (a) seldom or never make factual errors.
   (b) often make factual errors.

**8.** I find that I
   (a) seldom daydream during the day and really don't enjoy doing so when I do it.
   (b) frequently daydream during the day and enjoy doing so.

**9.** When working on a problem, I
   (a) prefer to follow the instructions or rules when they are given to me.
   (b) often enjoy circumventing the instructions or rules when they are given to me.

**10.** When I try to put something together, I prefer to have
   (a) step-by-step written instructions on how to assemble the item.
   (b) a picture of how the item is supposed to look once assembled.

**11.** I find that the person who irritates me the most is the one who appears to be
   (a) disorganized.
   (b) organized.

**12.** When an unexpected crisis comes up that I have to deal with, I
   (a) feel anxious about the situation.
   (b) feel excited by the challenge of the situation.

---

**SCORING KEY**

For items 1, 3, 5, 6, and 11, score as follows: a = 1, b = 0.

For items 2, 4, 7, 8, 9, 10, and 12, score as follows: a = 0, b = 1.

Your total score will range between 0 and 12.

---

## ANALYSIS AND INTERPRETATION

Decision making isn't all systematic logic. Good decision makers also have developed, through experience, an intuitive ability that complements rational analysis. This ability is particularly valuable when decision makers face high levels of uncertainty, when facts are limited, when there is little previous precedent, when time is pressing, or when there are multiple plausible alternatives to choose among and there are good arguments for each.

If you have an intuitive score greater than 8, you prefer situations where there is a lack of structure and rules. You can handle uncertainty, spontaneity, and openness. Whether this ability is a plus in your job depends to a great extent on the culture of your organization. Where rationality is highly valued, reliance on intuition is likely to be seen as a negative quality. In open and creative-type cultures, intuitive ability is more likely to be valued.

**More Self-Assessments**

To learn more about your skills, abilities, and interests, take the following self-assessments on the MyManagementLab®:

- I.A.4.—How Well Do I Handle Ambiguity?
- I.D.1.—Am I a Procrastinator?
- I.D.2.—How Do My Ethics Rate?
- III.C.1.—How Well Do I Respond to Turbulent Change? (This exercise also appears in Chapter 12 on pages 354–355.)
- IV.A.2.—Am I a Deliberate Decision Maker?

# Practise What You Have Learned

## DILEMMA

Suppose you are sitting at your desk examining a request a customer has just emailed to you. The customer is proposing a project that would be very lucrative for your company but has an extremely demanding time schedule over the next two weeks. Yesterday, one of your long-time employees gave two weeks' notice of his desire to leave the company and spend more time with his ailing mother.

Your employee is well qualified to meet the requirements of the request but it would force his last two weeks to be tremendously busy. How would you decide whether you should take the customer up on her request?

## BECOMING A MANAGER

- Pay close attention to decisions you make and how you make them.
- When you feel you have not made a good decision, assess how you could have made a better one. Which step of the decision-making process could you have improved?
- Work at developing good decision-making skills.
- Read books about decision making.
- Ask people you admire for advice on how they make good decisions.

## BE THE CONSULTANT: SOLVING PROBLEMS CREATIVELY

Creativity is a frame of mind. You need to expand your mind's capabilities—that is, open up your mind to new ideas. Every individual has the ability to improve his or her creativity, but many people simply don't try to develop that ability. In a global business environment, where changes are fast and furious, organizations desperately need creative people. The uniqueness and variety of problems that managers face demand that they be able to solve problems creatively.

### STEPS IN DEVELOPING THE SKILL

You can be more effective at solving problems creatively if you use the following 10 suggestions:[60]

1. THINK OF YOURSELF AS CREATIVE. Although this may be a simple suggestion, research shows that if you think you cannot be creative, you won't be. Believing in your ability to be creative is the first step in becoming more creative.

2. PAY ATTENTION TO YOUR INTUITION. Every individual has a subconscious mind that works well. Sometimes answers will come to you when you least expect them. Listen to that "inner voice." In fact, most creative people keep notepads near their beds and write down ideas when the thoughts come to them. That way they don't forget them.

3. MOVE AWAY FROM YOUR COMFORT ZONE. Every individual has a comfort zone in which certainty exists. But creativity and the known often do not mix. To be creative, you need to move away from the status quo and focus your mind on something new.

4. DETERMINE WHAT YOU WANT TO DO. Make sure you include taking time to understand a problem before attempting to try to resolve it, getting all the facts in mind, and trying to identify the most important ones.

5. LOOK FOR WAYS TO TACKLE THE PROBLEM. This process can be accomplished by setting aside a block of time

to focus on it; working out a plan for attacking it; establishing subgoals; imagining or actually using analogies wherever possible (e.g., could you approach your problem like a fish out of water and look at what the fish does to cope? Or can you use the things you have to do to find your way when it's foggy to help you solve your problem?); using different problem-solving strategies such as verbal, visual, mathematical, theatrical (e.g., you might draw a diagram of the decision or problem to help you visualize it better or you might talk to yourself out loud about the problem, telling it as you would tell a story to someone); trusting your intuition; and playing with possible ideas and approaches (e.g., look at your problem from a different perspective or ask yourself what someone else, such as your grandmother, might do if faced with the same situation).

6. LOOK FOR WAYS TO DO THINGS BETTER. Find new approaches by trying consciously to be original, not worrying about looking foolish, eliminating cultural taboos (such as gender stereotypes) that might influence your possible solutions, keeping an open mind, being alert to odd or puzzling facts, thinking of unconventional ways to use objects and the environment (e.g., thinking about how you could use newspaper or magazine headlines to help you be a better problem solver), discarding usual or habitual ways of doing things, and striving for objectivity by being as critical of your own ideas as you would be of those coming from someone else.

7. FIND SEVERAL RIGHT ANSWERS. Being creative means continuing to look for other solutions even when you think you have solved the problem. A better, more creative solution might be just around the corner.

8. BELIEVE IN FINDING A WORKABLE SOLUTION. Like believing in yourself, you also need to believe in your ideas. If you don't think you can find a solution, you probably won't.

9. BRAINSTORM WITH OTHERS. Creativity is not an isolated activity. Bouncing ideas off others creates synergy.

10. TURN CREATIVE IDEAS INTO ACTION. Coming up with creative ideas is only part of the process. Once the ideas are generated, they must be implemented. Keeping great ideas in your mind, or on papers that no one will read, does little to expand your creative abilities.

### PRACTISING THE SKILL

How many words can you make using the letters in the word brainstorm? (There are at least 95.)

## MANAGING WORKFORCE DIVERSITY: THE VALUE OF DIVERSITY IN DECISION MAKING

Have you decided what your major is going to be? How did you decide? Do you feel your decision is a good one? Is there anything you could have done differently to make sure that your decision was the best one?[61]

Making good decisions is tough! Managers are continuously making decisions—for example, developing new products, establishing weekly or monthly goals, implementing advertising campaigns, reassigning employees to different work groups, resolving customers' complaints, or purchasing new tablets for sales representatives. One important suggestion for making better decisions is to tap into the diversity of the work group. Drawing upon the ideas of diverse employees can prove valuable to a manager's decision making. Why? Diverse employees can provide fresh perspectives on issues. They can offer differing interpretations on how a problem is defined and may be more open to trying new ways of doing things. Diverse employees usually are more creative in generating alternatives and more flexible in resolving issues. Getting input from diverse sources increases the likelihood of finding creative and unique solutions.

Even though diversity in decision making can be valuable, it has drawbacks. The lack of a common perspective usually means that more time is spent discussing the issues. Communication may be a problem, particularly if language barriers are present. Seeking out diverse opinions can make the decision-making process more complex, confusing, and ambiguous. With multiple perspectives on the decision, it may also be difficult to reach a single agreement or to agree on specific actions. Although these drawbacks are valid concerns, the value of diversity in decision making outweighs the potential disadvantages.

When you have worked in teams, what advantages and disadvantages arose because of the diversity (or lack of diversity) in the group? What measures could be taken to make sure that diversity is an asset for a team, rather than something that causes problems?

# Team Exercises

## 3BL: THE TRIPLE BOTTOM LINE

A Canadian clothing company was losing market share to some of its U.S. competitors and began to outsource manufacturing of most of its products to Sri Lanka. This practice resulted in a negligible increase in product defects, but the cost savings were driving increased profitability by upwards of 15 percent per month. Management was thrilled, and the company shareholders were buoyed by the results.

An investigative journalism report uncovered some illegal practices at the Sri Lanka factory. Toxic effluent was being disposed of without proper handling and safeguard protections, and much of the waste was being dumped in back alleys and open spaces. Wages were paid on productivity targets, and basic pay was cut if management targets were not achieved. Intimidation and abuse was common when workers failed to reach production targets—in one example, 50 workers were locked in an unventilated room without access to toilet facilities, water, and food for over four hours as a punishment.

The report found that excessive overtime was an accepted practice, and workers were forced to work up to 130 hours per month in overtime, with a quarter of the employees not receiving any additional pay for their overtime. Three-quarters of the workers at this factory in Sri Lanka were young women from rural areas. They were told when recruited that the factories prefer them not to marry and were given pregnancy tests to weed out pregnant women. Sexual intimidation and abuse was common.

A decision that was having a positive impact on profit was turning out to be negative for people and the planet. What could the company do to deal with this situation?

### THINKING STRATEGICALLY ABOUT 3BL
There are eight steps that can be used to help navigate confusing ethical issues such as the Sri Lankan factory problems.

| 1) Recognize the ethical issue | Although labour practices may be more lax in Sri Lanka, the treatment of the workers is an ethical dilemma. |
|---|---|
| 2) Who will be affected? | Company employees and shareholders might be concerned, but the buck stops with the management team of the Canadian company. |
| 3) Get the facts. | The investigative report may have its own agenda. Get information from workers at the factory as well as the company running it on behalf of the Canadian company. |
| 4) Is it a case of right versus wrong? | Could you defend your choice to the broader public? To your friends and family? |

*(continued)*

(*continued*)

| 5) Is it a choice between two "goods" or between two "bads"? | Are there core values that are pitted against each other? Is it business needs (like staying in business) versus the needs of the broader community? Is it a truth versus loyalty situation (that exists for whistleblowers)? |
|---|---|
| 6) Apply ethical standards and principles to evaluate alternative courses of action. | Which option will produce the most good and do the least harm? Which option best serves the community as a whole? |
| 7) Make a decision. | You can bury yourself in facts and opinions, but at some point you just have to make the ethical decision. |
| 8) Act and reflect on the outcome. | How can you apply this learning to future decisions? What ethical dilemmas can we anticipate? |

## INDIVIDUAL VS. GROUP DECISIONS

Objective: To contrast individual and group decision making. Time: 15 minutes.

**Step 1:** You have 5 minutes to read the following story and individually respond to each of the 11 statements as either true, false, or unknown.

### THE STORY

A salesclerk had just turned off the lights in the store when a man appeared and demanded money. The owner opened a cash register. The contents of the cash register were scooped up, and the man sped away. A member of the police force was notified promptly.

### STATEMENTS ABOUT THE STORY

1. A man appeared after the owner had turned off his store lights. True, false, or unknown?

2. The robber was a man. True, false, or unknown?

3. The man did not demand money. True, false, or unknown?

4. The man who opened the cash register was the owner. True, false, or unknown?

5. The store owner scooped up the contents of the cash register and ran away. True, false, or unknown?

6. Someone opened a cash register. True, false, or unknown?

7. After the man who demanded the money scooped up the contents of the cash register, he ran away. True, false, or unknown?

8. The cash register contained money, but the story does not state how much. True, false, or unknown?

9. The robber demanded money of the owner. True, false, or unknown?

10. The story concerns a series of events in which only three persons are referred to: the owner of the store, a man who demanded money, and a member of the police force. True, false, or unknown?

11. The following events in the story are true: Someone demanded money; a cash register was opened; its contents were scooped up; a man dashed out of the store. True, false, or unknown?

**Step 2:** After you have answered the 11 questions individually, form groups of four or five members each. The groups have 10 minutes to discuss their answers and agree on the correct answers to each of the 11 statements.

**Step 3:** Your instructor will give you the correct answers. How many correct answers did you get at the conclusion of Step 1? How many did your group achieve at the conclusion of Step 2? Did the group outperform the average individual? The best individual? Discuss the implications of these results.

**Step 4:** Analyze your team's decision making by answering the following questions:

- Did you clearly identify the desired outcome?
- Were all members prepared to discuss the statements?
- Did you encourage open and active discussion of the story?
- Did you make and communicate guidelines for the decisions?
- Did you direct and manage the discussion?
- Did you get a commitment from all members of the team on the correct answers?

# Business Cases

## RESEARCH IN MOTION

Research in Motion (RIM) has been Canada's most successful and influential technology firm. It is hard to picture that a company that had a 44 percent share of the US market and whose main product was nicknamed "the Crackberry" could ever be facing such a moment of crisis.[62] A series of good decisions led to its success, and a series of poor ones led it to very dire circumstances in early 2012.

Jim Balsillie and Mike Lazaridis turned RIM into a powerhouse with massive revenue and unparalleled subscriber growth. The former co-CEOs believed in decision making by consensus, which was time consuming and thwarted innovation. Overconfidence, lack of focus on the business market, poor marketing, mass layoffs, and the PlayBook's failure to grab the market led RIM to replace the co-CEOs with Thorston Heins.

RIM is still doing very well in Asia, Africa, the Middle East, and parts of Europe, but its losses in the United States have been staggering—market share is down to less than 10 percent. The BlackBerry 10 is targeted for a late 2012 release and is anticipated to compete more directly with Apple and Samsung, the two companies that have surpassed RIM.

RIM has several major options on the table to consider. Heins has not ruled out selling the company. He could also split the company and sell off some of the assets. Licensing and partnerships appeal to Heins as a way to gain wider distribution for RIM's software platform. RIM could also choose to focus strictly on business users, the meat and potato part of its business. The last option is the status quo—waiting for the new BlackBerry 10 devices to rescue the company.

What should Thorsten Heins do? Why? Are there any other options that Heins should explore?

## CBC

# Bulldog Interactive Fitness

Holly Bond is the founder of Bulldog Interactive Fitness, a specialty gym designed with children in mind. Inspired by her own son Matthew, an overweight 13-year-old whom she claims was a casualty of the X-box generation, Holly is on a mission to fight childhood obesity. She is working hard to entice children to move off the couch, where they spend hours staring at the television or computer playing video games, and into her interactive fitness centre.

At Bulldog Interactive Fitness, children are attracted by the stimulation and challenge of video games, while being physically active at the same time. The Sony technology that is the backbone of this unique gym requires the gamer to ride a stationary bike uphill, groove hip hop style on a dance mat, and sword fight ninjas with superpowers. The children are enjoying the same video games they love, but they are getting their heart rates up and burning calories at the same time.

Holly and her husband James are trying to make money from an epidemic that is front and centre in the media—childhood obesity. With the decline in gym classes at schools and the increasing use of buses to transport children, the Bonds feel that schools are creating an environment of sick, stationary, unfit children. They envision a business that will fight against this trend of inactivity, increase fitness levels, and encourage a healthier lifestyle in the long run.

The Bonds are using television commercials to brand Bulldog Interactive Fitness and achieve their five-year plan of selling 1350 franchises. To reach this goal, they have to sell 20 new franchises per month. At a cost of $25 000 to enter the business, realizing their objective is going to be hard work. They have invested $250 000 into their business and hope to franchise it quickly, before someone else comes along to steal their idea.

James and Holly successfully operate two locations in Nova Scotia. They have sold one franchise in Toronto, but new franchise investors are not biting fast enough. Their benchmark is to have ten profitable locations up and running in order to drive them to the next level. Holly is encouraged by the 350 applica-

tions for a Bulldog Interactive Fitness franchise, but she knows the sale would be a lot more attractive with a big name partner to add marketing power. To achieve this partnership, Holly has been pursuing talks with X-box innovator Sony. Holly tried to use the Sony name in her previous advertising efforts, but was forced to withdraw Bulldog's connection with Sony because it had not been approved or officially endorsed. Since then, Holly has been chasing Sony executives and trying to sell them on the positive impact Bulldog Interactive Fitness is having on children.

The public relations executives at Sony finally agreed to have some dialogue with Bulldog Interactive Fitness about their future plans and business prospects, but no promotion or official arrangement has been reached. Holly invited Sony to attend the grand opening of their fifth franchise location, but no one attended. Undeterred, Holly is convinced that she will be able to secure a partnership with Sony and is certain they will see that her mission is worthwhile.

## QUESTIONS

### Interpret

1. What is the difference between corporate strategy and business strategy? What is competitive advantage, and where does it fit into strategy?
2. Of the three competitive strategies (cost leadership, differentiation, and focus) discussed in the text, which strategy is Bulldog Interactive Fitness pursuing?

### Analyze

3. Relate each step in the strategic management process to what you know about Bulldog Interactive Fitness from the case incident and video.

### Practise

4. In the video, while talking about growth opportunities, James Bond says, "One won't get you ten, but ten might get you one hundred." Explain what he means by this comment.
5. Using the Internet and other sources, identify two key competitors for Bulldog Interactive Fitness. Identify each company's sustainable competitive advantage.

*Source:* "Bulldog Fitness," *Venture's Dreamers and Schemers*, Show No. 6, Canadian Broadcasting Corporation, November 15, 2006.

## CBC

# Ben & Jerry's Ice Cream Dream

In May 1978, Ben Cohen and Jerry Greenfield completed a $5 correspondence course on ice-cream making and started Ben & Jerry's ice cream in a converted gas station in Burlington, Vermont. They gambled their life savings of $8000 on a dream. This pair of school friends set out to make Vermont's best ice cream, unaware that their efforts would turn into an empire of dairy delights. By 1984, Ben & Jerry's had sales of $4 million. By 1999, Ben & Jerry's was a proven success, with sales soaring to $237 million. In April 2000, Ben & Jerry's was acquired by the Anglo-Dutch corporation Unilever.

Ben & Jerry's operates on a corporate concept of *linked prosperity* anchored in three key parts to its mission statement. Its *product mission* calls for making, distributing, and selling "the finest quality all natural ice cream . . . with a continued commitment to incorporating wholesome, natural ingredients and promoting business practices that respect the earth." Its *economic mission* is "to operate the company on a sustainable financial basis of profitable growth," and its *social mission* is "to operate the company in a way that actively recognizes the central role that business plays in society by initiating innovative ways to improve the quality of life locally, nationally, and internationally."

The soundness of the *linked prosperity* concept is likely what motivated Morrie Baker and his real estate partner to risk over $1 million of their own money to develop Ben & Jerry's in Canada. But investors were worried that their $1 million could be eaten up very quickly. According to TheFranchiseMall.com, the total investment to open a single Ben & Jerry's franchise ranges from $173 300 to $438 900. Planning and decision making is critical. Where should the franchises be located? Climate and tourism are critical to their success. How much should be spent on a location? How much customer traffic is necessary to be profitable? Do the locations offer exclusivity, or would the location manager offer a site to competitors? These questions and many other aspects of planning a business are critically important.

Morrie Baker now owns 20 Canadian ice cream shops. He believes that success requires a combination of thoughtful strategy execution and accurate location selection. While Baker appears to be succeeding in Canada, it seems that elsewhere 10 percent of Ben & Jerry's shops close each year. Baker knows that a winning strategy requires the right decisions at the right times—within the confines of rationality!

## QUESTIONS

### Interpret

1. Managers tend to operate under conditions of bounded rationality. Explain.

2. Which step in the decision-making process presents the greatest risk?

### Analyze

3. Given the advances of information and communications technology, managerial decision making today is much easier because information is so quickly and readily available to aid in the decision-making process. Do you agree or disagree with this statement?

4. Which of the common decision-making biases and errors would most likely present the greatest risk to a manager deciding on a location for a Ben & Jerry's franchise?

### Practise

5. Using the Internet and other sources, identify some of the corporate social responsibility activities Ben & Jerry's has undertaken as a member of the Unilever company. What do you feel are the most important issues that affect the decision of the company to invest in these activities?

*Sources:* "Ben & Jerry's Ice Cream Moves into Canada," *Venture*, Canadian Broadcasting Corporation, January 30, 2005; Ben and Jerry's website, http://www.benjerry.com; "Ben & Jerry's Franchise," *The Franchise Mall*, http://www.thefranchisemall.com/franchises/details/10816-0-ben_and_jerrys.htm; Kathryn Tully, "My Liquidity Moment: Ben Cohen of Ben & Jerry's," *Financial Times*, June 23, 2010, http://www.ft.com/cms/s/0/f3a37bb4-7d20-11df-8845-00144feabdc0.html#axzz24hqIRXwK; Jon Entine, "Ben & Jerry's—Socially Responsiblle Meltdown?" *Ethical Corporation*, October 2006, p. 54, http://www.jonentine.com/ethical_corporation/2006_10_Ben_Jerrys.pdf.

CHAPTER

5

# Organizational Structure and Design

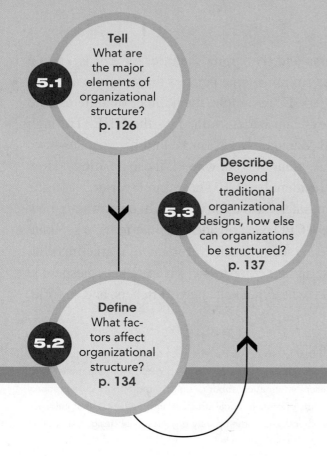

**Tell**
What are the major elements of organizational structure?
p. 126

**5.1**

**Describe**
Beyond traditional organizational designs, how else can organizations be structured?
p. 137

**5.3**

**Define**
What factors affect organizational structure?
p. 134

**5.2**

Maple Leaf Sports & Entertainment (MLSE) is a complex organization that owns the NHL's Toronto Maple Leafs, the NBA's Toronto Raptors, Major League Soccer's Toronto FC, the AHL's Toronto Marlies, Leafs TV, and Raptors NBA TV.[1] MLSE also owns Air Canada Centre (where the Maple Leafs and Raptors play their home games) and is a major investor in BMO Field (where the Toronto FC play their home games). Making that more complicated is the joint purchase of MLSE by Rogers and Bell, two fierce competitors. The Competition Bureau's approval requires a new management structure, with tough decisions regarding reporting relationships between the new president and CEO, and the two separate owners, Bell and Rogers.[2]

The new CEO's job will be more complex than it was before—it includes responsibility for the business affairs of each team (team operations, sales, marketing, finance, administration, event operations, broadcast, communications, and community development). Former CEO Richard Peddie was also responsible for the operation of Air Canada Centre, BMO Field, Ricoh Coliseum in Toronto, and General Motors Centre in Oshawa, Ontario. Reporting to both Bell and Rogers presents many challenges.

For MLSE to be successful, the management structure requires simplicity and clarity. What kind of organizational structure can support the

## Think About It

How do you run four sports teams and four sports facilities? Put yourself in the new CEO's shoes. How can the CEO continue to make Maple Leaf Sports & Entertainment successful? What organizational structure can best ensure MLSE's goals?

operations of the sports teams and the sports facilities? The CEO has a great deal of flexibility in determining some parts of the structure and less flexibility in determining others. For example, the number of athletes who can fill positions on a hockey team is determined by the NHL. Through the draft and trades, General Manager Brian Burke and his coaches have some ability to choose the particular players who fill these positions. How much feedback should the president and CEO have in player decisions?

MLSE also oversees ticket sales for the four teams. In determining how to manage ticket sales, the new CEO can consider whether to have separate ticket sales departments for each team, whether to include marketing with or separate from ticket sales, and whether to subdivide ticket salespeople into specialties: corporate sales, season tickets, playoff tickets, and so forth.

...................................................................................................................

Rogers and Bell's desire to make Maple Leaf Sports & Entertainment successful illustrates how important it is for managers to design an organizational structure that helps accomplish organizational goals and objectives. In this chapter, we present information about designing appropriate organizational structures. We look at the various elements of organizational structure and the factors that influence their design. We also look at some traditional and contemporary organizational designs, as well as organizational design challenges that today's managers face.

...................................................................................................................

# DEFINING ORGANIZATIONAL STRUCTURE

**5.1**

**Tell**
What are the major elements of organizational structure?

No other topic in management has undergone as much change in the past few years as that of organizing and organizational structure. Managers are questioning and re-evaluating traditional approaches to organizing work in their search for organizational structures that can achieve efficiency but also have the flexibility necessary for success in today's dynamic environment. Recall from Chapter 1 that **organizing** is defined as the process of creating an organization's structure. That process is important and serves many purposes (see Exhibit 5-1). The challenge for managers is to design an organizational structure that allows employees to work effectively and efficiently.

Just what is **organizational structure**? It is how job tasks are formally divided, grouped, and coordinated within an organization. When managers develop or change the structure, they are engaged in **organizational design**, a process that involves decisions about six key elements: work specialization, departmentalization, chain of command, span of control, centralization and decentralization, and formalization.[3]

---

**EXHIBIT 5-1    Purposes of Organizing**

- Divides work to be done into specific jobs and departments.
- Assigns tasks and responsibilities associated with individual jobs.
- Coordinates diverse organizational tasks.
- Clusters jobs into units.
- Establishes relationships among individuals, groups, and departments.
- Establishes formal lines of authority.
- Allocates and deploys organizational resources.

## Work Specialization

Adam Smith first identified division of labour and concluded that it contributed to increased employee productivity. Early in the twentieth century, Henry Ford applied this concept in an assembly line, where every Ford employee was assigned a specific, repetitive task.

Today we use the term **work specialization** to describe the degree to which tasks in an organization are subdivided into separate jobs. The essence of work specialization is that an entire job is not done by one individual but instead is broken down into steps, and each step is completed by a different person. Individual employees specialize in doing part of an activity rather than the entire activity.

During the first half of the twentieth century, managers viewed work specialization as an unending source of increased productivity, and for a time it was. Because it was not widely used, when work specialization *was* implemented, employee productivity rose. By the 1960s, however, it had become evident that a good thing could be carried too far. The point had been reached in some jobs where human diseconomies from work specialization— boredom, fatigue, stress, poor quality, increased absenteeism, and higher turnover—more than offset the economic advantages.

*When you are working in a team on a course project, does it make sense to specialize tasks? What are the advantages and disadvantages?*

**TODAY'S VIEW** Most managers today see work specialization as an important organizing mechanism but not as a source of ever-increasing productivity. They recognize the economies it provides in certain types of jobs, but they also recognize the problems it creates when carried to extremes, including job dissatisfaction, poor mental health, and a low sense of accomplishment.[4] McDonald's uses high work specialization to efficiently make and sell its products, and employees have precisely defined roles and standardized work processes. However, other organizations, such as Bolton, Ontario–based Husky Injection Molding Systems, and Ford Australia, have successfully increased job breadth and reduced work specialization. Still, specialization has its place in some organizations. No hockey team has anyone play both goalie and centre positions. Rather, players tend to specialize in their positions.

## Departmentalization

Does your college or university have an office of student affairs? A financial aid or student housing department? Once jobs have been divided up through work specialization, they have to be grouped back together so that common tasks can be coordinated. The basis on which jobs are grouped together is called **departmentalization**. Every organization will have its own specific way of classifying and grouping work activities. Exhibit 5-2 on page 128 shows the five common forms of departmentalization.

**Functional departmentalization** groups jobs by functions performed. This approach can be used in all types of organizations, although the functions change to reflect the organization's purpose and work. **Product departmentalization** groups jobs by product line. In this approach, each major product area is placed under the authority of a manager who is responsible for everything having to do with that product line. For example, Estée Lauder sells lipstick, eyeshadow, blush, and a variety of other cosmetics, represented by different product lines. The company's lines include Clinique

---

**organizing**
A management function that involves determining what tasks are to be done, who is to do them, how the tasks are to be grouped, who reports to whom, and where decisions are to be made.

**organizational structure**
How job tasks are formally divided, grouped, and coordinated within an organization.

**organizational design**
The process of developing or changing an organization's structure.

**work specialization**
The degree to which tasks in an organization are subdivided into separate jobs; also known as division of labour.

**departmentalization**
The basis on which jobs are grouped together.

**functional departmentalization**
Grouping jobs by functions performed.

**product departmentalization**
Grouping jobs by product line.

**EXHIBIT 5-2** The Five Common Forms of Departmentalization

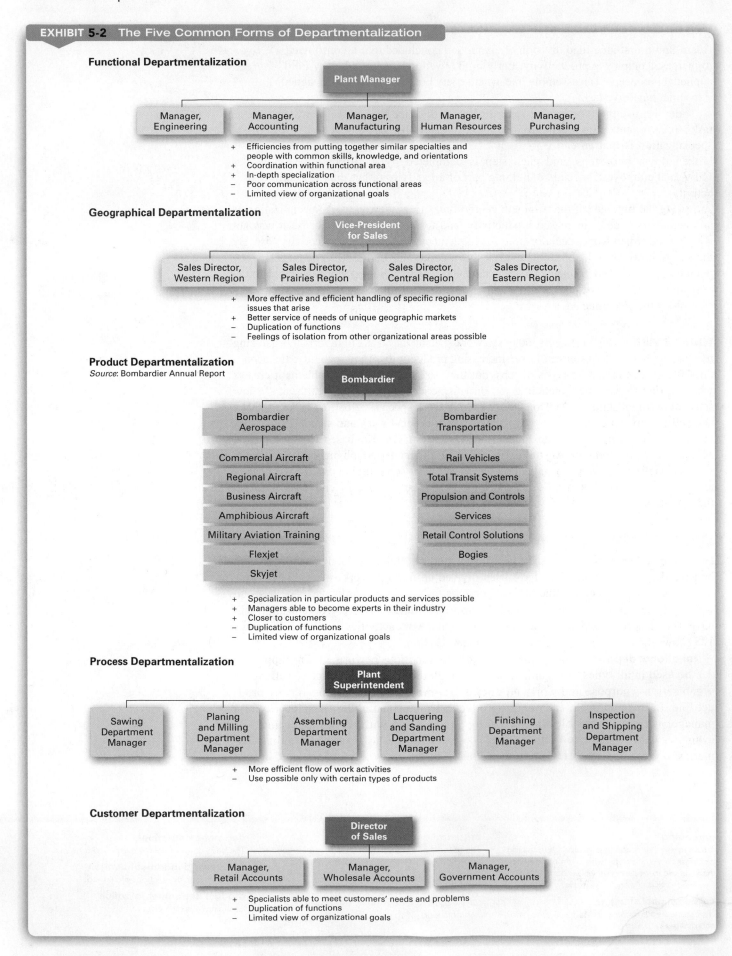

**Functional Departmentalization**

Plant Manager

- Manager, Engineering
- Manager, Accounting
- Manager, Manufacturing
- Manager, Human Resources
- Manager, Purchasing

+ Efficiencies from putting together similar specialties and people with common skills, knowledge, and orientations
+ Coordination within functional area
+ In-depth specialization
– Poor communication across functional areas
– Limited view of organizational goals

**Geographical Departmentalization**

Vice-President for Sales

- Sales Director, Western Region
- Sales Director, Prairies Region
- Sales Director, Central Region
- Sales Director, Eastern Region

+ More effective and efficient handling of specific regional issues that arise
+ Better service of needs of unique geographic markets
– Duplication of functions
– Feelings of isolation from other organizational areas possible

**Product Departmentalization**
*Source*: Bombardier Annual Report

Bombardier

Bombardier Aerospace
- Commercial Aircraft
- Regional Aircraft
- Business Aircraft
- Amphibious Aircraft
- Military Aviation Training
- Flexjet
- Skyjet

Bombardier Transportation
- Rail Vehicles
- Total Transit Systems
- Propulsion and Controls
- Services
- Retail Control Solutions
- Bogies

+ Specialization in particular products and services possible
+ Managers able to become experts in their industry
+ Closer to customers
– Duplication of functions
– Limited view of organizational goals

**Process Departmentalization**

Plant Superintendent

- Sawing Department Manager
- Planing and Milling Department Manager
- Assembling Department Manager
- Lacquering and Sanding Department Manager
- Finishing Department Manager
- Inspection and Shipping Department Manager

+ More efficient flow of work activities
– Use possible only with certain types of products

**Customer Departmentalization**

Director of Sales

- Manager, Retail Accounts
- Manager, Wholesale Accounts
- Manager, Government Accounts

+ Specialists able to meet customers' needs and problems
– Duplication of functions
– Limited view of organizational goals

and Origins, in addition to Canadian-created MAC Cosmetics and its own original line of Estée Lauder products, each of which operates as a distinct company. Similarly, MLSE treats the Raptors and the Maple Leafs as a separate product line in terms of the rest of its management and operations, with each team led by its own general manager.

**Geographical departmentalization** groups jobs on the basis of territory or geography such as the East Coast, Western Canada, or Central Ontario, or maybe by US, European, Latin American, and Asia–Pacific regions. **Process departmentalization** groups jobs on the basis of product or customer flow. In this approach, work activities follow a natural processing flow of products or even of customers. For example, many beauty salons have separate employees for shampooing, colouring, and cutting hair, all different processes for having one's hair styled. Finally, **customer departmentalization** groups jobs on the basis of customers who have common needs or problems that can best be met by having specialists for each. There are advantages to matching departmentalization to customer needs.

Large organizations often combine forms of departmentalization. For example, a major Canadian photonics firm organizes each of its divisions along functional lines: its manufacturing units around processes, its sales units around seven geographic regions, and its sales regions into four customer groupings.

**TODAY'S VIEW**   Two popular trends in departmentalization are the use of customer departmentalization and the use of cross-functional teams. Managers use customer departmentalization to monitor customers' needs and to respond to changes in those needs. Toronto-based Dell Canada is organized around four customer-oriented business units: home and home office; small business; medium and large business; and government, education, and health care. Burnaby, BC–based TELUS is structured around four customer-oriented business units: consumer solutions (focused on services to homes and individuals); business solutions (focused on services to small and medium-sized businesses and entrepreneurs); TELUS Québec (a TELUS company focused on services for the Quebec marketplace); and partner solutions (focused on services to wholesale customers, such as telecommunications carriers and wireless communications companies). Customer-oriented structures enable companies to better understand their customers and to respond faster to their needs.

Managers use **cross-functional teams**—teams made up of groups of individuals who are experts in various specialties and who work together—to increase knowledge and understanding for some organizational tasks. Scarborough, Ontario–based Aviva Canada, a leading property and casualty insurance group, puts together cross-functional catastrophe teams, with trained representatives from all relevant departments, to more quickly help policyholders when a crisis occurs. During the BC wildfires of summer 2003, the catastrophe team worked on both local and corporate issues, including managing information technology, internal and external communication, tracking, resourcing, and vendors. This type of organization made it easier to meet the needs of policyholders as quickly as possible.[5] We discuss the use of cross-functional teams more fully in Chapter 10.

TELUS, one of Canada's leading telecommunication companies, is structured around customer-oriented business units. A goal of this structure is to help the company improve customer response times.

---

**geographical departmentalization**
Grouping jobs on the basis of territory or geography.

**process departmentalization**
Grouping jobs on the basis of product or customer flow.

**customer departmentalization**
Grouping jobs on the basis of customers who have common needs or problems.

**cross-functional teams**
Work teams made up of individuals who are experts in various functional specialties.

## Chain of Command

Have you ever worked in an organization where the chain of command was not clear? What effect did this have on employees?

For many years, the chain-of-command concept was a cornerstone of organizational design. As you will see, it has far less importance today. But contemporary managers still need to consider its implications when deciding how best to structure their organizations.

The **chain of command** is the continuous line of authority that extends from upper organizational levels to the lowest levels and clarifies who reports to whom. It helps employees answer questions such as "Who do I go to if I have a problem?" or "To whom am I responsible?"

You cannot discuss the chain of command without discussing these other concepts: authority, responsibility, accountability, unity of command, and delegation. **Authority** refers to the rights inherent in a managerial position to tell people what to do and to expect them to do it.[6] To facilitate decision making and coordination, an organization's managers are part of the chain of command and are granted a certain degree of authority to meet their responsibilities. Some senior managers and CEOs are better at granting authority than others. For example, when Richard Peddie, former CEO of MLSE, hired Rob Babcock to be the general manager of the Raptors in 2004, some sports writers raised concerns over whether Babcock would have enough autonomy to do his job. Critics noted that Peddie "[had] a reputation for meddling with basketball operations."[7] When Babcock was fired in 2006, sports writers observed that many of his decisions were actually made by senior management.[8]

As managers coordinate and integrate the work of employees, those employees assume an obligation to perform any assigned duties. This obligation or expectation to perform is known as **responsibility**. Responsibility brings with it **accountability**, which is the need to report and justify work to a manager's superiors. Larry Tanenbaum, the Maple Leafs's minority co-owner, took the rare step of making a public apology to Maple Leaf fans by taking out full page letters in Toronto newspapers. "The Toronto Maple Leafs are a public trust with the greatest fans in the world," the letter reads. "We have fallen short of everyone's expectations, and for that we are sorry."[9]

The **unity of command** principle helps preserve the concept of a continuous line of authority. It states that every employee should receive orders from only one superior. Without unity of command, conflicting demands and priorities from multiple managers can create problems.

Because managers have limited time and knowledge, they may delegate some of their responsibilities to other employees. **Delegation** is the assignment of authority to another person to carry out specific duties, allowing the employee to make some of the decisions. Delegation is an important part of a manager's job, as it can ensure that the right people are part of the decision-making process. *Tips for Managers—How to Delegate Effectively* gives tips on how to do a better job of delegating.

To learn more about being an effective delegator, see *Developing Your Interpersonal Skills—Delegating* on page 150 at the end of the chapter.

# TIPS FOR MANAGERS

## How to Delegate Effectively

* Delegate the whole task.
* Select the right person.
* Ensure that authority equals responsibility.
* Give thorough instructions.
* Maintain feedback.
* Evaluate and reward performance.[10]

**LINE AND STAFF AUTHORITY** In many organizations, a distinction can be made between line and staff authority. **Line managers** are responsible for the essential activities of the organization, including production and sales. Line managers have the authority to issue orders to those in the chain of command. The president, the production manager, and the sales manager are examples of line managers. **Staff managers** work in the supporting activities of the organizations, such as human resources or accounting. Staff managers have advisory authority and cannot issue orders to those in the chain of command (except those in their own department). The vice-president of accounting, the human resources manager, and the marketing research manager are examples of staff managers. Mardi Walker, senior vice-president, People, for Maple Leaf Sports & Entertainment, may have recommendations about how the Raptors might win more games, but cannot expect that such recommendations to current General Manager Bryan Colangelo will be followed. However, as senior vice-president, People, Walker can give advice about managing employee benefits.

**TODAY'S VIEW**   Although early management theorists (Fayol, Weber, Taylor, and others) were enamoured with the concepts of chain of command, authority, responsibility, and unity of command, times have changed.[11] These concepts are far less important today. For example, at the Michelin plant in Tours, France, managers have replaced the top-down chain of command with "birdhouse" meetings, in which employees meet for five minutes at regular intervals throughout the day at a column on the shop floor and study simple tables and charts to identify production bottlenecks. Instead of being bosses, shop managers are enablers.[12] In addition, information technology has made such concepts less relevant today. In a matter of a few seconds, employees can access information that used to be available only to managers. Employees can communicate with anyone else in the organization without going through the chain of command.

## Span of Control

How many employees can a manager efficiently and effectively manage? This question of **span of control** is important because, to a large degree, it determines the number of levels and managers an organization needs. All things being equal, the wider or larger the span, the more efficient the organization. An example can show why.

Assume that we have two organizations, both of which have almost 4100 employees. As Exhibit 5-3 shows, if one organization has a uniform span of four and the other a span

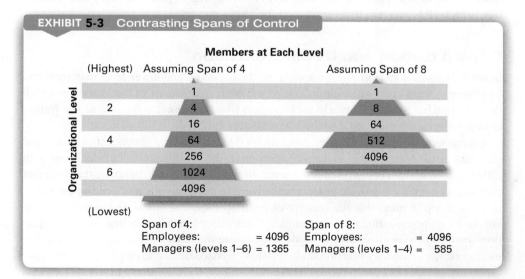

**EXHIBIT 5-3   Contrasting Spans of Control**

**Members at Each Level**

| Organizational Level | Assuming Span of 4 | Assuming Span of 8 |
|---|---|---|
| (Highest) | 1 | 1 |
| 2 | 4 | 8 |
| | 16 | 64 |
| 4 | 64 | 512 |
| | 256 | 4096 |
| 6 | 1024 | |
| (Lowest) | 4096 | |

Span of 4:
Employees:                = 4096
Managers (levels 1–6) = 1365

Span of 8:
Employees:                = 4096
Managers (levels 1–4) =  585

---

**chain of command**
The continuous line of authority that extends from the top of the organization to the lowest level and clarifies who reports to whom.

**authority**
The rights inherent in a managerial position to tell people what to do and to expect them to do it.

**responsibility**
The obligation or expectation to perform any assigned duties.

**accountability**
The need to report and justify work to a manager's superiors.

**unity of command**
The management principle that states every employee should receive orders from only one superior.

**delegation**
The assignment of authority to another person to carry out specific duties, allowing the employee to make some of the decisions.

**line managers**
Managers responsible for the essential activities of the organization, including production and sales.

**staff managers**
Managers who work in the supporting activities of the organizations (such as human resources or accounting).

**span of control**
The number of employees a manager can efficiently and effectively manage.

of eight, the wider span will have two fewer levels and approximately 800 fewer managers. If the average manager made $50 000 a year, the organization with the wider span would save more than $40 million a year in management salaries alone. Obviously, wider spans are more efficient in terms of cost. However, at some point, wider spans reduce *effectiveness*. When the span becomes too large, employee performance can suffer because managers may no longer have the time to provide the necessary leadership and support. The top performing manufacturing plants have up to 40 production workers per supervisor.[13] In a large call centre, that number can be as high as 50 customer service representatives per supervisor.

**TODAY'S VIEW**   The contemporary view of span of control recognizes that many factors influence the appropriate number of employees a manager can efficiently *and* effectively manage. These factors include the skills and abilities of the manager and the employees, and the characteristics of the work being done. For example, the more training and experience employees have, the less direct supervision they need. Therefore, managers with well-trained and experienced employees can function quite well with a wider span. Other contingency variables that determine the appropriate span include similarity of employee tasks, the complexity of those tasks, the physical proximity of subordinates, the degree to which standardized procedures are in place, the sophistication of the organization's information system, the strength of the organization's culture, and the preferred style of the manager.[14] Wider spans of control are also possible due to technology—it is easier for managers and their subordinates to communicate with each other, and there is often more information readily available to help employees perform their jobs.

The trend in recent years has been toward larger spans of control, which are consistent with managers' efforts to reduce costs, speed up decision making, increase flexibility, get closer to customers, and empower employees. However, to ensure that performance does not suffer because of these wider spans, organizations are investing heavily in employee training. Managers recognize that they can handle a wider span when employees know their jobs well or can turn to co-workers if they have questions.

## Centralization and Decentralization

In some organizations, top managers make all the decisions and lower-level managers and employees simply carry out their orders. At the other extreme are organizations in which decision making is pushed down to the managers who are closest to the action. The former organizations are centralized, and the latter are decentralized.

**Centralization** describes the degree to which decision making is concentrated at a single point in the organization. If top managers make the organization's key decisions with little or no input from below, then the organization is centralized. In contrast, the more that lower-level employees provide input or actually make decisions, the more **decentralization** there is. Keep in mind that the concept of centralization/decentralization is relative, not absolute—an organization is never completely centralized or decentralized. Few organizations could function effectively if all decisions were made by only a select group of top managers; nor could they function if all decisions were delegated to employees at the lowest levels. Nestlé uses decentralized marketing with centralized production, logistics, and supply chain management.[15]

**TODAY'S VIEW**   Most organizations start with a centralized model, where a founder makes all the decisions. As the businesses grow and diversify, their environments become complex. These businesses need to become more flexible and responsive, resulting in decentralized decision making. In large companies especially, lower-level managers are "closer to the action" and typically have more detailed knowledge about problems and how best to solve them than do top managers. For example, the Bank of Montreal's some 1000 branches are organized into "communities"—a group of branches within a limited geographical area. Each community is led by a community area manager, who typically works within a 20-minute drive of the other branches. This area manager can respond faster and more intelligently to problems in his or her community than could a senior executive in Toronto.

Another term for increased decentralization is **employee empowerment**, which means giving more decision-making authority to employees.

What determines whether an organization will move toward more centralization or decentralization? Companies facing dynamic environments are more likely to need to adapt quickly to change, and thus decentralize decision making. Stable environments allow for more rules and procedures, so decision making can be centralized more easily. A community college with one location is more likely to be centralized, while a college in a major metropolitan area with five campuses might treat each of the campuses as a separate unit and decentralize decision making to support a more complex environment.

## Formalization

**Formalization** refers to the degree to which jobs within the organization are standardized and the extent to which employee behaviour is guided by rules and procedures. If a job is highly formalized, the person doing that job has little freedom to choose what is to be done, when it is to be done, and how he or she does it. Employees can be expected to handle the same input in exactly the same way, resulting in consistent and uniform output. Organizations with high formalization have explicit job descriptions, numerous organizational rules, and clearly defined procedures covering work processes. On the other hand, where formalization is low, job behaviours are relatively unstructured, and employees have a great deal of freedom in how they do their work.

The degree of formalization varies widely among organizations and even within organizations. For example, at a newspaper, news reporters often have a great deal of discretion in their jobs. They may pick their news topics, find their own stories, research them the way they want to, and write them up, usually within minimal guidelines. In contrast, employees who lay out the newspaper pages do not have that type of freedom. They have constraints—both time and space—that standardize how they do their work.

Kingsey Falls, Quebec–based Cascades, a leading manufacturer of packaging products and tissue paper, uses decentralization effectively with more than 100 operating units located in Canada, the United States, and Europe.[16] Companies are treated as separate entities, based on product, and operate like a federation of small and medium-sized businesses. Each mill is accountable for its own bottom line, and employees are motivated through profit sharing in the profits generated by their own mill. The emphasis on decentralized, entrepreneurial management has been copied by other Canadian forest products companies, such as Domtar.

**TODAY'S VIEW** Although some formalization is important and necessary for consistency and control, many of today's organizations seem to be less reliant on strict rules and standardization to guide and regulate employee behaviour. Consider the following situation:

> It is 2:37 p.m. and a customer at a branch of a large national drugstore chain is trying to drop off a roll of film for same-day developing. Store policy states

that film must be dropped off by 2:00 p.m. for this service. The clerk knows that rules like this are supposed to be followed. At the same time, he wants to accommodate the customer, and he knows that the film could, in fact, be processed that day. He decides to accept the film and, by so doing, to violate the policy. He just hopes that his manager does not find out.[17]

Has this employee done something wrong? He did "break" the rule. But by breaking the rule, he actually brought in revenue and provided the customer good service: so good, in fact, that the customer may be satisfied enough to come back in the future.

Because such situations where rules may be too restrictive frequently arise, many organizations allow employees some freedom to make decisions they feel are best under the circumstances. However, this freedom does not mean that all organizational rules are thrown out the window. There *will* be rules that are important for employees to follow, and these rules should be explained so employees understand the importance of adhering to them. But for other rules, employees may be given some leeway in application.[18]

# ORGANIZATIONAL DESIGN DECISIONS

**Define**
What factors affect organizational structure?

**5.2**

All organizations do not have the same structures. A company with 30 employees is not going to look the same as one with 30 000 employees. But even organizations of comparable size do not necessarily have similar structures. What works for one organization may not work for another. How do managers decide what organizational structure to use? Organizational design decisions depend on certain contingency factors. In this section, we look at two generic models of organizational design and then at the contingency factors that favour each.

## Mechanistic and Organic Organizations

Dining in Vancouver can get you two very different experiences. At McDonald's, you will find a limited selection of menu items, most available daily. Employees are not expected to be decision makers. Rather, they are closely supervised and follow well-defined rules and standard operating procedures. Only one employee helps each customer. At Blue Water Café in downtown Vancouver, by contrast, there is no division of labour, and management does not dictate what the kitchen serves. Instead, the chef on duty creates a meal of his choice while you sit at the sushi bar and watch. The chef chooses the meal from the fresh fish of the day that he bought at the market earlier, so each day's menu can be quite original. Waiters work collaboratively, helping each other serve all customers, rather than being assigned to specific tables.

A **mechanistic organization** is a rigid and tightly controlled structure, much like that of McDonald's. It is characterized by high specialization, rigid departmentalization, a limited information network (mostly downward communication), narrow spans of control, little participation in decision making by lower-level employees, and high formalization.[19]

Mechanistic organizational structures tend to be efficiency machines and rely heavily on rules, regulations, standardized tasks, and similar controls. This organizational structure tries to minimize the impact of differing personalities, judgments, and ambiguity, because these human traits are seen as inefficient and inconsistent. Although no organization is totally mechanistic, almost all large corporations and government agencies have some mechanistic characteristics.

In direct contrast, **organic organization** is as highly adaptive and flexible a structure as the mechanistic organization is rigid and stable. Organic organizations have a division of labour, but the jobs people do are not standardized. Employees are highly trained and empowered to handle diverse job activities and problems, and these organizations frequently use cross-functional and cross-hierarchical teams. Employees in organic organizations require minimal formal rules and little direct supervision; instead, they rely on a free flow of information and a wide span of control. Their high levels of skills and training and the support provided by other team members make formalization and tight managerial controls unnecessary.

TAXI Canada is a major force in the creative marketing world. Its success is based on using an organic structure—lean and nimble. Even as the company faces rapid growth, managers want to retain the flexibility needed to generate great ideas. When an office gets too large, they open another office or set up in another city, allowing each office to operate organically.[20]

Organizations can display a mix of mechanistic and organic features. Wikipedia, the online encyclopedia, is known for its creation and editing of entries by anyone who has Internet access. In this way, it displays a very organic structure. However, behind the scenes a more mechanistic structure can be found, where individuals have some authority to monitor abuse and perform other functions to safeguard the credibility of entries and the website overall.

When is a mechanistic structure preferable, and when is an organic one more appropriate? Let us look at the main contingency factors influencing that decision.

## Contingency Factors

Top managers of most organizations typically put a great deal of thought into designing an appropriate structure. What that appropriate structure is depends on four contingency variables: the organization's strategy, size, technology, and degree of environmental uncertainty.

Why would a decentralized, free-wheeling, seemingly democratic website like Wikipedia need an organizational structure? Yet it has one.[21] At the bottom are 4.6 million registered English-language users, who are overseen by a group of about 1200 administrators, themselves overseen by a group called "bureaucrats." Above the bureaucrats are about 30 stewards, who can provide (and take away) special access status. Above the stewards is the seven-person Wikimedia Foundation Board of Trustees, "the ultimate corporate authority." At the top of the Wikipedia organizational chart is the "de facto leader," Jimmy Wales, a co-founder of Wikipedia.

**mechanistic organization**
An organizational design that is rigid and tightly controlled.

**organic organization**
An organizational design that is highly adaptive and flexible.

Because these variables can change over the life cycle of the organization, managers should consider from time to time whether the current organizational structure is best suited for the environment the organization is facing.

**STRATEGY AND STRUCTURE**   An organization's structure should facilitate the achievement of its goals. Because goals are influenced by the organization's strategies, strategy and structure should be closely linked. More specifically, structure should follow strategy. If managers significantly change the organization's strategy, they need to modify the structure to accommodate and support the change.

Most current strategy frameworks tend to focus on three dimensions:

- *Innovation.* An organization's drive to be on the cutting edge of its industry.
- *Cost minimization.* An organization's push to tightly control costs.
- *Imitation.* An organization's attempt to minimize risk and maximize profit opportunities by copying the market leaders.

What organizational structure works best with each dimension?[22] Innovators need the flexibility and free-flowing information of the organic structure, whereas cost minimizers seek the efficiency, stability, and tight controls of the mechanistic structure. Imitators use structural characteristics of both—the mechanistic structure to maintain tight controls and low costs, and the organic structure to mimic the industry's innovative directions.

**SIZE AND STRUCTURE**   Considerable evidence indicates that an organization's size significantly affects its structure.[23] For example, large organizations—those with 2000 or more employees—tend to have more specialization, departmentalization, centralization, and rules and regulations than do small organizations. However, the relationship is not linear. Beyond a certain point, size becomes a less important influence on structure as an organization grows. Why? Essentially, once an organization has around 2000 employees, the structure is already fairly mechanistic. Adding 500 employees to an organization with 2000 employees will not have much of an impact. On the other hand, adding 500 employees to an organization that has only 300 members is likely to result in a shift toward a more mechanistic structure.

**TECHNOLOGY AND STRUCTURE**   Every organization has at least one form of technology to convert its inputs into outputs. Employees at Whirlpool's Manaus, Brazil, facility build microwave ovens and air-conditioners on a standardized assembly line. Employees at FedEx Kinko's produce custom design and print jobs for individual customers. Employees at Bayer's facility in Karachi, Pakistan, make pharmaceutical products using a continuous-flow production line. Each of these organizations uses a different type of technology.

The initial interest in technology as a determinant of structure can be traced to the work of British scholar Joan Woodward.[24] She studied several small manufacturing firms in southern England to determine the extent to which organizational design elements were related to organizational success. Woodward was unable to find any consistent pattern until she segmented the firms into three categories based on the size of their production runs. The three categories, representing three distinct technologies, have increasing levels of complexity and sophistication. The first category, **unit production**, describes the production of items in units or small batches. The second category, **mass production**, describes large-batch manufacturing. The third and most technically complex group, **process production**, describes the production of items in continuous processes.

Since Woodward's initial work, numerous studies have been done on the technology–structure relationship. These studies generally demonstrate that organizations adapt their structures to their technology.[25] The processes or methods that transform an organization's inputs into outputs differ by their degree of routineness or standardization. In general, the more routine the technology, the more mechanistic the structure can be.

Organizations with more nonroutine technology, such as custom furniture building or online education, are more likely to have organic structures because the product delivery cannot be standardized.[26]

**ENVIRONMENTAL UNCERTAINTY AND STRUCTURE** In Chapter 2 we discussed an organization's environment and how the amount of uncertainty in that environment acts as a constraint on managerial discretion. Why should an organization's structure be affected by its environment? Because of environmental uncertainty! Some organizations face relatively stable and simple environments, while others face dynamic and complex environments. Because uncertainty threatens an organization's effectiveness, managers will try to minimize it. One way to reduce environmental uncertainty is through adjustments in the organization's structure.[27] The greater the uncertainty, the more an organization needs the flexibility offered by an organic structure. On the other hand, in a stable, simple environment, a mechanistic structure tends to be most effective.

**TODAY'S VIEW** The evidence on the environment–structure relationship helps explain why so many managers today are restructuring their organizations to be lean, fast, and flexible. Global competition, accelerated product innovation by competitors, and increased demands from customers for high quality and faster delivery are examples of dynamic environmental forces. Mechanistic organizations are not equipped to respond to rapid environmental change and environmental uncertainty. As a result, we are seeing a greater number of organizations designed to be more organic. However, a purely organic organization may not be ideal. One study found that organic structures may work more effectively if managers establish semistructures to govern "the pace, timing, and rhythm of organizational activities and processes." Introducing a bit of structure while keeping most of the flexibility of the organic structure may reduce operating costs.[28]

Interpret

## COMMON ORGANIZATIONAL DESIGNS

Maple Leaf Sports & Entertainment (MLSE) is divided into four operating units: MLSE, Toronto Raptors, Toronto Maple Leafs (Toronto Marlies is an affiliate), and Toronto FC. Before his retirement, Richard Peddie was the president and CEO of all four units.[29] The Raptors, the Maple Leafs, the Marlies, and Toronto FC all had and still have their own general managers who manage the day-to-day operations of the team, develop recruiting plans, and oversee training. The general managers report to the CEO, and have a number of managers who report to them. MLSE has a divisional structure, whereby its businesses operate separately, on a daily basis. The change in ownership with both Rogers and Bell onboard and the appointment of a new CEO may result in changes to the organizational design used by MLSE.

**5.3** Describe Beyond traditional organizational designs, how else can organizations be structured?

### Think About It

Why do organizations vary in the types of structures they have? How do organizations choose their structures? Why does Maple Leaf Sports & Entertainment have the structure it has? How will the MLSE structure change with the Rogers/Bell purchase?

What types of organizational designs exist in small businesses or in big companies such as Ford Canada, Corel, McCain Foods, Procter & Gamble, and eBay? When making organizational design decisions, managers can choose from traditional organizational designs and contemporary organizational designs.

---

**unit production**
The production of items in units or small batches.

**mass production**
The production of items in large batches.

**process production**
The production of items in continuous processes.

**EXHIBIT 5-4** Strengths and Weaknesses of Common Traditional Organizational Designs

| Structure | Strengths | Weaknesses |
|---|---|---|
| Simple structure | Fast; flexible; inexpensive to maintain; clear accountability. | Not appropriate as organization grows; reliance on one person is risky. |
| Functional structure | Cost-saving advantages from specialization (economies of scale, minimal duplication of people and equipment) and employees are grouped with others who have similar tasks. | Pursuit of functional goals can cause managers to lose sight of what is best for overall organization; functional specialists become insulated and have little understanding of what other units are doing. |
| Divisional structure | Focuses on results—division managers are responsible for what happens to their products and services. | Duplication of activities and resources increases costs and reduces efficiency. |

## Traditional Organizational Designs

In designing a structure to support the efficient and effective accomplishment of organizational goals, managers may choose to follow more traditional organizational designs. These designs—the simple structure, functional structure, and divisional structure—tend to be more mechanistic. Exhibit 5-4 summarizes the strengths and weaknesses of each design.

**SIMPLE STRUCTURE**  Most organizations start as entrepreneurial ventures with a simple structure consisting of owners and employees. A **simple structure** is an organizational structure with low departmentalization, wide spans of control, authority centralized in a single person, and little formalization.[30] This structure is most commonly used by small businesses in which the owner and manager are one and the same.

Most organizations do not remain simple structures. As an organization grows, it generally reaches a point where it has to add employees. As the number of employees rises, the structure tends to become more specialized and formalized. Rules and regulations are introduced, work becomes specialized, departments are created, levels of management are added, and the organization becomes increasingly bureaucratic. At this point, a manager might choose to organize around a functional structure or a divisional structure.

**FUNCTIONAL STRUCTURE**  A **functional structure** is an organizational structure that groups similar or related occupational specialties together. It is the functional approach to departmentalization applied to the entire organization. Revlon, for example, is organized around the functions of operations, finance, human resources, and product research and development.

**DIVISIONAL STRUCTURE**  The **divisional structure** is an organizational structure that consists of separate business units or divisions.[31] In this structure, each unit or division has relatively limited autonomy, with a division manager responsible for performance who has strategic and operational authority over his or her unit. In divisional structures, however, the parent corporation typically acts as an external overseer to coordinate and control the various divisions, and often provides support services such as financial and legal. As we noted earlier, Maple Leaf Sports & Entertainment has three divisions, including the two sports teams, the Raptors and the Maple Leafs.

## Contemporary Organizational Designs

Managers in contemporary organizations often find that traditional hierarchical designs are not appropriate for the increasingly dynamic and complex environments they face. In response to marketplace demands to be lean, flexible, and innovative, managers are developing creative ways to structure and organize work and to make their organizations more responsive to the needs of customers, employees, and other organizational constituents.[32] At the Canada Revenue Agency, the workforce is spread out, and employees rely on shared workspaces, mobile computing, and virtual private networks to get work done. Nevertheless, work gets done effectively and efficiently.[33] Exhibit 5-5 summarizes some of the newest concepts in organizational designs.

**TEAM STRUCTURE**  Larry Page and Sergey Brin, co-founders of Google, have created a corporate structure that "tackles most big projects in small, tightly focused teams."[34] In a **team structure**, the entire organization is made up of work groups or teams that perform the organization's work.[35] Employee empowerment is crucial in a team structure, because there is no line of managerial authority from top to bottom. Rather, employee teams are free to design work in the way they think is best. However, the teams are also held responsible for all work and performance results in their respective areas. Let us look at some examples of organizations that are organized around teams.

Whole Foods Market, the largest natural-foods grocer in the United States, now has seven stores in Ontario and BC. Each Whole Foods store is an autonomous profit centre composed of an average of 10 self-managed teams, each with a designated team leader. The team leaders in each store are a team; store leaders in each region are a team; and the company's six regional presidents are a team.[36] At the Sun Life Assurance Company of

#### EXHIBIT 5-5  Contemporary Organizational Designs

| Structure | Description | Advantages | Disadvantages |
|---|---|---|---|
| **Team** | A structure in which the entire organization is made up of work groups or teams. | Employees are more involved and empowered. Reduced barriers among functional areas. | No clear chain of command. Pressure on teams to perform. |
| **Matrix–Project** | Matrix is a structure that assigns specialists from different functional areas to work on projects but who return to their areas when the project is completed. Project is a structure in which employees continuously work on projects. As one project is completed, employees move on to the next project. | Fluid and flexible design that can respond to environmental changes. Faster decision making. | Complexity of assigning people to projects. Task and personality conflicts. |
| **Boundaryless** | A structure that is not defined by or limited to artificial horizontal, vertical, or external boundaries; includes *virtual* and *networked* types of organizations. | Highly flexible and responsive. Draws on talent wherever it is found. | Lack of control. Communication difficulties. |

**simple structure**
An organizational structure with low departmentalization, wide spans of control, authority centralized in a single person, and little formalization.

**functional structure**
An organizational structure that groups similar or related occupational specialties together.

**divisional structure**
An organizational structure that consists of separate business units or divisions.

**team structure**
An organizational structure in which the entire organization is made up of work groups or teams.

Canada (US) office in Wellesley Hills, Massachusetts, customer representatives work in eight-person teams trained to expedite all customer requests. When customers call in, they are not switched from one specialist to another, but to one of the teams who take care of every aspect of the customer's request. Together, team members work to make resolving insurance difficulties go much smoother.

In large organizations, the team structure complements what is typically a functional or divisional structure. This structural addition enables the organization to have the efficiency of a bureaucracy while providing the flexibility that teams provide. To improve productivity at the operating level, for example, Toyota's CAPTIN plant (based in Delta, BC), Motorola, and Xerox use self-managed teams extensively.[37]

*Have you ever had to work for two managers at the same time? Was this a positive or negative experience?*

**MATRIX AND PROJECT STRUCTURES**  Other popular contemporary designs are the matrix and project structures. The **matrix structure** is an organizational structure that assigns specialists from different functional departments to work on one or more projects led by project managers. Once a project is completed, the specialists return to their functional departments. Exhibit 5-6 shows an example of the matrix structure used in an aerospace firm. Along the top are the familiar organizational functions. The specific projects the firm is currently working on are listed along the left-hand side: aircraft, mission systems and avionics, engines and parts, and space technologies. Each project is managed by an individual who staffs his or her project with people from each of the functional departments. Adding this vertical dimension to the traditional horizontal functional departments in effect "weaves together" elements of functional and product departmentalization, creating a matrix arrangement. Another unique aspect of this design is that it creates a *dual chain of command*, which explicitly violates the classical organizing principle of unity of command.

How does a matrix structure work in reality? Employees in a matrix organization have two managers: their functional department manager and their product or project manager, who share authority. The project managers have authority over the functional members who are part of their project team in areas relative to the project's goals. However, decisions such as promotions, salary recommendations, and annual reviews remain the functional manager's responsibility. To work effectively, project and functional managers have to communicate regularly, coordinate work demands on employees, and resolve conflicts together.

Although the matrix structure continues to be an effective organizational structure choice for some organizations, many are using a **project structure**, in which employees

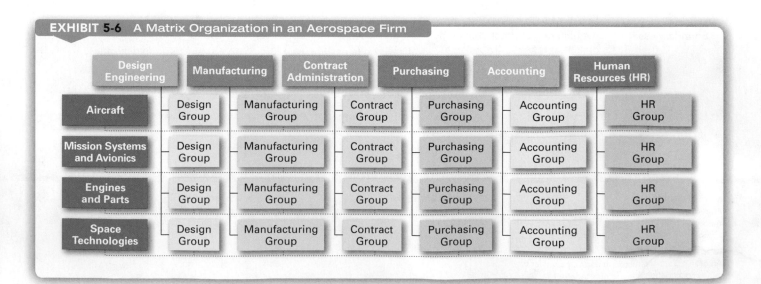

**EXHIBIT 5-6**   A Matrix Organization in an Aerospace Firm

| | Design Engineering | Manufacturing | Contract Administration | Purchasing | Accounting | Human Resources (HR) |
|---|---|---|---|---|---|---|
| **Aircraft** | Design Group | Manufacturing Group | Contract Group | Purchasing Group | Accounting Group | HR Group |
| **Mission Systems and Avionics** | Design Group | Manufacturing Group | Contract Group | Purchasing Group | Accounting Group | HR Group |
| **Engines and Parts** | Design Group | Manufacturing Group | Contract Group | Purchasing Group | Accounting Group | HR Group |
| **Space Technologies** | Design Group | Manufacturing Group | Contract Group | Purchasing Group | Accounting Group | HR Group |

continuously work on projects. Unlike the matrix structure, a project structure has no formal departments that employees return to at the completion of a project. Instead, employees take their specific skills, abilities, and experiences to other projects. All work in project-structured organizations is performed by teams of employees who become part of a project team because they have the appropriate work skills and abilities. For example, Oticon A/S, a Danish hearing-aid manufacturer, has no departments or employee job titles. All work is project based, and project teams form, disband, and form again as the work requires. Employees "join" project teams because they bring needed skills and abilities to that project. Once the project is completed, they move on to the next one.[38]

Project structures tend to be fluid and flexible organizational designs. This type of structure has no departmentalization or rigid organizational hierarchy to slow down decision making or taking action. Managers act as facilitators, mentors, and coaches. They "serve" the project teams by eliminating or minimizing organizational obstacles and by ensuring that the teams have the resources they need to effectively and efficiently complete their work.

**BOUNDARYLESS ORGANIZATIONS** Another approach to contemporary organizational design is the **boundaryless organization**, an organization whose design is not determined by a predefined structure. Instead the organization seeks to eliminate the chain of command, places no limits on spans of control, and replaces departments with empowered teams.[39] The term *boundaryless organization* was coined by Jack Welch, former chair of General Electric (GE), who wanted to eliminate vertical and horizontal boundaries within GE and break down external barriers between the company and its customers and suppliers. This idea may sound odd, but many successful organizations are finding they can operate more effectively in today's environment by remaining flexible and *un*structured: the ideal structure for them is *not* having a rigid, predefined structure. Instead, the boundaryless organization seeks to eliminate the chain of command, to have limitless spans of control, and to replace departments with empowered teams.[40]

What do we mean by "boundaries"? A typical organization has internal boundaries—horizontal boundaries imposed by work specialization and departmentalization, and vertical boundaries created by separating employees into organizational levels and hierarchies. The organization also has external boundaries, which separate the organization from its customers, suppliers, and other stakeholders. To minimize or eliminate these boundaries, managers might use virtual or network organizational structures.

How does a boundaryless organization operate in practice? General Electric is made up of a number of companies including GE Money, which provides financial services to consumers and retailers; GE Water & Process Technologies, which produces water treatment, wastewater treatment, and process systems products; GE Energy, which supplies technology to the energy industry; and NBC Universal Studios, a leading media and entertainment company. Anyone working in any division of GE can learn about opportunities available in the other business units and how to move into those units, if so desired. Mobility is one way a boundaryless organization functions for its employees. Outside the company, the boundaryless structure allows GE customers to ask factories to increase inventory when the customer needs more product. Thus, the customer makes a

---

**matrix structure**
An organizational structure that assigns specialists from different functional departments to work on one or more projects.

**project structure**
An organizational structure in which employees continuously work on projects.

**boundaryless organization**
An organization that is not defined by a chain of command, places no limits on spans of control, and replaces departments with empowered teams.

decision about inventory that was once made inside the organization. GE also encourages customers and suppliers to evaluate its service levels, giving direct and immediate feedback to employees.

**Virtual Organizations**   A **virtual organization** has elements of a traditional organization, but also relies on recent developments in information technology to get work done.[41] Thus, the organization could consist of a small core of full-time employees plus outside specialists hired on a temporary basis to work on opportunities that arise.[42] The virtual organization could also be composed of employees who work from their own home offices—connected by technology but perhaps occasionally getting together face-to-face. An example of a virtual organization is Strawberry Frog, an international advertising agency based in Amsterdam. The small administrative staff accesses a network of more than 100 people around the globe to complete advertising projects. By relying on this global web of freelancers, the company enjoys a network of talent without the overhead and structural complexity of a more traditional organization.

The inspiration for virtual organizations comes from the film industry. If you look at the film industry, people are essentially "free agents" who move from project to project applying their skills—directing, talent search, costuming, makeup, set design—as needed.

New Westminster, BC–based iGEN Knowledge Solutions uses its virtual form to bring technical solutions to its business clients. iGEN associates work from home offices connected by wireless technologies to solve client problems collaboratively. This structure allows faster idea implementation, product development, and service delivery. The company finds it easy to set up operations in different regions of the country without large overhead costs because of its virtual structure.

Some organizations are now testing out a new form of virtuality, using the virtual online world *Second Life* to create a different type of organization. Vancouver-based Davis LLP is the first Canadian law firm to have a presence in *Second Life*.[43] Lawyer Dani Lemon, whose online avatar (the digital version of a real person) is Lemon Darcy, said that "the online world gives [Davis LLP] an opportunity to interact with clients and meet new ones who are comfortable in that setting."

Lemon believes that being part of *Second Life* will bring new clients to Davis and give the company an opportunity to communicate in new ways. Several of her colleagues have joined her in this virtual office, including Sarah Dale-Harris (BarristerSolicitor Underwood), Pablo Guzman (PabloGuzman Little), Chris Bennett (IPand Teichmann), David Spratley (DaveS Blackadder), and Chris Metcalfe (IP Maximus).

Davis LLP's *Second City* office has a boardroom off the lobby that can be used for online conferences, a room containing recruiting information from Davis, and a library that will house online legal information. "I think it will be an evolving process," Lemon said of the online office. "We will use it as a networking tool and as a way to meet clients." The law firm plans to hold online events in *Second Life*, conduct seminars, and give talks that might be of value to potential clients.

**Network Organizations**   Another structural option for managers wanting to minimize or eliminate organizational boundaries is the **network organization**, which is a small core organization that outsources major business functions.[44] This approach allows organizations to concentrate on what they do best and to contract out other activities to companies that specialize in those activities. Many large organizations use the network structure to outsource manufacturing. Companies such as Cisco Systems, Nike, Ericsson, L.L.Bean, and Reebok have found that they can do business worth hundreds of millions of dollars without owning manufacturing facilities. San Jose, California–based Cisco Systems is essentially a research and development company that uses outside suppliers and independent manufacturers to assemble the Internet routers its engineers design. Similarly, Beaverton, Oregon–based Nike is a product development and marketing company that contracts with outside organizations to manufacture its athletic footwear. Mitel Networks designs computer equipment but outsources manufacturing and repair to BreconRidge, another Ottawa high tech firm.[45]

Pierre Nanterme is the CEO of Accenture, Ltd., an international consulting firm that is also a virtual organization. The company has no operational headquarters or branch offices. Its top-level executives are scattered around the world, and many of its employees spend their days travelling to or working with clients in their clients' offices. The company's culture is one of constant motion, and its managers thrive on personal contact with clients. As part of a global company, Accenture's managers and employees believe in spending time together in the countries where their clients are.

While many companies use outsourcing, not all are successful at it. Managers should be aware of some of the problems involved in outsourcing, such as the following:

- Choosing the wrong activities to outsource
- Choosing the wrong vendor
- Writing a poor contract
- Failing to consider personnel issues
- Losing control over the activity
- Ignoring the hidden costs
- Failing to develop an exit strategy (for either moving to another vendor or deciding to bring the activity back in-house)

A review of 91 outsourcing activities found that the two most likely reasons for an outsourcing venture failure were writing a poor contract and losing control of the activity.[46] Canadian managers say they are reluctant to outsource.[47] The PricewaterhouseCoopers (PwC) 2011 Business Insights survey[48] showed outsourcing as the lowest priority in terms of improving the competitiveness of Canadian businesses, while innovation and reducing costs were perceived as more important than outsourcing for dealing with volatility. In some cases, companies formerly used as outsourcers are now direct competitors due to globalization.

Analyze

---

**virtual organization**
An organization that has elements of a traditional organization, but also relies on recent developments in information technology to get work done.

**network organization**
A small core organization that outsources major business functions.

## Organizational Design Challenges

As managers look for organizational designs that will best support and facilitate employees doing their work efficiently and effectively in today's dynamic environment, certain challenges arise with which they must contend. These challenges include keeping employees connected, building a learning organization, and managing global structural issues.

**KEEPING EMPLOYEES CONNECTED** Many organizational design concepts were developed during the twentieth century, when work tasks were fairly predictable and constant, most jobs were full time and continued indefinitely, and work was done at an employer's place of business under a manager's supervision.[49] However, many organizations today are not like that, as you saw in our preceding discussion of virtual and network organizations. A major structural design challenge for managers is finding a way to keep widely dispersed and mobile employees connected to the organization. We cover information on motivating these employees in Chapter 9.

**BUILDING A LEARNING ORGANIZATION** Doing business in an intensely competitive global environment, managers at British retailer Tesco realize how important it is for stores to operate smoothly behind the scenes. At Tesco, they do so through the use of a proven tool—a set of software applications called Tesco in a Box, which promotes consistency in operations and acts as a way to share innovations. Tesco is an example of a learning organization, an organization that has developed the capacity to constantly learn, adapt, and change.[50] In a learning organization, employees continually acquire and share new knowledge and apply that knowledge in making decisions or doing their work. Some organizational theorists even go so far as to say that an organization's ability to learn and to apply that learning may be the only sustainable source of competitive advantage.[51]

What structural characteristics does a learning organization need? First, members of a learning organization must be able to share information and collaborate on work activities throughout the entire organization—across different functional specialties and even at different organizational levels. This sharing and collaboration requires that structural and physical barriers be minimal. In such a boundaryless environment, employees can work together and collaborate in doing the organization's work the best way they can and learn from each other. Second, because of the need to collaborate, teams tend to be an important feature of a learning organization's structural design. Employees work in teams empowered to make decisions about doing whatever work needs to be done and to resolve issues. With empowered employees and teams, the organization has little need for "bosses" to direct and control. Instead, managers serve as facilitators, supporters, and advocates.

**MANAGING GLOBAL STRUCTURAL ISSUES** Are there global differences in organizational structures? Are Australian organizations structured like those in Canada? Are German organizations structured like those in France or Mexico? Given the global nature of today's business environment, managers need to be familiar with the issues surrounding structural differences. Researchers have concluded that the structures and strategies of organizations worldwide are similar, "while the behavior within them is maintaining its cultural uniqueness."[52] What does this mean for designing effective and efficient structures? When designing or changing structure, managers may need to think about the cultural implications of certain design elements. One study showed that formalization—rules and bureaucratic mechanisms—may be more important in less economically developed countries and less important in more economically developed countries, where employees may have higher levels of professional education and skills.[53] Other structural design elements may be affected by cultural differences as well, such as chain of command and span of control.

## A Final Thought

No matter what structural design managers choose for their organization, the structure should help employees work in the most efficient and effective way possible to meet the organization's goals. After all, structure is simply a means to an end. To understand your reaction to organizational structure, see *Assess Your Skills—What Type of Organizational Structure Do I Prefer?* on pages 148–149 at the end of the chapter.

Practise

## Summary of Learning Objectives

**5.1** **What are the major elements of organizational structure?** Organizational structure is the formal arrangement of jobs within an organization. Organizational structures are determined by six key elements: work specialization, departmentalization, chain of command, span of control, centralization and decentralization, and formalization. Decisions made about these elements define how work is organized; how many employees managers supervise; where in the organization decisions are made; and whether employees follow standardized operating procedures or have greater flexibility in how they do their work.

For Maple Leaf Sports & Entertainment, separating the operation of the four sports teams because of the work specialization involved makes sense. For example, the general manager of the Raptors would not necessarily make good decisions about what the Maple Leafs should do to improve their game, even if Maple Leaf fans might disagree.

**5.2** **What factors affect organizational structure?** No one organizational structure is best. The appropriate structure depends on the organization's strategy (innovation, cost minimization, imitation), its size, the technology it uses (unit production, mass production, or process production), and the degree of environmental uncertainty the organization faces.

For Maple Leaf Sports & Entertainment, organizing its teams by industry makes sense—hockey, basketball, and soccer are different "industries" with different types of players. Because sports teams are governed by formal rules, the teams have more of a mechanistic structure than an organic one. Each team has a similar organizational structure, as size, technology, and environmental uncertainty would not differ in any meaningful way among the teams.

**5.3** **Beyond traditional organizational designs, how else can organizations be structured?** The traditional structures of organizations are simple, functional, and divisional. Contemporary organizational designs include team structure, matrix and project structures, and boundaryless organizations.

Maple Leaf Sports & Entertainment follows a traditional divisional structure for its sport teams. Other structures might be used to operate its sports facilities, such as a project structure or a boundaryless organization, because events and ticket sales can be managed in a variety of ways.

### SNAPSHOT SUMMARY

**5.1** **Defining Organizational Structure**
Work Specialization
Departmentalization
Chain of Command
Span of Control
Centralization and Decentralization
Formalization

**5.2** **Organizational Design Decisions**
Mechanistic and Organic Organizations
Contingency Factors

**5.3** **Common Organizational Designs**
Traditional Organizational Designs
Contemporary Organizational Designs
Organizational Design Challenges
A Final Thought

MyManagementLab® **Learning Resources**

# Resources

▼ **Explore and enhance your understanding of key chapter topics through the following online resources:**

- Student PowerPoints
- Audio Summary of Chapter
- ROLLS
- CBC Videos for Part 3
- MySearchLab

▶ Visit the **Study Plan** area to test your progress with **Pre-Tests** and **Post-Tests**.

▼ **Build on your knowledge and practise real-world applications using the following online activities:**

## Interpret

- Opening Case Activity: Organizing Key Terms
- Review and Apply: Solutions to Interpret section questions and activities
- Glossary Flashcards

## Analyze

- Opening Case Activity: Organizational Structure
- Review and Apply: Solutions to Analyze section questions and activities
- Self-Assessment Library

## Practise

- Opening Case Activity: How Organizational Structure Informs Organizational Strategy
- Review and Apply: Solutions to Practice section questions and activities
- Decision Making Simulation: Organizational Structure

# Interpret What You Have Read

1. Describe what is meant by the term *organizational design*.
2. In what ways can management departmentalize? When should one approach be considered over the others?
3. What is the difference between a mechanistic and an organic organization?
4. Why is a simple structure inadequate in large organizations?
5. Describe the characteristics of a boundaryless organizational structure.
6. Describe the characteristics of a learning organization. What are its advantages?

# Analyze What You Have Read

1. Which do you think is more efficient: a wide or a narrow span of control? What is an example of a company that would benefit from a narrow span of control? A wide span of control?
2. "An organization can have no structure." Do you agree or disagree with this statement? Explain.
3. Show how both the functional and matrix structures might create conflict within an organization.
4. Do you think the concept of organizational structure, as described in this chapter, is appropriate for charitable organizations? If yes, which organizational design do you believe to be most appropriate? If no, why not? Explain your position.
5. What effects do you think the characteristics of the boundaryless organization have on employees in today's contemporary organizations?
6. Why should structure follow strategy instead of the reverse?
7. What functions could your college or university outsource? Why?

# Assess Your Skills

## WHAT TYPE OF ORGANIZATIONAL STRUCTURE DO I PREFER?

For each of the following statements, circle your level of agreement or disagreement:[54]

1 = Strongly Disagree   2 = Moderately Disagree   3 = Neither Agree nor Disagree
4 = Moderately Agree   5 = Strongly Agree

I prefer to work in an organization where:

1. Goals are defined by those at higher levels.                                                    1 2 3 4 5
2. Clear job descriptions exist for every job.                                                       1 2 3 4 5
3. Top management makes important decisions.                                                        1 2 3 4 5
4. Promotions and pay increases are based as much on length of service as on level of performance.   1 2 3 4 5
5. Clear lines of authority and responsibility are established.                                     1 2 3 4 5
6. My career is pretty well laid out for me.                                                         1 2 3 4 5
7. I have a great deal of job security.                                                              1 2 3 4 5
8. I can specialize.                                                                                 1 2 3 4 5
9. My boss is readily available.                                                                     1 2 3 4 5
10. Organization rules and regulations are clearly specified.                                        1 2 3 4 5
11. Information rigidly follows the chain of command.                                                1 2 3 4 5
12. There is a minimal number of new tasks for me to learn.                                          1 2 3 4 5
13. Work groups incur little turnover in members.                                                    1 2 3 4 5
14. People accept the authority of a leader's position.                                              1 2 3 4 5
15. I am part of a group whose training and skills are similar to mine.                              1 2 3 4 5

**SCORING KEY**   Add up the numbers for each of your responses to get your total score.

### ANALYSIS AND INTERPRETATION

This instrument measures your preference for working in a mechanistic or an organic organizational structure.

Scores above 60 suggest that you prefer a mechanistic structure. Scores below 45 indicate a preference for an organic structure. Scores between 45 and 60 suggest no clear preference.

Because the trend in recent years has been toward more organic structures, you are more likely to find a good organizational match if you score low on this instrument. However, there are few, if any, pure organic structures. Therefore, very low scores may also mean that you are likely to be frustrated by what you perceive as overly rigid structures of rules, regulations, and boss-centred leadership. In general, however, low scores indicate that you prefer small, innovative, flexible, team-oriented organizations.

High scores indicate a preference for stable, rule-oriented, more bureaucratic organizations.

> ### More Self-Assessments
>
> To learn more about your skills, abilities, and interests, take the following self-assessments on the MyManagementLab®:
>
> - III.A.2.—How Willing Am I to Delegate?
> - III.A.3.—How Good Am I at Giving Performance Feedback?
> - IV.F.1.—Is My Workplace Political?
> - IV.F.2.—Do I Like Bureaucracy?

# Practise What You Have Learned

## DILEMMA

Choose an organization for which you have worked. How did the structure of your job and the organization affect your job satisfaction? Did the tasks within your job make sense? In what ways could they be better organized? What structural changes would you make to this organization? Would you consider making this a taller or flatter organization (that is, would you increase or decrease the span of control)? How would the changes you have proposed improve response to customers and your job satisfaction?

## BECOMING A MANAGER

- If you belong to a student organization or are employed, notice how various activities and events are organized through the use of work specialization, chain of command, authority, responsibility, and so forth.
- As you read current business periodicals, note what types of organizational structures businesses use and whether or not they are effective.
- Talk to managers about how they organize work and what they have found to be effective.
- Since delegating is part of decentralizing and is an important management skill, complete the *Developing Your Interpersonal Skills—Delegating* module on page 150 below. Then practise delegating in various situations.
- Look for examples of organizational charts (visual representations of organizations' structures) and use them to try to determine what structural design the organization is using.

## DEVELOPING YOUR DIAGNOSTIC AND ANALYTICAL SKILLS: A NEW KIND OF STRUCTURE

Admit it.[55] Sometimes the projects you are working on (school, work, or both) can get pretty boring and monotonous. Do you ever dream about having a magic button you could push to get someone else to do the boring, time-consuming stuff for you? At Pfizer, such a button is a reality for a large number of employees.

As a global pharmaceutical company, Pfizer is continually looking for ways to be more efficient and effective. The company's head of pfizerWorks (aka Office of the Future), Jordan Cohen, found that the "Harvard MBA staff we hired to develop strategies and innovate were instead Googling and making PowerPoints." Indeed, internal studies conducted to find out just how much time its valuable talent was spending on menial tasks was startling. The average Pfizer employee was spending 20 to 40 percent of his or her time on support work (creating documents, typing notes, doing research, manipulating data, scheduling meetings) and only 60 to 80 percent on knowledge work (strategy, innovation, networking, collaborating, critical thinking). The problem was not just at lower levels. Even the highest-level employees were affected. So Cohen began looking for solutions. The solution he chose turned out to be the numerous knowledge-process outsourcing companies based in India.

Initial tests of outsourcing support tasks did not go well. However, Cohen continued to tweak the process until everything worked. Now Pfizer employees can click the OOF (Office of the Future) button in Microsoft Outlook, and they are connected to an outsourcing company where a single worker in India receives the request and assigns it to a team.

The team leader calls the employee to clarify the request. The team leader then emails back a cost estimate for the requested work. At this point, the Pfizer employee can say yes or no. Cohen says that the benefits of OOF are unexpected. Time spent on data analysis has been cut—sometimes in half. The financial benefits are also impressive. Pfizer employees love it. "It's kind of amazing," Cohen says, "I wonder what they used to do."

### Questions

1. Describe and evaluate what Pfizer is doing.

2. What structural implications—good and bad—does this approach have? (Think in terms of the six organizational design elements.)

3. Do you think this arrangement would work for other types of organizations? Why or why not?

4. What role do you think organizational structure plays in an organization's efficiency and effectiveness? Explain.

## DEVELOPING YOUR INTERPERSONAL SKILLS: DELEGATING

### ABOUT THE SKILL

Managers get things done through other people. Because any manager's time and knowledge is limited, effective managers need to understand how to delegate. Delegation is the assignment of authority to another person to carry out specific duties. It allows an employee to make some of the decisions. Delegation should not be confused with participation. In participative decision making, authority is shared. In delegation, employees make decisions on their own.

### STEPS IN DEVELOPING THE SKILL

A number of actions differentiate the effective delegator from the ineffective delegator. You can be more effective at delegating if you use the following five suggestions:[56]

1. CLARIFY THE ASSIGNMENT. Determine what is to be delegated and to whom. You need to identify the person who is most capable of doing the task and then determine whether or not he or she has the time and motivation to do the task. If you have a willing and able employee, your responsibility is to provide clear information on what is being delegated, the results you expect, and any time or performance expectations you may have. Unless there is an overriding need to adhere to specific methods, you should specify only the results expected. Get agreement on what is to be done and the results expected, but let the employee decide the best way to complete the task.

2. SPECIFY THE EMPLOYEE'S RANGE OF DISCRETION. Every situation of delegation comes with constraints. Although you are delegating to an employee the authority to perform some task or tasks, you are not delegating unlimited authority. You are delegating authority to act on certain issues within certain parameters. You need to specify what those parameters are so that employees know, without any doubt, the range of their discretion.

3. ALLOW THE EMPLOYEE TO PARTICIPATE. One of the best ways to decide how much authority will be necessary to accomplish a task is to allow the employee who will be held accountable for the task to participate in that decision. Be aware, however, that allowing employees to participate can present its own set of potential problems as a result of employees' self-interests and biases in evaluating their own abilities.

4. INFORM OTHERS ABOUT THE DELEGATION. Delegation should not take place behind the scenes. Not only do the manager and employee need to know specifically what has been delegated and how much authority has been given, so does anyone else, both inside and outside the organization, who is likely to be affected by the employee's decisions and actions. Essentially, you need to communicate what has been delegated (the task and amount of authority) and to whom.

5. ESTABLISH FEEDBACK CHANNELS. To delegate without establishing feedback controls is to invite problems. The establishment of controls to monitor the employee's performance increases the likelihood that important problems will be identified and the task will be completed on time and to the desired specifications. Ideally, these controls should be determined at the time of the initial assignment. Agree on a specific time for the completion of the task and then set progress dates on which the employee will report back on how well he or she is doing and on any major problems that may have arisen. These controls can be supplemented with periodic checks to ensure that authority guidelines are not being abused, organizational policies are being followed, proper procedures are being met, and so forth.

### PRACTISING THE SKILL

Ricky Lee is the manager of the contracts group of a large regional office-supply distributor. His manager, Anne Zumwalt, has asked him to prepare, by the end of the month, the department's new procedures manual, which will outline the steps followed in negotiating contracts with office products manufacturers who supply the organization's products. Because Ricky has another major project he is working on, he went to Anne and asked her if it would be possible to assign the rewriting of the procedures manual to Bill Harmon, one of his employees who has worked in the contracts group for about three years. Anne said she had no problems with Ricky reassigning the project as long as Bill knew the parameters and the expectations for the completion of the project. Ricky is preparing for his meeting in the morning with Bill regarding this assignment. Prepare an outline of what Ricky should discuss with Bill to ensure the new procedures manual meets expectations.

# Team Exercises

## 3BL: THE TRIPLE BOTTOM LINE

### INTEGRATING SUSTAINABILITY INTO THE ORGANIZATIONAL STRUCTURE

Sustainability. Social responsibility. The environment. These concepts are buzzwords for regulators and stakeholders who put pressure on organizations to deal with 3BL issues, urging companies to determine how best to incorporate 3BL as part of their organizational structure.[57]

Organizations are concerned both with structure—where will 3BL decision-making authority reside?—and with the processes and flow of information across the organization. What kind of internal structure and support would magnify their 3BL efforts?

Organizations typically feature one of three 3BL structures.[58] The first is the traditional model, in which 3BL is an initiative or a few activities. Minimal resources are allocated to 3BL, and they may be spread across many departments or business units. The second is the federated model, where the organization has likely created a 3BL business unit and engaged an executive such as a Chief Sustainability Officer or a Chief Responsibility Officer. This unit is able to liaise with other business units and starts to align 3BL priorities with business strategy. The last model is an embedded structure, where 3BL is no longer a separate initiative but integrated into the company's business model, structure, and culture. Companies at this point view 3BL as a major source of competitive advantage.

### THINKING STRATEGICALLY ABOUT 3BL

Some best practices for ensuring 3BL success in an organization include the following:

- *Tie responsibility with senior executives.* You need more than "support" from the CEO— the CEO needs to drive the bus and set up a cross-functional 3BL committee with employee participation.
- *Establish regular target setting and reporting.* The focus on accountability builds traction within an organization.
- *Use employees, partners, and collaborators to leverage 3BL capabilities.* Achieve greater outcomes by working collaboratively with everyone in your sphere of influence.
- *Recruit 3BL change agents.* These champions of change will help embed a culture of concern for people, profit, and the planet.

## HOW IS YOUR SCHOOL ORGANIZED?

Every university or college displays a specific type of organizational structure. For example, if you are a business major, your classes are often housed in a department, school, or faculty of business. But have you ever asked why? Or is it something you just take for granted?

In Chapter 3 you had an opportunity to assess your college or university's strengths, weaknesses, and competitive advantage and see how these fit into its strategy. In this chapter, we have argued that structure follows strategy. Given your assessment in Chapter 3 (if you have not done so, you may want to refer to page 84 for the strategy part of this exercise), analyze your college or university's overall structure in terms of its degree of formalization, centralization/decentralization, and complexity. Look at the departmentalization that exists. Is your college or university more organic or mechanistic? How well does your college or university's structure fit with its strategy? Do the same thing for your college or university's size, technology, and environment. Assess its size, degree of technological routineness, and environmental uncertainty. Based on these assessments, what kind of structure would you predict that your college or university has? Does it have this structure now? Compare your findings with those of other classmates. Are there similarities in how each viewed the college or university? Differences? To what do you attribute these findings?

## BE THE CONSULTANT: THE NOVA SCOTIA ASSOCIATION OF SOCIAL WORKERS

The Nova Scotia Association of Social Workers (NSASW) contracted your management consulting firm to conduct an operational structure review.[59] The size of social worker governance councils varies across Canada, with larger associations like NSASW having professional staff to carry out association activities. The NSASW has a governance council of 30, as well as a Board of Examiners to provide oversight for the association. The Council is the governance body for the association and is responsible to follow the association By-Laws and the Social Workers Act of Nova Scotia. The Board is responsible for registration and renewal of provincial social workers, regulation of the members' practice to protect the public, and dealing with discipline and complaints. The Council and the Board have a difficult relationship, and staff roles, responsibilities, and reporting relationships are not clearly defined. The Executive Director complains about being stressed and overworked, and is not conducting performance evaluations. The membership has increased dramatically, putting a burden on the association's financial resources, staff, and volunteers.

Your analysis leads you to discover that Council meetings regularly run late and not all of the agenda items are accomplished. Consensus is almost impossible to reach, and decision making is ineffective at times. The Board plays a very valuable role in assuring the interests of the public and the profession are safeguarded, but no formal communication mechanism between the Board and the Council has been established.

You provided an interim report with many recommendations. Specifically, the Board has brought you in to discuss three of your recommendations:

1. Reduction of the governance council size to 15 members

2. Creation of a Liaison Committee to work with both the Council and the Board to develop a stronger working and reporting relationship

3. Formal approval of staff position descriptions by Council, with the Executive Director responsible for their implementation, to facilitate the Association's performance management system

What information will you provide to the Council to support your recommendations?

# Business Cases

## LEVITT-SAFETY LIMITED

Levitt-Safety Limited is Canada's largest specialist supplier of safety equipment and services.[60] Like many Canadian companies, it looked to emerging foreign markets for growth opportunities. However, globalization and outsourcing are no longer a one-way street. Foreign competitors are eyeing the Canadian market, because barriers to entry such as the North American regulatory and approval bodies are easier to navigate in Canada. To be successful in the Canadian marketplace, foreign companies need to spend a lot of time and money to build up their brands. Or they could form an alliance with a company like Levitt-Safety to piggyback on a brand that is already established and well known after 36 years of business.

Increased competition has led to downward pressure on profit margins. To counter this, CEO Bruce Levitt created an intermediary company to import their product and resell it to their distribution business. The company sales teams now have a much better understanding of inventory carrying costs, stock-outs, dead stock, and other often hidden costs. Levitt-Safety also has a separate manufacturing business, NL Technologies, run by Heidi Levitt, which has become a world leader in the manufacturing and design of mining technology.

Levitt-Safety has created an effective organizational structure, with an intermediary and a separately managed company. Levitt-Safety is looking at adding another brand that they can sell to others in the industry. Should Bruce Levitt set up another company or, instead, set up an alliance with a foreign company that would sell their product under the Levitt-Safety name?

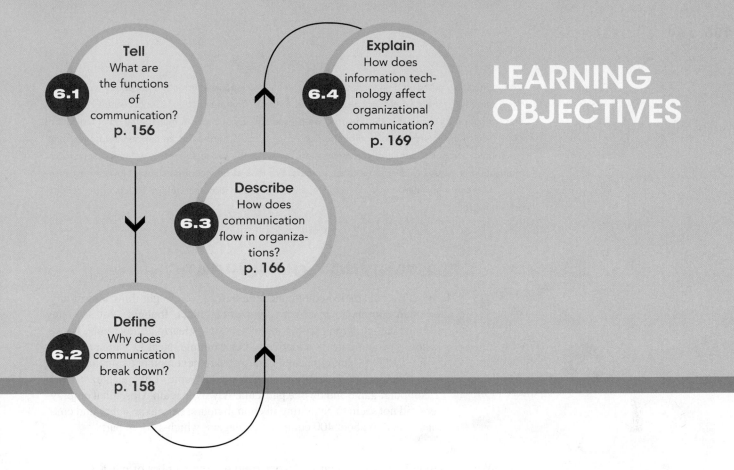

**Tell**
6.1
What are the functions of communication?
p. 156

**Explain**
6.4
How does information technology affect organizational communication?
p. 169

**Describe**
6.3
How does communication flow in organizations?
p. 166

**Define**
6.2
Why does communication break down?
p. 158

Significantly more than half of all Canadians use social networking. In 2011, 50 percent of online Canadians visited a social media site weekly, with more than a third accessing at least one site daily. Facebook and its close to 1 billion users is the leading site, with 86 percent of Canadian social media users on Facebook. In the last three years alone, Canadians have flocked to Twitter (from 1 percent to 20 percent) and LinkedIn (doubled during that time). Google+ signed up 10 million users in less than a month.[1]

Social media is now recognized as a multi-faceted tool by the business community. Some employers pre-screen job applicants by searching their Facebook and LinkedIn profiles or reading their Twitter feeds. "While the majority of Canadian companies are engaging in social media, most of them aren't combining the two fundamental pillars—posting information and monitoring what people are saying—with enough frequency to build lasting relationships with their customers," said Katie Delahaye Paine, CEO of KDPaine & Partners.[2] Some employers, such as the City of Toronto, have blocked the use of social media at work, while others are creating their own company networks on Facebook to allow employees to use social media as one of their communication tools.

## Think About It

Can social networking websites enhance communication in the workplace? How might social networking websites affect communication with customers and the broader community? What risks might Facebook use pose to graduating students looking for their first major job?

Communication between managers and employees provides the information necessary to get work done effectively and efficiently in organizations. As such, communication is fundamentally linked to managerial performance.[3] In this chapter, we present basic concepts in managerial communication. We describe the interpersonal communication process, distortions that can happen in interpersonal communication, the channels of communication, as well as the barriers to effective interpersonal communication and ways to overcome those barriers. We look at how communication flows in organizations, how communication networks operate, and how information technology affects organizational communication.

# UNDERSTANDING COMMUNICATION

**6.1**

**Tell**
What are the functions of communication?

If you have not studied communication before, you might think almost anyone can communicate effectively without much thought. Yet so many things can go wrong with communication—clearly not everyone knows how to communicate effectively. For example, Neal L. Patterson, chair and CEO of Cerner, a health care software development company based in Kansas City, probably wishes he could "replay" like a character in a computer game and do one particular day over again. Upset that employees did not seem to be putting in enough hours, he sent an angry and emotional email to about 400 company managers, which said, in part:

> We are getting less than 40 hours of work from a large number of our K.C.-based EMPLOYEES. The parking lot is sparsely used at 8 a.m.; likewise at 5 p.m. As managers, you either do not know what your EMPLOYEES are doing, or you do not CARE. You have created expectations on the work effort which allowed this to happen inside Cerner, creating a very unhealthy environment. In either case, you have a problem and you will fix it or I will replace you. . . . I will hold you accountable. You have allowed things to get to this state. You have two weeks. Tick, tock.[4]

Patterson had a message, and he wanted to get it out to his managers. Although the email was meant only for the company's managers, it was leaked and posted on a Yahoo! discussion site. The tone of the email surprised industry analysts, investors, and, of course, Cerner's managers and employees. The company's stock price dropped 22 percent over the next three days. Patterson apologized to his employees and acknowledged, "I lit a match and started a firestorm." Patterson's angry email is a good example of why individuals need to understand the importance of communication and the effect it can have.

The importance of effective communication for managers cannot be overemphasized. Everything a manager does involves communicating. Not *some* things, but everything! A manager cannot make a decision without information. That information has to be communicated. Once a decision is made, communication must again take place. Otherwise, no one would know that a decision was made. The best idea, the most creative suggestion, the best plan, or the most effective job redesign cannot take shape without communication. Managers need effective communication skills. We are not suggesting that good communication skills alone make a successful manager. We can say, however, that ineffective communication skills can lead to a continuous stream of managerial problems.

## What Is Communication?

**Communication** is the transfer and understanding of meaning. The first thing to note about this definition is the emphasis on the *transfer* of meaning. If no information or ideas have been conveyed, communication has not taken place. The speaker who is not heard or the writer who is not read has not communicated.

More importantly, however, communication involves the *understanding* of meaning. For communication to be successful, the meaning must be conveyed and understood. A letter written in Portuguese addressed to a person who does not read Portuguese cannot be considered communication until the letter is translated into a language the person does read and understand. Perfect communication, if such a thing exists, occurs when the receiver understands a transmitted thought or idea exactly as it was intended by the sender.

Another point to keep in mind is that *good* communication is often erroneously defined by the communicator as *agreement* with the message instead of clearly *understanding* the message.[5] If someone disagrees with us, many of us assume that the person just did not fully understand our position. In other words, many of us define good communication as having someone accept our views. But I can clearly understand what you mean and just *not* agree with what you say. Many times when a conflict has gone on for a long time, people will say the issue has not been resolved because the parties are not communicating effectively. That assumption reflects the tendency to think effective communication equals agreement.

The final point we want to make about communication is that it encompasses both **interpersonal communication**—communication between two or more people—and **organizational communication**—all the patterns, networks, and systems of communication within an organization. Both these types of communication are important to managers in organizations.

## Functions of Communication

Why is communication important to managers and organizations? It serves four major functions: control, motivation, emotional expression, and information.[6]

Communication acts to *control* member behaviour in several ways. As we know from Chapter 5, organizations have authority hierarchies and formal guidelines that employees are required to follow. For example, when employees are required to communicate any job-related grievance first to their immediate manager, or to follow their job description, or to comply with company policies, communication is being used to control. But informal communication also controls behaviour. When work groups tease or harass a member who is working too hard or producing too much (making the rest of the group look bad), they are informally controlling the member's behaviour.

Communication encourages *motivation* by clarifying to employees what is to be done, how well they are doing, and what can

If you have ever had a bad haircut, you have probably not forgotten the experience. You might have decided to never go to that stylist or salon again. But Dorys Belanger, owner of Montreal-based Au Premier Spa Urbain, says that a bad haircut should not be blamed on the stylist alone. Good communication, she says, is "fifty percent up to the hairdresser, fifty percent up to the client."

be done to improve performance if it is not up to par. As employees set specific goals, work toward those goals, and receive feedback on their progress, communication is required. Managers motivate more effectively if they show support for the employee by communicating constructive feedback, rather than mere criticism.

| **communication** | **interpersonal communication** | **organizational communication** |
|---|---|---|
| The transfer and understanding of meaning. | Communication between two or more people. | All the patterns, networks, and systems of communication within an organization. |

For many employees, their work group is a primary source of social interaction. The communication that takes place within the group is a fundamental mechanism by which members share frustrations and feelings of satisfaction. Communication, therefore, provides a release for *emotional expression* of feelings and for fulfillment of social needs.

Finally, individuals and groups need *information* to get things done in organizations. Communication provides that information.

No one of these four functions is more important than the others. For groups to work effectively, they need to maintain some form of control over members, motivate members to perform, provide a means for emotional expression, and make decisions. You can assume that almost every communication interaction that takes place in a group or organization is fulfilling one or more of these four functions.

Interpret

# INTERPERSONAL COMMUNICATION

**Define**

**6.2** Why does communication break down?

Facebook encourages online interaction rather than face-to-face communication.[7] Because Facebook users write rather than speak directly to each other, they may feel safer saying something on their Facebook page than they would in person. Individuals may also inadvertently incriminate themselves. The Ontario Provincial Police have used the site to find out about parties that might have illegal drug use and underage drinking. Facebook makes the police's job easy—party plans are instantly available on the site, along with directions to the location.

Before communication can take place, a purpose, expressed as a **message** to be conveyed, must exist. The message passes between a source (the sender) and a receiver. It is converted into symbols (called **encoding**) and passed by way of some medium (**channel**) to the receiver, who translates the sender's message (called **decoding**). Feedback is then passed

## Think About It

What effect will the growing use of online social networking sites have on people's ability to communicate face to face in the workplace as well as in life outside of work? Can online social networking lead people to forget to consider the consequences of their communication? What possible impact could this oversight have on their relations with co-workers (for both employees and managers)?

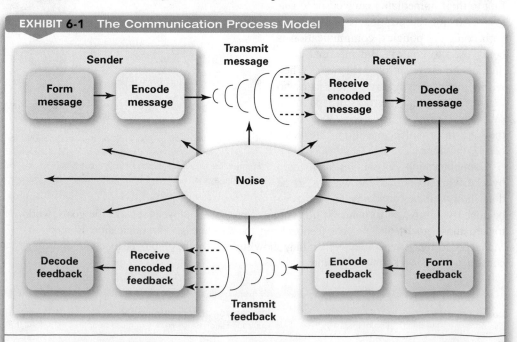

**EXHIBIT 6-1** The Communication Process Model

*Source:* McShane, *Canadian Organizational Behaviour* © 2008. McGraw Hill Ryerson; Reproduced with permission of McGraw-Hill Ryerson Ltd.

through a channel back to the sender, who decodes the feedback. The result is the transfer of meaning from one person to another.[8] Exhibit 6-1 illustrates the seven elements of the interpersonal **communication process**: the sender, the message, encoding, the channel, the receiver, decoding, and feedback. Note that **noise**—disturbances interfering with the transmission, receipt, or feedback of a message—can affect the entire process. Typical examples of noise include external factors such as illegible print, phone static, or background sounds of machinery or co-workers. Noise can also be the result of internal factors such as the receiver's inattention, as well as perceptions and personality traits of the receiver. Remember: Anything that interferes with understanding can be noise, and noise can create distortion at any point in the communication process.

## How Distortions Can Happen in Interpersonal Communication

Distortions can happen with the sender, the message, the channel, the receiver, or the feedback loop. Let us look at each of these things.

**SENDER**  A *sender* initiates a message by *encoding* a thought. Four conditions influence the effectiveness of that encoded message: the skills, attitudes, and knowledge of the sender, and the socio-cultural system. How? We will use ourselves, your textbook authors, as an example. If we do not have the required skills, our message will not reach you, the reader, in the form desired. Our success in communicating to you depends on our writing skills. In addition, any pre-existing ideas (attitudes) that we may have about numerous topics will affect how we communicate. For example, our attitudes about managerial ethics or the importance of managers to organizations influence our writing. Next, the amount of knowledge we have about a subject affects the message(s) we are transferring. We cannot communicate what we do not know; and if our knowledge is too extensive, our writing may not be understood by the readers either. Finally, the socio-cultural system in which we live influences us as communication senders. Our beliefs and values (all part of culture) act to influence what and how we communicate.

**MESSAGE**  The *message* itself can distort the communication process, regardless of the kinds of supporting tools or technologies used to convey it. A message is the actual physical product encoded by the source. It can be a written document, a speech, or even the gestures and facial expressions we make. The message is affected by the symbols used to transfer meaning (words, pictures, numbers, etc.), the content of the message itself, and the decisions that the sender makes in selecting and arranging both the symbols and the content. Noise can distort the communication process in any of these areas.

**CHANNEL**  The *channel* chosen to communicate the message also has the potential to be affected by noise. Whether it is a face-to-face conversation, an email message, or a company-wide memo, distortions can, and do, occur. Managers need to recognize that certain channels are more appropriate for certain messages. (Think back to how Cerner's CEO chose to communicate his frustration with his managers by email and whether that was an appropriate choice.) Obviously, if the office is on fire, a memo to convey that fact is inappropriate. If something is important, such as an employee's performance appraisal, a manager might want to use multiple channels—perhaps an oral review followed by a written letter summarizing the points. Using multiple channels to communicate a message decreases the potential for distortion. In general, the type of channel chosen will affect the extent

*Your instructor chooses to interact with all students via email, rather than hold office hours. How effective do you think email is as the channel of communication in this context?*

---

**message**
A purpose to be conveyed.

**encoding**
Converting a message into symbols.

**channel**
The medium a message travels along.

**decoding**
A receiver's translation of a sender's message.

**communication process**
The seven elements involved in transferring meaning from one person to another.

**noise**
Disturbances that interfere with the transmission, receipt, or feedback of a message.

to which accurate emotional expression can be communicated. For example, individuals often make stronger negative statements when using email than they would in a face-to-face conversation.[9] Additionally, individuals often give little thought to how their emails could be interpreted and assume that their intent will be readily apparent to the recipient, even though this is not always the case.[10]

**RECEIVER** The *receiver* is the individual to whom the message is directed. Before the message can be received, however, the symbols in it must be translated into a form that the receiver can understand. This step is called the *decoding* of the message. Just as the sender was limited by his or her skills, attitudes, knowledge, and socio-cultural system, so is the receiver. Just as the sender must be skillful in writing or speaking, so the receiver must be skillful in reading or listening. A person's knowledge influences his or her ability to receive. Moreover, the receiver's attitudes and socio-cultural background can distort the message. *Managing Workforce Diversity—The Communication Styles of Men and Women* on page 179 at the end of the chapter considers how men and women might hear messages differently.

**FEEDBACK LOOP** The final link in the communication process is a *feedback loop*. Feedback returns the message to the sender and provides a check on whether understanding has been achieved. Because feedback can be transmitted along the same types of channels as the original message, it faces the same potential for distortion. Many receivers forget their responsibility in the communication process: to give feedback. If you sit in a boring lecture but never discuss with the instructor ways that the delivery could be improved, you have not engaged in communication with your instructor.

When either the sender or the receiver fails to engage in the feedback process, the communication is effectively one-way communication. Two-way communication involves both talking and listening. Many managers communicate poorly because they fail to use two-way communication.

## Channels for Communicating Interpersonally

*Are there any guidelines on which communication channel is best for a given circumstance?*

Managers have a wide variety of communication channels from which to choose. Options include face-to-face, telephone, group meetings, formal presentations, memos, postal (snail) mail, fax machines, employee publications, bulletin boards, other company publications, audio- and videotapes, hotlines, email, computer conferences, voice mail, teleconferences, and videoconferences. All of these communication channels include oral or written symbols, or both. How do you know which to use? Managers can use 12 questions to help them evaluate appropriate communication channels for different circumstances.[11]

1. *Feedback.* How quickly can the receiver respond to the message?
2. *Complexity capacity.* Can the method effectively process complex messages?
3. *Breadth potential.* How many different messages can be transmitted using this method?
4. *Confidentiality.* Can communicators be reasonably sure their messages are received only by those for whom they are intended?
5. *Encoding ease.* Can the sender easily and quickly use this channel?
6. *Decoding ease.* Can the receiver easily and quickly decode messages?
7. *Time–space constraint.* Do senders and receivers need to communicate at the same time and in the same space?
8. *Cost.* How much does it cost to use this method?
9. *Interpersonal warmth.* How well does this method convey interpersonal warmth?
10. *Formality.* Does this method have the needed amount of formality?
11. *Scanability.* Does this method allow the message to be easily browsed or scanned for relevant information?
12. *Time of consumption.* Does the sender or receiver exercise the most control over when the message is dealt with?

Which channel a manager ultimately chooses should reflect the needs of the sender, the attributes of the message, the attributes of the channel, and the needs of the receiver. For example, if you need to communicate to an employee the changes being made in her job, face-to-face communication would be a better choice than a memo, because you want to be able to immediately address any questions and concerns that she might have. To find out more about face-to-face communication, see *Assess Your Skills—What's My Face-to-Face Communication Style?* on pages 176–177 at the end of the chapter.

We cannot leave the topic of interpersonal communication without looking at the role of **nonverbal communication**—that is, communication transmitted without words. Some of the most meaningful communications are neither spoken nor written. A loud siren or a red light at an intersection tells you something without words. When an instructor is teaching a class, she does not need words to know that her students are bored when their eyes glaze over or they begin to read the school newspaper in the middle of class. Similarly, when students start putting their papers, notebooks, and books away, the message is clear: Class time is just about over. The size of a person's office or the clothes he or she wears also convey messages to others. These examples are all forms of nonverbal communication. The best-known types of nonverbal communication are body language and verbal intonation.

**Body language** refers to gestures, facial expressions, and other body movements that convey meaning. A person frowning "says" something different from one who is smiling. Hand motions, facial expressions, and other gestures can communicate emotions or temperaments such as aggression, fear, shyness, arrogance, joy, and anger. Knowing the meaning behind someone's body movements and learning how to put forth your best body language can help you personally and professionally.[12] For example, studies indicate that those who maintain eye contact while speaking are viewed with more credibility than those whose eyes wander. People who make eye contact are also deemed more competent than those who do not.

*Does body language really affect how communication is received?*

Be aware that what is communicated nonverbally may be quite different from what is communicated verbally. A manager could say it is a good time to discuss a raise, but then keep looking at the clock. This nonverbal signal may indicate that the manager has other things to do right now. Thus, actions can often speak louder (and more accurately) than words.

A variety of popular books have been written to help interpret body language. However, use some care when interpreting nonverbal messages. For example, while it is often thought that crossing one's arms in front of one's chest shows resistance to a message, it might also mean the person is feeling cold.

**Verbal intonation** (more appropriately called *paralinguistics*) refers to the emphasis someone gives to words or phrases that conveys meaning. To illustrate how intonation can change the meaning of a message, consider the student who asks the instructor a question. The instructor replies, "What do you mean by that?" The student's reaction will vary, depending on the tone of the instructor's response. A soft, smooth vocal tone conveys interest and creates a different meaning from one that is abrasive and puts a strong emphasis on saying the last word. Most of us would view the first intonation as coming from someone sincerely interested in clarifying the student's concern, whereas the second suggests that the person is defensive or aggressive.

Remember that every oral communication also has a nonverbal message. This fact cannot be overemphasized. Why? Because the nonverbal component usually carries the greatest impact. People say, "It's not *what* you said, but *how* you said it." They respond to *how* something is said as well as *what* is said. Managers should keep this reality in mind as they communicate.

## Barriers to Effective Interpersonal Communication

In addition to the general distortions identified in the communication process, managers face other barriers to effective interpersonal communication.

---

**nonverbal communication**
Communication transmitted without words.

**body language**
Gestures, facial expressions, and other body movements that convey meaning.

**verbal intonation**
An emphasis given to words or phrases that conveys meaning.

Filtering, or shaping information to make it look good to the receiver, is not always intentional. John Seral, vice-president and chief information officer of GE Energy, noticed that "when the CEO asked how the quarter was looking, he got a different answer depending on whom he asked." Seral solved the problem by building a continuously updated database of the company's most important financial information. The database gives the CEO and also 300 company managers instant access to sales and operating figures on their PCs and BlackBerrys. Instead of dozens of analysts like the one pictured above compiling the information, the new system requires only six.

**FILTERING**  **Filtering** is the deliberate manipulation of information to make it appear more favourable to the receiver. For example, when an employee tells his or her manager what the manager wants to hear, that individual is filtering information. Does this happen much in organizations? Yes, it does! As information is communicated up through organizational levels, senders condense and synthesize it so those on top do not become overloaded with details. Those senders who are doing the condensing filter communications through their personal interests and their perceptions of what is important.

The extent of filtering tends to be a function of the number of vertical levels in the organization and the organizational culture. The more vertical levels an organization has, the more opportunities for filtering arise. As organizations become less dependent on strict hierarchical arrangements and instead use more collaborative, cooperative work arrangements, information filtering may become less of a problem. The ever-increasing use of email to communicate in organizations also reduces filtering, because intermediaries are bypassed and communication is more direct. Finally, the organizational culture encourages or discourages filtering by the type of behaviour it rewards. The more an organization rewards style and appearance, the more managers will be motivated to filter communications in their favour.

**EMOTIONS**  How a receiver feels when a message is received influences how he or she interprets it. You will often interpret the same message differently, depending on whether you are happy or upset. Distrust of the other person might lead to filtering. Extreme emotions are most likely to hinder effective communication. In such instances, we often disregard our rational and objective thinking processes and substitute emotional judgments. Try to avoid reacting to a message when you are upset because you are not likely to be thinking clearly.

**INFORMATION OVERLOAD**  A marketing manager goes on a week-long trip to Spain and does not have access to his email. On his return, he is faced with 1000 email messages. It is not possible to fully read and respond to each and every one of those messages without facing **information overload**—a situation in which information exceeds a person's processing capacity. Today's typical executive frequently complains of information overload. Email has added considerably to the number of hours worked per week, according to a recent study by Christina Cavanagh, professor of management communications at the University of Western Ontario's Richard Ivey School of Business.[13] Researchers calculate that 141 billion email messages circulate the globe each day. In 2001, that number was 5.1 billion email messages.[14] One researcher suggests that knowledge workers devote about 28 percent of their days to email.[15] The demands of keeping up with email, phone calls, faxes, meetings, and professional reading create an onslaught of data that is nearly impossible to process and assimilate. What happens when individuals have more information than they can sort and use? They tend to select out, ignore, pass over, or forget information. Or they may put off further processing until the overload situation is over. Regardless, the result is lost information and less effective communication.

**SELECTIVE PERCEPTION**  Individuals do not see reality; rather, they interpret what they see and call it "reality." These interpretations are based on an individual's needs, motivations, experience, background, and other personal characteristics. Individuals also project their interests and expectations when they are listening to others. For example, the employment interviewer who believes that young people spend too much time on leisure and social activities will have a hard time believing that young job applicants will work long hours.

**DEFENSIVENESS**  When people feel they are being threatened, they tend to react in ways that reduce their ability to achieve mutual understanding. They become defensive, engaging in behaviours such as verbally attacking others, making sarcastic remarks, being overly judgmental, and questioning others' motives.[16] When individuals interpret another's message as threatening, they often respond in ways that hinder effective communication.

**MENTAL MODELS**  We perceive the world in a certain way, and our mental model affects our communication. We form a frame of reference and assign certain meanings to a communication. This process might include filling in the missing pieces, which can limit the ability to receive the complete message.[17]

Previous experience with another person might also lead to communicators forming value judgments, A manager who feels his employee is always complaining may listen selectively to the employee or use negative nonverbal signals like frowning, causing the employee to become defensive.

**LANGUAGE**  Words have different meanings for different people. Age, education, and cultural background are three of the more obvious variables that influence the language a person uses and the definitions he or she gives to words. Television news anchor Peter Mansbridge and rap artist Nelly both speak English, but the language each uses is vastly different.

In an organization, employees typically come from diverse backgrounds and have different patterns of speech. Often employees who work for the same organization but in different departments have different **jargon**—specialized terminology or technical language that members of a group use to communicate among themselves. Keep in mind that while we may speak the same language, our use of that language is far from uniform. Senders tend to assume that the words and phrases they use mean the same to the receiver as they do to themselves. This assumption is incorrect and creates communication barriers. Knowing how each of us modifies the language would help minimize those barriers.

Should we look under "sushi" or "restaurants—Japanese" in the phone book when we decide we want raw fish for dinner? Paying attention to how people search for information online can give clearer insights into what organizations need to do to communicate more effectively.[18] The Internet has allowed Yellow Pages to better address user needs. "Now that we're seeing the trends through our online directories—the key words people use—it gives us a good idea of what they are looking for in the print book," said company spokeswoman Annie Marsolais.

Executives at Montreal-based Yellow Pages learned that they could produce better printed telephone directories by studying how online users searched for things such as sushi—demonstrating that customers and advertisers do not always think in the same categories.

---

**filtering**
The deliberate manipulation of information to make it appear more favourable to the receiver.

**information overload**
A situation in which information exceeds a person's processing capacity.

**jargon**
Specialized terminology or technical language that members of a group use to communicate among themselves.

**NATIONAL CULTURE** Communication differences can also arise from the different languages that individuals use to communicate and the national cultures they are part of. Interpersonal communication is not conducted the same way around the world. For example, compare countries that place a higher value on individualism (such as Canada) with countries in which the emphasis is on collectivism (such as Japan).[19]

In Canada, communication patterns tend to be oriented to the individual and clearly spelled out. Canadian managers rely heavily on memos, announcements, position papers, and other formal forms of communication to state their positions on issues. Supervisors may hoard information in an attempt to make themselves look good and as a way of persuading their employees to accept decisions and plans. For their own protection, lower-level employees often engage in this practice as well.

In collectivist countries, such as Japan, more interaction for its own sake takes place. The Japanese manager, in contrast to the Canadian manager, engages in extensive verbal consultation with subordinates over an issue first and draws up a formal document later to outline the agreement that was made. The Japanese value decisions by consensus, and open communication is an inherent part of the work setting. Also, face-to-face communication is encouraged.

Cultural differences can affect the way a manager chooses to communicate. These differences undoubtedly can be a barrier to effective communication if not recognized and taken into consideration.

Cultural differences also affect body language and such things as how closely people stand to each other. In China, it is not unusual for people to push to get ahead in queues and even step ahead of someone who has left too much space in line. In North America, there is an expectation that people will maintain a greater distance between one another and stay in their position in a lineup.

## TIPS FOR MANAGERS

### Communication with Diverse Individuals

* **Assume differences** until you establish similarity.

* Don't rush to evaluate—**observe** until you can confirm your interpretation.

* **Interpret** from the perspective of their culture instead of your own.

## Overcoming the Barriers

What can we do to overcome barriers to communication? The following suggestions should help make your interpersonal communication more effective.

**USE FEEDBACK** Many communication problems can be directly attributed to misunderstanding and inaccuracies. These problems are less likely to occur if individuals use the feedback loop in the communication process, either verbally or nonverbally.

If a speaker asks a receiver, "Did you understand what I said?" the response represents feedback. Good feedback should include more than yes-and-no answers. The speaker can ask a set of questions about a message to determine whether or not the message was received and understood as intended. Better yet, the speaker can ask the receiver to restate the message in his or her own words. If the speaker hears what was intended, understanding and accuracy should improve. Feedback also includes subtler methods than directly asking questions or having the receiver summarize the message. General comments can give the speaker a sense of the receiver's reaction to a message. To learn more about giving feedback, see *Assess Your Skills—How Good Am I at Giving Performance Feedback?* on pages 208–209 in Chapter 7.

Of course, feedback does not have to be conveyed in words. Actions *can* speak louder than words. A sales manager sends an email to his or her staff describing a new monthly sales report that all sales representatives will need to complete. If some of them do not turn in the new report, the sales manager has received feedback. This feedback suggests that the sales manager needs to clarify the initial communication. Similarly, when you are talking to people, you watch their eyes and look for other nonverbal clues to tell whether they are getting your message or not.

**SIMPLIFY LANGUAGE** Because language can be a barrier, managers should choose words and structure their messages in ways that will make those messages clear and understandable to the receiver. Remember, effective communication is achieved when a message is both received and *understood.* Understanding is improved by simplifying the language used in relation to the audience intended. For example, a hospital administrator should always try to communicate in clear, easily understood and specific terms. But the language used in messages to the emergency room staff needs to be purposefully different from that used with office employees. Jargon can facilitate understanding when used within a group of those who know what it means, but it can cause many problems when used outside that group. Being specific can also avert misunderstandings. Avoid phrases such as "as soon as possible" or "that may be hard to do," which may have completely different meanings for the two parties involved.

**LISTEN ACTIVELY** Do you know the difference between hearing and listening? When someone talks, we hear. But too often we do not listen. Listening is an active search for meaning, whereas hearing is passive. In listening, two people are engaged in thinking: the sender *and* the receiver.

Many of us are poor listeners. Why? Because careful listening is difficult. It is usually more satisfying to be on the offensive—that is, to be the one doing the talking. Listening, in fact, is often more tiring than talking. It demands intellectual effort. Unlike hearing, **active listening**, which is listening for full meaning without making premature judgments or interpretations, demands total concentration. The average person normally speaks at a rate of about 125 to 200 words per minute. However, the average listener can comprehend up to 400 words per minute.[20] The difference obviously leaves lots of idle time for the brain and opportunities for the mind to wander.

Active listening is enhanced by developing empathy with the sender—that is, by placing yourself in the sender's position. Because senders differ in attitudes, interests, needs, and expectations, empathy makes it easier to understand the actual content of a message. An empathetic listener reserves judgment on the message's content and carefully listens to what is being said. By organizing the information, the listener is better able to empathize with the sender. The goal is to improve your ability to receive the full meaning of a communication without having it distorted by premature judgments or interpretations. Other specific behaviours that active listeners demonstrate are listed in Exhibit 6-2. To learn

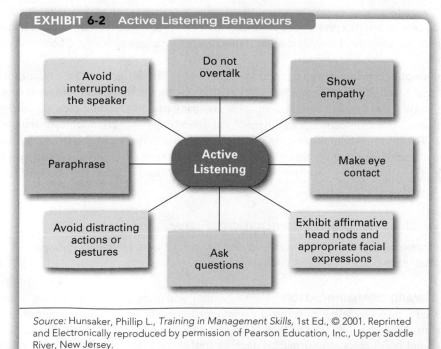

**EXHIBIT 6-2** Active Listening Behaviours

Avoid interrupting the speaker · Do not overtalk · Show empathy · Make eye contact · Exhibit affirmative head nods and appropriate facial expressions · Ask questions · Avoid distracting actions or gestures · Paraphrase · **Active Listening**

*Source:* Hunsaker, Phillip L., *Training in Management Skills,* 1st Ed., © 2001. Reprinted and Electronically reproduced by permission of Pearson Education, Inc., Upper Saddle River, New Jersey.

**active listening**
Listening for full meaning without making premature judgments or interpretations.

more about being an effective listener, see *Developing Your Interpersonal Skills—Active Listening* on pages 178–179 at the end of the chapter.

**CONSTRAIN EMOTIONS**   To assume that managers always communicate in a rational manner would be naive. We know that emotions can severely cloud and distort the transference of meaning. A manager who is emotionally upset over an issue is more likely to misconstrue incoming messages and fail to communicate clearly and accurately. What can the manager do? The simplest answer is to refrain from communicating until he or she has regained composure.

**WATCH NONVERBAL CUES**   If actions speak louder than words, it is important to watch your actions to make sure they align with and reinforce the words that go along with them. The effective communicator watches his or her nonverbal cues to ensure they convey the desired message.

## ORGANIZATIONAL COMMUNICATION

**6.3** **Describe** How does communication flow in organizations?

An understanding of managerial communication is not possible without looking at the fundamentals of organizational communication. In this section, we look at several important aspects of organizational communication including formal vs. informal communication, the direction of communication flow, and organizational communication networks.

### Formal vs. Informal Communication

Communication within an organization is often described as either formal or informal. **Formal communication** refers to communication that follows the official chain of command or is part of the communication required to do one's job. When a manager asks an employee to complete a task, he or she is communicating formally. So is the employee who brings a problem to the attention of his or her manager. Any communication that takes place within prescribed organizational work arrangements would be classified as formal.

**Informal communication** is communication that is not defined by the organization's structural hierarchy. When employees talk with each other in the lunchroom, as they pass in hallways, or as they are working out at the company exercise facility, they are engaging in informal communication. Employees form friendships and communicate with each other. The informal communication system fulfills two purposes in organizations: (1) it permits employees to satisfy their need for social interaction; (2) it can improve an organization's performance by creating alternative, and frequently faster and more efficient, channels of communication.

### Direction of Communication Flow

Organizational communication can flow downward, upward, laterally, or diagonally. Let us look at each of these types of communication.

**DOWNWARD COMMUNICATION**   Every morning and often several times a day, managers at UPS package delivery facilities gather employees for mandatory meetings that last precisely three minutes. During those 180 seconds, managers relay company announcements and go over local information such as traffic conditions or customer complaints. Each meeting ends with a safety tip. The three-minute meetings have proved so successful that many of the company's office employees are using the idea.[21]

Any communication that flows downward from managers to employees is **downward communication**. Downward communication is used to inform, direct, coordinate, and evaluate employees. When managers assign goals to their employees, they are using downward communication. Managers are also using downward communication when providing employees with job descriptions, informing them of organizational policies and procedures, pointing out problems that need attention, or evaluating and giving feedback on their performance. Downward communication can take place through any of the communication channels we described earlier. Managers can improve the quality of the feedback they give to employees if they follow the advice given in *Tips for Managers—Suggestions for Giving Feedback*.

**UPWARD COMMUNICATION**   Any communication that flows upward from employees to managers is **upward communication**. Managers rely on their employees for information. Reports are given to managers to inform them of progress toward goals and any current problems. Upward communication keeps managers aware of how employees feel about their jobs, their co-workers, and the organization in general. Managers also rely on it for ideas on how things can be improved. Some examples of upward communication include performance reports prepared by employees, suggestion boxes, employee attitude surveys, grievance procedures, manager–employee discussions, and informal group sessions in which employees have the opportunity to identify and discuss problems with their manager or even representatives of top management.

The extent of upward communication depends on the organizational culture. If managers have created a climate of trust and respect and use participative decision making or empowerment, there will be considerable upward communication as employees provide input to decisions. Ernst & Young encourages employees to evaluate the principals, partners, and directors on how well they create a positive work climate. A partner in the Montreal office was surprised to learn that people in her office found her a poor role model, and she took care to more carefully explain her actions as a result.[22] In a highly structured and authoritarian environment, upward communication still takes place, but is limited in both style and content.

# TIPS for MANAGERS

## Suggestions for Giving Feedback

Managers can use the following tips to give more effective feedback:

❋ Relate feedback to existing performance goals and clear expectations.

❋ Give **specific feedback** tied to observable behaviour or measurable results.

❋ Channel feedback toward **key result areas** and things the person can do something about.

❋ Give feedback **as soon as possible**.

❋ Give positive **feedback for improvement**, not just final results.

❋ Focus feedback on performance, not personalities.

❋ Speak directly and without judgment.

❋ Base feedback on accurate and credible information.[23]

## Suggestions for Receiving Feedback

Managers can use the following tips to receive feedback more effectively:

❋ Seek clarification and **specific examples**.

❋ Share your feelings about the message.

❋ Observe the **nonverbal cues** from the sender.

❋ Be open and avoid being **defensive**.

❋ Verify assumptions and **summarize**.

---

**formal communication**
Communication that follows the official chain of command or is part of the communication required to do one's job.

**informal communication**
Communication that is not defined by the organization's structural hierarchy.

**downward communication**
Communication that flows downward from managers to employees.

**upward communication**
Communication that flows upward from employees to managers.

**LATERAL COMMUNICATION** Communication that takes place among employees on the same organizational level is called **lateral communication**. In today's often chaotic and rapidly changing environment, lateral communication is frequently needed to save time and facilitate coordination. Cross-functional teams, for example, rely heavily on this form of communication. However, it can create conflicts if employees do not keep their managers informed about decisions they have made or actions they have taken.

**DIAGONAL COMMUNICATION** Communication that cuts across both work areas *and* organizational levels is **diagonal communication**. When an analyst in the credit department communicates directly with a regional marketing manager—note the different department and different organizational level—about a customer problem, they are engaging in diagonal communication. In the interest of efficiency and speed, diagonal communication can be beneficial. Email facilitates diagonal communication. In many organizations, any employee can communicate by email with any other employee, regardless of organizational work area or level. However, just as with lateral communication, diagonal communication has the potential to create problems if employees do not keep their managers informed.

## Organizational Communication Networks

The vertical and horizontal flows of organizational communication can be combined into a variety of patterns called **communication networks**. Exhibit 6-3 illustrates three common communication networks.

**TYPES OF COMMUNICATION NETWORKS** In the *chain* network, communication flows according to the formal chain of command, both downward and upward. The *wheel* network represents communication flowing between a clearly identifiable and strong leader and others in a work group or team. The leader serves as the hub through whom all communication passes. Finally, in the *all-channel* network, communication flows freely among all members of a work team.

As a manager, which network should you use? The answer depends on your goal. Exhibit 6-3 also summarizes the effectiveness of the various networks according to four criteria: speed, accuracy, the probability that a leader will emerge, and the importance of member satisfaction. One observation is immediately apparent: No single network is best for all situations. If you are concerned with high member satisfaction, the all-channel network is best; if having a strong and identifiable leader is important, the wheel facilitates this; and if accuracy is most important, the chain and wheel networks work best.

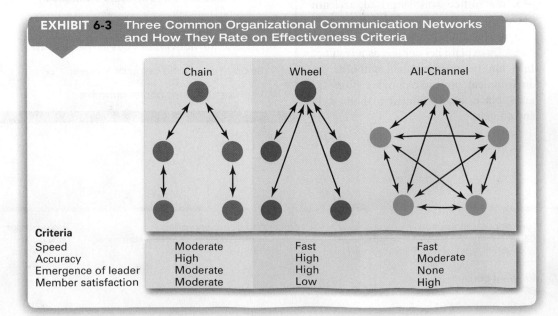

**EXHIBIT 6-3** Three Common Organizational Communication Networks and How They Rate on Effectiveness Criteria

|  | Chain | Wheel | All-Channel |
| --- | --- | --- | --- |
| **Criteria** | | | |
| Speed | Moderate | Fast | Fast |
| Accuracy | High | High | Moderate |
| Emergence of leader | Moderate | High | None |
| Member satisfaction | Moderate | Low | High |

**The Grapevine**  We cannot leave our discussion of communication networks without discussing the **grapevine**—the informal organizational communication network. The grapevine is active in almost every organization. Is it an important source of information? You bet! One survey reported that 75 percent of employees hear about matters first through rumours on the grapevine.[24]

What are the implications for managers? Certainly, the grapevine is an important part of any group or organization communication network and well worth understanding.[25] It identifies for managers those bewildering issues that employees consider important and anxiety-producing. It acts as both a filter and a feedback mechanism, picking up on the issues employees consider relevant. More importantly, from a managerial point of view, it *is* possible to analyze what is happening on the grapevine—what information is being passed, how information seems to flow along the grapevine, and which individuals seem to be key conduits of information on the grapevine. By being aware of the grapevine's flow and patterns, managers can stay on top of issues that concern employees and, in turn, can use the grapevine to disseminate important information. Since the grapevine cannot be eliminated, managers should "manage" it as an important information network.

Rumours that flow along the grapevine can never be entirely eliminated. Managers can minimize the negative consequences of rumours by limiting their range and impact. How? By communicating openly, fully, and honestly with employees, particularly in situations where employees may not like proposed or actual managerial decisions or actions. Open and honest communication with employees can affect the organization in various ways. A study by Watson Wyatt Worldwide concluded that effective communication "connects employees to the business, reinforces the organization's vision, fosters process improvement, facilitates change, and drives business results by changing employee behavior." For those companies that communicated effectively, total returns to shareholders were 57 percent higher over a five-year period than for companies with less effective communication. The study also showed that companies that were highly effective communicators were 20 percent more likely to report lower turnover rates.[26]

**Analyze**

# UNDERSTANDING INFORMATION TECHNOLOGY

**6.4**

**Explain**
How does information technology affect organizational communication?

Social networking websites such as Facebook and LinkedIn have become resources for employers seeking job candidates.[27] Companies large and small are using these resources to do research, form relationships, and fill positions. More than 350 companies broadcast their job listings to more than 10 million registered users of LinkedIn. A manager looking to fill a key position can use LinkedIn to view posted résumés and read an individual's postings, and can even "check out a competitor's site for potential candidates."

Brian Drum, president of executive search firm Drum Associates, uses social networking sites such as MySpace to see if there is any information about a job candidate's character that might suggest an

## Think About It

What impact does social media have on a company grapevine? Are there advantages to organizations in allowing employees to use social networking sites? If yes, do they outweigh the disadvantages?

---

**lateral communication**
Communication that takes place among employees on the same organizational level.

**diagonal communication**
Communication that cuts across both work areas and organizational levels.

**communication networks**
The variety of patterns of vertical and horizontal flows of organizational communication.

**grapevine**
The informal organizational communication network.

inability to perform reliably. "Sometimes all we find is meaningless chitchat," says Drum, "but once in a while we'll turn up something useful, like an unflattering picture or a piece of information that really shows what the person is made of."

Some businesses are not just using social networking sites for recruiting, however. They have also placed their own company profiles on such sites, allowing employees to interact with each other. They realize that a number of younger employees are using social networking sites, so they might as well encourage productive use of the medium.

Information technology is changing the way we live and work. Take the following three examples: In a number of countries, employees, managers, housewives, and teens use wireless interactive web phones to send email, surf the web, swap photos, and play computer games. Service technicians at Ajax, Ontario–based Pitney Bowes Canada use instant messaging rather than pagers, because "it's cheaper and it's two-way." The company knows when messages are received.[28] IBM's 398 000 employees regularly use instant messaging software for both communicating and workplace collaboration.[29]

The world of communication is not what it used to be. Managers are challenged to keep their organizations functioning smoothly while continually improving work operations *and* staying competitive, even though both the organization and the environment are changing rapidly. Although changing technology has been a significant source of the environmental uncertainty facing organizations, these same technological advances have enabled managers to coordinate the work efforts of employees in ways that can lead to increased efficiency and effectiveness. Information technology now touches every aspect of almost every company's business. The implications for the ways individuals communicate are profound.

## How Information Technology Affects Organizational Communication

Information technology has radically changed the way organizational members communicate. For example, it has

- significantly improved a manager's ability to monitor individual or team performance
- allowed employees to have more complete information to make faster decisions
- provided employees with more opportunities to collaborate and share information
- made it possible for employees to be fully accessible, any time, regardless of where they are

Several developments in information technology appear to have the most significant impact on current managerial communication: email, instant messaging, wikis and blogs, and social networking websites such as Facebook and LinkedIn.

*Have you ever emailed or instants messaged someone who was just in the next office? Does the reliance on technology make it harder or easier to communicate effectively with people?*

**EMAIL** Email is a quick and convenient way for organization members to share information and communicate. However, many people complain about email overload, and it is not always used effectively. A recent study found that opening nasty messages from your boss can harm your health over time.[30] While negative email messages from anyone had health consequences, those from superiors resulted in the most significant increase in a person's blood pressure.

Individuals should remember that email tends to be permanent, which means that a message sent in anger could come back to hurt the sender later on. Christina Cavanagh of the University of Western Ontario's Richard Ivey School of Business[31] suggests sleeping on angry emails before sending to be sure you are sending the right message. Email is also not necessarily private communication, and organizations often take the position that they have the right to read your email. To learn more about email communications protocols, see *Be the Consultant—Writing Better Emails* on page 180 at the end of the chapter.

**INSTANT MESSAGING** Instant messaging (IM) first became popular among teens and preteens who wanted to communicate online immediately with their friends. Now, it has moved to the workplace. IM provides immediate and collaborative communication and may replace the desk phone and email in the future.[32] However, IM has drawbacks. Unlike email, it requires users to be logged on to the organization's computer network in order to communicate with one another, which leaves the network open to security breaches. As a result, some organizations have limited which employees can use IM in the workplace.

**WIKIS AND BLOGS** Wikis and blogs are sites for open discussion and collaborative information sharing that have quickly replaced the company newsletter. Both can be used effectively internally and externally, allowing employees and customers to distribute and document information quickly.

**SOCIAL NETWORKING WEBSITES** Social networking websites such as Facebook, MySpace, and LinkedIn have drawn millions of subscribers who voluntarily post information about themselves that can be viewed by any other subscriber, unless the user deliberately sets privacy restrictions.

Employers and search firms are starting to check their clients' postings, and some even monitor employees to see if there is anything questionable in their character. Despite the public's concern that the government is not doing enough to protect individual privacy, many people feel free to post online information about themselves (flattering and unflattering), which is then readily accessible to anyone.

Some employers post job offerings on sites such as Facebook and LinkedIn; others post recruitment videos on sites such as YouTube. In a recent twist, some employers have conducted virtual interviews through *Second Life*, the online virtual community.[33] Job seekers create an "avatar," a computer-generated image that represents themselves, and then communicate with prospective employers through instant messaging. A recent virtual job fair on *Second Life* included employers Hewlett-Packard, Microsoft, Verizon, and Sodexho Alliance SA, a food and facilities-management services company.

Individuals who use websites such as Facebook may want to consider the lack of privacy such sites afford when it comes to employers and evaluations. Individuals may forget that once something has been posted to the web, it is difficult to erase. Although sharing photos of drunken partying may seem like a good idea, the portrait created might not leave a good impression on potential employers. As Deanna MacDougal, a partner at Toronto-based IQ Partners, notes, "If your potential employer Googles a name and sees your social life, that can be good but it can also hinder you. Even with password-protected sites, I think the youth need to be a little bit more careful." Geoff Bagg, president of Toronto-based The Bagg Group, adds: "I don't think you can segment your life and say, 'This is my private life and this is my work life.' They're all intertwined."[34]

Richard Branson, founder of the Virgin Group of Companies, discovered that employees were frustrated by delays in responses to text messages or faced a lack of understanding when lengthy emails were exchanged back and forth. Branson applies the Australian custom of "walkabout" as an effective management practice in the Virgin offices. He suggests engaging in random face-to-face interactions with employees to meet new people, get to know them better, and establish rapport. All of those things lead to better communication.[35]

## How Information Technology Affects Organizations

Employees—working in teams or as individuals—need information to make decisions and do their work. After describing the communication capabilities managers have at their disposal, it is clear that technology *can* significantly affect the way that organization members communicate, share information, and do their work. Information technology also creates opportunities for organizations. For example, colleges and universities now have the capability to offer online courses and degrees. Over time, these courses could decrease the number of students taught in face-to-face settings, while increasing the overall number of students who can be reached because of online methods of teaching.

Communication and the exchange of information among organization members are no longer constrained by geography or time. Collaborative work efforts among widely dispersed individuals and teams, information sharing, and the integration of decisions and work throughout an entire organization have the potential to increase organizational efficiency and effectiveness. While the economic benefits of information technology are obvious, managers must not forget to address the psychological drawbacks.[36] For example, what is the psychological cost of an employee being always accessible? Will there be increased pressure for employees to "check in" even during their off hours? How important is it for employees to separate their work lives and their personal lives? While these questions have no easy answers, they are issues that managers will have to face.

The widespread use of voice mail and email at work has led to some ethical concerns as well. These forms of communication are not necessarily private, because employers have access to them. The federal Privacy Act (which protects the privacy of individuals and provides individuals with the right to access personal information about themselves) and the Access to Information Act (which allows individuals to access government information) apply to all federal government departments, most federal agencies, and some federal Crown corporations. However, many private sector employees are not covered by privacy legislation. Only Quebec's Privacy Act applies to the entire private sector. Managers need to clearly convey to employees policies on such things as personal Internet and email use, and the extent to which their communications will be monitored.

## How Businesses Can Use Social Media

Social media is a peer-to-peer network based on some type of user profile, which allows people to connect with others who may share their interests, activities, or even contacts.

Practise

Google+ took 16 days to obtain 10 million users, a feat that took Facebook almost two years.[37] Why? Google+ gives users the ability to share status updates, photos, and contents within different "circles" of their choosing, such as business versus family. It also provides "hangouts," a new way to use social networking for video conferencing that may become a common practice for businesses. "Search Your World" is a social media quantum leap for the search engine, combining social media data as part of Google search queries, which will make search engine optimization (SEO) more challenging for businesses not embracing Google+.[38]

Because of this link, social networks can be created that allow companies to communicate with audiences in a much more personal way. Social media can play an integral role in engaging employees, consumers, suppliers, partners, and even investors. Building relationships and brand loyalty through social media can be faster and lower in cost than through traditional marketing.[39]

Organizations that use social media for employees to interact with management can make internal communication more stimulating, strengthening the culture of the organization and loyalty to the brand.[40]

Molson Coors used an internal blogging site (Yammer) to significantly improve its employee engagement. In Toronto, Yammer sold toques for Raising the Roof, resulting in $125 000 raised for the homeless. Molson Coors also created the Every Drop, Every Ripple campaign to encourage employees to pledge to reduce their personal water usage. The pledges were then shared socially on Facebook and Twitter.[41]

A sound social media strategy should be based on clear metrics benchmarks in terms of sales, brand awareness, and customer service.[42] Organizations need to plan in advance for criticisms and complaints, so that responses are quick and show that the company takes its customers' concerns seriously. A little preplanning can help turn a negative experience around when necessary.[43] See *Tips for Managers—Getting Started with Social Media* on how a business can get social media up and running.

## TIPS FOR MANAGERS

### Getting Started with Social Media

❋ Explore. What platforms are your customers and employees using?

❋ Listen. Use Google, Twitter, and Facebook to see what people are saying about your industry, your company, and your products.

❋ Create a strategy. What business goals can social media support?

❋ Choose the right platform. B2B customers are more likely to be reached via blogs, LinkedIn, and Twitter, while YouTube and Facebook are better for contact with consumers.

❋ Offer unique content. Provide insight on hot topics, VIP offers, or special deals.

❋ Manage the conversation. Nurture your brand ambassadors and follow up on all feedback.

❋ Coordinate channels. Ensure your social media platforms are linked with your website and other communication channels.

❋ Think mobile. Everything needs to be accessible on a mobile device.

❋ Build relationships. Stay connected in real time and build gradually.

*Source:* Debbie Dimoff, Vice President, Consulting, PricewaterhouseCoopers (PwC).[44]

Employers have now begun to use social media in the collective bargaining process to keep employees updated and to quash any false rumours. Unions use social media to gain support and to keep their members aware of what is happening on their side. "In collective bargaining . . . a lot of employers are using social media or controlled websites about the status of collective bargaining," says Len Polsky, a Calgary-based employment lawyer with MacPherson Leslie and Tyerman LLP. Polsky recalls one case where the union leadership negotiated agreements that the membership took issue with. "Had they taken advantage of social media in a greater way ... maybe the leadership could have aligned itself better with the members' thinking." [45]

# 6 Review and Apply

## Summary of Learning Objectives

**6.1 What are the functions of communication?**
Communication serves four major functions: control, motivation, emotional expression, and information. In the control function, communication sets out the guidelines for behaviour. Communication motivates by clarifying to employees what is to be done, how well they are doing, and what can be done to improve performance if it is not up to par. Communication provides an opportunity to express feelings and also fulfills social needs. Finally, communication provides the information to get things done in organizations.

Social media has allowed employers to learn more about potential employees, and some organizations have set up Facebook sites for employees to communicate with each other.

**6.2 Why does communication break down?** When a message passes between a sender and a receiver, it needs to be converted into symbols (called encoding) and passed to the receiver by some channel. The receiver translates (decodes) the sender's message. Feedback returns the message to the sender and provides a check on whether understanding has been achieved. At any point in this process, communication can be distorted by noise. Because feedback can be transmitted along the same types of channels as the original message, it faces the same potential for distortion. A variety of other factors can also affect whether the message is interpreted correctly, including the degree of filtering, the sender's or receiver's emotional state, and the degree of information overload (whether too much information is being sent).

With face-to-face communication, the receiver gains additional information through body language. The rise of online communication, through tools such as email and social networking sites such as Facebook, means that communication is often more ambiguous. It also becomes more difficult to know whether too much information has been revealed, because feedback mechanisms may not be as direct.

**6.3 How does communication flow in organizations?**
Communication can be formal or informal. Formal communication follows the official chain of command or is part of the communication required to do one's job. Informal communication is not defined by the organization's structural hierarchy. Communication can flow downward, upward, laterally to those at the same organizational level, or diagonally, cutting across both work areas and organizational levels.

Communication can also flow through networks and through the grapevine.

**6.4 How does information technology affect organizational communication?** Information technology allows managers and employees more access to each other and to customers and clients. It provides further opportunities for monitoring, as well as a greater ability to share information. Information technology also increases flexibility and responsiveness.

Although some workplaces have banned Facebook use, other employers have found ways to use Facebook as a source of information on job candidates and employees, and as a business communication tool. Many organizations are exploring how to benefit from Facebook, knowing that their younger employees are already widely using the social networking site.

### SNAPSHOT SUMMARY

**6.1 Understanding Communication**
What Is Communication?
Functions of Communication

**6.2 Interpersonal Communication**
How Distortions Can Happen in Interpersonal Communication
Channels for Communicating Interpersonally
Barriers to Effective Interpersonal Communication
Overcoming the Barriers

**6.3 Organizational Communication**
Formal vs. Informal Communication
Direction of Communication Flow
Organizational Communication Networks

**6.4 Understanding Information Technology**
How Information Technology Affects Organizational Communication
How Information Technology Affects Organizations
How Businesses Can Use Social Media

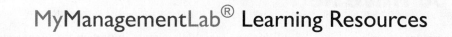

# MyManagementLab® Learning Resources

## Resources

▼ **Explore and enhance your understanding of key chapter topics through the following online resources:**

- Student PowerPoints
- Audio Summary of Chapter
- ROLLS
- CBC Videos for Part 3
- MySearchLab

▶ Visit the **Study Plan** area to test your progress with **Pre-Tests** and **Post-Tests**.

▼ **Build on your knowledge and practise real-world applications using the following online activities:**

## Interpret  ▶

- Opening Case Activity: Functions of Communication
- Review and Apply: Solutions to Interpret section questions and activities
- Glossary Flashcards

## Analyze ▶

- Opening Case Activity: Interpersonal and Everyday Interactions
- Review and Apply: Solutions to Analyze section questions and activities
- Self-Assessment Library

## Practise ▶

- Opening Case Activity: Impact of Communications in Today's Business
- Review and Apply: Solutions to Practice section questions and activities
- BizSkills Simulation: Business Communications
- Decision Making Simulation: Communication

# Interpret What You Have Read

1. What are the four functions of communication?
2. What steps can you take to make interpersonal communication more effective?
3. What can managers do to help determine which communication channel to use in a given circumstance?
4. Describe the barriers to effective interpersonal communication. How can they be overcome?
5. Which do you think is more important for a manager: speaking accurately or listening actively? Why?
6. How has social media changed communication?
7. How has information technology enhanced a manager's communication effectiveness?

# Analyze What You Have Read

1. "Ineffective communication is the fault of the sender." Do you agree or disagree with this statement? Explain your position.
2. Describe why effective communication can happen even without agreement between the communicating parties.
3. "As technology improves, employees will be working more, be more accessible to employers, and be suffering from information overload." Do you agree or disagree with this statement? Explain your position.
4. How might a manager use the grapevine to his or her advantage? Support your response.
5. Using what you have learned about active listening in this chapter, would you describe yourself as a good listener? Are there any areas in which you are deficient? If so, how could you improve your listening skills?

# Assess Your Skills

## WHAT'S MY FACE-TO-FACE COMMUNICATION STYLE?

For each of the following statements, circle the level of agreement or disagreement that you personally feel:[46]

1 = Strongly Disagree   2 = Moderately Disagree   3 = Neither Agree nor Disagree   4 = Moderately Agree
5 = Strongly Agree

| | |
|---|---|
| 1. I am comfortable with all varieties of people. | 1 2 3 4 5 |
| 2. I laugh easily. | 1 2 3 4 5 |
| 3. I readily express admiration for others. | 1 2 3 4 5 |
| 4. What I say usually leaves an impression on people. | 1 2 3 4 5 |
| 5. I leave people with an impression of me which they definitely tend to remember. | 1 2 3 4 5 |
| 6. To be friendly, I habitually acknowledge verbally others' contributions. | 1 2 3 4 5 |
| 7. I have some nervous mannerisms in my speech. | 1 2 3 4 5 |
| 8. I am a very relaxed communicator. | 1 2 3 4 5 |
| 9. When I disagree with somebody, I am very quick to challenge them. | 1 2 3 4 5 |
| 10. I can always repeat back to a person exactly what was meant. | 1 2 3 4 5 |
| 11. The sound of my voice is very easy to recognize. | 1 2 3 4 5 |
| 12. I leave a definite impression on people. | 1 2 3 4 5 |
| 13. The rhythm or flow of my speech is sometimes affected by nervousness. | 1 2 3 4 5 |
| 14. Under pressure I come across as a relaxed speaker. | 1 2 3 4 5 |
| 15. My eyes reflect exactly what I am feeling when I communicate. | 1 2 3 4 5 |
| 16. I dramatize a lot. | 1 2 3 4 5 |

17. Usually, I deliberately react in such a way that people know that I am listening to them.      1 2 3 4 5

18. Usually, I do not tell people much about myself until I get to know them well.      1 2 3 4 5

19. Regularly I tell jokes, anecdotes, and stories when I communicate.      1 2 3 4 5

20. I tend to gesture constantly when I communicate.      1 2 3 4 5

21. I am an extremely open communicator.      1 2 3 4 5

22. I am vocally a loud communicator.      1 2 3 4 5

23. In arguments I insist on very precise definitions.      1 2 3 4 5

24. In most social situations I generally speak very frequently.      1 2 3 4 5

25. I like to be strictly accurate when I communicate.      1 2 3 4 5

26. Because I have a loud voice, I can easily break into a conversation.      1 2 3 4 5

27. Often I physically and vocally act out when I want to communicate.      1 2 3 4 5

28. I have an assertive voice.      1 2 3 4 5

29. I readily reveal personal things about myself.      1 2 3 4 5

30. I am dominant in social situations.      1 2 3 4 5

31. I am very argumentative.      1 2 3 4 5

32. Once I get wound up in a heated discussion, I have a hard time stopping myself.      1 2 3 4 5

33. I am always an extremely friendly communicator.      1 2 3 4 5

34. I really like to listen very carefully to people.      1 2 3 4 5

35. Very often I insist that other people document or present some kind of proof for what they are arguing.      1 2 3 4 5

36. I try to take charge of things when I am with people.      1 2 3 4 5

37. It bothers me to drop an argument that is not resolved.      1 2 3 4 5

38. In most social situations I tend to come on strong.      1 2 3 4 5

39. I am very expressive nonverbally in social situations.      1 2 3 4 5

40. The way I say something usually leaves an impression on people.      1 2 3 4 5

41. Whenever I communicate, I tend to be very encouraging to people.      1 2 3 4 5

42. I actively use a lot of facial expressions when I communicate.      1 2 3 4 5

43. I very frequently exaggerate verbally to emphasize a point.      1 2 3 4 5

44. I am an extremely attentive communicator.      1 2 3 4 5

45. As a rule, I openly express my feelings and emotions.      1 2 3 4 5

**SCORING KEY**

**Step 1:** Reverse the score on items 7, 13, and 18 (1 = 5, 2 = 4, 3 = 3, etc.).

**Step 2:** Add together the scores on the following items to get a final total for each dimension. (Not every item is included in determining the dimensions.)

1. 24, 30, 36, 38 = _____ (Dominant)
2. 16, 19, 27, 43 = _____ (Dramatic)
3. 9, 31, 32, 37 = _____ (Contentious)
4. 15, 20, 39, 42 = _____ (Animated)
5. 4, 5, 12, 40 = _____ (Impression-leaving)
6. 7, 8, 13, 14 = _____ (Relaxed)
7. 10, 17, 34, 44 = _____ (Attentive)
8. 18, 21, 29, 45 = _____ (Open)
9. 3, 6, 33, 41 = _____ (Friendly)

### ANALYSIS AND INTERPRETATION

This scale measures the following dimensions of communication style:

Dominant—Tends to take charge of social interactions.

Dramatic—Manipulates and exaggerates stories and uses other stylistic devices to highlight content.

Contentious—Is argumentative.

Animated—Uses frequent and sustained eye contact and many facial expressions and gestures often.

Impression-leaving—Is remembered because of the communicative stimuli that are projected.

Relaxed—Is relaxed and void of nervousness.

Attentive—Makes sure that the other person knows that he or she is being listened to.

Open—Is conversational, expansive, affable, convivial, gregarious, unreserved, somewhat frank, definitely extroverted, and obviously approachable.

Friendly—Ranges from being unhostile to showing deep intimacy.

For each dimension, your score will range from 5 to 25. The higher your score for any dimension, the more that dimension characterizes your communication style. When you review your results, consider to what degree your scores aid or hinder your communication effectiveness. High scores for being attentive and open would almost always be positive qualities. A high score for contentiousness, on the other hand, could be a negative in many situations.

---

**More Self-Assessments**

To learn more about your skills, abilities, and interests, take the following self-assessments on the MyManagementLab®:

- II.A.2.—How Good Are My Listening Skills?

- III.A.3.—How Good Am I at Giving Performance Feedback? (This exercise also appears in Chapter 7 on pages 208–209.)

---

# Practise What You Have Learned

## DILEMMA

Think of a person with whom you have had difficulty communicating. Using the barriers to effective interpersonal communication as a start, analyze what has gone wrong with the communication process with that person. What can be done to improve communication? To what extent did sender and receiver problems contribute to the communication breakdown?

## BECOMING A MANAGER

- Practise debating with another student using a topic about which you both feel strongly but disagree (money, love, politics, ethics, etc.).
- Give your debate an "effective communication" rule: Before a person speaks, he or she must summarize what the other person just said and meant. If the sender does not agree with the summary, the receiver must try again.
- Pay attention to your own and others' nonverbal communication. Learn to notice the cues.

## DEVELOPING YOUR INTERPERSONAL SKILLS: ACTIVE LISTENING

### ABOUT THE SKILL

The ability to be an effective listener is often taken for granted. Hearing is often confused with listening, but hearing is merely recognizing sound vibrations. Listening is making sense of what we hear and requires paying attention, interpreting, and remembering. Effective listening is active rather than passive. Active listening is hard work and requires you to "get inside" the speaker's head in order to understand the communication from his or her point of view.

### STEPS IN DEVELOPING THE SKILL

You can be more effective at active listening if you use the following nine suggestions:[47]

1. MAKE EYE CONTACT. Making eye contact with the speaker focuses your attention, reduces the likelihood that you will be distracted, and encourages the speaker.

2. EXHIBIT AFFIRMATIVE NODS AND APPROPRIATE FACIAL EXPRESSIONS. The effective active listener shows interest in what is being said through nonverbal signals. Affirmative nods and appropriate facial expressions that signal interest in what is being said, when added to eye contact, convey to the speaker that you are really listening.

3. SHOW EMPATHY. Acknowledge the feelings of the speaker. The effective active listener uses phrases such as "You seem frustrated . . ." or "It sounds like you are feeling . . ."

4. AVOID DISTRACTING ACTIONS OR GESTURES. The other side of showing interest is avoiding actions that suggest your mind is elsewhere. When listening, do not look at your watch, shuffle papers, play with your pencil, or engage in similar distractions.

5. **ASK QUESTIONS.** The serious active listener analyzes what he or she hears and asks questions. This behaviour provides clarification, ensures understanding, and assures the speaker you are really listening.

6. **PARAPHRASE.** Restate in your own words what the speaker has said. The effective active listener uses phrases such as "What I hear you saying is . . ." or "Do you mean . . .?" Paraphrasing is an excellent control device to check whether or not you are listening carefully, as well as a control for accuracy of understanding.

7. **AVOID INTERRUPTING THE SPEAKER.** Let the speaker complete his or her thoughts before you try to respond. Do not try to second-guess where the speaker's thoughts are going. When the speaker is finished, you will know it.

8. **DO NOT OVERTALK.** Most of us would rather speak our own ideas than listen to what others say. While talking might be more fun and silence might be uncomfortable, you cannot talk and listen at the same time. The good active listener recognizes this fact and does not overtalk.

9. **MAKE SMOOTH TRANSITIONS BETWEEN THE ROLES OF SPEAKER AND LISTENER.** In most work situations, you are continually shifting back and forth between the roles of speaker and listener. The effective active listener makes transitions smoothly from speaker to listener and back to speaker.

**PRACTISING THE SKILL**

In student teams, develop a response to the following vignette that demonstrates active listening techniques such as showing empathy, asking questions, and paraphrasing.

You are the leader of a team that is halfway through completing a major class assignment. One of the team members asks to meet with you after class. She is very agitated when she sits down with you, but she manages to remain polite and fairly calm. "You allocate work to the team in a very unfair manner," she says. "Your deadlines are unrealistic, and you have assigned work that is unclear and unrealistic for us to complete. The whole team is angry with you, but no one wants to say anything since you are very close with the professor. This team project is not working and you have to change it." [48]

# MANAGING WORKFORCE DIVERSITY: THE COMMUNICATION STYLES OF MEN AND WOMEN

"You don't understand what I'm saying, and you never listen!" "You're making a big deal out of nothing." Have you said (or heard) these statements or ones like them when communicating with friends of the opposite sex?

Most of us probably have. Research shows that men and women tend to have different communication styles.[49] Let us look more closely at these differing styles and the problems that can arise, and try to suggest ways to minimize the barriers.

Deborah Tannen, professor of linguistics at Georgetown University, has studied the ways that men and women communicate, and reports some interesting differences. According to her research, men use talk to emphasize status, while women use it to create connection. Tannen states that communication between the sexes can be a continual juggling act to balance our conflicting needs for intimacy, which emphasizes closeness and commonality, and independence, which emphasizes separateness and differences. No wonder communication problems arise! Women hear and speak a language of connection and intimacy. Men hear and speak a language of status and independence. For many men, conversations are merely a way to preserve independence and maintain status in a hierarchical social order. For many women, however, conversations are a way to negotiate closeness and seek out support and confirmation. Let us look at a few examples of what Tannen has described.

Men frequently complain that women talk on and on about their problems. Women, however, criticize men for not listening. What is happening? When a man hears a woman talking about a problem, he frequently asserts his desire for independence and control by offering solutions. Many women, in contrast, view conversing about a problem as a way to promote closeness. The woman talks about a problem to gain support and connection, not to get the man's advice.

Here is another example: Men are often more direct than women in conversation. A man might say, "I think you're wrong on that point." A woman might say, "Have you looked at the marketing department's research report on that issue?" The implication in the woman's comment is that the report will point out the error. Men frequently misread women's indirectness as "covert" or "sneaky," but women are not as concerned as men with the status and one-upmanship that directness often creates.

Finally, men often criticize women for seeming to apologize all the time. Men tend to see the phrase "I'm sorry" as a sign of weakness because they interpret the phrase to mean the woman is accepting blame, when he may know she is not to blame. The woman also knows she is not at fault. She is typically using "I'm sorry" to express regret: "I know you must feel bad about this and I do too." Women learn to listen with empathy, which helps them maintain collaborative relationships.

What differences do you see in men's and women's communication styles? Have these differences ever gotten in the way of working together? Describe some of the issues you have encountered.

# Team Exercises

## 3BL: THE TRIPLE BOTTOM LINE

Ethical employers have been cautious about using Facebook and other social media sites for candidate screening due to legal restrictions against accessing information about a candidate's religious beliefs, sexual orientation, and health. However, many employers have been regularly accessing the social media profiles of job seekers to determine whether the candidate would fit in with their company, often rejecting candidates with inappropriate photos and status updates. This practice became a hot-button topic in the United States in March 2012 when the House of Representatives voted down an amendment that would have prohibited employers demanding access to Facebook accounts.

HR practitioners who use social media correctly find it to be a powerful candidate screening tool. Expanding into new mediums can really boost a company's recruitment and selection techniques. LinkedIn can be easily adapted to fit a company's strategy and is becoming the largest business network online. It and other sites like foursquare, Klout, and Google+ provide immediate access for recruitment and sourcing. These sites also supply employers with useful reference checking data, making it easier to verify the authenticity of references. The bigger sites like Facebook and LinkedIn allow employers to network and build relationships through referrals and shared contacts.

### THINKING STRATEGICALLY ABOUT 3BL

Social media is a terrific recruitment and selection tool when used ethically. Be aware, however, that it may not always predict future job behaviours. What social media can do is give managers some valuable information about a candidate's fit to their company.[50]

## WRITING BETTER EMAILS

### PURPOSE

To learn when to use the active or passive voice, when to be direct or indirect, and how to avoid jargon in emails.

| Active | Passive |
|---|---|
| • "The committee determined that the report was inconclusive." <br><br> • "I am writing the report." <br><br> • "Please contact Brian to discuss his concerns about your meeting." | • "It was determined by the committee that the report was inconclusive." <br><br> • "The report is being written by me." <br><br> • "It is suggested that your meeting with Brian was less than effective and that it would be appropriate that the matter had further discussions." |
| Direct | Indirect |
| • "I plan to reassign you to one of two different projects. Please let me know if you have any preferences on which application you would like to develop." <br><br> • "We have selected another candidate for the promotion. Thank you for your consideration." | • "We hope to develop two new applications this year. To best use your skills, I plan to reassign all team members to one of two different projects. Please let me know if you have any preferences." <br><br> • "Thank you for your hard work this quarter. Our selection of a candidate for promotion was taken very seriously. We considered your application very carefully, but another candidate was selected." |
| Clear | Jargon |
| • "When is the proposal expected?" <br><br> • "Be creative in meeting the target and make sure we're well organized." <br><br> • "Regarding" <br><br> • "To be clear" | • "What is the ETD of the RFP?" <br><br> • "Push the envelope; get our ducks in a row." <br><br> • "With reference to" <br><br> • "To tell the truth" |

### PROCEDURE

Form groups of five or six individuals. Prepare emails that are active, direct, and clear for each of the following four scenarios.

1. The company has been approached by a large competitor who wishes to acquire the company. Staff are worried the takeover might result in some employee layoffs within the next three months.

2. A customer has complained about an employee via email. You have investigated and found the complaint justified. How do you convey this to the employee?

3. Bonus decisions have been made. Not all individuals will receive a bonus.

4. An employee has gone above and beyond in meeting a customer's request. You want to acknowledge the employee's efforts.

# BE THE CONSULTANT: NAVIGATING THE WORKPLACE COMMUNICATION PROTOCOLS IN A TECHNOLOGY AGE

In 2000, faxing and letters were commonplace forms of communication in the office setting. Technology has advanced rapidly and changed the rules, but maintaining social protocols remains important. Poor etiquette and the excessive use of PDAs (personal digital assistants) and cell-phones have led to the term "cell-fishness." Here are some tips on how to be professional in the age of thumb typing and finger swiping.[51]

## SOCIAL MEDIA

- Do not gripe or jab at your company, even as a joke—the digital record is permanent.
- Accept Facebook requests from your superiors but not your subordinates.
- Keep your LinkedIn network primarily for business purposes.

## EMAIL

- Be discriminating with the urgent flag.
- Stay away from u, ttyl, 2nite, and other email slang.
- Avoid the one word responses "ok" and "thanks."
- Reply-all is not your friend.

## TEXTING/IM

- Forget the emoticons.
- Do not text or use IM for business purposes unless these forms of communication are a big part of your client's or company's culture—they are too informal.

- Keep in mind that throwing a "jk" after a jab does not make it less of a jab.

## VOICE MAIL

- Use office voice mail mainly to let people know how they can find you.
- Leave messages longer than the 5 second "Hey it's me, call me back" and shorter than 30 seconds.
- Be aware that caller ID is reducing the need for messages—more and more people do not retrieve their messages.

## TELEPHONE

- Consider the telephone when you need to deal with personal, complex, or multiple issues—voice can help you detect tone.
- Ensure that the background noise does not overwhelm the conversation.
- Never, never, ever call in the bathroom.

## FACE TO FACE

- Set your phone on vibrate unless you must receive a very important call, in which case ask the person if it is all right to leave the phone on.
- Do not check your phone every two minutes when you are with someone face to face.
- Do not be "cell-fish"—have an uninterrupted, focused conversation.

## BUSINESS CARDS

- Hand out your card only on request—it is not candy.
- Keep your hashtag, blog, and url off the card—just give basic contact information.

# Business Cases

## CISCO CANADA

Cisco Canada has embedded social media within its broader marketing strategy to drive brand awareness and engage customers and partners. Cisco started at the top with a social media governance strategy and provides ongoing social media training to staff. It created a team to manage content and its social media community. The team runs separately, but is integrated with public relations and marketing in order to leverage best practices.[52]

Tim Husband, digital marketing manager at Cisco Canada, emphasizes the importance of a local angle on its shared global content. "What's really important for us in Canada is that we're driving Canadian relevant content." [53] The Cisco road show is held in four cities across the country, and social media allows managers to engage customers before, during, and after the events. Social media also serves to enhance Cisco's corporate culture and recruiting efforts. Results from the 2011 Cisco Connected World Technology report suggests that college students would either choose not to work with a company that banned access to social media or would not follow the policy.[54]

Cisco has launched more visual collaboration solutions to support the increasing business needs for videoconferencing and the growth of the bring-your-own-device (BYOD) trend.[55] Richard McLeod, Cisco's senior director of business development, told Network World Canada that 90 percent of enterprises have begun or plan BYOD initiatives. By 2015, 200 million workers globally will take advantage of company-supplied desktop videoconferencing solutions.[56] The mobile environment and social media have Cisco envisioning a world where a user can move from IM to voice to video with a click or a swipe, both on a network and in the cloud.

Other than the number of fans and followers, what metrics can Cisco use to track the success of its social media campaigns? How can Cisco use social media for market intelligence and discovering sales opportunities?

# Business Cases

## SMALL BUSINESS SOCIAL MEDIA SUCCESS STORIES

Stanfield's underwear in Nova Scotia used social media to connect an established and older brand with a new generation. The family-run business has been churning out reliable underwear (a.k.a. tighty whities) but was not connecting with millennials. Stanfield's gamble was an online reality show stunt with an actor named Mark McIntyre who was confined to his apartment, wearing nothing all day but a fresh pair of the company's underwear. For every Facebook "like" that Stanfield's received, the company pledged $1 to the Canadian Cancer Society. As President Jon Stanfield notes, the stunt was a natural fit for a company in the business of protecting its customers' family jewels. CBC and other media were very receptive to the campaign, which led to 50 000 likes on Facebook, advertising awards, and people talking about Stanfield's underwear in a new and exciting way.

Wille Cromack, a principal with John Henry Bikes of North Vancouver, was skeptical about how Facebook and Twitter could be used to successfully retain clients and engage new customers. In keeping with the store's mission statement, Live to Ride, Cromack views the local community as a collection of clients. The company hosts events, biking excursions, and adventure camps for kids to build that community. However, a company Facebook and Twitter presence is boosting the company's community-building efforts. Its 12 000 Twitter followers are a "virtual club." Customer photos are posted on Facebook, and the client-community is further enhanced when customers tweet about their experiences.

Pythian, an Ottawa database services and consulting company, has succeeded in using social-media channels to bring skilled people to its doors, cutting out costly headhunters and recruiting agencies. Pythian needs highly skilled programmers and taps into them through its company blog and social media site LinkedIn. Employees contribute to Pythian's popular tech blog, a discussion about the database management sector that features real people and their stories in order to forge a real connection with readers. Pythian uses the blog and employee LinkedIn profiles to generate potential recruits. It has over 6000 participants in two LinkedIn groups used for networking and database discussions.

Pick a small business that you know well and indicate how you would use social media to help it grow its business. What kind of information would the business owner need to make a decision on your recommendation? How could a local food bank use social media effectively?

*Source:* Ivor Tossell and John Lorinc, "Six Canadian Companies Leading the Social Media Charge", *Globe and Mail*, May 3, 2012.

# CHAPTER 7 Human Resource Management

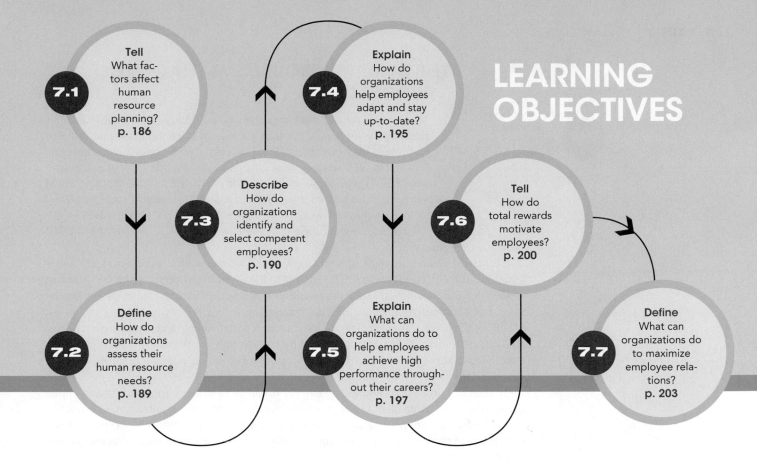

# LEARNING OBJECTIVES

**7.1** **Tell** What factors affect human resource planning? p. 186

**7.4** **Explain** How do organizations help employees adapt and stay up-to-date? p. 195

**7.3** **Describe** How do organizations identify and select competent employees? p. 190

**7.6** **Tell** How do total rewards motivate employees? p. 200

**7.2** **Define** How do organizations assess their human resource needs? p. 189

**7.5** **Explain** What can organizations do to help employees achieve high performance throughout their careers? p. 197

**7.7** **Define** What can organizations do to maximize employee relations? p. 203

The Calgary Chamber of Voluntary Organizations (CCVO) is the largest and strongest voluntary sector chamber in Canada and recently developed *A Guidebook for Building an Immigrant Workforce in the Nonprofit Sector* to help employers develop an inclusive strategy for attracting, recruiting, and retaining the most qualified candidates.[1] A future labour supply shortage looms in the nonprofit sector due to demographic shifts. Targeting immigrants can provide many benefits, including higher levels of skills and education, increased community responsiveness and representation, and lower recruitment and turnover costs.[2]

Alberta's nonprofit sector employs more than 100 000 staff,[3] but will face dramatic competition from the private and public sectors as baby boomers retire. Organizations need to make changes to their systems to overcome the challenges of attracting immigrants. A diversity strategy may require nonprofit employers to change aspects of their organizations as varied as their values, communication, branding, and recruitment advertising.

## Think About It

What are the barriers to hiring immigrants? What do employers need to do to build a more diverse workforce?

# THE HUMAN RESOURCE MANAGEMENT PROCESS

**7.1**

**Tell**
What factors affect human resource planning?

"Our people are our most important asset." Many organizations use this phrase, or something close to it, to acknowledge the important role that employees play in organizational success. These organizations also recognize that *all* managers must engage in some human resource management (HRM) activities—even in large ones that have a separate HRM department. Managers interview job candidates, orient new employees, and evaluate their employees' work performance. Because HR also involves appropriate ways of treating co-workers, even nonmanagers must be aware of basic HR principles and practices.

*Can* HRM be an important strategic tool? *Can* it help establish an organization's sustainable competitive advantage? The answer to these questions seems to be yes. Various studies have concluded that an organization's human resources can be a significant source of competitive advantage.[4] That conclusion is true for organizations around the world, not just for Canadian firms. The Human Capital Index, a comprehensive global study of more than 2000 firms conducted by consulting firm Watson Wyatt Worldwide, concluded that people-oriented HR gives an organization an edge by creating superior shareholder value.[5]

Human resource professionals are actively involved in strategy formulation and implementation. Thus, human resource practices must support the organization's distinctive competencies, its competitive advantage (for example, superior customer service, innovation, efficient production), and the long-term objectives of the organization (such as growth or market share).

Exhibit 7-1 introduces the key components of an organization's **human resource management process**, which consists of three key areas: *environmental factors* that impact HRM such as organizational culture, economic conditions, labour market issues, government legislation, and technology; *human resource requirements, and performance and reward factors* such as planning, recruitment, training, and total rewards;[6] and *employee relations factors* including employee engagement and occupational health and safety.

## Environmental Factors Affecting HRM

Notice in Exhibit 7-1 that the entire HRM process is influenced by the internal and external environments as well as the organization's strategy. Whatever effect the external environment has on the organization ultimately affects the organization's employees. We elaborated on the constraints that the environment puts on managers in Chapter 2. The external environmental factors that most directly influence the HRM process are economic conditions, labour market issues, government legislation, and technology. The key internal factor shaping an organization's ability to meet its strategic objectives is the organizational culture.

**ORGANIZATIONAL CULTURE** Culture consists of the organization's set of beliefs, values, and norms.[7] A positive **organizational culture** provides many benefits to an organization, including loyalty, commitment, direction, productivity, and retention. The Calgary Chamber of Voluntary Organizations suggests an inclusive workplace culture can be created through cross-cultural awareness and communication training, as well as through sessions where employees learn about different cultural practices.[8] StarTech of London, Ontario, has created an entrepreneurial culture by involving employees and ensuring that they enjoy what they do. "We bring in all employees to get their final input before finalizing our strategic plan," says co-founder Paul Seed.[9]

**ECONOMIC CONDITIONS** Canada's labour market features 18.7 million people, of which 14 million are employed full-time, 3.3 million part-time, and 1.4 million are unemployed.[10]

**EXHIBIT 7-1** The Human Resource Management Process

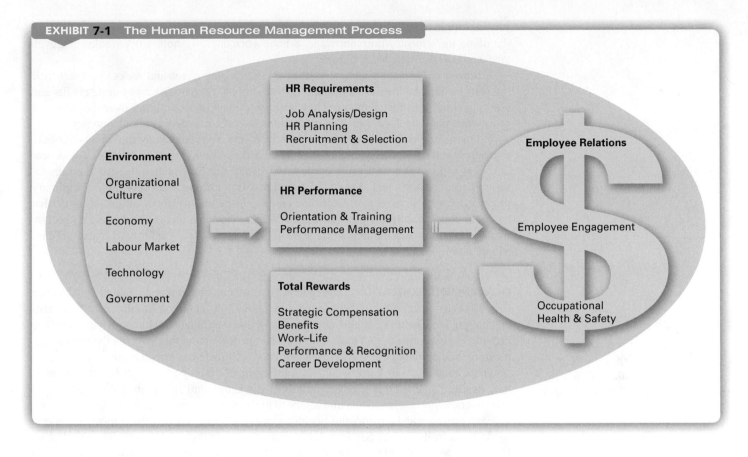

The ability of employers to recruit is dependent on local (and national) unemployment rates, competition in regional and local labour markets, and industry-specific labour market conditions. For example, hospitals across the country are facing a shortage of nurses, so provinces compete with each other, and recruitment, training, and retention strategies in this sector become more important. When the unemployment rate is high, employers have more potential employees to choose from.

**LABOUR MARKET ISSUES** According to the Canadian Chamber of Commerce, the number one concern of its members is "finding the right people to do the job," which has led to a skills shortage "crisis."[11] The Government of Canada is revamping its Skilled Worker Program to help fill vacancies in skilled trades.[12]

The Canadian population is aging. In 2010, the median age in Canada was 40 years, up from 26 years in 1971. Seniors make up the fastest-growing age group with close to 5 million Canadians aged 65 and older, a number expected to double by 2036. Over the next 10 years, 1 in 4 Canadian workers will be above 55 years old. The percentage of the population in this age group is growing rapidly due to the aging of the baby boom generation, high life expectancy, and a decreased fertility rate.[13] Canada also admits more immigrants per capita than any other country. According to the last census, the proportion of the population born outside the country was 20 percent in 2006.[14] These factors combine to provide challenges and opportunities for HR managers.

A unique labour market issue is unionization. In North America, many of the privileges that workers can count on are a result of the labour union movement. Government programs

**human resource management process**
Activities necessary for staffing the organization and sustaining high employee performance.

**organizational culture**
A system of shared values, norms, and beliefs held by organizational members that determines, in large degree, how employees act.

such as employment insurance, workers compensation, and pensions are a direct result of the union movement. Minimum wage, 8-hour work days, 40-hour work weeks, and even weekends off are also due to unions.[15]

A **labour union** is an organization that represents employees and seeks to protect their interests through collective bargaining. Labour unions try to improve pay and benefits and working conditions for members. They also try to have greater control over the rules and procedures covering issues such as promotions, layoffs, transfers, and outsourcing.

In unionized organizations, many HRM decisions are regulated by the terms of collective agreements, and management has much less flexibility in terms of HR policies, procedures, and practices. Collective agreements usually define such things as recruitment sources; criteria for hiring, promotions, and layoffs; training eligibility; and disciplinary practices. About 30 percent of Canadian employees belong to labour unions, a figure that has been consistent for the past 25 years.[16] Wages, working conditions, lack of respect by managers, unfair working hours, job security, and the desire for safer workplaces all contribute to unionization.

**GOVERNMENT LEGISLATION**  The federal government has greatly expanded its influence over HRM by enacting a number of laws and regulations including Employment Standards legislation, the Charter of Rights and Freedoms, and the Canadian Human Rights Act. The provincial governments also have their own labour legislation that governs the workplace, meaning that employment law in Canada involves 14 different jurisdictions.[17]

The Canada Labour Code establishes the right of employees to join labour unions if they desire. Part II of this legislation outlines the health and safety obligations of federal employers to prevent accidents and injury to their employees.

Each province and territory has health and safety regulations that cover most nonfederal workplaces in its region. Separate legislation covers workplace hazards. The Workplace Hazardous Materials Information System (WHMIS) is a comprehensive plan for providing information on the safe use of potentially hazardous materials in the workplace.

Employment standards legislation sets minimum employment standards in the private sector in Canada. It covers such things as the minimum age of employees, hours of work and overtime pay, minimum wages, equal pay, general holidays and annual vacations with pay, parental leave, and termination of employment.

The Charter of Rights and Freedoms and the Canadian Human Rights Act require employers to ensure that equal employment opportunities exist for job applicants and current employees. Decisions regarding who will be hired, for example, or which employees will be chosen for a management training program must be made without regard to race, sex, religion, age, colour, national origin, or disability.

Trying to balance the "shoulds and should-nots" of these laws often falls within the realm of employment equity. The Employment Equity Act creates four "protected categories"—women, Aboriginal peoples, people with disabilities, and visible minorities. These groups must not be discriminated against by federally regulated employers or any employers who receive federal contracts worth more than $200 000. Employment equity is intended to ensure that all citizens have an equal opportunity to obtain employment regardless of gender, race or ethnicity, or disabilities.

The intent of the Canada Labour Code, Occupational Health and Safety Act, employment standards legislation, the Charter of Rights and Freedoms, and the Canadian Human Rights Act is to ensure that all employees have a safe work environment, that they are not asked to work too many hours, that they have reasonable opportunities to be considered for jobs, and that pay for jobs is not discriminatory. Because an increasing number of workplace lawsuits are targeting supervisors, as well as their organizations, managers need to be aware of what they can and cannot do by law.[18]

**TECHNOLOGY**  Companies use technology in many areas of their operations, including HRM. Some companies utilize a *Human Resources Information System (HRIS)* to capture and manage employee data. An HRIS can help reduce administrative costs, provide information more quickly, ensure legal compliance, provide for better talent management and enhanced decision making, and streamline the entire people management function. By decreasing transactional activities, technology allows HR practitioners to increase their client and customer focus, solving problems and meeting their needs faster than was ever dreamed of previously. Technology can be a catalyst for innovation and productivity, providing organizations new ways to create value.[19] Technology also allows HR to strategically manage human capital proactively and has been shown to positively impact the organizational bottom line.[20]

Other technology applications for HRM include applicant tracking, performance management, elearning, online selection testing, computer monitoring, software-as-a-service (SaaS), and cloud computing.[21]

Oracle and SAP are examples of major companies that provide SaaS technologies, applications hosted by the vendor and made available via a network or the cloud.[22] Companies have to decide whether to rely on software and an internal HIRS or to utilize external vendors such as Oracle and SAP. HR practitioners work with these vendors to determine a system that aligns best with their needs, budget, and management requirements. Small firms can benefit from outsourcing or vendor applications as well, especially in payroll, talent management, and learning management solutions.

Mobile and self-service applications will lead to a consumer-driven user experience[23] that emphasizes efficiency and ease of use. Watson Wyatt consultants have identified other trends in technology, including:[24]

Interpret

- optimization of existing HR technology and systems
- enhanced focus on workforce analytics
- increased focus on reducing costs
- heightened data privacy issues

# HUMAN RESOURCE REQUIREMENTS

**7.2** — Define: How do organizations assess their human resource needs?

Canada will experience a shortage of 1 million skilled workers over the next 20 years, according to The Conference Board of Canada.[25] Aware of these predictions, managers at many companies are developing plans to ensure that they will have enough qualified people to fulfill their human resource needs. HR requirement planning involves job analysis and design, HR planning and recruitment, and selection. Managers begin human resource planning by reviewing the organization's current human resource status, usually through a *human resource inventory*. This information is taken from forms filled out by employees, and includes things such as name, education, training, prior employment, languages spoken, special capabilities, and specialized skills. Many firms have introduced HRIS to track employee information for policy and strategic needs. For example, these systems can be used for salary and benefits administration. They can also be used to track absenteeism, turnover, and health and safety data. More strategically, HRIS can be used to keep track of employee skills and education, and match these to ongoing needs of the organization.

## Job Analysis and Design

The initial part of HR requirement planning is **job analysis**, an assessment that defines jobs and the behaviours necessary to perform them. Information for a job analysis can be gathered by directly observing or videotaping individuals on the job, interviewing employees individually or in a group, having employees complete a structured questionnaire, having job "experts" (usually managers) identify a job's specific characteristics, or having employees record their daily activities in a diary or notebook.

**labour union**
An organization that represents employees and seeks to protect their interests through collective bargaining.

**job analysis**
An assessment that defines jobs and the behaviours necessary to perform them.

With information from the job analysis, managers develop or revise job descriptions and job specifications. A **job description** is a written statement of what a jobholder does, how the job is done, and why the job is done. It typically describes job content, environment, and conditions of employment. A **job specification** states the minimum qualifications that a person must possess to perform a given job successfully. It identifies the human traits, knowledge, skills, and attitudes needed to do the job effectively. The job description and the job specification are both important documents that aid managers in recruiting and selecting employees.

The second part of HR requirement planning is **job design**, which refers to specifics of how a job is organized. Various activites and duties are typically grouped together to allow for enhanced employee performance.[26] Grouping allows organizations to enrich, enlarge, or even rotate jobs. Job design can help an organization address problems such as work overload/underload, repetition, isolation, work design, and other risks related to breaks and excessive hours of work.

Having a better idea of the various tasks required in a position provides the employee with more control and a better understanding of the job process, and it allows the organization to reduce delays in filling vacant positions.

## Human Resource Planning

Through **human resource planning**, managers ensure that they have the right number and kinds of people in the right places at the right times, who are capable of effectively and efficiently performing assigned tasks. Through planning, organizations can avoid sudden talent shortages and surpluses.[27] Human resource planning can be condensed into two steps: (1) assessing current human resources; and (2) assessing future human resource needs and developing a program to meet those future needs.

## Meeting Future Needs

Future human resource needs are determined by the organization's mission, goals, and strategies. Demand for employees is a result of demand for the organization's products or services. On the basis of its estimate of total revenue, managers can attempt to establish the number and mix of employees needed to reach that revenue. In some cases, however, that situation may be reversed. When particular skills are necessary but in short supply, the availability of appropriate human resources determines revenues.

After they have assessed both current capabilities and future needs, managers are able to estimate human resource shortages—both in number and in type—and to highlight areas in which the organization will be overstaffed. Managers can then develop replacement charts for managerial positions to outline which employees are available to fill future managerial needs and to indicate who might be ready for promotion and who might need more training to move into upper-level positions. With all of this information, managers are ready to proceed to the next step in the HRM process.

## STAFFING THE ORGANIZATION

**7.3** Describe How do organizations identify and select competent employees?

To deal with recruiting issues, Scotiabank has developed a Careers webpage to target young graduates and encourage them to think about working for the bank.[28] "We looked at our audience and their primary medium is the Internet. We're matching the channels with the audience we're trying to attract," says Arlene Russell, vice-president of HR. The site gives corporate information, and users can do job searches and read about what makes Scotiabank a good employer.

### Think About It

How can using social media for recruitment bias decision making in the selection process? What steps can companies like Scotiabank take to avoid this bias?

Russell notes that e-recruiting is not the only way that the bank seeks job applicants. Scotiabank also uses print advertising and recruitment fairs, for example. "There are still strengths in all mediums and I think to really attract job seekers, you have to deliver on all the channels people want," says Russell. "The bottom line is you need to understand who you're speaking to and speak to them in the medium they're comfortable with."

Once managers know their current human resource status and their future needs, they can begin to do something about any shortages or excesses. If one or more vacancies exist, they can use the information gathered through job analysis to guide them in **recruitment**— that is, the process of locating, identifying, and attracting capable applicants.[29]

## Recruitment

At a career fair and expo at Edmonton City Centre mall, the Edmonton Police Service tried to convince high school students to consider a career with the police force. To show that there are many different opportunities in police service, they brought their vehicles, including police motorcycles and dirt bikes. Explains spokesperson Dean Parthenis, "People may have thought that once you become a police officer, you stay in that position on patrol for the rest of your life. You can if you like. But there's lots of opportunity to move around once you become a police officer."[30] Potential job candidates can be found through several sources, as Exhibit 7-2 shows.[31]

*How would you go about recruiting team members to work on a course project?*

Social networking offers organizations a chance to attract young, tech-savvy candidates through virtual recruitment booths, company Facebook pages, and even job postings through Twitter.

Web-based recruiting, or e-recruiting, has become a popular choice for organizations and applicants. After the Vancouver Police Department (VPD) examined what kinds of recruits would be needed over the next several years, the department decided to launch a recruitment seminar inside *Second Life*, the online alternative universe. The police recruiters created their own avatars (*Second Life* persona) dressed "in a specially designed VPD uniform, badge, belt, and radio." Inspector Kevin McQuiggen, head of the department's tech crimes division, explains why recruiting on *Second Life* makes sense: "If people are

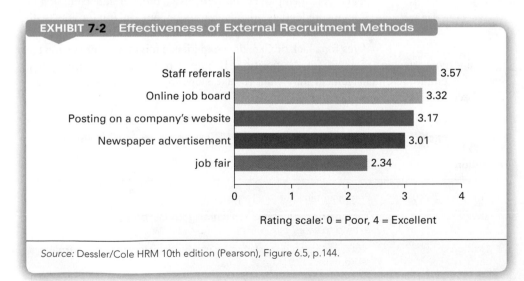

**EXHIBIT 7-2** Effectiveness of External Recruitment Methods

Staff referrals — 3.57
Online job board — 3.32
Posting on a company's website — 3.17
Newspaper advertisement — 3.01
job fair — 2.34

Rating scale: 0 = Poor, 4 = Excellent

*Source:* Dessler/Cole HRM 10th edition (Pearson), Figure 6.5, p.144.

**job description**
A written statement of what a jobholder does, how the job is done, and why the job is done.

**job specification**
A statement of the minimum qualifications that a person must possess to perform a given job successfully.

**job design**
The process of looking at a job to determine what set of tasks is is required, how they are done, and in what order.

**human resource planning**
The process by which managers ensure that they have the right number and kinds of people in the

right places at the right times, who are capable of effectively and efficiently performing assigned tasks.

**recruitment**
The process of locating, identifying, and attracting capable applicants.

The Vancouver Police Department has started recruiting through an online presence on *Second Life*. They created special avatars (shown here) to interview prospective candidates.

on *Second Life*, they're likely to be web-savvy, a quality the police department is looking for in new recruits." The department has seen an increasing number of Internet and technology-related crimes in recent years, and hiring people who can help detect those crimes would be an advantage to the Vancouver police.[32]

Although e-recruiting has been gaining in popularity (Scotiabank, for example, allows applicants to fill out information forms online and upload their résumés with the forms), employers use other recruitment sources as well. Burnaby, BC–based Electronic Arts Canada, following the lead of some other Canadian companies, decided to recruit at universities in recent years to win "the best and the brightest" from computer science programs.[33] Pat York, director of human resources, is pleased with the results, because the interviews have led to hires more than one-third of the time. Many companies continue to use print advertising and employment agencies.

Despite the popularity of new recruiting techniques, the majority of studies have found that employee referrals generally produce the best candidates.[34]

## Selection

Once the recruiting effort has developed a pool of candidates, the next step in the HRM process is to determine who is best qualified for the job. This step, called the **selection process**, is the process of screening job applicants to ensure that the most appropriate candidates are hired. Errors in hiring can have far-reaching implications, as the average cost of turnover can be as high as 150 percent of the employee's salary![35] Some selection practices may screen out applicants who have transferable skills. CCVO suggests that employers need to have a broader understanding of foreign credentials to avoid missing out on immigrants with valuable knowledge, skills, and abilities. Turning down candidates for a lack of Canadian experience might be overlooking the skills and competencies required for the position. If human resource planning shows a surplus of employees, management may want to take steps to reduce the organization's workforce, as Exhibit 7-3 demonstrates.

| EXHIBIT 7-3 | Workforce Reduction Options |
|---|---|
| **Option** | **Description** |
| Firing | Permanent involuntary termination |
| Layoffs | Temporary involuntary termination; may last only a few days or extend to years |
| Attrition | Not filling openings created by voluntary resignations or normal retirements |
| Transfers | Moving employees either laterally or downward; usually does not reduce costs but can reduce intraorganizational supply–demand imbalances |
| Reduced workweeks | Having employees work fewer hours per week, share jobs, or perform their jobs on a part-time basis |
| Early retirements | Providing incentives to older and more senior employees for retiring before their normal retirement dates |
| Job sharing | Having employees share one full-time position |

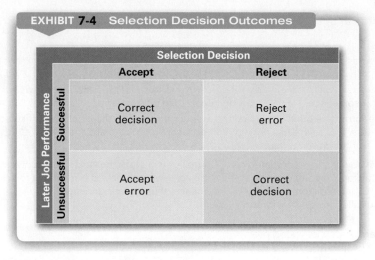

EXHIBIT **7-4** Selection Decision Outcomes

**WHAT IS SELECTION?**   Selection is an exercise in prediction. It seeks to predict which applicants will be successful if hired. *Successful* in this case means performing well on the criteria the organization uses to evaluate employees. In filling a sales position, for example, the selection process should be able to predict which applicants will generate a high volume of sales; for a position as a network administrator, it should predict which applicants will be able to effectively oversee and manage the organization's computer network.

Consider, for a moment, that any selection decision can result in four possible outcomes. As shown in Exhibit 7-4, two of these outcomes would be correct, and two would indicate errors.

A decision is correct when the applicant was predicted to be successful and proved to be successful on the job, or when the applicant was predicted to be unsuccessful and would have been so if hired. In the first case, we have successfully accepted; in the second case, we have successfully rejected.

Problems arise when errors are made by rejecting candidates who would have performed successfully on the job (reject errors) or by accepting those who ultimately perform poorly (accept errors). These problems can be significant. Given today's human resource laws and regulations, reject errors can cost more than the additional screening needed to find acceptable candidates. They can expose the organization to charges of discrimination, especially if applicants from protected groups are disproportionately rejected. The costs of accept errors include the cost of training the employee, the profits lost because of the employee's incompetence, the cost of severance, and the subsequent costs of further recruiting and screening. The major thrust of any selection activity should be to reduce the probability of making reject errors or accept errors while increasing the probability of making correct decisions. How do managers do this? By using selection procedures that are both valid and reliable.

**VALIDITY AND RELIABILITY**   Any selection device that a manager uses should demonstrate **validity**, a proven relationship between the selection device and some relevant job criterion. For example, the law prohibits managers from using a test score as a selection device unless there is clear evidence that, once on the job, individuals with high scores on the test outperform individuals with low test scores. The burden is on managers to show that any selection device they use to differentiate between applicants is related to job performance.

In addition to being valid, a selection device must also demonstrate **reliability**, which indicates whether the device measures the same thing consistently. For example, if a test is reliable, any single individual's score should remain fairly consistent over time, assuming that the characteristics being measured are also stable. No selection device can be effective

---

**selection process**
The process of screening job applicants to ensure that the most appropriate candidates are hired.

**validity**
The proven relationship that exists between the selection device and some relevant job criterion.

**reliability**
The ability of a selection device to measure the same thing consistently.

**EXHIBIT 7-5** Selection Devices

| Selection Device | Strengths | Weaknesses |
|---|---|---|
| Application forms | Relevant biographical data and facts that can be verified have been shown to be valid performance measures for some jobs.<br><br>When items on the form have been weighted to reflect job relatedness, this device has proved to be a valid predictor for diverse groups. | Usually only a couple of items on the form prove to be valid predictors of job performance and then only for a specific job.<br><br>Weighted-item applications are difficult and expensive to create and maintain. |
| Written tests | Tests of intellectual ability, spatial and mechanical ability, perceptual accuracy, and motor ability are moderately valid predictors for many semi-skilled and unskilled lower-level jobs in manufacturing.<br><br>Intelligence tests are reasonably good predictors for supervisory positions. | Intelligence and other tested characteristics can be somewhat removed from actual job performance, thus reducing their validity. |
| Performance-simulation tests | Tests are based on job analysis data and easily meet the requirement of job relatedness.<br><br>Tests have proven to be valid predictors of job performance. | They are expensive to create and administer. |
| Interviews | Interviews must be structured and well organized to be effective predictors.<br><br>Interviewers must use common questions to be effective predictors. | Interviewers must be aware of the legality of certain questions.<br><br>Interviews are subject to potential biases, especially if they are not well structured and standardized. |
| Background investigations | Verifications of background data are valuable sources of information. | Reference checks are essentially worthless as a selection tool. |
| Physical examinations | Physical exams have some validity for jobs with certain physical requirements. | Managers must be sure that physical requirements are job related and do not discriminate. |

if it is low in reliability. Using such a device would be like weighing yourself every day on an erratic scale. If the scale is unreliable—randomly fluctuating, say, four to seven kilos every time you step on it—the results will not mean much. To be effective predictors, selection devices must possess an acceptable level of consistency.

**TIPS FOR MANAGERS**

## Behavioural and Situational Questions

Situational interview questions feature some kind of scenario; the interviewer explains the scenario and then asks, "What would you do?" These questions test your judgment, knowledge, and/or ability.

Behavioural interview questions ask applicants how they handled job or life situations in the past. The idea is that past behaviour is the best predictor of future performance in similar situations. These types of questions have much higher validity in predicting future job performance.[37]

* Describe a time when you had to deal with a difficult customer.

* Tell me about a time that you had to meet two conflicting deadlines.

* Give me an example of a time when you had to conform to a policy with which you did not agree.

**TYPES OF SELECTION DEVICES** Managers can use a number of selection devices to reduce accept and reject errors. The best-known devices include application forms, written tests, performance-simulation tests, interviews, background investigations, and, in some cases, physical examinations. Exhibit 7-5 lists the strengths and weaknesses of each of these devices.[36]

**HR PERFORMANCE** To increase job satisfaction among employees and reduce turnover, organizations can provide a **realistic job preview (RJP)**. An RJP includes both positive and negative information about the job and the company. For example, in addition to the positive comments typically expressed during an interview, the job applicant might be told that there are limited opportunities to talk to co-workers during work hours, that promotional advancement is rare, or that work hours fluctuate so erratically that employees may be required to work during what are usually off hours (nights and weekends). Research indicates that applicants who have been given a realistic job preview hold lower and more realistic job expectations for the jobs they will be performing and are better able to cope with the frustrating elements of the job than are applicants who have been given only positive information.

Analyze

## ORIENTATION AND TRAINING

Thirty-year-old Roxann Linton is enthusiastic about her career at Scotiabank.[38] "Working with an international and diverse organization like Scotiabank, there are so many opportunities," says Linton. The young woman was chosen for Leading Edge, Scotiabank's fast-track leadership program. In the application process, she had to prepare a challenging business case analysis, go through psychometric testing, and be interviewed twice by a total of eight executives. The Leading Edge program prepares employees for senior management positions by rotating them through a series of assignments.

**7.4**

**Explain**
How do organizations help employees adapt and stay up-to-date?

### Think About It

What kinds of orientation and training methods do organizations use to help employees develop their skills and learn about their organizations?

Linton worked for the bank for about five years in the bank's internal audit department in Kingston, Jamaica. She then transferred to Halifax and worked in commercial banking. During the first 15 months of the Leading Edge program, Linton managed more than 100 people in the electronic banking contact centre. Her next assignment was as director of special projects at Scotia Cassels Investment Counsel, part of the bank's wealth management division. She launched a new corporate bond fund during her first three months in that assignment. She will have one more 12- to 18-month assignment in another part of the bank, and then she can start applying for vice-president positions.

Organizations have to introduce new members to the work they will do and to the organization. They do this through their orientation programs. As time goes by, employees may need to increase their skills. This need is handled through training. We review the strategies that organizations use for orientation and training below.

### Orientation

Did you participate in some type of organized introduction to campus life when you started college or university? If so, you might have been told about your school's rules and regulations, about the procedures for activities such as applying for financial aid, cashing a cheque, or registering for classes, and you were probably introduced to some of the campus administrators. A person starting a new job needs the same type of introduction to his or her job and to the organization. This introduction is called **orientation**.

There are two types of orientation. *Work unit orientation* familiarizes the employee with the goals of the work unit, clarifies how his or her job contributes to the unit's goals, and includes an introduction to his or her new co-workers. *Organization orientation* informs the new employee about the organization's objectives, history, philosophy, procedures, and rules. This information should include relevant human resource policies and benefits such as work hours, pay procedures, overtime requirements, and fringe benefits. In addition, a tour of the organization's work facilities is often part of the organization orientation.

---

**realistic job preview (RJP)**
A preview of a job that includes both positive and negative information about the job and the company.

**orientation**
The introduction of a new employee to his or her job and to the organization.

Managers have an obligation to make the integration of the new employee into the organization as smooth and as free of anxiety as possible. They need to openly discuss employee beliefs regarding mutual obligations of the organization and the employee.[39] It is in the best interests of the organization and the new employee to get the person up and running in the job as soon as possible. Successful orientation, whether formal or informal, results in an outsider–insider transition that makes the new member feel comfortable and fairly well adjusted, lowers the likelihood of poor work performance, and reduces the probability of a surprise resignation by the new employee only a week or two into the job.

## Training

Employee training is an important HRM activity. As job demands change, employee skills have to be altered and updated. In 2011, US business firms budgeted over $59 billion on workforce formal training.[40] Canadian companies spend far less than American firms on training and development—about $852 per employee compared with $1273 by the Americans in 2006.[41] Managers, of course, are responsible for deciding what type of training employees need, when they need it, and what form that training should take.

*Is college or university education enough for the workplace, or do you need more training?*

**TYPES OF TRAINING** When organizations invest in employee training, what are they offering? Some of the most popular types of training that organizations provide include information on sexual harassment, safety, management skills and development, and supervisory skills.[42] For many organizations, employee interpersonal skills training—communication, conflict resolution, team building, customer service, and so forth—is a high priority. Shannon Washbrook, director of training and development for Vancouver-based Boston Pizza International, says, "Our people know the Boston Pizza concept; they have all the hard skills. It's the soft skills they lack." To address that gap, Washbrook launched Boston Pizza College, a training initiative that uses hands-on, scenario-based learning about many interpersonal skills topics.[43] Technology-based training is becoming more popular. Exhibit 7-6 describes the major training methods that organizations utilize.

Infosys Technologies, India's fast-growing software company, has created Infosys University, one of the world's largest training centres, to train its new employees. The $120 million campus-like facility bans alcohol and offers only single-sex dorms, but has three movie theatres, a pool, a gym, and dozens of instructors. Online courses teach recruits everything from technical skills and team building to interpersonal communication and corporate etiquette. Says CEO Nandan Nilekani, "Companies haven't been investing enough in people. Rather than train them, they let them go. Our people are our capital. The more we invest in them, the more they can be effective."

**EXHIBIT 7-6**  Employee Training Methods

**Traditional Training Methods**

- *On-the-job*—Employees learn how to do tasks simply by performing them, usually after an initial introduction to the task.
- *Job rotation*—Employees work at different jobs in a particular area, getting exposure to a variety of tasks.
- *Mentoring and coaching*—Employees work with an experienced worker who provides information, support, and encouragement; also called *apprenticing* in certain industries.
- *Experiential exercises*—Employees participate in role playing, simulations, or other face-to-face types of training.
- *Workbooks/manuals*—Employees refer to training workbooks and manuals for information.
- *Classroom lectures*—Employees attend lectures designed to convey specific information.

**Technology-Based Training Methods**

- *CD-ROM/DVD/videotapes/audiotapes*—Employees use selected media to listen to information or watch demonstration of certain techniques.
- *Videoconferencing/teleconferencing/satellite TV*—Employees listen to or participate as information is conveyed or techniques demonstrated.
- *E-learning*—Internet-based learning in which employees participate in multimedia simulations or other interactive modules.

# PERFORMANCE MANAGEMENT

Managers need to know whether their employees are performing their jobs efficiently and effectively or whether improvement is needed. Employees are often compensated based on those evaluations.

**Explain**
What can organizations do to help employees achieve high performance throughout their careers?

**7.5**

## Performance Management System

Evaluating employee performance is part of a **performance management system**, which is a process of establishing performance standards and appraising employee performance in order to arrive at objective human resource decisions and to provide documentation in support of those decisions. Performance appraisal is a critical part of a performance management system. Some companies invest far more effort in it than others.

Performance appraisal is not easy to do, and many managers do it poorly. Both managers and employees often dread the appraisal process. A survey found that 41 percent of employees report having had a least one incident of being demotivated after feedback from their managers.[44] Performance appraisal can also be subject to politics, not unlike the 2002 Olympic Winter Games ice skating controversy in which the French judge was accused of manipulating her scores to enable the Russian skaters to win the gold over Canadians Jamie Salé and David Pelletier. Let us look at some different methods of doing performance appraisal.

*What techniques might you want to use if you had to evaluate the members of your student project group?*

**PERFORMANCE APPRAISAL METHODS**  Managers can choose from seven major performance appraisal methods. The advantages and disadvantages of each of these methods are shown in Exhibit 7-7.

**Written Essays**  The **written essay** is a performance appraisal method in which the evaluator writes out a description of an employee's strengths and weaknesses, past performance, and potential. The evaluator also makes suggestions for improvement.

**performance management system**
A process of establishing performance standards and evaluating performance in order to arrive at objective human resource decisions and to provide documentation in support of those decisions.

**written essay**
A performance appraisal method in which the evaluator writes out a description of an employee's strengths and weaknesses, past performance, and potential.

| EXHIBIT 7-7 | Advantages and Disadvantages of Performance Appraisal Methods | |
|---|---|---|
| Method | Advantage | Disadvantage |
| Written essays | Simple to use | More a measure of evaluator's writing ability than of employee's actual performance |
| Critical incidents | Rich examples; behaviourally based | Time-consuming; lack quantification |
| Graphic rating scales | Provide quantitative data; less time-consuming than others | Do not provide depth of job behaviour assessed |
| Behaviourally Anchored Rating Scales (BARS) | Focus on specific and measurable behaviours | Time-consuming; difficult to develop job behaviours |
| Multiperson comparisons | Compare employees with one another | Unwieldy with large number of employees; legal concerns |
| Management by Objectives (MBO) | Focuses on end goals; results oriented | Time-consuming |
| 360-degree feedback | Thorough | Time-consuming |

**Critical Incidents**  The use of **critical incidents** focuses the evaluator's attention on critical or key behaviours that separate effective from ineffective job performance. The evaluator writes down anecdotes describing what an employee did that was especially effective or ineffective. The key here is that only specific behaviours, not vaguely defined personality traits, are cited.

**Graphic Rating Scales**  One of the most popular performance appraisal methods is **graphic rating scales**. This method lists a set of performance factors such as quantity and quality of work, job knowledge, cooperation, loyalty, attendance, honesty, and initiative. The evaluator then goes down the list and rates the employee on each factor using an incremental scale, which usually specifies five points. A factor such as job knowledge, for example, might be rated from 1 ("poorly informed about work duties") to 5 ("has complete mastery of all phases of the job").

**Behaviourally Anchored Rating Scales**  Another popular performance appraisal method is **behaviourally anchored rating scales (BARS)**. These scales combine major elements from the critical incident and graphic rating scale approaches. The evaluator rates an employee according to items along a numeric scale, but the items are examples of actual job behaviours rather than general descriptions or traits.

**Multiperson Comparisons**  **Multiperson comparisons** compare one individual's performance with that of others.[45] Made popular by former General Electric (GE) CEO Jack Welch, this system rates employees as top performers (20 percent), middle performers (70 percent), or bottom performers (10 percent). Advocates of the system believe that by using this type of "rank and yank" appraisal, a company can rid itself of slackers and thus be more productive. However, critics say that the rankings unfairly penalize groups made up of star performers and hinder risk-taking and collaboration.[46] For example, Sprint used forced rankings for a year and discontinued the program because it found more effective ways to differentiate performance.[47] Are forced rankings a good idea or a bad idea? According to research, companies that used forced rankings and fired the bottom 5 percent to 10 percent of employees saw productivity increase by an impressive 16 percent over the first couple of years. However, in subsequent years, productivity gains dropped off considerably.[48] Companies are therefore questioning the wisdom of strict forced ranking. Even GE has been looking at ways to make its system more flexible and has encouraged its managers to use more common sense in assigning rankings.[49]

**Management by Objectives**  We previously introduced management by objectives (MBO) when we discussed planning in Chapter 3. MBO is also a mechanism for appraising performance. In fact, it is often used for assessing managers and professional employees.[50] With MBO, employees are evaluated according to how well they accomplish specific goals that have been established by them and their managers.

**360-Degree Feedback**    **360-degree feedback** is a performance appraisal method that uses feedback from multiple sources including supervisors, employees, co-workers, and customers. In other words, this appraisal uses information from the full circle of people with whom the employee interacts. Of the 101 large Canadian organizations surveyed by professors Mehrdad Debrayen and Stephane Brutus of the John Molson School of Business at Concordia University, 43 percent used 360-degree feedback.[51] Toronto-based Hill & Knowlton Canada, a public relations firm, uses 360-degree feedback to help employees learn what they need to do to get to the next level of the organization. The feedback has had the added benefit of reducing turnover to 18 percent.[52]

Users caution that although this method of appraisal is effective for career coaching and helping a manager recognize his or her strengths and weaknesses, it is not appropriate for determining pay, promotions, or terminations. Managers using 360-degree feedback also have to carefully consider the pros and cons of using anonymous evaluations.[53]

Not all organizations conduct performance evaluations; in particular, smaller organizations often do not. Consequently, it can be useful as an employee to ask your manager for an annual appraisal, if you do not routinely receive one. The feedback will allow you to determine your goals for the following year and identify anything for which you need improvement or training.

## What Happens When Performance Falls Short

So far, our discussion has focused on the performance management system. But what if an employee is not performing in a satisfactory manner? What can you do?

If, for some reason, an employee is not meeting his or her performance goals, a manager needs to find out why. If it is because the employee is mismatched for the job (a hiring error) or because he or she does not have adequate training, something relatively simple can be done: The manager can either reassign the individual to a job that better matches his or her skills, or train the employee to do the job more effectively. If the problem is associated not with the employee's abilities but with his or her desire to do the job, it becomes a **discipline** problem. In that case, a manager can try counselling and, if necessary, can take disciplinary action such as oral and written warnings, suspensions, and even termination.

**Employee counselling** is a process designed to help employees overcome performance-related problems. Rather than viewing the performance problem as something that needs to be punished (discipline), employee counselling attempts to uncover why employees have lost their desire or ability to work productively. More important, counselling is designed to find ways to fix the problem. In many cases, employees do not go from being productive one day to being unproductive the next. Rather, the change happens gradually and may be a function of what is occurring in their personal lives. Employee counselling attempts to assist employees in getting help to resolve whatever is bothering them.

---

**critical incidents**
A performance appraisal method in which the evaluator focuses on the critical or key behaviours that separate effective from ineffective job performance.

**graphic rating scales**
A performance appraisal method in which the evaluator rates an employee on a set of performance factors.

**behaviourally anchored rating scales (BARS)**
A performance appraisal method in which the evaluator rates an employee on examples of actual job behaviours.

**multiperson comparisons**
A performance appraisal method by which one individual's performance is compared with that of others.

**360-degree feedback**
A performance appraisal method that uses feedback from supervisors, employees, co-workers, and customers.

**discipline**
Actions taken by a manager to enforce an organization's standards and regulations.

**employee counselling**
A process designed to help employees overcome performance-related problems.

## TOTAL REWARDS

**7.6**

**Tell**
How do total rewards motivate employees?

Total rewards contains five components: strategic compensation, benefits, work–life balance, performance management, and career development. These elements do not operate in silos; rather, they can be combined in joint reward activities and strategies. The five components combine into one reward strategy that is integrated and results in happy, committed, and productive employees.[54] The total rewards model does not exist in a vacuum—rewards must be linked very closely with the organization's strategy.

### Strategic Compensation

*How would you know whether your employer was paying you fairly?*

Most of us expect to receive appropriate compensation from our employers. Therefore, developing an effective and appropriate compensation system is an important part of the HRM process.[55] Why? Because it helps attract and retain competent and talented individuals who help the organization accomplish its mission and goals. Compensation is typically the largest expense for an employer, so it becomes critical for compensation strategy to be directly linked with organizational strategy. An organization's compensation system has been shown to have an impact on its strategic performance and value creation.[56]

Managers must develop a compensation system that reflects the changing nature of work and the workplace in order to keep people motivated. Organizational compensation can include many different types of rewards and benefits such as base wages and salaries, wage and salary add-ons, incentive payments, as well as other benefits and services such as vacation time, extended health care, training allowances, and pensions. Benefits often amount to one-third or more of an individual's base salary and should be viewed by the employee as part of the total compensation package.

How do managers determine who gets paid $9 an hour and who gets $350 000 a year? Several factors influence the differences in compensation and benefit packages for different employees. Exhibit 7-8 summarizes these factors, which are both job-based and business- or industry-based.

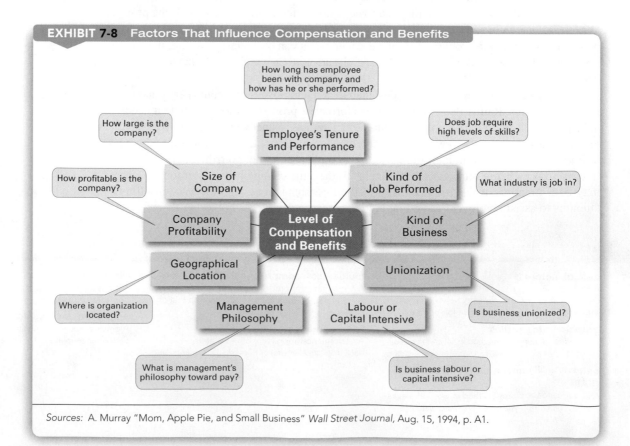

**EXHIBIT 7-8** Factors That Influence Compensation and Benefits

*Sources:* A. Murray "Mom, Apple Pie, and Small Business" *Wall Street Journal*, Aug. 15, 1994, p. A1.

Many organizations use an alternative approach to determining compensation called **skill-based pay**. In a skill-based pay system, an employee's job title does not define his or her pay category; skills do.[57] Research shows that these types of pay systems seem to be more successful in manufacturing organizations than in service organizations or organizations pursuing technical innovations.[58] Skill-based pay systems seem to mesh nicely with the changing nature of jobs and today's work environment. As one expert noted, "Slowly, but surely, we're becoming a skill-based society where your market value is tied to what you can do and what your skill set is. In this new world where skills and knowledge are what really count, it doesn't make sense to treat people as jobholders. It makes sense to treat them as people with specific skills and to pay them for these skills."[59] On the other hand, many organizations are using **variable pay** systems, in which an individual's compensation is contingent on performance—81 percent of Canadian and Taiwanese organizations use variable pay plans, and 78 percent of US organizations do.[60]

Although many factors influence the design of an organization's compensation system, flexibility is a key consideration. The traditional approach to paying people reflected a time of job stability when an employee's pay was largely determined by seniority and job level. Given the dynamic environments that many organizations face in which the skills that are absolutely critical to organizational success can change in a matter of months, the trend is to make pay systems more flexible and to reduce the number of pay levels. However, whatever approach managers take, they must establish a fair, equitable, and motivating compensation system that allows the organization to recruit and keep a productive workforce.

Executive compensation is a hot button topic in North America today, as the gap widens dramatically between workers and executives. In Canada, the average top CEO makes 189 times more than the average Canadian worker. In 1998, that figure was 105 times more. Executive compensation in the form of stock options and incentives is a key method of CEO recruitment. But as the wage gap widens, CEO compensation has become a much discussed topic and is considered to be an important factor contributing to the financial crisis of 2009.[61]

## Benefits

Benefits are programs and services meant to supplement the cash component of compensation. Some benefits, such as employment insurance, workers compensation, and the Canada Pension Plan, are mandatory. Other benefits a company may offer include time off with pay, savings and retirement programs, and supplementary health and life insurance. Employee services were traditionally a small part of total rewards but have increased with the aging workforce and lower job security. Employee services are divided between personal services such as counselling and employee assistance programs (EAPs), and job-related services such as childcare, food services, and family-friendly benefits, which are discussed in more detail as part of work–life balance.[62]

## Work–Life Balance

Professors Linda Duxbury of the Sprott School of Business at Carleton University and Chris Higgins of the University of Western Ontario are the leading Canadian researchers on the issue of work–life balance. Their research shows that employees are working long hours and are also increasingly being asked to work a number of unpaid hours a week. This work load affects employees' abilities to manage their family lives. In response, most major organizations have taken actions to make their workplaces more family-friendly by offering **family-friendly benefits**, which include

*What kinds of work–life balance issues are affecting your life right now?*

---

**skill-based pay**
A pay system that rewards employees for the job skills and competencies they can demonstrate.

**variable pay**
A pay system in which an individual's compensation is contingent on performance.

**family-friendly benefits**
Benefits that accommodate employees' needs for work–life balance.

Does being rigid about not offering flextime harm employers? Surrey, BC, mom Sheila Whitehead thinks so. She quit her job as a marketing manager for a pharmaceuticals company when she could not get the flextime she needed to spend more time with her four-year-old daughter Abigail and her other two young children. She says that employers are "missing out on incredibly talented people who simply don't want the rigid nine-to-five hours."

a wide range of work and family programs to help employees.[63] Companies have introduced programs such as on-site child care, summer day camps, flextime, job sharing, leaves for school functions, telecommuting, and part-time employment.

Work–life conflicts are as relevant to male employees with children and female employees without children as they are to female employees with children. Heavy workloads and increased travel demands, for example, are making it increasingly hard for many employees, male and female, to meet both work and personal responsibilities. A *Fortune* survey found that 84 percent of male executives surveyed said that "they'd like job options that let them realize their professional aspirations while having more time for things outside work." Also, 87 percent of these executives believed that any company that restructured top-level management jobs in ways that would both increase productivity and make more time available for life outside the office would have a competitive advantage in attracting talented employees.[64] Younger employees, particularly, put a higher priority on family and a lower priority on jobs, and are looking for organizations that give them more work flexibility.[65]

Today's progressive workplace is becoming more accommodating of the varied needs of a diverse workforce. It provides a wide range of scheduling options and benefits that give employees more flexibility at work and allow employees to better balance or integrate their work and personal lives. Despite these organizational efforts, work–life programs have room for improvement. Workplace surveys still show high levels of employee stress stemming from work–life conflicts. Large groups of women and minority employees remain unemployed or underemployed because of family responsibilities and bias in the workplace.[66] What can managers do?

Total rewards necessitate looking at the whole picture, and work–life balance must fit within the compensation and benefit strategy. Research has shown a significant, positive relationship between work–family initiatives and an organization's stock price.[67] Managers need to understand that people do differ in their preferences for work–family life scheduling options and benefits.[68] Some people prefer organizational initiatives that better *segment* work from their personal lives. Others prefer programs that facilitate *integration*. Flextime schedules segment because they allow employees to schedule work hours that are less likely to conflict with personal responsibilities. On the other hand, on-site child care integrates by blurring the boundaries between work and family responsibilities. People who prefer segmentation are more likely to be satisfied and committed to their jobs when offered options such as flextime, job sharing, and part-time hours. People who prefer integration are more likely to respond positively to options such as on-site child care, gym facilities, and company-sponsored family picnics.

## Performance and Recognition

Performance can be addressed through performance management as described earlier in the chapter, through pay-for-performance strategies, and through recognition. The goal of recognition is to reinforce positive behaviours either formally or informally. It can reinforce performance improvement and meet intrinsic needs for appreciation, positive communication, and feedback.[69]

## Career Development

The term *career* has several meanings. In popular usage, it can mean advancement ("she is on a management career track"), a profession ("he has chosen a career in accounting"), or a lifelong sequence of jobs ("his career has included 12 jobs in 6 organizations"). For our

**EXHIBIT 7-9** What Do College and University Grads Want from Their Jobs?

| Top Factors for Canadian Students | Top Factors for US Students | Top Factors for UK Students |
| --- | --- | --- |
| • Opportunities for advancement in position<br>• Good people to work with<br>• Good people to report to<br>• Work–life balance<br>• Initial salary | • Work–life balance<br>• Annual base salary<br>• Job stability and security<br>• Recognition for a job done well<br>• Increasingly challenging tasks<br>• Rotational programs | • International career opportunities<br>• Flexible working hours<br>• Variety of assignments<br>• Paid overtime |

purposes, we define a **career** as the sequence of positions held by a person during his or her lifetime.[70] Using this definition, we all have, or will have, a career. Moreover, the concept is as relevant to unskilled labourers as it is to software designers or physicians.

**MANAGING ONE'S CAREER** Downsizing, restructuring, and other organizational adjustments have brought us to one significant conclusion about career development: The individual—not the organization—is responsible for his or her own career! Individuals need to assume primary responsibility for career planning, career goal setting, and education and training.[71] Many employees will face the reality of layoffs at some point in their career. The secret is not to let it derail the long-term plan.

One of the first career decisions you have to make is career choice. The optimum career choice is one that offers the best match between what you want out of life and your interests, abilities, and market opportunities. Good career choice outcomes should result in a series of positions that give you an opportunity to be a good performer, make you want to maintain your commitment to your career, lead to highly satisfying work, and give you the proper balance between work and personal life. A good career match, then, is one in which you are able to develop a positive self-concept, to do work that you think is important, and to lead the kind of life you desire.[72] Exhibit 7-9 describes the factors Canadian, American, and UK college and university students and graduates are looking for in their jobs. As you look at these results, think about what is important to you. How would you have ranked these items?

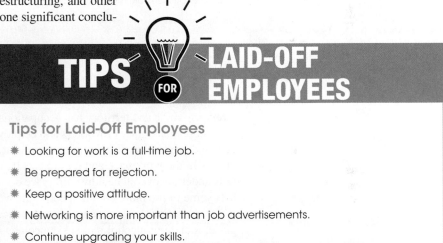

**TIPS FOR LAID-OFF EMPLOYEES**

**Tips for Laid-Off Employees**

* Looking for work is a full-time job.
* Be prepared for rejection.
* Keep a positive attitude.
* Networking is more important than job advertisements.
* Continue upgrading your skills.

# EMPLOYEE RELATIONS

Once an organization has attracted and motivated employees, retention becomes the next crucial component. Employee relations is the final part of the HRM process identified earlier in the chapter and completes the toolkit that is an effective and integrated model for the successful management of an organization's human resources.

**7.7** Define What can organizations do to maximize employee relations?

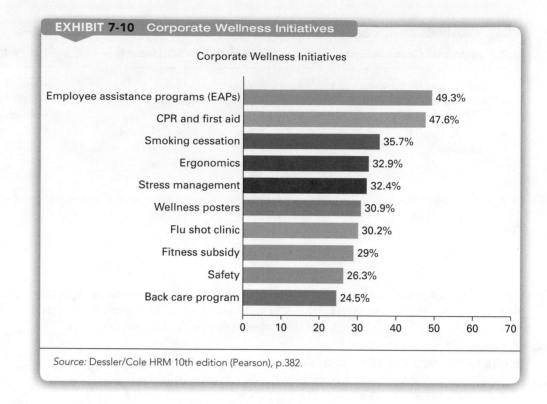

**EXHIBIT 7-10** Corporate Wellness Initiatives

Corporate Wellness Initiatives

| Initiative | Percentage |
|---|---|
| Employee assistance programs (EAPs) | 49.3% |
| CPR and first aid | 47.6% |
| Smoking cessation | 35.7% |
| Ergonomics | 32.9% |
| Stress management | 32.4% |
| Wellness posters | 30.9% |
| Flu shot clinic | 30.2% |
| Fitness subsidy | 29% |
| Safety | 26.3% |
| Back care program | 24.5% |

*Source:* Dessler/Cole HRM 10th edition (Pearson), p.382.

## Occupational Health and Safety

Every province and territory has occupational health and safety legislation, which is based on joint responsibility of workers and employers.[73] Both sides are meant to take reasonable care and precaution. Employers can prevent workplace accidents by reducing unsafe conditions in the workplace and unsafe acts by employees. Employee wellness is an area that falls under the overall healthy workplace desired by employers and employees. Exhibit 7-10 lists some of the more common corporate wellness initiatives.

Organizational performance can be reduced by several issues that can exist in the workplace, including alcohol and substance abuse, stress, repetitive strain injuries, workplace violence, and harassment.[74]

Sexual harassment is a serious issue in both public and private sector organizations. A survey by York University found that 48 percent of working women in Canada reported they had experienced some form of "gender harassment" in the year before they were surveyed.[75] Barbara Orser, a research affiliate with The Conference Board of Canada, notes that "sexual harassment is more likely to occur in workplace environments that tolerate bullying, intimidation, yelling, innuendo, and other forms of discourteous behaviour."[76]

## Employee Engagement

Employees in 2011 and beyond have experienced a severe economic downturn, have witnessed issues with governmental and personal debt, and have likely faced wage freezes, downsizing, and increased job demands. All of these factors combine to provide a new challenge for employers—keeping employees engaged.

The Conference Board of Canada published a report *Employee Engagement, A Review of Current Research and Its Implications*, in which it defined employee engagement as "a heightened emotional connection that an employee feels for his or her organization that influences him or her to exert greater discretionary effort to his or her work."[77] Organizations with high employee engagement likely have a high level of employee involvement, commitment to the organization, and job satisfaction.

Studies have proven that employee engagement leads to higher organizational perfor-mance.[78] Engaged employees are happier and and have more pride in their work. They are more likely to collaborate with co-workers, invest more effort and take additional respon-sibility, and remain with the organization than employees who are less engaged.[79]

The Conference Board summarized more than twelve major studies on employee engage-ment and discovered key drivers that were consistent in many of the reports. Exhibit 7-11 lists the eight most common drivers of employee engagement.

Practise

**EXHIBIT 7-11  Key Drivers of Employee Engagement**

| Key Driver | Checkpoint |
| --- | --- |
| Trust and integrity | How well do managers communicate and "walk the talk"? |
| Nature of the job | Is the job mentally stimulating day-to-day? |
| Line of sight between employee performance and company performance | Does the employee understand how his or her work contributes to the company's performance? |
| Career growth opportunities | Are there future opportunities for growth? |
| Pride about the company | How much self-esteem does the employee feel by being associated with the company? |
| Co-workers/team members | How well does the employee get along with his or her co-workers/team members? (These relationships significantly influence one's level of engagement.) |
| Employee development | Is the company making an effort to develop the employee's skills? |
| Relationship with one's manager | Does the employee value the relationship with his or her manager? |

*Source:* The Conference Board Inc.'s publication "Employee Engagement, A Review of Current Research and Its Implications," November 2006, John Gibbons.

# 7 Review and Apply

## Summary of Learning Objectives

 **7.1** **What factors affect human resource planning?** The human resource management (HRM) process consists of three key areas: *environmental factors* that impact HRM such as organizational culture, economic condi-tions, labour market issues, and technology; *human resource requirements, and performance and reward factors* such as planning, recruitment, training, and

total rewards;[80] and *employee relations factors* includ-ing health and safety and employee engagement.

Canada's workforce is aging and its demographics are changing, leading to projected employee skill shortages. CCVO recommends that nonprofit organizations need to include diversity initiatives as part of their HR management strategy.

**7.2** **How do organizations assess their human resource needs?** Human resource managers do a human resource inventory to discover what skills and capabilities current employees have. They map that inventory against what might be needed in the future, based on the organization's mission, goals, and strategies.

Organizations need to identify and assess the strengths and limitations of their employees. CCVO suggests using targeted training to overcome skill gaps in language, writing, presentation skills, communication, numeracy, and thinking skills.

**7.3** **How do organizations identify and select competent employees?** Organizations first need to assess their current and future needs for employees, to make sure they have enough of the right people to accomplish the organization's goals. When selecting new employees, organizations need to determine whether potential employees will be successful once they are on the job. To do this, managers use application forms, written tests, performance-simulation tests, interviews, background investigations, and, in some cases, physical examinations to screen employees. Managers also need to make sure that they do not engage in discrimination in the hiring process.

Organizations can develop more inclusive recruitment practices by advertising in various ethnic media sources and providing job descriptions without jargon or technical language.

**7.4** **How do organizations help employees adapt and stay up-to-date?** Organizations, particularly larger ones, have orientation programs for new employees. The orientation introduces the new employee to his or her job, and also to the organization. As job demands change, employees may need to have their skills updated through training programs. Companies use a variety of training methods, from on-the-job training to classroom work to technology-based training.

CCVO recommends having a mentor/buddy system so that new hires can ask existing employees various questions concerning behaviour in meetings, use of office materials, or even daily breaks.

**7.5** **What can organizations do to help employees achieve high performance throughout their careers?** Organizations should develop performance standards for employees and then evaluate employees on a regular basis. Through performance appraisal, employees learn whether they are performing effectively, or whether they need help to improve, including additional training.

Performance management ensures that employees are rewarded for excellence. It also helps establish career goals and adapt ongoing professional development plans.

**7.6** **How do total rewards motivate employees?** Total rewards contains five components: strategic compensation, benefits, work–life balance, performance management, and career development. These elements combine into one reward strategy that is integrated and results in happy, committed, and productive employees.

**7.7** **What can organizations do to maximize employee relations?** Once an organization has attracted and motivated employees, retention becomes the next crucial component. Employee relations is the final part of the HRM process identified earlier in the chapter and completes the toolkit that is an effective and integrated model for the successful management of an organization's human resources.

## SNAPSHOT SUMMARY

**7.1** **The Human Resource Management Process**
Environmental Factors Affecting HRM

**7.2** **Human Resource Requirements**
Job Analysis and Design
HR Planning

**7.3** **Staffing the Organization**
Recruitment
Selection

**7.4** **Orientation and Training**
Orientation
Training

**7.5** **Performance Management**
Performance Management System

**7.6** **Total Rewards**
Strategic Compensation
Benefits
Work–Life Balance
Performance and Recognition
Career Development

**7.7** **Employee Relations**
Occupational Health and Safety
Employee Engagement

## MyManagementLab® Learning Resources

# Resources

▼ **Explore and enhance your understanding of key chapter topics through the following online resources:**

- Student PowerPoints
- Audio Summary of Chapter
- ROLLS
- CBC Videos for Part 3
- MySearchLab

▶ Visit the **Study Plan** area to test your progress with **Pre-Tests** and **Post-Tests**.

▼ **Build on your knowledge and practise real-world applications using the following online activities:**

# Interpret

- Opening Case Activity: Planning for HR Requirements
- Review and Apply: Solutions to Interpret section questions and activities
- Glossary Flashcards

# Analyze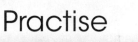

- Opening Case Activity: HR Requirements
- Review and Apply: Solutions to Analyze section questions and activities
- Self-Assessment Library

# Practise

- Opening Case Activity: The Selection Process
- Review and Apply: Solutions to Practice section questions and activities
- BizSkills Simulations:
  –Hiring a New Employee
  –Firing an Employee
  –Navigating Career Waters
- Decision Making Simulations:
  –HR & Diversity
  –Managing Your Career

# Interpret What You Have Read

1. Describe the environmental factors that most directly influence the human resource management process.

2. Contrast reject errors and accept errors. Which are more likely to open an employer to charges of discrimination? Why?

3. What is the relationship among job analysis, recruitment, and selection?

4. What are the two types of interview questions that employers should utilize?

5. What are the benefits and drawbacks of realistic job previews? (Consider this question from the perspective of both the organization and the employee.)

6. How are orientation and employee training alike? How are they different?

7. Describe three performance appraisal methods as well as the advantages and disadvantages of each.

8. What is skill-based pay?

9. How do recruitment, selection, orientation, and training directly affect workforce diversity?

# Analyze What You Have Read

1. Should an employer have the right to choose employees without government interference in the hiring process? Explain your position.

2. Do you think there are moral limits on how far a prospective employer should delve into an applicant's life by means of interviews, tests, and background investigations? Explain your position.

3. Studies show that women's salaries still lag behind men's, and even with equal opportunity laws and regulations women are paid about 73 percent of what men are paid. How would you design a compensation system that would address this issue?

4. Should managers offer flextime and other work–life balance initiatives? What special human resource management issues do these initiatives raise?

5. What are total rewards? How do the various components of total rewards lead to effective human resource management?

# Assess Your Skills

## HOW GOOD AM I AT GIVING PERFORMANCE FEEDBACK?

For each of the following pairs, identify the statement that most closely matches what you normally do when you give feedback to someone else.

1. **a.** Describe the behaviour.

   **b.** Evaluate the behaviour.

2. **a.** Focus on the feelings that the behaviour evokes.

   **b.** Tell the person what he or she should be doing differently.

3. **a.** Give specific instances of the behaviour.

   **b.** Generalize.

4. **a.** Deal only with behaviour that the person can control.

   **b.** Sometimes focus on something the person can do nothing about.

5. **a.** Tell the person as soon as possible after the behaviour.

   **b.** Sometimes wait too long.

6. **a.** Focus on the effect the behaviour has on me.

   **b.** Try to figure out why the individual did what he or she did.

7. **a.** Balance negative feedback with positive feedback.

   **b.** Sometimes focus only on the negative.

8. **a.** Do some soul searching to make sure that the reason I am giving the feedback is to help the other person or to strengthen our relationship.

   **b.** Sometimes give feedback to punish, win, or dominate the other person.

**SCORING KEY** Total the number of "a" responses, and then total the number of "b" responses, and then form an a/b ratio. For instance, if you have 6 "a" responses and 2 "b" responses, your a/b ratio would be 6/2.

### ANALYSIS AND INTERPRETATION

Along with listening skills, feedback skills comprise the other primary component of effective communication. This instrument is designed to assess how good you are at providing feedback.

In this assessment instrument, the "a" responses are your self-perceived strengths and the "b" responses are your self-perceived weaknesses. By looking at the proportion of your "a" and "b" responses, you will be able to see how effective you feel you are when giving feedback and determine where your strengths and weaknesses lie. For instance, an a/b ratio of 8/0, 7/1, or 6/2 suggests relatively strong feedback skills. In contrast, ratios of 3/5, 2/6, 1/7, or 0/8 indicate significant self-perceived weaknesses that can

be improved upon. To work on improving your feedback skills, see M. London, *Job Feedback: Giving, Seeking, and Using Feedback for Performance Improvement* (Lawrence Erlbaum, 2003).

---

**More Self-Assessments**

To learn more about your skills, abilities, and interests, take the following self-assessments on the MyManagementLab®:

- I.B.3.–How Satisfied Am I With My Job?
- III.B.3.–Am I Experiencing Work–Family Conflict?

---

# Practise What You Have Learned

## DILEMMA

Your instructor has asked class members to form teams to work on a major class project. You have worked on teams before and have not always been pleased with the results. This time you are determined to have a good team experience. You have reason to believe that effective performance management might make a difference.

You also know that evaluating performance and giving feedback are important. You have heard that organizations are using competencies as the basis for managing performance. A competency is a combination of knowledge, skills, and abilities (KSAs) used to improve performance. For example, negotiation or effective communications are competencies that are desirable in a group context.

With all of this in mind, write up a list of competencies that you would expect to find in strong team members.

## BECOMING A MANAGER

- Using the Internet, research different companies that interest you and check out what required competencies they list in their job descriptions.
- If you are working, note what types of competencies you see in your managers. What do they do that seems to be effective? Ineffective? What can you learn from this?

## DEVELOPING YOUR DIAGNOSTIC AND ANALYTICAL SKILLS: DEALING WITH A DIFFICULT PERSON

Document your answers to the following questions about someone with whom you are not getting along. Implement your written action plan for how you will adapt your behaviour to influence this negative relationship.

1. Your typical approach has not been successful. Describe your approach.

2. What, in your opinion, is this person's personality and behavioural style?

3. How does this person react to your style?

4. What way(s) could you modify your behaviour to improve your relationship with this person?

5. Outline a specific action plan for your next meeting with this person.

## DEVELOPING YOUR INTERPERSONAL SKILLS: INTERVIEWING

### ABOUT THE SKILL

The interview is used almost universally as part of the employee selection process. Not many of us have ever been hired without having gone through one or more interviews. Interviews can be valid and reliable selection tools, but they need to be structured and well organized.

### STEPS IN DEVELOPING THE SKILL

You can be an effective interviewer by using the following eight suggestions for interviewing job candidates:[81]

1. REVIEW THE JOB DESCRIPTION AND JOB SPECIFICATIONS. Be sure that prior to the interview you have reviewed pertinent information about the job. Why? Because this will provide you with valuable information with which to assess the job candidate. Furthermore, knowing the relevant job requirements will help eliminate interview bias.

2. PREPARE A STRUCTURED SET OF SITUATIONAL AND BEHAVIOURAL QUESTIONS THAT YOU WANT TO ASK ALL JOB APPLICANTS. By having a set of prepared questions, you are able to better compare all candidates' answers against a common base. Use a standardized evaluation form.

3. **BEFORE MEETING A CANDIDATE, REVIEW HIS OR HER APPLICATION FORM AND RÉSUMÉ.** By doing this preparation, you will be able to create a complete picture of the candidate in terms of what is represented on the résumé or application and what the job requires. You can also begin to identify areas to explore during the interview: Areas that are not clearly defined on the résumé or application but are essential to the job can become a focal point in your discussion with the candidate.

4. **OPEN THE INTERVIEW BY PUTTING THE APPLICANT AT EASE AND PROVIDING A BRIEF PREVIEW OF THE TOPICS TO BE DISCUSSED.** Interviews are stressful for job candidates. If you indicate up front that you want a successful outcome for both of you and engage in a bit of small talk at the beginning, you can give the candidate time to adjust to the interview setting. By providing a preview of topics to come, you are giving the candidate an agenda, which helps the candidate begin to frame what he or she will say in response to your questions.

5. **ASK YOUR QUESTIONS AND LISTEN CAREFULLY TO THE CANDIDATE'S ANSWERS.** Select follow-up questions that flow naturally from the answers given. Focus on the candidate's responses as they relate to information you need to ensure that the person meets your job requirements. If you are still uncertain, use a follow-up question to probe further for information.

6. **GIVE THE CANDIDATE A CHANCE TO ASK QUESTIONS.** Typically, at the start of the interview, you would let candidates know there will be an opportunity to ask questions at the end, or, if you prefer, throughout the interview.

7. **CLOSE THE INTERVIEW BY TELLING THE APPLICANT WHAT IS GOING TO HAPPEN NEXT.** Applicants are anxious about the status of your hiring decision. Be upfront with candidates regarding others who will be interviewed and the remaining steps in the hiring process. Let the person know your time frame for making a decision. In addition, tell the applicant how you will notify him or her about your decision.

8. **WRITE YOUR EVALUATION OF THE APPLICANT WHILE THE INTERVIEW IS STILL FRESH IN YOUR MIND.** Do not wait until the end of the day, after interviewing several people, to write your analysis of each candidate. Memory can (and often will) fail you! The sooner after an interview you write down your impressions, the better chance you have of accurately noting what occurred in the interview and your perceptions of the candidate.

### PRACTISING THE SKILL

You can also be effective at being interviewed through practice and preparation.

Review and update your résumé. Then ask several friends who are employed in management-level positions or are taking management training programs to critique it. Ask them to explain their comments and to make any changes that they think will improve your résumé.

Now inventory your interpersonal and technical skills, and any practical experiences that do not show up in your résumé. Draft a set of leading questions you would like to be asked in an interview that would give you a chance to discuss the unique qualities and attributes you could bring to a job.

# Team Exercises

## 3BL: THE TRIPLE BOTTOM LINE

Human Resource Management is part of the solution when it comes to the Triple Bottom Line. Consider the following benefits that accrue in the three main areas of 3BL:

### PEOPLE

Immigrants provide innovation, creativity, and high levels of skills and education.

### PROFIT

Inclusive workplaces feature higher job satisfaction and lower recruiting and turnover costs.

### PLANET

A broader labour supply pool provides long-term sustainability and avoids the necessity of meeting labour shortages with higher compensation and benefit packages.

### THINKING STRATEGICALLY ABOUT 3BL

The New Brunswick government has invested more than $5 million in its Aboriginal population. In January 2010, it invested $1 million for Aboriginal students to complete post-secondary education.[82] This investment was followed in October 2011 with $4 million for an employment training program in information and communications technology.[83] These strategic initiatives are meant to address a labour shortage and increase First Nations participation in the workforce. What other strategies could the government use to enhance employment opportunities for Aboriginal peoples?

## NETWORKING: THE 30-SECOND COMMERCIAL

Networking is a skill that can be very valuable for students to use for job hunting and making contacts. Think of it as building relationships with a variety of people whom you may be able to help or receive help from in the future. Before attending a networking event, you should learn to develop your "30 second commercial."[84] This tool is like an elevator pitch, which is a quick summary of you, an organization, or even a product/service. The name suggests that it should be possible to deliver the summary in the time span of an elevator ride. Venture capitalists on shows like CBC's *Dragon's*

Den[85] often judge the quality of an idea by the quality of its elevator pitch and will ask entrepreneurs for their elevator pitches in order to quickly weed out bad ideas and weak teams. Your 30-second commercial can be used in many situations, such as job interviewing and even dating!

When you meet a potential contact, you should state your purpose early in the conversation. Your initial discussion should be brief and to the point. You are meeting this person because they are in the field/industry you want to explore, so your goal is not to get a job but to obtain information from them about the industry.

Here are two templates that you can use to build a 30-second commercial. You have five minutes to create your commercial. Divide into pairs, greet each other with a firm, professional handshake, and take turns saying your commercial. Circulate among other students and practise your commercial. Obtain written feedback from one classmate.

## OPTION A

- Your Name
- Your current status (*student, program, school*)
- What were your major accomplishments? (*academic or work, list 3 and results*)
- What do you want to do next? (*seek information on this industry, learn more about role X, learn more about the organization, etc.*)

## OPTION B

- I'm (*name*). I'm a (*_ year student*) with (*university, college, school*). Most recently, I worked at (*company*) as a (*job title*), where I (*list a few duties*). Whether at school or in the workplace, I bring three key strengths to the table: (___, ___, ___). At this time, I am seeking (*information, background, details, etc.*) in this field as I am considering a career in this industry.

Continue to polish and develop your personal 30-second commercial—you never know when it may come in handy.

For more information, see Julia McKinnell, "The Introvert's Guide to Networking," *Maclean's*, August 26, 2010, and Derek Sankey, "Don't Overlook 'Face Time' in Job Search," *Ottawa Citizen*, November 16, 2011.

## BE THE CONSULTANT

You have been hired by a company to give some guidance on their job interview questions. A lawyer told managers of the company that several of their questions do not meet Canadian legislation requirements and provided them with sample revised questions. Turn the remainder of the bad questions into good interview questions.

| No | Instead |
|---|---|
| What is your age? | Are you of legal working age? |
| Do you have kids? | Are there any restrictions on your ability to travel as necessary? |
| Are you a Canadian citizen? | Are you legally entitled to work in Canada? |
| What are your strengths and weaknesses? | |
| Tell me about yourself. | |
| Why should I hire you for this job? | |
| What interests you about our company? | |
| Do you ever abuse alcohol or drugs? | |
| If you were a *Lost* character, who would you be? | |
| Do you get along well with people? | |

# Business Cases

## WELLINGTON WEST

Bay Street is the centre of Canada's financial district, but a Winnipeg-based brokerage firm proved that having its headquarters in Toronto was not a requirement for success. Wellington West started as a small investment boutique, formed a financial services division and an energy and mining investment division, and grew to become one of Canada's sparkling success stories. Few companies have been named to both the 50 Best Managed Companies in Canada and the 50 Best Employers in Canada, but Wellington West did it numerous times.[86]

Wellington West derived its competitive advantage from three areas: a client-centric approach, its unique organizational culture, and employee ownership.[87] The company's culture allowed it to draw employees seeking an alternative to large Canadian banks, opting instead for a large firm that operates like a boutique.[88] Wellington West became a firm that was built both for and by financial advisors. Another major core principle was employee ownership. More than

90 percent of the 650 employees became shareholders.[89] Founder and CEO Charlie Spiring summed it up as follows: "Ownership is a powerful thing. No one washes a rental car."

The growth that Wellington West achieved was astounding. In 1994, the company had one office, revenue of $2.5 million, and managed $250 million worth of assets. By 2008, Wellington West had 51 offices and $133 million in revenue, and was managing over $10 billion worth of client assets.[90] The success started from the top, and CEO Spiring was named to Canada's Top 40 Under 40 and won an Entrepreneur of the Year award from Ernst & Young.

Ultimately, Wellington West's success led to it being a popular target for acquisition. In 2011, the energy and investment mining arm of Wellington West was acquired by National Bank. National Bank Financial co-CEO Ricardo Pascoe said the $333 million acquisition would allow the company to pursue a leadership position in investment banking for mid-cap energy and mining companies in Canada. "What we're really going after," he said, "is Wellington West's client relationship and their research coverage."[91]

In late August 2012, Wellington West Financial Services was acquired by Manulife Financial. "This transaction allows us to build on our position as one of Canada's premier investment firms and reflects our commitment to independent financial advice in Canada," said Rick Annaert, chief executive of Manulife Securities. "There is a natural cultural fit between our two firms."[92]

What can National Bank and Manulife do to maintain Wellington West's strong corporate culture that has traditionally been somewhat "anti-bank"?

## CBC

# Tamarack Lake Electric Boat Company

Meet Montgomery Gisborne, a graduate of Ryerson University in Toronto, Ontario, with a rich history in electric vehicles. Since 1994, Gisborne has served on the executive of the Electric Vehicle Society, Canada's largest electric vehicle organization. In 1996, he constructed an electric car to compete in the 1997 American Tour de Sol Solar & Electric Car Rally and placed tenth out of 50 entrants. His electric car placed first in 2003.

Gisborne formed the Tamarack Lake Electric Boat Company in 2005 to bring electric boats to the market. The Loon was a custom-designed, six-metre pontoon-style prototype—a boat designed with 738 watts of solar panels overhead, serving as both a source of solar energy and a roof. With a cruising speed of 5 knots (9.3 km/h), the six-metre, eight-passenger Loon weighed in at 1000 kilograms, slightly heavier than a gas-powered version. Today, Tamarack Lake Electric Boat Company offers the commercial version of the Loon (6.7 metres, 1000 watt [peak] solar array, with a top speed of 8 knots [14.8 km/h]) and the Osprey (9.75 metres, 2000 watt [peak] solar array, with the same top speed as the Loon).

Montgomery Gisborne has a lot of money riding on the successful commercialization of the electric boat—over a quarter of a million dollars to be more precise. At $35 000 per Loon, almost twice the price of a comparable gasoline engine–powered equivalent, it could be a tough sell, requiring a seasoned sales professional. The trouble is, Gisborne is not only the salesperson, but he is also the production engineer, the web page designer, and the advertising and promotions manager: it's a one-person show. No small surprise that when he received his first order for twelve boats, his eighteen hour days were not long enough!

Personally scrambling to come up with enough materials to construct twelve Loons was a challenge. But Gisborne's efforts were followed by disappointment when the buyer who ordered the boats was restricted to purchasing only five boats by his foreign government. Gisborne recognized that he could no longer do

it all himself, so he hired some local talent to assist in the production of the boats and a part-time publicist to promote his creations. The publicity work has paid off, generating a significant order from Australia as well as deals coming in on the Internet.

Now the question is: Which organizational structure will best suit the Tamarack Lake Electric Boat Company?

## QUESTIONS

### Interpret

1. Tamarack Lake Electric Boat Company is a start-up company. Many contemporary organizational designs do not lend themselves to the reality of start-ups. In your view, which of the contemporary organizational designs are inappropriate? Explain.

2. Which approach to decision making—centralized or decentralized—would be most beneficial for Tamarack Lake Electric Boat Company? Support your answer.

### Analyze

3. Do you feel that a concerted effort to involve key stakeholders would offer the Tamarack Lake Electric Boat Company a sustainable competitive advantage?

4. One possible organizational structure for the Tamarack Lake Electric Boat Company would be to hire a small number of full-time employees who contract out certain aspects of the work such as hull fabrication, electronic components, boat interior components, advertising, accounting, and final assembly. Many aspects of running the company could be undertaken remotely. Would a network organization be an option for the Tamarack Lake Electric Boat Company?

### Practise

5. Organizational structure refers to the formal arrangement of jobs within an organization. Suppose you have been retained to develop an organizational structure for the Tamarack Lake Electric Boat Company. First, discuss which of the purposes of organizing support the need for an organizational structure in this company. Second, given the need for flexibility, adaptability, and nimbleness in this start-up company, which organizational design would you recommend for the company at the moment and why?

*Sources:* "Solar Boat," *Venture's Dreamers and Schemers*, Show No. 1, Canadian Broadcasting Corporation, October 11, 2006; Tamarack Lake Electric Boat Company website, http://www.tamarackelectricboats.com.

# CHAPTER 8 Leadership

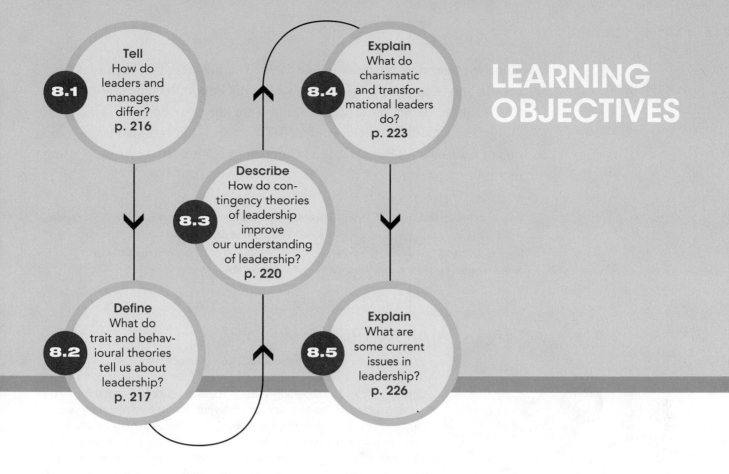

## LEARNING OBJECTIVES

**8.1** Tell
How do leaders and managers differ?
p. 216

**8.4** Explain
What do charismatic and transformational leaders do?
p. 223

**8.3** Describe
How do contingency theories of leadership improve our understanding of leadership?
p. 220

**8.2** Define
What do trait and behavioural theories tell us about leadership?
p. 217

**8.5** Explain
What are some current issues in leadership?
p. 226

When Rossana Di Zio Magnotta first started Vaughan, Ontario–based Festa Juice with her husband Gabe, the company sold imported grape juice to people who were making wine at home.[1] A scientist by training, Magnotta helped with the technical side of the business by applying biochemistry and microbiology to winemaking. Her intention was to offer free advice about winemaking to her customers, even testing some of their samples to see how they could improve their wine.

Magnotta's scientific background did not impress her customers, however, who were mainly first-generation Italian and Portuguese men. They had trouble believing a Canadian woman (even if she had Italian ancestry) could possibly know how to make wine. "They would say they were 'born in the grapes,' and start talking to me about the old country," she said.

Rather than feel undermined by the questioning of her winemaking ability, Magnotta decided to win over her customers by writing a step-by-step guide to winemaking, "Making Wine the Festa Way." The booklet was translated into Italian and Spanish, and was given away to every Festa Juice purchaser.

Because of the helpful advice Magnotta provided, it was not too long before customers started asking the company to sell wine, rather than juice and advice. After much consideration, the husband and wife team decided to buy Charal Winery, which had a license and a few pieces of equipment, although no land. They renamed the company Magnotta Winery and

### Think About It

What does it mean to be a leader for today's organizations? Put yourself in Rossana Di Zio Magnotta's shoes: What kinds of challenges does she face as a leader in the winery business?

launched their new business in late 1990. The business has been very successful and is now the third-largest winery in Ontario. Its net earnings were $2.6 million on net sales of $24 million for the year ending January 31, 2009. The winery has received over 3000 awards and has also been voted one of Canada's 50 Best Managed Companies eight years in a row, starting in 1999.

Why is leadership so important? Because leaders in organizations are the ones who make things happen.

If leadership is so important, it is only natural to ask: What differentiates leaders from nonleaders? What is the most appropriate style of leadership? What can you do if you want to be seen as a leader? In this chapter, we try to answer these and other questions about what it means to be a leader.

## MANAGERS VS. LEADERS

**Tell**
How do leaders and managers differ?

**8.1**

Let us begin by clarifying the distinction between managers and leaders. *Leadership* and *management* are two terms that are often confused and typically viewed as separate. What is the difference between them?

Manager and leaders act in different but complementary ways. Leaders cope with change so as to transform organizations, while managers cope with the complexity of keeping organizations running effectively and efficiently. As organizations deal with much more rapid change, management and leadership are seen as integrated roles rather than separate functions.[2] Exhibit 8-1 illustrates the basic distinction between managers and leaders. **Leaders** provide vision and strategy to the organization; managers implement that vision and strategy, coordinate and staff the organization, and handle day-to-day problems. **Leadership** is the process of influencing individuals or groups toward the achievement of goals.

Can managers be leaders? Should leaders be managers? Because no one yet has shown that leadership ability is a handicap to a manager, we believe that all managers should

**EXHIBIT 8-1**  Distinctions Between Managers and Leaders

| | Managers | Leaders |
|---|---|---|
| What is to be done? | Planning and budgeting | Creating a vision and setting direction |
| Who is going to do it? | Organizing and staffing | Aligning people to the vision |
| How can we make it happen? | Controlling and problem solving | Motivating people |

*Source:* Reprinted with permission from "What Leaders Really Do" by John P. Kotter.  Harvard Business Review. May 1990 Copyright © 1990 by Harvard Business Publishing; all rights reserved.

ideally be leaders. One of the major functions of management is to lead. However, not all leaders have the capabilities or skills of effective managers, and thus not all leaders should be managers. An individual who can set vision and strategy is not necessarily able to plan, organize, and control. Mark Henderson, president and CEO of Ericsson Canada, believes that "managers and leaders don't have all the answers, but strong leadership seems to utilize the knowledge of the employees and the collective power of their motivation and experience."[3]

## EARLY LEADERSHIP THEORIES

When Rossana Di Zio Magnotta and her husband, Gabe, decided to start Magnotta Winery, their intention was to sell their wine through the Liquor Control Board of Ontario (LCBO).[4] Their timing for the opening of the business could not have been worse. The economy was in the midst of a downturn. As Magnotta explains, "On December 7, 1990, we opened up shop and immediately got hit with the recession that was rolling across the country." At the same time, the LCBO informed Magnotta and her husband that there was no room in the stores to shelve Magnotta wine. These obstacles had not been part of their business planning.

**8.2 Define** What do trait and behavioural theories tell us about leadership?

### Think About It

A president and CEO of any company has to manage people effectively. Are there specific traits or behaviours that leaders such as Rossana Di Zio Magnotta should have?

Magnotta and her husband ended up waging a 10-year battle with the LCBO. She explains, "We had no choice; it was either fight or die."

Leadership has been of interest since the early days of people gathering together in groups to accomplish goals. However, it was not until the early part of the twentieth century that researchers began to study leadership. These early leadership theories focused on the *leader* (trait theories) and how the *leader interacted* with his or her group members (behavioural theories).

### Trait Theories

Leadership research in the 1920s and 1930s focused on leader traits—characteristics that might be used to differentiate leaders from nonleaders. The intent was to isolate traits that leaders possessed and nonleaders did not. Some of the traits studied included physical stature, appearance, social class, emotional stability, fluency of speech, and sociability. Despite the best efforts of researchers, it proved to be impossible to identify a set of traits that would *always* differentiate leaders (the person) from nonleaders. Maybe it was a bit optimistic to think that there could be consistent and unique traits that would apply universally to all effective leaders, whether they were in charge of Toyota Motor Corporation, the Moscow Ballet, Ted's Outfitters Shop, or Queen's University. However, more recent attempts to identify traits consistently associated with leadership (the process, not the person) have been more successful. Eight traits associated with effective leadership include drive, the desire to lead, honesty and integrity, self-confidence, cognitive and emotional intelligence, job-relevant knowledge, and extroversion.[5] These traits are briefly described in Exhibit 8-2.

*Think about some of the managers you have encountered. How did their traits affect whether they were good or bad managers?*

---

**leader**
Someone who can influence others and provide vision and strategy to the organization.

**leadership**
The process of influencing individuals or groups toward the achievement of goals.

**EXHIBIT 8-2** Eight Traits Associated with Leadership

1. **Drive.** Leaders exhibit a high effort level. They have a relatively high desire for achievement; they are ambitious; they have a lot of energy; they are tirelessly persistent in their activities; and they show initiative.

2. **Desire to lead.** Leaders have a strong desire to influence and lead others. They demonstrate the willingness to take responsibility.

3. **Honesty and integrity.** Leaders build trusting relationships between themselves and followers by being truthful or nondeceitful and by showing high consistency between word and deed.

4. **Self-confidence.** Followers look to leaders for an absence of self-doubt. Leaders, therefore, need to show self-confidence in order to convince followers of the rightness of their goals and decisions.

5. **Cognitive intelligence.** Leaders need to be intelligent enough to gather, synthesize, and interpret large amounts of information, and they need to be able to create visions, solve problems, and make correct decisions.

6. **Emotional intelligence.** Leaders need to be aware of their emotions and those of others, and they need to be able to use those emotions effectively when making decisions.

7. **Job-relevant knowledge.** Effective leaders have a high degree of knowledge about the company, industry, and technical matters. In-depth knowledge allows leaders to make well-informed decisions and to understand the implications of those decisions.

8. **Extroversion.** Leaders are energetic, lively people. They are sociable, assertive, and rarely silent or withdrawn.

*Sources:* S. A. Kirkpatrick and E. A. Locke, "Leadership: Do Traits Really Matter?" *Academy of Management Executive.* May 1991, pp. 48–60; and T. A. Judge, J. E. Bono, R. Iiies and M. Werner, "Personality and Leadership: A Qualitative and Quantitative Review," *Journal of Applied Psychology,* Aug. 2002, pp. 765–780.

Researchers have begun organizing traits around the Big Five personality framework.[6] They have found that most of the dozens of traits that emerged in various leadership reviews fall under one of the Big Five personality traits (extroversion, agreeableness, conscientiousness, emotional stability, and openness to experience). This approach has resulted in consistent and strong support for traits as predictors of leadership.

Conservative MP Steven Fletcher (Charleswood–St. James–Assiniboia, Manitoba) is driven to be a leader. Left a quadriplegic after a car accident when he was 23, Fletcher was determined to take charge of his life. He won his first political campaign to become president of the University of Manitoba Students' Union. He later became president of the Progressive Conservative Party of Manitoba. When he was elected MP, he defeated his riding's incumbent Liberal candidate. Fletcher says many of his constituents are not aware that he is quadriplegic until they meet him.

Researchers agreed that traits alone were not sufficient to explain effective leadership, because explanations based solely on traits ignored the interactions of leaders and their group members as well as situational factors. Possessing the appropriate traits only made it more likely that an individual would be an effective leader. Therefore, leadership research from the late 1940s to the mid-1960s concentrated on the preferred behavioural styles that leaders demonstrated. Researchers wondered whether there was something unique in what effective leaders *did*—in other words, in their *behaviour*.

## Behavioural Theories

**Behavioural theories** of leadership identify behaviours that differentiate effective leaders from ineffective leaders. Researchers hoped that the behavioural theories approach would provide more definitive answers about the nature of leadership than did the trait theories. Studies on thousands of leadership behaviours distilled down to two main aspects: people-oriented and task-oriented behaviours.[7]

**UNIVERSITY OF IOWA STUDIES** The University of Iowa studies (conducted by Kurt Lewin and his associates) explored three leadership styles.[8] The **autocratic style** describes a leader who tends to centralize authority, dictate work methods, make unilateral decisions, and limit employee participation. The **democratic style** describes a leader who tends to involve employees in decision making, delegate authority, encourage participation in deciding work methods and goals, and use feedback as an opportunity for coaching employees. The **laissez-faire style** describes a leader who generally gives the group complete freedom to make decisions and complete the work in whatever way it sees fit. Aaron Regent, president and CEO of Barrick Gold Corporation, believes that "sometimes leadership is about leading, sometimes it's about following, and sometimes it's just about getting out of the way."[9]

Lewin and his associates researched which one of the three leadership styles was most effective. Their results seemed to indicate that the democratic style contributed to both good quantity and quality of work. Had the answer to the question of the most effective leadership style been found? Unfortunately, it was not that simple. Later studies of the autocratic and democratic styles showed mixed results. The democratic style sometimes produced higher performance levels than the autocratic style, but at other times it produced lower or equal performance levels. More consistent results were found, however, when a measure of subordinate satisfaction was used. Group members' satisfaction levels were generally higher under a democratic leader than under an autocratic one.[10] To learn more about your leadership style, see *Assess Your Skills—What's My Leadership Style?* on pages 236–238 at the end of the chapter.

Now leaders faced a dilemma! Should they focus on achieving higher performance or on achieving higher member satisfaction? This recognition of the dual nature of a leader's behaviour—that is, focusing on the task and on the people—was a key characteristic of successful leaders.

Behavioural studies support the idea that people-oriented behaviours are related to follower satisfaction, motivation, and leader effectiveness, while production-oriented behaviours are slightly more strongly related to performance by the leader, the group, and the organization.

Interpret

---

**behavioural theories**
Leadership theories that identify behaviours that differentiate effective leaders from ineffective leaders.

**autocratic style**
A leadership style where the leader tends to centralize authority, dictate work methods, make unilateral decisions, and limit employee participation.

**democratic style**
A leadership style where the leader tends to involve employees in decision making, delegate authority, encourage participation in deciding work methods and goals, and use feedback as an opportunity for coaching employees.

**laissez-faire style**
A leadership style where the leader tends to give the group complete freedom to make decisions and complete the work in whatever way it sees fit.

**Describe**

How do contingency theories of leadership improve our understanding of leadership?

**8.3**

# CONTINGENCY THEORIES OF LEADERSHIP

Contingency theories of leadership developed after it became clear that identifying traits or key behaviours was not enough to understand what made good leaders. Contingency researchers considered whether different situations required different styles of leadership. To illustrate how situations might affect the ability to lead, consider the fate of an American who was recruited to run Canadian companies. Successful Texas oilman J. P. Bryan was given two chances to restore profitability at Canadian companies—Gulf Canada Resources (now ConocoPhillips) and Canadian 88 Energy (which later became Esprit Exploration)—and failed in both attempts.[11] This example suggests that one's leadership style may need to be adjusted for different companies and employees, and perhaps even for different countries, an observation consistent with research findings that not all leaders can lead in any situation.[12]

*Do you know what your leadership style is? What impact might your style have on how you lead?*

In this section, we examine two contingency theories of leadership—Hersey and Blanchard's Situational Leadership® and path-goal theory. Both of these theories focus on the relationship of the leader to followers, and there is broad support for the idea that this relationship is important.[13] Each theory attempts to answer *if-then* contingencies (that is, *if* this is the situation, *then* this is the best leadership style to use).

## Hersey and Blanchard's Situational Leadership®

Paul Hersey and Ken Blanchard developed a leadership theory that has gained a strong following among management development specialists.[14] This contingency theory of leadership, called **Situational Leadership® (SL)**, focuses on followers' readiness. Hersey and Blanchard argue that successful leadership is achieved by selecting the right leadership style, which is contingent on the level of the followers' readiness. Before we proceed, we need to clarify two points: Why a leadership theory focuses on the followers, and what is meant by the term *readiness*.

The emphasis on the followers in leadership effectiveness reflects the reality that the followers are the ones who accept or reject the leader. Regardless of what the leader does, effectiveness depends on the actions of his or her followers. This fact is an important dimension that has been overlooked or underemphasized in most leadership theories. **Readiness**, as defined by Hersey and Blanchard, refers to the extent to which people have the ability and willingness to accomplish a specific task.

SL uses the same two leadership dimensions that Fred Fiedler, a psychologist at the University of Washington who pioneered the study of leadership behaviours, identified in his contingency model of leadership: task and relationship behaviours. However, Hersey and Blanchard go a step further by considering each as either high or low and then combining them into four specific leadership styles (see Exhibit 8-3 on page 221), described as follows:

- *Telling* (high task–low relationship): The leader defines roles and tells people what, how, when, and where to do various tasks.
- *Selling* (high task–high relationship): The leader provides both directive and supportive behaviour.
- *Participating* (low task–high relationship): The leader and follower share in decision making; the main role of the leader is facilitating and communicating.
- *Delegating* (low task–low relationship): The leader provides little direction or support.

The final component in SL theory is follower readiness, described in four stages:

- *R1:* People are both *unable* and *unwilling* to take responsibility for doing something. They are neither competent nor confident.
- *R2:* People are *unable* but *willing* to do the necessary job tasks. They are motivated but currently lack the appropriate skills.
- *R3:* People are *able* but *unwilling* to do what the leader wants.
- *R4:* People are both *able* and *willing* to do what is asked of them.

**EXHIBIT 8-3** Hersey and Blanchard's Situational Leadership®

SL essentially views the leader–follower relationship as similar to that of a parent and child. Just as a parent needs to give up control as a child becomes more mature and responsible, so, too, should a leader. As followers reach high levels of readiness, the leader responds not only by continuing to decrease control over their activities, but also by continuing to decrease relationship behaviour. SL says if followers are *unable* and *unwilling* to do a task, the leader needs to give clear and specific directions; if followers are *unable* and *willing,* the leader needs to display high task orientation to compensate for the followers' lack of ability and high relationship orientation to get followers to "buy into" the leader's desires; if followers are *able* and *unwilling,* the leader needs to use a supportive and participative style; and if employees are both *able* and *willing,* the leader does not need to do much.

SL has intuitive appeal. It acknowledges the importance of followers and builds on the logic that leaders can compensate for ability and motivational limitations in their followers. Yet research efforts to test and support the theory generally have been disappointing.[15] Why? Possible explanations include internal inconsistencies in the model itself as well as problems with research methodology. So despite its appeal and wide popularity, any endorsement of the SL theory should be made with caution.

## Path-Goal Theory

Currently, one of the most respected approaches to understanding leadership is **path-goal theory**, which states that a leader's job is to assist his or her followers in attaining their goals and to provide the necessary direction and support to ensure that their goals are compatible with the overall objectives of the group or organization. Developed by University of Toronto Professor Martin Evans in the late 1960s, the path-goal theory was subsequently expanded upon by Robert House (formerly at the University of Toronto and now at the

**Situational Leadership® (SL)**
A leadership theory that focuses on the readiness of followers.

**readiness**
The extent to which people have the ability and willingness to accomplish a specific task.

**path-goal theory**
A leadership theory that says the leader's job is to assist his or her followers in attaining their goals and to provide the necessary direction and/or support to ensure that their goals are compatible with the overall objectives of the group or organization.

Wharton School of Business). Path-goal theory is a contingency model of leadership that takes key elements from the expectancy theory of motivation (see Chapter 9, page 255).[16] The term *path-goal* is derived from the belief that effective leaders clarify the path to help their followers get from where they are to the achievement of their work goals and make the journey along the path easier by reducing roadblocks and pitfalls.

Path-goal theory identifies four leadership behaviours:

- *Directive leader.* Leader lets subordinates know what is expected of them, schedules work to be done, and gives specific guidance on how to accomplish tasks.
- *Supportive leader.* Leader is friendly and shows concern for the needs of followers.
- *Participative leader.* Leader consults with group members and uses their suggestions before making a decision.
- *Achievement-oriented leader.* Leader sets challenging goals and expects followers to perform at their highest level.

In contrast to Fiedler's view that a leader could not change his or her behaviour, House assumed that leaders are flexible. In other words, path-goal theory assumes that the same leader can display any or all of these leadership styles, depending on the situation.

Path-goal theory proposes two situational or contingency variables that moderate the leadership behaviour–outcome relationship: *environmental* factors that are outside the control of the follower (including task structure, formal authority system, and the work group) and factors that are part of the personal characteristics of the *follower* (including locus of control, experience, and perceived ability). Environmental factors determine the type of leader behaviour required if subordinate outcomes are to be maximized; personal characteristics of the follower determine how the environment and leader behaviour are interpreted. The theory proposes that leader behaviour will not be effective if it is redundant with what the environmental structure is providing or is incongruent with follower characteristics. Exhibit 8-4 gives some illustrations of leadership behaviour tailored to the situation.

Research on the path-goal theory is generally encouraging. Although not every study has found support, the majority of the evidence supports the logic underlying the theory.[17] In summary, employee performance and satisfaction are likely to be positively influenced when the leader compensates for shortcomings in either the employee or the work setting.

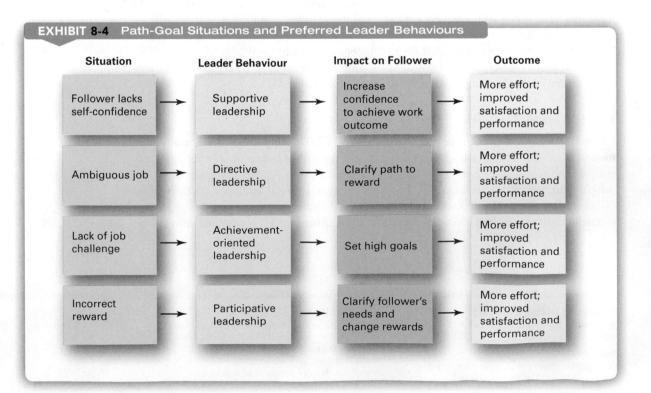

**EXHIBIT 8-4** Path-Goal Situations and Preferred Leader Behaviours

| Situation | Leader Behaviour | Impact on Follower | Outcome |
|-----------|------------------|--------------------|---------|
| Follower lacks self-confidence | Supportive leadership | Increase confidence to achieve work outcome | More effort; improved satisfaction and performance |
| Ambiguous job | Directive leadership | Clarify path to reward | More effort; improved satisfaction and performance |
| Lack of job challenge | Achievement-oriented leadership | Set high goals | More effort; improved satisfaction and performance |
| Incorrect reward | Participative leadership | Clarify follower's needs and change rewards | More effort; improved satisfaction and performance |

However, if the leader spends time explaining tasks when they are already clear or when the employee has the ability and experience to handle them without interference, the employee is likely to see such directive behaviour as redundant or even insulting.

## LEADING CHANGE

When the Liquor Control Board of Ontario (LCBO) decided not to give Magnotta Winery any shelf space, Rossana Di Zio Magnotta and her husband, Gabe, settled on two strategies.[18] They decided to sell the wine themselves and also wage a battle against the LCBO.

**8.4**

**Explain** What do charismatic and transformational leaders do?

### Think About It

Mobilizing people to work toward a leader's vision is a difficult task. How do leaders such as Rossana Di Zio Magnotta get individuals to support their vision and help carry it out?

To gain customers, the Magnottas used an innovative marketing strategy, selling their wine at significantly less than the price of similar quality wine at the LCBO. Their strategy got publicity in the newspapers, and soon people were travelling to their winery in Vaughan, Ontario, to purchase wine.

The battle against the LCBO lasted 10 years, but eventually the LCBO started carrying some Magnotta icewines.

Most of the leadership theories presented so far in this chapter have described **transactional leaders**—leaders who guide or motivate their followers in the direction of established goals by clarifying role and task requirements.[19] But another kind of leadership is needed for leading change in organizations. Two types of leadership have been identified in situations where leaders have inspired change: charismatic–visionary leadership and transformational leadership.

### Charismatic–Visionary Leadership

Jeff Bezos, founder and CEO of Amazon.com, is a person who exudes energy, enthusiasm, and drive.[20] He is fun-loving (his legendary laugh has been described as a flock of Canada geese on nitrous oxide), but has pursued his vision for Amazon with serious intensity and has demonstrated an ability to inspire his employees through the ups and downs of a rapidly growing company. Bezos is what we call a **charismatic leader**—an enthusiastic, self-confident leader whose personality and actions influence people to behave in certain ways.

*Have you ever encountered a charismatic leader? What was this person like?*

**CHARACTERISTICS OF CHARISMATIC LEADERS**   Several authors have attempted to identify the personal characteristics of charismatic leaders.[21] The most comprehensive analysis identified five such characteristics that differentiate charismatic leaders from noncharismatic ones: Charismatic leaders have a vision, are able to articulate that vision, are willing to take risks to achieve that vision, are sensitive to both environmental constraints and follower needs, and exhibit behaviours that are out of the ordinary.[22]

**EFFECTS OF CHARISMATIC LEADERSHIP**   What can we say about the charismatic leader's effect on his or her followers? An increasing body of evidence shows impressive correlations between charismatic leadership and high performance and satisfaction among followers.[23] Research indicates that people who work for charismatic leaders are motivated to

---

**transactional leaders**
Leaders who guide or motivate their followers in the direction of established goals by clarifying role and task requirements.

**charismatic leader**
An enthusiastic, self-confident leader whose personality and actions influence people to behave in certain ways.

exert extra work effort and express greater satisfaction, because they like their leaders.[24] One of the most cited studies of the effects of charismatic leadership was done at the University of British Columbia in the early 1980s by Jane Howell (now at the University of Western Ontario) and Peter Frost.[25] They found that those who worked under a charismatic leader generated more ideas, produced better results, reported higher job satisfaction, and showed stronger bonds of loyalty. Howell concludes, "Charismatic leaders know how to inspire people to think in new directions."[26]

Charismatic leadership also affects overall company performance. Robert House and colleagues studied 63 American and 49 Canadian companies (including Nortel Networks, Molson, Gulf Canada, and Manulife Financial) and found that "between 15 and 25 percent of the variation in profitability among the companies was accounted for by the leadership qualities of their CEO."[27] Charismatic leaders led more profitable companies. However, a recent study of the impact of a charismatic CEO on subsequent organizational performance found no relationship.[28] Despite this finding, charisma is still believed to be a desirable leadership quality.

Charismatic leadership may have a downside, however, as we see from the recent accounting scandals and high-profile bankruptcies of North American companies. WorldCom's Bernard Ebbers and Enron's Kenneth Lay "seemed almost a breed apart, blessed with unique visionary powers" when their companies' stock prices were growing at phenomenal rates in the 1990s.[29] After the scandals, however, there was some agreement that CEOs with less vision and more ethical and corporate responsibility might be more desirable.

**BECOMING CHARISMATIC**   Can people learn to be charismatic leaders? Or are charismatic leaders born with their qualities? Although a small number of experts still think that charisma cannot be learned, most believe that individuals can be trained to exhibit charismatic behaviours.[30] For example, researchers have succeeded in teaching undergraduate students to "be" charismatic. How? The students were taught to articulate a sweeping goal, communicate high performance expectations, exhibit confidence in the ability of subordinates to meet those expectations, and empathize with the needs of their subordinates; they learned to project a powerful, confident, and dynamic presence; and they practised using a captivating and engaging voice tone. The researchers also trained the student leaders to use charismatic nonverbal behaviours including leaning toward the follower when communicating, maintaining direct eye contact, and having a relaxed posture and animated facial expressions. In groups with these "trained" charismatic leaders, members had higher task performance, higher task adjustment, and better adjustment to the leader and to the group than did group members who worked in groups led by noncharismatic leaders.

One last thing we need to say about charismatic leadership: it may not always be needed to achieve high levels of employee performance. Charismatic leadership may be most appropriate when the follower's task has an ideological purpose or when the environment involves a high degree of stress and uncertainty.[31] For this reason, charismatic leaders most often surface in the arenas of politics, religion, or war; or when a business firm is starting up or facing a survival crisis. For example, Martin Luther King Jr. used his charisma to bring about social equality through nonviolent means, and Steve Jobs achieved unwavering loyalty and commitment from Apple Computer's employees by articulating a vision of a company that would become a world leader.

**VISIONARY LEADERSHIP**   Although the term *vision* is often linked with charismatic leadership, **visionary leadership** goes beyond charisma—it is the ability to create and articulate a realistic, credible, and attractive vision of the future that improves on the present situation.[32] This vision, if properly selected and implemented, is so energizing that it "in effect jump-starts the future by calling forth the skills, talents, and resources to make it happen."[33]

A vision should offer clear and compelling imagery that taps into people's emotions and inspires enthusiasm to pursue the organization's goals. It should be able to generate possibilities that are inspirational and unique, and offer new ways of doing things that are clearly better for the organization and its members. Visions that are clearly articulated and have powerful imagery are easily grasped and accepted. For example, Michael Dell (founder of Dell) created a vision of a business that sells and delivers a finished personal computer directly to a customer in less than a week. The late Mary Kay Ash's vision of women as entrepreneurs selling products that improved their self-image guided her cosmetics company, Mary Kay Cosmetics.

What skills do visionary leaders have? Once the vision is identified, these leaders appear to have three skills that are related to effectiveness in their visionary roles.[34] First is the *ability to explain the vision to others* by making the vision clear in terms of required goals and actions through clear oral and written communication. The second skill is the *ability to express the vision not just verbally but through behaviour*, which requires behaving in ways that continuously convey and reinforce the vision. The third skill is the *ability to extend or apply the vision to different leadership contexts*. For example, the vision has to be as meaningful to the people in accounting as it is to those in production, and to employees in Halifax as it is to those in Toronto.

## Transformational Leadership

Some leaders are able to inspire followers to transcend their own self-interests for the good of the organization and are capable of having a profound and extraordinary effect on their followers. These individuals are **transformational leaders**. Examples include Frank Stronach, chair of Aurora, Ontario–based Magna International; and Mogens Smed, CEO of Calgary-based DIRTT (Doing It Right This Time) and former CEO of SMED International. Prime Minister Stephen Harper was named *Time* magazine's 2006 Canadian Newsmaker of the Year, in part because of his transformational style. *Time* contributing editor Stephen Handelman explained the choice as follows: "[Harper] has set himself the messianic tasks of remaking Canadian federalism by curbing Ottawa's spending powers and overhauling Canada's health care and social welfare system." Handelman predicted that should Harper win a Conservative majority in the next election, "he may yet turn out to be the most transformational leader since Trudeau."[35]

Transformational leaders pay attention to the concerns and developmental needs of individual followers; they change followers' awareness of issues by helping those followers look at old problems in new ways; and they are able to excite, arouse, and inspire followers to put out extra effort to achieve group goals.[36]

Transformational leaders turn followers into believers on a vision, working toward what they believe is really important. "Part of a leader's role is to set the vision for the company and to communicate that vision to staff to get their buy-in," explains Dave Anderson of WorkSafeBC.[37] Transformational leadership is more than charisma, since the transformational leader attempts to empower followers to question not only established views but even those views held by the leader.[38]

The evidence supporting the superiority of transformational leadership over transactional leadership is overwhelmingly impressive. Studies that looked at managers in different settings, including the military and business, found that transformational leaders were evaluated as more effective, higher performers, and more promotable than their transactional counterparts.[39] In addition, evidence indicates that transformational leadership is strongly correlated with lower turnover rates, higher productivity, and higher employee satisfaction.[40] Finally, subordinates of transformational leaders may trust their leaders and their organizations more and feel that they are being fairly treated, which in turn may positively influence their work motivation (see Chapter 9).[41] However, transformational leadership should be used with some caution in non-North American contexts, because its effectiveness may be affected by cultural values concerning leadership.[42]

---

**visionary leadership**
The ability to create and articulate a realistic, credible, and attractive vision of the future that improves on the present situation.

**transformational leaders**
Leaders who inspire followers to transcend their own self-interests for the good of the organization, and who have a profound and extraordinary effect on their followers.

# CURRENT ISSUES IN LEADERSHIP

**8.5**

**Explain**
What are some current issues in leadership?

When Rossana Di Zio Magnotta first started trying to help her customers learn how to make wine, she ran into a significant hurdle.[43] Her customers, many of whom were first-generation Italian and Portuguese male immigrants, did not believe that a woman could know how to make wine. They constantly told her stories that implied that they knew more about winemaking than she did.

Magnotta knew that if she simply asserted her knowledge, her customers might become resentful. Instead, she wrote a step-by-step guide on winemaking and then started distributing it with each purchase of winemaking materials. This way, her customers would not feel threatened by her expertise and were able to make better wine. The booklet significantly increased her business. "One Italian would bring three of his brothers, and when I got one Portuguese guy I got five of his cousins, so all of a sudden my business became an instant success," she explains. All by leading behind the scenes.

> ## Think About It
>
> Do men and women lead differently? Do men and women face different challenges in moving to the top of an organization? What factors might have affected Rossana Di Zio Magnotta's ability to be seen as an effective leader?

In this section, we look at some of the issues that leaders face today, including managing power, developing trust, providing moral leadership, providing online leadership, and understanding gender differences in leadership.

## Managing Power

Where do leaders get their power—that is, their capacity to influence work actions or decisions? Five sources of leader power have been identified: legitimate, coercive, reward, expert, and referent.[44]

**Legitimate power** and authority are the same. Legitimate power represents the power a leader has as a result of his or her position in the organization. People in positions of authority are also likely to have reward and coercive power, but legitimate power is broader than the power to coerce and reward.

**Coercive power** is the power that rests on the leader's ability to punish or control. Followers react to this power out of fear of the negative results that might occur if they do not comply. As a manager, you typically have some coercive power, such as being able to suspend or demote employees or to assign them work they find unpleasant or undesirable.

**Reward power** is the power to give positive benefits or rewards. These rewards can be anything that another person values. In an organizational context, that might include money, favourable performance appraisals, promotions, interesting work assignments, friendly colleagues, and preferred work shifts or sales territories.

**Expert power** is influence that is based on expertise, special skills, or knowledge. As jobs have become more specialized, managers have become increasingly dependent on staff "experts" to achieve the organization's goals. If an employee has skills, knowledge, or expertise that is critical to the operation of a work group, that person's expert power is enhanced.

Finally, **referent power** is the power that arises because of a person's desirable resources or personal traits. If I admire and identify with you, you can exercise power over me because I want to please you. Referent power develops out of admiration of another and a desire to be like that person. If you admire someone to the point of modelling your behaviour and attitudes after him or her, that person has referent power over you.

Most effective leaders rely on several different forms of power to affect the behaviour and performance of their followers. For example, Lieutenant Commander Geoffrey Wadley, commanding officer of one of Australia's state-of-the-art submarines, the HMAS *Sheean,* employs different types of power in managing his crew and equipment. He gives orders to the crew (legitimate), praises them (reward), and disciplines those who commit infractions (coercive). As an effective leader, he also strives to have expert power (based on his expertise and knowledge) and referent power (based on his being admired) to influence his crew.[45]

## Developing Trust

After union members reluctantly agreed to $850 million a year in concessions that they believed were necessary to keep their company from bankruptcy in 2004, Air Canada's employees were stunned at president and CEO Robert Milton's after-the-fact disclosure of lucrative compensation policies and pension protections designed to retain key executives. Milton and his chief restructuring officer, Calin Rovinescu, were to receive one percent of the airline's shares, potentially worth an estimated $21 million, if the proposed takeover by Victor Li was successful. Any trust that employees had in Milton's ability to lead the airline into the future was eroded. In the end, the deal with Li collapsed when union members could not agree to further concessions relating to their pension plans.[46]

Milton's behaviour illustrates how fragile leader trust can be. In today's uncertain environment, an important consideration for leaders is building trust and credibility. Before we can discuss ways leaders can build trust and credibility, we have to know what trust and credibility are and why they are so important.

The main component of credibility is honesty. Surveys show that honesty is consistently singled out as the number-one characteristic of admired leaders. According to James Kouzes and Barry Posner, eminent scholars and leadership coaches, "Honesty is absolutely essential to leadership. If people are going to follow someone willingly, whether it be into battle or into the boardroom, they first want to assure themselves that the person is worthy of their trust." In addition to being honest, credible leaders are competent and inspiring.[47] They are personally able to effectively communicate their confidence and enthusiasm. Thus, followers judge a leader's **credibility** in terms of his or her honesty, competence, and ability to inspire.

Trust is closely entwined with the concept of credibility, and, in fact, the terms are often used interchangeably. **Trust** is defined as the belief in the integrity, character, and ability of a person. Followers who trust a leader are willing to be vulnerable to the leader's actions because they are confident that their rights and interests will not be abused.[48] Research has identified five dimensions that make up the concept of trust:[49]

- *Integrity:* Honesty and truthfulness
- *Competence:* Technical and interpersonal knowledge and skills
- *Consistency:* Reliability, predictability, and good judgment in handling situations
- *Loyalty:* Willingness to protect a person, physically and emotionally
- *Openness:* Willingness to share ideas and information freely

Of these five dimensions, integrity seems to be the most critical when someone assesses another's trustworthiness.[50] However, both integrity and competence were seen in our earlier discussion of leadership traits as consistently associated with leadership.

Workplace changes have reinforced why such leadership qualities are so important. For example, the trend toward empowerment and self-managed work teams has reduced or eliminated many of the traditional control mechanisms used to monitor employees. If a work team is free to schedule its own work, evaluate its own performance, and even make

---

**legitimate power**
The power a leader has as a result of his or her position in the organization.

**coercive power**
The power a leader has through his or her ability to punish or control.

**reward power**
The power a leader has to give positive benefits or rewards.

**expert power**
The influence a leader has based on his or her expertise, special skills, or knowledge.

**referent power**
The power a leader has because of his or her desirable resources or personal traits.

**credibility**
The degree to which someone is perceived as honest, competent, and able to inspire.

**trust**
The belief in the integrity, character, and ability of a person.

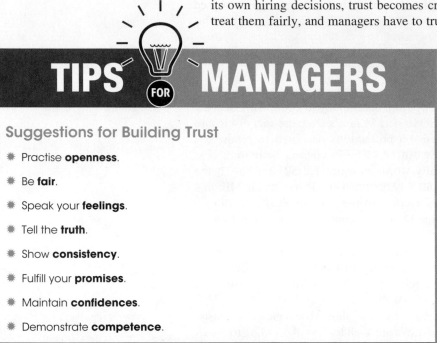

## TIPS FOR MANAGERS

### Suggestions for Building Trust

* Practise **openness**.

* Be **fair**.

* Speak your **feelings**.

* Tell the **truth**.

* Show **consistency**.

* Fulfill your **promises**.

* Maintain **confidences**.

* Demonstrate **competence**.

its own hiring decisions, trust becomes critical. Employees have to trust managers to treat them fairly, and managers have to trust employees to conscientiously fulfill their responsibilities.

Also, leaders have to increasingly lead others who may not be in their immediate work group—members of cross-functional teams, individuals who work for suppliers or customers, and perhaps even people who represent other organizations through strategic alliances. These situations do not allow leaders the luxury of falling back on their formal positions for influence. Many of these relationships, in fact, are fluid and fleeting; the ability to develop trust quickly is crucial to the success of the relationship.

Why is it important that followers trust their leaders? Research has shown that trust in leadership is significantly related to positive job outcomes, including job performance, job satisfaction, and organizational commitment.[51] Given the importance of trust in effective leadership, how should leaders build trust? See *Tips for Managers—Suggestions for Building Trust.*[52]

### Providing Ethical Leadership

The topic of leadership and ethics has received surprisingly little attention. Only recently have ethics and leadership researchers begun to consider the ethical implications of leadership.[53] Visit your local bookstore and you will find quite a few books on ethics and leadership. Why now? One reason is a growing general interest in ethics throughout the field of management. Another, without a doubt, is the recent corporate and government financial scandals that have increased the public's and politicians' concerns about ethical standards.

Ethics is part of leadership in a number of ways. For example, transformational leaders have been described as fostering moral virtue when they try to change the attitudes and behaviours of followers.[54] We can also see an ethical component to charisma. Unethical leaders may use their charisma to enhance their power over followers and use that power for self-serving purposes. On the other hand, ethical leaders may use their charisma in more socially constructive ways to serve others.[55] We also see a lack of ethics when leaders abuse their power and give themselves large salaries and bonuses while, at the same time, they seek to cut costs by laying off employees. Of course, trust, which is important to ethical behaviour, explicitly deals with the leadership traits of honesty and integrity.

Analyze

As we have seen recently, leadership is not value-free. Providing moral leadership involves addressing the *means* that a leader uses in trying to achieve goals, as well as the content of those goals. As a recent study concluded, ethical leadership is more than being ethical; it is reinforcing ethics through organizational mechanisms such as communication and the reward system.[56] Thus, before we judge any leader to be effective, we should consider both the moral content of his or her goals *and* the means used to achieve those goals.

*Would you expect your job as a leader to be more difficult if employees are working from home, connected by computer?*

### Providing Online Leadership

How do you lead people who are physically separated from you and where interactions are essentially reduced to written online communications? Pat O'Day, manager of a five-person virtual team at KPMG International, understands the challenges of providing online leadership. To help his team be more effective,

O'Day says, "We communicate through email and conference calls and meet in person four times a year."[57]

What little research has been done in online leadership has focused on managing virtual teams.[58] This research suggests there are three fundamental challenges in providing online leadership: communication, performance management, and trust.

**COMMUNICATION**   In a virtual setting, leaders may need to learn new communication skills in order to be seen as effective. To effectively convey online leadership, managers must realize they have choices in the words, structure, tone, and style of their online communications and be alert to expressions of emotions. In face-to-face communications, harsh *words* can be softened by nonverbal action. A smile and comforting gestures, for example, can lessen the blow behind words such as *disappointed*, *unsatisfactory*, *inadequate*, or *below expectations*. In online interactions, that nonverbal aspect does not exist.

The *structure* of words in online communication has the power to motivate or demotivate the receiver. Is the message made up of full sentences or just phrases? The latter is likely to be seen as curt and more threatening. Similarly, a message in ALL CAPS is the equivalent of shouting.

Leaders also need to be sure the *tone* of their message correctly conveys the emotions they want to send. Is the message formal or informal? Does it convey the appropriate level of importance or urgency? Is the leader's writing style consistent with his or her oral style? For example, if a leader's written communication is more formal than his or her oral style, it will likely create confusion for employees and hinder the effectiveness of the message.

Online leaders must also choose a *style*. Do they use emoticons, abbreviations, jargon, and the like? Do they adapt their style to their audience? Observation suggests that some managers have difficulty adjusting to computer-based communications. For instance, they use the same style with their bosses that they use with their staff. Or they selectively use online communication to "hide" when delivering bad news. Finally, online leaders need to develop the skills of "reading between the lines" in the messages they receive so they can decipher the emotional components.

**PERFORMANCE MANAGEMENT**   Another challenge of online leadership is managing performance. How? By defining, facilitating, and encouraging it.[59] As leaders *define* performance, they must ensure that all members of a virtual team understand the team's goals, their responsibilities in achieving those goals, and how goal achievement is going to be assessed. There should be no surprises or uncertainties about performance expectations. Although these issues are important managerial responsibilities in all situations, they are particularly critical in virtual work environments because there are no face-to-face interactions to convey expectations or address performance problems.

Online leaders also have a responsibility to *facilitate* performance. Facilitating involves reducing or eliminating obstacles to successful performance and providing adequate resources to get the job done. This task can be particularly challenging, especially if the virtual team is global, since the physical distance separating the leader and the team means it is not easy to get team members the resources they may need.

Finally, online leaders are responsible for *encouraging* performance by providing sufficient rewards that virtual employees really value. As we will see in Chapter 9, motivating employees can be difficult, even in work settings where there is face-to-face interaction. In a virtual setting, the motivational challenge can be even greater because the leader is not there in person to encourage, support, and guide. What can online leaders do? They can ask virtual employees what rewards are most important to them—pay, benefits, technology upgrades, opportunities for professional development, and so forth. Then, they can make sure the rewards are provided in a timely manner after major work goals have been achieved. Finally, any rewards program must be perceived as fair. This expectation is not any different from that of leaders in nonvirtual settings—employees want and expect rewards to be distributed fairly.

**TRUST**   The final challenge of providing online leadership is the trust issue. In a virtual setting, there are numerous opportunities to violate trust. One possible trust issue is whether the system is being used to monitor and evaluate employees. The technology is there to do so, but leaders must consider whether that is really the best way to influence employee behaviour. T. J. Rodgers, founder and CEO of Cypress Semiconductor, found out the hard way that it might not be.[60] He built an in-house system that tracked goals and deadlines. If a department missed its target, the software shut down its computers and cancelled the manager's next paycheque. After realizing the system encouraged dishonesty, Rodgers ditched it. The experience made him understand that it was more important to create a culture in which trust among all participants is expected and required. In fact, the five dimensions of trust we described earlier—integrity, competence, consistency, loyalty, and openness—would be vital to the development of such a culture.

## Team Leadership

Since leadership is increasingly taking place within a team context and more organizations are using work teams, the role of the leader in guiding team members is gaining importance. The role of team leader *is* different from the traditional leadership role. Many leaders are not equipped to handle the change to employee teams. As one consultant noted, "Even the most capable managers have trouble making the transition because all the command-and-control type things they were encouraged to do before are no longer appropriate. There's no reason to have any skill or sense of this."[61] This same consultant estimated that "probably 15 percent of managers are natural team leaders; another 15 percent could never lead a team because it runs counter to their personality—that is, they're unable to sublimate their dominating style for the good of the team. Then there's that huge group in the middle: Team leadership doesn't come naturally to them, but they can learn it."[62]

The challenge for many managers is learning how to become an effective team leader. They have to learn skills such as having the patience to share information, being able to trust others and to give up authority, and understanding when to intervene. Effective team leaders have mastered the difficult balancing act of knowing when to leave their teams alone and when to get involved. New team leaders may try to retain too much control at a time when team members need more autonomy, or they may abandon their teams at times when team members need support and help.[63] (To learn more about teams, see *Assess Your Skills—How Good Am I at Building and Leading a Team?* on pages 292–293 in Chapter 10.)

One study of organizations that had reorganized themselves around employee teams found certain common responsibilities of all leaders. These tasks included coaching, facilitating, handling disciplinary problems, reviewing team and individual performance, training, and communication.[64] However, a more meaningful way to describe the team leader's job is to focus on two priorities: (1) managing the team's external boundary and (2) facilitating the team process.[65] These priorities entail four specific leadership roles (see Exhibit 8-5).

Team leaders are *liaisons with external constituencies*, which may include upper management, other organizational work teams, customers, or suppliers. The leader represents the team to other constituencies, secures needed resources, clarifies others' expectations of the team, gathers information from the outside, and shares that information with team members.

*What has been your biggest challenge when trying to lead team members?*

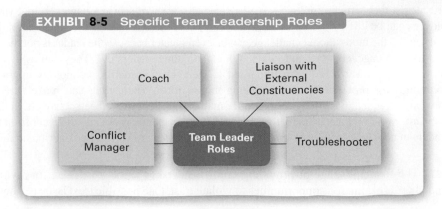

**EXHIBIT 8-5** Specific Team Leadership Roles

When Eva Aariak spoke to the Nunavut legislative assembly to explain why she should be elected the territory's premier, she emphasized that her leadership style included the ability to listen and encourage others to share their ideas. She considers herself a team player, which will work well with the territory's consensus style of government built from the principles of parliamentary democracy and Aboriginal values.

Team leaders are *troubleshooters*. When the team has problems and asks for assistance, team leaders sit in on meetings and try to help resolve the problems. Troubleshooting rarely involves technical or operational issues, because the team members typically know more about the tasks being done than does the leader. The leader is most likely to contribute by asking penetrating questions, helping the team talk through problems, and getting needed resources to tackle problems.

Team leaders are *conflict managers*. They help identify issues such as the source of the conflict, who is involved, the issues, the resolution options available, and the advantages and disadvantages of each. By getting team members to address questions such as these, the leader minimizes the disruptive aspects of intrateam conflicts.

Finally, team leaders are *coaches*. They clarify expectations and roles, teach, offer support, and do whatever else is necessary to help team members keep their work performance high.

## Understanding Gender Differences and Leadership

There was a time when the question "Do males and females lead differently?" could be accurately characterized as a purely academic issue—interesting, but not very relevant. That time has certainly passed! Many women now hold management positions, and many more around the world will continue to join the management ranks. Women filled 20 percent of senior management roles globally in 2011 (down from 24 percent in 2009).[66] They are highly involved in smaller companies. Industry Canada reports that in 2007, 47 percent of all small to medium-sized enterprises had some degree of female ownership.[67] Moreover, a study by the Canadian Imperial Bank of Commerce estimates that since 1989, women-run businesses have increased 60 percent faster than those run by men.[68]

In other economically developed countries, the percentage of female managerial/administrative employees is as follows: Australia—37 percent; France—39 percent; Germany—38 percent; China—17 percent; Poland—36 percent; and Sweden—32 percent.[69] Misconceptions about the relationship between leadership and gender can adversely affect hiring, performance evaluation, promotion, and other human resource decisions for both men and women. For example, evidence indicates that a "good" manager is still perceived as predominantly masculine.[70] A warning before we proceed: This topic is controversial. If male and female styles differ, is one inferior? If there is a difference, is one gender more effective in leading than the other? These are important questions and we will address them shortly.

A number of studies focusing on gender and leadership style have been conducted.[71] Their general conclusion is that males and females *do* use different styles. Specifically, women tend to adopt a more democratic or participative style. Women are more likely to encourage participation, share power and information, and attempt to enhance followers' self-worth. They lead through inclusion and rely on their charisma, expertise, contacts, and interpersonal skills to influence others. Women tend to use transformational leadership, motivating others by transforming their self-interest into organizational goals. Men are more likely to use a directive, command-and-control style. They rely on formal position authority for their influence. Men use transactional leadership, handing out rewards for good work and punishment for bad.[72] However, the above findings have an interesting qualifier. The tendency of female leaders to be more democratic than males declines when women are in male-dominated jobs. In such jobs, apparently, group norms and male stereotypes influence women, and they are likely to act more autocratically.[73]

Another issue to consider is how male and female leaders are perceived in the workplace. A recent study sheds some light on this topic.[74] One major finding of this research was that men consider women to be less skilled at problem solving, which is one of the qualities often associated with effective leadership. Another finding was that both men and women believed women to be superior to men at "take care" behaviours and men superior to women at "take charge" behaviours. Such gender-based stereotyping creates challenges both for organizations and for leaders within those organizations. Organizations need effective leaders at all levels, but they need to ensure that stereotypical perceptions do not limit who those leaders might be.[75]

Although it is interesting to see how male and female leadership styles differ, a more important question is whether they differ in effectiveness. Some researchers have shown that males and females tend to be equally effective as leaders,[76] but an increasing number of studies have shown that women executives, when rated by their peers, employees, and bosses, score higher than their male counterparts on a wide variety of measures, including getting extra effort from subordinates and overall effectiveness in leading. Subordinates also reported more satisfaction with the leadership given by women.[77] Based on a summary of five studies, female managers performed better at motivating others, fostering communication, producing high quality work, and listening to others.[78] Why these differences? One possible explanation is that in today's organizations, flexibility, teamwork and partnering, trust, and information sharing are rapidly replacing rigid structures, competitive individualism, control, and secrecy. In these types of workplaces, effective managers must use more social and interpersonal behaviours. They listen, motivate, and provide support to their people. They inspire and influence rather than control. Women seem to do those things better than men.[79] See Exhibit 8-6 for some sage advice from several of Canada's best female corporate leaders.

**EXHIBIT 8-6  Lessons from Canada's Female Leaders**

| | |
|---|---|
| Tamara Vrooman, CEO, Vancity | "When leaders believe what they are saying and have confidence, others are inspired to want to follow them." |
| Elyse Allan, president and CEO, GE Canada | "Leadership is about conviction and a sense of responsibility, that you don't give up halfway through." |
| Mandy Shapansky, president and CEO, Xerox Canada | "You can't be afraid of failure. Failure is a sign you're pushing the envelope or you're trying to innovate." |
| Ellen Moore, president and CEO, Chubb Insurance Co. of Canada | "You need to be able to set a clear course, something that is consistent so people understand where you're taking them." |

*Source:* Reproduced with permission.

Yale graduate Indra Nooyi, who played in an all-girl rock band while growing up in Chennai, India, is the savvy, irreverent chair and CEO of PepsiCo Inc. Joining PepsiCo as chief strategist 15 years ago to help turn around the company, she has doubled net profits to over $5.6 billion by focusing on better nutrition and promoting workforce diversity. "Indra can drive as deep and hard as anyone I've ever met," says former CEO Roger Enrico, "but she can do it with a sense of heart and fun." Nooyi still sings in the office and sometimes even goes barefoot at work.

Although women seem to rate highly on those leadership skills needed to succeed in today's dynamic global environment, we do not want to fall into the same trap as the early leadership researchers who tried to find the "one best leadership style" for all situations. We know that there is no one *best* style for all situations. Instead, which leadership style is effective will depend on the situation. Even if men and women differ in their leadership styles, we should not assume that one is always preferable to the other.

*Tips for Future Leaders* gives some suggestions for being a better leader.

Practise

## Tips for Future Leaders

✳ People work **with** you, not **for** you.

✳ **Spend time with people** at all levels and positions in the organization.

✳ Create a culture of **caring**—people do not care how much you know until they know how much you care.

✳ **Be persistent**. Re-evaluate and re-invent yourself.

✳ Support your organization's people. Look for the **good**, not the bad.

✳ Energize your team with a vision. Create a sense of **urgency**.

# 8 Review and Apply

## Summary of Learning Objectives

**8.1** **How do leaders and managers differ?** Managers are appointed to their positions. They have formal authority; this authority gives them their ability to influence employees. In contrast, leaders can be appointed or can emerge from within a work group. They provide vision and strategy and are able to influence others for reasons beyond formal authority. Though ideally all managers should be leaders, not all leaders can be managers, because they do not all have the ability to plan, organize, and control.

Rossana Di Zio Magnotta has demonstrated the ability to both lead and manage at Magnotta Winery.

**8.2** **What do trait and behavioural theories tell us about leadership?** Researchers agree that traits alone are not sufficient for explaining effective leadership. Possessing the appropriate traits makes it only more likely that an individual would be an effective leader. In general, behavioural theories have identified useful behaviours that managers should have, but the research could not identify when these behaviours were most useful.

Rossana Di Zio Magnotta notes that one of her most useful leadership traits is being tough and willing to stand up to adversity.

**8.3** **How do contingency theories of leadership improve our understanding of leadership?** Contingency theories acknowledge that different situations require different leadership styles. The theories suggest that leaders may need to adjust their style to the needs of different organizations and employees, and perhaps different countries.

**8.4** **What do charismatic and transformational leaders do?** While most leaders are transactional, guiding followers to achieve goals by clarifying role and task requirements, charismatic and transformational leaders inspire and influence their followers. Charismatic leaders are enthusiastic and self-confident leaders whose personality and actions motivate followers. They are known for having and articulating a vision, and for being willing to take risks to achieve that vision. Transformational leaders turn followers into believers on a mission, and encourage followers to go beyond their own self-interests for the greater good. Transformational leadership is more than charisma, since the transformational leader attempts to empower followers to question established views, even those views held by the leader.

Rossana Di Zio Magnotta found that motivating customers to help resolve the winery's dispute with the Liquor Control Board of Ontario reinforced the idea that the wines should be carried in the stores. By mobilizing customers, she caught the attention of the LCBO.

**8.5** **What are some current issues in leadership?** The major leadership issues today include managing power, developing trust, providing moral leadership, providing online leadership, and understanding gender differences and leadership.

Rossana Di Zio Magnotta's experience with Italian and Portuguese male customers illustrates the differences men and women can face in the workplace. She had to find a way to make her male customers comfortable with her expertise, something a man in her position would probably not have had to do.

### SNAPSHOT SUMMARY

**8.1** **Managers vs. Leaders**

**8.2** **Early Leadership Theories**
Trait Theories
Behavioural Theories

**8.3** **Contingency Theories of Leadership**
Hersey and Blanchard's Situational Leadership®
Path-Goal Theory

**8.4** **Leading Change**
Charismatic–Visionary Leadership
Transformational Leadership

**8.5** **Current Issues in Leadership**
Managing Power
Developing Trust
Providing Ethical Leadership
Providing Online Leadership
Team Leadership
Understanding Gender Differences and Leadership

# MyManagementLab® Learning Resources

## Resources

Explore and enhance your understanding of key chapter topics through the following online resources:

- Student PowerPoints
- Audio Summary of Chapter
- ROLLS
- CBC Videos for Part 4
- MySearchLab

Visit the **Study Plan** area to test your progress with **Pre-Tests** and **Post-Tests**.

Build on your knowledge and practise real-world applications using the following online activities:

### Interpret

- Opening Case Activity: Identifying Leaders
- Review and Apply: Solutions to Interpret section questions and activities
- Glossary Flashcards

### Analyze

- Opening Case Activity: How and Why Leaders Are Formed
- Review and Apply: Solutions to Analyze section questions and activities
- Self-Assessment Library

### Practise

- Opening Case Activity: Comparing Leadership Styles
- Review and Apply: Solutions to Practice section questions and activities
- Decision Making Simulations:
  - Leadership
  - The Leadership Imperative
  - Responsibility, Authority & Delegation

# Interpret What You Have Read

1. Discuss the strengths and weaknesses of the trait theory of leadership.
2. Discuss when the laissez-faire decision-making style is more appropriate than the democratic style.
3. What is the importance of charisma in leadership?
4. What are the two contingency variables of the path-goal theory of leadership?
5. What similarities, if any, can you find between Hersey and Blanchard's Situational Leadership®, and path-goal theory?
6. What sources of power are available to leaders? Which ones are most effective?
7. What are the five dimensions of trust?

# Analyze What You Have Read

1. "All managers should be leaders, but not all leaders should be managers." Do you agree or disagree with this statement? Support your position.
2. "It is more important to get work done than to worry about how your team is feeling." Do you agree or disagree with this statement?
3. Do you think that most managers in real life use a contingency approach to increase their leadership effectiveness? Discuss.
4. Trust is crucial to leading a group effectively. Discuss a time when a leader did not have the trust of the group you were in and how it affected the group's performance.
5. "Charismatic leadership is always appropriate in organizations." Do you agree or disagree? Support your position.
6. What kinds of campus activities could a full-time student do that might lead to the perception that he or she is a charismatic leader? In pursuing those activities, what might the student do to enhance this perception of being charismatic?

# Assess Your Skills

## WHAT IS MY LEADERSHIP STYLE?

The following items describe aspects of leadership behaviour. Respond to each item according to the way you would be most likely to act if you were the leader of a work group. Use this scale for your responses:

A = Always
F = Frequently
O = Occasionally
S = Seldom
N = Never

1. I would most likely act as the spokesperson of the group.    A F O S N
2. I would encourage overtime work.    A F O S N
3. I would allow group members complete freedom in their work.    A F O S N
4. I would encourage the use of uniform procedures.    A F O S N
5. I would permit group members to use their own judgment in solving problems.    A F O S N
6. I would stress being ahead of competing groups.    A F O S N
7. I would speak as a representative of the group.    A F O S N
8. I would needle group members for greater effort.    A F O S N

9. I would try out my ideas in the group.                                                A F O S N

10. I would let group members do their work the way they think best.                     A F O S N

11. I would be working hard for a promotion.                                             A F O S N

12. I would be able to tolerate postponement and uncertainty.                           A F O S N

13. I would speak for the group when visitors were present.                             A F O S N

14. I would keep the work moving at a rapid pace.                                        A F O S N

15. I would turn group members loose on a job and let them go to it.                     A F O S N

16. I would settle conflicts when they occur in the group.                              A F O S N

17. I would get swamped by details.                                                     A F O S N

18. I would represent the group at outside meetings.                                    A F O S N

19. I would be reluctant to allow group members any freedom of action.                  A F O S N

20. I would decide what should be done and how it should be done.                       A F O S N

21. I would push for increased production.                                              A F O S N

22. I would let some group members have authority that I should keep.                   A F O S N

23. Things would usually turn out as I predicted.                                       A F O S N

24. I would allow the group a high degree of initiative.                                A F O S N

25. I would assign group members to particular tasks.                                   A F O S N

26. I would be willing to make changes.                                                 A F O S N

27. I would ask group members to work harder.                                           A F O S N

28. I would trust group members to exercise good judgment.                              A F O S N

29. I would schedule the work to be done.                                               A F O S N

30. I would refuse to explain my actions.                                               A F O S N

31. I would persuade group members that my ideas are to their advantage.                A F O S N

32. I would permit the group to set its own pace.                                       A F O S N

33. I would urge the group to beat its previous record.                                 A F O S N

34. I would act without consulting the group.                                           A F O S N

35. I would ask that group members follow standard rules and regulations.               A F O S N

**SCORING KEY**

1. Circle the numbers 8, 12, 17, 18, 19, 30, 34, and 35.

2. Write a 1 in front of the circled number if you responded Seldom or Never.

3. Also write a 1 in front of any remaining (uncircled) items if you responded Always or Frequently to these.

4. Circle the 1s that you have written in front of the following questions: 3, 5, 8, 10, 15, 18, 19, 22, 24, 26, 28, 30, 32, 34, and 35.

5. Count the circled 1s. This is your score for "Concern for People."

6. Count the uncircled 1s. This is your score for "Task."

### ANALYSIS AND INTERPRETATION

This leadership instrument taps the degree to which you are task or people oriented. Task orientation is concerned with getting the job done, whereas people orientation focuses on group interactions and the needs of individual members.

The cutoff scores separating high and low scores are approximately as follows. For task orientation, high is a score above 10; low is below 10. For people orientation, high is a score above 7; low is below 7.

The best leaders are ones who can balance their task/people orientation to various situations. A high score on both would indicate this balance. If you are too task oriented, you tend to be autocratic. You get the job done but at a high emotional cost. If you are too people oriented, your leadership style may be overly laissez-faire. People are likely to be happy in their work but sometimes at the expense of productivity.

Your score should also help you put yourself in situations that increase your likelihood of success. Evidence indicates that when employees are experienced and know their jobs well, they tend to perform best with a people-oriented leader. If you are people oriented, then this is a favourable situation for you. But if you are task oriented, you might want to pass on this situation.

### More Self-Assessments

To learn more about your skills, abilities, and interests, take the following self-assessments on the MyManagementLab®:

- II.B.2.–How Charismatic Am I?
- II.B.4.–Do Others See Me as Trustworthy?
- II.B.6.–How Good Am I at Building and Leading a Team? (This exercise also appears in Chapter 10 on pages 292–293.)

# Practise What You Have Learned

## DILEMMA

You have worked hard at your organization and were rewarded with a promotion. What you may not have prepared for is the difficult situation of workplace friends now reporting to you. Fortunately experts indicate that you can both maintain those friendships and use them to be a better manager.[80]

## BECOMING A MANAGER

- Meet with each of your friends individually to discuss any concerns they may have.
- Do not create new boundaries—remind the team that you have not changed and that you are still there for support and advice
- Do not assume that people will be resentful. Many will be very happy for you, and you can deal with the others on a one-on-one basis.
- Avoid venting about the new position with your friends.
- Offer your friends support and time and space to adapt to the changes.

## DEVELOPING YOUR DIAGNOSTIC AND ANALYTICAL SKILLS: RADICAL LEADERSHIP

Ricardo Semler, CEO of Semco Group of São Paulo, Brazil, is considered by many to be a radical. He has never been the type of leader that most people would expect to be in charge of a multimillion-dollar business.[81] Why? Semler breaks all the traditional "rules" of leading and managing. He is the ultimate hands-off leader who does not even have an office at the company's headquarters. As the "leading proponent and most tireless evangelist" of participative management, Semler says his philosophy is simple: Treat people like adults and they will respond like adults.

Underlying the participative management approach is the belief that "organizations thrive best by entrusting employees to apply their creativity and ingenuity in service of the whole enterprise and to make important decisions close to the flow of work, conceivably including the selection and election of their bosses." According to Semler, his approach works well. But how does it work in reality?

At Semco, most of the trappings of organizations and management are absent. There are no organization charts, no long-term plans, no statements of corporate values, no dress codes, and no written rules or policy manuals. The company's 3000 employees decide their work hours and their pay levels. Subordinates decide who their bosses will be and also review their bosses' performance. The employees elect the corporate leadership and decide most of the company's new strategic initiatives. Each person has one vote—including Ricardo Semler.

At one of the company's plants outside São Paulo, there are no supervisors telling employees what to do. On any given day, an employee may decide to "run a grinder or drive a forklift, depending on what needs to be done." João Vendramin Neto, who is in charge of Semco's manufacturing, says that "the workers know the organization's objectives and they use common sense to decide for themselves what they should do to hit those goals."

Why did Semler decide that his form of radical leadership was necessary, and does it work? Semler did not pursue such radical self-governance out of some altruistic ulterior motive. Instead, he felt it was the only way to build an organization that was flexible and resilient enough to flourish in chaotic and turbulent times. He maintains that this approach has enabled Semco to survive the roller-coaster nature of Brazilian politics and the Brazilian economy. Although the country's political leadership and economy have gone from one extreme to another and countless Brazilian banks and companies have failed, Semco has survived. Not just survived—prospered. Semler says, "If you look at Semco's numbers, we've grown 27.5 percent a year for 14 years."

Semler attributes this fact to flexibility—of his company and, most importantly, of his employees.

### Questions

1. Describe Ricardo Semler's leadership style. What do you think the advantages and drawbacks of his style might be?
2. What challenges might a radically "hands-off" leader face? How could those challenges be addressed?
3. How could future leaders be identified in this organization? Would leadership training be important to this organization? Discuss.
4. What could other businesses learn from Semler's approach to leadership?

## Team Exercises

### 3BL: THE TRIPLE BOTTOM LINE

The Centre for Creative Leadership conducted a study of executives entitled "Leadership and the Triple Bottom Line."[82] The study found that the top five leadership competencies necessary for adopting 3BL approaches are:

- Long term view (20 percent)
- Communication (15 percent)
- Influence (11 percent)
- Scanning the external environment (9 percent)
- Collaboration (8 percent)

The respondents further identified the importance of creating an organizational culture where 3BL approaches were accepted and aligned with strategy, values, rewards, and recognition. Beyond the cultural support, leaders must model 3BL behaviours in their professional and personal lives to successfully achieve organizational support. What other competencies do you think are important for leaders to be effective at maximizing the triple bottom line?

### THINKING STRATEGICALLY ABOUT 3BL

A 3BL strategy is not enough. Organizations must develop the leadership capacity to manage 3BL opportunities and challenges. The leaders surveyed suggested that success with 3BL would come through an integrated approach, with key stakeholder involvement and a balanced perspective of long-term strategy and short-term results. Pick a small and medium-sized business in your community. Who are the key stakeholders you would recommend involving in order to support 3BL? Which of those stakeholders would be most opposed to 3BL?

### THE PRE–POST LEADERSHIP ASSESSMENT

#### OBJECTIVE

To compare characteristics intuitively related to leadership with leadership characteristics found in leadership theory.

#### PROCEDURE

Identify three people (e.g., friends, relatives, previous boss, public figures) whom you consider outstanding leaders. List why you feel each individual is a good leader. Compare your lists of the three people. Which traits, if any, are common to all three? Your instructor will lead the class in a discussion of leadership characteristics based on your lists. Students will call out what they identified, and your instructor will write the traits on the chalkboard. When all students have shared their lists, class discussion will focus on the following questions:

- What characteristics consistently appeared on students' lists?
- Were these characteristics more trait oriented or behaviour oriented?
- In what situations were these characteristics useful?
- What, if anything, does this exercise suggest about leadership attributes?

### BE THE CONSULTANT: HIRING ETHICAL LEADERS

Your consulting firm has been chosen to develop questions that might help organizations select more ethical leaders. You are very familiar with behavioural interview questions that generally start with "tell me about a time when you…" or "give me an example of a situation in which you . . ."

You feel that four key areas where ethical leadership may come into difficulty are compromise, conflicting values, time pressure, and formal rules. In business situations, compromise is often necessary for things to happen. Sometimes that compromise might be a situation where your values were not in line with organizational values. Often leaders have to come to quick decisions or use a more informal style where they bend the rules to get something done.

Develop behavioural questions for the four areas mentioned previous page:

| Compromise | |
|---|---|
| Conflicting values | |
| Time pressure | |
| Bending the rules | |

What are other areas requiring ethical leadership?

# Business Cases

## ENBRIDGE

Canada's Outstanding CEO of the Year for 2011 was Patrick Daniel, CEO and president of Calgary-based Enbridge Inc., Canada's largest crude oil pipeline company.[83] Leadership of Enbridge is like that of many companies. Enbridge's strategy focuses on a combination of high growth, low risk, and steady income—a simple sounding proposition that is very hard to maintain. As a result, Daniel indicates that Enbridge has been both aggressive and cautious. "We go after everything, but we are very disciplined and conservative."

Daniel has worked in Canada's energy sector for four decades, but his last year has been the most tumultuous. Lower energy prices, increased competition through deregulation, public interest group criticism over pipeline projects, and an Enbridge oil spill in Michigan have all created a perfect storm through which Daniel must navigate. Enbridge's Northern Gateway project has polarized extremes. Support is high with think tanks, policy forums, politicians, and business leaders. Opposition is also high with First Nations groups, special interest groups, and environmental watchdogs all legitimately concerned with an environmentally sound and effective way to transport crude oil and natural gas. The NIMBY principle (Not In My Back Yard) is also at odds with pipeline development. Daniel recounts earlier days where landowners felt it was their obligation to provide the right of way to serve Canadian development. That sentiment has changed dramatically. Daniel believes a key leadership competency in his position is patience—being able to calmly discuss all sides of the issue with various stakeholders.

Canada's single biggest export is crude oil and it is going almost exclusively to one market. Daniel has been pushing for a national energy strategy encompassing development and sustainability. How should companies like Enbridge work with the Canadian government and the energy industry to develop markets outside of the United States?

# CHAPTER 9

## Motivating Employees

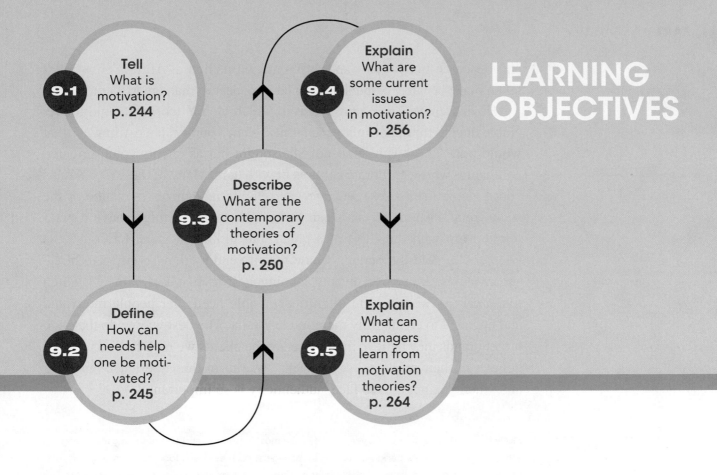

**Tell**
What is motivation?
p. 244

9.1

**Explain**
What are some current issues in motivation?
p. 256

9.4

**Describe**
What are the contemporary theories of motivation?
p. 250

9.3

**Define**
How can needs help one be motivated?
p. 245

9.2

**Explain**
What can managers learn from motivation theories?
p. 264

9.5

# LEARNING OBJECTIVES

How do you expand an independent consulting business without the money to hire staff? [1]

Grail Noble of Toronto-based Yellow House Events brought a Gen Y intern into her home office in 2006. That 23-year-old college graduate, who became her first employee later that year, convinced Noble to adopt a new corporate culture to harness the energy and quality work of Generation Y (those born between the late 1970s and the turn of the century). Six years later, Yellow House's revenue growth of 2395 percent had it ranking number 16 on *Profit* magazine's Top 200 fastest growing companies. [2]

Gen Ys, sometimes called Millennials, are often stereotyped as self-absorbed, impatient, flighty, and so gratuitously confident they think they can run a company after a few days on the job. This tech-immersed age group has no doubt caused sleepless nights among many CEOs, because Gen Ys represent the future of the workforce. With an aging population and looming labour shortages, companies can ill afford to ignore these young people and their habits and desires.

But Gen Y is not as scary as it seems. As Noble's experiences demonstrate, tapping into their needs and motivations can unleash tremendous productivity. Since she started targeting young talent, Yellow House's revenue has grown from less than $200 000 in 2005 to $2.7 million last year. Yellow House has landed new clients—including Virgin Mobile, Revlon,

## Think About It

What motivates Gen Y employees to work at Yellow House? What has Grail Noble done to increase employee motivation?

**243**

and Research In Motion—and differentiated its brand. All this growth has taken place because Noble has learned how best to manage Millennials.

Having created an environment in which Gen Y workers could thrive, Noble hunted for opportunities to harness their youthful energy in ways that would put Yellow House ahead. She sought out as clients youth-oriented companies whose corporate cultures fit with hers. Many of these firms' marketing departments skew younger, and Noble recognizes the value of the social relationships her staff can forge with them. "I might have a great relationship with the CEO of a client, but ultimately most CEOs let the people who hold the budget decide which vendors they're going to hire," she explains. Moreover, event planning is a high-stakes game in which much can go wrong—and often does. Noble needs her people motivated and engaged to create truly memorable affairs. The best way to do that is to target brands they believe in. "Those are the clients we look for, because we believe in their product," says Noble. "We're in the experience business, and when you get face to face, authenticity is so important."

..................................................................................................................

Motivating and rewarding employees is one of the most important, and one of the most challenging, activities that managers perform. Successful managers, such as Grail Noble, understand that what motivates them personally may have little or no effect on others. Just because *you* are motivated by being part of a cohesive work team or by challenging work, do not assume everyone feels the same. Effective managers who want their employees to put forth maximum effort recognize that they need to know how and why employees are motivated and to tailor their motivational practices to satisfy the needs and wants of those employees.

In this chapter, we first look at some early motivation theories and then at contemporary theories. We finish by looking at several current motivation issues and present practical suggestions that managers can use to motivate employees.

..................................................................................................................

## WHAT IS MOTIVATION?

**Tell**
What is motivation?

**9.1**

All managers need to be able to motivate their employees, and that requires an understanding of what motivation is. Many people incorrectly view motivation as a personal trait—a trait that some people have and others do not. Our knowledge of motivation tells us that we cannot label people that way. What we *do* know is that motivation is the result of the interaction between a person and a situation. Certainly, individuals differ in motivational drive but, overall, motivation varies from situation to situation. For example, your level of motivation probably differs among the various courses you take each term. As we analyze the concept of motivation, keep in mind that the level of motivation varies both between individuals and within individuals at different times.

**Motivation** refers to an individual's willingness to exert high levels of effort to reach organizational goals, conditioned by the degree to which that effort satisfies some individual need. Although, in general, motivation refers to effort exerted toward any goal, here it refers to organizational goals because our focus is on work-related behaviour.

The three key elements in the definition of motivation are effort, organizational goals, and need. The *effort* element is a measure of intensity or drive.[3] A motivated person tries hard. But high levels of effort are unlikely to lead to favourable job performance unless the effort is channelled in a direction that benefits the organization.[4] Therefore we must consider the

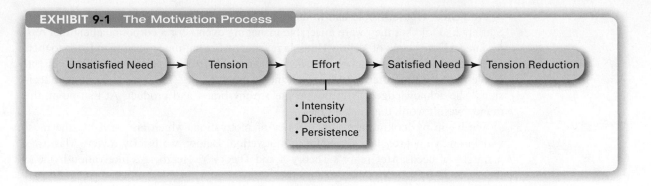

**EXHIBIT 9-1** The Motivation Process

Unsatisfied Need → Tension → Effort → Satisfied Need → Tension Reduction

• Intensity
• Direction
• Persistence

quality of the effort as well as its intensity. Effort that is directed toward, and consistent with, *organizational goals* is the kind of effort that we should be seeking. Finally, we will treat motivation as a *need-satisfying* process, as shown in Exhibit 9-1.

A **need** is an internal state that makes certain outcomes appear attractive. An unsatisfied need creates tension, which an individual reduces by exerting effort. Because we are interested in work behaviour, this tension-reduction effort must be directed toward organizational goals. Therefore, inherent in our definition of motivation is the requirement that the individual's needs be compatible with the organization's goals. When the two do not match, individuals may expend high levels of effort that run counter to the interests of the organization. Incidentally, this situation is not all that unusual. Some employees regularly spend a lot of time talking with friends at work to satisfy their social need. They exert a great deal of effort, but little, if any, is being directed toward work.

*What motivates you?*

Finding ways to motivate employees to achieve high levels of performance is an important organizational problem, and managers keep looking for a solution. A Canadian Policy Research Network[5] survey found that only 40 percent of Canadians are very satisfied with their jobs. Equally, only 40 percent of American workers were satisfied with key elements of their current jobs, although 80 percent reported a hesitant overall satisfaction,[6] while 54 percent of Danish workers reported high satisfaction.[7] In light of these results, it is no wonder that both academic researchers and practising managers want to understand and explain employee motivation.

## EARLY THEORIES OF MOTIVATION

Grail Noble of Yellow House was interested in recognizing the unique characteristics of Gen Y employees.[8] She attended conferences and conducted research on the habits of today's younger workers. She learned that they wanted to be empowered on the job and also to work within an entrepreneurial culture. Noble adopted an open-book financial policy and treated her staff as owners of Yellow House.

**9.2**

**Define**
How can needs help one be motivated?

**Think About It**

What kinds of needs do employees have? Why might an employee lack passion for the work they are doing?

---

**motivation**
An individual's willingness to exert high levels of effort to reach organizational goals, conditioned by the degree to which that effort satisfies some individual need.

**need**
An internal state that makes certain outcomes appear attractive.

At Yellow House, Noble had to make a tough decision to drop a lucrative customer. Staffers had told her they were miserable managing events for a corporate client that represented a large chunk of Yellow House's revenue. After calling a meeting to listen to their concerns, observing their email exchanges, and noting her own experiences with the client, Noble fired the firm after completing all the assigned work. "That was a very tough decision," she acknowledges. "But my people are my brand and product. At that point, the money wasn't worth their unhappiness."

We begin by looking at needs theories of motivation, which are probably the most widely known approaches to employee motivation. Below, we briefly review Maslow's hierarchy of needs, McGregor's Theory X and Theory Y, Herzberg's motivation-hygiene theory, and McClelland's theory of needs.

## Maslow's Hierarchy of Needs Theory

The best-known theory of motivation is probably Abraham Maslow's **hierarchy of needs theory**.[9] Maslow (1908–1970), an American psychologist at Brandeis University, proposed that within every person is a hierarchy of five needs:

1. **Physiological needs**. Food, drink, shelter, sexual satisfaction, and other physical requirements.
2. **Safety needs**. Security and protection from physical and emotional harm, as well as assurance that physical needs will continue to be met.
3. **Social needs**. Affection, belongingness, acceptance, and friendship.
4. **Esteem needs**. Internal esteem factors such as self-respect, autonomy, and achievement, and external esteem factors such as status, recognition, and attention.
5. **Self-actualization needs**. Growth, achieving one's potential, and self-fulfillment; the drive to become what one is capable of becoming.

Maslow argued that each level in the needs hierarchy must be substantially satisfied before the next one is activated. He further suggested that once a need is substantially satisfied, it no longer motivates behaviour. In other words, as each need is largely fulfilled, the next need becomes dominant. As Exhibit 9-2 illustrates, an individual moves up the needs hierarchy. In terms of motivation, Maslow's theory proposed that no need is ever fully satisfied, but a substantially satisfied need will no longer motivate an individual. According to Maslow, therefore, if you want to motivate someone, you need to understand what level that person has reached on the hierarchy and satisfy needs at or above that level.

Tough financial times can shift employee needs back to the lower levels of the pyramid such as safety needs. In late 2008 and throughout 2009, Yellow House's revenue dropped by 50 percent as companies across North America slashed their event budgets. Instead of drawing up a recovery plan herself, Noble sat down with her staff and asked a simple question: "What are we going to do to overcome this?"

Together, Noble and her team came up with several ideas, ultimately deciding to create a list of target clients—growing brands the Yellow Housers admired—and to send each

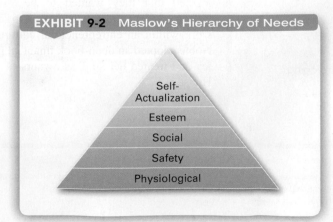

**EXHIBIT 9-2** Maslow's Hierarchy of Needs

one a tiny money tree as a sign of good luck during the recession. One of those firms was youth-focused Virgin Mobile. "They loved the money tree and made a connection with the staffer who dropped it off," Noble recalls. Virgin Mobile asked for a meeting with Yellow House, whose staff quickly impressed the prospective client with their engagement and knowledge of music and pop culture. As a result, Virgin signed on as one of Yellow House's flagship clients, helping Noble's firm recover much of the revenue lost to the recession. Because Noble focused on meeting the safety needs of her employees, she was able to turn the company around.

The practical significance of Maslow's theory is widely accepted.[10] However, Maslow provided no empirical support for his theory, and several studies that sought to validate it could not.[11]

## McGregor's Theory X and Theory Y

Are individuals intrinsically or extrinsically motivated? Douglas McGregor (1906–1964), a management professor at the Massachusetts Institute of Technology (MIT) Sloan School of Management, tried to uncover the answer to this question through his discussion of Theory X and Theory Y.[12] **Extrinsic motivation** comes from outside the person and includes such things as pay, bonuses, and other tangible rewards. **Intrinsic motivation** reflects an individual's internal desire to do something, and motivation comes from interest, challenge, and personal satisfaction. Individuals show intrinsic motivation when they deeply care about their work, look for ways to improve the work, and are fulfilled by doing it well.[13]

*Do you need to be rewarded by others or are you a self-motivator?*

McGregor's **Theory X** offers an essentially negative view of people. The theory assumes that employees have little ambition, dislike work, want to avoid responsibility, and need to be closely controlled to work effectively. It suggests that people are almost exclusively driven by extrinsic motivators. **Theory Y** offers a positive view. This theory assumes that employees can exercise self-direction, accept and actually seek out responsibility, and consider work a natural activity. It suggests that people are more intrinsically motivated. McGregor believed that Theory Y assumptions best captured the true nature of employees and should guide management practice. He proposed that participation in decision making, responsible and challenging jobs, and good group relations would maximize employee motivation.

Our knowledge of motivation tells us that neither theory alone fully accounts for employee behaviour. What we know is that motivation is the result of the interaction of the individual and the situation. Individuals differ in their basic motivational drive. As well, while you may find completing a homework assignment boring, you might enthusiastically plan a surprise party for a friend. These points underscore the idea that the level of motivation varies both *between* individuals and *within* individuals at different times. They also suggest that managers should try to make sure that situations are motivating for employees.

---

**hierarchy of needs theory**
Maslow's theory proposing a hierarchy of five human needs: physiological, safety, social, esteem, and self-actualization; as each need becomes satisfied, the next need becomes dominant.

**physiological needs**
A person's need for food, drink, shelter, sexual satisfaction, and other physical requirements.

**safety needs**
A person's need for security and protection from physical and emotional harm, as well as assurance that physical needs will continue to be met.

**social needs**
A person's need for affection, belongingness, acceptance, and friendship.

**esteem needs**
A person's need for internal esteem factors such as self-respect, autonomy, and achievement, and external esteem factors such as status, recognition, and attention.

**self-actualization needs**
A person's need to grow and become what he or she is capable of becoming.

**extrinsic motivation**
Motivation that comes from outside the person and includes such things as pay, bonuses, and other tangible rewards.

**intrinsic motivation**
Motivation that comes from the person's internal desire to do something, due to such things as interest, challenge, and personal satisfaction.

**Theory X**
The assumption that employees have little ambition, dislike work, want to avoid responsibility, and must be closely controlled to perform effectively.

**Theory Y**
The assumption that employees can exercise self-direction, accept and seek out responsibility, and consider work a natural activity.

**EXHIBIT 9-3** Herzberg's Motivation-Hygiene Theory

| Motivators | Hygiene Factors |
|---|---|
| • Achievement | • Supervision |
| • Recognition | • Company policy |
| • Work itself | • Relationship with |
| • Responsibility |   supervisor |
| • Advancement | • Working conditions |
| • Growth | • Salary |
| | • Relationship with peers |
| | • Personal life |
| | • Relationship with |
| |   subordinates |
| | • Status |
| | • Security |

| Extremely Satisfied | Neutral | Extremely Dissatisfied |

## Herzberg's Motivation-Hygiene Theory

Frederick Herzberg (1923–2000), American psychologist and University of Utah professor of management, proposed the **motivation-hygiene theory**. According to Herzberg's theory, intrinsic factors are related to job satisfaction and motivation, whereas extrinsic factors are related to job dissatisfaction.[14] Believing that individuals' attitudes toward work determined success or failure, Herzberg investigated the question "What do people want from their jobs?" He asked people for detailed descriptions of situations in which they felt exceptionally good or bad about their jobs. These findings are shown in Exhibit 9-3.

Herzberg concluded from his analysis that the replies people gave when they felt good about their jobs were significantly different from the replies they gave when they felt bad. Certain characteristics were consistently related to job satisfaction (factors on the left side of the exhibit), and others to job dissatisfaction (factors on the right side). Those factors associated with job satisfaction were intrinsic and included things such as achievement, recognition, and responsibility. When people felt good about their work, they tended to attribute these characteristics to themselves. On the other hand, when they were dissatisfied with their work, they tended to cite extrinsic factors such as supervision, company policy, interpersonal relationships, and working conditions.

Herzberg thought the data also suggested that the opposite of satisfaction was not dissatisfaction, as had been traditionally believed. Removing dissatisfying characteristics from a job would not necessarily make that job more satisfying (or motivating). As shown in Exhibit 9-4, Herzberg proposed that his findings indicated the existence of a dual continuum: The opposite of "satisfaction" is "no satisfaction," and the opposite of "dissatisfaction" is "no dissatisfaction."

Herzberg believed the factors that led to job satisfaction were separate and distinct from those that led to job dissatisfaction. Therefore, managers who sought to eliminate factors that created job dissatisfaction could bring about workplace harmony but not necessarily

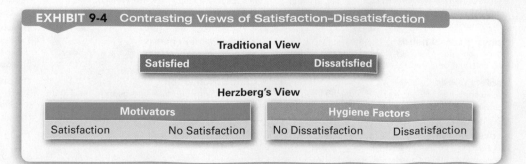

**EXHIBIT 9-4** Contrasting Views of Satisfaction–Dissatisfaction

**Traditional View**

| Satisfied | Dissatisfied |

**Herzberg's View**

| Motivators | Hygiene Factors |
|---|---|
| Satisfaction    No Satisfaction | No Dissatisfaction    Dissatisfaction |

Langley, BC–based Pazmac Enterprises uses insights from Herzberg's theory to organize its workplace.[15] Pazmac employees enjoy perks often associated with the high-tech industry, including an on-site swimming pool, personal trainers, weekly yoga classes, and professional counselling services. Unlike most machine shops, Pazmac is spotlessly clean, with a tastefully designed lunchroom and a plush men's washroom. Owner Steve Scarlett clearly considers both hygiene and motivator factors in dealing with his employees. His strategy has paid off. The company has had very little employee turnover in recent years, and several employees have worked there for more than 15 years.[16]

motivation. The extrinsic factors that eliminate job dissatisfaction were called **hygiene factors**. When these factors are adequate, people will not be dissatisfied, but they will not be satisfied (or motivated) either. To motivate people in their jobs, Herzberg suggested emphasizing **motivators**, the intrinsic factors such as achievement, recognition, and challenge that increase job satisfaction.

Herzberg's theory enjoyed wide popularity from the mid-1960s to the early 1980s, but criticisms arose concerning his procedures and methodology. Although today we say the theory is simplistic, it has had a strong influence on how we currently design jobs.

Noble learned that Gen Y staffers have a blurry line between work and personal life. If they are engaged in their jobs, they are perfectly willing to log long hours in the office or take client calls at 11 p.m.—provided they can update their Facebook status and make personal calls at any hour of the workday. (Noble is usually the last person in the office each morning and sometimes has to kick staffers out at night.) "They don't see their work selves as different from their social selves," she explains. "What can be difficult is that they care more about where they work, what they're working on, and who they're working with than did past generations."

Creating a fitting work environment has required Noble to make some adjustments. While she prefers working in silence, her young hires like to crank Top 40 tunes and create a veritable party atmosphere as they work. Noble found that it took time to allow herself to forget her workers' ages and relative lack of experience, and simply trust their ability to get a job done. Naturally, the Yellow House's home office did not suffice for long. Gen Y staffers typically enjoy working in funky, open-concept spaces, so the company soon moved into an airy office in a nineteenth-century building in Toronto's Distillery Historic District.

---

**motivation-hygiene theory**
Herzberg's theory that intrinsic factors are related to job satisfaction and motivation, whereas extrinsic factors are related to job dissatisfaction.

**hygiene factors**
Factors that eliminate job dissatisfaction, but do not motivate.

**motivators**
Factors that increase job satisfaction and motivation.

## McClelland's Theory of Needs

American psychological theorist David McClelland (1917–1998) and his Harvard associates proposed the **theory of needs**. This theory maintains that work performance is motivated by three acquired (not innate) needs:[17] the **need for achievement (nAch)**, which is the drive to excel, to achieve in relation to a set of standards, and to strive to succeed; the **need for power (nPow)**, which is the need to make others behave in a way that they would not have behaved otherwise; and the **need for affiliation (nAff)**, which is the desire for friendly and close interpersonal relationships. Of these three needs, the need for achievement has been the most researched. What does this research show?

People with a high need for achievement are striving for personal achievement rather than for the trappings and rewards of success. They have a desire to do something better or more efficiently than it has been done before.[18] These people prefer jobs that offer personal responsibility for finding solutions to problems. They like to receive rapid and unambiguous feedback on their performance in order to tell whether they are improving and to be able to set moderately challenging goals. High achievers avoid what they perceive to be very easy or very difficult tasks. A high need to achieve does not necessarily lead to becoming a good manager, especially in large organizations, because high achievers focus on their *own* accomplishments, while good managers emphasize helping *others* accomplish their goals.[19] McClelland showed that employees can be trained to stimulate their achievement need by being in situations where they have personal responsibility, feedback, and moderate risks.[20]

The other two needs in this theory have not been researched as extensively as the need for achievement. However, we do know that the best managers tend to be high in the need for power and low in the need for affiliation.[21]

While needs theories give us some insights into motivating employees, they do not provide a complete picture of motivation. Moreover, additional needs seem to motivate some employees. For example, employees are increasingly feeling the need for work–life balance. They need time to take care of their loved ones while managing their workloads. Having some time during the day when one can at least see nature may be another important need. Research suggests that being exposed to nature (even just being able to see some trees from your office window) has many beneficial effects. A lack of such exposure can actually impair well-being and performance.[22] We now turn to some contemporary theories of motivation that explain the processes managers can use to motivate employees. (See also *Assess Your Skills - What Rewards Do I Value Most?* on pages 268–269 at the end of the chapter.)

## CONTEMPORARY THEORIES OF MOTIVATION

**Describe**

**9.3** What are the contemporary theories of motivation?

One of the challenges of motivating employees is linking productivity to rewards. Companies like Yellow House Events have to link productivity to rewards to ensure employees feel motivated.

The theories we discuss in this section represent contemporary explanations of employee motivation. Although they may not be as well known as some of the older theories we just discussed, they do have reasonable degrees of valid research support.[23] What are the contemporary theories of motivation? We look at four: four-drive theory, reinforcement theory, equity theory, and expectancy theory.

### Four-Drive Theory

**Four-drive theory** is a holistic theory developed by Harvard Business School professors Paul Lawrence and Nitin Nohria. It describes motivation in four categories: the drive to acquire, to bond, to learn and to defend.[24] These drives interact with each other in varying degrees, depending on the individual and his or her external circumstances. The first three drives are

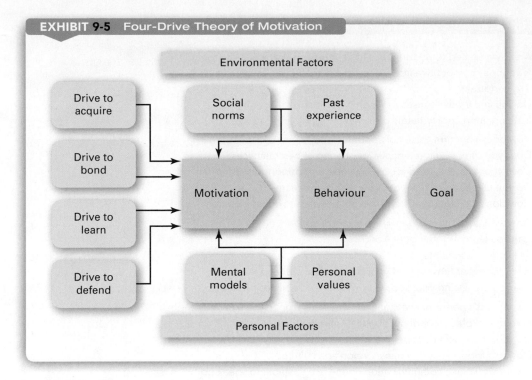

**EXHIBIT 9-5** Four-Drive Theory of Motivation

considered "proactive" in the sense that we are always trying to fulfill them, independent of each other. The domination of one drive over the others can lead to a lack of balance in an employee's personal and work life. Exhibit 9-5 presents the four-drive theory.

The **drive to acquire** is the competitive drive for material goods, status, accomplishments, and power. This drive can lead to both greater performance and negative competition, so organizations can use the drive to bond to help minimize unhealthy competition.

The **drive to bond** is the social side of the equation, whereby we try to bond with others and engage in mutually beneficial relationships. These individual relationships can grow to include cooperation and collaboration with groups and teams in the workplace, especially when supported with team-based rewards and challenging goals.

The **drive to learn** is the drive to satiate curiosity and understand ourselves and the world around us. This drive is part of our need for growth and self-actualization discussed earlier. A work environment that allows for exploration can provide higher satisfaction, and learning new skills can be of greater importance than pay to some employees.

The **drive to defend** is all about self-protection. You may have faced the "fight-or-flight" response when defending yourself from danger, but perhaps also in relationships or dealing with your belief systems. This drive is the only reactive one and is typically triggered by threats. Communication can be used to correct employee misinformation that might cause unintentional threats in the workplace.

Most companies focus on the drive to acquire though pay and incentives, but often do not consider the impact of the other drives on employee engagement and motivation. Recognizing that employees want to bond, organizations could plan effective team-building activities that are more than just lip service and give the team a few hours of

---

**theory of needs**
McClelland's theory that the needs for achievement, power, and affiliation are major motives in work.

**need for achievement (nAch)**
The drive to excel, to achieve in relation to a set of standards, and to strive to succeed.

**need for power (nPow)**
The need to make others behave in a way that they would not have behaved otherwise.

**need for affiliation (nAff)**
The desire for friendly and close interpersonal relationships.

**four-drive theory**
The theory that behaviour is influenced by our innate drives to acquire, bond, learn, and defend.

**drive to acquire**
The drive to seek, take control of, and retain objects and personal experiences.

**drive to bond**
The drive to form social relationships with others.

**drive to learn**
The drive to satisfy our curiosity and understand ourselves and the world around us.

**drive to defend**
The drive to protect ourselves both physically and socially.

**EXHIBIT 9-6** Organizational Implications of Four-Drive Theory

| Drive to acquire | • Are rewards tied to performance in your organization?<br>• Is your pay competitive internally and externally?<br>• Are performance expectations clearly defined?<br>• Do you know what constitutes high performance in your firm?<br>• Is recognition appropriately provided for your performance? |
|---|---|
| Drive to bond | • How does your firm value collaboration and teamwork?<br>• Does your firm's culture encourage sharing of best practices?<br>• Does your firm provide support networks and opportunities for networking?<br>• Do you feel strongly that you are a part of the team?<br>• How does management show that it cares about you on a personal level? |
| Drive to learn | • Does your work interest you?<br>• Can you learn new things at work?<br>• Are your assignments varied and challenging?<br>• How does your firm support your personal growth and learning?<br>• Are you enhancing your knowledge, skills, and abilities as part of your work? |
| Drive to defend | • Is your firm's performance management system open, transparent, and fair?<br>• Is your workplace free of hostility and intimidation?<br>• Do your managers treat people with respect?<br>• Do you support your company's vision and culture?<br>• Is your workplace communication open—are you able to speak up? |

fun. We discussed the importance of efficiency and effectiveness in Chapter 1. However, organizations focused exclusively on efficiency through automation and standardization may be jeopardizing the drive to learn. They should instead spend more time on improving effectiveness and on how they structure their jobs and projects. A strong vision and corporate culture can provide employees with higher motivation that connects with their drive to defend. Exhibit 9-6 describes some of the organizational implications of four-drive theory.

The four-drive theory is based on substantive research on emotions and neural processes.[25] However it does not sufficiently explain learned needs, and some critics argue that other drives could be included.

## Reinforcement Theory

**Reinforcement theory**, as proposed by Harvard psychologist B. F. Skinner (1904–1990), suggests that behaviour is influenced by consequences. It argues that external consequences, or **reinforcers**, if given immediately following a behaviour, increase the probability that the behaviour will be repeated.

Reinforcement theory focuses solely on what happens to a person when he or she takes some action. According to Skinner, reinforcement theory can be explained as follows: People will most likely engage in desired behaviours if they are rewarded for doing so; these rewards are most effective if they immediately follow a desired behaviour, and behaviour that is not rewarded, or is punished, is less likely to be repeated.[26]

In keeping with reinforcement theory, managers can influence employees' behaviour by reinforcing actions they deem desirable. However, the emphasis is on positive reinforcement, which means managers should ignore, not punish, unfavourable behaviour. Even though punishment eliminates undesired behaviour faster than nonreinforcement, its effect is often only temporary and may result in workplace conflicts, absenteeism, and turnover. Research has shown that reinforcement is an important influence on employee behaviour, but it is not the only explanation for differences in employee motivation.[27]

## Equity Theory

The term *equity* is related to the concept of fairness and equal treatment compared with others who behave in similar ways. Considerable evidence demonstrates that employees compare their job inputs and outcomes relative to others' and that inequities influence the degree of effort employees exert.[28]

**Equity theory**, developed by workplace and behavioural psychologist John Stacey Adams, proposes that employees perceive what they get from a job situation (outcomes) in relation to what they put into it (inputs) and then compare their input–outcome ratio with the input–outcome ratio of relevant others (see Exhibit 9-7). If employees perceive their ratio as equal to that of relevant others, a state of equity exists. In other words, they perceive that their situation is fair—that justice prevails. However, if the ratio is perceived as unequal, inequity exists, and they view themselves as under- or overrewarded. Not all inequity (or equity) is real. It is the individual's *perception* that determines the equity of the situation.

What will employees do when they perceive an inequity? Equity theory proposes that employees might (1) distort either their own or others' inputs or outcomes, (2) behave in some way to induce others to change their inputs or outcomes, (3) behave in some way to change their own inputs or outcomes, (4) choose a different comparison person, or (5) quit their jobs. These types of employee reactions have generally proved to be accurate.[29] A review of the research consistently confirms the equity thesis: Whenever employees perceive inequity, they will act to correct the situation.[30] The result might be lower or higher productivity, improved or reduced quality of output, increased absenteeism, or voluntary resignation.

> *Have you ever thought someone else's pay was unfair compared with yours?*

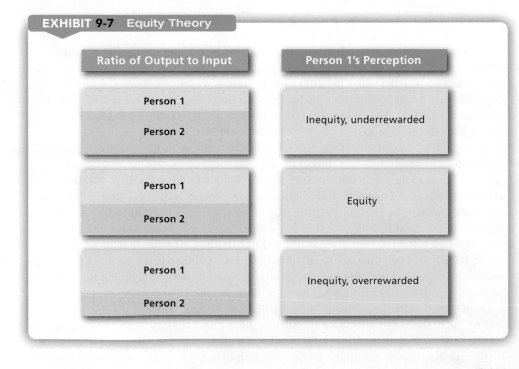

**EXHIBIT 9-7   Equity Theory**

| Ratio of Output to Input | Person 1's Perception |
|---|---|
| Person 1 / Person 2 | Inequity, underrewarded |
| Person 1 / Person 2 | Equity |
| Person 1 / Person 2 | Inequity, overrewarded |

**reinforcement theory**
The theory that behaviour is influenced by consequences.

**reinforcers**
Consequences that, when given immediately following a behaviour, increase the probability that the behaviour will be repeated.

**equity theory**
The theory that an employee compares his or her job's input–outcome ratio with that of relevant others and then responds to correct any inequity.

When Toronto city councillors voted themselves an 8.9 percent pay raise in 2007, they were not thinking about possible budget shortfalls. Instead, they were responding to the idea that they were underpaid compared to other government decision makers who performed duties similar to their own. As councillors for the largest city in the country, with the largest budget, they were advised by a consulting firm that they should rank in the "top 25 percent of salaries for councillors across the country." Their salary before the raise was one of the lowest in the country.

The **referent** against which individuals compare themselves is an important variable in equity theory.[31] Three referent categories have been defined: other, system, and self. The *other* category includes other individuals with similar jobs in the same organization but also includes friends, neighbours, or professional associates. On the basis of what they hear at work or read about in newspapers or trade journals, employees compare their pay with that of others. The *system* category includes organizational pay policies and procedures, and the administration of the system. Whatever precedents have been established by the organization regarding pay allocation are major elements of this category. The *self* category refers to the input–outcome ratio that is unique to the individual. It reflects personal experiences and contacts, and is influenced by criteria such as previous jobs or family commitments. The choice of a particular set of referents is related to the information available about the referents as well as to their perceived relevance. At Surrey, BC–based Back in Motion Rehab, management decided that the highest-paid director's base salary should be less than two times the salary of the average staff member.[32] Because this policy uses the average staff member's pay as a referent, it sends the message that the output of the average staff member is truly valued.

Originally, equity theory focused on **distributive justice**, which is the perceived fairness of the amount and allocation of rewards among individuals. More recent research has focused on looking at issues of **procedural justice**, which is the perceived fairness of the process used to determine the distribution of rewards. This research shows that distributive justice has a greater influence on employee satisfaction than procedural justice, while procedural justice tends to affect an employee's organizational commitment, trust in his or her boss, and intention to stay or quit.[33] What are the implications for managers? They should consider openly sharing information on how allocation decisions are made, follow consistent and unbiased procedures, and engage in similar practices to increase the perception of procedural justice. Employees who have an increased perception of procedural justice are likely to view their bosses and the organization as positive, even if they are dissatisfied with pay, promotions, and other personal outcomes.

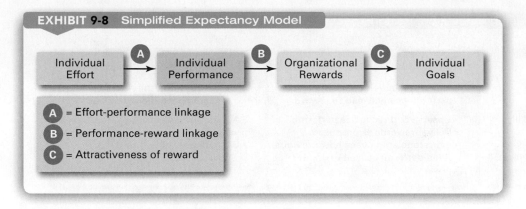

**EXHIBIT 9-8** Simplified Expectancy Model

Individual Effort → **A** → Individual Performance → **B** → Organizational Rewards → **C** → Individual Goals

**A** = Effort-performance linkage
**B** = Performance-reward linkage
**C** = Attractiveness of reward

## Expectancy Theory

The most comprehensive and widely accepted explanation of employee motivation to date is the expectancy theory, developed by Victor Vroom, professor at the Yale School of Management.[34] Although the theory has its critics,[35] most research evidence supports it.[36]

**Expectancy theory** states that an individual tends to act in a certain way based on the expectation that the act will be followed by a given outcome and on the attractiveness of that outcome to the individual. It includes three variables or relationships (see Exhibit 9-8):

- *Expectancy, or effort–performance linkage.* The probability perceived by the individual that exerting a given amount of effort will lead to a certain level of performance.
- *Instrumentality, or performance–reward linkage.* The degree to which the individual believes that performing at a particular level is instrumental in attaining the desired outcome.
- *Valence, or attractiveness of reward.* The importance that the individual places on the potential outcome or reward that can be achieved on the job. Valence considers both the goals and needs of the individual.

This explanation of motivation might sound complex, but it really is not. It can be summed up in these questions: How hard do I have to work to achieve a certain level of performance, and can I actually achieve that level? What reward will I get for working at that level of performance? How attractive is the reward to me, and does it help me achieve my goals? Whether you are motivated to put forth effort (that is, to work) at any given time depends on your particular goals and your perception of whether a certain level of performance is necessary to attain those goals.

The key to expectancy theory is understanding an individual's goal and the link between effort and performance, between performance and rewards, and finally, between rewards and individual goal satisfaction. Expectancy theory recognizes that there is no universal principle for explaining what motivates individuals and thus stresses that managers need to understand why employees view certain outcomes as attractive or unattractive. After all, we want to reward individuals with those things they value as positive. Expectancy theory also emphasizes expected behaviours. Do employees know what is expected of them and how they will be evaluated? Finally, the theory is concerned with perceptions; reality is irrelevant. An individual's own perceptions of performance, reward, and goal outcomes, not the outcomes themselves, will determine his or her motivation (level of effort). Exhibit 9-9 suggests how managers might increase employee motivation, using expectancy theory.

**referents**
Those things individuals compare themselves against in order to assess equity.

**distributive justice**
Perceived fairness of the amount and allocation of rewards among individuals.

**procedural justice**
Perceived fairness of the process used to determine the distribution of rewards.

**expectancy theory**
The theory that an individual tends to act in a certain way based on the expectation that the act will be followed by a given outcome and on the attractiveness of that outcome to the individual.

**EXHIBIT 9-9** Steps to Increasing Motivation, Using Expectancy Theory

| Improving Expectancy | Improving Instrumentality | Improving Valence |
|---|---|---|
| **Improve the ability of the individual to perform** | **Increase the individual's belief that performance will lead to reward** | **Make sure that the reward is meaningful to the individual** |
| • Make sure employees have skills for the task.<br>• Provide training.<br>• Assign reasonable tasks and goals. | • Observe and recognize performance.<br>• Deliver rewards as promised.<br>• Indicate to employees how previous good performance led to greater rewards. | • Ask employees what rewards they value.<br>• Give rewards that are valued. |

### Integrating Contemporary Theories of Motivation

We have presented four contemporary motivation theories. You might be tempted to view them independently, but doing so would be a mistake. Many of the ideas underlying the theories are complementary, and you will better understand how to motivate people if you see how the theories fit together.[37]

Four-drive theory suggests that jobs and workplaces should provide an opportunity to fulfill the drives to acquire, bond, learn, and defend. The drives should be kept in balance, so that employees are not overly influenced by any one drive.

Expectancy theory predicts that an employee will exert a high level of effort if he or she perceives that there is a strong relationship between effort and performance, performance and rewards, and rewards and satisfaction of personal goals. Each of these relationships is, in turn, influenced by certain factors. The level of individual performance is determined not only by the level of individual effort, but also by the individual's ability to perform and by whether the organization has a fair and objective performance evaluation system. The performance–reward relationship will be strong if the individual perceives that it is performance (rather than seniority, personal favourites, or some other criterion) that will be rewarded. The final link in expectancy theory is the rewards–goal relationship. Needs theories come into play at this point. Motivation is high to the degree that the rewards an individual receives for his or her high performance satisfy the dominant needs consistent with his or her individual goals.

Rewards also play a key part in equity theory. Individuals will compare the rewards (outcomes) they have received from the inputs or efforts they made with the input–outcome ratio of relevant others. Any inequities may influence the effort expended.

Interpret

Reinforcement theory says that behaviour is influenced by consequences, which is consistent with expectancy theory. The theory argues that when consequences are given immediately following a behaviour, the behaviour is more likely to be repeated. Thus, much like expectancy theory, the emphasis is on linking rewards (consequences) directly to performance.

## CURRENT ISSUES IN MOTIVATION

**Explain**
**9.4** What are some current issues in motivation?

One of the challenges managers face is how to motivate many different employee groups: students, new graduates, mothers returning to the workplace, and ethnic minorities. Some companies find that older female employees want flexible hours and stimulating work, but are not looking to be promoted. Young college graduates working in head office, on the other hand, want a challenging, well-paid career and time to pursue personal interests and family life. Many employees want managers who help them.[38]

### Think About It

What factors need to be considered when motivating employees who have very different needs? What can employers do to motivate young people?

To keep her Yellow House staff engaged, Noble regularly solicits their opinions on almost everything, including new hires; she allows at least two employees to participate in interviews to ensure a candidate is a good cultural fit. She also offers pay increases before each employee's annual performance review; as a result, no one has asked for a raise, and Yellow House has lost only one employee to a competitor.

So far, we have covered a lot of the theoretical bases of employee motivation. Understanding and predicting employee motivation continues to be one of the most popular areas in management research. However, even current studies of employee motivation are influenced by several significant workplace issues—issues such as motivating a diverse workforce, designing effective rewards programs, and improving work–life balance. Let us take a closer look at each of these issues.

## Motivating a Diverse Workforce

To maximize motivation in today's workforce, managers need to think in terms of *flexibility*. For example, studies tell us that men place more importance on having autonomy in their jobs than do women. In contrast, the opportunity to learn, convenient and flexible work hours, and good interpersonal relations are more important to women.[39] Baby Boomers may need more flextime as they manage the needs of their children and their aging parents. Gen-Xers want employers to add to their experience so they can develop portable skills. Meanwhile, Gen-Yers want more opportunities and the ability to work in teams.[40] Managers need to recognize that what motivates a single mother with two dependent children who is working full time to support her family may be very different from what motivates a single part-time employee or an older employee who is working only to supplement his or her retirement income. A wide array of rewards is needed to motivate employees with such diverse needs.

**MOTIVATING EMPLOYEES FROM DIVERSE CULTURES** In today's global business environment, managers cannot automatically assume that motivational programs that work in one location are going to work in others. Most current motivation theories were developed in the United States by Americans about Americans.[41] The most obviously American characteristic in these theories is the strong emphasis on individualism and quality-of-life cultural characteristics. For example, both goal-setting and expectancy theories emphasize goal accomplishment as well as rational and individual thought. Let us look at several theories to see if there is any cross-cultural transferability.

Maslow's hierarchy of needs proposes that people start at the physiological level and then move progressively up the hierarchy in order. This hierarchy, if it has any application at all, aligns with American culture. In countries such as Japan, Greece, and Mexico, where uncertainty-avoidance characteristics are strong (that is, individuals prefer structured situations), security needs would be on the top of the needs hierarchy. Countries that score high on quality-of-life characteristics (that is, individuals value relationships and are concerned with the welfare of others)—Denmark, Sweden, Norway, the Netherlands, and Finland—would have social needs on top.[42] We would predict, for example, that group work will motivate employees more when a country's culture scores high on quality-of-life characteristics.

Equity theory has a relatively strong following in the United States. Given that US-style reward systems are based on the assumption that employees are highly sensitive to equity in reward allocations, the theory's popularity is not surprising. In the United States, equity is meant to closely tie pay to performance. However, recent evidence suggests that in collectivist cultures (where individuals expect that others will look after and protect them), especially in the former socialist countries of Central and Eastern Europe, employees expect rewards to reflect their individual needs as well as their performance.[43] Moreover, consistent with a legacy of communism and centrally planned economies, employees exhibit a greater "entitlement" attitude—that is, they expect outcomes to be greater than their inputs.[44] These findings suggest that US-style pay practices may need modification, especially in Russia and other former communist countries, in order to be perceived as fair by employees.

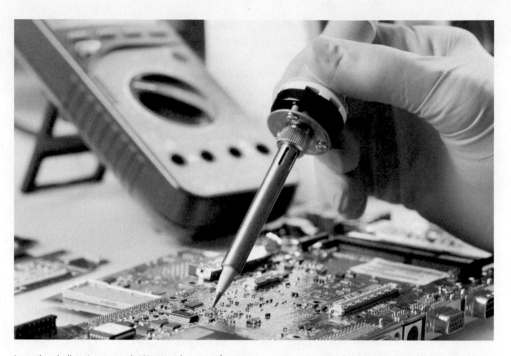

It can be challenging to apply Western theories of motivation to Japanese employees repairing computer chips. The use of a soldering iron to quickly and delicately repair tiny computer chips is so extraordinarily precise that only a few thousand of all Japan's workers are honoured with the title of "super technician" or supaa ginosha. These workers receive certificates and pins, but seldom money.

Despite these cross-cultural differences in motivation, do not assume there are no cross-cultural consistencies. For example, the desire for interesting work seems important to almost all employees, regardless of their national culture. In a study of seven countries, employees in Belgium, Britain, Israel, and the United States ranked "interesting work" number one among 11 work goals, and this factor was ranked either second or third in Japan, the Netherlands, and Germany.[45] Similarly, in a study comparing job-preference outcomes among graduate students in the United States, Canada, Australia, and Singapore, growth, achievement, and responsibility were rated the top three and had identical rankings.[46] Both of these studies suggest some universality to the importance of intrinsic factors identified by Herzberg in his motivation-hygiene theory. Another recent study examining workplace motivation trends in Japan also seems to indicate that Herzberg's model is applicable to Japanese employees.[47]

**MOTIVATING MINIMUM-WAGE EMPLOYEES**  Suppose that in your first managerial position after graduating, you are responsible for managing a work group composed of minimum-wage employees. Offering more pay to these employees for high levels of performance is out of the question: Your company just cannot afford it.[48] In addition, many of these employees may have limited education and skills. What are your motivational options at this point? One of the toughest motivational challenges facing many managers today is how to achieve high performance levels from minimum-wage employees.

One trap we often fall into is thinking that people are motivated only by money. Although money is important as a motivator, it is not the only reward that people seek and that managers can use. What are some other types of rewards? Many companies use employee recognition programs such as employee of the month, quarterly employee performance award ceremonies, or other celebrations of employee accomplishment. For instance, at many fast-food restaurants such as McDonald's and Wendy's, you will often see plaques hanging in prominent places that feature the "Crew Member of the Month." These types of programs highlight employees whose performance has been of the type and level the organization wants to encourage. Many managers also recognize the power of praise, but you need to be sure that these "pats on the back" are sincere and done for the right reasons; otherwise, employees can interpret such actions as manipulative.

We know from the motivation theories presented earlier that rewards are only part of the motivation equation. We need to look at other elements such as empowerment and career development assistance. We can look to the expectancy theory for these insights. In service industries such as travel and hospitality, retail sales, child care, and maintenance, where pay for front-line employees generally does not get much higher than the minimum-wage level, successful companies are empowering these front-line employees with more authority to address customers' problems. By providing these opportunities to minimum-wage employees, you are preparing them for the future—one that ideally promises better pay. For many, this type of reward system is a strong motivator![49]

**MOTIVATING PROFESSIONAL AND TECHNICAL EMPLOYEES**   In contrast to a generation ago, the typical employee today is more likely to be a highly trained professional with a post-secondary degree than a blue-collar factory worker. What special concerns should managers be aware of when trying to motivate a team of engineers at London, Ontario–based EllisDon, software designers at Vancouver-based Electronic Arts, or a group of consultants at Accenture?

Professionals are typically different from nonprofessionals.[50] They have a strong and long-term commitment to their field of expertise. Their loyalty is more often to their profession than to their employer. To keep current in their field, they need to regularly update their knowledge, and because of their commitment to their profession they rarely define their workweek as 8:00 a.m. to 5:00 p.m., five days a week.

What motivates professionals? Money and promotions typically are low on their priority list. Why? They tend to be well paid and enjoy what they do. In contrast, job challenge tends to be ranked high. They like to tackle problems and find solutions. Their chief reward in their jobs is the work itself. Professionals also value support. They want others to think that what they are working on is important.[51] That may be true for all employees, but professionals tend to be focused on their work as their central life interest, whereas nonprofessionals typically have other interests outside work that can compensate for needs not met on the job. The preceding points imply that managers should provide professional and technical employees with new assignments and challenging projects. Give them autonomy to follow their interests and allow them to structure their work in ways they find productive. Reward them with educational opportunities—training, workshops, conferences—that allow them to keep current in their field and to network with their peers. Also reward them with recognition. Managers should ask questions and engage in other actions that demonstrate to their professional and technical employees that they are sincerely interested in what their employees are doing.

To attract, motivate, and retain employees, Google offers many different perks, including chef-prepared food, a gym, a masseuse, on-site car washes, haircuts, dry cleaning, free on-site doctor and dentist, and child care next door.

**MOTIVATING CONTINGENT WORKERS** As many full-time jobs have been eliminated through downsizing and other organizational restructurings, the number of openings for part-time, contract, and other forms of temporary work have increased. Contingent workers do not have the security or stability that permanent employees have, and they do not identify with the organization or display the commitment that other employees do. Temporary workers also typically get little or no benefits such as health care or pensions.[52]

There is no simple solution for motivating contingent employees. For that small set of individuals who prefer the freedom of their temporary status—for example, some students, working mothers, retirees—the lack of stability may not be an issue. Temporariness might also be preferred by highly compensated physicians, engineers, accountants, or financial planners who do not want the demands of a full-time job. But these are the exceptions. For the most part, temporary employees are not temporary by choice.

What will motivate involuntarily temporary employees? An obvious answer is the opportunity to become a permanent employee. In cases in which permanent employees are selected from a pool of temps, the temps will often work hard in hopes of becoming permanent. A less obvious answer is the opportunity for training. The ability of a temporary employee to find a new job is largely dependent on his or her skills. If the employee sees that the job he or she is doing can help develop marketable skills, then motivation is increased. From an equity standpoint, a manager should also consider the repercussions of mixing permanent and temporary workers when pay differentials are significant. When temps work alongside permanent employees who earn more, and get benefits, too, for doing the same job, the performance of temps is likely to suffer. Separating such employees or perhaps minimizing interdependence between them might help managers decrease potential problems.[53]

## Designing Effective Rewards Programs

Employee rewards programs play a powerful role in motivating for appropriate employee behaviour. In this section, we look at how managers can design effective rewards programs by using employee recognition programs and pay-for-performance programs. First, though, we should examine the issue of the extent to which money motivates.

**THE ROLE OF MONEY** The most commonly used reward in organizations is money. As one author notes, "Money is probably the most emotionally meaningful object in contemporary life: only food and sex are its close competitors as common carriers of such strong and diverse feelings, significance, and strivings."[54]

Little research attention has been given to individual differences in people's feelings about money, although some studies indicate that money is not employees' top priority.[55] A survey of 2000 Canadians discovered that trustworthy senior management and a good balance between work and personal or family life mattered more than pay or benefits when it came to employee satisfaction.[56] In another survey that looked at Canadian attitudes about work, one respondent explained, "Of course money is important, but that's not what's going to make you jump out of bed in the morning." Another noted, "Everyone here would take more money and more time off—that's a given. But some of the things that really make the job a good or bad one are your relations with your boss."[57]

A number of studies suggest that an individual's attitude toward money is correlated with personality traits and demographic factors.[58] People who value money score higher on "attributes like sensation seeking, competitiveness, materialism, and control." People who desire money score higher on self-esteem, need for achievement, and Type A personality measures. Men seem to value money more than women. These studies suggest that individuals who value money will be more motivated by it than individuals who value other things.

What these findings suggest is that when organizations develop reward programs, they need to consider very carefully what individuals value.

**EMPLOYEE RECOGNITION PROGRAMS** **Employee recognition programs** provide managers with opportunities to give employees personal attention and express interest, approval, and appreciation for a job well done.[59] These programs can take many forms. For instance, you can personally congratulate an employee in private for a good job. You can send a handwritten note or an email message acknowledging something positive that the employee has done. For employees with a strong need for social acceptance, you can publicly recognize accomplishments. To enhance group cohesiveness and motivation, you can celebrate team successes, perhaps by throwing a pizza party to celebrate a team's accomplishments.

One of the consistent themes that has emerged in the 13 years that Hewitt Associates has studied the 50 Best Companies to work for in Canada is the importance of recognition. A large number of the winning companies show appreciation for their employees frequently and visibly.[60]

**PAY-FOR-PERFORMANCE PROGRAMS** What's in it for me? That is a question every person consciously or unconsciously asks before engaging in any form of behaviour. Our knowledge of motivation tells us that people act in order to satisfy some need. Before they do anything, they look for a payoff or reward. Although organizations may offer many different rewards, most of us are concerned with earning an amount of money that allows us to satisfy our needs and wants. In fact, a large body of research suggests that pay is far more motivational than some motivation theorists such as Maslow and Herzberg suggest.[61] Because pay is an important variable in motivation, we need to look at how we can use pay to motivate high levels of employee performance. This concern explains the logic behind pay-for-performance programs.

**Pay-for-performance programs** are variable compensation plans that pay employees on the basis of a performance measure.[62] Piece-rate pay plans, wage-incentive plans, profit-sharing, and lump-sum bonuses are examples. What differentiates these forms of pay from more traditional compensation plans is that instead of paying a person for time on the job, pay is adjusted to reflect a performance measure. Performance measures might include such things as individual productivity, team or work-group productivity, departmental productivity, or the overall organization's profit performance.

Pay for performance is probably most compatible with expectancy theory. Specifically, if motivation is to be maximized, individuals should perceive a strong relationship between their performance and the rewards they receive. If rewards are allocated only on nonperformance factors—such as seniority, job title, or across-the-board pay raises—then employees are likely to reduce their efforts.

Pay-for-performance programs are popular; the number of employees affected by variable-pay plans has been rising in Canada. A 2007 survey of 314 firms by Hewitt Associates found that 80 percent of respondents had variable-pay programs in place, compared with 43 percent in 1994.[63] Pay-for-performance programs are more common for non-unionized employees than unionized ones, although more than 30 percent of unionized companies had such plans in 2002.[64] Prem Benimadhu, former vice-president of governance and human resource management with The Conference Board of Canada, noted, "Canadian unions have been very allergic to variable compensation."[65] In addition to wage uncertainty, employees may object to pay for performance if they feel that factors out of their control might affect the extent to which bonuses are possible.[66]

About 22 percent of Japanese companies have company-wide pay-for-performance plans.[67] However, one Japanese company, Fujitsu, dropped its performance-based program after eight years because it proved to be "flawed and a poor fit with Japanese culture."[68]

**employee recognition programs**
Reward programs that provide managers with opportunities to give employees personal attention and express interest, approval, and appreciation for a job well done.

**pay-for-performance programs**
Variable compensation plans that pay employees on the basis of some performance measure.

Management found that some employees set goals as low as possible for fear of falling short. Others set extremely short-term goals. As a result, Fujitsu executives felt that ambitious projects that could produce hit products were being avoided.

Do pay-for-performance programs work? The evidence is mixed, at best.[69] One recent study that followed the careers of 1000 top economists found that they put in more effort early in their careers, at a time when productivity-related incentives had a larger impact.[70] A recent study of Finnish white-collar employees found that higher levels of payment and more frequent payments positively affected productivity, while lower levels of payment did not improve productivity.[71] A recent study in Canada looked at both unionized and non-unionized workplaces, and found that variable-pay plans resulted in "increased productivity, a safer work environment, a better understanding of the business by employees, and little risk of employees losing base pay," according to Prem Benimadhu.[72] But there are also studies that question the effectiveness of pay-for-performance approaches, suggesting they can lead to less group cohesiveness in the workplace.[73]

If the organization uses work teams, managers should consider group-based performance incentives that will reinforce team effort and commitment. But whether these programs are individual based or team based, managers do need to ensure that they are specific about the relationship between an individual's pay and his or her expected level of appropriate performance. Employees must clearly understand exactly how performance—theirs and the organization's—translates into dollars on their paycheques.[74] Ottawa-based Lee Valley Tools uses quarterly newsletters to employees to let them know how much profit is forecast. The newsletter helps employees understand how hard work will pay off for them. Robin Lee, the company's president, says that "sharing information and profits promotes an atmosphere in which hard work, innovation, and efficiency pay off for everybody."[75]

The weak link between pay and performance is nowhere more evident than in the final type of rewards program we are going to look at—employee stock options.

**STOCK OPTION PROGRAMS** Executive bonus and stock option programs have come under fire because they seem to fly in the face of the belief that executive pay aligns with the organization's performance. What are stock option programs and what are they designed to do?

**Stock options** are a financial incentive that gives employees the right to purchase shares of company stock at some time in the future, at a set price. The original idea behind employee stock option plans was to turn employees into owners and give them strong motivation to work hard to make the company successful.[76] If the company was successful, the value of the stock went up, making the stock options valuable. In other words, there was a link between performance and reward. The popularity of stock options as a motivational and compensation tool skyrocketed during the dot-com boom in the late 1990s. Because many dot-coms could not afford to pay employees the going market-rate salaries, stock options were offered as performance incentives. As long as the market was rising, employees were willing to give up large salaries in exchange for stock options. However, when stock prices tanked in 2001, many individuals who joined and stayed with a dot-com for the opportunity to get rich through stock options found those stock options had become worthless. The declining stock market became a powerful demotivator.

Despite the risk of potential lost value and the widespread abuse of stock options, managers might want to consider them as part of their overall motivational program. An appropriately designed stock option program can be a powerful motivational tool for the entire workforce.[77]

Analyze

## Improving Work–Life Balance

While many employees continue to work an eight-hour day, five days a week, with fixed start and end times, organizations have started to implement programs to help employees manage their lives outside work. Many of the work–life balance programs that organizations have implemented are a response to the varied needs of a diverse workforce.

In addition to helping with errands and meals, contemporary companies are looking at a variety of scheduling options, including flextime, job sharing, and telework to help employees balance work and personal life.

**FLEXIBLE WORK SCHEDULES**   Many organizations have developed flexible work schedules that recognize different needs. For instance, a **compressed workweek** is a workweek in which employees work longer hours per day but fewer days per week. The most common form is four 10-hour days (a 4/40 program). However, organizations could design other types of schedules to fit employees' needs. Another alternative is **flexible work hours** (also popularly known as **flextime**), a scheduling option in which employees are required to work a specific number of hours per week but are free to vary those hours within certain limits. In a flextime schedule, all employees are required to be on the job for certain common core hours, but starting, ending, and lunch-hour times are flexible. Flextime is one of the most desired benefits among employees.[78] Employers have responded; a survey shows that 82 percent of Canadian employers expect to have flexible work arrangements by 2015 if not earlier.

**JOB SHARING**   Another scheduling option that can be effective in motivating a diverse workforce is **job sharing**—the practice of having two or more people split a full-time job. This type of job schedule might be attractive to individuals who want to work but do not want the demands and hassles of a full-time position.

**TELEWORK**   Another alternative made possible by information technology is telecommuting or **telework**, in which employees work away from their office, usually at home, and are linked to the workplace by computer and other technology. Since many jobs are computer

According to a 2010 Workopolis study, 53 percent of Canadian workers want a telework option to decrease commuting time and increase productivity.[79]

---

**stock options**
A financial incentive that gives employees the right to purchase shares of company stock at some time in the future, at a set price.

**compressed workweek**
A workweek in which employees work longer hours per day but fewer days per week.

**flexible work hours (flextime)**
A scheduling option in which employees are required to work a specific number of hours per week but are free to vary those hours within certain limits.

**job sharing**
The practice of having two or more people split a full-time job.

**telework**
A job arrangement in which employees work at home and are linked to the workplace by computer and other technology.

and Internet oriented, this job arrangement might be considered ideal for some people as there is no commuting, the hours are flexible, there is freedom to dress as you please, and there are few or no interruptions from colleagues. However, keep in mind that some employees miss the informal interactions at work that satisfy their social needs and provide a source of new ideas.

**Explain**
What can managers learn from motivation theories?

**9.5**

# FROM THEORY TO PRACTICE: SUGGESTIONS FOR MOTIVATING EMPLOYEES

We have covered a lot of information about motivation in this chapter. If you are a manager concerned with motivating your employees, what specific recommendations can you draw from the theories and issues discussed so far? Although there is no simple, all-encompassing set of guidelines, the following suggestions draw on what we know about motivating employees:

- *Recognize individual differences.* Almost every contemporary motivation theory recognizes that employees are not identical. They have different needs, attitudes, personalities, and other important individual variables. Managers may not be giving enough consideration to what employees really want in terms of pay and benefits from the workplace. A recent survey of 446 employers by Western Compensation and Benefits Consultants found that 94 percent listed competitive base salary as an important incentive. Only 52 percent of employers listed flexible scheduling as a good incentive.[80] Meanwhile, a Statistics Canada survey found that employees want "challenging work, continuous learning, flexible work arrangements, and better communication with their employers."[81] Eighty-seven percent of companies in the Western Compensation survey reported having difficulties attracting new employees in 2006. Companies may need to pay more attention to what their employees say that they want.
- *Match people to jobs.* A great deal of evidence demonstrates the motivational benefits of carefully matching people to jobs. For example, high achievers should have jobs that let them participate in setting moderately challenging goals and give them autonomy and feedback. Also, keep in mind that not everybody is motivated by jobs that are high in autonomy, variety, and responsibility.
- *Individualize rewards.* Because employees have different needs, what acts as a reinforcer for one may not for another. Managers should use their knowledge of employee differences to individualize the rewards they control, such as pay, promotions, recognition, desirable work assignments, autonomy, and participation.
- *Link rewards to performance.* Managers need to make rewards contingent on performance. Rewarding factors other than performance will reinforce only those other factors. Important rewards such as pay increases and promotions should be given for the attainment of specific goals. Managers should also look for ways to increase the visibility of rewards, making them potentially more motivating.
- *Check the system for equity.* Employees should perceive that rewards or outcomes are equal to the inputs. On a simple level, experience, ability, effort, and other obvious inputs should explain differences in pay, responsibility, and other obvious outcomes. Remember that one person's equity is another's inequity, so an ideal reward system should weigh inputs differently in arriving at the proper rewards for each job.
- *Use recognition.* Use the power of recognition. In an economy where cost-cutting and layoffs are widespread (as we are experiencing in the current economy), recognition is a low-cost means to reward employees, and it is a reward that most employees consider valuable.

- *Don't ignore money.* It is easy to get so caught up in setting goals, creating interesting jobs, and providing opportunities for participation that you forget that money is a major reason why most people work. Some studies indicate that money is not the top priority of employees. Professor Graham Lowe at the University of Alberta and a colleague found that relationships in the workplace are more important than pay or benefits in determining job satisfaction.[82] Nevertheless, the allocation of performance-based wage increases, piecework bonuses, and other pay incentives is important in determining employee motivation. We are not saying that managers should focus solely on money as a motivational tool; rather, we are simply stating the obvious—if money is removed as an incentive, people are not going to show up for work. The same cannot be said for removing performance goals, enriched work, or participation.

Practise

# 9 Review and Apply

## Summary of Learning Objectives

**9.1 What is motivation?** Motivation refers to an individual's willingness to exert high levels of effort to reach organizational goals, conditioned by the degree to which that effort satisfies some individual need.

At Yellow House Events, one key way to motivate employees was to target brands that the employees believed in.

**9.2 How can needs help motivation?** According to needs theories, individuals have needs that, when fulfilled, will motivate them to perform well. While the theories do not account for all aspects of motivation, they do inform managers that individuals have different needs that should be considered when developing reward plans.

Yellow House Events discovered that as their Gen Y employees aged, they developed different needs, and the company tried to address these needs to keep the employees motivated.

**9.3 What are the contemporary theories of motivation?** Equity theory proposes that employees compare their rewards and their productivity with others, and then determine whether they have been treated fairly. Individuals who perceive that they are underrewarded will try to adjust their behaviour to correct this imbalance. Expectancy theory explores the link between people's belief in whether they can do the work assigned, their belief in whether they will get the rewards promised, and the extent to which the reward is something they value. Most research evidence supports expectancy theory.

Noble offers her staff pay increases in advance of their annual performance review, ensuring that employees do not have to ask for raises or move to competitors for more salary.

**9.4 What are some current issues in motivation?** Current issues in motivation include motivating a diverse workforce, designing effective rewards programs, and improving work–life balance.

One of Yellow House Events' challenges was motivating employees who did not like working for certain lucrative clients. Noble would occasionally "fire" clients to ensure that employees were motivated by the events that they were planning.

**9.5 What can managers learn from motivation theories?** Managers can motivate employees by recognizing individual differences, matching people to jobs, individualizing rewards, linking rewards to performance, checking the system for equity, using recognition, and not ignoring that money is a major reason why most people work.

Noble has worked hard to recognize the different needs of Gen Y employees and has allowed them to have flexible hours and blast music in the workplace. The company also has its employees participate in interviews for new hires to help keep current employees committed to the organization.

### SNAPSHOT SUMMARY

**9.1 What Is Motivation?**

**9.2 Early Theories of Motivation**
Maslow's Hierarchy of Needs Theory
McGregor's Theory X and Theory Y
Herzberg's Motivation-Hygiene Theory
McClelland's Theory of Needs

**9.3 Contemporary Theories of Motivation**
Four-Drive Theory
Reinforcement Theory
Equity Theory
Expectancy Theory
Integrating Contemporary Theories of Motivation

**9.4 Current Issues in Motivation**
Motivating a Diverse Workforce
Designing Effective Rewards Programs
Improving Work–Life Balance

**9.5 From Theory to Practice: Suggestions for Motivating Employees**

## MyManagementLab® Learning Resources

# Resources

▼ **Explore and enhance your understanding of key chapter topics through the following online resources:**

- Student PowerPoints
- Audio Summary of Chapter
- ROLLS
- CBC Videos for Part 4
- MySearchLab

▶ Visit the **Study Plan** area to test your progress with **Pre-Tests** and **Post-Tests**.

▼ **Build on your knowledge and practise real-world applications using the following online activities:**

# Interpret 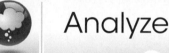 ▶

- Opening Case Activity: Theory Factors of Success
- Review and Apply: Solutions to Interpret section questions and activities
- Glossary Flashcards

# Analyze  ▶

- Opening Case Activity: Meeting Expectations
- Review and Apply: Solutions to Analyze section questions and activities
- Self-Assessment Library

# Practise ▶

- Opening Case Activity: Job Profiles and Motivation
- Review and Apply: Solutions to Practice section questions and activities
- Decision Making Simulation: Motivation

# Interpret What You Have Read

1. How do needs affect motivation?
2. Contrast lower-order and higher-order needs in Maslow's needs hierarchy.
3. Describe the three needs in McClelland's theory of needs.
4. Describe the four drives in Lawrence and Nohria's four-drive theory of motivation.
5. What are some possible consequences of employees' perceiving an inequity between their inputs and outcomes and those of others?
6. What are some advantages of using pay-for-performance programs to motivate employee performance? Are there drawbacks? Explain.
7. What are the advantages of flextime from an employee's perspective? From management's perspective?
8. What can organizations do to create more motivating environments for their employees?

# Analyze What You Have Read

1. Most of us have to work for a living, and a job is a central part of our lives. Why then do managers have to worry about employee motivation issues?
2. What role would money play in (1) the hierarchy of needs theory, (2) motivation-hygiene theory, (3) equity theory, and (4) expectancy theory?
3. If you accept Theory Y assumptions, how would you be likely to motivate employees? What would you do if you accept Theory X assumptions?
4. What difficulties do you think workforce diversity causes for managers who are trying to use equity theory?
5. Describe a task you have done recently for which you exerted a high level of effort. Explain your behaviour using the following motivation approaches: (1) the hierarchy of needs theory, (2) motivation-hygiene theory, (3) equity theory, and (4) expectancy theory.
6. Describe several means that you might use to motivate (1) minimum-wage employees working for a small company that makes tortillas or (2) professional and technical employees working for a software design firm. Which of your suggestions do you think is best? Support your position.
7. Many job design experts who have studied the changing nature of work say that people do their best work when they are motivated by a sense of purpose rather than by the pursuit of money. Do you agree? Explain your position.

# Assess Your Skills

## WHAT REWARDS DO I VALUE MOST?

Below are 10 work-related rewards. For each, identify the number that best describes the value that a particular reward has for you personally. Use the following scale to express your feelings:

1 = No Value at All   2 = Slight Value   3 = Moderate Value   4 = Great Value   5 = Extremely Great Value

| | |
|---|---|
| **1.** Good pay | 1 2 3 4 5 |
| **2.** Prestigious title | 1 2 3 4 5 |
| **3.** Vacation time | 1 2 3 4 5 |
| **4.** Job security | 1 2 3 4 5 |
| **5.** Recognition | 1 2 3 4 5 |
| **6.** Interesting work | 1 2 3 4 5 |
| **7.** Pleasant conditions | 1 2 3 4 5 |
| **8.** Chances to advance | 1 2 3 4 5 |
| **9.** Flexible schedule | 1 2 3 4 5 |
| **10.** Friendly co-workers | 1 2 3 4 5 |

**SCORING KEY**   To assess your responses, prioritize them into groups. Put all the rewards you gave a 5 together. Do the same for your other responses. The rewards you gave 5s or 4s are the ones that you most desire and that your employer should emphasize with you.

**ANALYSIS AND INTERPRETATION**

What motivates you does not necessarily motivate me, so employers that want to maximize employee motivation should determine what rewards each employee individually values. This instrument can help you understand which work-related rewards have the greatest value to you. Compare the rewards that your employer offers with your scores. The greater the disparity, the more you might want to consider looking for opportunities at another organization with a reward structure that better matches your preferences.

> **More Self-Assessments**
>
> To learn more about your skills, abilities, and interests, take the following self-assessments on the MyManagementLab®:
>
> - I.C.1–What Motivates Me?
> - I.C.4–What's My View on the Nature of People?
> - IV.B.1–Am I Engaged?

# Practise What You Have Learned

## DILEMMA

You are in a team with six other management students and you have a major case analysis due in four weeks. The case project will count for 25 percent of the course mark. You are the team leader. Several team members are having difficulty motivating themselves to get started on the project. Identify ways you could motivate your team members, using needs theories, expectancy theory, and equity theory. How will you motivate yourself?

## BECOMING A MANAGER

- Start paying attention to times when you are highly motivated and times when you are not as motivated. What accounts for the difference?
- When working on teams for class projects or on committees in student organizations, try different approaches to motivating others.
- If you are working, assess which of the four drives are strongest in motivating you at your job.
- As you visit various businesses, note what, if any, employee recognition programs these businesses use.
- Talk to practising managers about their approaches to employee motivation. What have they found works?

## DEVELOPING YOUR DIAGNOSTIC AND ANALYTICAL SKILLS: TWENTY-FIRST-CENTURY FACTORY TOWN

ATCO Structures & Logistics is building a town in empty farmland about 100 km north of Regina.[83] BHP Billiton is opening the largest potash mine in the world in 2015, and the ATCO town will hold approximately 2500 employees, about 80 percent of whom are likely to be male. This $350 million complex will be open from 2015 to 2022, after which BHP will replace the topsoil and remove the roadways, restoring the land for future agricultural uses.

Work camps are common in mining, and traditionally they have featured shared rooms and group washrooms. ATCO is approaching their temporary town differently. Facilities will include 500 single bedrooms, each equipped with a bathroom, Wi-Fi, flat-screen TV, and mini-fridge. Lecture halls used for training during the day will provide broadcasts of hockey games and UFC fights, as well as card and video game tournaments. Worker priorities are changing, and ATCO is building a 20 000 square foot fitness facility with a gym, two squash courts, a weight room, and an indoor running track with 360-degree window views. In a quintessentially Canadian move, ATCO is also putting in a full-sized outdoor hockey rink.

To keep employees occupied and stem the potential substance abuse problem featured in some camps, one out of every five residents at the facility will be there to look after the workers, including cooking, cleaning, maintenance, and security.

### Questions

1. What is it like to work at one of BHP Billiton's mining camps? (Hint: Go to BHP Billiton's website and click on People and Careers.) What is your assessment of the company's philosophy toward employees?

2. What do you think is ATCO's biggest challenge in keeping employees occupied while living in a huge work camp?

3. If you were managing a team of potash miners and tradespeople, how would you keep them motivated?

## DEVELOPING YOUR INTERPERSONAL SKILLS: MAXIMIZING EMPLOYEE EFFORT

### ABOUT THE SKILL

There is no simple, all-encompassing set of motivational guidelines, but the following suggestions draw on the essence of what we know about motivating employees.[84]

### STEPS IN DEVELOPING THE SKILL

You can be more effective at motivating employees if you apply the following eight suggestions:

1. RECOGNIZE INDIVIDUAL DIFFERENCES. Almost every contemporary motivation theory recognizes that employees are not homogeneous. They have different

needs. They also differ in terms of attitudes, personality, and other important individual variables.

2. MATCH PEOPLE TO JOBS. A great deal of evidence demonstrates the motivational benefits of carefully matching people to jobs. People who lack the necessary skills to perform successfully will be disadvantaged. Redesign jobs to enhance motivation.

3. USE GOALS. You should ensure that employees have hard, specific goals and feedback on how well they are doing in pursuit of those goals. Employees will be more committed if goals are clear and set through participation.

4. ENSURE THAT GOALS ARE PERCEIVED AS ATTAINABLE. Regardless of whether goals are actually attainable, employees who see goals as unattainable will reduce their effort. Be sure, therefore, that employees feel confident that increased effort can lead to achieving performance goals.

5. INDIVIDUALIZE REWARDS AND ENSURE THEY ARE TIMELY. Because employees have different needs, what acts as a reinforcer for one may not do so for another. Use your knowledge of employee differences to individualize the rewards over which you have control. Some of the more obvious rewards that you can allocate include pay, promotions, autonomy, and the opportunity to participate in goal setting and decision making.

6. LINK REWARDS TO PERFORMANCE. You need to make rewards contingent on performance. Rewarding factors other than performance will reinforce only the importance of those other factors. Key rewards such as pay increases and promotions should be given for the attainment of employees' specific goals. Linking rewards to

performance increases effort-performance and performance-reward expectancies.

7. CHECK THE SYSTEM FOR EQUITY. Employees should perceive that rewards or outcomes are equal to the inputs given. On a simplistic level, experience, ability, effort, and other obvious inputs should explain differences in pay, responsibility, and other obvious outcomes.

8. LINK PAY WITH PERFORMANCE. It is easy to get so caught up in setting goals, creating interesting jobs, and providing opportunities for participation that you forget that money is a major reason why most people work. Thus, the allocation of performance-based wage increases, piecework bonuses, employee stock ownership plans, and other pay incentives are important in determining employee motivation.

**PRACTISING THE SKILL**

Employees at Radialpoint in Montreal can get their laundry washed, dried, and folded for them at work. At trucking company Groupe Robert, based in Rougemont, Quebec, employees are entered into monthly draws for concerts and shows; each employee receives a Christmas food basket; and birthday cards are personally signed by the CEO. At Brantford, Ontario–based S. C. Johnson & Son, employees and their families can take holidays at the company's resort in the Muskokas. The company also provides an on-site massage therapist. All of these companies believe that there is more to rewards than just cash.

All of the following traditional and offbeat benefits are currently offered at various Canadian firms. Rank-order them for yourself, putting those that are most likely to motivate you at the top of your list. Now look at your top five choices. How do you think you will rank them in 10 years? Why?

| | | | |
|---|---|---|---|
| Flextime | Dental insurance | Pets at work | Company car |
| Telework | Vision insurance | Fitness memberships | Subsidized cafeteria |
| Paid vacation | Life insurance | On-site daycare | Annual birthday gift |
| Management development plan | Retirement plan | Clothing allowance | Transportation voucher |
| Family picnics and parties | Profit sharing/stock purchase plan | Children's college/ university tuition | Benefits for unmarried domestic partners |
| Paid sick days | Daily naptime | Tuition refund | Free snacks and candy |
| Child and elder care referral services | Flexible spending plan | Non work-related courses | Ability to keep frequent flier miles |
| Bring Your Own Device (BYOD) | Employee assistance program | Laundry/dry cleaning service | Company-sponsored teams |

# Team Exercises

## 3BL: THE TRIPLE BOTTOM LINE

Corporate sustainability practices can have a positive impact on recruitment, retention, and employee engagement. Towers Perrin's 2007 Global Workforce Study shows that a

firm's reputation for social responsibility (including environmental work) is one of the top ten drivers of employee engagement worldwide.[85] How do employers engage employees in their sustainability efforts? Some of the steps include public sustainability goals, senior executive support, as well as training, policies, and programs which integrate sustainability into employee roles performance.

### THINKING STRATEGICALLY ABOUT 3BL

There are many ways to motivate employees to modify their behaviour and actions to become more sustainable.

- Recognition
- Management feedback
- Salary and bonuses
- Benefits
- Competition/peer inducements
- Modified job requirements
- Opportunities for growth

All of these incentives need to be aligned with organizational goals or there will be incongruence and any behavioural changes will be short-lived. Different organizations could use combinations of the above incentives that fit their culture. For example, Intel ties corporate sustainability goals to their annual performance bonus.[86] Which of the above incentives would have the greatest impact on your behaviour?

## HOW CAN YOU MOTIVATE OTHERS?

This exercise is designed to increase your awareness of how and why you motivate others and to help you focus on the needs of those you are attempting to motivate.

### STEP 1

Break into groups of five to seven people. Each group member is to respond individually to the following situations:

Situation 1: You are the owner and president of a 50-employee organization that provides call-centre services to a number of local businesses. Your company has two major units. Customer care answers questions from customers about malfunctioning technology (computers, cellphones, and home networks). Sales and marketing makes telemarketing calls to people's homes. Employees who work in sales and marketing phone people and try to sell them cellphone plans and/or Internet access at reduced prices. They also conduct market research via phone, calling people to ask them to answer survey questions. Employees who work in customer care often receive calls from irate customers who are having technical difficulties. Employees who work in sales and marketing often encounter irate people when they phone to sell them something or conduct a survey, particularly at dinner time. Your goal is to motivate all 50 employees to their highest level of effort.

Task 1: Look at the table listing 10 factors you could use to motivate your employees. Rank the factors from most important to least important (1 to 10), placing your rankings in the Task 1 column.

Situation 2: Consider now that you are one of the 50 employees who have been given insight into what motivates you.

Task 2: As an employee, look again at the factors listed in the table and think about what would motivate you most effectively. Again, rank the factors from most important to least important (1 to 10), and place your rankings in the Task 2 column.

### STEP 2

Each member should share his or her prioritized lists (the lists from Tasks 1 and 2) with the other members of the group.

### STEP 3

After each member has presented his or her lists, the group should respond to the following questions:

1. Are each individual's lists (Task 1 and Task 2) similar or dissimilar to the others? What do the differences or similarities suggest to you?

2. What have you learned about how and why to motivate others, and how can you apply this information?

| Work Factor | Task 1 Rank | Task 2 Rank |
| --- | --- | --- |
| Recognition for customer accomplishments | | |
| A variety of tasks (sales and customer service) | | |
| Seeing the results of my work | | |
| Opportunity for advancement | | |
| Being compensated for enhanced performance | | |
| A comfortable physical working environment | | |
| Opportunities for advancement | | |
| Job security | | |
| Equity in access to benefits | | |
| Interesting work | | |

## BE THE CONSULTANT

Microfinance institutions (MFIs) provide financial services to poor and low-income individuals (microfinance), includ-ing microcredit, savings, money transfers, insurance, and payment services.[87] A local MFI has engaged your consulting firm to advise them on the benefits of incorporating sustainability practices internally and with clients.

Particularly, they are interested in your firm answering the following questions:

1. How will sustainability practices increase the motivation of their employees?

2. How can sustainability provide added value to their clients?

3. How will sustainability practices of their clients lead to decreased credit risk?

4. Which stakeholders might put pressure on MFIs to have better sustainability performance?

# Business Cases

## BEST BUY

Customer-centricity.[88] That concept is the new strategic focus that Brad Anderson, CEO of Best Buy, is betting on to keep the company from becoming a retailing casualty like Woolworth or Kmart. What is customer-centricity? Simply put, it is figuring out which customers are the most profitable and doing whatever it takes to please them so they want to come back often and spend money. As the biggest consumer electronics retailer in North America, Best Buy has a lot at stake. Its 100 000-plus employees will play a crucial role in this new approach, which shifts the focus from "pushing gadgets to catering to customers."

"At Best Buy, People Are the Engines That Drive Our Success." That sentence is the up-front-and-central slogan on the company's web-based career centre. To Best Buy, it is not just an empty slogan either. The company has tried to create an environment in which employees, wherever they are, have numerous opportunities to learn, work, play, and achieve. One way Best Buy can do that is by providing facts and figures to employees on everything from new technology to industry changes to company actions. At store meetings or on the intranet, employees can get the information they need to do their jobs and do them well.

Like many other companies, Best Buy has "struggled to meet the demands of its business—how to do things better, faster, and cheaper than its competitors—with an increasingly stressed-out workforce." Its culture has always rewarded long hours and sacrifice. One manager used a plaque to recognize the employee "who turns on the lights in the morning and turns them off at night." However, that approach has been taking its toll on employees. Best Buy is having difficulty retaining its best and brightest managers and executives.

Anderson wants to know why the company does not have an "innovative incentive program to foster our innovative culture." He has come to you for advice. What is the best way for the company to get employees on board so that they will be more customer-centric in their approach?

# Understanding Groups and Teams

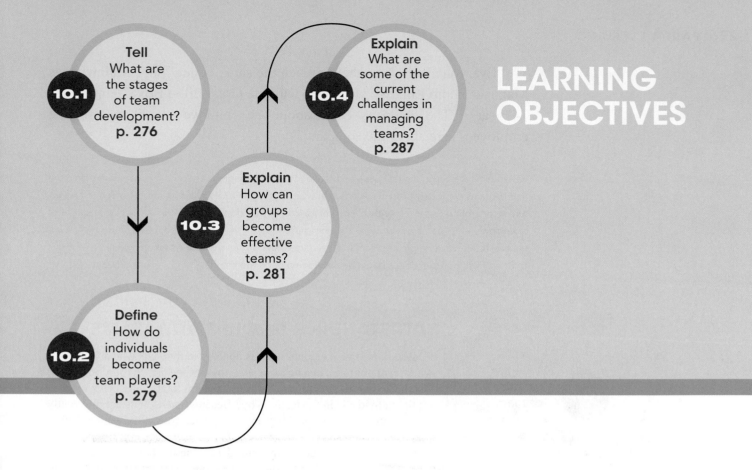

# LEARNING OBJECTIVES

**Tell**
What are the stages of team development?
p. 276
**10.1**

**Explain**
What are some of the current challenges in managing teams?
p. 287
**10.4**

**Explain**
How can groups become effective teams?
p. 281
**10.3**

**Define**
How do individuals become team players?
p. 279
**10.2**

The Great Little Box Company Ltd.[1] (GLBC) of Vancouver, BC, started in 1982 with a 5000 square foot plant in Burnaby and only three employees. Total sales in the first year were $80 000. Today the company sells that in less than a day. "We fill more orders in an hour now than we did that first month," says founder Robert Meggy.

In Canada, the corrugated packaging industry is dominated by a handful of large, multinational companies. GLBC is the largest regional firm in Western Canada, turning out more than 150 000 cardboard boxes daily. Meggy attributes the company's success to his 170 employees, who are committed to providing the company's customers with good service, quick turnaround, and on-time delivery. "If you keep your staff happy, they will keep your customers happy," says James Palmer, vice-president of sales and marketing.

GLBC encourages and supports its employees through ongoing skills training, and career and personal development. Their employee profit-sharing plan reflects a commitment to employee empowerment, motivation, and employee success.

GLBC has an "open-book" process, whereby it shares its corporate and financial information with all employees. The monthly meetings provide an opportunity for employee input and for recognizing and rewarding employees for their efforts. "It's important to share the financials with everyone," says Meggy. "We want employees to run the company like their own business."

## Think About It

What makes a team different from any group of people? Robert Meggy learned that a top sales and marketing department was essential to the company's success. He brought on a new type of sales person who happened to be an exceptional team player. "This changed my opinion about sales people completely," said Meggy. "So now I make sure I get very good sales people in place."

"Everyone works together to reach the same target," says Maintenance Manager Philip Lim, who has been with the Great Little Box Company for 14 years. "The company cares about the employees and, in turn, the employees care about the company."

Work teams are one of the realities—and challenges—of managing in today's dynamic global environment. Teams are widely used in Canada. Thousands of organizations have made the move to restructure work around teams rather than individuals. Why? What do these teams look like? What stages of development do teams go through? Like the challenge Robert Meggy faced, how can business owners create effective employee teams? These are a few of the types of questions we answer in this chapter. First, however, let us begin by developing our understanding of group/team behaviour.

# UNDERSTANDING GROUPS AND TEAMS

**10.1**

**Tell**
What are the stages of team development?

Because most organizational work is done by individuals who are part of a work team or group, managers need to understand team/group behaviour. The behaviour of a team is not simply the sum total of the behaviours of all the individuals in the team. Why? Because individuals act differently in teams than they do when they are alone. Therefore, if we want to understand organizational behaviour more fully, we need to study teams.

Though teams and groups can differ depending on their purpose, we use "groups" and "teams" interchangeably in our theoretical discussions below (conforming to how scholars have written their research) because we are discussing teams or groups in the workplace. Interchanging these terms simply underscores that the processes for groups and teams are similar, although formal work teams/groups involve more synergy.

## What Is a Team?

Most of you are already familiar with teams, especially if you have watched organized sports events. Although a sports team has many of the same characteristics as a work team, work teams *are* different from informal groups and have their own unique traits. **Work teams** are two or more interacting and interdependent individuals whose members work intensely on a specific, common goal using their positive **synergy** (combined efforts that are greater than the sum of individual efforts), individual and mutual accountability, and complementary skills. In a work team, the combined individual efforts of team members result in a level of performance that is greater than the sum of those individual inputs, by generating positive synergy through coordinated effort. Exhibit 10-1 provides some examples of different types of teams in today's organizations.

## Informal Groups

Employees also belong to *informal groups*. Unlike work teams or groups, these informal groups have no need or opportunity to engage in collective work that requires joint effort. Informal groups are social and occur naturally in the workplace in response to the need for social contact. For example, three employees from different departments who regularly eat lunch together are an informal group. Informal groups tend to form around friendships and common interests.

Google's website explains the company looks for exceptional people, and one of the skills they need is the ability to work as a team member. "We work in small teams, which we believe promotes spontaneity, creativity, and speed," the company says, "and team achievements are highly valued." Pictured here are some of Google's employees playing cricket at its research and development (R&D) centre in India.

**EXHIBIT 10-1** Types of Teams in Organizations

| Team Type | Description | Example |
|---|---|---|
| Cross-functional teams | Employees who are experts in various functions; task interdependence is limited as each member works with other employees in different departments. | Calgary-based Canadian Pacific Railway (CPR) uses cross-functional teams to figure out ways to cut costs. All the functional areas affected by the cost cutting are represented. |
| Problem-solving teams | Employees from the same department or functional area who are trying to improve work activities or solve specific problems. | The RCMP uses a drug task force separate from its main policing operations to address issues related to the manufacture, sale, and use of illegal drugs. |
| Self-managed teams | Employees with high autonomy who are responsible for an entire work process or segment. Unlike a problem-solving team, the team is also responsible for managing itself. | Muskoseepi Park in Grand Prairie, Alberta, is operated by a self-managed team whose members are accountable to each other and do not have direct daily supervision. |
| Advisory teams | Teams that provide feedback and recommendations to organizational decision makers. | Nova Scotia Business Inc. uses an advisory team to keep on top of community issues throughout the province. |
| Virtual teams | Teams that use information technologies to link physically dispersed members. | Microsoft's staff in Richmond, BC, are part of a virtual team with members in Redmond, Washington, and other global centres. |

## Stages of Team Development

Team development is a dynamic process. Most teams and groups are in a continual state of change, although there is a general pattern that describes how most of them develop. Professor Bruce Tuckman of Ohio State University developed a five-stage model of small group development.[2] As shown in Exhibit 10-2, these five stages are *forming, storming, norming, performing,* and *adjourning.*

Stage I, **forming**, has two aspects. First, people join the team either because of a work assignment or for some other benefit desired (such as status, self-esteem, affiliation, power, or security).

Once the team's membership is in place, the second part of the forming stage begins: the task of defining the team's purpose, structure, and leadership. This phase is characterized by a great deal of uncertainty. Members are "testing the waters" to determine what types of behaviour are acceptable. This stage is complete when members begin to think of themselves as part of a team.

Stage II, **storming**, is one of intragroup conflict. Members accept the existence of the team but resist the control that the team imposes on individuality. Further, there is conflict over who will control the team. When this stage is complete, there will be a relatively clear hierarchy of leadership within the team and agreement on the team's direction. Conflict helps the team clarify roles and leads to some level of belonging for team members, although teams with major problems can sometimes get stuck in this stage.

Stage III is one in which close relationships develop and the team demonstrates cohesiveness. There is now a strong sense of team identity and camaraderie. This **norming** stage is complete when the team structure solidifies and the team has assimilated a common set of expectations of what defines correct member behaviour. Members are involved and begin to support each other.

*Have you ever noticed the stages a team goes through in learning how to work together?*

---

**work team**
Two or more interacting and interdependent individuals whose members work intensely on a specific, common goal using their positive synergy, individual and mutual accountability, and complementary skills.

**synergy**
Combined efforts that are greater than the sum of individual efforts.

**forming**
The first stage of team development in which people join the group and then define the team's purpose, structure, and leadership.

**storming**
The second stage of team development, which is characterized by intragroup conflict.

**norming**
The third stage of team development, which is characterized by close relationships and cohesiveness.

**EXHIBIT 10-2** Stages of Team Development

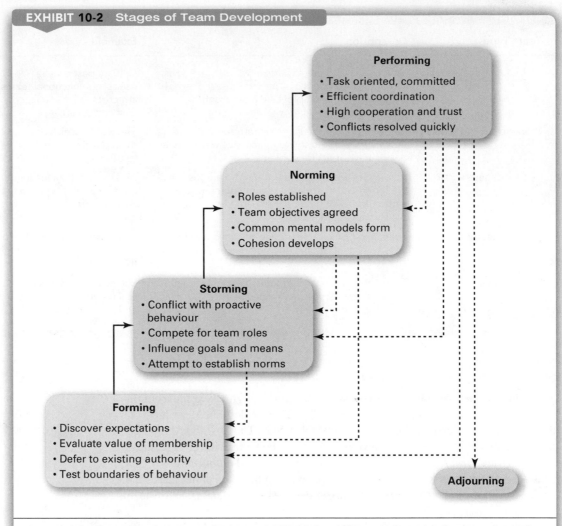

**Performing**
- Task oriented, committed
- Efficient coordination
- High cooperation and trust
- Conflicts resolved quickly

**Norming**
- Roles established
- Team objectives agreed
- Common mental models form
- Cohesion develops

**Storming**
- Conflict with proactive behaviour
- Compete for team roles
- Influence goals and means
- Attempt to establish norms

**Forming**
- Discover expectations
- Evaluate value of membership
- Defer to existing authority
- Test boundaries of behaviour

**Adjourning**

*Source:* McShane, *Canadian Organizational Behaviour* © 2008. McGraw Hill Ryerson. Reproduced with permission of McGraw-Hill Ryerson Ltd.

Stage IV is **performing**. The team structure at this point is fully functional and accepted by team members. Team energy has moved from getting to know and understand each other to performing the task at hand. Team purpose and roles are clear, and achievement leads to pride and high productivity.

Performing is the last stage in the development of permanent work teams. Temporary teams—such as project teams, task forces, and similar groups that have a limited task to perform—have a fifth stage, **adjourning**. In this stage, the team prepares to disband. High levels of task performance are no longer the team's top priority. Instead, attention is directed at wrapping up activities, perhaps with some sort of ceremony to help members seek closure. Responses of team members vary at this stage. Some are upbeat, basking in the team's accomplishments. Others may be saddened by the loss of camaraderie and friendships gained during the work team's life.

Many of you have probably experienced each of these stages in working on a class team project. Team members are selected and then meet for the first time. There is a "feeling out" period to assess what the team is going to do and how it is going to do it. This phase is usually rapidly followed by a battle for control: Who is going to be in charge? Once this issue is resolved and a "hierarchy" agreed on, the team identifies specific aspects of the task, who is going to do them, and dates by which the assigned work needs to be completed. General expectations are established and agreed on by each member. These decisions form the foundation for what you hope will be a coordinated team effort culminating in a project well done. Once the team project is completed and turned in, the team breaks up. Of course, some teams do not get far beyond the first or second stage; these teams typically have serious interpersonal conflicts, turn in disappointing work, and get lower grades.

Should you assume from the preceding discussion that a team becomes more effective as it progresses through the first four stages? Some researchers argue that effectiveness of work teams increases at advanced stages, but that is not always the case.[3] Also, teams do not always proceed clearly from one stage to the next. Sometimes, in fact, several stages may be going on simultaneously, as when teams are storming and performing at the same time. Individuals within a team may also be at different stages, with some performing while others are still in the forming or norming stage. When individuals are shy, they may take longer to reach the performing stage, and it may be helpful for team members to support and encourage each other through the stages. Teams sometimes regress to previous stages. Therefore, do not assume that all teams precisely follow this development process or that Stage IV (performing) is always the most desirable stage. Instead, think of this model as a general framework, which emphasizes that teams are dynamic entities. A framework can help you better understand the problems and issues that are most likely to surface during a team's life.

Interpret

# TURNING INDIVIDUALS INTO TEAM PLAYERS

Robert Meggy recognized that the latest tools and equipment were only useful in providing on-time delivery if the people using them were effective team players. GLBC created HR systems to support the belief that the company's greatest assets are its people. This approach led to low turnover, higher morale, and increased teamwork.

**Define**
**10.2** How do individuals become team players?

### Think About It

What does it take to turn an individual into a team player?

So far, we have made a strong case for the value and growing popularity of work teams, but not every employee is inherently a team player. Some people prefer to be recognized for their individual achievements. In some organizations, too, work environments are such that only the strong survive. Creating teams in such an environment may meet some resistance. Countries differ in terms of the degree to which individuals are encouraged by societal institutions to be integrated into groups. Teams fit well in countries that score high on collectivism, where working together is encouraged. But what if an organization wants to introduce teams into an individualistic society like that of Canada? The job becomes more difficult.

## The Challenges of Creating Team Players

One substantial barrier to work teams is the individual resistance that may exist. Employees' success, when they are part of teams, is no longer defined in terms of individual performance. Instead, success is a function of how well the team as a whole performs. To perform well as team members, individuals must be able to communicate openly and honestly with one another, to confront differences and resolve conflicts, and to place lower priority on personal goals for the good of the team. For many employees, these demands are difficult and sometimes impossible assignments.

The challenge of creating team players will be greatest when the national culture is highly individualistic and the teams are being introduced into an established organization

---

**performing**
The fourth stage of team development, in which the team structure is fully functional and accepted by team members.

**adjourning**
The final stage of team development for temporary teams, in which members are concerned with wrapping up activities rather than task performance.

that has historically valued individual achievement.[4] These organizations prospered by hiring and rewarding corporate stars, and they bred a competitive work climate that encouraged individual achievement and recognition. In this context, employees can experience culture shock caused by a sudden shift in the focus to teamwork.[5]

Team players do not just appear. A lot of hard work is required to get team members to gel. That is why baseball teams, like the Toronto Blue Jays, go to spring training every year—to prepare themselves as a team for the upcoming season.

In contrast, the challenge for management is less demanding when teams are introduced in places in which employees have strong collectivist values—such as Japan or Mexico. The challenge of forming teams will also be less in new organizations that use teams as their initial means of structuring work. For instance, Saturn Corporation (an American organization owned by General Motors) was designed around teams from its start. Everyone at Saturn was hired on the understanding that they would be working in teams, and the ability to be a good team player was a hiring prerequisite. *Managing Workforce Diversity—The Challenge of Managing Diverse Teams* on page 294 considers how you can help team members from different cultures work together more effectively.

## What Roles Do Team Members Play?

A **role** refers to a set of expected behaviour patterns attributed to someone who occupies a given position in a social unit. In a group, individuals are expected to perform certain roles because of their positions in the group. **Task-oriented roles** tend to be oriented toward task accomplishment, while **maintenance roles** are oriented toward maintaining group member satisfaction and relationships.[6] Think about groups that you have been in and the roles that you played. Were you continually trying to keep the group focused on getting its work done? If so, you were filling a task accomplishment role. Or were you more concerned that group members had the opportunity to offer ideas and that they were satisfied with the experience? If so, you were performing a maintenance role to preserve the harmony of the group. Both roles are important to the ability of a group to function effectively and efficiently, and some group members are flexible and play both roles. One study found that the most effective teams had a leader who performed both the task-oriented and the maintenance roles.[7] In some groups, unfortunately, there are people who take on neither role, and participate very little in the team functions. It is not helpful if there are too many people who do not take on a role.

## Shaping Team Behaviour

Several options are available for managers who are trying to turn individuals into team players. The three most popular ways include proper selection, employee training, and rewarding the appropriate team behaviours. Let us look at each of these.

**SELECTION**   Some individuals already possess the interpersonal skills to be effective team players. When hiring team members, in addition to checking on the technical skills required to successfully perform the job, the organization should ensure that applicants can fulfill team roles.

As we have mentioned before, some applicants have been socialized around individual contributions and, consequently, lack team skills, as might some current employees whose jobs are being restructured into teams. When faced with such candidates, a manager can do several things. First, and most obvious, if a candidate's team skills are woefully lacking, do not hire that candidate. If successful performance requires interaction, rejecting such a candidate is appropriate. On the other hand, a good candidate with only some basic team skills can be hired on a probationary basis and required to undergo training to shape him or her into a team player. If the skills are not learned or practised, the individual may have to be let go for failing to master the skills necessary for performing successfully on the job.

**TRAINING**   Performing well in a team involves a set of behaviours. As we discussed in the preceding chapter, new behaviours can be learned. Even a large portion of people who were raised on the importance of individual accomplishment can be trained to become team players. Training specialists can conduct workshops that allow employees to experience the satisfaction that teamwork can provide. The workshops usually cover such topics as team problem solving, communications, negotiations, conflict resolution, and coaching skills. It is not unusual, too, for these employees to be exposed to the five stages of team development that we discussed earlier.[8] At Verizon Communications, for example, trainers focus on how a team goes through various stages before it gels. Employees are reminded of the importance of patience, because teams take longer to do some things—such as make decisions—than do employees acting alone.[9]

**REWARDS** The organization's reward system needs to encourage cooperative efforts rather than competitive ones. For example, Lockheed Martin Aeronautics Company has organized its 20 000-plus employees into teams. Rewards are structured to return a percentage increase in the bottom line to the team members on the basis of achievements of the team's performance goals.

Promotions, pay raises, and other forms of recognition should be given to employees who are effective collaborative team members. Recognition of teamwork does not mean that individual contribution is ignored, but rather that it is balanced with selfless contributions to the team. Examples of behaviours that should be rewarded include training new colleagues, sharing information with teammates, helping resolve team conflicts, and mastering new skills in which the team is deficient.[10] Finally, managers cannot forget the inherent rewards that employees can receive from teamwork. Work teams provide camaraderie. It is exciting and satisfying to be an integral part of a successful team. The opportunity to engage in personal development and to help teammates grow can be a very satisfying and rewarding experience for employees.[11]

# TURNING GROUPS INTO EFFECTIVE TEAMS

Robert Meggy believes that building teamwork improves the bottom line and is key to attracting and retaining good employees. Employees working together effectively understand each other's jobs and make fewer mistakes.

**10.3** Explain How can groups become effective teams?

## Think About It

How can managers create effective teams?

Employees are strongly encouraged to attend company social functions, and those who do not usually end up leaving during their first year. Meggy says that employees need to be interested in the people with whom they work, "and if you're not interested in that, you're not interested in the company—because people make up the company."

Teams are not automatic productivity enhancers; they can also be disappointments. The challenge is to create effective teams. Effective teams have a number of characteristics, which we review below. In addition, teams need to build group cohesiveness, manage group conflict, and prevent social loafing to perform well. For more insights into creating effective teams, see *Developing Your Interpersonal Skills—Creating Effective Teams* on page 294 at the end of the chapter.

---

**role**
A set of expected behaviour patterns attributed to someone who occupies a given position in a social unit.

**task-oriented roles**
Roles performed by group members to ensure that group tasks are accomplished.

**maintenance roles**
Roles performed by group members to maintain good relations within the group.

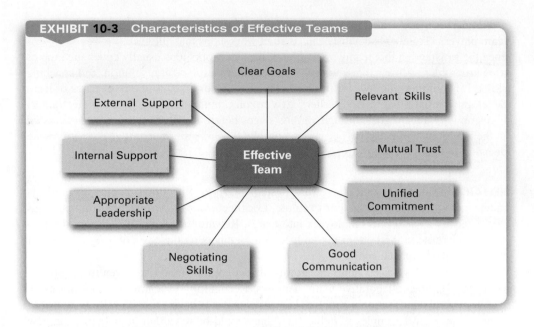

**EXHIBIT 10-3** Characteristics of Effective Teams

## Characteristics of Effective Teams

*How do you build an effective team? Have you ever done so?*

Research on teams provides insights into the characteristics associated with effective teams.[12] Let us look more closely at these characteristics, which are shown in Exhibit 10-3.

**CLEAR GOALS**  High-performance teams have a clear understanding of the goals to be achieved. Members are committed to the team's goals; they know what they are expected to accomplish and understand how they will work together to achieve these goals.

**RELEVANT SKILLS**  Effective teams are composed of competent individuals who have the necessary technical and interpersonal skills to achieve the desired goals while working well together. This last point is important, since not everyone who is technically competent has the interpersonal skills to work well as a team member.

**MUTUAL TRUST**  Effective teams are characterized by high levels of mutual trust among members. Members believe in each other's ability, character, and integrity. But as you probably know from personal relationships, trust is fragile. For team members to have mutual trust, they must believe that the team is capable of getting the task done and that "the team will not harm the individual or his or her interests."[13] Maintaining this trust requires careful attention by managers.

**UNIFIED COMMITMENT**  Unified commitment is characterized by dedication to the team's goals and a willingness to expend extraordinary amounts of energy to achieve them. Members of an effective team exhibit intense loyalty and dedication to the team and are willing to do whatever it takes to help their team succeed.

**GOOD COMMUNICATION**  Not surprisingly, effective teams are characterized by good communication. Members convey messages, verbally and nonverbally, to each other in ways that are readily and clearly understood. Also, feedback helps to guide team members and to correct misunderstandings. Like a couple who have been together for many years, members on high-performing teams are able to quickly and efficiently share ideas and feelings.

**NEGOTIATING SKILLS**  Effective teams are continually making adjustments as to who does what. This flexibility requires team members to possess negotiating skills. Since

As Roger Fisher and William Ury explain in their book *Getting to Yes*, win-win negotiation has four rules: one, separate the people from the issue; two, focus on interests and information, not positions; three, generate numerous alternatives; and four, develop an objective standard on which to base results of the negotiation.

problems and relationships are regularly changing in teams, members need to be able to confront and reconcile differences.

**APPROPRIATE LEADERSHIP**   Effective leaders can motivate a team to follow them through the most difficult situations. How? By clarifying goals, demonstrating that change is possible by overcoming inertia, increasing the self-confidence of team members, and helping members to more fully realize their potential. Increasingly, effective team leaders act as coaches and facilitators. They help guide and support the team but do not control it. See also *Assess Your Skills—How Good Am I at Building and Leading a Team?* on pages 292–293 at the end of the chapter.

**INTERNAL AND EXTERNAL SUPPORT**   The final condition necessary for an effective team is a supportive climate. Internally, the team should have a sound infrastructure, which means having proper training, a clear and reasonable measurement system that team members can use to evaluate their overall performance, an incentive program that recognizes and rewards team activities, and a supportive human resource system. The right infrastructure should support members and reinforce behaviours that lead to high levels of performance. Externally, managers should provide the team with the resources needed to get the job done.

## Building Group Cohesiveness

Intuitively, it makes sense that groups in which there is a lot of internal disagreement and lack of cooperation are less effective in completing their tasks than are groups in which members generally agree, cooperate, and like each other. Research in this area has focused on **group cohesiveness**, or the degree to which members are attracted to each other and share the group's goals. Cohesiveness is important because studies have shown it to be related to a group's productivity.[14]

**group cohesiveness**
The degree to which group members are attracted
to each other and share the group's goals.

Research has generally shown that highly cohesive groups are more effective than less cohesive ones.[15] However, this relationship between cohesiveness and effectiveness is more complex. A key moderating variable is the degree to which the group's attitude aligns with its goals or with the goals of the organization.[16] The more cohesive a group is, the more its members will follow its goals. If the goals are desirable (e.g., high output, quality work, cooperation with individuals outside the group), a cohesive group is more productive than a less cohesive group. But if cohesiveness is high and attitudes are unfavourable, productivity decreases. If cohesiveness is low and goals are supported, productivity increases, but not as much as when both cohesiveness and support are high. When cohesiveness is low and goals are not supported, cohesiveness has no significant effect on productivity.

Most studies of cohesiveness focus on *socio-emotional cohesiveness*: the "sense of togetherness that develops when individuals derive emotional satisfaction from group participation."[18] There is also *instrumental cohesiveness*: the "sense of togetherness that develops when group members are mutually dependent on one another because they believe they could not achieve the group's goal by acting separately." Teams need to achieve a balance between these two types of cohesiveness to function well. *Tips for Managers— Increasing Group Cohesiveness* indicates how to increase both socio-emotional and instrumental cohesiveness.

## TIPS FOR MANAGERS

### Increasing Group Cohesiveness

Increasing socio-emotional cohesiveness

* Keep the group relatively **small**.
* Strive for a **favourable public image** to increase the status and prestige of belonging.
* Encourage interaction and cooperation.
* Emphasize members' **common characteristics** and interests.
* **Point out environmental threats** (e.g., competitors' achievements) to rally the group.

Increasing instrumental cohesiveness

* Regularly update and clarify the group's goal(s).
* Give every group member a **vital "piece of the action."**
* Channel each group member's special talents toward the **common goal(s)**.
* Recognize and equitably reinforce every member's contributions.
* Frequently remind group members **they need each other** to get the job done.[17]

Analyze

## Managing Group Conflict

Another important group process is how a group manages conflict. As a group performs its assigned tasks, disagreements inevitably arise. When we use the term **conflict**, we are referring to *perceived* differences that result in some form of interference or opposition. Whether the differences are real or not is irrelevant. If people in a group perceive that differences exist, then there is conflict. Our definition encompasses the full range of conflict—from subtle or indirect acts to overt acts such as strikes, riots, or wars.

Over the years, three different views have evolved regarding conflict.[19] One view argues that conflict must be avoided—that it indicates a problem within the group. We call this **the traditional view of conflict**. A second view, the **human relations view of conflict**, argues that conflict is a natural and inevitable outcome in any group and need not be negative but, rather, has the potential to be a positive force in contributing to a group's performance. The third and most recent perspective proposes that not only can conflict be a positive force in a group, but also that some conflict is *absolutely necessary* for a group to perform effectively. This third approach is called the **interactionist view of conflict**.

The interactionist view does not suggest that all conflicts are good. Some conflicts are seen as supporting the goals of the work group and improving its performance; these are **functional conflicts** of a constructive nature. Other conflicts are destructive and prevent a group from achieving its goals. These are **dysfunctional conflicts**. Exhibit 10-4 on page 285 illustrates the challenge facing managers. They want to create an environment in which there is healthy conflict that will help the group reach a high level of performance.

**EXHIBIT 10-4** Conflict and Group Performance

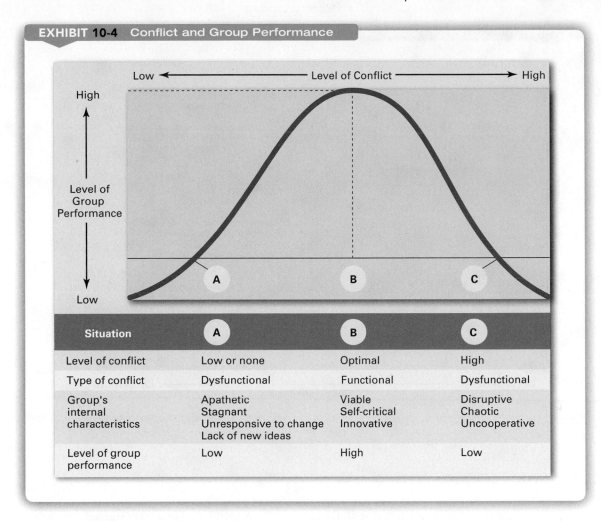

| Situation | A | B | C |
|---|---|---|---|
| Level of conflict | Low or none | Optimal | High |
| Type of conflict | Dysfunctional | Functional | Dysfunctional |
| Group's internal characteristics | Apathetic Stagnant Unresponsive to change Lack of new ideas | Viable Self-critical Innovative | Disruptive Chaotic Uncooperative |
| Level of group performance | Low | High | Low |

What differentiates functional from dysfunctional conflict? The evidence indicates that you need to look at the *type* of conflict.[20] Three types have been identified: task, relationship, and process.

**Task conflict** relates to the content and goals of the work. **Relationship conflict** is based on interpersonal relationships. **Process conflict** relates to how the work gets done. Studies demonstrate that relationship conflicts are almost always dysfunctional. Why? It appears that the friction and interpersonal hostilities inherent in relationship conflicts increase personality clashes and decrease mutual understanding, thereby hindering the completion of organizational tasks. On the other hand, low levels of process conflict and low-to-moderate levels of task conflict are functional. For process conflict to be productive, it must be kept to a minimum. Intense arguments about who should do what become dysfunctional when they create uncertainty about task roles, increase the time taken to complete tasks, and lead to members working at cross-purposes. A low-to-moderate level of task conflict consistently demonstrates a positive effect on group performance because it stimulates discussions of ideas that help

**conflict**
Perceived differences that result in some form of interference or opposition.

**traditional view of conflict**
The view that all conflict is bad and must be avoided.

**human relations view of conflict**
The view that conflict is a natural and inevitable outcome in any group and has the potential to be a positive force in contributing to a group's performance.

**interactionist view of conflict**
The view that some conflict is absolutely necessary for a group to perform effectively.

**functional conflicts**
Conflicts that support the goals of the work group and improve its performance.

**dysfunctional conflicts**
Conflicts that are destructive and prevent a group from achieving its goals.

**task conflict**
Conflict over content and goals of the work.

**relationship conflict**
Conflict based on interpersonal relationships.

**process conflict**
Conflict over how the work gets done.

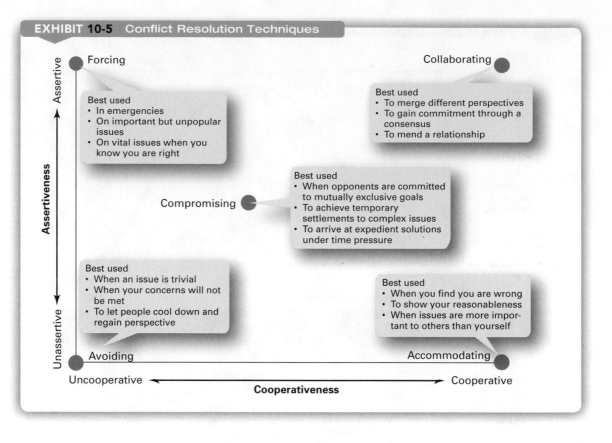

**EXHIBIT 10-5** Conflict Resolution Techniques

**Forcing**

Best used
- In emergencies
- On important but unpopular issues
- On vital issues when you know you are right

**Collaborating**

Best used
- To merge different perspectives
- To gain commitment through a consensus
- To mend a relationship

**Compromising**

Best used
- When opponents are committed to mutually exclusive goals
- To achieve temporary settlements to complex issues
- To arrive at expedient solutions under time pressure

Best used
- When an issue is trivial
- When your concerns will not be met
- To let people cool down and regain perspective

**Avoiding**

Best used
- When you find you are wrong
- To show your reasonableness
- When issues are more important to others than yourself

**Accommodating**

Assertiveness — Assertive / Unassertive

Cooperativeness — Uncooperative / Cooperative

groups be more innovative.[21] Because we have yet to devise a sophisticated measuring instrument for assessing whether a given task, relationship, or process conflict level is optimal, too high, or too low, the manager must make intelligent judgments.

When group conflict becomes dysfunctional, what can managers do? They can select from five conflict-resolution options: avoiding, accommodating, forcing, compromising, and collaborating.[22] (See Exhibit 10-5 for a description of each of these techniques.) Keep in mind that no one option is ideal for every situation. Which approach to use depends on the manager's desire to be more or less cooperative and more or less assertive.

## Preventing Social Loafing

One of the more important findings related to group size is **social loafing**, which is the tendency of individuals to expend less effort when working with others than when working individually.[23] Social loafing is much more likely to happen in larger groups. This finding directly challenges the logic that the group's productivity should at least equal the sum of the productivity of each group member. What causes social loafing? It may be caused by a belief that others in the group are not doing their fair share. If you see others as lazy or inept, you can re-establish equity by reducing your effort. Another explanation is the dispersion of responsibility. Because the results of the group cannot be attributed to any one person, the relationship between an individual's input and the group's output is clouded. In such situations, individuals may be tempted to become "free riders" and coast on the group's efforts. In other words, there will be a reduction in efficiency when individuals think that their contribution cannot be measured.

For managers, the implications of social loafing are significant. When managers use collective work situations to enhance morale and teamwork, they must also have a way to identify individual efforts. If this is not done, they must weigh the potential losses in productivity from using groups against any possible gains in employee satisfaction.[24]

# CURRENT CHALLENGES IN MANAGING TEAMS

Managers also face some current challenges in managing global teams. They also have to determine when it is best to use a team.

**10.4**

**Explain**
What are some of the current challenges in managing teams?

## Managing Global Teams

Two characteristics of today's organizations are obvious: (1) they are global; and (2) work is increasingly done by groups or teams. This reality means that any manager is likely, at some point in time, to have to manage a global team. What do we know about managing global teams? We know there are both drawbacks and benefits in using global teams (see Exhibit 10-6). We will look at some of the issues associated with managing global teams.

**GROUP MEMBER RESOURCES IN GLOBAL TEAMS** In global organizations, understanding the relationship between group performance and group member resources is more challenging because of the unique cultural characteristics represented by members of a global team. In addition to recognizing team members' abilities, skills, knowledge, and personality, managers need to be familiar with and clearly understand the cultural characteristics of the groups and the group members they manage.[25] For example, is the global team from a culture in which uncertainty avoidance is high? If so, members will not be comfortable dealing with unpredictable and ambiguous tasks. Also, as managers work with global teams, they need to be aware of the potential for stereotyping, which has been shown to be a problem with global teams.[26]

**GROUP STRUCTURE** Some of the structural areas where we see differences in managing global teams include conformity, status, social loafing, and cohesiveness.

**Conformity** Research suggests that conformity to social norms tends to be higher in collectivist cultures than in individualistic cultures.[27] Despite this, however, groupthink (discussed in Chapter 4) tends to be less of a problem in global teams because members are less likely to feel pressured to conform to the ideas, conclusions, and decisions of the group.[28]

---

**EXHIBIT 10-6** Drawbacks and Benefits of Global Teams

**Drawbacks**

- Dislike or mistrust team members
- Increased personal conflict
- Stereotyping
- Communication problems

**Benefits**

- Greater diversity of ideas
- Less groupthink
- Increased attention on understanding others' ideas, perspectives, etc.

*Source:* N. Adler, *International Dimensions in Organizational Behaviour,* 4th Ed (Cincinnati, OH; South-Western College Publishing, 2002) pp. 141–147.

---

**social loafing**
The tendency of individuals to expend less effort when working collectively than when working individually.

**Status**   The importance of status varies among cultures. The French, for example, are extremely status conscious. Also, countries differ on the criteria that confer status. Status for Latin Americans and Asians tends to come from family position and formal roles held in organizations. In contrast, although status is important in countries such as Canada and Australia, it tends to be less "in your face," and is usually based on accomplishments rather than on titles and family history. Managers should be sure to understand who and what holds status when interacting with people from a culture different from their own. A Canadian manager who does not understand that office size is not a measure of a Japanese executive's position or who fails to grasp the importance the British place on family genealogy and social class is likely to unintentionally offend others and lessen his or her interpersonal effectiveness.

**Social loafing**   Social loafing has a Western bias and is most prevalent in individualistic cultures, such as Canada and the United States, which are dominated by self-interest. It is not consistent with collectivistic societies, in which individuals are motivated by in-group goals. In studies comparing employees from the United States with employees from the People's Republic of China and Israel (both collectivistic societies), the Chinese and Israelis did not tend to engage in social loafing. In fact, they actually performed better in a group than when working alone.[29]

**Cohesiveness**   Cohesiveness is another group structural element where managers may face special challenges. In a cohesive group, members are unified and "act as one." There is a great deal of camaraderie and group identity is high. In global teams, however, cohesiveness is often more difficult to achieve because of higher levels of mistrust, miscommunication, and stress.[30]

**GROUP PROCESSES**   The processes global teams use to do their work can be particularly challenging for managers. Communication problems often arise because not all team members may be fluent in the team's working language. This language barrier can lead to inaccuracies, misunderstandings, and inefficiencies.[31] However, research has also shown that a multicultural global team is better able to make use of the diversity of ideas represented if a wide range of information is used.[32]

Managing conflict in global teams, especially when those teams are virtual teams, is not easy. Conflict in multicultural teams can interfere with how information is used by the team. However, research shows that in collectivistic cultures, a collaborative conflict management style can be most effective.[33]

**THE MANAGER'S ROLE**   Despite the challenges associated with managing global teams, there are things managers can do to provide the group with an environment in which efficiency and effectiveness are enhanced.[34] First, because communication skills are vital, managers should focus on developing those skills. As we have said earlier, managers also need to consider cultural differences when deciding what type of global team to use. For example, evidence suggests that self-managed teams have not fared well in Mexico largely due to that culture's low tolerance for ambiguity and uncertainty, and employees' strong respect for hierarchical authority.[35] Finally, managers must be sensitive to the unique differences of each member of the global team. But, it is also important that team members be sensitive to each other.

*Do you ever find you are tired of working in a team?*

## Beware! Teams Are Not Always the Answer

Despite considerable success in the use of teams, they are not necessarily appropriate in all situations. Teamwork takes more time and often more resources than individual work; it has increased communication demands, and an increased number of conflicts to be managed and meetings to be run. In the rush to enjoy the benefits of teams, some managers have introduced them into situations in which the work is better done by individuals. A 2003 study by Statistics Canada found that the introduction of teamwork lowered job turnover in the service industries, for both high- and low-skilled employees. However, manufacturing companies experienced higher job turnover if they introduced teamwork and formal teamwork training, compared with not doing so (15.8 percent vs. 10.7 percent).[36]

How do you know if the work of your group would be better done in teams? Three questions can help determine whether a team fits the situation:[37]

- *Can the work be done better by more than one person?* Simple tasks that do not require diverse input are probably better left to individuals.
- *Does the work create a common purpose or set of goals for the people in the group that is more than the sum of individual goals?* For example, many new-car dealer service departments have introduced teams that link customer service personnel, mechanics, parts specialists, and sales representatives. Such teams can better manage collective responsibility for ensuring that customer needs are properly met.
- *Are the members of the group interdependent?* Teams make sense where there is interdependence between tasks; where the success of the whole depends on the success of each one; and where the success of each one depends on the success of the others. Soccer, for example, is an obvious *team* sport because of the interdependence of the players. Swim teams, by contrast, are not really teams, but groups of individuals whose total performance is merely the sum of the individual performances.

Researchers have outlined the conditions under which organizations would find teams more useful: "when work processes cut across functional lines; when speed is important (and complex relationships are involved); when the organization mirrors a complex, differentiated, and rapidly changing market environment; when innovation and learning have priority; when the tasks that have to be done require online integration of highly interdependent performers."[38]

Practise

## Summary of Learning Objectives

 **10.1** **What are the stages of team development?** The five stages are forming, storming, norming, performing, and adjourning. These stages describe how teams evolve over time, although teams do not necessarily go through these stages in a completely linear fashion. Some researchers argue that the effectiveness of work teams increases at advanced stages, but the reality is not that simple. The assumption may be generally true, but what makes a team effective is a complex issue. Instead, think of this model as a general framework of how teams develop.

GLBC uses formal recognition programs to recognize team success, helping teams bond by receiving cash awards for ideas to help resolve a problem or improve a work process. Employees collaborate in teams on these ideas and have saved the company more than $500 000.

**10.2** **How do individuals become team players?** Many individuals resist being team players. To improve the odds that a team will function well, managers can select the right people to be on a team, train individuals in how to work on teams, and make sure that rewards encourage individuals to be cooperative team players.

GLBC's daily production meetings and weekly departmental meetings ensure a two-way communication with employees. Employees take the meetings very seriously and are able to speak freely with a high level of trust. This practice has led to employees working together to provide both positive and constructive feedback.

**10.3** **How can groups become effective teams?** The characteristics associated with effective teams include clear goals, relevant skills, mutual trust, unified commitment, good communication, negotiating skills, appropriate leadership, and internal and external support. To be effective, teams also need to build group cohesiveness, manage group conflict, and prevent social loafing.

GLBC also uses company awards to motivate employees to pull together. They initiated a BOX Event (Big Outrageous eXtravaganza), wherein the company sets realistic and stretch goals. If the team is able to meet its overall profit target or "stretch goal" for the year, Meggy takes all employees on an all-expenses paid trip to an exciting destination such as Las Vegas or Mexico.

**10.4** **What are some of the current challenges in managing teams?** Managers face a variety of challenges in managing global teams. The cultural differences of the team members may lead to more conflict, at least initially. As well, there may be an increase in communication difficulties. Another challenge that managers face is to consider whether a team is really necessary to get the work done.

### SNAPSHOT SUMMARY

 **10.1** **Understanding Groups and Teams**
What Is a Team?
Informal Groups
Stages of Team Development

 **10.2** **Turning Individuals into Team Players**
The Challenges of Creating Team Players
What Roles Do Team Members Play?
Shaping Team Behaviour

 **10.3** **Turning Groups into Effective Teams**
Characteristics of Effective Teams
Building Group Cohesiveness
Managing Group Conflict
Preventing Social Loafing

**10.4** **Current Challenges in Managing Teams**
Managing Global Teams
Beware! Teams Are Not Always the Answer

# MyManagementLab® Learning Resources

## Resources

Explore and enhance your understanding of key chapter topics through the following online resources:

- Student PowerPoints
- Audio Summary of Chapter
- ROLLS
- CBC Videos for Part 4
- MySearchLab

Visit the **Study Plan** area to test your progress with **Pre-Tests** and **Post-Tests**.

Build on your knowledge and practise real-world applications using the following online activities:

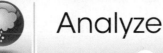

## Interpret

- Opening Case Activity: Group and Team Formation
- Review and Apply: Solutions to Interpret section questions and activities
- Glossary Flashcards

## Analyze

- Opening Case Activity: Examining Team Functionality
- Review and Apply: Solutions to Analyze section questions and activities
- Self-Assessment Library

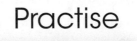

## Practise

- Opening Case Activity: Redesigning Teams
- Review and Apply: Solutions to Practice section questions and activities
- BizSkills Simulation: Team Management
- Decision Making Simulations:
  –Teams
  –Virtual Teams

# Interpret What You Have Read

1. Contrast (1) self-managed and cross-functional teams; and (2) virtual and face-to-face teams.

2. What are some of the ways that virtual teams can enhance productivity?

3. What problems might surface in teams during each of the five stages of team development?

4. Describe three ways managers can try to encourage individuals to become team players.

5. Why do you believe mutual trust is important in developing high-performing work teams?

6. Why might a manager want to stimulate conflict in a group or team? How could conflict be stimulated?

# Analyze What You Have Read

1. How do you explain the rapidly increasing popularity of work teams in countries such as Canada and the United States, whose national cultures place a high value on individualism?

2. Think of a team to which you belong (or have belonged). Trace its development through the five stages of team development shown in Exhibit 10-2 on page 278. How closely did its development parallel the team development model? How might the team development model have been used to improve the team's effectiveness?

3. All work teams are work groups, but not all work groups are work teams. Do you agree or disagree with this statement? Discuss.

4. Would you prefer to work alone or as part of a team? Why? Support your response with data from your self-assessments.

5. Describe a situation in which individuals, acting independently, outperform teams in an organization.

# Assess Your Skills

## HOW GOOD AM I AT BUILDING AND LEADING A TEAM?

Use the following rating scale to respond to the 18 statements on building and leading an effective team:[39]

> 1 = Strongly Disagree   2 = Disagree   3 = Slightly Disagree   4 = Slightly Agree
> 5 = Agree   6 = Strongly Agree

1. I am knowledgeable about the different stages of development that teams can go through in their life cycles.　　1 2 3 4 5 6

2. When a team forms, I make certain that all team members are introduced to one another at the outset.　　1 2 3 4 5 6

3. When the team first comes together, I provide directions, answer team members' questions, and clarify goals, expectations, and procedures.　　1 2 3 4 5 6

4. I help team members establish a foundation of trust among one another and between themselves and me.　　1 2 3 4 5 6

5. I ensure that standards of excellence, not mediocrity or mere acceptability, characterize the team's work.　　1 2 3 4 5 6

6. I provide a great deal of feedback to team members regarding their performance.　　1 2 3 4 5 6

7. I encourage team members to balance individual autonomy with interdependence among other team members.　　1 2 3 4 5 6

8. I help team members become at least as committed to the success of the team as to their own personal success.　　1 2 3 4 5 6

9. I help members learn to play roles that assist the team in accomplishing its tasks as well as building strong interpersonal relationships.    1 2 3 4 5 6

10. I articulate a clear, exciting, passionate vision of what the team can achieve.    1 2 3 4 5 6

11. I help team members become committed to the team vision.    1 2 3 4 5 6

12. I encourage a win/win philosophy in the team; that is, when one member wins, every member wins.    1 2 3 4 5 6

13. I help the team avoid groupthink or making the group's survival more important than accomplishing its goal.    1 2 3 4 5 6

14. I use formal process management procedures to help the group become faster, more efficient, and more productive, and to prevent errors.    1 2 3 4 5 6

15. I encourage team members to represent the team's vision, goals, and accomplishments to outsiders.    1 2 3 4 5 6

16. I diagnose and capitalize on the team's core competence.    1 2 3 4 5 6

17. I encourage the team to achieve dramatic breakthrough innovations as well as small continuous improvements.    1 2 3 4 5 6

18. I help the team work toward preventing mistakes, not just correcting them after the fact.    1 2 3 4 5 6

**SCORING KEY**   To calculate your total score, add up your scores on the 18 individual items.

## ANALYSIS AND INTERPRETATION

The authors of this instrument propose that it assesses team development behaviours in 5 areas: diagnosing team development (statements 1, 16); managing the forming stage (2–4); managing the norming stage (6–9, 13); managing the storming stage (10–12, 14, 15); and managing the performing stage (5, 17, 18). Your score will range between 18 and 108, with higher scores indicating greater ability at building and leading an effective team.

Based on a norm group of 500 business students, the following can help estimate where you are in relation to others:

Total score of 95 or more = You are in the top quartile
72–94 = You are in the second quartile

60–71 = You are in the third quartile
Less than 60 = You are in the bottom quartile

### More Self-Assessments

To learn more about your skills, abilities, and interests, take the following self-assessments on the MyManagementLab®:

- II.A.2.–How Good Are My Listening Skills?
- II.B.4.–Do Others See Me as Trustworthy?

# Practise What You Have Learned

## DILEMMA

One of your instructors has just informed your class that you will be working on a new major assignment worth 30 percent of your course mark. The assignment is to be done in teams of seven. Realistically you will need to function as a virtual team, because each of you has a different work and class schedule, so that there is almost no time when more than three people could meet face to face. As you know, virtual teams have benefits, but they can also face problems. How will you build group cohesiveness in this team? What norms might help the team function, and how should the norms be decided? What will you do to prevent social loafing?

## BECOMING A MANAGER

How to manage a virtual team:

- What do we need to operate as an effective virtual team?
- What should our team start doing?
- What should our team stop doing?
- How should our team monitor our progress?
- What are our virtual team meeting protocols?
- What are our technology protocols?
- What are our roles, expectations, goals, and behaviour standards?
- How should our group manage conflict?

# DEVELOPING YOUR INTERPERSONAL SKILLS: CREATING EFFECTIVE TEAMS

## ABOUT THE SKILL

A team is different from a group because its members are committed to a common purpose, have a set of specific performance goals, and hold themselves mutually accountable for the team's results. Teams can produce outputs that are greater than the sum of the individual contributions of its members. The primary force that makes a work group an effective team—that is, a real high-performing team—is its emphasis on performance.

## STEPS IN DEVELOPING THE SKILL

Managers and team leaders have a significant impact on a team's effectiveness. You can be more successful at creating an effective team if you use the following nine suggestions:[40]

1. **ESTABLISH A COMMON PURPOSE.** An effective team needs a common purpose to which all members aspire. This purpose is a vision and is broader than any specific goals. The common purpose provides direction, momentum, and commitment for team members.

2. **ASSESS TEAM STRENGTHS AND WEAKNESSES.** Team members will have different strengths and weaknesses. Knowing these strengths and weaknesses can help the team leader build on the strengths and compensate for the weaknesses.

3. **DEVELOP SPECIFIC INDIVIDUAL GOALS.** Specific individual goals help lead team members to achieve higher performance. In addition, specific goals facilitate clear communication and help maintain the focus on getting results.

4. **GET AGREEMENT ON A COMMON APPROACH FOR ACHIEVING GOALS.** Goals are the ends a team strives to attain. Defining and agreeing on a common approach ensures the team's unity regarding the means for achieving those ends.

5. **ENCOURAGE ACCEPTANCE OF RESPONSIBILITY FOR BOTH INDIVIDUAL AND TEAM PERFORMANCE.** Successful teams make members individually and jointly accountable for the team's purpose, goals, and approach. Members understand what they are individually responsible for and what they are jointly responsible for.

6. **BUILD MUTUAL TRUST AMONG MEMBERS.** When there is trust, team members believe in the integrity, character, and ability of each other. When trust is lacking, members are unable to depend on each other. Teams that lack trust tend to be short-lived.

7. **MAINTAIN AN APPROPRIATE MIX OF TEAM MEMBER SKILLS AND PERSONALITIES.** Team members come to the team with different skills and personalities. To perform effectively, teams need three types of skills. First, teams need people with technical expertise. Next, they need people with problem-solving and decision-making skills to identify problems, generate alternatives, evaluate those alternatives, and make competent choices. Finally, teams need people with good interpersonal skills.

8. **PROVIDE NEEDED TRAINING AND RESOURCES.** Team leaders need to make sure that their teams have both the training and the resources they need to accomplish their goals.

9. **CREATE OPPORTUNITIES FOR SMALL ACHIEVEMENTS.** Building an effective team takes time. Team members have to learn to think and work as a team. New teams cannot be expected to hit home runs every time they come to bat, especially at the beginning. Instead, team members should be encouraged to try for small achievements first.

## PRACTISING THE SKILL

You are the leader of a five-member project team that has been assigned the task of moving your engineering firm into the new booming area of high-speed rail construction. You and your team members have been researching the field, identifying specific business opportunities, negotiating alliances with equipment vendors, and evaluating high-speed rail experts and consultants from around the world. Throughout the process, Tonya, a highly qualified and respected engineer, has challenged everything you say during team meetings and in the workplace. For example, at a meeting two weeks ago, you presented the team with a list of 10 possible high-speed rail projects that had been identified by the team, and started evaluating your organization's ability to compete for them. Tonya contradicted virtually all your comments, questioned your statistics, and was quite pessimistic about the possibility of contracts. After this latest display of displeasure, two other group members, Liam and Ahmed, came to you and complained that Tonya's actions were damaging the team's effectiveness. You originally put Tonya on the team for her unique expertise and insight. What should you say to Tonya, and how can you help get the team on the right track to reach its full potential?

# MANAGING WORKFORCE DIVERSITY: THE CHALLENGE OF MANAGING DIVERSE TEAMS

Understanding and managing teams composed of people who are similar can be difficult. Add in diverse members and managing teams can be even more of a challenge. However, the benefits to be gained from the diverse perspectives, skills, and abilities often more than offset the extra effort.[41] How can you meet the challenge of coordinating a diverse work team? It is important to stress four critical interpersonal behaviours: understanding, empathy, tolerance, and communication.

You know that people are not the same, yet they need to be treated fairly and equitably. Differences (cultural, physical, or other) can cause people to behave in different ways.

Team leaders need to understand and accept these differences. Each and every team member should be encouraged to do the same.

Empathy is closely related to understanding. As a team leader, you should try to understand others' perspectives.

Tolerance is another important interpersonal behaviour in managing diverse teams. Even though you understand that people are different and you empathize with them, accepting different perspectives or behaviours is not easy. But it is important to be tolerant in dealing with diverse ages, gender, and cultural backgrounds—to allow team members the freedom to be themselves. Part of being tolerant is being open-minded about different values, attitudes, and behaviours.

Finally, open communication is vital in managing a diverse team. Diversity problems may intensify if people are afraid or unwilling to openly discuss issues that concern them. Communication within a diverse team needs to be two-way. If a person wants to know whether a certain behaviour is offensive to someone else, it is best to ask. Likewise, a person who is offended by someone else's behaviour should explain his or her concerns and ask that person to stop. As long as these communication exchanges are handled in a nonthreatening, low-key, and friendly manner, they generally will have positive outcomes. Finally, it helps to have an atmosphere within the team that supports and celebrates diversity.

Put yourself in the place of an Asian woman who has joined a team of Caucasian and Hispanic men. How can you be made to feel more welcome and comfortable with the team? As the Asian woman, what could you do to help the team get along well together and also help your transition to the team?

# Team Exercises

## 3BL: THE TRIPLE BOTTOM LINE

Richard Branson, founder of the Virgin Group of companies, decided that an entrepreneurial approach to sustainability would be most effective if based on a team model. Branson established a charitable foundation and sought involvement from everyone working with the Virgin Group. Rather than simply write cheques to charities, Virgin employees wanted to be a true partner to charitable organizations and leverage internal operations for sustainability.

Virgin Unite was launched as an integral part of the Virgin Group, rather than a charitable arm. Employees wanted it to be a way of connecting people and entrepreneurial ideas to make sustainability happen. Virgin Unite would provide the means for the groups to connect with each other. Virgin employees join with leaders and workers at existing businesses who are concerned with making profit while helping people and the planet.

## THINKING STRATEGICALLY ABOUT 3BL

The focus on entrepreneurial sustainability is a new way of doing business, where people are willing to say "screw business as usual" and look beyond financial profit as the only driving force for companies like Virgin. How would you apply entrepreneurial sustainability to a large Canadian company like Tim Hortons? What nonprofit associations could it partner with to become more sustainable?

*Source:* Richard Branson, "How Virgin Unite Connects Philanthropy with Entrepreneurialism," *Canadian Business*, February 20, 2012.

## BE THE CONSULTANT: CONDUCTING EFFECTIVE MEETINGS

A team meeting can be of vital importance to the success of your academic projects. Conducting effective meetings takes diligence and practice. Here are some tips.

| | |
|---|---|
| 1. Prepare for the meeting. | • Plan the meeting carefully: who, what, when, where, why and how many?<br>• Distribute the agenda and any relevant materials before the meeting.<br>• Begin the meeting with the agenda and get all participants to agree on the items/expectations.<br>• Review action items from previous meetings. |
| 2. Ensure the Chair is prepared. | • Vary the chairs of meetings to involve members more effectively.<br>• Discussions and behaviours become predictable with one chair—mix it up for creativity and participation. |
| 3. Maintain the focus. | • Encourage problem solving and explore various alternatives.<br>• Encourage conflict of ideas, not personalities.<br>• Do not allow any member to manipulate the agenda. |
| 4. Establish ground rules. | • Encourage participation by all - draw out the quiet ones and quiet the talkative ones.<br>• Stay on track and maintain momentum.<br>• Allow people to fill different roles (harmonizers, gatekeepers and compromisers). |

*(continued)*

*(continued)*

| | |
|---|---|
| 5. Maximize the chair's role. | • Start on time, set clear time limits.<br>• Use a note taker and time keeper as required.<br>• The leader stimulates and controls the discussion, keeps the meeting on task, and summarizes all the points discussed.<br>• Get feedback *during* the meeting to optimize meeting processes and norms. |
| 6. Ensure effective decision making. | • Groups typically vote or reach consensus; consensus is more difficult and time-consuming but provides the best decision-making.<br>• Summarize agreements.<br>• Even if individuals don't 100% agree with the decision, they are more likely to support it (or less likely to oppose it) when their opinions have been heard.<br>• Identify additional data needed to make decisions. |
| 7. Clarify deliverables and next steps. | • Evaluate the meeting.<br>• End the meeting by clarifying what happens next.<br>• What actions need to follow, who is responsible, and by when?<br>• Schedule the next meeting before you leave.<br>• Follow up on action items after the meeting. |

# Business Cases

## ONTARIO REALTY CORPORATION

The Ontario Realty Corporation (ORC) manages real estate for the Ontario public service. Greg Dadd was CEO when the decision was made to build up his team's abilities in delivering top-notch customer service.

Dadd held a three-day retreat for his managers to "take a look at what they wanted to accomplish at ORC, involve people in sharing information, and develop solutions that we all owned." The retreat was used to facilitate discussions on continuous improvement and involved people across every region and all functional areas. Break-out groups were used to brainstorm, look at issues from fresh perspectives, and build networks with other colleagues.

ORC made the retreat even more tactical by inviting a key client to discuss what they were looking for in customer service. The client's perspective was used as a litmus test when solutions were proposed during the retreat. Dadd was able to build a stronger team as a result of the retreat. He put together all the customer service solutions in a work plan during the retreat so that momentum was not lost and the ORC team was committed to following through.

ORC recently merged with Infrastructure Ontario as a cost savings measure. Is it time for another retreat?

*Source: Ontario Realty Corporation (ORC) Annual Report 2005–2006* (Toronto, ON: ORC, 2006).

**CBC**

# Leading With Integrity: Quova's Marie Alexander

Quova Inc. is an Internet geo-location company founded in 1999 and headquartered in Mountain View, California. Quova's expertise lies in enabling online businesses to instantly identify where a visitor to their website is geographically located. Online companies, including broadcasters, e-retailers, and banks, integrate Quova's geo-location data into their web applications to target advertising, detect fraud, and comply with local laws. Quova provides detailed demographic and other data with accuracy of 99.9 percent at the country level and up to 98.2 percent accuracy at the state level.

Quova was a privately held company with 70 employees before being acquired as a wholly owned subsidiary of Neustar, Inc. in October, 2010. Quova has worked with some impressive companies such as BBC Worldwide and Continental Airlines. Such a fast-paced, leading-edge organization, competing in a dynamic and creative environment, requires strong leadership.

Meet Marie Alexander, president and chief executive officer of Quova Inc. Marie has a diverse academic background, including multiple degrees in business administration and music therapy, as well as a plethora of experience, ranging from amusement park management to working in mental institutions. At first glance, Ms. Alexander may appear to be an unusual choice for effective leadership at Quova. However, in Marie's opinion, her various experiences and unique educational background have shaped her leadership style and make her the optimal choice to successfully lead Quova in a dynamic and ever-changing competitive environment.

A recognized expert in Internet geo-location, Marie Alexander believes that leadership is behavioural. She prac-tises a form of "hands-under" leadership—a nurturing style that helps followers understand and reach their potential by "lifting and catching" them. Ms. Alexander, who believes in leading with compassion, interprets conflict among subordinates with a unique perspective. According to Marie, conflict is a positive aspect of organizational behaviour and demonstrates organizational growth. Without conflict, passive aggressiveness could prevail and silently, but certainly, destroy an organization.

## QUESTIONS

### Interpret

1. What is the difference between leadership and management?

2. What are the eight traits associated with effective leadership?

### Analyze

3. Marie Alexander believes that leadership is behavioural. How are behavioural theories of leadership different from trait theories? Of the three leadership styles from the University of Iowa studies, would you consider Marie Alexander to be an autocratic, democratic, or laissez-faire leader?

4. How is Marie Alexander's form of "hands-under" leadership consistent with path-goal theory?

### Practise

5. Suppose that a major security leak in Quova's systems were to be discovered such that site visitors could be located and subsequently targeted by criminals. How might Marie Alexander publicly lead this company to preserve the support and confidence of investors, customers, and other key stakeholders?

*Source:* "Leading with Integrity" (video), Pearson Prentice Hall Management Video Library.

## CBC

# Work–Life Balance: Canadian Voices and the British Experiment

A survey on work–life balance reveals that Canadians are feeling stressed at work. Millions of workers are struggling, and failing, to balance the demands they face at home with the growing demands of their work. Companies are spending millions of dollars in benefits, while the costs of absenteeism are soaring near $3 billion a year.

Over 10 000 Canadian workers were surveyed, and only 5 percent were able to say anything positive about their employer. Many employees lament that their organizations do not encourage participation in flexibility programs; they believe that taking advantage of these programs would be career limiting.

Linda Duxbury, a management expert, says there must be a change in attitude toward productivity; efficiency gains are not proportional to the number of hours clocked. Managers who are unable to transition to a supportive environment will be displaced as the workplace is demanding change.

Human Resources Minister Jane Stewart agrees that businesses have to do what is right for the long-term health of the workforce. She says many Canadians are taking advantage of extended maternity leave benefits, and there is an 80 percent increase in the number of dads staying home under the new Parental Benefit program. She also trusts that the Compassionate Leave program, designed to support working Canadians who have to care for sick or elderly dependents, will offer some of the flexibility demanded by workers in the face of an aging population.

## OPPORTUNITY 2000

The British culture is facing a crisis: A culture notorious for long working hours is burned out, and the outlook in the workforce is pessimistic. The British government is trying to assist workers in their efforts to rebalance through *The Challenge Fund*, $26 million to help businesses make their employees happier. British Telecom has been advocating work–life balance for 20 years. The company has about 6300 home-workers whose productivity levels are 20 percent higher than that of their colleagues working at the office. These home-workers take significantly fewer sick days and do not require expensive office space, all of which have saved the company over $125 million a year. The lesson is that longer hours do not necessarily pay off.

Lynne Copp, organizational development consultant and change coach, recommends giving employees three paid days of emergency leave, time which can be taken a few hours at a time, whenever needed. This initiative reduced the tendency for employees to take a full sick day. Trusting the staff has paid off. On average, employees took off only a single day of their emergency time, saving companies thousands of dollars. Copp says that new graduates are driving the cultural change. A recent UK study revealed that job flexibility is the top priority for today's job applicants.

## QUESTIONS

### Interpret

1. What is meant by work–life balance? What efforts have contemporary organizations made to help struggling employees achieve this balance? Why?

2. Understanding and predicting employee motivation continues to be one of the most popular areas in management research. What are the five levels of needs in Maslow's hierarchy of needs? What are some current workplace issues that influence employee motivation?

### Analyze

3. What lessons can British Telecom (BT) teach Canadian businesses about work–life balance and productivity?

4. What initiatives has the Canadian government taken to support the work–life balance concerns of today's employees? How else might the government foster a stronger, caring culture in today's corporate environment?

### Practise

5. If you are a manager concerned with a motivation problem at your workplace, what specific recommendations can you draw from theories and issues discussed in the text and the CBC video case?

*Source:* "Work–Life Special: Canadian Voices/The British Experiment," *Venture,* Show No. 896, Canadian Broadcasting Corporation, January 19, 2003.

# CHAPTER 11

# Foundations of Control

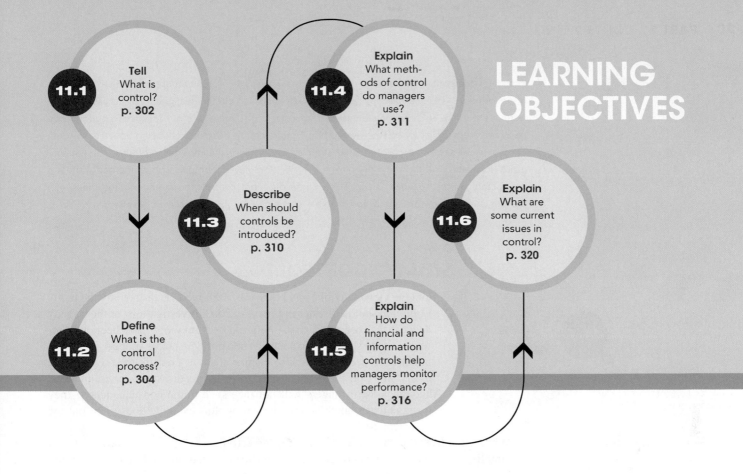

**11.1**
Tell
What is
control?
p. 302

**11.4**
Explain
What methods of control
do managers
use?
p. 311

**11.3**
Describe
When should
controls be
introduced?
p. 310

**11.6**
Explain
What are
some current
issues in
control?
p. 320

**11.2**
Define
What is the
control
process?
p. 304

**11.5**
Explain
How do
financial and
information
controls help
managers monitor
performance?
p. 316

# LEARNING OBJECTIVES

Curling is an iconic national pastime played by more than one million Canadians. The Canadian men's team is ranked #1 in the world, and the women's team is #2. During the 2010 Olympic games in Vancouver, the men's and women's curling finals were two of the top five most watched events on CTV.[1]

In the mid 2000s, the Canadian Curling Association (CCA) was facing a seven figure deficit and hired Greg Stremlaw as their new CEO in 2007. The CCA adopted a new policy governance model and began a top-down restructuring program that focused on financial controls and the association's bottom line. Stremlaw created a new business plan with clear operational objectives. The new strategies have led to a large increase in sponsorship from companies such as Tim Hortons, Ford, and Great Western Brewery.[2]

The CCA established two major financial controls that have put the association back on firm footing and helped turn the major deficit into a $3 425 230 surplus in 2011–2012. Stremlaw established a long-term financial reserve fund to protect the CCA against future financial problems and also began a curling assistance program to support the grassroots network of curling centres and member associations.

## Think About It

What is organizational control? Look at the decisions that Greg Stremlaw made. How did he use control to turn around the financial fortunes of the Canadian Curling Association?

In today's competitive global marketplace, managers want their organizations to achieve high levels of performance, and one way they can do that is by searching out the best practices successful organizations are using. By comparing themselves against the best, managers look for specific performance gaps and areas for improvement—areas where better controls over the work being done are needed.

As we will see in this chapter, Greg Stremlaw understands the importance of management controls. No matter how thorough the planning, a decision may still be poorly implemented without a satisfactory control system in place. This chapter describes controls for monitoring and measuring performance. It also looks at how to create a well-designed organizational control system.

## WHAT IS CONTROL?

**11.1** Tell What is control?

Both the viewing public and NASA officials were devastated by the tragic *Columbia* shuttle disaster in February 2003. Investigations of the tragedy suggest that organizational safety controls may not have been as thorough as they should have been.[3] When problems were spotted, managers might have been too quick to dismiss them as non-life-threatening, and in this situation that choice may have led to disastrous consequences. Although most managers will not face such tragic consequences if they ignore signs that something may be wrong, this example does point out the importance of control.

What is **control**? It is the process of monitoring activities to ensure that they are being accomplished as planned, and correcting any significant deviations. All managers should be involved in the control function, even if their units are performing as planned. Managers cannot really know whether their units are performing properly until they have evaluated what activities have been done and compared the actual performance with the desired standard.[4] An effective control system ensures that activities are completed in ways that lead to the attainment of the organization's goals. The criterion that determines the effectiveness of a control system is how well it facilitates goal achievement. The more a control system helps managers achieve their organization's goals, the better the system.[5]

### Performance Standards

To achieve control, performance standards must exist. These standards are the specific goals created during the planning process. **Performance** is the end result of an activity. Whether that activity is hours of intense practice before a concert or race, or carrying out job responsibilities as efficiently and effectively as possible, performance is what results from that activity.

Managers are concerned with **organizational performance**—the accumulated end results of all the organization's work activities. It is a complex but important concept. Managers need to understand the factors that contribute to a high level of organizational performance. After all, they do not want (or intend) to manage their way to mediocre performance. They *want* their organizations, work units, or work groups to achieve high levels of performance, no matter what mission, strategies, or goals are being pursued.

### Measures of Organizational Performance

All managers must know what organizational performance measures will give them the information they need. The most frequently used organizational performance measures include organizational productivity, organizational effectiveness, and industry and company rankings.

**ORGANIZATIONAL PRODUCTIVITY** **Productivity** is the overall output of goods or services produced divided by the inputs needed to generate that output. Organizations strive to be productive. They want the most goods and services produced using the least amount of inputs. Output is measured by the sales revenue an organization receives when those goods and services are sold (selling price × number sold). Input is measured by the costs of acquiring and transforming the organizational resources into the outputs.

**ORGANIZATIONAL EFFECTIVENESS**   In Chapter 1, we defined managerial effectiveness as goal attainment. Can the same interpretation apply to organizational effectiveness? Yes, it can. **Organizational effectiveness** is a measure of how appropriate organizational goals are and how well an organization is achieving those goals. It is a common performance measure used by managers in designing strategies, work processes, and work activities, and in coordinating the work of employees.

**INDUSTRY AND COMPANY RANKINGS**   There is no shortage of different types of industry and company rankings. The rankings for each list are determined by specific performance measures. For example, the companies listed in *Report on Business Magazine*'s Top 1000 are measured by assets. They are ranked according to after-tax profits in the most recent fiscal year, excluding extraordinary gains or losses.[6] The companies listed in the 50 Best Employers in Canada are ranked based on answers given by managers to a leadership team survey, an employee opinion survey, and a human resource survey designed by Hewitt Associates, a compensation and benefits consultant.[7] The companies listed in the *PROFIT* 200: Canada's Fastest Growing Companies are ranked based on their percentage sales growth over the past five years. Private and publicly traded companies that are over 50 percent Canadian-owned and are headquartered in Canada nominate themselves, and then *PROFIT* editors collect further information about eligible companies.[8]

## Why Is Control Important?

Planning can be done, an organizational structure can be created to efficiently facilitate the achievement of goals, and employees can be motivated through effective leadership. Still, there is no assurance that activities are going as planned and that the goals managers are seeking are, in fact, being attained. Control is important, therefore, because it is the final link in the four management functions. Control is the only way managers know whether organizational goals are being met and, if not, the reasons why. The value of the control function lies in its relation to planning, empowering employees, and protecting the organization and workplace.

*How can control help a team perform better on a course project?*

In Chapter 3, we described goals as the foundation of planning. Goals give specific direction to managers. However, just stating goals or having employees accept your goals is no guarantee that the necessary actions to accomplish those goals have been taken. As the old saying goes, "The best-laid plans often go awry." The effective manager needs to follow up to ensure that what others are supposed to do is, in fact, being done and that their goals are, in fact, being achieved. In reality, managing is an ongoing process, and controlling activities provide the critical link back to planning (see Exhibit 11-1). If managers did not control, they would have no way of knowing whether their goals and plans were on target and what future actions to take.

---

**control**
The process of monitoring activities to ensure that they are being accomplished as planned, and correcting any significant deviations.

**performance**
The end result of an activity.

**organizational performance**
The accumulated end results of all the organization's work activities.

**productivity**
The overall output of goods or services produced divided by the inputs needed to generate that output.

**organizational effectiveness**
A measure of how appropriate organizational goals are and how well an organization is achieving those goals.

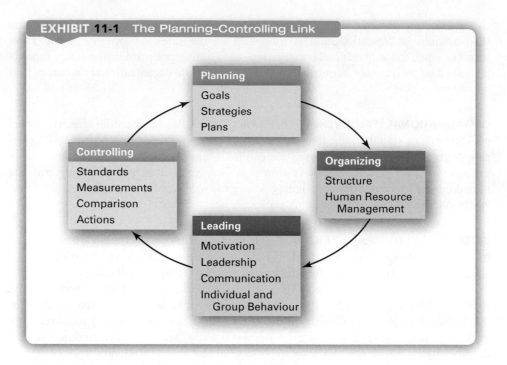

**EXHIBIT 11-1** The Planning-Controlling Link

Another reason control is important is employee empowerment. Many managers are reluctant to empower their employees because they fear employees will do something wrong for which the manager will be held responsible. Thus, many managers are tempted to do things themselves and avoid empowering. This reluctance, however, can be reduced if managers develop an effective control system that provides information and feedback on employee performance.

The final reason that managers control is to protect the organization and the physical workplace.[9] Given today's environment, with heightened security alerts and surprise financial scandals, managers must have plans in place to protect the organization's employees, data, and infrastructure.

# THE CONTROL PROCESS

**11.2**

**Define**
What is the control process?

The **control process** is a three-step process: measuring actual performance, comparing actual performance against a standard, and taking managerial action to correct deviations or inadequate standards (see Exhibit 11-2). The control process for managers is similar to what you might do as a student at the beginning of the term: set goals for yourself for studying and marks, and then evaluate your performance after midterms, determining whether you have studied enough or need to study more in order to meet whatever goals you set for your marks. (To learn more about how proactive you are, see *Assess Your Skills—How Proactive Am I?* on pages 330–331 at the end of the chapter.)

## Measuring Performance

To determine what actual performance is, a manager must acquire information about it. The first step in control, then, is measuring. Let us consider how we measure and what we measure.

**HOW WE MEASURE** Four sources of information frequently used by managers to measure actual performance are personal observations, statistical reports, oral reports, and written reports. In the workplace, personal observation is sometimes known as management by

**EXHIBIT 11-2** The Control Process

Step 1 — Measuring Actual Performance

GOALS
Organizational
Divisional
Departmental
Individual

Comparing Actual Performance Against Standard — Step 2

Step 3 — Taking Managerial Action

walking around. It can provide hands-on and detailed coverage of activities, but is time consuming and distracting when it comes to employees. Reports provide a more complete data source but may suffer when it comes to interpretation and subjective factors. For most managers, using a combination of approaches increases both the number of input sources and the probability of getting reliable information.

**WHAT WE MEASURE**   *What* we measure is probably more critical to the control process than *how* we measure. Why? The selection of the wrong criteria can result in serious dysfunctional consequences. Besides, what we measure determines, to a great extent, what people in the organization will attempt to excel at.[10] For example, if employees are evaluated by the number of big-ticket items they sell, they may not help customers who are looking for less expensive items.

Some control criteria are applicable to any management situation. For example, because all managers, by definition, coordinate the work of others, criteria such as employee satisfaction or turnover and absenteeism rates can be measured. Most managers also have budgets set in dollar costs for their areas of responsibility. Keeping costs within budget is, therefore, a fairly common control measure. However, any comprehensive control system needs to recognize the diversity of activities that managers do. A production manager at a paper tablet manufacturer might use measures such as quantity of paper tablets produced per day and per labour-hour, scrap rate, and/or percentage of rejects returned by customers. On the other hand, the manager of an administrative unit in a government agency might use the number of client requests processed per hour or the average time required to process paperwork. Marketing managers often use measures such as percentage of market held, average dollars per sale, number of customer visits per salesperson, or number of customer impressions per advertising medium.

Most jobs and activities can be expressed in tangible and measurable terms. However, when a performance indicator cannot be stated in quantifiable terms, managers should use subjective measures. Although subjective measures have significant limitations, they are better than having no standards at all and ignoring the control function. If an activity is important, the excuse that it is difficult to measure is unacceptable.

**control process**
A three-step process that includes measuring actual performance, comparing actual performance against a standard, and taking managerial action to correct deviations or inadequate standards.

**EXHIBIT 11-3** Sales Performance Figures for July, Beer Unlimited

| Brand | (number of cases) Standard | Actual | Over (Under) |
|---|---|---|---|
| Premium Lager (Okanagan Spring, Vernon, BC) | 1075 | 913 | (162) |
| India Pale Ale (Alexander Keith's, Halifax) | 800 | 912 | 112 |
| Maple Brown Ale (Upper Canada Brewery, Toronto) | 620 | 622 | 2 |
| Blanche de Chambly (Brasseries Unibroue, Quebec) | 160 | 110 | (50) |
| Full Moon (Alley Kat, Edmonton) | 225 | 220 | (5) |
| Black Cat Lager (Paddock Wood Brewing, Saskatoon, Saskatchewan) | 80 | 65 | (15) |
| Bison Blonde Lager (Agassiz, Winnipeg) | 170 | 286 | 116 |
| **Total cases** | **3130** | **3128** | **(2)** |

## Comparing Performance Against Standard

The comparing step determines the degree of variation between actual performance and the standard. Although some variation in performance can be expected in all activities, it is critical to determine the acceptable **range of variation**. Deviations that exceed this range become significant and need the manager's attention. In the comparison stage, managers are particularly concerned with the size and direction of the variation. An example can help make this concept clearer.

Chris Tanner is sales manager for Beer Unlimited, a distributor of specialty beers in the Prairies. Tanner prepares a report during the first week of each month that describes sales for the previous month, classified by brand name. Exhibit 11-3 displays both the sales goal (standard) and the actual sales figures for the month of July.

Should Tanner be concerned about July's sales performance? Sales were a bit higher than originally targeted, but does that mean there were no significant deviations? Even though overall performance was generally quite favourable, he may need to examine several brands more closely. However, the number of brands that deserve attention depends on what he believes to be *significant*. How much variation should Tanner allow before corrective action is taken?

The deviation on three brands (Maple Brown Ale, Full Moon, Black Cat Lager) is very small and does not need special attention. On the other hand, are the shortages for Premium Lager and Blanche de Chambly brands significant? That is a judgment Tanner must make. Premium Lager sales were 15 percent below his goal. This deviation is significant and needs attention. He should look for a cause. In this instance, Tanner attributes the decrease to aggressive advertising and promotion programs by the big domestic producers, Anheuser-Busch and Miller. Because Premium Lager is his company's number-one selling microbrew, it is most vulnerable to the promotion clout of the big domestic producers. If the decline in sales of Premium Lager is more than a temporary slump (that is, if it happens again next month), then Tanner will need to cut back on inventory stock.

An error in understating sales can be as troublesome as an overstatement. For example, is the surprising popularity of Bison Blonde Lager (up 68 percent) a one-month anomaly, or is this brand becoming more popular with customers? If the brand is increasing in popularity, Tanner will want to order more product to meet customer demand, so as not to run short and risk losing customers. Again, he will have to interpret the information and make a decision. Our Beer Unlimited example illustrates that both overvariance and undervariance in any comparison of measures may require managerial attention.

**BENCHMARKING OF BEST PRACTICES**   We first introduced the concept of benchmarking in Chapter 3. Remember that **benchmarking** is the search for the best practices among competitors or noncompetitors that lead to their superior performance. The **benchmark** is the standard of excellence against which to measure and compare.[11] At its most fundamental level, benchmarking means learning from others.[12] As a tool for monitoring and measuring organizational performance, benchmarking can be used to help identify specific performance gaps and potential areas for improvement.[13] To ensure the company is on track, Montreal-based BouClair, a home-decorating store, benchmarks everything against past performance and also against what other leading retailers are doing. "If a particular department or category is up 40 percent in sales over last year but we said we expected it to grow at 60 percent, then we are going to investigate and find out why," Gerry Goldberg, president and CEO, says.[14] "Then we look at our own same-store sales increases and compare them to the best companies out there. That's how we measure our efficiency and our productivity."

Managers should not look just at external organizations for best practices. It is also important for them to look inside their organization for best practices that can be shared. Research shows that best practices frequently already exist within an organization but usually go unidentified and unused.[15] In today's environment, organizations striving for high performance levels cannot afford to ignore such potentially valuable information. Some companies have already recognized the potential of internally benchmarking best practices as a tool for monitoring and measuring performance. For example, to improve diversity within the company, Saskatoon, Saskatchewan–based Yanke Group, a trucking company, is committed to hiring Aboriginal peoples and people with disabilities. Yanke reviews its employment equity benchmarks quarterly.[16] Toyota Motor Corporation developed a suggestion-screening system to prioritize best practices based on potential impact, benefits, and difficulty of implementation. General Motors sends employees—from upper management to line employees—to different plants where they learn about internal and external best practices.[17] Exhibit 11-4 provides a summary of what managers must do to implement an internal benchmarking best-practices program.

---

**EXHIBIT 11-4**   **Steps to Successfully Implement an Internal Benchmarking Best-Practices Program**

1. *Connect best practices to strategies and goals.* The organization's strategies and goals should dictate what types of best practices might be most valuable to others in the organization.

2. *Identify best practices throughout the organization.* Organizations must have a way to find out what practices have been successful in different work areas and units.

3. *Develop best-practices reward and recognition systems.* Individuals must be given an incentive to share their knowledge. The reward system should be built into the organization's culture.

4. *Communicate best practices throughout the organization.* Once best practices have been identified, that information needs to be shared with others in the organization.

5. *Create a best-practices knowledge-sharing system.* There needs to be a formal mechanism for organizational members to continue sharing their ideas and best practices.

6. *Nurture best practices on an ongoing basis.* Create an organizational culture that reinforces a "we can learn from everyone" attitude and emphasizes sharing information.

*Source:* T. Leahy, "Extracting Diamonds in the Rough," *Business Finance*, Aug. 2000, pp. 33–37.

---

**range of variation**
The acceptable degree of variation between actual performance and the standard.

**benchmarking**
The search for the best practices among competitors or noncompetitors that lead to their superior performance.

**benchmark**
The standard of excellence against which to measure and compare.

Toronto-based Celestica redesigned its manufacturing process to cut waste. It did so by watching how factory workers carried out their duties, and then designing more efficient processes. Workers at its Monterrey, Mexico, plant "reduced equipment setup time by 85 percent, shortened time between receiving an order and shipping it by 71 percent, reduced floor space used by 34 percent, reduced consumables by 25 percent, reduced scrap by 66 percent and reduced the investment in surface-mount technology (SMT) lines by 49 percent."

## Taking Managerial Action

The third and final step in the control process is taking managerial action. Managers can choose among three possible courses of action: They can do nothing; they can correct the actual performance; or they can revise the standard. Because "doing nothing" is fairly self-explanatory, let us look more closely at the other two options.

**CORRECT ACTUAL PERFORMANCE** If the source of the performance variation is unsatisfactory work, the manager will want to take corrective action. Examples of such corrective action might include changing strategy, structure, compensation practices, or training programs; redesigning jobs; or firing employees.

A manager who decides to correct actual performance has to make another decision: Should immediate or basic corrective action be taken? **Immediate corrective action** corrects problems at once to get performance back on track. **Basic corrective action** looks at how and why performance has deviated and then proceeds to correct the source of deviation. It is not unusual for managers to rationalize that they do not have the time to take basic corrective action and therefore must be content to perpetually "put out fires" with immediate corrective action. Effective managers, however, analyze deviations and, when the benefits justify it, take the time to pinpoint and correct the causes of variance.

To return to our Beer Unlimited example, taking immediate corrective action on the negative variance for Premium Lager, Chris Tanner might contact the company's retailers and have them immediately drop the price on Premium Lager by 5 percent. However, taking basic corrective action would involve more in-depth analysis by Tanner. After assessing how and why sales deviated, he might choose to increase in-store promotional efforts, increase the advertising budget for this brand, or reduce future purchases from the brewery. The action Tanner takes will depend on the assessment of the brand's potential profitability.

**REVISE THE STANDARD** Possibly, the variance was a result of an unrealistic standard—the goal may have been too high or too low. In such instances, the standard needs corrective attention, not the performance. For example, if individuals are exceeding the standard, or have no difficulty meeting the standard, perhaps the standard should be raised. In our example, Chris Tanner might need to raise the sales goal (standard) for Bison Blonde Lager to reflect its growing popularity.

The more troublesome problem is revising a performance standard downward. If an employee, work team, or work unit falls significantly short of reaching its goal, their natural response is to shift the blame for the variance to the goal. For example, students who make a low grade on a test often attack the grade cut-off standards as too high. Rather than acknowledge that their performance was inadequate, students argue that the standards are unreasonable. Similarly, salespeople who fail to meet their monthly quotas may attribute the failures to unrealistic quotas. It may be true that when a standard is too high, it can result in a significant variation and may even contribute to demotivating those employees being measured. But keep in mind that if employees or managers do not meet the standard, the first thing they are likely to attack is the standard. If you believe that the standard is realistic, fair, and achievable, hold your ground. Explain your position, reaffirm to the employee, team, or unit that you expect future performance to improve, and then take the necessary corrective action to turn that expectation into reality.

## Summary of Managerial Decisions

Exhibit 11-5 summarizes the manager's decisions in the control process. Standards evolve out of goals that are developed during the planning process. These goals provide the basis

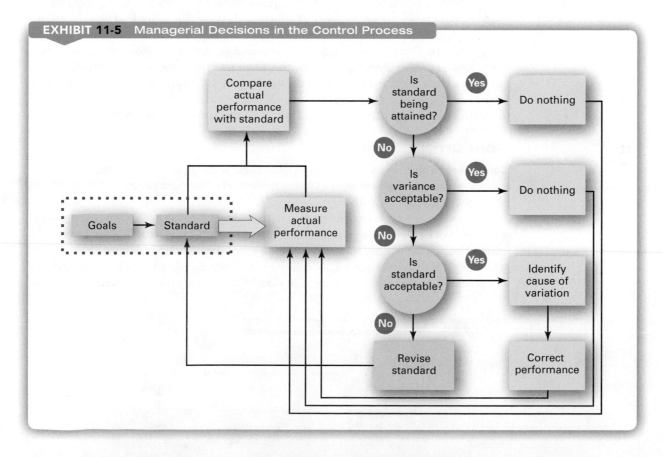

**EXHIBIT 11-5** Managerial Decisions in the Control Process

---

**immediate corrective action**
Corrective action that corrects problems at once to get performance back on track.

**basic corrective action**
Corrective action that looks at how and why performance deviated and then proceeds to correct the source of deviation.

for the control process, which is essentially a continuous flow between measuring, comparing, and taking managerial action. Depending on the results of comparing, a manager's decision about what course of action to take might be to do nothing, revise the standard, or correct the performance.

# WHEN TO INTRODUCE CONTROL

**11.3** **Describe** When should controls be introduced?

Managers can implement controls *before* an activity begins, *during* the time the activity is going on, and *after* the activity has been completed. The first type is called *feedforward control,* the second is *concurrent control,* and the last is *feedback control* (see Exhibit 11-6).

## Feedforward Control

The most desirable type of control—**feedforward control**—prevents anticipated problems since it takes place before the actual activity.[18] Let us look at some examples of feedforward control.

When McDonald's Canada opened its first restaurant in Moscow, it sent company quality control experts to help Russian farmers learn techniques for growing high-quality potatoes and to help bakers learn processes for baking high-quality breads. Why? Because McDonald's strongly emphasizes product quality no matter what the geographical location. It wants a cheeseburger in Moscow to taste like one in Winnipeg. Still another example of feedforward control is the scheduled preventive maintenance programs on aircraft done by airlines. These programs are designed to detect and prevent structural damage that might lead to an accident.

The key to feedforward controls is taking managerial action *before* a problem occurs. Feedforward controls are desirable because they allow managers to prevent problems rather than having to correct them later after the damage (such as poor-quality products, lost customers, lost revenue, and so forth) has already been done. Unfortunately, these controls require timely and accurate information that often is difficult to obtain. As a result, managers frequently end up using the other two types of control.

*When working on a project, do you anticipate problems ahead of time or wait until they occur?*

## Concurrent Control

**Concurrent control**, as its name implies, takes place while an activity is in progress. When control is enacted while the work is being performed, management can correct problems before they become too costly.

The best-known form of concurrent control is direct supervision. When managers use **management by walking around**, a term used to describe a manager who is out in the work area and interacting directly with employees, they are using concurrent control. When a manager directly oversees the actions of employees, he or she can monitor their actions and correct problems as they occur. Although, obviously, some delay occurs between the activity

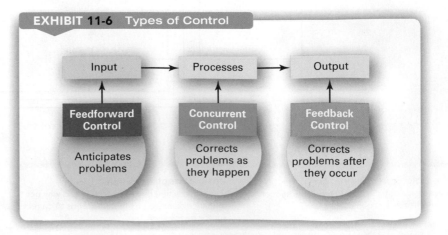

**EXHIBIT 11-6** Types of Control

Input → Processes → Output

Feedforward Control — Anticipates problems

Concurrent Control — Corrects problems as they happen

Feedback Control — Corrects problems after they occur

and the manager's corrective response, the delay is minimal. Problems usually can be addressed before much resource waste or damage has been done. Also, technical equipment (computers, computerized machine controls, and so forth) can be programmed for concurrent controls. You may have experienced concurrent control when using a computer program such as word-processing software that alerts you to misspelled words or incorrect grammatical usage as you type. In addition, many organizational quality programs rely on concurrent controls to inform employees if their work output is of sufficient quality to meet standards.

## Feedback Control

The most popular type of control relies on feedback. In **feedback control**, the control takes place *after* the activity is done. For example, when McDonald's executives learned that a suspected criminal ring had allegedly stolen millions of dollars in top prizes in their customer games, the theft was discovered through feedback control.[19] Even though the company took corrective action once the problem was discovered, the damage had already occurred.

*Have you used feedback with team members after completing a team project?*

As the McDonald's example shows, the major drawback of this type of control is that by the time the manager has the information, the problems have already occurred—leading to waste or damage. But for many activities, feedback is the only viable type of control available. Financial statements are an example of feedback controls. If, for example, the income statement shows that sales revenues are declining, the decline has already occurred. At this point, the manager's only option is to try to determine why sales have decreased and to correct the situation.

Feedback controls have two advantages.[20] First, feedback provides managers with meaningful information on how effective their planning efforts were. Feedback that indicates little variance between standard and actual performance is evidence that the planning was generally on target. If the deviation is significant, a manager can use that information when formulating new plans to make them more effective. Second, feedback control can enhance employee motivation. People want information on how well they have performed and feedback control provides that information. However, managers should be aware of recent research that suggests individuals raise their goals when they receive positive feedback but lower their goals when they receive negative feedback.[21] (To learn how to give feedback effectively, see *Developing Your Interpersonal Skills—Providing Feedback* on pages 331–332 at the end of the chapter.)

Interpret

## METHODS OF CONTROL

The Canadian Curling Association implemented a new corporate governance structure. They followed John Carver's Policy Governance® model of board leadership, which required the CCA to be governed in an organized, planned, and highly disciplined manner.[22]

**11.4** Explain
What methods of control do managers use?

### Think About It

What methods of control are available to managers? How do managers introduce controls? What impact might controls have on employees?

Ideally, every organization would like to efficiently and effectively reach its goals. Does this mean that the control systems organizations use are identical? In other words, would Matsushita, the Canadian Curling Association,

---

**feedforward control**
A type of control that focuses on preventing anticipated problems, since it takes place before the actual activity.

**concurrent control**
A type of control that takes place while an activity is in progress.

**management by walking around**
A term used to describe a manager who is out in the work area and interacting directly with employees.

**feedback control**
A type of control that takes place after a work activity is done.

**EXHIBIT 11-7** Characteristics of Three Approaches to Designing Control Systems

| Type of Control | Characteristics |
| --- | --- |
| Market | Uses external market mechanisms, such as price competition and relative market share, to establish standards used in system. Typically used by organizations whose products or services are clearly specified and distinct and that face considerable marketplace competition. |
| Bureaucratic | Emphasizes organizational authority. Relies on administrative and hierarchical mechanisms, such as rules, regulations, procedures, policies, standardization of activities, well-defined job descriptions, and budgets to ensure that employees exhibit appropriate behaviours and meet performance standards. |
| Clan | Regulates employee behaviour by the shared values, norms, traditions, rituals, beliefs, and other aspects of the organization's culture. Often used by organizations in which teams are common and technology is changing rapidly. |

and WestJet Airlines have the same types of control systems? Probably not. There are generally three approaches to designing control systems: market, bureaucratic, and clan controls (see Exhibit 11-7).[23]

## Market Control

**Market control** is an approach to control that emphasizes the use of external market mechanisms, such as price competition and relative market share, to establish the standards used in the control system. Organizations that use the market control approach often have divisions set up as profit centres and evaluated by the percentage of total corporate profits contributed. For instance, at Japan's Matsushita, which supplies a wide range of products throughout the world, the various divisions (audiovisual and communication networks, components and devices, home appliances, and industrial equipment) are evaluated according to the profit each generates.

## Bureaucratic Control

Another approach to control is **bureaucratic control**, which emphasizes organizational authority and relies on administrative rules, regulations, procedures, and policies. The CCA provides a good example of bureaucratic control. The achievement of financial profit is part of the culture at the nonprofit association. The mandate is slightly different than for a corporation, however, because all the money CCA generates is fed back into the sport of curling. Greg Stremlaw is given freedom to run the association as he sees fit, but the board governance model expects him to adhere closely to budgets and to stay within corporate guidelines.

## Clan Control

**Clan control** is an approach to control in which employee behaviour is regulated by the shared values, norms, traditions, rituals, beliefs, and other aspects of the organization's culture. While market control relies on external standards and bureaucratic control is based on strict hierarchical mechanisms, clan control is dependent on the individuals and the groups in the organization (the clan) to identify appropriate and expected behaviours and performance measures. At Calgary-based WestJet Airlines, individuals are well aware of the expectations regarding appropriate work behaviour and performance standards, and employees are encouraged to keep costs low.[24]

Most organizations do not rely totally on just one of these approaches to design an appropriate control system. Instead, they choose to emphasize either bureaucratic or clan control, and then add some market control measures. The key is to design an appropriate control system that helps the organization efficiently and effectively reach its goals. We consider clan culture in more detail than the other types of control systems because it provides control that is both more flexible and more enduring than either market or bureaucratic control. As we mentioned earlier, clan control is regulated by organizational culture. When employees are guided by a strong set of organizational values and norms, they can be empowered to make decisions that will benefit the organization in the long run.

WestJet has a much better profit margin than Air Canada and its other rivals. Founder and former CEO Clive Beddoe introduced a generous profit-sharing plan to ensure that employees felt personally responsible for the profitability of the airline. The company's accountants insist that profit-sharing turns employees into "cost cops" looking for waste and savings. WestJet encourages teamwork and gives employees a lot of freedom to determine and carry out their day-to-day duties. The company saves $2.5 million annually in cleaning costs by having everyone work together.

**ORGANIZATIONAL CULTURE** **Organizational culture** is a system of shared meaning and beliefs held by organizational members that determines, in large degree, how they act. It represents a common perception held by an organization's members that influences how they behave. In every organization, there are values, symbols, rituals, myths, and practices that have evolved over time.[25] These shared values and experiences mainly determine what employees perceive and how they respond to their world.[26] When faced with problems or issues, the organizational culture—the "way we do things around here"—influences what employees can do and how they conceptualize, define, analyze, and resolve issues.

*How does the culture of your college or university differ from that of your high school?*

Our definition of organizational culture implies three things:

- Culture is a *perception.* Individuals perceive the organizational culture on the basis of what they see, hear, or experience within the organization.
- Culture is *shared.* Even though individuals may have different backgrounds or work at different organizational levels, they tend to describe the organization's culture in similar terms.
- Culture is a *descriptive* term. Culture is concerned with how members perceive the organization, not with whether they like it. It describes rather than evaluates.

Research suggests there are seven dimensions that capture the essence of an organization's culture.[27] These dimensions are described in Exhibit 11-8. Each dimension ranges

---

**market control**
An approach to control that emphasizes the use of external market mechanisms, such as price competition and relative market share, to establish the standards used in the control system.

**bureaucratic control**
An approach to control that emphasizes organizational authority and relies on administrative rules, regulations, procedures, and policies.

**clan control**
An approach to control in which employee behaviour is regulated by the shared values, norms, traditions, rituals, beliefs, and other aspects of the organization's culture.

**organizational culture**
A system of shared values, norms, and beliefs held by organization members that determines, in large degree, how employees act.

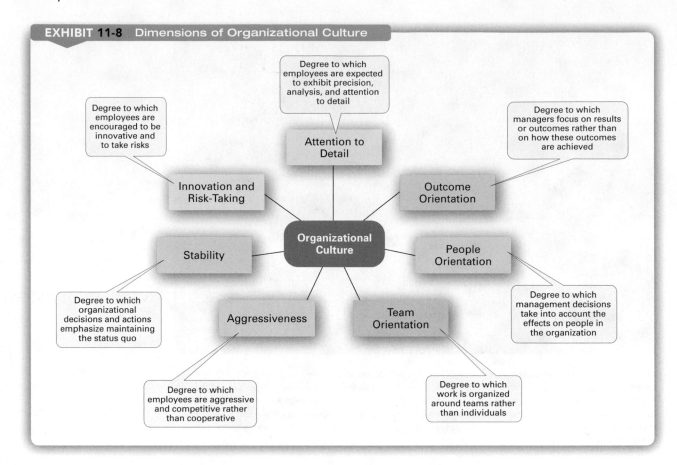

**EXHIBIT 11-8** Dimensions of Organizational Culture

Attention to Detail
Degree to which employees are expected to exhibit precision, analysis, and attention to detail

Innovation and Risk-Taking
Degree to which employees are encouraged to be innovative and to take risks

Outcome Orientation
Degree to which managers focus on results or outcomes rather than on how these outcomes are achieved

Organizational Culture

Stability
Degree to which organizational decisions and actions emphasize maintaining the status quo

People Orientation
Degree to which management decisions take into account the effects on people in the organization

Aggressiveness
Degree to which employees are aggressive and competitive rather than cooperative

Team Orientation
Degree to which work is organized around teams rather than individuals

from low (not very typical of the culture) to high (very typical of the culture). Appraising an organization on these seven dimensions gives a composite picture of the organization's culture. In many organizations, one of these cultural dimensions is often emphasized more than the others and essentially shapes the organization's personality and the way organization members work. For example, at Sony Corporation the focus is on product innovation. The company "lives and breathes" new-product development (outcome orientation), and employees' work decisions, behaviours, and actions support that goal. In contrast, WestJet Airlines has made its employees a central part of its culture (people orientation). However, its admission in 2006 of engaging in corporate espionage against Air Canada may cause employees to question WestJet's corporate values.

**STRONG VS. WEAK CULTURES**   Although all organizations have cultures, not all cultures have an equal impact on employees' behaviours and actions. **Strong cultures**—cultures in which the key values are deeply held and widely shared—have a greater influence on employees than do weak cultures. The more employees accept the organization's key values and the greater their commitment to those values, the stronger the culture is.

Whether an organization's culture is strong, weak, or somewhere in between depends on factors such as the size of the organization, how long it has been around, how much turnover there has been among employees, and the intensity with which the culture began.

Some organizations do not make clear what is important and what is not. This lack of clarity is a characteristic of weak cultures. In such organizations, culture is unlikely to greatly influence managers. Most organizations, however, have moderate to strong cultures. There is relatively high agreement on what is important, what defines "good" employee behaviour, what it takes to get ahead, and so forth. *Tips for Managers—Creating a More Ethical Culture* provides some suggestions for managers who want to build and maintain a more ethical culture in the workplace.

A growing body of evidence suggests that strong cultures are associated with high organizational performance.[28] It is easy to understand why a strong culture enhances performance.

After all, when values are clear and widely accepted, employees know what they are supposed to do and what is expected of them. They are able to act quickly to take care of problems, preventing any potential performance decline. However, the drawback is that the same strong culture might prevent employees from trying new approaches, especially during periods of rapid change.[29] Strong cultures do not always yield *positive* results.[30] Enron had a very strong and unethical culture. It enabled employees and top management to engage in unethical behaviour that was concealed from public scrutiny.

**TIPS FOR MANAGERS**

**Creating a More Ethical Culture**

✳ Be a **visible role model**.

✳ Communicate **ethical expectations**.

✳ Provide **ethics training**.

✳ Visibly **reward ethical acts and punish unethical ones**.

✳ Provide **protective mechanisms** so employees can discuss ethical dilemmas and report unethical behaviour without fear.

**DEVELOPING AN ORGANIZATION'S CULTURE**  An organization's culture is derived from the founders' philosophy. The culture, in turn, strongly influences the selection criteria used to hire new employees. Clan control requires careful selection and socialization of employees who will support the organization's culture, both of which include making sure to manage diversity in the workforce.

The actions of the current top managers set the general expectations as to what is acceptable behaviour and what is not. Through the socialization process, new employees learn the organization's way of doing things. If socialization is successful, new employees will learn the values of the organization and behave accordingly, and the organization's culture will be preserved.

**HOW EMPLOYEES LEARN CULTURE**  Culture is transmitted to employees in a number of ways. The most significant are stories, rituals, material symbols, and language.

**Stories**  An organization's "stories" typically are related to significant people or events, such as the organization's founders, rule breaking, reactions to past mistakes, and so forth.[31] They help employees learn the culture by anchoring the present in the past, providing explanations and legitimacy for current practices, and showing what is important to the organization.[32]

**Rituals**  An organization's rituals are repetitive sequences of activities that express and reinforce the values of the organization, the goals that are most important, and the people who are most important.[33] One well-known ritual is Walmart's company chant that employees say at the beginning of each workday.

**Material Symbols**  An organization's material symbols convey to employees who is important, the degree of equality desired by top management, and the kinds of behaviour (for example, risk-taking, conservative, authoritarian, participative, individualistic, and so on) that are expected and appropriate. The layout of an organization's facilities, how employees dress, the types of automobiles provided to top executives, and the availability of corporate aircraft are examples of material symbols.

**Language**  Many organizations and units within organizations use language as a way to identify members of a culture. By learning this language, members attest to their acceptance

**strong cultures**
Organizational cultures in which the key values are deeply held and widely shared.

**EXHIBIT 11-9** Managerial Decisions Affected by Organizational Culture

**Planning**

- The degree of risk that plans should contain
- Whether plans should be developed by individuals or teams
- The degree of environmental scanning in which management will engage

**Leading**

- The degree to which managers are concerned with increasing employee job satisfaction
- The appropriate leadership style(s)
- Whether all disagreements—even constructive ones—should be eliminated

**Organizing**

- How much autonomy should be designed into employees' jobs
- Whether tasks should be done by individuals or in teams
- The degree to which department managers interact with each other

**Controlling**

- Whether to impose external controls or to allow employees to control their own actions
- What criteria should be emphasized in employee performance evaluations
- What repercussions will result from exceeding one's budget

of the culture and their willingness to help preserve it. New employees are frequently overwhelmed with acronyms and jargon that, after a short period of time, become a natural part of their language. Once learned, the language acts as a common denominator to unite members of a given culture.

Analyze

**HOW CULTURE AFFECTS MANAGERS**  An organization's culture does more than influence employee behaviour; it also constrains a manager's decision-making options in all management functions. Exhibit 11-9 shows the major areas of a manager's job that are affected by the culture in which he or she operates.

# FINANCIAL AND INFORMATION CONTROLS

**11.5 Explain** How do financial and information controls help managers monitor performance?

The Canadian Curling Association had a deficit of more than a million dollars in the mid 2000s. Thanks to the introduction of financial and information controls as part of a governance overhaul, the CCA had a $3 425 230 surplus in 2011–2012.

One of the primary purposes of every business is to earn a profit. To achieve this goal, managers need financial controls and accurate information. Managers might, for example, carefully analyze quarterly income statements for excessive expenses. They might also perform several financial ratio tests to ensure that sufficient cash is available to pay ongoing expenses, debt levels have not risen too high, and assets are being used productively. Or they might look at newer financial control tools such as EVA (economic value added) to see if the company is creating economic value. Managers can control information and use it to control other organizational activities.

**Think About It**

How can managers use financial and information controls to make sure that their organizations are performing well?

## Traditional Financial Control Measures

Traditional financial control measures include ratio analysis and budget analysis. Exhibit 11-10 summarizes some of the most popular financial ratios used in organizations. Liquidity ratios measure an organization's ability to meet its current debt obligations. Leverage ratios examine the organization's use of debt to finance its assets and whether it is able to meet the interest payments on the debt. Activity ratios assess how efficiently the firm is using its assets. Finally, profitability ratios measure how efficiently and effectively the firm is using its assets to generate profits.

| EXHIBIT 11-10 | Popular Financial Ratios | | |
|---|---|---|---|
| **Objective** | **Ratio** | **Calculation** | **Meaning** |
| **Liquidity** | Current ratio | $\dfrac{\text{Current assets}}{\text{Current liabilities}}$ | Tests the organization's ability to meet short-term obligations |
| | Acid test | $\dfrac{\text{Current assets less inventories}}{\text{Current liabilities}}$ | Tests liquidity more accurately when inventories turn over slowly or are difficult to sell |
| **Leverage** | Debt to assets | $\dfrac{\text{Total debt}}{\text{Total assets}}$ | The higher the ratio, the more leveraged the organization |
| | Times interest earned | $\dfrac{\text{Profits before interest and taxes}}{\text{Total interest charges}}$ | Measures how far profits can decline before the organization is unable to meet its interest expenses |
| **Activity** | Inventory turnover | $\dfrac{\text{Sales}}{\text{Inventories}}$ | The higher the ratio, the more efficiently inventory assets are being used |
| | Total asset turnover | $\dfrac{\text{Sales}}{\text{Total assets}}$ | The fewer assets used to achieve a given level of sales, the more efficiently management is using the organization's total assets |
| **Profitability** | Profit margin on sales | $\dfrac{\text{Net profit after taxes}}{\text{Total sales}}$ | Identifies the profits that various products are generating |
| | Return on investment | $\dfrac{\text{Net profit after taxes}}{\text{Total assets}}$ | Measures the efficiency of assets to generate profits |

These ratios are calculated using information from the organization's two primary financial statements: the balance sheet and the income statement. They compare two figures and express them as a percentage or ratio. Because you have undoubtedly discussed these ratios in introductory accounting and finance courses, or you will in the near future, we are not going to elaborate on how they are calculated. Instead, we mention these ratios only briefly here to remind you that managers use such ratios as internal control devices for monitoring how efficiently and profitably the organization uses its assets, debt, inventories, and the like.

Budgets are used for control as they provide managers with quantitative standards against which to measure and compare resource consumption. By pointing out deviations between standard and actual consumption, they become control tools. If the deviations are judged to be significant enough to require action, the manager will want to examine what has happened and try to uncover the reasons behind the deviations. With this information, he or she can take whatever action is necessary. For example, if you use a personal budget for monitoring and controlling your monthly expenses, you might find one month that your miscellaneous expenses were higher than you had budgeted for. At that point, you might cut back spending in another area or work extra hours to try to get more income.

## Other Financial Control Measures

In addition to the traditional financial tools, managers are using measures such as EVA (economic value added) and MVA (market value added). The fundamental concept behind these financial tools is that companies are supposed to take in capital from investors and make it worth more. When managers do that, they have created wealth. When they take in capital and make it worth less, they have destroyed wealth.

**Economic value added (EVA)** is a tool that measures corporate and divisional performance. It is calculated by taking after-tax operating profit minus the total annual cost of

**economic value added (EVA)**
A financial tool that measures corporate and divisional performance, calculated by taking after-tax operating profit minus the total annual cost of capital.

capital.[34] EVA is a measure of how much economic value is being created by what a company does with its assets, less any capital investments the company has made in its assets. As a performance control tool, EVA focuses managers' attention on earning a rate of return over and above the cost of capital. About 30 percent of Canadian companies use EVA, including Montreal-based Rio Tinto Alcan, Montreal-based Domtar, Markham, Ontario–based Robin Hood Multifoods, and Montreal-based cable company Cogeco.[35] When EVA is used as a performance measure, employees soon learn that they can improve their organization's or business unit's EVA either by using less capital (figuring out how to spend less) or by investing capital in high-return projects (projects that will bring in more money, with fewer expenses). Former Molson CEO Daniel O'Neill was well rewarded for EVA improvement to the company in 2002. He "closed several breweries, laid off hundreds of staff, and slashed overhead costs, using the savings to modernize remaining breweries," all of which sent Molson shares soaring. O'Neill received a $2.4 million bonus for his efforts.[36]

**Market value added (MVA)** adds a market dimension. It is a tool that measures the stock market's estimate of the value of a firm's past and expected capital investment projects. If the company's market value (value of all outstanding stock plus the company's debt) is greater than all the capital invested in it (from shareholders, bondholders, and retained earnings), it has a positive MVA, indicating that managers have created wealth. If the company's market value is less than all the capital invested in it, the MVA will be negative, indicating that managers have destroyed wealth. Studies have shown that EVA is a predictor of MVA and that consecutive years of positive EVA generally lead to a high MVA.[37]

To understand that EVA and MVA measure different things, let us consider three companies that had the highest MVA in the United States in 2006 and the amount of wealth they created for their shareholders (in US dollars): General Electric ($281 billion), Exxon Mobil ($223 billion), and Microsoft ($221 billion). While these three companies had relatively similar MVA, they had very different real profits (measured by EVA). Exxon Mobil had the highest EVA ($28.9 billion), followed by Microsoft ($9.1 billion), and then GE ($8.2 billion). Microsoft, with a lower MVA than General Electric, delivered a higher EVA.[38]

## Information Controls

In April 2007, Gordon Bobbitt found hundreds of phone records from Rogers littering the streets of Toronto. These records contained contact information, financial details, and, in some cases, social insurance numbers. This case was just one instance of consumer records that were not handled properly. Earlier in 2007, CIBC and retailer TJX Companies (operator of Winners and HomeSense) had breaches of security with consumer data. In 2006, the RCMP processed about 7800 cases of identity theft, which represented $16.3 million in individual losses.[39]

There are two ways to view information: (1) as a tool to help managers control other organizational activities and (2) as an organizational area that managers need to control. Let us look first at information as a control tool.

**HOW IS INFORMATION USED IN CONTROLLING?** Information is critical to monitoring and measuring an organization's activities and performance. Managers need the right information at the right time and in the right amount. Without information, they would find it difficult to measure, compare, and take action as part of the controlling process. Inaccurate, incomplete, excessive, or delayed information will seriously impede performance.

For example, in measuring actual performance, managers need information about what is happening within their area of responsibility and what the standards are. They need this information to compare actual performance with the standard and to help them determine acceptable ranges of variation within these comparisons. Managers rely on information to help them develop appropriate courses of action if there are or are not significant deviations between actual and standard performance. Information can also be used to control costs, as Air Canada discovered when they improved their maintenance procedures. Mechanics were given tablet-sized display screens mounted on their trucks and connected to a wireless local area network. In this way, information about required repairs became easily available, and the display was large enough to show maintenance diagrams when needed.

The technology significantly improved maintenance productivity. Mechanics spent less time travelling back and forth to the hangar to get additional parts, since they could determine what they needed more quickly. Mechanics could also make sure that parts were waiting when planes landed, so simple repairs could be performed without delaying flights.

As you can see, information is an important tool in monitoring and measuring organizational performance. Most of the information tools that managers use arise out of the organization's management information system.

Although there is no universally agreed-upon definition of a **management information system (MIS)**, we will define it as a system used to provide management with needed information on a regular basis. In theory, this system can be manual or computer-based, although all current discussions focus on computer-supported applications. The term *system* in MIS implies order, arrangement, and purpose. Further, an MIS focuses specifically on providing managers with *information*, not merely *data*. These two points are important and require elaboration.

A library provides a good analogy. Although it can contain millions of volumes, a library does not do users much good if they cannot find what they want quickly. That is why librarians spend a great deal of time cataloguing a library's collections and ensuring that materials are returned to their proper locations. Organizations today are like well-stocked libraries. There is no lack of data. There is, however, an inability to process the data so that the right information is available to the right person when he or she needs it. Likewise, a library is almost useless if it has the book you need immediately but either you cannot find it or the library takes a week to retrieve it from storage. An MIS, on the other hand, has organized data in some meaningful way and can access the information in a reasonable amount of time. **Data** are raw, unanalyzed facts, such as numbers, names, or quantities. Raw unanalyzed facts are relatively useless to managers. When data are analyzed and processed, they become **information**. An MIS collects data and turns them into relevant information for managers to use.

**CONTROLLING INFORMATION**  As critically important as an organization's information is to everything it does, managers must have comprehensive and secure controls in place to protect that information. Such controls can range from data encryption to system firewalls to data backups, and include other techniques as well.[40] Problems can lurk in places that an organization might not even have considered, such as search engines. Sensitive, defamatory, confidential, or embarrassing organizational information has found its way into search engine results. For example, detailed monthly expenses and employee salaries on the National Speleological Society's website turned up in a Google search.[41] Laptop computers are also proving to be a weak link in an organization's data security. For example, Boston-based mutual fund company Fidelity Investments disclosed that a stolen laptop had the personal information of almost 200 000 current and former Hewlett-Packard employees.[42] Even RFID (radio frequency identification) tags, now being used by more and more organizations to track and control products, may be vulnerable to computer viruses.[43] Needless to say, whatever information controls are used must be monitored regularly to ensure that all possible precautions are in place to protect the organization's important information.

---

**market value added (MVA)**
A financial tool that measures the stock market's estimate of the value of a firm's past and expected capital investment projects.

**management information system (MIS)**
A system used to provide management with needed information on a regular basis.

**data**
Raw, unanalyzed facts.

**information**
Processed and analyzed data.

# CURRENT ISSUES IN CONTROL

**11.6** Explain
What are some current issues in control?

The Canadian Curling Association, like virtually all nonprofit organizations, has a board of directors that looks after the interests of members. In recent years, corporate governance has come under scrutiny because of corporate scandals. Many boards were not overseeing management as well as they might have.

The CCA used Carver's Policy Governance® model to strengthen its board policies in recent years. The primary duty of the CCA board is to "approve, monitor and provide guidance on the strategic planning process." While the president and CEO and senior management team create the strategic plan, the board has to review and approve it. The board's role also includes identifying the principal risks of the CCA's business and managing and monitoring these risks, as well as approving CCA's strategic plans, annual budget, and financial plans.

> ### Think About It
>
> Why has corporate governance become so important in recent years? What are the advantages of having a strong corporate board? Would there be any disadvantages?

The employees of Tempe, Arizona–based Integrated Information Systems thought there was nothing wrong with exchanging copyrighted digital music over a dedicated office server they had set up. Like office betting on college basketball games, it was technically illegal, but harmless—or so they thought. But after the company had to pay a $1.5 million settlement to the Recording Industry Association of America, managers wished they had controlled the situation better.[44]

Control is an important managerial function. What types of control issues do today's managers face? We look at five: balanced scorecard, corporate governance, cross-cultural differences, workplace concerns, and customer interactions.

## Balanced Scorecard

The balanced scorecard approach to performance measurement was introduced as a way to evaluate organizational performance from more than just the financial perspective.[45] The **balanced scorecard** is a performance measurement tool that examines four areas that contribute to an organization's performance: financial, customer, internal business process, and learning and growth assets. Exhibit 11-11 illustrates how the balanced scorecard is measured. The financial area looks at activities that improve the short- and long-term performance of the organization. The customer area looks at the customer's view of the organization, whether customers return, and whether they are satisfied. The internal business process looks at how production and operations, such as order fulfillment, are carried out. The learning and growth area looks at how well the company's employees are being managed for the company's future.

According to this approach, managers should develop goals in each of the four areas and then measure to determine if these goals are being met. For example, a company might include cash flow, quarterly sales growth, and return on investment (ROI) as measures for success in the financial area. It might include percentage of sales coming from new products as a measure of customer goals. It might include dollars spent toward training, or number of courses taken by employees, as a measure of learning and growth. The intent of the balanced scorecard is to emphasize that all of these areas are important to an organization's success and that there should be a balance among them.

Although a balanced scorecard makes sense, managers still tend to focus on areas that drive their organization's success.[46] Their scorecards reflect their strategies. If those strategies centre on the customer, for example, then the customer area is likely to get more attention than the other three areas. Yet you really cannot focus on measuring only one performance area because, ultimately, other performance areas will be affected.

Many companies are starting to use the balanced scorecard as a control mechanism, including Bell Canada, British Airways, and Hilton Hotels. The Ontario Hospital Association uses a scorecard for 89 hospitals, designed to evaluate four main areas: clinical

**EXHIBIT 11-11** The Balanced Scorecard

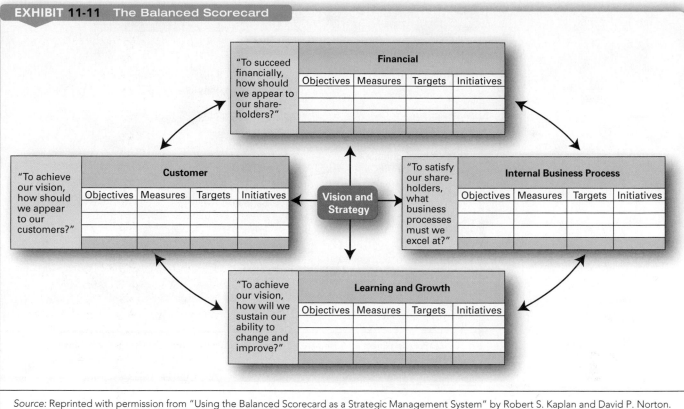

*Source:* Reprinted with permission from "Using the Balanced Scorecard as a Strategic Management System" by Robert S. Kaplan and David P. Norton. *Harvard Business Review,* Jan. 1996. Copyright © 1996 by Harvard Business Publishing; all rights reserved..

use and outcomes, financial performance and financial condition of the hospital, patient satisfaction, and how the hospital is investing for the future. The scorecard is purposefully designed to recognize the synergies among each of these measures. After hospitals are evaluated on the scorecard measures, the results of the scorecard evaluations are made available to patients, giving them an objective basis for choosing a hospital. The association provides the reports on its website.[47]

## Corporate Governance

Although Andrew Fastow, Enron's former chief financial officer, had an engaging and persuasive personality, that still does not explain why Enron's board of directors failed to raise even minimal concerns about management's questionable accounting practices. The board even allowed Fastow to set up off-balance-sheet partnerships for his own profit at the expense of Enron's shareholders.

**Corporate governance,** the system used to govern a corporation so that the interests of corporate owners are protected, failed abysmally at Enron, as it did at many of the other companies caught in recent financial scandals. In the aftermath of these scandals, there have been increased calls for better corporate governance. Two areas in which corporate governance is being reformed are the role of boards of directors and financial reporting. The concern over corporate governance exists in Canada and globally.[48] For example, 75 percent of senior executives at US and Western European corporations expect their boards of directors to take a more active role in improving corporate governance.[49]

**balanced scorecard**
A performance measurement tool that looks at four areas that contribute to an organization's performance: financial, customer, internal business process, and learning and growth assets.

**corporate governance**
The system used to govern a corporation so that the interests of corporate owners are protected.

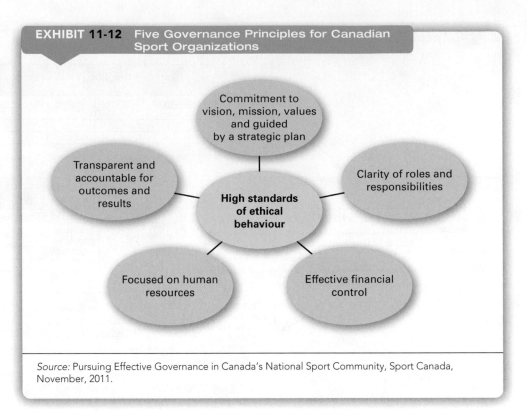

**EXHIBIT 11-12** Five Governance Principles for Canadian Sport Organizations

*Source:* Pursuing Effective Governance in Canada's National Sport Community, Sport Canada, November, 2011.

**THE ROLE OF BOARDS OF DIRECTORS** The original purpose of a board of directors was to have a group, independent from management, looking out for the interests of shareholders who, because of the corporate structure, were not involved in the day-to-day management of the organization. However, it has not always worked that way in practice. Board members often enjoy a cozy relationship with managers in which board members "take care" of the CEO and the CEO "takes care" of the board members.

This quid pro quo arrangement is changing. In the United States, since the passage of the Sarbanes-Oxley Act in 2002, demands on board members of publicly traded companies in the United States have increased considerably.[50] The Canadian Securities Administrators rules, which came into effect in March 2004, strive to tighten board responsibility somewhat, though these rules are not as stringent as those developed in the United States. To help sport organizations govern their affairs more effectively, Sport Canada developed five governance principles for Canadian sport organizations (see Exhibit 11-12 for a list of five governance principles).[51]

**FINANCIAL REPORTING** In addition to expanding the role of boards of directors, the Canadian Securities Administrators rules require more financial disclosure by organizations, but, unlike the Sarbanes-Oxley Act of the United States, do not require senior managers to provide a qualitative assessment of an organization's internal compliance control. Still, these types of changes should lead to somewhat better information—information that is more accurate and reflective of the firm's financial condition.

## Cross-Cultural Differences

The concepts of control that we have discussed so far are appropriate for an organization whose units are not geographically separated or culturally distinct. But what about global organizations? Will control systems be different, and what should managers know about adjusting controls for cross-cultural differences?

Methods of controlling people and work can be quite different in different countries. The differences we see in organizational control systems of global organizations are primarily in the measurement and corrective action steps of the control process. In a global corporation, managers of foreign operations tend to be less directly controlled by the home office, if for no other reason than that distance keeps managers from being able to observe work directly. Because distance creates a tendency to formalize controls, the home office of a global company often relies on extensive formal reports for control. The global company may also use the power of information technology to control work activities. For instance, the Japanese-based retailer Seven & i Holdings, which owns the 7-Eleven convenience store chain, uses automated cash registers not only to record sales and monitor inventory, but also to schedule tasks for store managers and to track managers' use of the built-in analytical graphs and forecasts. If managers do not use them enough, they are told to increase their activities.[52]

Technology's impact on control is most evident in comparisons of technologically advanced nations with those that are less technologically advanced. In countries such as Canada, the United States, Japan, Great Britain, Germany, and Australia, global managers use indirect control devices—especially computer-generated reports and analyses—in addition to standardized rules and direct supervision to ensure that work activities are going as planned. In less technologically advanced countries, managers tend to rely more on direct supervision and highly centralized decision making as means of control.

Also, constraints on what corrective actions managers can take may affect managers in foreign countries, because laws in some countries do not allow managers the option of closing facilities, laying off employees, taking money out of the country, or bringing in a new management team from outside the country.

Finally, another challenge for global companies in collecting data for measurement and comparison is comparability. For instance, a company's manufacturing facility in Mexico might produce the same products as a facility in Scotland. However, the Mexican facility might be much more labour intensive than its Scottish counterpart (to take strategic advantage of lower labour costs in Mexico). If the top-level executives were to control costs by, for example, calculating labour costs per unit or output per employee, the figures would not be comparable. Global managers must address these types of control challenges.

## Workplace Concerns

Today's workplace presents considerable control challenges for managers. From monitoring employees' computer use at work to protecting the workplace from disgruntled employees, managers must control the workplace to ensure that the organization's work can be carried out efficiently and effectively as planned. In this section, we look at two major workplace concerns: workplace privacy and employee theft.

**WORKPLACE PRIVACY** If you work, do you think you have a right to privacy at your workplace? What can your employer find out about you and your work? You might be surprised by the answers!

Employers can (and do), among other things, read your email (even those marked "personal" or "confidential"), tap your telephone, monitor your work by computer, store and review computer files, and monitor you in an employee washroom or dressing room. These actions are not all that uncommon. Nearly 57 percent of Canadian companies have Internet-use policies restricting employees' personal use of the Internet.[53] Employees of the City of Vancouver are warned that their computer use is monitored, and a desktop agent icon of a spinning head reminds them that they are being watched.

Why do managers feel they must monitor what employees are doing? A big reason is that employees are hired to work, not to surf the web checking stock prices, placing bets at online casinos, or shopping for presents for family or friends. An Ipsos-Reid poll found Canadians spend 1.6 billion hours a year online at work for personal reasons, an average of 4.5 hours a week per employee.[54] That lost time represents a significant cost to businesses. Conservative estimates suggest that personal use of the Internet at work costs Canadian businesses more than $16 billion annually in lost productivity.[55]

Another reason that managers monitor employee email and computer use is that they do not want to risk being sued for creating a hostile workplace environment because of offensive messages or an inappropriate image displayed on a co-worker's computer screen. Concern about racial or sexual harassment is one of the reasons why companies might want to monitor or keep backup copies of all email. This electronic record can help establish what actually happened and can help managers react quickly.[56]

Finally, managers want to ensure that company secrets are not being leaked.[57] Although protecting intellectual property is important for all businesses, it is especially important in high-tech industries. Managers need to be certain that employees are not, even inadvertently, passing information on to others who could use that information to harm the company.

Even with the workplace monitoring that managers can do, Canadian employees do have some protection through the Criminal Code, which prohibits unauthorized interception of electronic communication. The Personal Information Protection and Electronic Documents Act, which went into effect in early 2004, gives employees some privacy protection, but it does not make workplace electronic monitoring illegal. Under existing laws, if an individual is aware of a corporate policy of surveillance and does not formally object, or remains at the job, the monitoring is acceptable.[58] Unionized employees may have a bit more privacy with respect to their computers. The Canada Labour Code requires employers operating under a collective agreement to disclose information about plans for technological change. This information might provide unions with an opportunity to bargain over electronic surveillance.

Because of the potentially serious costs, and given the fact that many jobs now entail work that involves using a computer, many companies are developing and enforcing workplace monitoring policies. The responsibility for workplace monitoring falls on managers, who must develop some type of viable workplace monitoring policy. What can managers do to maintain control in a way that is not demeaning to employees? They should develop a clear and unambiguous computer-use policy and make sure that every employee knows about it. For example, managers should tell employees upfront that their computer use may be monitored at any time and provide clear and specific guidelines as to what constitutes acceptable use of company email systems and the web. The Bank of Montreal blocks access to "some of the dubious sites that are high risk," such as Playboy.com and other pornographic sites. The bank has developed policies about appropriate and inappropriate use of the Internet, which are emailed to all employees several times a year.[59]

**EMPLOYEE THEFT** Would you be surprised to find out that up to 75 percent of Canadian organizations have reported experiencing employee theft and fraud?[60] It is a costly problem. Air Canada, which has run a campaign against employee theft, noted that the airline "is right in line with industry standards for employee theft, and that means as much as 9 percent of stock such as office supplies and on-board products is taken each year."[61] A 2008 Retail Council of Canada study found that 87 percent of small and medium-sized businesses experienced some sort of theft. Another study pegged the cost of employee theft for Canadian retail businesses at $3 billion, or 1.5 percent of all sales.[62]

**Employee theft** is defined as any unauthorized taking of company property by employees for their personal use.[63] It can range from embezzlement to fraudulent filing of expense reports to removing equipment, parts, software, and office supplies from company premises. While retail businesses have long faced serious potential losses from employee theft, loose financial controls at start-ups and small companies and the ready availability of information technology have made employee stealing an escalating problem in all kinds and sizes of organizations. Employee theft is a control issue. Managers need to educate themselves about this problem and be prepared to deal with it.[64]

Why do employees steal? The answer depends on whom you ask.[65] Experts in various fields—industrial security, criminology, clinical psychology—all have different perspectives. Industrial security people propose that people steal because the opportunity

**EXHIBIT 11-13** Control Measures for Deterring or Reducing Employee Theft or Fraud

| Feedforward | Concurrent | Feedback |
|---|---|---|
| Use careful prehiring screening. | Treat employees with respect and dignity. | Make sure employees know when theft or fraud has occurred—not naming names but letting people know this is not acceptable. |
| Establish specific policies defining theft and fraud and discipline procedures. | Openly communicate the costs of stealing. | Use the services of professional investigators. |
| Involve employees in writing policies. | Let employees know on a regular basis about their successes in preventing theft and fraud. | Redesign control measures. |
| Educate and train employees about the policies. | Use video surveillance equipment if conditions warrant. | Evaluate your organization's culture and the relationships of managers and employees. |
| Have professionals review your internal security controls. | Install "lock-out" options on computers, telephones, and email. | |
| | Use corporate hotlines for reporting incidents. | |
| | Set a good example. | |

presents itself through lax controls and favourable circumstances. Criminologists say it is because people have financial pressures (such as personal financial problems) or vice-based pressures (such as gambling debts). Clinical psychologists suggest that people steal because they can rationalize whatever they are doing as correct and appropriate behaviour ("everyone does it," "they had it coming," "this company makes enough money and they will never miss anything this small," "I deserve this for all that I put up with," and so forth).[66] Although each of these approaches provides compelling insights into employee theft and has been instrumental in program designs to deter it, unfortunately employees continue to steal.

What can managers do to deter or reduce employee theft or fraud? We can use the concepts of feedforward, concurrent, and feedback controls to identify actions managers can take.[67] Exhibit 11-13 summarizes several possible control measures.

## Customer Interactions

Every month, each local branch of Enterprise Rent-a-Car conducts telephone surveys with customers.[68] Each branch earns a ranking based on the percentage of its customers who say they were "completely satisfied" with their last Enterprise experience—a level of satisfaction referred to as "top box." Top box performance is important to Enterprise because completely satisfied customers are far more likely to be repeat customers. By using this service–quality index measure, employees' careers and financial aspirations are linked with the organizational goal of providing consistently superior service to each and every customer. Managers at Enterprise understand the connection between employees and customers, and the importance of controlling these interactions.

Customer service is probably the best area to see the link between planning and controlling. If a company proclaims customer service as one of its goals, it quickly and clearly becomes apparent whether or not that goal is being achieved by seeing how satisfied

**employee theft**
Any unauthorized taking of company property by employees for their personal use.

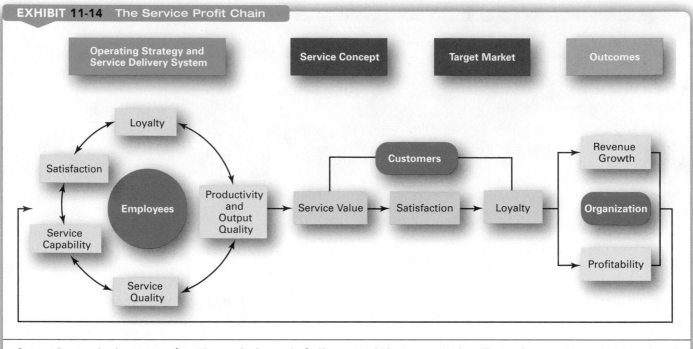

**EXHIBIT 11-14** The Service Profit Chain

One of the many ways in which L.L.Bean controls interactions with its customers is by providing outstanding customer service. Not only are the company's store staff and telephone order takers trained to handle all inquiries with exceptional courtesy and efficiency, but also every item purchased, from clothing to kayaks, is 100 percent guaranteed. Continuing a tradition of customer satisfaction that is almost 100 years old, L.L.Bean promises to accept returns for refund or replacement of "anything purchased from us at any time" if it is not completely satisfactory in every way.

customers are with their service. How can managers control the interactions between the goal and the outcome when it comes to customers? The concept of a service profit chain can help (see Exhibit 11-14).

The **service profit chain** is the service sequence from employees to customers to profit.[69] According to this concept, the company's strategy and service delivery system influences how employees serve customers—their attitudes, behaviours, and service capability. Service capability, in turn, enhances how productive employees are in providing service and the quality of that service. The level of employee service productivity and service quality influences customer perceptions of service value. When service value is high, it has a positive impact on customer satisfaction, which leads to customer loyalty. Customer loyalty, in turn, improves organizational revenue growth and profitability.

What does the concept of a service profit chain mean for managers? Managers who want to control customer interactions should work to create long-term and mutually beneficial relationships among the company, employees, and customers. How? By creating a work environment that not only enables employees to deliver high levels of quality service, but also makes them feel they are capable of delivering top-quality service. In such a service climate, employees are motivated to deliver superior service.

WestJet Airlines is a good example of the service profit chain in action. WestJet is the most consistently profitable Canadian airline, and its customers are fiercely loyal. This situation has been achieved because the company's operating strategy (hiring, training, rewards and recognition, teamwork, and so forth) is built around customer service. Employees consistently deliver outstanding service value to customers, and WestJet's customers reward the company by coming back. Through efficiently and effectively controlling these customer interactions, companies such as WestJet and Enterprise have succeeded.

Practise

# 11 Review and Apply

## Summary of Learning Objectives

 **What is control?** Control is the process of monitoring activities to ensure that they are being accomplished as planned and of correcting any significant deviations. Managers can measure a variety of performances, but the most frequently used ones are organizational productivity, organizational effectiveness, and industry rankings.

When Greg Stremlaw joined the Canadian Curling Association, he and the Board immediately changed the culture to run the nonprofit association like a business, while introducing financial controls to help turn the association's fortunes around.

 **What is the control process?** The control process is a three-step process: measuring actual performance, comparing actual performance against a standard, and taking managerial action to correct deviations or inadequate standards.

**11.3 When should controls be introduced?** Managers can implement controls before an activity begins (feedforward control), during the time the activity is going on (concurrent control), and after the activity has been completed (feedback control).

**11.4 What methods of control do managers use?** There are three different approaches to designing control systems: market, bureaucratic, and clan control. Market control emphasizes the use of external market mechanisms, such as price competition and relative market share, to establish the standards used in the control system. Bureaucratic control emphasizes organizational authority and relies on administrative rules, regulations, procedures, and policies. Under clan control, employee behaviours are regulated by the shared values, norms, traditions, rituals, beliefs, and other aspects of the organization's culture.

**service profit chain**
The service sequence from employees to customers to profit.

Control is often needed to improve organizational performance, as Greg Stremlaw found when he took over the CCA and had to shrink the association's large deficit.

**11.5 How do financial and information controls help managers monitor performance?** Financial ratio analysis allows managers to monitor how efficiently and profitably the organization uses its assets, debt, inventories, and the like. Budget analysis provides managers with quantitative standards against which to measure and compare resource consumption. Economic value added (EVA) is a tool that measures corporate and divisional performance, while market value added (MVA) measures the stock market's estimate of the value of a firm's past and expected capital investment projects. Information may be used both as a tool to help managers control other organizational activities and as an organizational area that managers need to control.

At the CCA, Greg Stremlaw uses traditional financial controls, as well as other measures, including the brand impressions and value produced by the CCA through sponsorship and the www.curling.ca platform.

**11.6 What are some current issues in control?** Important current issues in control include the balanced scorecard (looking at financial, customer, internal business process, and learning and growth assets), corporate governance, cross-cultural differences, workplace concerns, and customer interactions.

The CCA has a board of directors that looks after the interests of members. The primary duty of the CCA board is to "approve, monitor and provide guidance on the strategic planning process." The board also approves CCA's strategic plans, annual budget, and financial plans.

## SNAPSHOT SUMMARY

**What Is Control?**
Performance Standards
Measures of Organizational Performance
Why Is Control Important?

**The Control Process**
Measuring Performance
Comparing Performance Against Standard
Taking Managerial Action
Summary of Managerial Decisions

**When to Introduce Control**
Feedforward Control
Concurrent Control
Feedback Control

**Methods of Control**
Market Control
Bureaucratic Control
Clan Control

**Financial and Information Controls**
Traditional Financial Control Measures
Other Financial Control Measures
Information Controls

**Current Issues in Control**
Balanced Scorecard
Corporate Governance
Cross-Cultural Differences
Workplace Concerns
Customer Interactions

# MyManagementLab® Learning Resources

## Resources

▼ **Explore and enhance your understanding of key chapter topics through the following online resources:**

- Student PowerPoints
- Audio Summary of Chapter
- ROLLS
- CBC Videos for Part 5
- MySearchLab

▶ Visit the **Study Plan** area to test your progress with **Pre-Tests** and **Post-Tests**.

▼ **Build on your knowledge and practise real-world applications using the following online activities:**

## Interpret

- Opening Case Activity: Types of Control
- Review and Apply: Solutions to Interpret section questions and activities
- Glossary Flashcards

## Analyze

- Opening Case Activity: Controlling and Organizational Culture
- Review and Apply: Solutions to Analyze section questions and activities
- Self-Assessment Library

## Practise

- Opening Case Activity: Consequences of Lack of Controls
- Review and Apply: Solutions to Practice section questions and activities
- Decision Making Simulation: Controlling

# Interpret What You Have Read

1. What is the role of control in management?
2. What are three approaches to designing control systems?
3. Explain the source of an organization's culture and how that culture is maintained.
4. Describe how culture is transmitted to employees.
5. Name four methods managers can use to acquire information about actual organizational performance.
6. Contrast immediate and basic corrective action.
7. What are the advantages and disadvantages of feed-forward control?
8. Describe the financial control measures managers can use.
9. What can management do to implement a bench-marking best-practices program?
10. What challenges do managers of global organizations face with their control systems?

# Analyze What You Have Read

1. How are planning and control linked? Is the control function linked to the organizing and leading functions of management? Explain.
2. Why is feedback control the most popular type of control? Justify your response.
3. How could you use the concept of control in your own personal life? Be specific. (Think in terms of feedforward, concurrent, and feedback controls as well as controls for the different areas of your life.)
4. Why is it that what is measured is probably more critical to the control process than how it is measured?
5. When do electronic surveillance devices such as computers, video cameras, and telephone monitoring step over the line from "effective management controls" to "intrusions on employee rights"?
6. What would an organization have to do to change its dominant control approach from bureaucratic to clan? From clan to bureaucratic?
7. "Every individual employee in the organization plays a role in controlling work activities." Do you agree or do you think control is something that only managers are responsible for? Explain.

# Assess Your Skills

## HOW PROACTIVE AM I?

For each of the following statements, circle the level of agreement or disagreement that you personally feel:[70]

> 1 = Strongly Disagree   2 = Moderately Disagree   3 = Slightly Disagree   4 = Neither Agree nor Disagree
> 5 = Slightly Agree   6 = Moderately Agree   7 = Strongly Agree

1. I am constantly on the lookout for new ways to improve my life.   1 2 3 4 5 6 7
2. I feel driven to make a difference in my community, and maybe the world.   1 2 3 4 5 6 7
3. I tend to let others take the initiative to start new projects.   1 2 3 4 5 6 7
4. Wherever I have been, I have been a powerful force for constructive change.   1 2 3 4 5 6 7
5. I enjoy facing and overcoming obstacles to my ideas.   1 2 3 4 5 6 7
6. Nothing is more exciting than seeing my ideas turn into reality.   1 2 3 4 5 6 7
7. If I see something I don't like, I fix it.   1 2 3 4 5 6 7
8. No matter what the odds, if I believe in something I will make it happen.   1 2 3 4 5 6 7
9. I love being a champion for my ideas, even against others' opposition.   1 2 3 4 5 6 7
10. I excel at identifying opportunities.   1 2 3 4 5 6 7
11. I am always looking for better ways to do things.   1 2 3 4 5 6 7
12. If I believe in an idea, no obstacle will prevent me from making it happen.   1 2 3 4 5 6 7

13. I love to challenge the status quo.                1 2 3 4 5 6 7

14. When I have a problem, I tackle it head-on.         1 2 3 4 5 6 7

15. I am great at turning problems into opportunities.  1 2 3 4 5 6 7

16. I can spot a good opportunity long before others can. 1 2 3 4 5 6 7

17. If I see someone in trouble, I help out in any way I can. 1 2 3 4 5 6 7

**SCORING KEY**   Add up the numbers for each of your responses to get your total score.

## ANALYSIS AND INTERPRETATION

This instrument assesses proactive personality. Research finds that the proactive personality is positively associated with entrepreneurial intentions.

Your proactive personality score will range between 17 and 119. The higher your score, the stronger your proactive personality. High scores on this questionnaire suggest you have strong inclinations toward becoming an entrepreneur.

### More Self-Assessments

To learn more about your skills, abilities, and interests, take the following self-assessments on the MyManagementLab®:

- I.E.2.–What Time of Day Am I Most Productive?
- II.B.5.–How Good Am I at Disciplining Others?
- III.A.2.–How Willing Am I to Delegate?
- III.A.3.–How Good Am I at Giving Performance Feedback? (This exercise also appears in Chapter 7 on pages 208–209.)

# Practise What You Have Learned

## DILEMMA

Your parents have let you know they are expecting a big party for their twenty-fifth wedding anniversary and have put you in charge of planning it. Develop a timeline for carrying out the project and then identify ways to monitor progress toward getting the party planned. How will you know that your plans have been successful? At what critical points do you need to examine your plans to make sure that everything is on track?

## BECOMING A MANAGER

- Identify the types of controls you use in your own personal life and whether they are feedforward, concurrent, or feedback controls.
- When preparing for major class projects, identify some performance measures that you can use to help you determine whether or not the project is going as planned.
- Try to come up with some ways to improve your personal efficiency and effectiveness.

## DEVELOPING YOUR INTERPERSONAL SKILLS: PROVIDING FEEDBACK

### ABOUT THE SKILL

In this chapter, we introduced several suggestions for providing feedback. One of the more critical feedback sessions will occur when you, as a manager, are using feedback control to address performance issues.

### STEPS IN DEVELOPING THE SKILL

You can be more effective at providing feedback if you use the following 10 suggestions:[71]

1. **SCHEDULE THE FEEDBACK SESSION IN ADVANCE AND BE PREPARED.** One of the biggest mistakes you can make is to treat feedback control lightly. Simply calling in an employee and giving feedback that is not well organized serves little purpose for you or your employee. For feedback to be effective, you must plan ahead. Identify the issues you wish to address and cite specific examples to reinforce what you are saying. Set aside the time for the meeting with the employee. Make sure that what you do is done in private and can be completed without interruptions. That may mean closing your office door (if you have one), holding phone calls, and the like.

2. **PUT THE EMPLOYEE AT EASE.** Regardless of how you feel about the feedback, you must create a supportive climate for the employee. Recognize that giving and receiving feedback can be an emotional event, even when the feedback is positive. By putting your employee at ease, you begin to establish a supportive environment in which understanding can take place.

3. **MAKE SURE THE EMPLOYEE KNOWS THE PURPOSE OF THE FEEDBACK SESSION.** What is the purpose of the meeting?

That is something any employee will wonder. Clarifying what you are going to do sets the appropriate stage for what is to come.

4. **FOCUS ON SPECIFIC RATHER THAN GENERAL WORK BEHAVIOURS.** Feedback should be specific rather than general. General statements are vague and provide little useful information—especially if you are attempting to correct a problem.

5. **KEEP COMMENTS IMPERSONAL AND JOB-RELATED.** Feedback should be descriptive rather than judgmental or evaluative, especially when you are giving negative feedback. No matter how upset you are, keep the feedback job-related and never criticize someone personally because of an inappropriate action. You are censuring job-related behaviour, not the person.

6. **SUPPORT FEEDBACK WITH HARD DATA.** Tell your employee how you came to your conclusion about his or her performance. Hard data help your employees identify with specific behaviours. Identify the "things" that were done correctly and provide a detailed critique. If you do need to criticize, state the basis of your conclusion that a good job was not completed.

7. **DIRECT THE NEGATIVE FEEDBACK TOWARD WORK-RELATED BEHAVIOUR THAT THE EMPLOYEE CONTROLS.** Negative feedback should be directed toward work-related behaviour that the employee can do something about. Suggest what he or she can do to improve the situation. This practice helps take the sting out of the criticism and offers guidance to an individual who understands the problem but does not know how to resolve it.

8. **LET THE EMPLOYEE SPEAK.** Get the employee's perceptions about what you are saying, especially if you are addressing a problem. Of course, you are not looking for excuses, but you need to be empathetic to the employee and hear his or her side. Letting the employee speak involves your employee and just might provide information you were unaware of.

9. **ENSURE THAT THE EMPLOYEE HAS A CLEAR AND FULL UNDERSTANDING OF THE FEEDBACK.** Feedback must be concise and complete enough that your employee clearly and fully understands what you have said. Consistent with active listening techniques, have your employee rephrase the content of your feedback to check whether it fully captures your meaning.

10. **DETAIL A FUTURE PLAN OF ACTION.** Performing does not stop simply because feedback occurred. Good performance must be reinforced and new performance goals set. However, when performance deficiencies have been identified, time must be devoted to helping your employee develop a detailed, step-by-step plan to correct the situation. This plan includes what has to be done, when, and how you will monitor the activities. Offer whatever assistance you can to help the employee, but make it clear that it is the employee, not you, who has to make the corrections.

## PRACTISING THE SKILL

This exercise can help you learn how managers could use feedback control when starting a project. Think of a skill you would like to acquire or improve, or a habit you would like to break. Perhaps you would like to learn a foreign language, start exercising, quit smoking, ski better, or spend less. For the purpose of this exercise, assume you have three months to make a start on your project and all the necessary funds. Draft a plan of action that outlines what you need to do, when you need to do it, and how you will know that you have successfully completed each step of your plan. Be realistic, but do not set your sights too low either. Review your plan. What outside help or resources will you require? How will you get them? Add these to your plan. Ask someone to follow the steps in your plan. What modifications did the person suggest you make, if any?

# Team Exercises

## 3BL: THE TRIPLE BOTTOM LINE

Germany's Siemens has been doing business in Canada for 100 years and recently made a radical change to move away from nuclear energy to focus on green power, sustainable cities, and health care.[72] The move started when the German government announced it would stop its nuclear power plants, all built by Siemens. The German action was a response to the 2011 nuclear disaster in Fukushima, Japan, which focused attention on the high risk posed by nuclear power. In Canada, Siemens made a $20 million investment in a wind turbine blade manufacturing facility in Tillsonburg, Ontario.[73] Recently Siemens signed an agreement with the Ontario government to develop projects such as smart-grid electric vehicles, wind and solar power, water treatment, and energy conservation.[74] Siemens has developed a model for Canadian cities to enhance their environmental performance. The city finances the necessary energy-saving measures, with the savings in energy and operational costs guaranteed by Siemens. To date, more than 6500 buildings have been modernized with savings of $2 billion and a carbon reduction of 9 million tonnes.[75]

Siemens is an example of an industry giant working collaboratively with Canadian municipal governmental partners to achieve sustainability in green energy. Vancouver recently adopted an "EcoDensity Charter," which focuses on limiting sprawl, reducing the carbon footprint, and expanding housing options.[76]

### THINKING STRATEGICALLY ABOUT 3BL

Companies like Siemens that are looking at green power instead of nuclear energy might put in place several measures of energy performance such as pollution prevention, process safety, employee health and safety, and customer perception targets. These measures provide them with a way of evaluating their move away from nuclear energy. What kind of measures could you put in place to gauge community perceptions concerning Siemens' switch to green power? How could the Canadian nuclear industry convince Siemens to continue using nuclear energy?

## BE THE CONSULTANT: APPLYING FEEDFORWARD, CONCURRENT, AND FEEDBACK CONTROLS

You will be assigned one or more of the following tasks:

1. You are a consultant to a manager of a small retail clothing store. Over the past six months, the manager has noticed that a significant amount of inventory has gone missing. The manager is not sure whether it is employees or customers who are taking things from the store. The manager has a somewhat limited budget, but wants to know what possibilities there are for controlling inventory. You have agreed to present a set of recommendations, identifying feedforward, concurrent, and feedback mechanisms that the manager might use.

2. You are a student in a business program at a local college or university. Several of your professors have expressed an interest in developing some specific controls to minimize opportunities for students to cheat on homework assignments and exams. Because you find cheating offensive, you and some other students have volunteered to write a report outlining some suggestions that might be used to control possible cheating (1) before it happens, (2) while in-class exams or assignments are being completed, and (3) after it has happened.

3. Devise control measures for each of the tasks involved in delivering a beverage to a Starbucks customer. Determine whether the measure is a feedforward, concurrent, or a feedback control.

Be prepared to present your suggestions before the rest of the class.

# Business Cases

## FACEBOOK

The "Hacker Way" is Facebook's organizational culture, and it originates with CEO Mark Zuckerberg. The culture is equal parts egalitarian, risk-taking, collaborative, innovative, driven and irreverent.[77] In 2008, Facebook started a process called Bootcamp to encapsulate their culture for new employees. Facebook grows so rapidly—more than 1000 employees have been hired since January 2011—that Bootcamp provides a hands-on glimpse into the company's values and culture.

Bootcamp is a six-week journey for every engineering hire, no matter how senior, which includes one-on-one sessions with mentors and in-depth talks from senior engineers. New hires unlearn old habits as they work on real software bugs right from day one. The program helps show them the ropes and initiates them into Facebook's urgent, do-it-now culture.[78] Joel Seligstein, Facebook's Bootcamp "Yoda," describes the program as learning "to think about how to attack challenges and how to meet people."[79] The result of Bootcamp is a culture that teaches employees how to act and react, how to tackle problems independently, and how to take risks to keep Facebook growing rapidly and successfully.

One new recruit was working on a software bug and crashed part of Facebook. But the company culture is very tolerant of failure, as evidenced by their "Move Fast and Break Things" motto. Slogans like "We Hack Therefore We Are" are plastered everywhere around the office. Bootcamp helps keep Facebook nimble, and the culture of constant change helps provide its competitive advantage over rivals. It is not uncommon for employees to walk right up to Mark Zuckerberg to talk about an engineering fix or a company problem. The organizational structure is kept purposefully flat, so that Zuckerberg remains hands-on with Facebook. Periodically, Facebook has all-night "Hackathons," where engineers try out new software ideas that often become company products.[80]

# CHAPTER 12 Managing Change

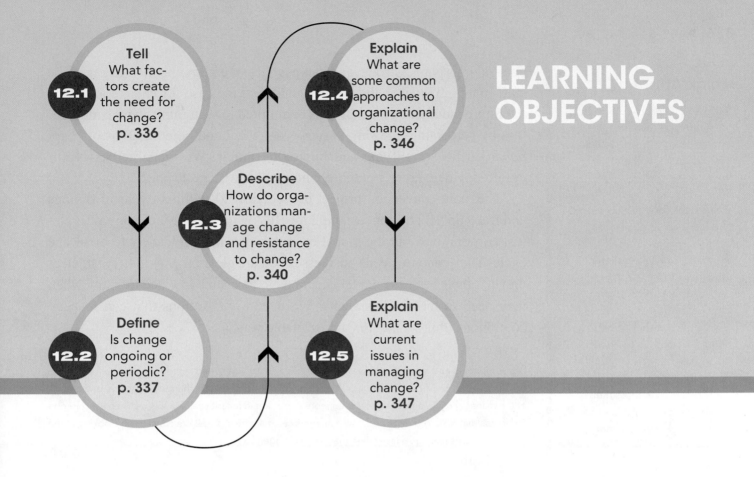

## LEARNING OBJECTIVES

**Tell** What factors create the need for change? p. 336
**12.1**

**Explain** What are some common approaches to organizational change? p. 346
**12.4**

**Describe** How do organizations manage change and resistance to change? p. 340
**12.3**

**Define** Is change ongoing or periodic? p. 337
**12.2**

**Explain** What are current issues in managing change? p. 347
**12.5**

Fiona MacLeod has more than 20 years of international change management experience. Most recently, she was responsible for restructuring the US convenience retail business for London-based British Petroleum (BP). BP is the third largest global energy company and one of six "big oil" companies, with vertically integrated operations to drill for, refine, and market petroleum products.[1]

MacLeod's project followed three previous unsuccessful initiatives to improve efficiency. She needed to put a change in place that would last, so she started by clarifying the US business purpose: a secure position in the marketplace for years to come. Her plan was to convert BP's 1000 US retail outlets from company-owned to franchises, with a revamped brand and new marketing programs. Selling the stores would cut 10 000 jobs at BP, without any guarantee that the new franchise owners would hire current BP employees. The conversion would take approximately 18 months, so keeping staff motivated to reduce overhead and improve operations was a huge challenge, given their uncertainty about their future employment prospects. MacLeod noted that "our people were displaying the classic signs of change fatigue.... People were very jaded" and lacked confidence that they could make things better.[2]

MacLeod's team asked for employee feedback on the business case for reorganization, and communicated monthly performance objectives and

## Think About It

MacLeod is surprised by how many change management programs consume massive resources but ultimately fail to solve the problems for which they were created.[6] The reason for this failure is the focus on "big splashes" instead of continuous improvement. Like a dieter who loses weight and then later puts it all back on, if change is not sustainable than it will not stick. What should leaders do to understand the change that is required in their organization? How can leaders then develop a long-term plan for change and work to keep the program on track?

cost-savings plans. Strong leadership and clear communication engaged the staff to a high level as they truly understood the case for change and what the future would look like. BP was committed to sustaining change momentum by celebrating the simple successes. MacLeod noted that "people got rewarded for simplifying and improving things. We made heroes of our day-to-day deliverers, not those who make the biggest splash."[3]

The store conversion project produced $700 million a year in savings and freed up $1.2 billion in capital for BP.[4] Ultimately, MacLeod said, "Not just corporations, but the global economy depends on leaders to break the cycle. The economy needs businesses that are clear on why they exist, clear on what their business model is, and have measures in place to know when they need to make adjustments. We need organizations that can manage continuous improvement in a predictable way."[5]

Big companies and small businesses, universities and colleges, and governments at all levels are being forced to significantly change the way they do things. Although change has always been a part of the manager's job, it has become even more important in recent years. In this chapter, we describe the forces that lead to change and how managers can manage change. We conclude by looking at the critical concerns managers face when managing change today.

## FORCES FOR CHANGE

**Tell**
**12.1** What factors create the need for change?

If it were not for change, the manager's job would be relatively easy. Planning would be simple because tomorrow would be no different from today. The issue of effective organizational design would also be solved, because the environment would be free from uncertainty and there would be no need to adapt. Similarly, decision making would be dramatically streamlined—the outcome of each alternative could be predicted with almost certain accuracy. The manager's job would, indeed, be simplified if, for example, competitors did not introduce new products or services, if customers did not demand new and improved products, if government regulations were never modified, or if employees' needs never changed. But that is not the way it is. Change is an organizational reality.[7] Managing change is an integral part of every manager's job. In Chapter 2, we pointed out the external and internal forces that constrain managers. These same forces also bring about the need for change. Let us look briefly at these forces.

### External Forces

*Are there external forces that might suggest to you that your college or university could think about doing things differently?*

The external forces that create the need for change come from various sources. In recent years, the *marketplace* has affected companies such as Yahoo! with ever-intensifying competition from Google, MySpace, and Ask Jeeves. These companies constantly adapt to changing consumer desires as they develop new search capabilities. Target's entry into the Canadian market will have a major impact on existing competitors, who must consider change as a way of adapting to new competition.

*Government laws and regulations* are a frequent impetus for change. For example, the Canadian Generally Accepted Accounting Principles (GAAP) have been replaced by the International Financial Reporting Standards (IFRS). This change requires Canadian publicly accountable companies to change the way they disclose financial information and enact corporate governance to allow for greater transparency in financial reporting.

*Technology* also creates the need for change. For example, technological improvements in diagnostic equipment have created significant economies of scale for hospitals. Assembly-line technology in other industries is changing dramatically as organizations replace human labour with robots. In the greeting card industry, email and the Internet have changed the way people exchange greeting cards. The move from locally installed to web-based software and computing will create a major shift for companies. The cloud will provide lower costs, higher efficiency, and greater innovation, but may increase security concerns.[8]

The fluctuation in *labour markets* also forces managers to change. Organizations that need certain kinds of employees must change their human resource management activities to attract and retain skilled employees in the areas of greatest need. For example, health care organizations facing severe nursing shortages have had to change the way they schedule work hours.

*Economic changes,* of course, affect almost all organizations. For example, global recessionary pressures force organizations to become more cost-efficient. But even in a strong economy, uncertainties about interest rates, federal budget deficits, and currency exchange rates create conditions that may force organizations to change.

## Internal Forces

In addition to the external forces just described, internal forces also create the need for change. These internal forces tend to originate primarily from the internal operations of the organization or from the impact of external changes.

A redefinition or modification of an organization's *strategy* often introduces a variety of changes. For instance, when British Petroleum (BP) struggled to salvage its reputation after the devastating Gulf of Mexico oil spill in 2010, safety and risk management became a major focal point in their corporate strategy. Previously their strategy had a much smaller 3BL component, but with the need to repair its image, BP acted quickly and sold off major assets to pay for the Gulf cleanup.[9]

An organization's *workforce* is rarely static. Its composition changes in terms of age, education, ethnic background, sex, and so forth. Take, for example, an organization in which a large number of older executives, for financial reasons, decide to continue working instead of retiring. There might be a need to restructure jobs in order to retain and motivate younger managers. The compensation and benefits system might also need to be adapted to reflect the needs of this older workforce.

The introduction of new *equipment* represents another internal force for change. Employees may have their jobs redesigned, need to undergo training on how to operate the new equipment, or be required to establish new interaction patterns within their work groups.

Finally, *employee attitudes* such as job dissatisfaction may lead to increased absenteeism, more voluntary resignations, and even labour strikes. Such events often lead to changes in management policies and practices.

## TWO VIEWS OF THE CHANGE PROCESS

For years Yahoo!—which helped give birth to the commercial Internet in 1994—dominated the Internet services market.[10] By 2005, however, the company started to lose its competitive edge.

The company, well known for its banner and video ads, was targeted by both Google (who bought online ad firm DoubleClick) and Microsoft (who bought digital marketing firm aQuantive). Yahoo! tried to make a deal with Facebook but was not successful, while Google bought the leading video-sharing site YouTube. Yahoo!'s response to competition has been comparatively slow, although it did buy 80 percent of advertising network RightMedia in April 2007.[11]

**12.2**

**Define**
Is change ongoing or periodic?

**Think About It**

How does change happen in organizations? What happens if companies do not recognize change as a constant process, as Yahoo! failed to do?

Because Yahoo! delayed its response to competition from Google, it faced even bigger challenges. In 2007, Google was worth $158 billion on the stock market, while Yahoo! was valued at $42 billion. Yahoo struggled to compete with Google in social media, so formed partnerships with Facebook and Twitter. Yahoo has since changed gears and entered a search agreement with Microsoft, moving from being the biggest search engine to a hub content provider.[12]

We can use two very different metaphors to describe the change process.[13] One metaphor envisions the organization as a large ship crossing calm waters. The ship's captain and crew know exactly where they are going because they have made the trip many times before. Change comes in the form of an occasional storm, a brief distraction in an otherwise calm and predictable trip. In the other metaphor, the organization is seen as a small raft navigating a raging river with uninterrupted white-water rapids. Aboard the raft are half a dozen people who have never worked together before, who are totally unfamiliar with the river, who are unsure of their eventual destination, and who, as if things were not bad enough, are travelling at night. In the white-water rapids metaphor, change is an expected and natural state, and managing change is a continuous process. These two metaphors present very different approaches to understanding and responding to change. Let us take a closer look at each one.

## The Calm Waters Metaphor

Up until the late 1980s, the calm waters metaphor more or less described the situation that managers faced. This metaphor is best illustrated by the three-step description of the change process developed by Kurt Lewin, often recognized as the founder of social psychology (see Exhibit 12-1).[14]

According to Lewin, successful change can be planned and requires *unfreezing* the status quo, *changing* to a new state, and *refreezing* to make the change permanent. The status quo can be considered an equilibrium state. To move from this equilibrium, unfreezing is necessary. Unfreezing can be thought of as preparing for the needed change. It can be achieved by increasing the *driving forces,* which are forces that drive change and direct behaviour away from the status quo; decreasing the *restraining forces,* which are forces that resist change and push behaviour toward the status quo; or combining the two approaches. Driving forces include the environmental changes discussed earlier, but could also be the introduction of new competitors or technologies. Driving forces create the necessary urgency for change, but are often not enough to overcome employee resistance to change without strategies to reduce the restraining forces. Employee involvement would be one example of a strategy geared toward enhancing organizational change efforts.[15]

Once unfreezing is done, the change itself can be implemented. However, merely introducing change does not ensure that the change will take hold. The new situation needs to

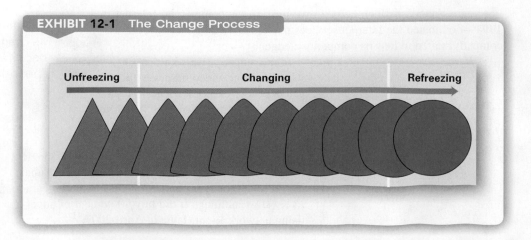

**EXHIBIT 12-1    The Change Process**

Unfreezing          Changing          Refreezing

be *refrozen* so that it can be sustained over time. Unless this last step is taken, there is a strong chance that the change will be short-lived as employees revert back to the old equilibrium state—that is, the old ways of doing things. The objective of refreezing, then, is to stabilize the new situation by reinforcing the new behaviours.

Note how Lewin's three-step process treats change simply as a break in the organization's equilibrium state. The status quo has been disturbed, and change is necessary to establish a new equilibrium state. However, a calm waters environment is not what most managers face today.[16]

## The White-Water Rapids Metaphor

The white-water rapids metaphor is consistent with our discussion of uncertain and dynamic environments in Chapters 2 and 3. It is also consistent with a world that is increasingly dominated by information, ideas, and knowledge.[17] We can see how the metaphor applies to Microsoft, which is currently facing an uncertain and dynamic environment after dominating the software industry for many years.

To get a feeling of what managing change might be like when you have to continuously manoeuvre in uninterrupted and uncertain rapids, consider attending a college or university that has the following rules: Courses vary in length. Unfortunately, when you sign up, you do not know how long a course will run. It might go for 2 weeks or 30 weeks. Furthermore, the instructor can end a course any time he or she wants, with no prior warning. If that is not bad enough, the length of the class changes each time it meets: Sometimes the class lasts 20 minutes; other times it runs for 3 hours. The time of the next class meeting is set by the instructor during this class. There is one more thing. All exams are unannounced, so you have to be ready for a test at any time. To succeed in this type of environment, you would have to be incredibly flexible and able to respond quickly to changing conditions. Students who are overly structured, slow to respond, or uncomfortable with change would not survive.

Growing numbers of managers are coming to accept that their jobs are very much like what students would face in such a college or university. The stability and predictability of the calm waters metaphor do not exist. Disruptions in the status quo are not occasional and temporary, and they are not followed by a return to calm waters. Many managers never get out of the rapids. They face constant change, bordering on chaos.

Is the white-water rapids metaphor an exaggeration? No! Although you would expect this type of chaotic and dynamic environment in high-tech industries, even organizations in non-high-tech industries are faced with constant change.

To learn about your response to working in a changing workplace, see *Assess Your Skills—How Well Do I Respond to Turbulent Change?* on pages 354–355 at the end of the chapter.

## Putting the Two Views in Perspective

Does *every* manager face a world of constant and chaotic change? No, but the number who do not is dwindling. Managers in such businesses as telecommunications, computer software, and women's clothing have long confronted a world of white-water rapids. These managers used to envy their counterparts in industries such as banking, utilities, oil exploration, publishing, and air transportation, where the environment was historically more stable and predictable. However, those days of stability and predictability are long gone!

Today, any organization that treats change as an occasional disturbance in an otherwise calm and stable world runs a great risk. Too much is changing too fast for an organization or its managers to be complacent. It is no longer business as usual. Managers must be ready to efficiently and effectively manage the changes facing their organizations or their work areas. Nevertheless, managers have to be certain that change is the right thing to do at any given time.

When Dr. George Saleh switched his medical practice to a digital paperless system, the initial results were chaotic. After a few months, however, Dr. Saleh found himself seeing the same number of patients in less time, reducing his secretarial expenses, and being reimbursed by insurance companies in days instead of months. He can access patient records from home or the hospital, search his patient database to find out who is taking which drug, and spend time asking patients important questions. The new system "has made me a better doctor," he says. "It has changed the way I work every day."

## MANAGING CHANGE

**12.3** **Describe** How do organizations manage change and resistance to change?

BP's Head of Safety and Operations, Mark Bly, led a four-month independent investigation featuring a team of over 50 technical and other specialists drawn from inside BP and externally. The subsequent report found no single cause for the explosion and fire that killed 11 people and led to the Gulf of Mexico oil spill in 2010.[18]

BP's Group Chief Executive Robert (Bob) Dudley implemented all the recommendations in an effort to improve the safety of its operations. "It will be incumbent on everyone at BP to embrace and implement the changes necessary to ensure that a tragedy like this can never happen again," Dudley said.[19]

> **Think About It**
>
> What industry changes might come from BP's report on the causes of the oil spill?

### What Is Organizational Change?

Most managers, at one point or another, will have to make changes in some aspects of their workplace. We classify these changes as **organizational change**—any alteration of people, structure, or technology. Organizational changes often need someone to act as a catalyst and assume the responsibility for managing the change process—that is, a **change agent**. Who can be change agents?

We assume that changes are initiated and coordinated by a manager within the organization. However, the change agent could be a nonmanager—for example, a change specialist from the HR department or even an outside consultant with expertise in change implementation. For major system-wide changes, an organization often hires outside consultants to provide advice and assistance. Because they are from the outside, they offer an objective perspective that insiders may lack. However, outside consultants are usually at a disadvantage because they have a limited understanding of the organization's history, culture, operating procedures, and people. Outside consultants are also likely to initiate more drastic change than insiders would (which can be either a benefit or a disadvantage) because they do not have to live with the repercussions after the change is implemented. In contrast, internal managers who act as change agents may be more thoughtful, but possibly overcautious, because they must live with the consequences of their decisions.

As change agents, managers are motivated to initiate change because they are committed to improving their organization's performance. Initiating change involves identifying what types of changes might be needed and putting the change process in motion. But managing organizational change has another key aspect. Managers must manage employee resistance to change. What types of organizational change might managers need to make, and how do managers deal with resistance to change?

### Types of Change

What *can* a manager change? The manager's options fall into three categories: structure, technology, and people (see Exhibit 12-2). Changing *structure* includes any alteration in authority relations, coordination mechanisms, employee empowerment, job redesign, or similar structural variables. Changing *technology* encompasses modifications in the way work is performed or the methods and equipment that are used. Changing *people* refers to changes in employee attitudes, expectations, perceptions, and behaviour.

**CHANGING STRUCTURE** We discussed organizational structure issues in Chapter 5. Managers' organizing responsibilities in the sphere of structure include such activities as choosing the organization's formal design, allocating authority, and determining the degree of formalization. Once those structural decisions have been made, however, they are not final. Changing conditions or changing strategies brings about the need to make structural changes.

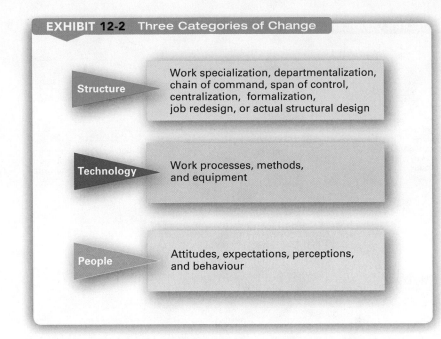

**EXHIBIT 12-2** Three Categories of Change

**Structure** → Work specialization, departmentalization, chain of command, span of control, centralization, formalization, job redesign, or actual structural design

**Technology** → Work processes, methods, and equipment

**People** → Attitudes, expectations, perceptions, and behaviour

What options does a manager have for changing structure? The manager has the same ones we introduced in our discussion of organizational structure and design. A few examples should make this clear. Recall from Chapter 5 that an organization's structure is defined in terms of work specialization, departmentalization, chain of command, span of control, centralization and decentralization, and formalization. Managers can alter one or more of these *structural elements.*

Another option would be to make major changes in the actual *structural design.* For example, the design change might involve a shift from a functional to a product structure or the creation of a project structure design. The Department of Fisheries and Oceans (DFO) has successfully used co-management in the Atlantic region, with management teams featuring representatives from industry, key stakeholders, and the broader community.[20] Some government agencies and private organizations are looking to new organizational ventures, forming public–private partnerships (P3s) to deal with change. BC's Canada Line, a rail-based rapid transit line built between Vancouver International Airport and downtown Vancouver before the 2010 Olympic Winter Games, was the first BC P3 project to launch. These partnerships are adept at reducing risk and obtaining better long-term financing.

**CHANGING TECHNOLOGY** Managers can also change the technology used to convert inputs into outputs. This type of change generally involves the introduction of new equipment, tools, or methods; automation (replacing certain tasks done by people with machines); or computerization.

**CHANGING PEOPLE** Changing people—changing their attitudes, expectations, perceptions, and behaviours—is not easy. Yet, for over 30 years now, academic researchers and actual managers have been interested in finding ways for individuals and groups within organizations to work together more effectively. The term **organizational development (OD)**, although occasionally used to refer to all types of change in an organization, essentially describes techniques or programs that are meant to change people and the nature and

Interpret

---

**organizational change**
Any alteration of people, structure, or technology in an organization.

**change agent**
Someone who acts as a catalyst and assumes the responsibility for managing the change process.

**organizational development (OD)**
Techniques or programs meant to change people and the nature and quality of interpersonal work relationships.

**EXHIBIT 12-3** Organizational Development Techniques

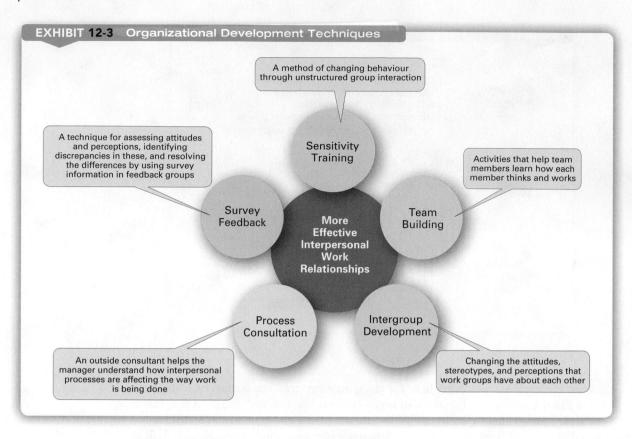

quality of interpersonal work relationships.[21] The most popular OD techniques are described in Exhibit 12-3. The common thread in these techniques is that each seeks to bring about changes in the organization's people. For example, executives at Scotiabank, Canada's second-largest bank, knew that the success of a new customer sales and service strategy depended on changing employee attitudes and behaviours. Managers used different OD techniques during the strategic change including team building, survey feedback, and intergroup development. One indicator of how well these techniques worked in getting people to change was that every branch in Canada implemented the new strategy on or ahead of schedule.[22]

## Making Change Happen Successfully

When changes are needed, who makes them happen? Who manages them? Although you may think change is the responsibility of top managers, actually managers at *all* organizational levels are involved in the change process. Employees may not be aware of all the external driving forces for change, which means that managers must inform them about changes in competition, consumer preferences, government regulations and other aspects of the external environment. Employees who are aware that the company is facing adversity are more likely to change their habits to help transform the situation.[23]

Even with the involvement of all levels of managers in change efforts, change processes do not always work the way they should. In fact, a global study of organizational change concludes that "Hundreds of managers from scores of US and European companies [are] satisfied with their operating prowess . . . [but] dissatisfied with their ability to implement change."[24] One of the reasons change fails is that managers do not really know how to introduce change in organizations. Professor John Kotter of Harvard Business School identifies a number of places where managers make mistakes when leading change. These mistakes are illustrated in Exhibit 12-4 on page 343. We should also note that recent research emphasizes the need in change processes to manage the "hard stuff" as well as the "soft" or people issues in order to be successful.[25]

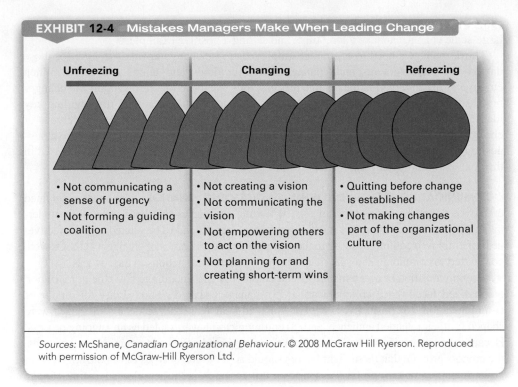

**EXHIBIT 12-4  Mistakes Managers Make When Leading Change**

| Unfreezing | Changing | Refreezing |
| --- | --- | --- |
| • Not communicating a sense of urgency<br>• Not forming a guiding coalition | • Not creating a vision<br>• Not communicating the vision<br>• Not empowering others to act on the vision<br>• Not planning for and creating short-term wins | • Quitting before change is established<br>• Not making changes part of the organizational culture |

*Sources:* McShane, *Canadian Organizational Behaviour.* © 2008 McGraw Hill Ryerson. Reproduced with permission of McGraw-Hill Ryerson Ltd.

How can managers make change happen successfully? Managers can increase the likelihood of making change happen successfully in three ways. First, they should focus on making the organization ready for change. Exhibit 12-5 summarizes the characteristics of organizations that are ready for change.

Second, managers need to understand their own role in the change process. Managers facilitate change by creating a simple, compelling statement of the need for change; communicating constantly and honestly throughout the process; getting as much employee participation as possible; respecting employees' apprehension about the change but encouraging them to be flexible; removing those who resist but only after all possible attempts have been

**EXHIBIT 12-5  Characteristics of Change-Capable Organizations**

- *Link the present and the future.* Think of work as more than an extension of the past; think about future opportunities and issues, and factor them into today's decisions.

- *Make learning a way of life.* Change-friendly organizations excel at knowledge sharing and management.

- *Actively support and encourage day-to-day improvements and changes.* Successful change can come from the small changes as well as the big ones.

- *Ensure diverse teams.* Diversity ensures that things won't be done the way they are always done.

- *Encourage mavericks.* Since their ideas and approaches are outside the mainstream, mavericks can help bring about radical change.

- *Shelter breakthroughs.* Change-friendly organizations have found ways to protect those breakthrough ideas.

- *Integrate technology.* Use technology to implement changes.

- *Build and deepen trust.* People are more likely to support changes when the organization's culture is trusting and managers have credibility and integrity.

made to get their commitment to the change; aiming for short-term change successes since large-scale change can take a long time; and setting a positive example.[26]

Third, managers need to encourage employees to be change agents—to look for those day-to-day improvements and changes that individuals and teams can make. When employees are involved in the change process, they are more likely to support the changes required. Employees also have the front-line knowledge that is crucial to providing key ideas. For example, a recent study of organizational change found that 77 percent of changes at the work-group level were reactions to a specific, current problem or to a suggestion from someone outside the work group; and 68 percent of those changes occurred in the course of employees' day-to-day work.[27]

**COMMUNICATING EFFECTIVELY WHEN UNDERGOING CHANGE**  One study examined employee communications programs in 10 leading companies that had successfully undertaken major restructuring programs.[28] Eight factors were found to be related to the effectiveness of employee communications in these companies during times of change: (1) CEOs were committed to communication; (2) management matched their actions to their words; (3) two-way communication between managers and employees was encouraged; (4) the organization emphasized face-to-face communication; (5) managers shared responsibility for employee communication; (6) positive ways were found to deal with bad news; (7) messages were shaped for their intended audience; and (8) communication was treated as an ongoing process. Because the companies studied came from a variety of industries and organizational settings, the authors propose that these eight factors should apply to many types of organizations.

Perhaps the most important lesson from this research is that employees facing change need to be told what is happening and why, in very direct language, in order to reduce their fears. Good communication makes the process of change go more smoothly.

**GLOBAL ORGANIZATIONAL DEVELOPMENT**  Much of what we know about global organizational development (OD) practices has come from North American research. However, managers need to recognize that some OD techniques, although effective in North American organizations, may not be appropriate for organizations or organizational divisions based in other countries.[29] For example, a study of OD interventions showed that "multirater (survey) feedback as practised in the United States is not embraced in Taiwan" because the cultural value of "saving face is simply more powerful than the value of receiving feedback from subordinates."[30] What is the lesson for managers? Before using the same techniques to implement behavioural changes, especially across different countries, managers need to be sure that they have taken into account cultural characteristics and whether the techniques "make sense for the local culture."

## Managing Resistance to Change

Change can be a threat to people in an organization. Organizations can build up inertia that motivates people to resist changing their status quo, even though change might be beneficial. Why do people resist change and what can be done to minimize their resistance?

**WHY PEOPLE RESIST CHANGE**  Resistance to change is well documented.[31] Why *do* people resist change? An individual is likely to resist change for the following reasons: uncertainty, habit, concern over personal loss, team dynamics, and the belief that the change is not in the organization's best interest.[32]

Change replaces the known with ambiguity and uncertainty. When you finish school, you will be leaving an environment where you know what is expected of you to join an organization where things are uncertain. Employees in organizations are faced with similar uncertainty and sometimes fear what they do not know. For example, when quality control methods based on sophisticated statistical models are introduced into manufacturing plants, many quality control inspectors have to learn new methods. Some inspectors may fear they will be unable to do so and might, therefore, develop a negative attitude toward the change or behave poorly if required to use those new methods.

Another cause of resistance is that we do things out of habit. Every day, when you go to school or work, you probably go the same way. If you are like most people, you find a single route and use it regularly. Human beings are creatures of

*How would you feel if your company, two years after you started there, changed the software you used to enter your contract and sales information?*

habit. Life is complex enough—we do not want to have to consider the full range of options for the hundreds of decisions we make every day. To cope with this complexity, we rely on habits or programmed responses. When confronted with change, this tendency to respond in our accustomed ways becomes a source of resistance. Employees need to be forced out of their comfort zones when their habits are no longer organizationally appropriate.[33]

The third cause of resistance is the fear of losing something already possessed. Change threatens the investment you have already made in the status quo. The more people have invested in the current system, the more they resist change. Why? They fear the loss of status, money, authority, friendships, personal convenience, or other economic benefits that they value. This factor helps explain why older employees tend to resist change more than younger employees. Older employees have generally invested more in the current system and thus have more to lose by changing.

Team dynamics such as norms and values may also conflict with the organizational changes needed, and the behaviours of the members will serve to discourage individuals from embracing the change.[34]

A final cause of resistance is a person's belief that the change is incompatible with the goals and interests of the organization. An employee who believes that a proposed new job procedure will reduce product quality or productivity can be expected to resist the change.

**TECHNIQUES FOR REDUCING RESISTANCE**  When managers see resistance to change as dysfunctional, they can choose from a variety of actions to deal with it.[35] Exhibit 12-6 shows how to manage resistance at the unfreezing, changing, and refreezing stages. Actions include communicating the reasons for change, getting input from employees, choosing the timing of change carefully, and showing management support for the change process. Providing support to employees to deal with the stress of the change is also important. The actions a manager chooses depend on the type and source of the resistance. In general, resistance is likely to be lower if managers involve people in the change, offer training where needed, and are open to revisions once the change has been implemented. For more suggestions on reducing resistance, see *Developing Your Interpersonal Skills—Managing Resistance to Change* on page 356 at the end of the chapter.

Analyze

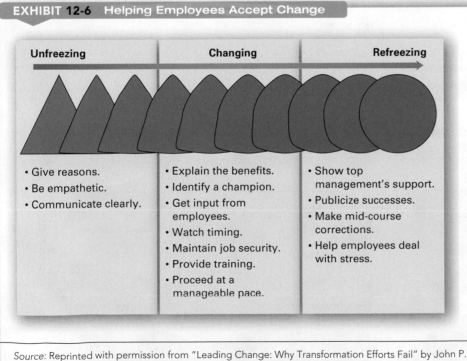

**EXHIBIT 12-6  Helping Employees Accept Change**

| Unfreezing | Changing | Refreezing |
|---|---|---|
| • Give reasons.<br>• Be empathetic.<br>• Communicate clearly. | • Explain the benefits.<br>• Identify a champion.<br>• Get input from employees.<br>• Watch timing.<br>• Maintain job security.<br>• Provide training.<br>• Proceed at a manageable pace. | • Show top management's support.<br>• Publicize successes.<br>• Make mid-course corrections.<br>• Help employees deal with stress. |

*Source:* Reprinted with permission from "Leading Change: Why Transformation Efforts Fail" by John P. Kotter. *Harvard Business Review*, March 1995. Copyright © 1995 by Harvard Business Publishing; all rights reserved..

**12.4** Explain What are some common approaches to organizational change?

# COMMON APPROACHES TO ORGANIZATIONAL CHANGE

Change occurs daily in organizations. There are many common approaches to organizational change, but action research and appreciative inquiry are two of the leading approaches.[36]

## Action Research

Kurt Lewin's action research approach has a problem-solving view that change is based on changing employee attitudes and behaviours along with collecting data to diagnose the organizational problems in more detail. This approach relies on Lewin's earlier discussion on *unfreezing* the status quo, *changing* to a new state, and *refreezing* to make the change permanent.

Typically an outside consultant is the original change agent. Employees are highly involved in data collection and analysis, and the nature and timing of the change are determined. Once the change is introduced, organizational and team systems are then redesigned to support the refreezing process. Action research is highly participative and employees work with the consultant to understand the changes required and build commitment.[37] Exhibit 12-7 illustrates the action research approach.

## Appreciative Inquiry

Appreciative inquiry (AI) is a more positive approach than action research. AI begins by investigating what the organization is doing well. Searching for the organization's strengths can help create a vision of what it could become. Like parents who focus on highlighting the positive aspects of a child's behaviour instead of the negative, AI uncovers successful events and teams within an organization and uses that knowledge as a guidepost for the change effort.[38] Canadian Tire successfully launched a major AI effort, which solicited feedback from employees across the country to come up with six key values that defined "The Canadian Tire Way." Employees used AI to visualize a positive future for Canadian Tire.[39] The four stages of AI are illustrated in Exhibit 12-8.

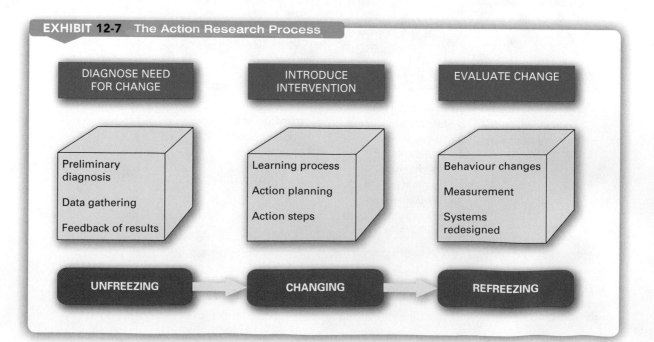

**EXHIBIT 12-7    The Action Research Process**

DIAGNOSE NEED FOR CHANGE

INTRODUCE INTERVENTION

EVALUATE CHANGE

Preliminary diagnosis

Data gathering

Feedback of results

Learning process

Action planning

Action steps

Behaviour changes

Measurement

Systems redesigned

UNFREEZING → CHANGING → REFREEZING

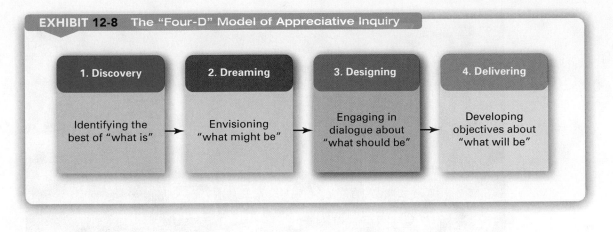

**EXHIBIT 12-8** The "Four-D" Model of Appreciative Inquiry

| 1. Discovery | 2. Dreaming | 3. Designing | 4. Delivering |
|---|---|---|---|
| Identifying the best of "what is" | Envisioning "what might be" | Engaging in dialogue about "what should be" | Developing objectives about "what will be" |

# CURRENT ISSUES IN MANAGING CHANGE

After the Gulf of Mexico oil spill, one of the biggest challenges facing Robert Dudley, BP's new group chief executive, was moving the company into new growth areas. Dudley lined up more than 30 projects around the world, including ventures in Russia, India, and Canada. Company shares have recovered well over half the value lost when they plunged after the spill.[40]

**12.5** — **Explain** What are current issues in managing change?

BP introduced new safety standards, which have enabled employees to stop operations several times when corrective action was needed. "We are rewarding people for doing that," said Dudley, "This is part of the cultural change." Dudley also pointed out that the entire industry needs to change to prevent another devastating deepwater oil spill like the one BP suffered. "I believe the industry also has a responsibility to change."[41]

**Think About It**

What can companies do to stimulate and nurture innovation?

Today's change issues—changing organizational culture and handling employee stress—are critical concerns for managers. What can managers do to change an organization's culture when that culture no longer supports the organization's mission? What can managers do to handle the stress created by today's dynamic and uncertain environment? We look at these issues in this section.

## Changing Organizational Culture

When W. James McNerney Jr. became CEO of 3M Company, he brought with him managerial approaches from his old employer, General Electric. He soon discovered that what was routine at General Electric was unheard of at 3M. For example, he was the only one who showed up at meetings without a tie. His blunt, matter-of-fact, and probing style of asking questions caught many 3M managers off guard. McNerney soon realized that he would need to address the cultural issues before tackling any needed organizational changes.[42]

If an organization's culture is made up of relatively stable and permanent characteristics (see Chapter 11), it tends to be very resistant to change.[43] A culture takes a long time to form; once established, it tends to become entrenched. Strong cultures are particularly resistant to change because employees have become deeply committed to them.

The explosion of the space shuttle *Columbia* in 2003 highlights how difficult changing an organization's culture can be. An investigation into the explosion found that the causes were remarkably similar to the reasons given for the *Challenger* disaster 17 years earlier.[44] Although foam striking the shuttle was the technical cause, NASA's organizational culture was the real problem. Joseph Grenny, a NASA engineer, noted that "The NASA

The toy industry is very competitive and picking the next great toy is not easy. Still, Toronto-based Spin Master is better than most at finding the most innovative new toys. Co-CEOs Anton Rabie and Ronnen Harary and Executive Vice-President Ben Varadi rely on intuition. They have also created a "culture of ideas," and pick everyone's brains for new ideas, "from inventors and licensing companies to distributors and retailers around the world." They give a prize to one employee each month for the best idea.

culture does not accept being wrong." The culture does not accept that "there's no such thing as a stupid question." Instead, "the humiliation factor always runs high."[45] Consequently, people do not speak up. As this example shows, if, over time, a certain culture becomes inappropriate to an organization and a handicap to management, there may be little a manager can do to change it, especially in the short run. Even under favourable conditions, cultural changes have to be viewed in years, not weeks or even months.

**UNDERSTANDING THE SITUATIONAL FACTORS** What "favourable conditions" might facilitate cultural change? The evidence suggests that cultural change is most likely to take place when most or all of the following conditions exist:

- *A dramatic crisis occurs.* A crisis can be the shock that weakens the status quo and makes people start thinking about the relevance of the current culture. Examples are a surprising financial setback, the loss of a major customer, or a dramatic technological innovation by a competitor.
- *Leadership changes hands.* New top leadership, who can provide an alternative set of key values, may be perceived as more capable of responding to the crisis than the old leaders were. Top leadership includes the organization's chief executive but might include all senior managers.
- *The organization is young and small.* The younger the organization, the less entrenched its culture. Similarly, managers can communicate new values more easily in a small organization than in a large one.
- *The culture is weak.* The more widely held the values and the higher the agreement among members on those values, the more difficult it will be to change. Conversely, weak cultures are more receptive to change than are strong ones.[46]

These situational factors help explain why a company such as Microsoft faces challenges in reshaping its culture. For the most part, employees like the old ways of doing things and do not always see the company's problems as critical.

**HOW CAN CULTURAL CHANGE BE ACCOMPLISHED?** Now we ask the question: If conditions are right, how do managers go about changing culture? The challenge is to unfreeze the current culture, implement the new "ways of doing things," and reinforce those new values. No single action is likely to have the impact necessary to change something that is widely accepted and highly valued. Thus, there needs to be a comprehensive and coordinated strategy for managing cultural change, as shown in *Tips for Managers—Strategies for Managing Cultural Change*.

As you can see, these suggestions focus on specific actions that managers can take to change the ineffective culture. Following these suggestions, however, is no guarantee that a manager's change efforts will succeed. Organizational members do not quickly let go of values they understand that have worked well for them in the past. Managers must, therefore, be patient. Change, if it comes, will be slow, and managers must stay constantly alert to protect against any return to old familiar practices and traditions.

## TIPS FOR MANAGERS

### Strategies for Managing Cultural Change

* Set the tone through management behaviour. Managers, particularly top management, need to be **positive role models**.
* Create new stories, symbols, and rituals to replace those currently in vogue.
* Select, promote, and support employees who **adopt the new values** that are sought.
* **Redesign socialization processes** to align with the new values.
* Change the reward system to **encourage acceptance** of a new set of values.
* Replace unwritten norms with **formal rules and regulations** that are tightly enforced.
* **Shake up current subcultures** through transfers, job rotation, and/or terminations.
* Work to get peer-group consensus through **employee participation** and creation of a climate with a high level of trust.

## Handling Employee Stress

As a student, you have probably experienced stress when finishing class assignments and projects, taking exams, or finding ways to pay rising tuition costs, which may mean juggling a job and school. Then, there is the stress associated with getting a decent job after graduation. Even after you have landed that job, your stress is not likely to stop. For many employees, organizational change creates stress. A dynamic and uncertain environment characterized by mergers, restructurings, forced retirements, and downsizing has created a large number of employees who are overworked and stressed out.[47] According to the Vanier Institute of the Family, employees' stress-related disorders cost Canadian businesses an estimated $12 billion per year.[48] A 2011 Ipsos-Reid survey conducted for sanofi-aventis Canada showed that workplace stress was bad enough to cause 35 percent of those surveyed to say that it had made them physically ill.[49] In this section, we review what stress is, what causes it, how to identify its symptoms, and what managers can do to reduce it.

**WHAT IS STRESS?** **Stress** is the adverse reaction people have to excessive pressure placed on them from extraordinary demands, constraints, or opportunities.[50] Let us look more closely at what stress is. Stress is not necessarily bad. Although often discussed in a negative context, stress does have a positive value, particularly when it offers a potential gain. Functional stress enables an athlete, stage performer, or employee to perform at his or her highest level in crucial situations.

However, stress is more often associated with fear of loss. When you take a test at school or have your annual performance review at work, you feel stress because you know that there can be either positive or negative outcomes. A good performance

*What are the things that cause you stress?*

**stress**
The adverse reaction people have to excessive pressure placed on them from extraordinary demands, constraints, or opportunities.

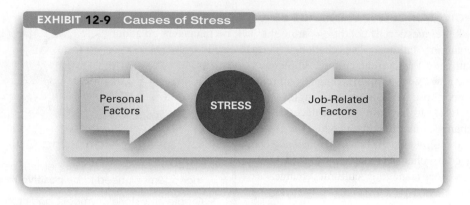

EXHIBIT 12-9 Causes of Stress

review may lead to a promotion, greater responsibilities, and a higher salary. But a poor review may keep you from getting the promotion. An extremely poor review might lead to your being fired.

Just because the conditions are right for stress to surface does not always mean it will. Stress is highest for individuals who are uncertain whether they will win or lose and lowest for individuals who think that winning or losing is a certainty. In addition, if winning or losing is unimportant, there is no stress. An employee who believes that keeping a job or earning a promotion is unimportant will experience no stress before a performance review.

**CAUSES OF STRESS** As shown in Exhibit 12-9, the causes of stress can be found in issues related to the organization or in personal factors that evolve out of the employee's private life. Clearly, change of any kind has the potential to cause stress. It can present opportunities, constraints, or demands. Moreover, changes are frequently created in a climate of uncertainty and around issues that are important to employees. It is not surprising, then, that change is a major stressor.

**SYMPTOMS OF STRESS** What signs indicate that an employee's stress level might be too high? Stress shows itself in a number of ways. For example, an employee who is experiencing a high level of stress may become depressed, accident prone, or argumentative; may have difficulty making routine decisions; may be easily distracted, and so on. As Exhibit 12-10 shows, stress symptoms can be grouped under three general categories: physical, psychological, and behavioural. Of these, the physical symptoms are least relevant to managers. Of greater importance are the psychological and behavioural symptoms, since these directly affect an employee's work.

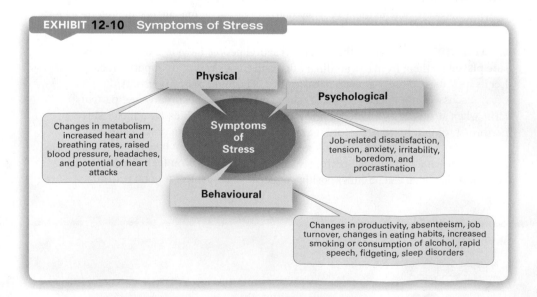

EXHIBIT 12-10 Symptoms of Stress

In Japan, there is a stress phenomenon called karoshi (pronounced kah-roe-she), which is translated literally as "death from overwork." During the late 1980s, "several high-ranking Japanese executives still in their prime years suddenly died without any previous sign of illness."[51] As public concern increased, even the Japanese Ministry of Labour got involved, and the Ministry now publishes statistics on the number of karoshi deaths. As Japanese multinational companies expand operations to China, Korea, and Taiwan, it is feared that the karoshi culture may follow.

**REDUCING STRESS**   As we mentioned earlier, not all stress is dysfunctional. Since stress can never be totally eliminated from a person's life, either off the job or on, managers are concerned with reducing the stress that leads to dysfunctional work behaviour. How? Through controlling certain organizational factors to reduce organizational stress, and to a more limited extent, offering help for personal stress.

Things managers can do in terms of organizational factors begin with employee selection. Managers need to make sure that an employee's abilities match the job requirements. When employees are in over their heads, their stress levels typically will be high. A realistic job preview during the selection process can minimize stress by reducing ambiguity about job expectations. Improved organizational communications will keep ambiguity-induced stress to a minimum. Similarly, a performance planning program such as management by objectives (see Chapter 3) will clarify job responsibilities, provide clear performance goals, and reduce ambiguity through feedback. Job redesign is also a way to reduce stress. If stress can be traced to boredom or to work overload, jobs should be redesigned to increase challenge or to reduce the workload. Redesigns that increase opportunities for employees to participate in decisions and to gain social support have also been found to reduce stress.[52]

Stress from an employee's personal life raises two problems. First, this type of stress is difficult for the manager to control directly. Second, there are ethical considerations. Specifically, does the manager have the right to intrude—even in the subtlest ways—in an employee's personal life? If the manager believes intervention is ethical and the employee is receptive, there are a few approaches the manager can consider. Employee *counselling* can provide stress relief. Employees often want to talk to someone about their problems, and the organization—through its managers, in-house human resource counsellors, or free or low-cost outside professional help—can meet that need. Companies such as BC Hydro and the University of British Columbia are just two of many organizations that provide extensive counselling services for their employees. A *time management program* can help employees sort out their priorities if their personal lives suffer from a lack of planning that, in turn, creates stress.[53]

Still another approach is organizationally sponsored *wellness programs*. For example, Montreal-based Ericsson Canada, a telecommunications firm, insists that all employees take holidays at minimum in week-long increments. Peter Buddo, vice-president of human resources, explains his company's policy: "One day off a week is not going to do anyone any good." Hamilton, Ontario–based Dofasco's employees have access to three gyms, one at the plant, and the other two a 15-minute drive from the plant. There are 4000 visits a month to the three gyms combined. Montreal-based Hewlett-Packard Canada gives all of its employees ergonomics training so that they will sit properly at their computer screens and avoid neck, shoulder, and arm injuries from keyboarding. The company also has four subsidized on-site fitness centres for staff in the Toronto area. Employees pay $20 a month to use the centres at any time of the day to take breaks and reduce stress.[54]

Practise

## Summary of Learning Objectives

**12.1 What factors create the need for change?**
Organizations are confronted with the need for change from both external and internal forces. Externally, the marketplace, government laws and regulations, technology, labour markets, and economic changes all put pressure on organizations to change. Internally, organizations may decide to change strategies. The introduction of new equipment can also lead to change. The workforce, both in terms of composition and attitudes, can also lead to demands for change.

Change has been a big part of the BP culture. The Gulf of Mexico oil spill was one of the more major forces of change that BP has ever faced. It featured pressure from stockholders, government, the general public, and special interest groups concerned about the widespread environmental damage.

**12.2 Is change ongoing or periodic?** Up until the late 1980s, change was viewed as periodic, something that could be planned and managed readily. In between periods of change, organizations "stayed the course." In more recent years, environments have become more uncertain and dynamic, which has led to more continuous demands for change.

Fiona MacLeod viewed change at BP in a more continuous fashion to avoid the dangerous focus on "big splashes."

**12.3 How do organizations manage change and resistance to change?** Managers can change an organization's structure, technology, and people. People tend to resist change for a variety of reasons. The main reason is that change replaces the known with ambiguity and uncertainty. As well, people do not necessarily like to change their habits; they may fear losing something already possessed (e.g., status, money, friendships); team dynamics might work against the change; and they may believe that the change could actually reduce product quality or productivity.

BP is constantly developing and using new technologies to recover oil and gas more safely and efficiently. Employees must be involved in any redesign so that they can more quickly adapt to the changes required.

**12.4 What are some common approaches to organizational change?** Action research looks at solving some organizational problem by researching and diagnosing the need for change, introducing the intervention, and then changing employee attitudes and behaviours to stabilize the change. Appreciative inquiry focuses more on the positive side to create future success through analysis of organizational

strengths. The four steps are discovery, dreaming, designing and delivering.

BP was the first major oil company to break with the oil industry's stance that oil production and greenhouse gas emissions were not connected. This type of major change forced the company to re-evaluate its own energy use as well as its CO2 emissions.

**12.5 What are current issues in managing change?** One main consideration in managing change is determining how to introduce change in an existing organizational culture. An organization's culture can make it difficult to introduce change because employees are often committed to old ways of doing things. The other major consideration is how to deal with employee stress while undergoing change.

One of Robert Dudley's main goals at BP was to return to a sense of calm and confidence. The company reintroduced a dividend program that had been suspended since the oil spill. This action signalled to employees that the worst of the crisis was over and helped them to deal with their stress.

## SNAPSHOT SUMMARY

**12.1 Forces for Change**
External Forces
Internal Forces

**12.2 Two Views of the Change Process**
The Calm Waters Metaphor
The White-Water Rapids Metaphor
Putting the Two Views in Perspective

**12.3 Managing Change**
What Is Organizational Change?
Types of Change
Making Change Happen Successfully
Managing Resistance to Change

**12.4 Common Approaches to Organizational Change**
Action Research
Appreciative Inquiry

**12.5 Current Issues in Managing Change**
Changing Organizational Culture
Handling Employee Stress

## MyManagementLab® Learning Resources

# Resources

**Explore and enhance your understanding of key chapter topics through the following online resources:**

- Student PowerPoints
- Audio Summary of Chapter
- ROLLS
- CBC Videos for Part 5
- MySearchLab

Visit the **Study Plan** area to test your progress with **Pre-Tests** and **Post-Tests**.

**Build on your knowledge and practise real-world applications using the following online activities:**

# Interpret

- Opening Case Activity: Types of Change
- Review and Apply: Solutions to Interpret section questions and activities
- Glossary Flashcards

# Analyze

- Opening Case Activity: Change Situations and Resistance
- Review and Apply: Solutions to Analyze section questions and activities
- Self-Assessment Library

# Practise

- Opening Case Activity: Change Simulations
- Review and Apply: Solutions to Practice section questions and activities
- Decision Making Simulations:
  –Human Resources Management
  –Organizational Culture
  –Change

# Interpret What You Have Read

1. Define organizational change.
2. Discuss the external and internal forces for change.
3. Why is handling change an integral part of every manager's job?
4. Describe Lewin's three-step change process. How is it different from the change process needed in the white-water rapids metaphor of change?

5. Describe two approaches to managing organizational change.
6. Discuss what it takes to make change happen successfully.
7. Explain why people resist change and how resistance might be managed.

# Analyze What You Have Read

1. Who are change agents? Do you think that a low-level employee could act as a change agent? Explain.
2. Why is organizational development planned change? Explain how planned change is important for organizations in today's dynamic environment.
3. Which organization—DaimlerChrysler or Apple—do you think would have more difficulty changing its culture? Explain your position.
4. "Managers have a responsibility to their employees who are suffering serious ill effects from work-related stress." Do you agree or disagree with the statement? Support your position.

5. Do you think changes can occur in an organization without a champion to foster new and innovative ways of doing things? Explain.
6. How would an organization decide between action research and appreciative inquiry? Explain briefly how each brings about organizational change.
7. Organizations typically have limits to how much change they can absorb. As a manager, what signs would you look for that might suggest that your organization has exceeded its capacity to change?

# Assess Your Skills

## HOW WELL DO I RESPOND TO TURBULENT CHANGE?

Listed below are a set of statements describing the characteristics of a managerial job.[55] If your job had these features, how would you react to them? Use the following rating scale for your answers:

> 1 = This feature would be very unpleasant for me.
>
> 2 = This feature would be somewhat unpleasant for me.
>
> 3 = I would have no reaction to this feature one way or another; or it would be about equally enjoyable and unpleasant.
>
> 4 = This feature would be enjoyable and acceptable most of the time.
>
> 5 = I would enjoy this feature very much; it's completely acceptable.

1. I regularly spend 30 to 40 percent of my time in meetings.  1 2 3 4 5

2. A year and a half ago, my job did not exist, and I have been essentially inventing it as I go along.  1 2 3 4 5

3. The responsibilities I either assume or am assigned consistently exceed the authority I have for discharging them.  1 2 3 4 5

4. I am a member of a team and I have no more authority than anyone else on the team.  1 2 3 4 5

5. At any given moment in my job, I have on the average about a dozen phone calls or emails to be returned.  1 2 3 4 5

6. My job performance is evaluated not only by my boss but also by my peers and subordinates.  1 2 3 4 5

7. About three weeks a year of formal management training is needed in my job just to stay current.  1 2 3 4 5

8. My job consistently brings me into close working contact at a professional level with people of many races, ethnic groups, and nationalities, and of both sexes.  1 2 3 4 5

9. For many of my work colleagues, English is their second language.  1 2 3 4 5

10. My boss is from another country and has been in this country only for six months.  1 2 3 4 5

11. There is no objective way to measure my effectiveness.  1 2 3 4 5

12. I report to three different bosses for different aspects of my job, and each has an equal say in my performance appraisal.  1 2 3 4 5

13. On average, about one-third of my time is spent dealing with unexpected emergencies that force all scheduled work to be postponed.  1 2 3 4 5

14. On average, I spend about a week every month out of town on business.  1 2 3 4 5

15. I frequently have to work until 8 p.m. to get my day's work completed.  1 2 3 4 5

16. When I have a meeting with the people who report to me, at least one or two will participate by phone or electronic conferencing.  1 2 3 4 5

17. The degree I earned in preparation for this type of work is now obsolete, and I probably should go back for another degree.  1 2 3 4 5

18. My job requires me to read 100 to 200 pages per week of technical materials.  1 2 3 4 5

19. My department is so interdependent with several other departments in the organization that all distinctions about which departments are responsible for which tasks are quite arbitrary.  1 2 3 4 5

20. I am unlikely to get a promotion anytime in the near future.  1 2 3 4 5

21. There is no clear career path for me in this job and organization.  1 2 3 4 5

22. During the period of my employment here, either the entire organization or the division I worked in has been reorganized every year or so.  1 2 3 4 5

23. While I have many ideas about how to make things work better, I have no direct influence on either the business policies or the personnel policies that govern my division.  1 2 3 4 5

24. My organization is a defendant in an antitrust suit, and if the case comes to trial I will probably have to testify about some decisions that were made a few years ago.  1 2 3 4 5

25. Sophisticated new technological equipment and software are continually being introduced into my division, necessitating constant learning on my part.  1 2 3 4 5

26. The computer I have in my office can be monitored by my bosses without my knowledge.  1 2 3 4 5

**SCORING KEY**   To calculate your tolerance of change score, add up your responses to all 26 items.

## ANALYSIS AND INTERPRETATION

This instrument describes a number of characteristics of the changing workplace. The higher your score, the more comfortable you are with change.

The author of this instrument suggests an "average" score is around 78. If you scored over 100, you seem to be accepting the "new" workplace fairly well. If your score was below 70, you are likely to find the manager's job in the twenty-first century unpleasant, if not overwhelming.

### More Self-Assessments

To learn more about your skills, abilities, and interests, take the following self-assessments on the MyManagementLab®:

- I.A.4—How Well Do I Handle Ambiguity?
- I.A.5—How Creative Am I?
- III.C.2—How Stressful Is My Life?
- III.C.3—Am I Burned Out?

# Practise What You Have Learned

## DILEMMA

Think of something you would like to change in your personal life. It could be your study habits, your fitness and nutrition, the way you interact with others, or anything else of interest to you. What values and assumptions have encouraged the behaviour that currently exists (the one you want to change)? What driving and restraining forces can you address in order to make the desired change?

## BECOMING A MANAGER

- Accept the change instead of resisting it, and find the potential benefits and new opportunities the change may bring.
- Familiarize yourself with the new aspects as quickly as possible, but be patient and recognize that you cannot master everything at once.
- Be organized. Make a list of what needs to be done to make the change happen, and focus on one change at a time.
- Ask "How?" rather than "Why?" "How can I use the support of others to facilitate the transition?" Change can be intimidating, but asking the right questions can make you more comfortable with what is going on around you.
- Gain back control. Change can take control away from you, so stare down your challenges.

## DEVELOPING YOUR INTERPERSONAL SKILLS: MANAGING RESISTANCE TO CHANGE

Kurt Lewin's force field analysis model was discussed earlier in the chapter. This exercise will help you apply the model to a real-life situation.[56] Lewin suggests that whenever driving forces are greater than restraining forces, the status quo will change.

### ABOUT THE SKILL

Driving forces are both attitudes to change and the emotions surrounding those attitudes. Developing your emotional intelligence will help you understand the forces operating within you and others.

### STEPS IN DEVELOPING THE SKILL

The following steps can be used as a guide to following Lewin's force field analysis.

1. CLARIFY YOUR VISION OF THE CHANGE YOU WANT TO SEE. Write down the goal you have for a particular situation (school success, health and nutrition, career development, etc.). The vision of the desired future will help you clarify the goal.

2. LIST THE DRIVING FORCES. Record the forces that are favourable to the change you would like to achieve. List them in the first column of a four-column chart.

3. LIST THE RESTRAINING FORCES. Record the forces that oppose your change or might limit your effectiveness. List these in the third column.

4. RATE THE DRIVING AND RESTRAINING FORCES. In column two, rate each driving force from 1 (weak) to 5 (strong); in column four rate each restraining force from 1 (weak) to 5 (strong).

5. DEVELOP A STRATEGY. Decide which of the forces could be influenced most easily. Come up with a strategy to strengthen the driving forces or weaken the restraining forces. Note that reducing the impact of restraining forces is often easier. If you look at your ratings, can you figure out a way to raise the scores of the driving forces or reduce the scores of the restraining forces?

6. DEVELOP YOUR ACTION PLAN. What steps can you take that will have the greatest impact? Identify the resources you will need and come up with a basic implementation plan.

## PRACTISING THE SKILL

You are the regional manager of two successful restaurants that employ bartenders and servers. One of the restaurants is downtown and the other is in a highly populated suburb. Each of the teams of bartenders and servers tends to work almost exclusively with others doing the same job. Servers in the downtown restaurant earn less pay and have no duties behind the bar. Servers in the suburban restaurant often fill in behind the bar.

In your professional reading, you have come across the concept of cross-training restaurant staff and giving them more varied responsibilities, which in turn has been shown to improve customer satisfaction while lowering costs. You call the two team leaders, Sue and Scott, into your office to explain that you want the bartending teams to move to this approach. To your surprise, both team leaders are both opposed to the idea.

Sue says she and the other downtown bartenders feel they are needed in the main bar, where they fill the most vital role in the restaurant. They have developed special talents in mixology and pouring, and often work in difficult and stressful circumstances with a much younger clientele. The downtown bartenders think the suburban bartenders have relatively easy jobs for the pay they receive, since they also spend time serving customers in the restaurant.

Scott, the leader of the suburban bartenders, tells you his group believes the downtown bartenders lack the special training and extra experience required to work with the senior IT executives who frequent their restaurant, as well as the special skills needed to serve and tend bar. The bartenders claim they have heavier responsibilities and do more exacting work, because they have responsibilities as servers as well.

What should you do about your idea to introduce more cross-training for the restaurant teams?

# Team Exercises

## 3BL: THE TRIPLE BOTTOM LINE

### HOW CAN COMPANIES MAKE THE CHANGE TOWARD SUSTAINABILITY?

Moving toward the triple bottom line requires vision from the outset. Businesses move to sustainability in an attempt to improve economic performance, enhance corporate image, reduce the environmental impact of their actions, and attract and retain top employees. External forces for change certainly can have a strong influence on the move to sustainability, but companies need to be able to drive this process even when the external forces are not apparent.

An important first step is to decide how much of the organization should be involved in 3BL. Sustainability can be implemented in all facets of the organization, but often the best place to start is with its products and services.[57] Westport Innovations of Vancouver, for example, develops environmental technologies and services that enable vehicles to operate on clean-burning alternative fuels.[58] Companies need to look at their products to see if they can be made from nontoxic, renewable materials, or even if there is another use for their product. Nike Grind[59] uses recycled shoes to make sport surfaces like playgrounds. Other areas where companies can consider sustainability include processes, its business model, and the supplier value chain.[60]

Functional areas of a company can implement sustainability in their processes and practices. The facilities team of Ottawa's Algonquin College designed the largest Leadership in Environmental and Energy Design (LEED) Platinum certified building in Canada as part of the new Centre for Construction Excellence.[61] Human resource departments can build their 3BL presence through recruitment and training. Finance departments can provide more detailed reporting of sustainability initiatives.

The last piece of the puzzle is having the right change leadership in place. Earlier in the chapter, change agents were discussed. 3BL change agents would be charged with facilitating training and education, gathering 3BL resources, linking employees to experts, coordinating meetings, and problem-solving 3BL issues.

### THINKING PRACTICALLY ABOUT 3BL

How can companies demonstrate leadership to the industry concerning the need for 3BL?

Walmart Canada held a Green Business Summit in Vancouver in 2010. The Summit demonstrated to the attendees that all businesses could work together to accelerate change toward triple bottom line goals. The outcome was ShareGreen.ca, an open website where companies and individuals can share cases studies of green business practices with a positive impact on return-on-investment (ROI).[62]

## OVERCOMING RESISTANCE TO CHANGE

### OBJECTIVES

- To explore resistance to change.
- To investigate the planning necessary to overcome resistance.

### THE SITUATION

You have been promoted to HR Manager in a large IT organization with three divisions: a helpdesk staffing agency, a network consulting branch, and a software development unit. There are three VPs, and each administers one of the divisions. The VP of the software development unit has been struggling.

The president has just informed you that he will be emailing staff in the software division tomorrow to announce he is consolidating the software development and the network consulting under one division. Only one of the VPs will run the two divisions, and the other VP will become a manager and report to the VP. Two supervisors will report to the manager. All employees from the former separate divisions will report to the two supervisors.

The president is well respected in industry for his technical ability, and you have established a strong working relationship with him over the past five years. He has grown the company from 25 employees to over 2000 in the last ten years. He has developed a reputation for making quick decisions that have led to issues such as a lack of coordination, frustrated staff, and even high turnover. This decision is his alone, and he has not obtained feedback or involved anyone else in the decision. He has asked you to create a draft email to staff outlining all of the changes. You have some experience with managing change at a previous company and have decided that you will provide some recommendations to the president by tomorrow on how to manage his desired consolidation more effectively.

### PROCEDURE

1. Divide into groups of five to seven—you are acting as the HR Manager in the scenario.

2. Each group should identify the forces causing resistance to that change in the scenario.

3. Each group should develop a set of recommendations for the president.

4. Reassemble the class and hear each group's recommendations and explanations.

5. After each group has presented, the other consulting groups should pose probing questions about the presenting group's recommendations.

## BE THE CONSULTANT: THE CELESTIAL AEROSPACE COMPANY

### OBJECTIVES

- To illustrate how forces for change and stability must be managed in organizations.
- To illustrate the effects of alternative change techniques on the relative strength of forces for change and forces for stability.

### THE SITUATION

The marketing division of the Celestial Aerospace Company (CAP) has gone through two major reorganizations in the past seven years. Initially, the structure changed from a functional to a matrix form (see Chapter 5), which did not satisfy some functional managers nor did it lead to organizational improvements. The managers complained that the structure confused the authority and responsibility relationships. In reaction to these complaints, senior management returned to the functional form, which maintained market and project teams managed by project managers with a few general staff personnel. No functional specialists were assigned to these groups. After the change, problems began to surface. Project managers complained they could not obtain the necessary assistance from functional staff. It not only took more time to obtain assistance but also created problems in establishing stable relationships with functional staff members. Because these problems affected customer service, project managers demanded a change in the organizational structure.

Faced with these complaints and demands from project managers, senior management is pondering yet another reorganization for the division. They have requested an outside consultant (you) to help them in their reorganization plan—one that will provide some stability to the structure, address their issues, and help the organization achieve its strategic goals.

### PROCEDURE

1. Divide into groups of five to seven and take the role of consultants.

2. Each group should identify the forces necessitating the change and the resistance to that change in the company.

3. Each group should develop a set of strategies for dealing with the resistance to change and for implementing those strategies.

4. Reassemble the class and hear each group's recommendations and explanations.

5. After each group has presented, the other consulting groups should pose probing questions about the presenting group's recommendations.

# Business Cases

## 1-800-GOT-JUNK?

Eighteen thousand expired cans of sardines.[63] Fifty garden gnomes. A mechanical bull. Trophies from a nudist colony. These objects are just some of the weird items that Vancouver-based 1-800-GOT-JUNK? customers have asked the uniformed people in the freshly scrubbed blue trucks to haul away. Company founder and CEO Brian Scudamore discovered a lucrative niche between "trash cans and those big green bins dropped off by" the giant waste haulers. But even in such an uncomplicated business as hauling people's junk, Scudamore must be concerned with managing change and innovation.

1-800-GOT-JUNK? is an award-winning company with a corporate staff of about 300 individuals. "With a vision of creating the 'FedEx' of junk removal," says Scudamore, "I dropped out of university with just one year left to become a full-time JUNKMAN! Yes, my father, a liver transplant surgeon, was not impressed, to say the least." However, in 2011, the company had more than 200 franchises and system-wide revenues were over $100 million.[64] Not surprisingly, Scudamore's father is a little more understanding these days about his son's business! Since 1997, the company has grown exponentially. The company made the list of *Entrepreneur* magazine's 100 fastest-growing franchises in 2005 and 2006. It was named one of the Best Employers in Canada by *Canadian Business*, and Scudamore won the International Franchise Association's Entrepreneur of the Year award.

Hauling junk would be, to most people's minds at least, a pretty simple business. However, the company Scudamore founded is a "curious hybrid." It has been described as a blend of "old economy and new economy." The company's service—hauling away trash—has been done for hundreds, if not thousands, of years. But 1-800-GOT-JUNK? also relies heavily on up-to-date information technology and has the kind of organizational culture that most people associate with high-tech start-ups. The company uses its 1-800-GOT-JUNK? call centre to do the booking and dispatching for all its franchise partners. The franchise partners also use the company's proprietary intranet and customer-relationship management site—dubbed JunkNet—to access schedules, customer information, real-time reports, and so forth. According to Scudamore's philosophy, this approach allowed franchise partners to "work on the business" instead of "work in the business." On any given day, all a franchisee has to do is open up JunkNet to see the day's schedule. If a new job comes in during a workday, the program automatically sends an alert to the franchisee. Needless to say, the company's franchisees tend to be quite tech-savvy. In fact, some of them have installed GPS devices in their trucks to help find the most efficient routes on a job. Others use online navigation sites. With the price of gas continuing to increase, this type of capability is important.

1-800-GOT-JUNK? has a culture that would rival any high-tech start-up. The head office is known as the Junktion. Grizzly, Scudamore's dog, comes to the office every day and helps employees relieve stress by playing catch anytime, anywhere. Each morning at exactly 10:55, all employees at the Junktion meet for a five-minute huddle, where they share good news, announcements, metrics, and problems they are encountering. Visitors to the Junktion have to join the group huddle too. One of the most conspicuous features of the Junktion is the "Vision Wall," which contains the varied outputs of Scudamore's brainstorms. Other members of the executive team have visions for the company's future as well. Periodically they will wander through the offices of Genome Sciences Centre, the tenant occupying the space above them, to visualize a future when Got-Junk? has expanded so sufficiently that it will take over that office space. Company franchisees are also encouraged to take initiative and be creative. For example, the Toronto franchise, which has 12 trucks, sometimes gets a blue truck motorcade going down Yonge Street through the heart of the city as a way to be noticed and to publicize its services. Despite the company's success to date, Scudamore is wondering whether he is prepared to face whatever changes may happen in the environment in the years to come. How would you advise him to be a "change-capable" organization?

## PRAIRIE GENERAL HOSPITAL

When you think about the significant changes that have occurred in people's lives over the past five decades, clearly the advances in medical science would be at the top of such a list. Diseases have been eradicated, and medical procedures and devices have helped save thousands of lives. But do not be too quick to conclude that the health care industry is a model of innovation and efficiency.[65]

Hospitals, in general, have one of the most archaic and costly operating systems of any group of large organizations. Nearly 95 percent of all hospitals currently use procedures and record-keeping systems that were implemented more than 50 years ago. Many doctors and technicians prefer to function the way they have always done. Individuals in this industry have been highly reluctant to accept and use new technologies.

Doctors and hospital administrators at Prairie General Hospital, however, refuse to be part of "the old guard." Consider the following incident that happened in the emergency room at Prairie General. A middle-aged patient was brought in by his wife to the emergency room (ER). The patient, who was very overweight, was complaining of shortness of breath and dizziness. Although the patient claimed he was fine, his wife made him go to the hospital. Immediately

the staff at Prairie General went to work. While nurses hooked the patient up to heart monitoring equipment and checked his vital signs, a resident wheeled over an emergency room cart, which contained a laptop computer. Logging in the patient's identification number, the ER doctor noticed that the patient had had an electrocardiogram (EKG) in the past year. By reviewing the past EKG records and comparing them with current heart monitoring results, the doctor determined the patient was in the middle of a heart attack. Within 10 minutes of seeing the patient, doctors had determined that he was suffering from a blocked artery. Clot-busting drugs were swiftly administered, and the patient was immediately taken to the cardiac lab where an emergency angioplasty was performed to open up the clogged artery. Within a day, the patient was back on his feet and ready to go home. In most other hospitals, the patient might not have been so lucky!

Prairie General is unusual in the health care industry. This hospital is investing money in technology that enables it to provide better service at a lower cost. Through its system, called CareWeb, more than 1 million patient records are available. Each of these records contain all previous medical orders, such as lab test results and prescriptions, for every patient. When a patient comes to the hospital, that individual's health history is easily retrievable and can be used to assist in the current diagnosis.

What has been the effect of this technology change on Prairie General? The system is saving the hospital more than $1 million each year. It has reduced errors in patient care by more than 90 percent, and reduced prescription errors and potential adverse drug interactions by more than 50 percent. Patient charts are now available in moments rather than hours or days. Patients are discharged more than 30 minutes faster than they had been before CareWeb was implemented.

Cost savings, time savings, increased patient care, and saved lives—all these benefits make you wonder why every hospital is not making such changes!

### Questions

1. Describe the types of changes that have occurred at Prairie General in terms of structure, technology, and people. Cite examples.

2. Why do you think the medical profession resists changing to systems such as CareWeb? Explain.

3. Assume you were going to make a presentation to a group of hospital staff (doctors and administrators) on why they should invest in technology such as CareWeb. How would you attempt to overcome their resistance to change and their attitude about continuing to do what they have always done? Discuss.

# CBC

# Eco-Preneurs: Easywash, the World's Most Eco-friendly Carwash Company

The average Canadian washes his or her car three times per month; this number contributes to a carwash market valued at $3.5 billion. That represents a lot of money *and* a lot of water! Laura-Lee Normandeau and Geoff Baker's Vancouver, BC, company Easywash would like a piece of that financial pie, but in a way that is environmentally friendly and preserves a lot of that water. In a single year, the Easywash system would save 24 million litres of clean drinking water now being used to wash cars, recycling nearly 85 percent of water used in the wash process from its own well.

This start-up company was formed with a view to franchise, the expectation being that each Easywash franchise would command a selling price of between $1 million and $2.5 million. Easywash would provide the franchisee with assistance in setting up the carwash, a full training package on running the operation, marketing materials, and ongoing support. The challenge is that while carwashes are capital intensive by nature, in Canada they are dominated by oil companies. Land costs are very high and there are few financing opportunities. Undaunted, Normandeau and Baker have gambled everything, with $1.25 million from 60 shareholders and debt servicing payments of $30 000 per month on $3.5 million. Construction costs on the initial site were originally budgeted at $1.5 million, but have gone considerably over budget to around $2.3 million.

Like most environmentally friendly businesses and services, Easywash has discovered that going green is not cost-free. Would customers be willing to pay a bit more for an environmentally friendly car wash? While the franchise featured an express wash for $5 including taxes (the lowest price carwash in the marketplace), covering the operational costs and servicing the capital costs of the franchise would require an enormous number of carwashes at $5. Also, the full-service wash was significantly more expensive than its less green competitors.

Going bankrupt proved to be the only way through which the company could be restarted with a different debt/equity structure.

The Easywash story suggests that a number of key controls are needed to ensure viability; both the controls and viability appear to be in question.

## QUESTIONS

### Interpret

1. Controlling refers to the process of monitoring activities to ensure that they are being accomplished as planned and correcting any significant deviations. Discuss which of the activities undertaken by Easywash could have benefited from more effective control. What types of control could have assisted the company?

2. Discuss the benchmarking activities that Easywash may have been expected to undertake.

### Analyze

3. Traditional financial control measures include ratio analysis and budget analysis. Referring to the popular financial ratios presented in the text, which of those ratios, when calculated for Easywash, would be expected to reflect poor performance?

4. Discuss the types of controls that Easywash could put in place that would capture management's need to control before, during, and after a customer washes a car.

### Practise

5. "Going green" is an admirable goal, but many customers are not willing to pay for it. Environmentally friendly, leading-edge companies such as Easywash represent considerably more risk than their less environmentally friendly competition and therefore require a much higher level of control. Do you agree with this statement?

*Sources:* "Green Business: Easywash," *Fortune Hunters,* Season 1, Canadian Broadcasting Corporation, January 12, 2008; Brian Morton, "Eco-friendly Carwash Hopes to Attract Investors by Appearance on TV Show," *Vancouver Sun,* January 16, 2008.,

## CBC

# NB Power and Protest

In October 2009, New Brunswick Premier Shawn Graham announced a new deal with Hydro Quebec. This new deal, according to Graham, would lower industrial power rates by 23 percent and freeze residential rates for five years. In his view, it was a good deal. The $4.8 billion agreement with Hydro Quebec would give Quebec exclusive control over the province's transmission lines and a near monopoly over lucrative energy markets in the United States.

This Quebec control angered neighbouring Atlantic Provinces and drew harsh criticism in New Brunswick. Residents simply did not want to lose control of their public utilities. Equally important, residents stated they wanted a voice in any type of transaction that would affect their future.

The Voice of the People rally, held in Fredericton, was organized to denounce the sale of NB Power assets to Hydro Quebec. The number of critics was growing and included some members of Premier Shawn Graham's own political party. Among those discontent with the agreement was Newfoundland and Labrador Premier Danny Williams, who shared his belief that the deal was an attempt by the province of Quebec to get a stranglehold on access to US markets.

As a result of the wide-spread anger the proposed deal generated, Premier Graham re-negotiated the deal, keeping ownership of the transmission lines and public utilities. However, the revised agreement does give Hydro Quebec the right to use the transmission lines to move power to the United States, which means Quebec will own the bulk of New Brunswick hydro-electric facilities.

Despite the re-vamped and scaled back power deal, people are still upset. The government later announced it would allow public hearings on the deal, but admitted that the hearings would have no effect on the outcome. Protestors are saying that Graham's deal grossly undervalues the power assets of New Brunswick and must be stopped by removing Graham's government from office. If voters have their way, Shawn Graham's party will be the first "one-term" party in office in New Brunswick's history.

## QUESTIONS

### Interpret

1. What external forces create the need for change? What internal forces create the need for change?

2. Compare the calm waters metaphor to the white-water rapids metaphor for describing the change process.

### Analyze

3. What mistakes do managers make when leading change? In this situation, why do you think Premier Shawn Graham was unable to implement the change successfully?

4. Why do people resist change, even when the change is beneficial? What was beneficial about the new deal with Hydro Quebec? Why were residents resisting the deal?

### Practise

5. How can managers help employees accept change? What might Premier Shawn Graham have done to help his constituents and other leaders embrace his proposed deal?

*Source:* "NB Power Energy, NB Power Protest," *The National*, CBC News, January 20 and March 20, 2010.

# Endnotes

## CHAPTER 1

**1.** Based on S. Whittaker, "The Junk Man Cometh," *Gazette* (Montreal), June 5, 2006, p. B1; and M. Haiken, "Employees: The Ultimate Partners," *Business 2.0 Magazine*, November 27, 2006; "Press Kit," 1-800-Got-Junk? website, www.1800gotjunk.com/us_en/Files/PRESS_KIT.pdf.

**2.** J. Beer, "Q&A: Brian Scudamore, founder/CEO, 1-800-Got-Junk?" *Canadian Business*, May 7, 2012, http://www.canadianbusiness.com/article/81127—q-a-brian-scudamore-founder-ceo-1-800-got-junk.

**3.** Based on S. Whittaker, "The Junk Man Cometh," *Gazette* (Montreal), June 5, 2006, p. B1; and M. Villano, "Making a Cache of Cash Cleaning Up Others' Trash," *Globe and Mail*, May 5, 2006, p. G7.

**4.** J. Beer, "Q&A: Brian Scudamore, founder/CEO, 1-800-Got-Junk?" *Canadian Business*, May 7, 2012, http://www.canadianbusiness.com/article/81127—q-a-brian-scudamore-founder-ceo-1-800-got-junk.

**5.** K. A. Tucker and V. Allman, "Don't Be a Cat-and-Mouse Manager," *Gallup Business Journal*, http://businessjournal.gallup.com/content/12574/dont-be-a-cat-and-mouse-manager.aspx.

**6.** See the *Tenth Annual Survey of Canada's Most Respected Corporations*, conducted by Ipsos-Reid and sponsored by KPMG, which asks 250 of Canada's leading CEOs to indicate which corporations they most respect in eight categories, http://www.rbc.com/newsroom/pdf/CMRC2004En.pdf.

**7.** "WorkUSA 2004/2005: Effective Employees Drive Financial Results," Watson Wyatt Worldwide, Washington, DC.

**8.** D. J. Campbell, "The Proactive Employee: Managing Workplace Initiative," *Academy of Management Executive*, August 2000, pp. 52–66.

**9.** J. S. McClenahen, "Prairie Home Champion," *IndustryWeek*, October 2005, pp. 45–47.

**10.** P. Drucker, *Management: Tasks, Responsibilities, Practices* (New York: Harper & Row, 1974).

**11.** H. Fayol, *Industrial and General Administration* (Paris: Dunod, 1916).

**12.** J. Beer, "Q&A: Brian Scudamore, founder/CEO, 1-800-Got-Junk?" *Canadian Business*, May 7, 2012, http://www.canadianbusiness.com/article/81127—q-a-brian-scudamore-founder-ceo-1-800-got-junk.

**13.** For a comprehensive review of this question, see C. P. Hales, "What Do Managers Do? A Critical Review of the Evidence," *Journal of Management*, January 1986, pp. 88–115.

**14.** H. Mintzberg, *The Nature of Managerial Work* (New York: Harper & Row, 1973); and J. T. Straub, "Put on Your Manager's Hat," *USA Today*, October 29, 2002.

**15.** S. J. Carroll and D. A. Gillen, "Are the Classical Management Functions Useful in Describing Managerial Work?" *Academy of Management Review*, January 1987, p. 48.

**16.** H. Koontz, "Commentary on the Management Theory Jungle—Nearly Two Decades Later," in *Management: A Book of Readings*, 6th ed., eds. H. Koontz, C. O'Donnell, and H. Weihrich (New York: McGraw-Hill, 1984); S. J. Carroll and D. A. Gillen, "Are the Classical Management Functions Useful in Describing Managerial Work?" *Academy of Management Review*, January 1987, p. 48; and P. Allan, "Managers at Work: A Large-Scale Study of the Managerial Job in New York City Government," *Academy of Management Journal*, September 1981, pp. 613–619.

**17.** E. White, "Firms Step Up Training for Front-Line Managers," *Wall Street Journal*, August 27, 2007, p. B3.

**18.** R. L. Katz, "Skills of an Effective Administrator," *Harvard Business Review*, September–October 1974, pp. 90–102.

**19.** D. Nebenzahl, "People Skills Matter Most," *Gazette* (Montreal), September 20, 2004, p. B1.

**20.** J. Beer, "Q&A: Brian Scudamore, founder/CEO, 1-800-Got-Junk?" *Canadian Business*, May 7, 2012, http://www.canadianbusiness.com/article/81127—q-a-brian-scudamore-founder-ceo-1-800-got-junk.

**21.** H. G. Barkema, J. A. C. Baum, and E. A. Mannix, "Management Challenges in a New Time," *Academy of Management Journal*, October 2002, pp. 916–930; M. A. Hitt, "Transformation of Management for the New Millennium," *Organizational Dynamics*, Winter 2000, pp. 7–17; T. Aeppel, "Power Generation," *Wall Street Journal*, April 7, 2000, p. A11; "Rethinking Work," *Fast Company*, April 2000, p. 253; "Workplace Trends Shifting over Time," *Springfield News Leader*, January 2, 2000, p. 7B1; "Expectations: The State of the New Economy," *Fast Company*, September 1999, pp. 251–264; T. J. Tetenbaum, "Shifting Paradigms: From Newton to Chaos," *Organizational Dynamics*, Spring 1998, pp. 21–33; T. A. Stewart, "Brain Power: Who Owns It, How They Profit from It," *Fortune*, March 17, 1997, pp. 105–110; G. P. Zachary, "The Right Mix," *Wall Street Journal*, March 13, 1997, p. A11; W. H. Miller, "Leadership at a Crossroads," *IndustryWeek*, August 19, 1996, pp. 42–56; M. Scott, "Interview with Dee Hock," *Business Ethics*, May–June 1996, pp. 37–41; J. O. C. Hamilton, S. Baker, and B. Vlasic, "The New Workplace," *BusinessWeek*, April 29, 1996, pp. 106–117.

**22.** Industry Canada, *Key Small Business Statistics, July 2012*. http://www.ic.gc.ca/eic/site/061.nsf/eng/h_02689.html.

**23.** Industry Canada, *Key Small Business Statistics, July 2012*. http://www.ic.gc.ca/eic/site/061.nsf/eng/h_02689.html.

**24.** Industry Canada, *Key Small Business Statistics, July 2012*. http://www.ic.gc.ca/eic/site/061.nsf/eng/h_02689.html.

**25.** Industry Canada, *Key Small Business Statistics, July 2012*. http://www.ic.gc.ca/eic/site/061.nsf/eng/h_02689.html.

**26.** Canada Post, *2010 Annual Report: Making Necessary Change*, http://www.canadapost.ca/cpo/mc/assets/pdf/aboutus/annualreport/ar_2010-e.pdf.

**27.** Based on J. B. Miner and N. R. Smith, "Decline and Stabilization of Managerial Motivation Over a 20-Year Period," *Journal of Applied Psychology*, June 1982, pp. 297–305; and J. B. Miner, B. Ebrahimi, and J. M. Wachtel, "How Deficiencies in Motivation to Manage Contribute to the United States' Competitiveness Problem (and What Can Be Done About It)," *Human Resource Management*, Fall 1995, pp. 363–386.

**28.** Bob Willard, *The Sustainability Advantage* (Gabriola Island, BC: New Society Publishers, 2002), p. 6.

**29.** See Shopify, "Shopify Marks Fifth Anniversary," Press Release, September 13, 2011, http://www.shopify.com/press/articles/shopify-marks-fifth-anniversary.html.

**30.** See K. Chow, "Fastest-Growing Companies: Shopify," *Business Journal*, May 16, 2011, http://www.obj.ca/Other/Special-Reports/2011-05-16/article-2507771/FASTEST-GROWING-COMPANIES%3A-Shopify/1.

**31.** See "The World's 50 Most Innovative Companies: Top 10 Retail," *Fast Company*, http://www.fastcompany.com/most-innovative-companies/2012/industry/retail#shopify.

**32.** See K. Chow, "Fastest-Growing Companies: Shopify," *Business Journal*, May 16, 2011, http://www.obj.ca/Other/Special-Reports/2011-05-16/article-2507771/FASTEST-GROWING-COMPANIES%3A-Shopify/1; Shopify, "Shopify Announces Build-A-Business Competition," Press Release, 2012, http://www.shopify.com/press/articles/shopify-announces-build-a-business-competition.html.

**33.** See FuEL Awards, "Meet the Judges," http://www.fuelawards.ca/judges.

**34.** See Shopify, "Quit Your Day Job. Work at Shopify," Shopify Careers, www.shopify.com/careers.

**35.** See Shopify, "Shopify Announces $7 Million Series A Funding from Bessemer, FirstMark, and Felicis," Press Release, December 13, 2010, http://www.shopify.com/press/articles/7-million-series-a-funding.html.

**36.** See Shopify, "Shopify Announces $7 Million Series A Funding from Bessemer, FirstMark, and Felicis," Press Release, December 13, 2010, http://www.shopify.com/press/articles/7-million-series-a-funding.html.

## SUPPLEMENT 1

**1.** See M. Ayyagari, T. Beck, and A. Demirgüç-Kunt, *Small and Medium Enterprises Across the Globe: A New Database*. World Bank: World Bank Policy Research Working Paper Series #3127 (2003); *Small and Medium-sized Enterprise Financing in Canada* (Ottawa: Industry Canada, Statistics Canada, and Finance Canada, 2003); *Key Small Business Statistics* (Ottawa: Industry Canada, July 2005); Diane Guillemette, *Small and Medium-sized Enterprise Outlook,* National Research Council of Canada (NRC) publication no. 47566 (Ottawa: NRC, 2004); and *Key Small Business Financing Statistics* (Ottawa: Industry Canada, Statistics Canada, and Finance Canada, August 2005).

**2.** See M. Ayyagari, T. Beck, and A. Demirgüç-Kunt, *Small and Medium Enterprises Across the Globe: A New Database*. World Bank: World Bank Policy Research Working Paper Series #3127 (2003); *Small and Medium-sized Enterprise Financing in Canada* (Ottawa: Industry Canada, Statistics Canada, and Finance Canada, 2003); *Key Small Business Statistics* (Ottawa: Industry Canada, July 2005); Diane Guillemette, *Small and Medium-sized Enterprise Outlook,* National Research Council of Canada (NRC)

publication no. 47566 (Ottawa: NRC, 2004); and *Key Small Business Financing Statistics* (Ottawa: Industry Canada, Statistics Canada, and Finance Canada, August 2005).

**3.** See Royal Bank of Canada, *Annual Small Business Survey* (2005); and TD Canada Trust, *Small Business Survey* (2011).

**4.** See Royal Bank of Canada, *Annual Small Business Survey* (2005); and TD Canada Trust, *Small Business Survey* (2011).

**5.** *Key Small Business Financing Statistics* (Ottawa: Industry Canada, Statistics Canada, and Finance Canada, August 2005); *Key Small Business Statistics* (Ottawa: Industry Canada, July 2005); Organisation for Economic Co-operation and Development (OECD), *Promoting Entrepreneurship and Innovative SMEs in a Global Economy*, 2nd OECD Conference of Ministers Responsible for Small and Medium-sized Enterprises (SMEs), Istanbul, June 2004; and J. Baldwin, L. Brian, and R. Dupuy, *Failure Rates for New Canadian Firms: New Perspectives on Entry and Exit*, (Ottawa: Statistics Canada, 2000).

**6.** *Key Small Business Financing Statistics* (Ottawa: Industry Canada, Statistics Canada, and Finance Canada, August 2005); *Small and Medium-sized Enterprise Financing in Canada,* (Ottawa: Industry Canada, Statistics Canada, and Finance Canada, 2003).

**7.** Industry Canada, *Key Small Business Statistics, July 2012*, (Ottawa: Industry Canada, July 2012), http://www.ic.gc.ca/eic/site/061.nsf/eng/h_02689.html.

**8.** National Survey of Nonprofit and Voluntary Organizations (NSVO) 2003 and 2004. See also M. H. Hall, M. L. de Witt, D. Lasby, D. McIver, T. Evans, C. Johnson, et al., *Cornerstones of Community: Highlights of the National Survey of Nonprofit and Voluntary Organizations, 2003 revised*, Catalogue no. 61-533. (Ottawa: Statistics Canada, 2005).

**9.** Imagine Canada, "The Nonprofit and Voluntary Sector in Canada," http://www.imaginecanada.ca/files/www/en/nsnvo/sector_in_canada_factsheet.pdf; Statistics Canada, *Satellite Account of Non-profit Institutions and Volunteering, 2007*, Catalogue no. 13-015-X (Ottawa: Statistics Canada, 2009), p. 11, http://www.statcan.gc.ca/pub/13-015-x/13-015-x2009000-eng.pdf.

**10.** Imagine Canada, "The Nonprofit and Voluntary Sector in Canada," http://www.imaginecanada.ca/files/www/en/nsnvo/sector_in_canada_factsheet.pdf; Statistics Canada, *Satellite Account of Non-profit Institutions and Volunteering, 2007*, Catalogue no. 13-015-X (Ottawa: Statistics Canada, 2009), p. 11, http://www.statcan.gc.ca/pub/13-015-x/13-015-x2009000-eng.pdf.

**11.** Imagine Canada, "The Nonprofit and Voluntary Sector in Canada," http://www.imaginecanada.ca/files/www/en/nsnvo/sector_in_canada_factsheet.pdf; Statistics Canada, *Satellite Account of Non-profit Institutions and Volunteering, 2007*, Catalogue no. 13-015-X (Ottawa: Statistics Canada, 2009), p. 11, http://www.statcan.gc.ca/pub/13-015-x/13-015-x2009000-eng.pdf.

**12.** Imagine Canada, "The Nonprofit and Voluntary Sector in Canada," http://www.imaginecanada.ca/files/www/en/nsnvo/sector_in_canada_factsheet.pdf; Statistics Canada, *Satellite Account of Non-profit Institutions and Volunteering, 2007*, Catalogue no. 13-015-X (Ottawa: Statistics Canada, 2009), p. 11, http://www.statcan.gc.ca/pub/13-015-x/13-015-x2009000-eng.pdf.

**13.** Imagine Canada, "National Survey of Nonprofit & Voluntary Organizations," http://library.imaginecanada.ca/sector_research/statistics/nsnvo.

**14.** See Policy Research Initiative (PRI), *What We Need to Know about the Social Economy* (Ottawa: Policy Research Initiative, 2005).

**15.** J. R. Baldwin, E. Gray, J. Johnson, J. Proctor, M. Raliquzza-man, and D. Sabourin, *Failing Concerns: Business Bankruptcy in Canada*, Catalogue No. 61-525-WPE (Ottawa: Statistics Canada, 1997).

**16.** See National Survey of Nonprofit and Voluntary Organizations (NSVO) 2003 and 2004.

**17.** See National Survey of Nonprofit and Voluntary Organizations (NSVO) 2003 and 2004; M. H. Hall, M. L. de Witt, D. Lasby, D. McIver, T. Evans, C. Johnson, et al., *Cornerstones of Community: Highlights of the National Survey of Nonprofit and Voluntary Organizations, 2003 revised*, Catalogue no. 61–533. (Ottawa: Statistics Canada, 2005); R. Saunders, *Passion and Commitment under Stress: Human Resource Issues in Canada's Nonprofit Sector. A Synthesis Report* (Ottawa: Canadian Policy Research Networks, 2004); M. H. Hall, A. Andrukow, C. Barr, K. Brock, M. de Witt, D. Embuldeniya, L. Jolin, D. Lasby, B. Lévesque, E. Malinsky, S. Stowe, Y. Vaillancourt, *The Capacity to Serve: A Qualitative Study of the Challenges Facing Canada's Nonprofit and Voluntary Organizations*, (Toronto: Canadian Centre for Philanthropy, 2003); L. J. Roberts, *Caught in the Middle: What Small, Nonprofit Organizations Need to Survive and Flourish*, (Ottawa: Voluntary Sector Initiative (VSI), 2001).

**18.** Equinox Management Consultants Ltd., *Gaps in SME Financing: An Analytical Framework* (Ottawa: Industry Canada, February 2002); *Key Small Business Financing Statistics* (Ottawa: Industry Canada, Statistics Canada, and Finance Canada, August 2005); *Small and Medium-sized Enterprise Financing in Canada* (Ottawa: Industry Canada, Statistics Canada, and Finance Canada, 2003); Organisation for Economic Co-operation and Development (OECD), *Promoting Entrepreneurship and Innovative SMEs in a Global Economy*, 2nd OECD Conference of Ministers Responsible for Small and Medium-sized Enterprises (SMEs), Istanbul, June 2004.

**19.** John R. Baldwin, *Innovation: The Key to Success in Small Firms*, Catalogue no. 76. (Ottawa: Statistics Canada, February 1995); Zoltan Acs, Randall K. Morck, and Bernard Yeung, *Small Firms, Globalization, and Canadian Public Policy*. Joint Series of Competitiveness No. 20. January 2000; Organisation for Economic Co-operation and Development (OECD), *Promoting Entrepreneurship and Innovative SMEs in a Global Economy*, 2nd OECD Conference of Ministers Responsible for Small and Medium-sized Enterprises (SMEs), Istanbul, June 2004;

**20.** Organisation for Economic Co-operation and Development (OECD), *Promoting Entrepreneurship and Innovative SMEs in a Global Economy*, 2nd OECD Conference of Ministers Responsible for Small and Medium-sized Enterprises (SMEs), Istanbul, June 2004; Jean Guinet, *Networks, Partnerships, Clusters and Intellectual Property Rights: Opportunities and Challenges for Innovative SMEs in a Global Economy*, Report to the 2nd OECD Conference of Ministers Responsible for Small and Medium-sized Enterprises (SMEs), Istanbul, June 2004; M. Feldman, J. Francis, J. Bercovitz, "Creating a Cluster While Building a Firm: Entrepreneurs and the Formation of Industrial Clusters," *Regional Studies* 39, no. 1 (2005), pp. 129–141.

## CHAPTER 2

**1.** Adam Waterous, "The Keystone XL Delay was a Gift to Canada," *Globe and Mail*, April 4, 2012, http://www.theglobean-dmail.com/news/opinions/opinion/the-keystone-xl-delay-was-a-gift-to-canada/article2391122/.

**2.** TransCanada. "Keystone XL Pipeline Project," TransCanada Corporation, http://www.transcanada.com/keystone.html.

**3.** AP, "Thwarted on US Oil Pipeline, Canada Looks to China," *Canadian Business*, January 29, 2012, http://www.canadianbusi-ness.com/article/68160—thwarted-on-us-oil-pipeline-canada-looks-to-china.

**4.** "Obama Changes Course, Fast-tracks Keystone Pipeline," *CTV News*, http://www.ctv.ca/CTVNews/TopStories/20120322/keystone-pipeline-announcement-120322/#ixzz2PQn5ISXc.

**5.** T. M. Hout, "Are Managers Obsolete?" *Harvard Business Review*, March–April 1999, pp. 161–168; and J. Pfeffer, "Management as Symbolic Action: The Creation and Maintenance of Organizational Paradigms," in *Research in Organizational Behavior*, vol. 3, eds. L. L. Cummings and B. M. Staw (Greenwich, CT: JAI Press, 1981), pp. 1–52.

**6.** Adam Waterous, "The Keystone XL Delay was a Gift to Canada," *Globe and Mail*, April 4, 2012, http://www.theglobean-dmail.com/news/opinions/opinion/the-keystone-xl-delay-was-a-gift-to-canada/article2391122/.

**7.** AP, "Thwarted on US Oil Pipeline, Canada Looks to China," *Canadian Business*, January 29, 2012, http://www.canadianbusi-ness.com/article/68160—thwarted-on-us-oil-pipeline-canada-looks-to-china.

**8.** "Bottled Water in Canada," *Euromonitor International*, http://www.euromonitor.com/bottled-water-in-canada/report.

**9.** Anne Kingston, "Green Report: It's So Not Cool," *Macleans*, May 14, 2007. http://www.macleans.ca/article.jsp?content=20070514_105163_105163.

**10.** Joe Cressy, "Celebrating the Beginning of the End of Bottled Water in Canada," *rabble.ca*, December 2, 2009, http://rabble.ca/news/2009/12/celebrating-beginning-end-bottled-water-canada.

**11.** J. S. Harrison and C. H. St. John, "Managing and Partnering With External Stakeholders," *Academy of Management Executive*, May 1996, pp. 46–60.

**12.** A. J. Hillman and G. D. Keim, "Shareholder Value, Stakeholder Management, and Social Issues: What's the Bottom Line?" *Strategic Management Journal*, March 2001, pp. 125–139; and J. Kotter and J. Heskett, *Corporate Culture and Performance* (New York: Free Press, 1992).

**13.** G. Lamphier, "Alberta Oil Exports Threatened by Surging U.S. Output," *Ottawa Citizen*, April 19, 2012; G. Lamphier, "Cheap Natural Gas Can Work to Alberta's Advantage," *Edmonton Journal*, April 28, 2012, p. B1.

**14.** T. S. Mescon and G. S. Vozikis, "Federal Regulation—What Are the Costs?" *Business*, January–March 1982, pp. 33–39.

**15.** J. Thorpe, "Inter-Provincial Trade Barriers Still a Concern for Executives 'Handicapping Country Economically,'" *Financial Post* (*National Post*), September 13, 2004, p. FP2.

**16.** R. Annan, for Goodmans LLP, "Merger Remedies in Canada," *Competition Bureau*, November 4, 2005, http://www.competitionbureau.gc.ca/eic/site/cb-bc.nsf/vwapj/richard-annan.pdf/$file/richard-annan.pdf.

**17.** See "Frito Lay Eliminating Trans Fat from Some Snacks," *Halifax Live.com*, February 23, 2004, http://www.halifaxlive.com/snack_02232004_769.php.

18. See "Banning Bad Fats," *CBC News*, November 6, 2006, http://www.cbc.ca/news/background/fats/banning_badfats.html.

19. G. Bonnell, "Food Industry Rushes to Drop Trans Fats," *Calgary Herald*, March 11, 2004, p. D1.

20. Statistics Canada, "Population by Sex and Age Group," CANSM, Table 051-001, September 28, 2011, http://www.statcan.gc.ca/tables-tableaux/sum-som/l01/cst01/demo10a-eng.htm.

21. Dave Collyer, President, Canadian Association of Petroleum Producers (CAPP), "Canadian Oil and Gas Industry Outlook—Opportunities & Challenges," (presentation to the Association of Professional Engineers and Geoscientists of Alberta [APEGA], Calgary, April 19, 2012); Global Clean Energy Congress and Exhibition, Calgary, November 1–3, 2011, http://www.capp.ca/getdoc.aspx?dt=PDF&docID=206748; Oil & Gas Sector Outlook 2012, Supplement to *Canadian Business*, April 30, 2012.

22. Canadian Association of Petroleum Producers (CAPP), "2010 Responsible Canadian Energy Report," www.rce2010.ca.

23. Sustainable Development Technology Canada (SDTC), "Clean Technologies Help Green the Patch," SDTC Information Feature, *Globe and Mail*, February 27, 2012.

24. C. Gillis and A. Kingston, "The Great Pet Food Scandal," *Maclean's*, April 30, 2007, www.macleans.ca/business/companies/article.jsp?content=20070430_104326_104326; "Company Overview of Menu Foods Income Fund," *Bloomberg Businessweek*, http://investing.businessweek.com/research/stocks/snapshot/snapshot.asp?capId=3206215; D. George-Cosh, "Menu Foods Hammered as Customer Walks," *Globe and Mail*, June 13, 2007, p. B15.

25. "Is Corporate Canada Being 'Hollowed Out'?" *CBC News*, May 27, 2007, http://www.cbc.ca/news/background/mergers/hollowed-out.html.

26. "Global 500, Countries, Canada," *CNN Money*, http://money.cnn.com/magazines/fortune/global500/2011/countries/Canada.html.

27. "Global 500," *CNN Money*, http://money.cnn.com/magazines/fortune/global500/2011/.

28. A. Shama, "Management Under Fire: The Transformation of Management in the Soviet Union and Eastern Europe," *Academy of Management Executive* 7, no. 1 (1993), pp. 22–35.

29. World Trade Organization (WTO), *WTO Policy Issues for Parliamentarians* (Geneva: WTO, 2001), p. 1, www.wto.org/english/res_e/booksp_e/parliamentarians_e.pdf.

30. B. Mitchener, "A New EU, But No Operating Manual," *Wall Street Journal*, December 16, 2002, p. A10.

31. Statistics Canada, "Imports, Exports and Trade Balance of Goods on a Balance-of-Payment Basis, by Country or Country Grouping," CANSIM, Table 228-0003, May 10, 2005, http://www.statcan.gc.ca/tables-tableaux/sum-som/l01/cst01/gblec02a-eng.htm.

32. See Standing Committee on Foreign Affairs, *Mexico: Canada's Other NAFTA Partner*, vol. 3, March 2004, http://www.parl.gc.ca/Content/SEN/Committee/373/fore/rep/rep03mar04-e.htm; Foreign Affairs and International Trade Canada, "The NAFTA's Impact," http://www.international.gc.ca/trade-agreements-accords-commerciaux/agr-acc/nafta-alena/nafta5_section04.aspx?lang=en&view=d.

33. Association of Southeast Asian Nations (ASEAN), "Gross Domestic Product in ASEAN, at Current Prices (Nominal), in US Dollars," Table 5, Macroeconomic Indicators, February 15, 2011, www.aseansec.org/stat/Table5.pdf.

34. Council of Canadians, "Trans-Pacific Partnership," http://www.canadians.org/trade/issues/TPP/index.html.

35. BRICS, Fourth BRICS Summit, New Delhi, March 29, 2012, http://www.bricsindia.in/.

36. This section is based on materials from the World Trade Organization website, www.wto.org.

37. G. Abramovich, "Google's China Syndrome," *DM News*, June 20, 2006, www.dmnews.com/cms/dm-news/search-marketing/37089.html.

38. G. Hofstede, *Culture's Consequences: International Differences in Work-Related Values*, 2nd ed. (Thousand Oaks, CA: Sage, 2001), pp. 9–15; and G. Hofstede, "The Cultural Relativity of Organizational Practices and Theories," *Journal of International Business Studies*, Fall 1983, pp. 75–89.

39. Hofstede called this dimension masculinity versus femininity, but we have changed his terms because of their strong sexist connotation.

40. The five usual criticisms and Hofstede's responses (in parentheses) are: (1) Surveys are not a suitable way to measure cultural differences (answer: they should not be the only way); (2) Nations are not the proper units for studying cultures (answer: they are usually the only kind of units available for comparison); (3) A study of the subsidiaries of one company cannot provide information about entire national cultures (answer: what was measured were differences among national cultures; any set of functionally equivalent samples can supply information about such differences); (4) The IBM data are old and therefore obsolete (answer: the dimensions found are assumed to have centuries-old roots; they have been validated against all kinds of external measurements; recent replications show no loss of validity); (5) Four or five dimensions are not enough (answer: additional dimensions should be statistically independent of the dimensions defined earlier; they should be valid on the basis of correlations with external measures; candidates are welcome to apply). See A. Harzing and G. Hofstede, "Planned Change in Organizations: The Influence of National Culture," in *Research in the Sociology of Organizations*, p. 14; P. A. Bamberger, M. Erez, and S. B. Bacharach, eds. *Cross Cultural Analysis of Organizations*, (Greenwich, CT: JAI Press, 1996), pp. 297–340.

41. G. Hofstede, *Culture's Consequences: Comparative Values, Behaviors, Institutions and Organizations Across Nations*, 2nd ed. (Thousand Oaks, CA: Sage, 2001).

42. Based on C. Gillis and A. Kingston, "The Great Pet Food Scandal," *Maclean's*, April 30, 2007, www.macleans.ca/business/companies/article.jsp?content=20070430_104326_104326; and D. Barboza and A. Barrionuevo, "Filler in Animal Feed Is Open Secret in China," *New York Times*, April 30, 2007.

43. C. A. Barlett and S. Ghoshal, *Managing Across Borders: The Transnational Solution*, 2nd ed. (Boston: Harvard Business School Press, 2002); and N. J. Adler, *International Dimensions of Organizational Behavior*, 4th ed. (Cincinnati, OH: South-Western College Publishing, 2002), pp. 9–11.

44. D. A. Aaker, *Developing Business Strategies*, 5th ed. (New York: John Wiley & Sons, 1998); and J. A. Byrne, "Borderless Management," *BusinessWeek*, May 23, 1994, pp. 24–26.

45. G. A. Knight and S. T. Cavusgil, "A Taxonomy of Born-Global Firms," *Management International Review* 45, no. 3

(2005), pp. 15–35; S. A. Zahra, "A Theory of International New Ventures: A Decade of Research," *Journal of International Business Studies*, January 2005, pp. 20–28; and B. M. Oviatt and P. P. McDougall, "Toward a Theory of International New Ventures," *Journal of International Business Studies*, January 2005, pp. 29–41.

**46.** Brendan B. Read, "More Bell(s) Tolling for Indian Outsourcing," *TMCnet.com*, http://call-center-software.tmcnet.com/topics/call-center-services/articles/50740-more-bells-tolling-indian-outsourcing.htm; Vikas Bajaj, "A New Capital of Call Centers," *New York Times*, November 25, 2011, http://www.nytimes.com/2011/11/26/business/philippines-overtakes-india-as-hub-of-call-centers.html?pagewanted=all.

**47.** Mega Brands Inc., *Annual Report 2006*, http://www.megabrands.com/media/pdf/corpo/en/reports/2006_annual_report_en.pdf; Mega Brands Inc., "Mega Brands Reports Fourth Quarter and 2011 Results," Press Release, March 12, 2012, http://www.megabrands.com/media/pdf/corpo/en/PressReleaseQ4-20110314.pdf.

**48.** Industry Canada, International Trade, Canadian Economy (NAICS 11-91), http://www.ic.gc.ca/eic/site/cis-sic.nsf/eng/h_00029.html.

**49.** Derek Sankey, "U.S. Franchisors Eye Canada for Growth," *Financial Post*, November 17, 2009.

**50.** L. Frost, "Starbucks Lures French Café Society," *Associated Press*, January 16, 2004.

**51.** "How the Music Industry's Transformation Is Paving the Way for Monetization Opportunities," *Seeking Alpha*, November 26, 2010, http://seekingalpha.com/article/238741-how-the-music-industry-s-transformation-is-paving-the-way-for-monetization-opportunities.

**52.** "How the Music Industry's Transformation Is Paving the Way for Monetization Opportunities," Seeking Alpha, November 26, 2010, http://seekingalpha.com/article/238741-how-the-music-industry-s-transformation-is-paving-the-way-for-monetization-opportunities.

**53.** O. Ward, "Pop Goes Globalization," *Toronto Star*, March 13, 2004, p. A18.

**54.** A. Kreamer, "America's Yang Has a Yen for Asia's Yin," *Fast Company*, July 2003, p. 58; D. Yergin, "Globalization Opens Door to New Dangers," *USA Today*, May 28, 2003, p. 11A; K. Lowrey Miller, "Is It Globaloney?" *Newsweek*, December 16, 2002, pp. E4–E8; L. Gomes, "Globalization Is Now a Two-Way Street—Good News for the U.S.," *Wall Street Journal*, December 9, 2002, p. B1; J. Kurlantzick and J. T. Allen, "The Trouble with Globalism," *U.S. News & World Report*, February 11, 2002, pp. 38–41; J. Guyon, "The American Way," *Fortune*, November 26, 2001, pp. 114–120.

**55.** J. Guyon, "The American Way," *Fortune*, November 26, 2001, pp. 114–120.

**56.** OccupyWallStreet website, http://occupywallst.org/; Occupy Movement page, *The Guardian*, http://www.guardian.co.uk/world/occupy-movement; Forum on "Understanding the Occupy Movement: Perspectives from the Social Sciences," *Berkeley Journal of Sociology*, http://bjsonline.org/2011/12/understanding-the-occupy-movement-perspectives-from-the-social-sciences/; "Opinion Roundup: What Has the Occupy Movement Accomplished?" *CBC News*, November 23, 2011, http://www.cbc.ca/news/canada/story/2011/11/23/f-occupy-movement.html.

**57.** Adapted from G. M. Spreitzer, M. W. McCall Jr., and J. D. Mahoney, "Early Identification of International Executive Potential," *Journal of Applied Psychology*, February 1997, pp. 6–29.

**58.** M. A. Prospero, "Attitude Adjustment," *Fast Company*, December 2005, p. 107; D. Roberts and M. Arndt, "It's Getting Hotter in the East," *BusinessWeek*, August 22/29, 2005, pp. 78–81; M. Champion, "Scotland Looks East for Labor," *Wall Street Journal*, July 7, 2005, p. A11; L. Bower, "Cultural Awareness Aids Business Relations," *Springfield Business Journal*, April 4–10, 2005, p. 59; R. Rosmarin, "Mountain View Masala," *Business* 2.0, March 2005, pp. 54–56; and P.-W. Tam, "Culture Course," *Wall Street Journal*, May 25, 2004, pp. B1+.

**59.** C. Harvey and M. J. Allard, *Understanding and Managing Diversity: Readings, Cases, and Exercises*, 2nd ed. (Upper Saddle River, NJ: Prentice Hall, 2002); P. L. Hunsaker, *Training in Management Skills* (Upper Saddle River, NJ: Prentice Hall, 2001); and J. Greenberg, *Managing Behavior in Organizations: Science in Service to Practice*, 2nd ed. (Upper Saddle River, NJ: Prentice Hall, 1999).

**60.** Information from INDITEX company website, www.inditex; and M. Helft, "Fashion Fast-Forward," *Business* 2.0, May 2002, pp. 60–66.

**61.** Denise Deveau, "Cleaning Up in Pet Stores," *Financial Post*, April 2, 2012; Earth Rated PoopBags website, ww.poopbags.ca.

**62.** Pet Food Association of Canada, "Pet Food Industry in Canada," http://www.pfac.com/about/industry/index.html.

## CHAPTER 3

**1.** See Maple Leaf Foods, "Maple Leaf Foods Proceeding with Final Phase of Value Creation Plan," (Press Release, October 19, 2011) http://investor.mapleleaf.ca/phoenix.zhtml?c=88490&p=irol-newsArticle&ID=1619258&highlight=.

**2.** V. Pilieci, "The Lost Generation of Business Talent," *Vancouver Sun*, May 2, 2001, pp. D1, D9.

**3.** See, for example, J. A. Pearce II, K. K. Robbins, and R. B. Robinson Jr., "The Impact of Grand Strategy and Planning Formality on Financial Performance," *Strategic Management Journal*, March–April 1987, pp. 125–134; L. C. Rhyne, "Contrasting Planning Systems in High, Medium, and Low Performance Companies," *Journal of Management Studies*, July 1987, pp. 363–385; J. A. Pearce II, E. B. Freeman, and R. B. Robinson Jr., "The Tenuous Link Between Formal Strategic Planning and Financial Performance," *Academy of Management Review*, October 1987, pp. 658–675; D. K. Sinha, "The Contribution of Formal Planning to Decisions," *Strategic Management Journal*, October 1990, pp. 479–492; N. Capon, J. U. Farley, and J. M. Hulbert, "Strategic Planning and Financial Performance: More Evidence," *Journal of Management Studies*, January 1994, pp. 22–38; C. C. Miller and L. B. Cardinal, "Strategic Planning and Firm Performance: A Synthesis of More Than Two Decades of Research," *Academy of Management Journal*, March 1994, pp. 1649–1685; and P. J. Brews and M. R. Hunt, "Learning to Plan and Planning to Learn: Resolving the Planning School/Learning School Debate," *Strategic Management Journal*, December 1999, pp. 889–913.

**4.** H. Mintzberg, *The Rise and Fall of Strategic Planning* (New York: Free Press, 1994).

**5.** H. Mintzberg, *The Rise and Fall of Strategic Planning* (New York: Free Press, 1994).

**6.** H. Mintzberg, *The Rise and Fall of Strategic Planning* (New York: Free Press, 1994).

**7.** G. Hamel and C. K. Prahalad, *Competing for the Future* (Boston: Harvard Business School Press, 1994).

**8.** D. Miller, "The Architecture of Simplicity," *Academy of Management Review*, January 1993, pp. 116–138.

**9.** R. Molz, "How Leaders Use Goals," *Long Range Planning*, October 1987, p. 91.

**10.** P. N. Romani, "MBO by Any Other Name Is Still MBO," *Supervision*, December 1997, pp. 6–8; and A. W. Schrader and G. T. Seward, "MBO Makes Dollar Sense," *Personnel Journal*, July 1989, pp. 32–37.

**11.** P. N. Romani, "MBO by Any Other Name Is Still MBO," *Supervision*, December 1997, pp. 6–8; and R. Rodgers and J. E. Hunter, "Impact of Management by Objectives on Organizational Productivity," *Journal of Applied Psychology*, April 1991, pp. 322–336.

**12.** For additional information on goals, see, for example, P. Drucker, *The Executive in Action* (New York: HarperCollins Books, 1996), pp. 207–214; and E. A. Locke and G. P. Latham, *A Theory of Goal Setting and Task Performance* (Upper Saddle River, NJ: Prentice Hall, 1990).

**13.** See Entrepreneur (Roynat Capital business profiles), "Air Transat A. T. Inc.," *National Post*, September 24, 2012, www2.canada.com/nationalpost/entrepreneur/transat.html.

**14.** J. D. Hunger and T. L. Wheelen, *Strategic Management*, 7th ed. (Upper Saddle River, NJ: Prentice Hall, 2000).

**15.** J. R. Schermerhorn Jr. and B. Wright, *Management*, 2nd Canadian Edition (Mississauga, ON: Wiley, 2011).

**16.** J. R. Schermerhorn Jr. and B. Wright, *Management*, 2nd Canadian Edition (Mississauga, ON: Wiley, 2011).

**17.** J. R. Schermerhorn Jr. and B. Wright, *Management*, 2nd Canadian Edition (Mississauga, ON: Wiley, 2011).

**18.** P. J. Brews and M. R. Hunt, "Learning to Plan and Planning to Learn: Resolving the Planning School/Learning School Debate," *Strategic Management Journal*, December 1999, pp. 889–913.

**19.** Paul J. H. Schoemaker and Cornelius A. J. M. van der Heijden, "Integrating Scenarios into Strategic Planning at Royal Dutch/Shell," *Planning Review* 20, no. 3 (1992), pp. 41–46.

**20.** F. Jossi, "Take a Peek Inside," *HR Magazine*, June 2002, pp. 46–52; and R. A. Martins, "Continuous Improvement Strategies and Production Competitive Criteria: Some Findings in Brazilian Industries," *Total Quality Management*, May 2001, pp. 281–291.

**21.** See http://www.mapleleaf.ca/en/corporate/company-info/overview/ (accessed Nov 14, 2011).

**22.** J. W. Dean Jr. and M. P. Sharfman, "Does Decision Process Matter? A Study of Strategic Decision-Making Effectiveness," *Academy of Management Journal*, April 1996, pp. 368–396.

**23.** See Marina Strauss and Jacquie McNish, "With Target, Canada's Retail Landscape Set for Massive Makeover," *Globe and Mail*, January 13, 2011, www.theglobeandmail.com/globe-investor/with-target-canadas-retail-landscape-set-for-massive-makeover/article1868308/.

**24.** Based on A. A. Thompson, Jr., A. J. Strickland III, and J. E. Gamble, *Crafting and Executing Strategy*, 14th ed. (New York: McGraw-Hill Irwin, 2005).

**25.** J. Magretta, "Why Business Models Matter," *Harvard Business Review*, May 2002, pp. 86–92.

**26.** M. Carpenter, G. Sanders, K. Harling, *Strategic Management*, Canadian ed. (Pearson, 2012).

**27.** See WorkSafeBC, "Our Vision, Mission, and Guiding Principles," http:// www.worksafebc.com/about_us/our_mandate/vision_mission_guiding_principles/default.asp).

**28.** C. K. Prahalad and G. Hamel, "The Core Competence of the Corporation," *Harvard Business Review*, May–June 1990, pp. 79–91.

**29.** See P&G, "Core Strengths," http://www.pg.com/en_US/company/core_strengths.shtml.

**30.** See Kevin O'Marah and Debra Hofman, "The AMR Supply Chain Top 25 for 2010," *Gartner*, June 2, 2010, http://www.gartner.com/DisplayDocument?id=1379613.

**31.** See, for example, H. J. Cho and V. Pucik, "Relationship Between Innovativeness, Quality, Growth, Profitability, and Market Value," *Strategic Management Journal* 26, no. 6 (2005), pp. 555–575; W. F. Joyce, "Building the 4+2 Organization," *Organizational Dynamics*, May 2005, pp. 118–129; R. S. Kaplan and D. P. Norton, "Measuring the Strategic Readiness of Intangible Assets," *Harvard Business Review*, February 2004, pp. 52–63; C. M. Fiol, "Managing Culture as a Competitive Resource: An Identity-Based View of Sustainable Competitive Advantage," *Journal of Management*, March 1991, pp. 191–211; T. Kono, "Corporate Culture and Long-Range Planning," *Long Range Planning*, August 1990, pp. 9–19; S. Green, "Understanding Corporate Culture and Its Relation to Strategy," *International Studies of Management and Organization*, Summer 1988, pp. 6–28; C. Scholz, "Corporate Culture and Strategy—The Problem of Strategic Fit," *Long Range Planning*, August 1987, pp. 78–87; and J. B. Barney, "Organizational Culture: Can It Be a Source of Sustained Competitive Advantage*?*" *Academy of Management Review*, July 1986, pp. 656–665.

**32.** K. E. Klein, "Slogans That Are the Real Thing," *BusinessWeek Online*, www.businessweek.com, August 4, 2005; and T. Mucha, "The Payoff for Trying Harder," *Business 2.0*, July 2002, pp. 84–85.

**33.** A. Carmeli and A. Tischler, "The Relationships Between Intangible Organizational Elements and Organizational Performance," *Strategic Management Journal* 25, no. 13, December 2004, pp. 1257–1278; P. W. Roberts and G. R. Dowling, "Corporate Reputation and Sustained Financial Performance," *Strategic Management Journal*, December 2002, pp. 1077–1093; and C. J. Fombrun, "Corporate Reputations as Economic Assets," in *Handbook of Strategic Management*, ed. M. A. Hitt, R. E. Freeman, and J. S. Harrison (Malden, MA: Blackwell Publishers, 2001), pp. 289–312.

**34.** "Johnson & Johnson Ranks No. 1 in National Corporate Reputation Survey for Seventh Consecutive Year," Harris Interactive Press Release, www.harrisinteractive.com, December 7, 2005.

**35.** See Marina Strauss, "For Indigo CEO, It's Time to Think Outside the Book," *Globe and Mail*, November 9, 2011, http://www.theglobeandmail.com/globe-investor/for-indigo-ceo-its-time-to-think-outside-the-book/article2231354/.

**36.** M. Carpenter, G. Sanders, K. Harling, *Strategic Management*, Canadian ed. (Pearson, 2012), p. 75.

**37.** H. Mintzberg, "The Strategy Concept I: Five Ps for Strategy," *California Management Review*, Fall 1987, pp. 11–24.

**38.** Based on A. A. Thompson, Jr., A. J. Strickland III, and J. E. Gamble, *Crafting and Executing Strategy*, 14th ed. (New York: McGraw-Hill Irwin, 2005).

**39.** Based on A. A. Thompson, Jr., A. J. Strickland III, and J. E. Gamble, *Crafting and Executing Strategy*, 14th ed. (New York: McGraw-Hill Irwin, 2005).

**40.** See Walmart Canada, "Walmart Canada to Open 40 Super-centres in the Coming Fiscal Year," (Press release, January 26, 2011), www.walmartcanada.ca/Pages/Press%20Releases/Article/169/188/21.

**41.** M. Bustillo, "New Chief at Wal-Mart Looks Abroad For Growth," *Wall Street Journal*, February 2, 2009, p. B1.

**42.** P. Marck, "Tim Hortons Brews Up Record Sales: No Holes in Doughnut Business in Canada," *Edmonton Journal*, January 7, 2004, p. A1.

**43.** See XM Canada, "Sirius Canada and XM Canada Complete Merger," June 21, 2011, www.xmradio.ca/about/merger.cfm.

**44.** G. Pitts, "Small Is Beautiful, Conglomerates Signal," *Globe and Mail*, April 1, 2002,pp. B1, B4; Brookfield Asset Management website, www.brookfield.com; and *Brookfield Asset Management 2006 Annual Report*, www.brookfield.com/userfiles/file/Annual Reports/2006/2006 AnnualReport.pdf.

**45.** V. Ramanujam and P. Varadarajan, "Research on Corporate Diversification: A Synthesis," *Strategic Management Journal* 10 (1989), pp. 523–551. See also A. Shleifer and R. W. Vishny, "Takeovers in the 1960s and 1980s: Evidence and Implications," in *Fundamental Issues in Strategy*, ed. R. P. Rumelt, D. E. Schendel, and D. J. Teece (Boston: Harvard Business School Press, 1994).

**46.** Based on A. A. Thompson, Jr., A. J. Strickland III, and J. E. Gamble, *Crafting and Executing Strategy*, 14th ed. (New York: McGraw-Hill Irwin, 2005).

**47.** J. A. Pearce, II, "Retrenchment Remains the Foundation of Business Turnaround," *Strategic Management Journal* 15 (1994), pp. 407–417.

**48.** See, for example, M. E. Porter, *Competitive Strategy: Techniques for Analyzing Industries and Competitors* (New York: Free Press, 1980); M. E. Porter, *Competitive Advantage: Creating and Sustaining Superior Performance* (New York: Free Press, 1985); G. G. Dess and P. S. Davis, "Porter's (1980) Generic Strategies as Determinants of Strategic Group Membership and Organizational Performance," *Academy of Management Journal*, September 1984, pp. 467–488; G. G. Dess and P. S. Davis, "Porter's (1980) Generic Strategies and Performance: An Empirical Examination With American Data—Part I: Testing Porter," *Organization Studies* 7, no. 1 (1986), pp. 37–55; G. G. Dess and P. S. Davis, "Porter's (1980) Generic Strategies and Performance: An Empirical Examination With American Data—Part II: Performance Implications," *Organization Studies* 7, no. 3 (1986), pp. 255–261; M. E. Porter, "From Competitive Advantage to Corporate Strategy," *Harvard Business Review*, May–June 1987, pp. 43–59; A. I. Murray, "A Contingency View of Porter's 'Generic Strategies,'" *Academy of Management Review*, July 1988, pp. 390–400; C. W. L. Hill, "Differentiation Versus Low Cost or Differentiation and Low Cost: A Contingency Framework," *Academy of Management Review*, July 1988, pp. 401–412; I. Bamberger, "Developing Competitive Advantage in Small and Medium-Sized Firms," *Long Range Planning*, October 1989, pp. 80–88; D. F. Jennings and J. R. Lumpkin, "Insights Between Environmental Scanning Activities and Porter's Generic Strategies: An Empirical Analysis," *Strategic Management Journal* 18, no. 4 (1992), pp. 791–803; N. Argyres and A. M. McGahan, "An Interview with Michael Porter," *Academy of Management Executive*, May 2002, pp. 43–52; and A. Brandenburger, "Porter's Added Value: High Indeed!" *Academy of Management Executive*, May 2002, pp. 58–60.

**49.** A. Brandenburger and B. Nalebuff, *Co-Opetition* (New York, NY: Currency/Doubleday, 1996).

**50.** M. Carpenter, G. Sanders, K. Harling, *Strategic Management*, Canadian ed. (Pearson, 2012).

**51.** See Vancity, *Vancity 2010 Annual Report*, https://www.vancity.com/SharedContent/documents/pdfs/Vancity_2010_Annual Report.pdf.

**52.** D. Miller and J. Toulouse, "Strategy, Structure, CEO Personality, and Performance in Small Firms," *American Journal of Small Business*, Winter 1986, pp. 47–62.

**53.** C. W. L. Hill, "Differentiation versus Low Cost or Differentiation and Low Cost: A Contingency Framework," *Academy of Management Review*, July 1988, pp. 401–412; R. E. White, "Organizing to Make Business Unit Strategies Work," in *Handbook of Business Strategy*, 2nd ed., ed. H. E. Glass (Boston: Warren Gorham and Lamont, 1991), pp. 24.1–24.14; D. Miller, "The Generic Strategy Trap," *Journal of Business Strategy*, January–February 1991, pp. 37–41; S. Cappel, P. Wright, M. Kroll, and D. Wyld, "Competitive Strategies and Business Performance: An Empirical Study of Select Service Businesses," *International Journal of Management*, March 1992, pp. 1–11; and J. W. Bachmann, "Competitive Strategy: It's O.K. to Be Different," *Academy of Management Executive*, May 2002, pp. 61–65.

**54.** See CBC News, "Air Canada's Zip Shut Down," September 8, 2004, www.cbc.ca/news/business/story/2004/09/08/zip_040908.html.

## CHAPTER 4

**1.** Derek Sankey, "Women Embrace Franchising", *Financial Post*, March 26, 2012, http://www.canada.com/technology/Women+embrace+franchising/6378913/story.html.

**2.** See "Canadian Franchise Statistics and Information," *Franshiseek Canada*, http://www.franchiseek.com/Canada/Franchise_Canada_Statistics.htm.

**3.** See Nurse Next Door™, "What Makes Us Unique," http://www.nursenextdoorfranchise.com/what-makes-us-unique/.

**4.** I. Wylie, "Who Runs This Team Anyway?" *Fast Company*, April 2002, pp. 32–33.

**5.** D. A. Garvin and M. A. Roberto, "What You Don't Know About Making Decisions," *Harvard Business Review*, September 2001, pp. 108–116.

**6.** W. Pounds, "The Process of Problem Finding," *Industrial Management Review*, Fall 1969, pp. 1–19.

**7.** P. C. Nutt, *Why Decisions Fail: Avoiding the Blunders and Traps That Lead to Debacles* (San Francisco, CA: Berrett-Koehler Publishers, 2002).

**8.** See Canadian Franchise Association (CFA), "Canadian Franshise Association Identifies Hot Sector Trends in Franchising for 2008," CFA Media Release, http://www.cfa.ca/News/CFA_Media_Releases/CFAMediaRelease01070801.aspx.

**9.** See Nurse Next Door™, "The Investment," http://www.nursenextdoorfranchise.com/the-investment/; Derek Sankey,"Women Embrace Franchising," *Financial Post*, March 26, 2012, http://www.canada.com/technology/Women+embrace+franchising/6378913/story.htm.

**10.** See H. A. Simon, "Rationality in Psychology and Economics," *Journal of Business*, October 1986, pp. 209–224; A. Langley, "In Search of Rationality: The Purposes Behind the Use of Formal

Analysis in Organizations," *Administrative Science Quarterly*, December 1989, pp. 598–631.

**11.** See, for example, J. G. March, *A Primer on Decision Making* (New York: Free Press, 1994), pp. 8–25; and A. Langley, H. Mintzberg, P. Pitcher, E. Posada, and J. Saint-Macary, "Opening Up Decision Making: The View from the Black Stool," *Organization Science*, May–June 1995, pp. 260–279.

**12.** See N. McK. Agnew and J. L. Brown, "Bounded Rationality: Fallible Decisions in Unbounded Decision Space," *Behavioral Science*, July 1986, pp. 148–161; B. E. Kaufman, "A New Theory of Satisficing," *Journal of Behavioral Economics*, Spring 1990, pp. 35–51; and D. R. A. Skidd, "Revisiting Bounded Rationality," *Journal of Management Inquiry*, December 1992, pp. 343–347.

**13.** See Karen Christensen, "Questions for Dolly Chugh," *Rotman Magazine,* Winter 2009, p. 89; K. Milkman, D. Chugh, and M. Bazerman "How Can Decision Making Be Improved?," *Perspectives on Psychological Science* 4, no. 4 (2009), pp. 379–383, http://www.hbs.edu/research/pdf/08-102.pdf; D. Chugh and M. Bazerman, "Bounded Awareness —What You Fail To See Can Hurt You," *Mind and Society* 6, no. 1 (2007), pp. 1–18.

**14.** W. Cole, "The Stapler Wars," *Time Inside Business*, April 2005, p. A5.

**15.** See K. R. Hammond, R. M. Hamm, J. Grassia, and T. Pearson, "Direct Comparison of the Efficacy of Intuitive and Analytical Cognition in Expert Judgment," in *IEEE Transactions on Systems, Man, and Cybernetics* SMC-17 no. 5 (1987): pp. 753–770; W. H. Agor, ed., *Intuition in Organizations* (Newbury Park, CA: Sage Publications, 1989); O. Behling and N. L. Eckel, "Making Sense Out of Intuition," *The Executive*, February 1991, pp. 46–47; L. A. Burke and M. K. Miller, "Taking the Mystery Out of Intuitive Decision Making," *Academy of Management Executive*, October 1999, pp. 91–99; A. L. Tesolin, "How to Develop the Habit of Intuition," *Training & Development*, March 2000, p. 76; and T. A. Stewart, "How to Think with Your Gut," *Business* 2.0, November 2002, pp. 98–104.

**16.** A. Dijksterhuis, M. W. Bos, L. F. Nordgren, R. B. van Baaren, "On Making the Right Choice: The Deliberation-Without-Attention Effect," *Science*, 311, no. 5763 (February 17, 2006), pp. 1005–1007.

**17.** S. Maich, "Promises, Promises but Tax Bill Grows," *Financial Post* (*National Post*), June 1, 2004, p. FP1.

**18.** K. R. Brousseau, M. J. Driver, G. Hourihan, and R. Larsson, "The Seasoned Executive's Decision-Making Style," *Harvard Business Review*, February 2006, pp. 111–121.

**19.** A. J. Rowe, J. D. Boulgarides, and M. R. McGrath, *Managerial Decision Making, Modules in Management Series* (Chicago: SRA, 1984), pp. 18–22.

**20.** C. Shaffran, "Mind Your Meeting: How to Become the Catalyst for Culture Change," *Communication World*, February–March 2003, pp. 26–29.

**21.** I. L. Janis, *Victims of Groupthink* (Boston: Houghton Mifflin, 1972); R. J. Aldag and S. Riggs Fuller, "Beyond Fiasco: A Reappraisal of the Groupthink Phenomenon and a New Model of Group Decision Processes," *Psychological Bulletin*, May 1993, pp. 533–552; T. Kameda and S. Sugimori, "Psychological Entrapment in Group Decision Making: An Assigned Decision Rule and a Groupthink Phenomenon," *Journal of Personality and Social Psychology*, August 1993, pp. 282–292.

**22.** R. G. Vleeming, "Machiavellianism: A Preliminary Review," *Psychology Reports*, February 1979, pp. 295–310.

**23.** See Richard Branson, "What Steve Jobs Taught Me By Kicking My Butt," *Canadian Business*, September 22, 2011, http://www.canadianbusiness.com/article/46349—branson-what-steve-jobs-taught-me-by-kicking-my-butt.

**24.** Based on J. Brockner, *Self Esteem at Work* (Lexington, MA: Lexington Books, 1988), Chapters 1–4.

**25.** See, for example, L. K. Michaelson, W. E. Watson, and R. H. Black, "A Realistic Test of Individual vs. Group Consensus Decision Making," *Journal of Applied Psychology* 74, no. 5 (1989), pp. 834–839; R. A. Henry, "Group Judgment Accuracy: Reliability and Validity of Postdiscussion Confidence Judgments," *Organizational Behavior and Human Decision Processes*, October 1993, pp. 11–27; P. W. Paese, M. Bieser, and M. E. Tubbs, "Framing Effects and Choice Shifts in Group Decision Making," *Organizational Behavior and Human Decision Processes*, October 1993, pp. 149–165; N. J. Castellan Jr., ed., *Individual and Group Decision Making* (Hillsdale, NJ: Lawrence Erlbaum Associates, 1993); and S. G. Straus and J. E. McGrath, "Does the Medium Matter? The Interaction of Task Type and Technology on Group Performance and Member Reactions," *Journal of Applied Psychology*, February 1994, pp. 87–97.

**26.** E. J. Thomas and C. F. Fink, "Effects of Group Size," *Psychological Bulletin*, July 1963, pp. 371–384; F. A. Shull, A. L. Delbecq, and L. L. Cummings, *Organizational Decision Making* (New York: McGraw-Hill, 1970), p. 151; A. P. Hare, *Handbook of Small Group Research* (New York: Free Press, 1976); M. E. Shaw, *Group Dynamics: The Psychology of Small Group Behavior*, 3rd ed. (New York: McGraw-Hill, 1981); P. Yetton and P. Bottger, "The Relationships Among Group Size, Member Ability, Social Decision Schemes, and Performance," *Organizational Behavior and Human Performance*, October 1983, pp. 145–159.

**27.** A. Kleingeld, H. Van Tuijl, and J.A. Algera, "Participation in the Design of Performance Management Systems: A Quasi-Experimental Field Study," *Journal of Organizational Behaviour* 25, no.7 (2004), pp. 831–854.

**28.** S. McShane and S. Steen, *Canadian Organizational Behaviour*, 7th ed. (Toronto, ON: McGraw-Hill, 2009), pp.165–166.

**29.** D. Kahneman and A. Tversky, "Judgment Under Uncertainty: Heuristics and Biases," *Science* 185 (1974), pp. 1124–1131.

**30.** Information for this section is taken from S. P. Robbins, *Decide & Conquer* (Upper Saddle River, NJ: Financial Times/Prentice Hall, 2004).

**31.** See, for example, B. M. Staw, "The Escalation of Commitment to a Course of Action," *Academy of Management Review*, October 1981, pp. 577–587; D. R. Bobocel and J. P. Meyer, "Escalating Commitment to a Failing Course of Action: Separating the Roles of Choice and Justification," *Journal of Applied Psychology*, June 1994, pp. 360–363; C. F. Camerer and R. A. Weber, "The Econometrics and Behavioral Economics of Escalation of Commitment: A Re-examination of Staw's Theory," *Journal of Economic Behavior and Organization*, May 1999, pp. 59–82; V. S. Rao and A. Monk, "The Effects of Individual Differences and Anonymity on Commitment to Decisions," *Journal of Social Psychology*, August 1999, pp. 496–515; and G. McNamara, H. Moon, and P. Bromiley, "Banking on Commitment: Intended and Unintended Consequences of an Organization's Attempt to Attenuate Escalation of Commitment," *Academy of Management Journal*, April 2002, pp. 443–452.

**32.** K. Davis and W. C. Frederick, *Business and Society: Management, Public Policy, Ethics*, 5th ed. (New York: McGraw-Hill, 1984), pp. 28–41, 76.

**33.** G. F. Cavanagh, D. J. Moberg, and M. Valasquez, "The Ethics of Organizational Politics," *Academy of Management Journal*, June 1981, pp. 363–374. See also F. N. Brady, "Rules for Making Exceptions to Rules," *Academy of Management Review*, July 1987, pp. 436–444, for an argument that the theory of justice is redundant with the prior two theories. See also T. Donaldson and T. W. Dunfee, "Toward a Unified Conception of Business Ethics: Integrative Social Contracts Theory," *Academy of Management Review*, April 1994, pp. 252–284; M. Douglas, "Integrative Social Contracts Theory: Hype Over Hypernorms," *Journal of Business Ethics*, July 2000, pp. 101–110; and E. Soule, "Managerial Moral Strategies—In Search of a Few Good Principles," *Academy of Management Review*, January 2002, pp. 114–124, for discussions of integrative social contracts theory.

**34.** E. Soule, "Managerial Moral Strategies—In Search of a Few Good Principles," *Academy of Management Review*, January 2002, p. 117.

**35.** F. D. Sturdivant, *Business and Society: A Managerial Approach*, 3rd ed. (Homewood, IL: Richard D. Irwin, 1985), p. 128.

**36.** L. Bogomolny, "Good Housekeeping," *Canadian Business*, March 1, 2004, pp. 87–88; and Royal Bank of Canada (RBC), "Community & Sustainability," *RBC website*, http://www.rbc.com/community-sustainability/index.html.

**37.** See Industry Canada, "Corporate Social Responsibility," http://www.ic.gc.ca/eic/site/csr-rse.nsf/eng/rs00129.html.

**38.** W. Dabrowski, "Tighter Guidelines Issued on Disclosure: Canada's 'Sarbanes,'" *Financial Post* (*National Post*), March 30, 2004, p. FP1.

**39.** L. Bogomolny, "Good Housekeeping," *Canadian Business*, March 1, 2004, pp. 87–88.

**40.** Terry Eyden, "Global Survey on Business Ethics," *Accounting Web*, June 21, 2012, http://www.accountingweb.com/article/global-survey-business-ethics/219380; and J. Alexander, "On the Right Side," *World Business*, January–February 1997, pp. 38–41.

**41.** P. Richter, "Big Business Puts Ethics in Spotlight," *Los Angeles Times*, June 19, 1986, p. 29.

**42.** F. R. David, "An Empirical Study of Codes of Business Ethics: A Strategic Perspective" (paper presented at the 48th Annual Academy of Management Conference, Anaheim, California, August 1988).

**43.** P.S. Ridge, "Ethics Programs Aren't Stemming Employee Misconduct," *Wall Street Journal*, May 11, 2000, p. A1.

**44.** L. Bogomolny, "Good Housekeeping," *Canadian Business*, March 1, 2004, pp. 87–88.

**45.** A. K. Reichert and M. S. Webb, "Corporate Support for Ethical and Environmental Policies: A Financial Management Perspective," *Journal of Business Ethics*, May 2000; G. R. Weaver, L. K. Trevino, and P. L. Cochran, "Corporate Ethics Programs as Control Systems: Influences of Executive Commitment and Environmental Factors," *Academy of Management Journal*, February 1999, pp. 41–57; G. R. Weaver, L. K. Trevino, and P. L. Cochran, "Integrated and De-coupled Corporate Social Performance: Management Commitments, External Pressures, and Corporate Ethics Practices," *Academy of Management Journal*, October 1999, pp. 539–552; and B. Z. Posner and W. H. Schmidt, "Values and the American Manager: An Update," *California Management Review*, Spring 1984, pp. 202–216.

**46.** L. Nash, "Ethics Without the Sermon," *Harvard Business Review*, November–December 1981, p. 81.

**47.** See, for example, R. A. Buccholz, *Essentials of Public Policy for Management*, 2nd ed. (Upper Saddle River, NJ: Prentice Hall, 1990).

**48.** M. Friedman, *Capitalism and Freedom* (Chicago: University of Chicago Press, 1962); and M. Friedman, "The Social Responsibility of Business Is to Increase Profits," *New York Times Magazine*, September 13, 1970, p. 33.

**49.** J. Bakan, *The Corporation* (Toronto: Big Picture Media Corporation, 2003).

**50.** Information from the Avon's website on its Corporate Citizenship, http://avoncompany.com/corporatecitizenship/breastcancer.html.

**51.** E. P. Lima, "Seeding a World of Transformation," *Industry-Week*, September 6, 1999, pp. 30–31.

**52.** E. White, "PR Firms Advise Corporations on Social Responsibility Issues," *Wall Street Journal*, November 13, 2002, p. B10.

**53.** The Triple Bottom Line was first introduced in J. Elkington, *Cannibals with Forks: The Triple Bottom Line of 21st Century Business* (Stony Creek, CT: New Society Publishers, 1998).

**54.** See, for example, A. B. Carroll, "The Pyramid of Corporate Social Responsibility: Toward the Moral Management of Organizational Stakeholders," *Business Horizons*, July–August 1991, pp. 39–48.

**55.** This section has been influenced by E. Gatewood and B. Carroll, "The Anatomy of Corporate Social Response," *Business Horizons*, September–October 1981, pp. 9–16.

**56.** See, for example, P. Cochran and R. A. Wood, "Corporate Social Responsibility and Financial Performance," *Academy of Management Journal*, March 1984, pp. 42–56; K. Aupperle, A. B. Carroll, and J. D. Hatfield, "An Empirical Examination of the Relationship Between Corporate Social Responsibility and Profitability," *Academy of Management Journal*, June 1985, pp. 446–463; J. B. McGuire, A. Sundgren, and T. Schneeweis, "Corporate Social Responsibility and Firm Financial Performance," *Academy of Management Journal*, December 1988, pp. 854–872; D. M. Georgoff and J. Ross, "Corporate Social Responsibility and Management Performance" (paper presented at the National Academy of Management Conference, Miami, Florida, August 1991); S. A. Zahra, B. M. Oviatt, and K. Minyard, "Effects of Corporate Ownership and Board Structure on Corporate Social Responsibility and Financial Performance" (paper presented at the National Academy of Management Conference, Atlanta, Georgia, August 1993); "Social Responsibility and the Bottom Line," *Business Ethics*, July–August 1994, p. 11; D. B. Turban and D. W. Greening, "Corporate Social Performance and Organizational Attractiveness to Prospective Employees," *Academy of Management Journal*, June 1996, pp. 658–672; S. A. Waddock and S. B. Graves, "The Corporate Social Performance–Financial Performance Link," *Strategic Management Journal*, April 1997, pp. 303–319; and S. L. Berman, A. C. Wicks, S. Kotha, and T. M. Jones, "Does Stakeholder Orientation Matter? The Relationship Between Stakeholder Management Models and Firm Financial Performance," *Academy of Management Journal*, October 1999, pp. 488–506.

**57.** D. J. Wood and R. E. Jones, "Stakeholder Mismatching: A Theoretical Problem in Empirical Research on Corporate Social

Performance," *International Journal of Organizational Analysis* 3, no. 3 (1995), pp. 229–267.

**58.** See A. A. Ullmann, "Data in Search of a Theory: A Critical Examination of the Relationships Among Social Performance, Social Disclosure, and Economic Performance of U.S. Firms," *Academy of Management Review*, July 1985, pp. 540–557; R. E. Wokutch and B. A. Spencer, "Corporate Saints and Sinners: The Effects of Philanthropic and Illegal Activity on Organizational Performance," *California Management Review*, Winter 1987, pp. 62–77; R. Wolfe and K. Aupperle, "Introduction to Corporate Social Performance: Methods for Evaluating an Elusive Construct," ed. J. E. Post, *Research in Corporate Social Performance and Policy* 13 (1991), pp. 265–268; and D. J. Wood and R. E. Jones, "Stakeholder Mismatching: A Theoretical Problem in Empirical Research on Corporate Social Performance," *International Journal of Organizational Analysis* 3 (1995), pp. 229–267.

**59.** D. Macfarlane, "Why Now?" *Report on Business Magazine*, March 2004, pp. 45–46.

**60.** J. V. Anderson, "Mind Mapping: A Tool for Creative Thinking," *Business Horizons*, January–February 1993, pp. 42–46; M. Loeb, "Ten Commandments for Managing Creative People," *Fortune*, January 16, 1995, pp. 135–136; M. Henricks, "Good Thinking," *Entrepreneur*, May 1996, pp. 70–73; H.-S.Choi and L. Thompson, "Old Wine in a New Bottle: Impact of Membership Change on Group Creativity," *Organizational Behavior and Human Decision Processes* 98, no. 2 (2005), pp. 121–132; R. Florida and J. Goodnight, "Managing for Creativity," *Harvard Business Review* 83, no. 7 (2005), pp. 124+; L. L. Gilson, J. E. Mathieu, C. E. Shalley, and T. M. Ruddy, "Creativity and Standardization: Complementary or Conflicting Drivers of Team Effectiveness?" *Academy of Management Journal* 48, no. 3 (2005), pp. 521–531; and K. G. Smith, C. J. Collins, and K. D. Clark, "Existing Knowledge, Knowledge Creation Capability, and the Rate of New Product Introduction in High-Technology Firms," *Academy of Management Journal* 48, no. 2 (2005), pp. 346–357.

**61.** Information for this box comes from B. C. McDonald and D. Hutcheson, "Dealing With Diversity Is Key to Tapping Talent," *Atlanta Business Chronicle*, December 18, 1998, p. 45A1; P. M. Elsass and L. M. Graves, "Demographic Diversity in Decision-Making Groups: The Experience of Women and People of Color," *Academy of Management Review*, October 1997, pp. 946–973; and N. J. Adler, ed., *International Dimensions of Organizational Behavior*, 4th ed. (Cincinnati, OH: South-Western College Publishing, 2001).

**62.** See Joe Castaldo, "How Management Has Failed at RIM," *Canadian Business*, January 19, 2012, http://www.canadianbusiness.com/article/66599—how-management-has-failed-at-rim; Joe Castaldo, "Can This Man Save RIM," *Canadian Business*, March 5, 2012, http://money.ca.msn.com/investing/canadian-business/can-this-man-save-rim-thorsten-heins-stay-the-course-plan; Iain Marlow, "What's Behind RIM's Marketing Missteps?" *Globe and Mail*, May 2, 2012, http://www.theglobeandmail.com/technology/tech-news/whats-behind-rims-marketing-missteps/article4105346/; Susan Krashinsky, "RIM's Marketing Challenge: Revive the CrackBerry Addiction," *Globe and Mail*, January 24, 2012, http://www.theglobeandmail.com/report-on-business/industry-news/marketing/rims-marketing-challenge-revive-the-crackberry-addiction/article1360018/; Iain Marlow, "'Pragmatic, Operational-Type Guy' Takes Over Reins at RIM," *Globe and Mail*, January 23, 2012, http://m.theglobeandmail.com/globe-investor/pragmatic-operational-type-guy-takes-over-reins-at-rim/article554464/; and Iain Marlow and Omar El Akkad, "RIM's Hard Choices: Five Ways To Rescue Canada's Tech Icon," *Globe and Mail*, April 14, 2012, http://www.theglobeandmail.com/technology/rims-hard-choices-five-ways-to-rescue-canadas-tech-icon/article4210441/.

## CHAPTER 5

**1.** Based on "Company Facts," Air Canada Centre, www.theaircanadacentre.com/corporate/CompanyFacts.asp; City of Toronto, "BMO Field Opens at Exhibition Place," News Release, May 11, 2007, http://wx.toronto.ca/inter/it/newsrel.nsf/9da959222128b9e885256618006646d3/41b84cf6c5ef64fe852572db004bc010?OpenDocument; MLSE, "Bell Completes Acquisition of Ownership Interest in Maple Leaf Sports & Entertainment," and "Rogers Completes Maple Leaf Sports & Entertainment Transaction," Press Releases, August 22, 2012, http://www.mlse.com/mlse_statement_082212.aspx; Toronto FC, "Toronto FC—Our Brief History and Bright Future," Toronto FC website, http://www.torontofc.ca/content/history; and Ricoh Coliseum "Contact Us," www.ricohcoliseum.com/contact/.

**2.** See, for example Bruce Dowbiggin, "Wrinkles Remain in Future MLSE Management Structure," *Globe and Mail*, May 3, 2012, http://www.theglobeandmail.com/sports/bruce-dowbiggin/wrinkles-remain-in-future-mlse-management-structure/article2422190/; Jeff Beer, "The Real Reason Rogers and Bell Bought MLSE," *Canadian Business*, January 19, 2012, http://www.canadianbusiness.com/article/66597—the-real-reason-rogers-and-bell-bought-mlse; Tara Perkins and Jacqueline Nelson, "Competition Bureau Clears BCE-Rogers Acquisition of MLSE Stake, *Globe and Mail*, May 2, 2012, http://www.theglobeandmail.com/globe-investor/competition-bureau-clears-bce-rogers-acquisition-of-mlse-stake/article2420539/; and Bruce Dowbiggin, "MLSE Deal: A Typical Canadian Compromise," *Globe and Mail*, December 11, 2011, http://www.theglobeandmail.com/sports/bruce-dowbiggin/mlse-deal-a-typical-canadian-compromise/article2267542/.

**3.** See, for example, R. L. Daft, *Organization Theory and Design*, 6th ed. (St. Paul, MN: West Publishing, 1998).

**4.** S. Melamed, I. Ben-Avi, and M. S. Green, "Objective and Subjective Work Monotony: Effects on Job Satisfaction, Psychological Distress, and Absenteeism in Blue-Collar Workers," *Journal of Applied Psychology*, February 1995, pp. 29–42.

**5.** W. Hillier, "BC Forest Fires: A Time of Need," *Canadian Underwriter* 72, no. 1 (2004), pp. 22–23.

**6.** For a discussion of authority, see W. A. Kahn and K. E. Kram, "Authority at Work: Internal Models and Their Organizational Consequences," *Academy of Management Review*, January 1994, pp. 17–50.

**7.** B. Arthur, "Peddie Gives New GM 'Autonomy' for Change," *National Post*, June 8, 2004, p. S2.

**8.** M. Grange, "So What, Exactly, Has Changed?" *Globe and Mail*, March 11, 2006, p. S1.

**9.** James Mirtle, "Leafs Ownership Apologizes to Fans for 'Unacceptable' End to Season," *Globe and Mail*, April 9, 2012, http://www.theglobeandmail.com/sports/hockey/leafs-beat/leafs-ownership-apologizes-to-fans-for-unacceptable-end-to-season/article2396502/.

**10.** Tips for Managers based on R. L. Daft, *The Leadership Experience*, 3e. © 2005 South-Western, a part of Cengage Learning, Inc. Reproduced by permission, www.cengage.com/permissions.

**11.** R. Ashkenas, "Simplicity-Minded Management," *Harvard Business Review*, December 2007, pp. 101–109; and P. Glader, "It's Not Easy Being Lean," *Wall Street Journal*, June 19, 2006, pp. B1+.

**12.** R. C. Morais, "The Old Lady Is Burning Rubber," *Forbes*, November 26, 2007, pp. 146–150.

**13.** D. Drickhamer, "Lessons from the Leading Edge," *Industry Week*, February 21, 2000, pp. 23–26.

**14.** D. Van Fleet, "Span of Management Research and Issues," *Academy of Management Journal*, September 1983, pp. 546–552.

**15.** See, for example, Nestlé's website, www.nestle.com; Ben Worthen, "Nestlé's Enterprise Resource Planning (ERP) Odyssey," *CIO*, May 15, 2002, http://www.cio.com/article/31066/Nestl_eacute_s_Enterprise_Resource_Planning_ERP_Odyssey.

**16.** Based on L. Millan, "Who's Scoffing Now? The Lemaire Brothers Started Out Using Recycled Fibre in One Small Paper Mill in Rural Quebec," *Canadian Business*, March 27, 1998, pp. 74–77; Cascades Inc.,"Profile," www.cascades.com/profile; and Cascades Inc., *Resolutely Cascades: 2008 Annual Report*, http://www.cascades.com//client_file/upload/pdf/rapports/2008_annuel_an.pdf.

**17.** E. W. Morrison, "Doing the Job Well: An Investigation of Pro-Social Rule Breaking," *Journal of Management*, February 2006, pp. 5–28.

**18.** E. W. Morrison, "Doing the Job Well: An Investigation of Pro-Social Rule Breaking," *Journal of Management*, February 2006, pp. 5–28.

**19.** T. Burns and G. M. Stalker, *The Management of Innovation* (London: Tavistock, 1961); and D. A. Morand, "The Role of Behavioral Formality and Informality in the Enactment of Bureaucratic Versus Organic Organizations," *Academy of Management Review*, October 1995, pp. 831–872.

**20.** See the Taxi website, http://taxi.ca/; P. Lavoie, "Taxi," *Campaign*, October 12, 2007; and L. Sylvain, "Taxi Deconstructed," *Strategy*, June 2007, http://strategyonline.ca/2007/06/01/taxidecon-20070601/.

**21.** J. Dee, "All the News That's Fit to Print Out," *New York Times Magazine*, July 1, 2007, pp. 34–39.

**22.** See, for example, R. E. Miles and C. C. Snow, *Organizational Strategy, Structure, and Process* (New York: McGraw-Hill, 1978); D. Miller, "The Structural and Environmental Correlates of Business Strategy," *Strategic Management Journal*, January–February 1987, pp. 55–76; H. L. Boschken, "Strategy and Structure: Reconceiving the Relationship," *Journal of Management*, March 1990, pp. 135–150; H. A. Simon, "Strategy and Organizational Evolution," *Strategic Management Journal*, January 1993, pp. 131–142; R. Parthasarthy and S. P. Sethi, "Relating Strategy and Structure to Flexible Automation: A Test of Fit and Performance Implications," *Strategic Management Journal* 14, no. 6 (1993), pp. 529–549; D. C. Galunic and K. M. Eisenhardt, "Renewing the Strategy-Structure-Performance Paradigm," in *Research in Organizational Behavior*, vol. 16, ed. B. M. Staw and L. L. Cummings (Greenwich, CT: JAI Press, 1994), pp. 215–255; and D. Jennings and S. Seaman, "High and Low Levels of Organizational Adaptation: An Empirical Analysis of Strategy, Structure, and Performance," *Strategic Management Journal*, July 1994, pp. 459–475.

**23.** See, for example, P. M. Blau and R. A. Schoenherr, *The Structure of Organizations* (New York: Basic Books, 1971); D.

S. Pugh, "The Aston Program of Research: Retrospect and Prospect," in *Perspectives on Organization Design and Behavior*, ed. A. H. Van de Ven and W. F. Joyce, pp. 135–166 (New York: John Wiley, 1981); and R. Z. Gooding and J. A. Wagner III, "A Meta-Analytic Review of the Relationship Between Size and Performance: The Productivity and Efficiency of Organizations and Their Subunits," *Administrative Science Quarterly*, December 1985, pp. 462–481.

**24.** J. Woodward, *Industrial Organization: Theory and Practice* (London: Oxford University Press, 1965).

**25.** See, for example, C. Perrow, "A Framework for the Comparative Analysis of Organizations," *American Sociological Review*, April 1967, pp. 194–208; J. D. Thompson, *Organizations in Action* (New York: McGraw-Hill, 1967); J. Hage and M. Aiken, "Routine Technology, Social Structure, and Organizational Goals," *Administrative Science Quarterly*, September 1969, pp. 366–377; and C. C. Miller, W. H. Glick, Y. D. Wang, and G. P. Huber, "Understanding Technology-Structure Relationships: Theory Development and Meta-Analytic Theory Testing," *Academy of Management Journal*, June 1991, pp. 370–399.

**26.** D. Gerwin, "Relationships Between Structure and Technology," in *Handbook of Organizational Design*, vol. 2, ed. P. C. Nystrom and W. H. Starbuck, pp. 3–38 (New York: Oxford University Press, 1981); and D. M. Rousseau and R. A. Cooke, "Technology and Structure: The Concrete, Abstract, and Activity Systems of Organizations," *Journal of Management*, Fall–Winter 1984, pp. 345–361.

**27.** F. E. Emery and E. Trist, "The Causal Texture of Organizational Environments," *Human Relations*, February 1965, pp. 21–32; P. Lawrence and J. W. Lorsch, *Organization and Environment: Managing Differentiation and Integration* (Boston: Harvard Business School, Division of Research, 1967); and M. Yasai-Ardekani, "Structural Adaptations to Environments," *Academy of Management Review*, January 1986, pp. 9–21.

**28.** L. A. Perlow, G. A. Okhuysen, and N. P. Repenning, "The Speed Trap: Exploring the Relationship Between Decision Making and Temporal Context," *Academy of Management Journal* 45, 2002, pp. 931–995.

**29.** Based on "Management, Maple Leaf Sports & Entertainment," #RaptorsCamp on nba.com, www.nba.com/raptors/news/mlsel_management.html; "Gilbert Named Marlies Head Coach," Press Release, marlies.ca, July 27, 2006, www.torontomarlies.com/news/News.asp?story_id=14; and "Marlies Home Opener Oct. 6," Press Release, June 18, 2007, marlies.ca, www.torontomarlies.com/news/news.asp?story_id=433.

**30.** H. Mintzberg, *Structure in Fives: Designing Effective Organizations* (Upper Saddle River, NJ: Prentice Hall, 1983), p. 157.

**31.** R. J. Williams, J. J. Hoffman, and B. T. Lamont, "The Influence of Top Management Team Characteristics on M-Form Implementation Time," *Journal of Managerial Issues*, Winter 1995, pp. 466–480.

**32.** See, for example, R. E. Hoskisson, C. W. L. Hill, and H. Kim, "The Multidivisional Structure: Organizational Fossil or Source of Value?" *Journal of Management* 19, no. 2 (1993), pp. 269–298; I. I. Mitroff, R. O. Mason, and C. M. Pearson, "Radical Surgery: What Will Tomorrow's Organizations Look Like?" *Academy of Management Executive*, February 1994, pp. 11–21; T. Clancy, "Radical Surgery: A View from the Operating Theater," *Academy of Management Executive*, February 1994, pp. 73–78; M. Hammer, "Processed Change: Michael Hammer

Sees Process as 'the Clark Kent of Business Ideas'—A Concept That Has the Power to Change a Company's Organizational Design," *Journal of Business Strategy*, November–December 2001, pp. 11–15; D. F. Twomey, "Leadership, Organizational Design, and Competitiveness for the 21st Century," *Global Competitiveness*, Annual 2002, pp. S31–S40; and G. J. Castrogiovanni, "Organization Task Environments: Have They Changed Fundamentally Over Time?" *Journal of Management* 28, no. 2 (2002), pp. 129–150.

**33.** T. Starner, "Room for Improvement," *IQ Magazine*, March–April 2003, pp. 36–37.

**34.** Q. Hardy, "Google Thinks Small," *Forbes*, November 14, 2005, pp. 198–202.

**35.** See, for example, H. Rothman, "The Power of Empowerment," *Nation's Business*, June 1993, pp. 49–52; B. Dumaine, "Payoff from the New Management," *Fortune*, December 13, 1993, pp. 103–110; J. A. Byrne, "The Horizontal Corporation," *BusinessWeek*, December 20, 1993, pp. 76–81; J. R. Katzenbach and D. K. Smith, *The Wisdom of Teams* (Boston: Harvard Business School Press, 1993); L. Grant, "New Jewel in the Crown," *U.S. News & World Report*, February 28, 1994, pp. 55–57; D. Ray and H. Bronstein, *Teaming Up: Making the Transition to a Self-Directed Team-Based Organization* (New York: McGraw Hill, 1995); and D. R. Denison, S. L. Hart, and J. A. Kahn, "From Chimneys to Cross-Functional Teams: Developing and Validating a Diagnostic Model," *Academy of Management Journal*, December 1996, pp. 1005–1023.

**36.** C. Fishman, "Whole Foods Is All Teams," *Fast Company, Greatest Hits*, vol. 1, 1997, pp. 102–113.

**37.** W. Hillier, "BC Forest Fires: A Time of Need," *Canadian Underwriter*, January 2004, pp. 22–23.

**38.** P. LaBarre, "This Organization Is Dis-Organization," *Fast Company*, www.fastcompany.com/magazine/03/oticon.html.

**39.** See, for example, G. G. Dess et al., "The New Corporate Architecture," *Academy of Management Executive*, August 1995, pp. 7–20.

**40.** For additional readings on boundaryless organizations, see M. Hammer and S. Stanton, "How Process Enterprises Really Work," *Harvard Business Review*, November–December 1999, pp. 108–118; T. Zenger and W. Hesterly, "The Disaggregation of Corporations: Selective Intervention, High-Powered Incentives, and Modular Units," *Organization Science* 8 (1997), pp. 209–222; R. Ashkenas, D. Ulrich, T. Jick, and S. Kerr, *The Boundaryless Organization: Breaking the Chains of Organizational Structure* (San Francisco: Jossey-Bass, 1997); R. M. Hodgetts, "A Conversation With Steve Kerr," *Organizational Dynamics*, Spring 1996, pp. 68–79; and J. Gebhardt, "The Boundaryless Organization," *Sloan Management Review*, Winter 1996, pp. 117–119. For another view of boundaryless organizations, see B. Victor, "The Dark Side of the New Organizational Forms: An Editorial Essay," *Organization Science*, November 1994, pp. 479–482.

**41.** S. C. Certo and S. T. Certo, *Modern Management*, 10th edition, (Upper Saddle River, NJ: Prentice Hall, 2006), p. 316; P. M. J. Christie and R. R. Levary, "Virtual Corporations: Recipe for Success," *Industrial Management*, July/August 1998, pp. 7–11; and C. C. Snow, R. E. Miles, and H. J. Coleman Jr., "Managing 21st Century Network Organizations," *Organizational Dynamics*, Winter, 1992, pp. 5–20.

**42.** See, for example, W. H. Davidow and M. S. Malone, *The Virtual Corporation* (New York: HarperCollins, 1992); H.

Chesbrough and D. Teece, "When Is Virtual Virtuous? Organizing for Innovation," *Harvard Business Review*, January–February 1996, pp. 65–73; G. G. Dess, A. Rasheed, K. J. McLaughlin, and R. L. Priem, "The New Corporate Architecture," *Academy of Management Executive*, August 1995, pp. 7–20; M. Sawhney and D. Parikh, "Break Your Boundaries," *Business* 2.0, May 2000, pp. 198–207; D. Pescovitz, "The Company Where Everybody's a Temp," *New York Times Magazine*, June 11, 2000, pp. 94–96; W. F. Cascio, "Managing a Virtual Workplace," *Academy of Management Executive*, August 2000, pp. 81–90; D. Lyons, "Smart and Smarter," *Forbes*, March 18, 2002, pp. 40–41; and B. Hedberg, G. Dahlgren, J. Hansson, and N. Goran Olve, *Virtual Organizations and Beyond: Discovering Imaginary Systems* (New York: John Wiley, 2001).

**43.** Based on G. Shaw, "Vancouver Law Firm Opens Virtual Branch Office," *Vancouver Sun*, September 26, 2007, p. F4.

**44.** R. E. Miles and C. C. Snow, "Causes of Failures in Network Organizations," *California Management Review* 34, no. 4 (1992), pp. 53–72; R. E. Miles and C. C. Snow, "The New Network Firm: A Spherical Structure Built on Human Investment Philosophy," *Organizational Dynamics*, Spring 1995, pp. 5–18; C. Jones, W. Hesterly, and S. Borgatti, "A General Theory of Network Governance: Exchange Conditions and Social Mechanisms," *Academy of Management Review*, October 1997, pp. 911–945; and R. E. Miles, C. C. Snow, J. A. Mathews, G. Miles, and H. J. Coleman, "Organizing in the Knowledge Age: Anticipating the Cellular Form," *Academy of Management Executive*, November 1997, pp. 7–24.

**45.** SMTnet, "Mitel Outsources Manufacturing to New Company," News Release, September 7, 2001, http://www.smtnet.com/news/index.cfm?fuseaction=view_news&news_id=1884.

**46.** J. Barthelemy and D. Adsit, "The Seven Deadly Sins of Outsourcing," *Academy of Management Executive* 17, no. 2 (2003), pp. 87–100.

**47.** K. Restivo, "Most Canadian Tech Firms Prefer Not to Outsource, Study Shows," *Financial Post* (*National Post*), June 11, 2004, p. FP5.

**48.** PricewaterhouseCoopers LLP, *Embracing the New: The Business Insights® Survey of Canadian Private Companies 2011*, http://www.pwc.com/ca/en/private-company/publications/business-insights-2011-10-en.pdf.

**49.** C. E. Connelly and D. G. Gallagher, "Emerging Trends in Contingent Work Research," *Journal of Management*, November 2004, pp. 959–983.

**50.** P. Olson, "Tesco's Landing," *Forbes*, June 4, 2007, pp. 116–118; and P. M. Senge, *The Fifth Discipline: The Art and Practice of Learning Organizations* (New York: Doubleday, 1990).

**51.** D. A. Garvin, A. C. Edmondson, and F. Gino, "Is Yours a Learning Organization?" *Harvard Business Review*, March 2008, pp. 109–116; A. N. K. Chen and T. M. Edgington, "Assessing Value in Organizational Knowledge Creation: Considerations for Knowledge Workers," *MIS Quarterly*, June 2005, pp. 279–309; K. G. Smith, C. J. Collins, and K. D. Clark, "Existing Knowledge, Knowledge Creation Capability, and the Rate of New Product Introduction in High-Technology Firms," *Academy of Management Journal*, April 2005, pp. 346–357; R. Cross, A. Parker, L. Prusak, and S. P. Borgati, "Supporting Knowledge Creation and Sharing in Social Networks," *Organizational Dynamics*, Fall 2001, pp. 100–120; M. Schulz, "The Uncertain Relevance of Newness: Organizational Learning and Knowledge

Flows," *Academy of Management Journal*, August 2001, pp. 661–681; G. Szulanski, "Exploring Internal Stickiness: Impediments to the Transfer of Best Practice within the Firm," *Strategic Management Journal*, Winter Special Issue, 1996, pp. 27–43; and J. M. Liedtka, "Collaborating Across Lines of Business for Competitive Advantage," *Academy of Management Executive*, April 1996, pp. 20–37.

**52.** N. M. Adler, *International Dimensions of Organizational Behavior*, 4th ed. (Cincinnati, OH: South-Western College Publishing), 2002, p. 66.

**53.** P. B. Smith and M. F. Peterson, "Demographic Effects on the Use of Vertical Sources of Guidance by Managers in Widely Differing Cultural Contexts," *International Journal of Cross Cultural Management*, April 2005, pp. 5–26.

**54.** Based on J. F. Veiga and J. N. Yanouzas, *The Dynamics of Organization Theory: Gaining a Macro Perspective* (St. Paul, MN: West, 1979), pp. 158–160.

**55.** FAST COMPANY by A. Cohen. Copyright 2008 by Mansueto Ventures LLC. Reproduced with permission of Mansueto Ventures LLC in the format Textbook via Copyright Clearance Center.

**56.** Based on P. L. Hunsaker, *Training in Management Skills* (Upper Saddle River, NJ: Prentice Hall, 2001), pp. 135–136 and 430–432; R. T. Noel, "What You Say to Your Employees When You Delegate," *Supervisory Management*, December 1993, p. 13; and S. Caudron, "Delegate for Results," *IndustryWeek*, February 6, 1995, pp. 27–30.

**57.** See, for example, Deloitte, "Organizing for Corporate Responsibility and Sustainability: How a Company's Organizational Structure and Governance Models Can Support CS&R Success," Deloitte Development LLC, 2009, http://www.corpgov.deloitte.com/site/us/board-governance/corporate-responsibility-and-sustainability/; Canadian Business for Social Responsibility (CBSR) and the Network for Business Sustainability, *Embedding Sustainability in Organizational Culture—Framework and Best Practices* (report emerging from the workshop "Embedding Sustainability into Corporate Cultures," presented February 23, 2010, in Toronto, Ontario, by CBSR and Network for Business Sustainability), http://www.cbsr.ca/sites/default/files/file/CultureReport_Final.pdf; Kathee Rebernak, "Where Sustainability Lives: A Path to Integration and Innovation," *Environmental Leader*, July 12, 2009, http://www.environmentalleader.com/2009/07/12/where-sustainability-lives-a-path-to-integration-and-innovation/.

**58.** Deloitte, "Organizing for Corporate Responsibility and Sustainability: How a Company's Organizational Structure and Governance Models Can Support CS&R Success," Deloitte Development LLC, 2009, http://www.corpgov.deloitte.com/site/us/board-governance/corporate-responsibility-and-sustainability/.

**59.** See the Nova Scotia Association of Social Workers (NSASW) website, http://www.nsasw.org; NSASW, "Board of Examiners Annual Report," January 1–December 31, 2010, http://www.nsasw.org/files/File/Board%20of%20Examiners/BOARD%20OF%20EXAMINERS-2011.pdf; and Richard G. Ramsay Management Consultants Inc., *The Nova Scotia Association of Social Workers: Organization Structure Review, Final Report*, October, 2009, http://www.nsasw.org/inner.php?id=70.

**60.** See, for example, Northern Light Technologies, "About Us," http://www.nltinc.com/about.html; Levitt-Safety, "About Us," http://www.levitt-safety.com/Company/AboutUs/tabid/61/De-

fault.aspx; and "As I See It," Interview with Bruce Levitt of Levitt-Safety Limited in *Embracing the New: The Business Insights® Survey of Canadian Private Companies 2011*, PricewaterhouseCoopers LLP, p. 25, http://www.pwc.com/ca/en/private-company/publications/business-insights-2011-10-en.pdf.

## CHAPTER 6

**1.** Les Faber, "Canadian Social Media Statistics 2011," *WebFuel*, July 20, 2011, http://www.webfuel.ca/canada-social-media-statistics-2011/.

**2.** CNW, "Less Than a Fifth of Canadian Companies Use Social Media Effectively," *Canadian Newswire*, August 30, 2011, http://www.newswire.ca/en/story/832943/less-than-a-fifth-of-canadian-companies-use-social-media-effectively.

**3.** T. Dixon, *Communication, Organization, and Performance* (Norwood, NJ: Ablex Publishing Corporation, 1996), p. 281; P. G. Clampitt, *Communicating for Managerial Effectiveness* (Newbury Park, CA: Sage Publications, 1991); and L. E. Penley, E. R. Alexander, I. E. Jernigan, and C. I. Henwood, "Communication Abilities of Managers: The Relationship to Performance," *Journal of Management*, March 1991, pp. 57–76.

**4.** "Electronic Invective Backfires," *Workforce*, June 2001, p. 20; and E. Wong, "A Stinging Office Memo Boomerangs," *New York Times*, April 5, 2001, p. C11.

**5.** C. O. Kursh, "The Benefits of Poor Communication," *Psychoanalytic Review*, Summer–Fall 1971, pp. 189–208.

**6.** W. G. Scott and T. R. Mitchell, *Organization Theory: A Structural and Behavioral Analysis* (Homewood, IL: Richard D. Irwin, 1976).

**7.** Based on A. Shimo, "Why Is T.O. the Capital of Facebook?" *Toronto Star*, June 30, 2007, p. ID3; and "City of Toronto Disconnects Workers from Facebook," *CBCnews.ca*, May 10, 2007, www.cbc.ca/technology/story/2007/05/10/facebook-toronto-city.html.

**8.** D. K. Berlo, *The Process of Communication* (New York: Holt, Rinehart & Winston, 1960), pp. 30–32.

**9.** T. R. Kurtzberg, C. E. Naquin, and L. Y. Belkin, "Electronic Performance Appraisals: The Effects of E-Mail Communication on Peer Ratings in Actual and Simulated Environments," *Organizational Behavior and Human Decision Processes* 98, no. 2 (2005), pp. 216–226.

**10.** J. Kruger, N. Epley, J. Parker, and Z.-W. Ng, "Egocentrism Over E-Mail: Can We Communicate as Well as We Think?" *Journal of Personality and Social Psychology* 89, no. 6 (2005), pp. 925–936.

**11.** P. G. Clampitt, *Communicating for Managerial Effectiveness* (Newbury Park, CA: Sage Publications, 1991).

**12.** A. Warfield, "Do You Speak Body Language?" *Training & Development*, April 2001, pp. 60–61; D. Zielinski, "Body Language Myths," *Presentations*, April 2001, pp. 36–42; and "Visual Cues Speak Loudly in Workplace," *Springfield News-Leader*, January 21, 2001, p. 8B.

**13.** C. Cavanagh, *Managing Your E-Mail: Thinking Outside the Inbox* (Hoboken, NJ: John Wiley & Sons, 2003).

**14.** K. Macklem, "You've Got Too Much Mail," *Maclean's*, January 30, 2006, pp. 20–21.

**15.** K. Macklem, "You've Got Too Much Mail," *Maclean's*, January 30, 2006, pp. 20–21.

**16.** D. K. Berlo, *The Process of Communication* (New York: Holt, Rinehart & Winston, 1960), p. 103.

**17.** P.N. Johnson-Laird, "Mental Models and Deduction," *Trends in Cognitive Sciences* 5, no. 10 (2001).

**18.** Based on G. Robertson, "Goodbye, Buttonhole Makers. Hello, Tapas," *Globe and Mail*, May 22, 2007, p. B1.

**19.** A. Mehrabian, "Communication Without Words," *Psychology Today*, September 1968, pp. 53–55.

**20.** See, for example, S. P. Robbins and P. L. Hunsaker, *Training in Interpersonal Skills*, 3rd ed. (Upper Saddle River, NJ: Prentice Hall, 2003); M. Young and J. E. Post, "Managing to Communicate, Communicating to Manage: How Leading Companies Communicate with Employees," *Organizational Dynamics*, Summer 1993, pp. 31–43; J. A. DeVito, *The Interpersonal Communication Book*, 6th ed. (New York: HarperCollins, 1992); and A. G. Athos and J. J. Gabarro, *Interpersonal Behavior* (Upper Saddle River, NJ: Prentice Hall, 1978).

**21.** O. Thomas, "Best-Kept Secrets of the World's Best Companies: The Three Minute Huddle," *Business* 2.0, April 2006, p. 94.

**22.** V. Galt, "Top-Down Feedback," *Vancouver Sun*, February 15, 2003, pp. E1, E2.

**23.** Tips for Managers based on R. Kreitner and A. Kinicki, *Organizational Behavior*, 6th ed. (New York: McGraw-Hill/Irwin, 2004), p. 335. Reprinted by permission of McGraw-Hill Education.

**24.** Cited in "Heard It Through the Grapevine," *Forbes*, February 10, 1997, p. 22.

**25.** See, for example, A. Bruzzese, "What to Do About Toxic Gossip," *USA Today*, March 15, 2001, http://www.usatoday.com/careers/news/usa050.htm; N. B. Kurland and L. H. Pelled, "Passing the Word: Toward a Model of Gossip and Power in the Workplace," *Academy of Management Review*, April 2000, pp. 428–438; N. DiFonzo, P. Bordia, and R. L. Rosnow, "Reining in Rumors," *Organizational Dynamics*, Summer 1994, pp. 47–62; M. Noon and R. Delbridge, "News from Behind My Hand: Gossip in Organizations," *Organization Studies* 14, no. 1 (1993), pp. 23–26; and J. G. March and G. Sevon, "Gossip, Information and Decision Making," in *Decisions and Organizations*, ed. G. March (Oxford: Blackwell, 1988), pp. 429–442.

**26.** Watson Wyatt Worldwide, *Effective Communication: A Leading Indicator of Financial Performance–2005/2006 Communication ROI Study* (Washington, DC: Watson Wyatt Worldwide, 2006).

**27.** B. McCrea, "A New Kind of Hookup," *Black Enterprise*, July 2007, p. 52.

**28.** G. Buckler, "Instant Messaging Replacing Pagers in the Enterprise," *Computing Canada*, March 26, 2004, p. 18.

**29.** J. Rohwer, "Today, Tokyo: Tomorrow, the World," *Fortune*, September 18, 2000, pp. 140–152; J. McCullam and L. Torres, "Instant Enterprising," *Forbes*, September 11, 2000, p. 28; J. Guyon, "The World Is Your Office," *Fortune*, June 12, 2000, pp. 227–234; S. Baker, N. Gross, and I. M. Kunii, "The Wireless Internet," *BusinessWeek*, May 29, 2000, pp. 136–144; and R. Lieber, "Information Is Everything …" *Fast Company*, November 1999, pp. 246–254.

**30.** M. Vallis, "Nasty E-mail from the Boss May Mean More Sick Days," *National Post*, January 9, 2004, pp. A1, A9. Study was done by George Fieldman, a psychologist at Buckingham-

shire Chilterns University College, and presented at the 2004 Annual Occupational Psychology Conference of the British Psychological Society.

**31.** Derived from P. Kuitenbrouwer, "Office E-Mail Runs Amok," *Financial Post*, October 18, 2001, p. FP11.

**32.** See, for example, Jabra, *GenM: Defining the Workforce of Tomorrow*, 2012, http://campaigns.jabra.com/eCards/UK/6339_4_Jabra_GenM_Study_Booklet_final.pdf; Contact Centre Live, "Research Identifies Growing Mobile Work Culture & Frustration with Solutions Provided by IT Depts," March 13, 2012, http://www.callcentreclinic.com/news/market-research/research-identifies-growing-mobile-work-culture—frustration-with-solutions-provided-by-it-depts—46575.htm.

**33.** Information on *Second Life* based on A. Athavaley, "A Job Interview You Don't Have to Show Up For," *Wall Street Journal*, June 20, 2007, p. D1.

**34.** "Be Careful About Your E-Trail," *Prince George Citizen*, June 22, 2007, p. 36.

**35.** R. Branson, "It's No Wonder They Don't Understand You," *Canadian Business*, September 8, 2011, http://www.canadian-business.com/article/43982—branson-it-s-no-wonder-they-don-t-understand-you.

**36.** K. Hafner, "For the Well Connected, All the World's an Office," *New York Times*, March 30, 2000, p. D11.

**37.** Kelly Robertson, "Adoption of Google+ Essential for Canadian Businesses," *Canadian Business Journal*, February 12, 2012, http://www.cbj.ca/index.php?news=7859.

**38.** Kelly Robertson, "Adoption of Google+ Essential for Canadian Businesses", *Canadian Business Journal*, February 12, 2012, http://www.cbj.ca/index.php?news=7859.

**39.** Debbie Dimoff, "Connecting with Social Media" PricewaterhouseCoopers LLP, 2011, http://www.pwc.com/ca/en/private-company/lets-talk/social-media.jhtml.

**40.** Jennifer Vivian, "Molson Coors Canada Incorporates Social Media into Its Employee Engagement Approach to Drive Performance, Productivity and Bottom Line Results," *Social Media for Business Performance*, February 6, 2012, http://smbp.uwaterloo.ca/2012/02/molson-coors-canada-incorporates-social-media-into-its-employee-engagement-approach-to-drive-performance-productivity-and-bottom-line-results/.

**41.** Molson Coors, "Every Drop Every Ripple," http://www.everydropeveryripple.com.

**42.** "Pros and Cons of Social Media," *Canadian Business Network*, http://www.canadabusiness.ca/eng/page/2655/.

**43.** "Pros and Cons of Social Media," *Canadian Business Network*, http://www.canadabusiness.ca/eng/page/2655/.

**44.** Debbie Dimoff, "Connecting with Social Media" PricewaterhouseCoopers LLP, 2011, http://www.pwc.com/ca/en/private-company/lets-talk/social-media.jhtml.

**45.** Derek Sankey, "Employers, Unions Making More Use of Social Media," *Postmedia News*, May 8, 2012, http://www.canada.com/business/Employers+unions+making+more+social+media/6547875/story.html.

**46.** Adapted from R. Norton, "Foundation of a Communicator Style Construct," *Human Communication Research*, 4, 1978, pp. 99–112.

**47.** Based on C. R. Rogers and R. E. Farson, *Active Listening* (Chicago: Industrial Relations Center of the University of

Chicago, 1976); and P. L. Hunsaker, *Training in Management Skills* (Upper Saddle River, NJ: Prentice Hall, 2001), pp. 61–62.

**48.** S. McShane and S. Steen, *Canadian Organizational Behaviour*, 8th ed. (Toronto, ON: McGraw-Hill Ryerson Ltd. Canada, 2012), Team Exercise 9.3 Active Listening.

**49.** J. Langdon, "Differences Between Males and Females at Work," *USA Today*, February 5, 2001, www.usatoday.com; J. Manion, "He Said, She Said," *Materials Management in Health Care*, November 1998, pp. 52–62; G. Franzwa and C. Lockhart, "The Social Origins and Maintenance of Gender Communication Styles, Personality Types, and Grid-Group Theory," *Sociological Perspectives* 41, no. 1 (1998), pp. 185–208; and D. Tannen, *Talking from 9 to 5: Women and Men in the Workplace* (New York: Avon Books, 1995).

**50.** Greg Moran, "Using Social Media in Assessment & Selection," *North America Business Review*, April 16, 2012, http://www.businessreviewcanada.ca/marketing/social-media/using-social-media-in-assessment-selection.

**51.** "Workplace Communication Protocol, 2011 edition," *Canadian Business*, November 21, 2011.

**52.** Based on information from Cisco, "Social@CiscoCanada," http://www.cisco.com/web/CA/socialmedia/index.html.

**53.** Etan. Vlessing, "Social Media in the Enterprise: Cisco Canada Drives Brand Awareness," TELUS Talks Business, January 18, 2012, http://community.telustalksbusiness.com/blogs/talk_business/2012/01/18/social-media-in-the-enterprise-cisco-canada-drives-brand-awareness.

**54.** Cisco, *2011 Cisco Connected World Technology Report*, http://www.cisco.com/en/US/netsol/ns1120/index.html.

**55.** Paolo Del Mibletto, "Cisco Ushers in People-Centric Collaboration," *CDN*, March 3, 2012, http://www.itbusiness.ca/it/client/en/cdn/News.asp?id=66738.

**56.** Paolo Del Mibletto, "Cisco Ushers in People-Centric Collaboration," *CDN*, March 3, 2012, http://www.itbusiness.ca/it/client/en/cdn/News.asp?id=66738.

## CHAPTER 7

**1.** See the Calgary Chamber of Voluntary Organizations (CCVO) website, www.calgarycvo.org.

**2.** A. Burrowes and J. Coe, *Beyond the Boomers: A Guidebook for Building an Immigrant Workforce in the Nonprofit Sector* (Calgary, AB: CCVO, 2011), http://www.calgarycvo.org/sites/default/files/resources/201107_CCVO_DiversityWorkbook.pdf.

**3.** R. Roach, *The Nonprofit and Voluntary Sector in Alberta: Regional Highlights of the National Survey of Nonprofit and Voluntary Organizations*, (Toronto ON: Imagine Canada, 2006).

**4.** See, for example, Y. Y. Kor and H. Leblebici, "How Do Interdependencies Among Human-Capital Deployment, Development, and Diversification Strategies Affect Firms' Financial Performance?" *Strategic Management Journal*, October 2005, pp. 967–985; D. E. Bowen and C. Ostroff, "Understanding HRM–Firm Performance Linkages: The Role of the 'Strength' of the HRM System," *Academy of Management Review*, April 2004, pp. 203–221; R. Batt, "Managing Customer Services: Human Resource Practices, Quit Rates, and Sales Growth," *Academy of Management Journal*, June 2002, pp. 587–597; A. S. Tsui, J. L. Pearce, L. W. Porter, and A. M. Tripoli, "Alternative Approaches to the Employee–Organization Relationship: Does Investment in

Employees Pay Off?" *Academy of Management Journal*, October 1997, pp. 1089–1121; M. A. Huselid, S. E. Jackson, and R. S. Schuler, "Technical and Strategic Human Resource Management Effectiveness As Determinants of Firm Performance," *Academy of Management Journal*, January 1997, pp. 171–188; J. T. Delaney and M. A. Huselid, "The Impact of Human Resource Management Practices on Perceptions of Organizational Performance," *Academy of Management Journal*, August 1996, pp. 949–969; B. Becker and B. Gerhart, "The Impact of Human Resource Management on Organizational Performance: Progress and Prospects," *Academy of Management Journal*, August 1996, pp. 779–801; M. J. Koch and R. G. McGrath, "Improving Labor Productivity: Human Resource Management Policies Do Matter," *Strategic Management Journal*, May 1996, pp. 335–354; and M. A. Huselid, "The Impact of Human Resource Management Practices on Turnover, Productivity, and Corporate Financial Performance," *Academy of Management Journal*, June 1995, pp. 635–672.

**5.** "Maximizing the Return on Your Human Capital Investment: The 2005 Watson Wyatt Human Capital Index® Report," "WorkAsia 2004/2005: A Study of Employee Attitudes in Asia," and "European Human Capital Index 2002," Watson Wyatt Worldwide (Washington, D.C.).

**6.** See WorldatWork®, *Total Rewards Model*, (WorldatWork®, 2011), http://www.worldatwork.org/waw/adimLink?id=28330&nonav=y.

**7.** Adapted from Gareth Morgan, *Images of Organization*, (Thousand Oaks, CA: Sage Publications, 2006).

**8.** A. Burrowes and J. Coe, *Beyond the Boomers: A Guidebook for Building an Immigrant Workforce in the Nonprofit Sector* (Calgary, AB: CCVO, 2011), http://www.calgarycvo.org/sites/default/files/resources/201107_CCVO_DiversityWorkbook.pdf.

**9.** Deloitte Canada, "Congratulations to Canada's 50 Best Managed Companies," *National Post*, February 21, 2011.

**10.** Statistics Canada, "Labour Force Survey, August 2012," *The Daily* (Statistics Canada), http://www.statcan.gc.ca/daily-quotidien/120907/dq120907a-eng.htm.

**11.** Peter O'Neill, "Chamber Seeks Changes to EI to Combat Skills Shortage Crisis; President Says Ottawa Believes Its Own 'Propaganda'' About the State of the Economy; 'Competitiveness' Should Be Its Mandate," *Vancouver Sun*, February 8, 2012: C2; Canadian Chamber of Commerce, "Taking on the Top 10 Barriers to Canadian Competitiveness," *Connect!*, February 8, 2012, http://www.chamber.ca/index.php/en/news/C197/taking-on-the-top-10-barriers-to-canadian-competitiveness; and Canadian Chamber of Commerce, "Top 10 Barriers to Competitiveness," *Connect!*, http://chambertop10.ca.

**12.** Working in Canada, "Canada Targets Skilled Trades," http://www.workingin-canada.com/visa/skills-in-demand/canada-targets-skilled-trades.

**13.** Human Resources and Skills Development Canada, "Canadians in Context—Aging Population," http://www4.hrsdc.gc.ca/.3ndic.1t.4r@-eng.jsp?iid=33.

**14.** Human Resources and Skills Development Canada, "Canadians in Context—Aging Population," http://www4.hrsdc.gc.ca/.3ndic.1t.4r@-eng.jsp?iid=33.

**15.** See, for example, The Ontario Federation of Labour's Workers Under 30 Committee, "Myths About Unions," http://youth.ofl.ca/index.php/myths/; Lawrence Mishel and Matthew Walters,

*How Unions Help All Workers* (Washington, DC: Economic Policy Institite, 2003); A. Jilani, "Report: Five Things Unions Have Done for All Americans," *Think Progress*, March 5, 2011, http://thinkprogress.org/politics/2011/03/05/148930/top-five-things-unions/?mobile=nc.

**16.** Statistics Canada, "Unionization: Unionized Rates in First Half of 2006 and 2007," http://www.statcan.gc.ca/pub/75-001-x/topics-sujets/unionization-syndicalisation/unionization-syndicalisation-2007-eng.htm.

**17.** G. Dessler and N. Cole, *Human Resources Management in Canada*, 10th ed. (Toronto, ON: Pearson Prentice-Hall).

**18.** S. Armour, "Lawsuits Pin Target on Managers," *USA Today*, October 1, 2002, www.usatoday.com.

**19.** See, for example, C. Sleezer, T. Wentling, and R. Cude, eds., *Human Resource Development and Information Technology: Making Global Connections* (Norwell, MA: Kluwer Academic Publishers, 2001), pp. 89–104; W. F. Cascio, "From Business Partner to Driving Business Success: The Next Step in the Evolution of HR Management," in *The Future of Human Resource Management: 64 Thought Leaders Explore the Critical HR Issues of Today and Tomorrow,* M. Losey, S. Meisinger, and D. Ulrich, eds. (Hoboken, NJ: John Wiley & Sons, 2005), pp. 103–109; B. Luck, *Innovation of Technology: Business for a New Century*, 2010, http://www.scribd.com/?doc/?27947709/?Innovation-of-Technology-in-Business-Slides; and A. Walker, "Best Practices in HR Technology," in A. Walker and T. Perrin, eds., *Web-based Human Resources: The Technologies and Trends That Are Transforming HR* (New York, NY: McGraw-Hill, 2001), pp. 3–14.

**20.** W. Brockbank, "If HR Were Really Strategically Proactive: Present and Future Directions in HR's Contribution to Competitive Advantage," *Human Resource Management*, Winter 1999.

**21.** D. Sankey, "Technologies Extend HR Reach," *Ottawa Citizen*, November 9, 2011, http://www2.canada.com/ottawacitizen/story.html?id=a6638454-3711-422e-9c0e-1a40d1ac52f2.

**22.** D. Sankey, "Technologies Extend HR Reach," *Ottawa Citizen*, November 9, 2011, http://www2.canada.com/ottawacitizen/story.html?id=a6638454-3711-422e-9c0e-1a40d1ac52f2.

**23.** D. Vanheukelom, "HR Tech's Future (and Present) in the Cloud," *Canadian HR Reporter*, October 10, 2011, http://www.hrreporter.com/articleview/11414-hr-techs-future-and-present-in-the-cloud.

**24.** "HRIS in 2010 (or Sooner!): Experts Predict Use of Wrist Mounted Devised, Virtual HR Access, and HR Voice Recognition", *Managing HR Information Systems*, February 2002, pp.1–4.

**25.** E. Beauchesne, "Skills Training Rebounds: But Labour Shortage May Still Be Looming," *Telegram*, November 21, 2003, p. D1.

**26.** G. Dessler and N. Cole, *Human Resources Management in Canada*, 10th ed. (Toronto, ON: Pearson Prentice-Hall).

**27.** J. Sullivan, "Workforce Planning: Why to Start Now," *Workforce*, September 2002, pp. 46–50.

**28.** Based on A. Tomlinson, "The Many Benefits of Online Job Boards," *Canadian HR Reporter*, July 15, 2002, pp. 17–18. The Career webpage can be found at http://www.scotiabank.com/ca/en/0,,178,00.html.

**29.** T. J. Bergmann and M. S. Taylor, "College Recruitment: What Attracts Students to Organizations?" *Personnel*, May–June 1984, pp. 34–46; and A. S. Bargerstock and G. Swanson, "Four Ways to Build Cooperative Recruitment Alliances," *HR Magazine*, March 1991, p. 49.

**30.** F. Loyie, "Police in a Rush to Lure New Recruits," *Edmonton Journal*, April 24, 2004, p. B3.

**31.** S. Burton and D. Warner, "The Future of Hiring—Top 5 Sources for Recruitment Today," *Workforce Vendor Directory*, 2002, p. 75.

**32.** C. Eustace, "VPD: Virtual Police Department," *Vancouver Sun*, May 29, 2007, pp. A1–A2.

**33.** G. Shaw, "An Offer That's Hard to Refuse," *Vancouver Sun*, November 12, 2003, p. D5.

**34.** See, for example, J. P. Kirnan, J. E. Farley, and K. F. Geisinger, "The Relationship Between Recruiting Source, Applicant Quality, and Hire Performance: An Analysis by Sex, Ethnicity, and Age," *Personnel Psychology*, Summer 1989, pp. 293–308; and R. W. Griffeth, P. Hom, L. Fink, and D. Cohen, "Comparative Tests of Multivariate Models of Recruiting Sources Effects," *Journal of Management* 23, no. 1 (1997), pp. 19–36.

**35.** Hub Pages, "The Average Cost of Employee Turnover," July 26, 2008, http://lifeislikethat.hubpages.com/hub/The-Average-Cost-of-Employee-Turnover.

**36.** G. W. England, *Development and Use of Weighted Application Blanks*, rev. ed. (Minneapolis: Industrial Relations Center, University of Minnesota, 1971); J. J. Asher, "The Biographical Item: Can It Be Improved?" *Personnel Psychology*, Summer 1972, p. 266; G. Grimsley and H. F. Jarrett, "The Relation of Managerial Achievement to Test Measures Obtained in the Employment Situation: Methodology and Results," *Personnel Psychology*, Spring 1973, pp. 31–48; E. E. Ghiselli, "The Validity of Aptitude Tests in Personnel Selection," *Personnel Psychology*, Winter 1973, p. 475; I. T. Robertson and R. S. Kandola, "Work Sample Tests: Validity, Adverse Impact, and Applicant Reaction," *Journal of Occupational Psychology* 55, no. 3 (1982), pp. 171–183; A. K. Korman, "The Prediction of Managerial Performance: A Review," *Personnel Psychology*, Summer 1986, pp. 295–322; G. C. Thornton, *Assessment Centers in Human Resource Management* (Reading, MA: Addison-Wesley, 1992); C. Fernandez-Araoz, "Hiring Without Firing," *Harvard Business Review*, July–August, 1999, pp. 108–120; and A. M. Ryan and R. E. Ployhart, "Applicants' Perceptions of Selection Procedures and Decisions: A Critical Review and Agenda for the Future," *Journal of Management* 26, no. 3 (2000), pp. 565–606.

**37.** See, for example, T. Janz, L. Hellervik, D. Gilmore. *Behavior Description Interviewing* (Newton, MA: Allyn and Bacon Publishers, 1986); S. J. Motowidlo, G. W. Carter, M. D. Dunnette, et al., "Studies of the Structured Behavioral Interview," *Journal of Applied Psychology* 77, no. 5 (1992), pp. 571–587; M. A. McDaniel, D. Whetzel, F. L. Schmidt, S. D. Maurer, "The Validity of Employment Interviews: A Comprehensive Review and Meta-Analysis," *Journal of Applied Psychology* 79, no. 4, (1994), pp. 599–616; and T. Janz, "Initial Comparisons of Patterned Behavior-Based Interviews Versus Unstructured Interviews," *Journal of Applied Psychology* 67, no. 5 (1982), pp. 577–580.

**38.** A. Wahl, "People Power," *Canadian Business*, March 29–April 11, 2004, p. 58.

**39.** C. L. Cooper, "The Changing Psychological Contract at Work: Revisiting the Job Demands–Control Model," *Occupational and Environmental Medicine*, June 2002, p. 355; D. M. Rousseau and S. A. Tijoriwala, "Assessing Psychological Contracts: Issues, Alternatives and Measures," *Journal of Organizational Behavior* 19, S1 (1998), pp. 679–695; and S. L. Robinson, M. S. Kraatz, and D. M. Rousseau, "Changing Obligations and the Psychological Contract: A Longitudinal Study," *Academy of Management Journal*, February 1994, pp. 137–152.

**40.** "2011 Industry Report," *Training Magazine*, November 2011, www.trainingmag.com.

**41.** D. Sankey, "Canadian Companies Skimp on Training," *National Post*, June 27, 2007: p. WK3.

**42.** H. Dolezalek, "2005 Industry Report," *Training*, December 2005, pp. 14–28.

**43.** B. Hall, "The Top Training Priorities for 2003," *Training*, February 2003, p. 40.

**44.** S. Purba, "When Reviews Deserve a Failing Grade," *Globe and Mail*, June 11, 2004, p. C1

**45.** K. Clark, "Judgment Day," *U.S. News & World Report*, January 13, 2003, pp. 31–32; E. E. Lawler III, "The Folly of Forced Ranking," *Strategy & Business*, Third Quarter 2002, pp. 28–32; K. Cross, "The Weakest Links," *Business2.Com*, June 26, 2001, pp. 36–37; J. Greenwald, "Rank and Fire," *Time*, June 18, 2001, pp. 38–39; D. Jones, "More Firms Cut Workers Ranked at Bottom to Make Way for Talent," *USA Today*, May 30, 2001, p. B11; and M. Boyle, "Performance Reviews: Perilous Curves Ahead," *Fortune*, May 28, 2001, pp. 187–188.

**46.** J. McGregor, "The Struggle to Measure Performance," *BusinessWeek*, January 9, 2006, pp. 26–28.

**47.** D. Jones, "Study: Thinning Herd from Bottom Helps," *USA Today*, March 14, 2005, p. 1B.

**48.** S. E. Cullen, P. K. Bergey, and L. Aiman-Smith, "Forced Distribution Rating Systems and the Improvement of Workforce Potential: A Baseline Simulation," *Personnel Psychology*, Spring 2005, pp. 1–32.

**49.** J. McGregor, "The Struggle to Measure Performance," *BusinessWeek*, January 9, 2006, pp. 26–28.

**50.** R. D. Bretz Jr., G. T. Milkovich, and W. Read, "The Current State of Performance Appraisal Research and Practice: Concerns, Directions, and Implications," *Journal of Management*, June 1992, p. 331.

**51.** M. Debrayen and S. Brutus, "Learning from Others' 360-Degree Experiences," *Canadian HR Reporter*, February 10, 2003, pp. 18–19.

**52.** M. Johne, "It's Good PR to Keep Employees Loyal," *Globe and Mail*, September 20, 2002, p. C1.

**53.** M. A. Peiperl, "Getting 360° Feedback Right," *Harvard Business Review*, January 2001, pp. 142–147.

**54.** Based on WorldatWork®, *Total Rewards Model*, (WorldatWork®, 2011), http://www.worldatwork.org/waw/ adimLink?id=28330&nonav=y.

**55.** This section based on R. I. Henderson, *Compensation Management in a Knowledge-Based World*, 9th ed. (Upper Saddle River, NJ: Prentice Hall, 2003).

**56.** L. R. Gomez-Mejia, "Structure and Process of Diversification, Compensation Strategy, and Firm Performance," *Strategic Management Journal* 13 no. 5 (1992), pp. 381–397; and E. Montemayor, "Congruence Between Pay Policy and Competitive Strategy in High-Performing Firms," *Journal of Management* 22, no. 6 (1996), pp. 889–908.

**57.** E. E. Lawler III, G. E. Ledford Jr., and L. Chang, "Who Uses Skill-Based Pay and Why," *Compensation & Benefits Review*, March–April 1993, p. 22; G. E. Ledford, "Paying for the Skills,

Knowledge and Competencies of Knowledge Workers," *Compensation & Benefits Review*, July–August 1995, pp. 55–62; C. Lee, K. S. Law, and P. Bobko, "The Importance of Justice Perceptions on Pay Effectiveness: A Two-Year Study of a Skill-Based Pay Plan," *Journal of Management* 26, no. 6 (1999), pp. 851–873.

**58.** J. D. Shaw, N. Gupta, A. Mitra, and G. E. Ledford Jr., "Success and Survival of Skill-Based Pay Plans," *Journal of Management*, February 2005, pp. 28–49.

**59.** M. Rowland, "It's What You Can Do That Counts," *New York Times*, June 6, 1993, p. F17.

**60.** Information from Hewitt Associates Studies, "Hewitt Study Shows Pay-for-Performance Plans Replacing Holiday Bonuses," December 6, 2005; "Salaries Continue to Rise in Asia Pacific," Hewitt Annual Study Reports, November 23, 2005; and CLA Personnel, "Hewitt Associates Study Reveals Salary Increases Remain Flat," Info CLA, http://www.clapersonnel.ca/ en_employ_articles_details.asp?id=2086.

**61.** "Gap Between What CEOs and Workers Earn Widening, *Global News*, May 3, 2012, http://www.globalnews. ca/6442633782/story.html; and "CEOS vs the 99%: No Contest When It Comes to Pay," News Release, Canadian Centre for Policy Alternatives, January 3, 2012, http://www.policyalternatives.ca/newsroom/news-releases/ceos-vs-99-no-contest-when-it-comes-pay.

**62.** Based on G. Dessler and N. Cole, *Human Resources Management in Canada*, 10th ed. (Toronto, ON: Pearson Prentice-Hall), Chapter 13.

**63.** C. Oglesby, "More Options for Moms Seeking Work–Family Balance," *CNN.com*, May 10, 2001.

**64.** J. Miller and M. Miller, "Get A Life!" *Fortune*, November 28, 2005, pp. 108–124.

**65.** M. Elias, "The Family-First Generation," *USA Today*, December 13, 2004, p. 5D.

**66.** F. Hansen, "Truths and Myths About Work/Life Balance," *Workforce*, December 2002, pp. 34–39.

**67.** M. M. Arthur, "Share Price Reactions to Work–Family Initiatives: An Institutional Perspective," *Academy of Management Journal*, August 2003, pp. 497–505.

**68.** N. P. Rothbard, T. L. Dumas, and K. W. Phillips, "The Long Arm of the Organization: Work–Family Policies and Employee Preferences for Segmentation," paper presented at the 61st Annual Academy of Management meeting, Washington, D.C., August 2001.

**69.** Based on WorldatWork®, *Total Rewards Model*, (Worldat Work®, 2011), http://www.worldatwork.org/waw/ adimLink?id=28330&nonav=y.

**70.** D. E. Super and D. T. Hall, "Career Development: Exploration and Planning," in *Annual Review of Psychology*, vol. 29, eds. M. R. Rosenzweig and L. W. Porter (Palo Alto, CA: Annual Reviews, 1978), p. 334.

**71.** M. Cianni and D. Wnuck, "Individual Growth and Team Enhancement: Moving Toward a New Model of Career Development," *Academy of Management Executive*, February 1997, pp. 105–115.

**72.** D. E. Super, "A Life-Span Life Space Approach to Career Development," *Journal of Vocational Behavior*, Spring 1980, pp. 282–298. See also E. P. Cook, and M. Arthur, *Career Theory*

*Handbook* (Upper Saddle River, NJ: Prentice Hall, 1991), pp. 99–131; and L. S. Richman, "The New Worker Elite," *Fortune*, August 22, 1994, pp. 56–66.

**73.** Based on G. Dessler and N. Cole, *Human Resources Management in Canada*, 10th ed. (Toronto, ON: Pearson Prentice-Hall), Chapter 14.

**74.** Based on G. Dessler and N. Cole, *Human Resources Management in Canada*, 10th ed. (Toronto, ON: Pearson Prentice-Hall), Chapter 14.

**75.** "Employers Underestimate Extent of Sexual Harassment, Report Says," *Vancouver Sun*, March 8, 2001, p. D6.

**76.** "Employers Underestimate Extent of Sexual Harassment, Report Says," *Vancouver Sun*, March 8, 2001, p. D6.

**77.** John Gibbons, *Employee Engagement A Review of Current Research and Its Implications* (Ottawa, ON: The Conference Board of Canada, November 2006).

**78.** J. K. Harter, F. L. Schmidt, T. L. Hayes, "Business-Unit-Level Relationship Between Employee Satisfaction, Employee Engagement, and Business Outcomes: A Meta-Analysis," *Journal of Applied Psychology* 87, no. 2, (2002), pp. 268–279.

**79.** J. A. LePine, A. Erez, and D. E. Johnson, "The Nature and Dimensionality of Organizational Citizenship Behavior: A Critical Review and Meta-Analysis," *Journal of Applied Psychology* 87, no. 1 (2002), pp. 52–65.

**80.** See WorldatWork®, *Total Rewards Model*, (WorldatWork®, 2011), http://www.worldatwork.org/waw/adimLink?id=28330&nonav=y.

**81.** Based on S. P. Robbins and D. A. DeCenzo, *Fundamentals of Management*, 4th ed. (Upper Saddle River, NJ: Prentice Hall, 2004), p. 194.

**82.** Communications New Brunswick, "New Initiatives to Help Aboriginal Students Pursue Post-Secondary Education," Government of New Brunswick News Release, January 6, 2010, http://www.gnb.ca/cnb/news/pet/2010e0007pe.htm.

**83.** "New Brunswick Invests in Training for Aboriginal Peoples," *Canadian HR Reporter*, October 7, 2911, http://www.hrreporter.com/articleprint.aspx?articleid=11403.

**84.** Laura A. DeCarlo, "The 30-Second Commercial: What's Unique About You?" The Global Career Services Network, http://www.careerdirectors.com/members/articles/I01.pdf.

**85.** *Dragon's Den*, Canadian Broadcasting Corporation, http://www.cbc.ca/dragonsden/.

**86.** Wellington West, *Rock Steady, Annual Report 2008*, http://www.wellwest.ca/documents/reports/WW_AR_2008.pdf.

**87.** Wellington West, *Rock Steady, Annual Report 2008*, http://www.wellwest.ca/documents/reports/WW_AR_2008.pdf.

**88.** Wellington West, *Rock Steady, Annual Report 2008*, http://www.wellwest.ca/documents/reports/WW_AR_2008.pdf.

**89.** M. Cash, "Steady Growth Brings $333-M Payoff—National Bank Buys Wellington West," *Winnipeg Free Press*, May 27, 2011, http://www.winnipegfreepress.com/business/steady-growth-brings-333-m-payoff-122710338.html.

**90.** Wellington West, *Rock Steady, Annual Report 2008*, http://www.wellwest.ca/documents/reports/WW_AR_2008.pdf.

**91.** M. Cash, "Steady Growth Brings $333-M Payoff—National Bank Buys Wellington West," *Winnipeg Free Press*, May 27, 2011, http://www.winnipegfreepress.com/business/steady-growth-brings-333-m-payoff-122710338.html.

**92.** A. Hopkins, "Manulife Buys Financial Planning Firm Wellington West," Reuters, August 29, 2012, http://www.reuters.com/article/2012/08/29/us-manulife-wellingtonwest-idUS-BRE87S11F20120829; "Manulife Acquires Wellington West Arm," *Winnipeg Free Press*, August 30, 2012, http://www.winnipegfreepress.com/business/manulife-acquires-wellington-west-arm-167960166.html.

## CHAPTER 8

**1.** Based on "Magnotta: Breaking New Ground with Innovative Marketing Strategies," Industry Canada, http://www.ic.gc.ca/eic/site/061.nsf/eng/rd02457.html; S. Fife, "Break the Competitive Roadblock: Three Canadian Success Stories," *Canadian Business*, May 18, 2007, www.canadianbusiness.com; G. Stimmell, "Wine's Scrappy Duo," *Toronto Star*, January 24, 2007, p. D4; "Canada's Most Award-Winning Magnotta Winery," December 8, 2008, http://thewineladies.com; and "Magnotta Winery Corporation Announces January 31, 2009 Annual Results," *Marketwire*, April 30, 2009, www.marketwire.com.

**2.** See, for example, "Feature Interview with Peter Drucker," *Training & Development Magazine* (September 1998); J. Kotter, "What Leaders Really Do", *Harvard Business Review* 68 (1990), pp. 103–111; and H. Mintzberg, In Conversation, *CBC Ideas*, The Canadian Broadcasting Corporation, 1999.

**3.** "Portraits in Leadership 2011," *Canadian Business* and the Ted Rogers Leadership Centre, Ryerson University, www.canadian-business.com/portraits.

**4.** Based on "Magnotta: Breaking New Ground with Innovative Marketing Strategies," Industry Canada, http://www.ic.gc.ca/eic/site/061.nsf/eng/rd02457.html; S. Fife, "Break the Competitive Roadblock: Three Canadian Success Stories," *Canadian Business*, May 18, 2007, www.canadianbusiness.com; G. Stimmell, "Wine's Scrappy Duo," *Toronto Star*, January 24, 2007, p. D4; "Canada's Most Award-Winning Magnotta Winery," December 8, 2008, http://thewineladies.com; and "Magnotta Winery Corporation Announces January 31, 2009 Annual Results," *Marketwire*, April 30, 2009, www.marketwire.com.

**5.** See S. A. Kirkpatrick and E. A. Locke, "Leadership: Do Traits Matter?" *Academy of Management Executive*, May 1991, pp. 48–60; and T. A. Judge, J. E. Bono, R. Ilies, and M. Werner, "Personality and Leadership: A Qualitative and Quantitative Review," *Journal of Applied Psychology*, August 2002, pp. 765–780.

**6.** See T. A. Judge, J. E. Bono, R. Ilies, and M. Werner, "Personality and Leadership: A Review" (paper presented at the 15th Annual Conference of the Society for Industrial and Organizational Psychology, New Orleans, 2000); T. A. Judge, J. E. Bono, R. Ilies, and M. W. Gerhardt, "Personality and Leadership: A Qualitative and Quantitative Review," *Journal of Applied Psychology*, August 2002, pp. 765–780; and D. A. Hofmann and L. M. Jones, "Leadership, Collective Personality, and Performance," *Journal of Applied Psychology* 90, no. 3 (2005), pp. 509–522.

**7.** P. G. Northhouse, *Leadership: Theory and Practice*, 3rd ed. (Thousand Oaks, CA: Sage, 2004), Chapter 4; and G. A. Yukl, *Leadership in Organizations*, 3rd ed. (Englewood Cliffs, NJ: Prentice Hall, 1994), Chapter 3.

**8.** K. Lewin and R. Lippitt, "An Experimental Approach to the Study of Autocracy and Democracy: A Preliminary Note," *Sociometry* 1 (1938), pp. 292–300; K. Lewin, "Field Theory and Experiment in Social Psychology: Concepts and Methods,"

*American Journal of Sociology* 44 (1939), pp. 868–896; K. Lewin, R. Lippitt, and R. K. White, "Patterns of Aggressive Behavior in Experimentally Created Social Climates," *Journal of Social Psychology* 10 (1939), pp. 271–301; and R. Lippitt, "An Experimental Study of the Effect of Democratic and Authoritarian Group Atmospheres," *University of Iowa Studies in Child Welfare* 16 (1940), pp. 43–95.

9. "Portraits in Leadership 2011," *Canadian Business* and the Ted Rogers Leadership Centre, Ryerson University, www.canadianbusiness.com/portraits.

10. B. M. Bass, *Stogdill's Handbook of Leadership* (New York: Free Press, 1981), pp. 289–299.

11. R. McQueen, "The Long Shadow of Tom Stephens: He Branded MacBlo's Crew as Losers, Then Made Them into Winners," *Financial Post* (*National Post*), June 22, 1999, pp. C1, C5.

12. A. J. Mayo and N. Nohria, "Zeitgeist Leadership," *Harvard Business Review* 83, no. 10 (2005), pp. 45–60.

13. H. Wang, K. S. Law, R. D. Hackett, D. Wang, and Z. X. Chen, "Leader–Member Exchange as a Mediator of the Relationship Between Transformational Leadership and Followers' Performance and Organizational Citizenship Behavior," *Academy of Management Journal* 48, no. 3 (June 2005), pp. 420–432.

14. P. Hersey and K. Blanchard, "So You Want to Know Your Leadership Style?" *Training & Development*, February 1974, pp. 1–15; and P. Hersey and K. Blanchard, *Management of Organizational Behavior: Leading Human Resources*, 8th ed. (Englewood Cliffs, NJ: Prentice Hall, 2001).

15. See, for example, C. F. Fernandez and R. P. Vecchio, "Situational Leadership Theory Revisited: A Test of an Across-Jobs Perspective," *Leadership Quarterly* 8, no. 1 (1997), pp. 67–84; and C. L. Graeff, "Evolution of Situational Leadership Theory: A Critical Review," *Leadership Quarterly* 8, no. 2 (1997), pp. 153–170.

16. R. J. House, "A Path-Goal Theory of Leader Effectiveness," *Administrative Science Quarterly*, September 1971, pp. 321–338; R. J. House and T. R. Mitchell, "Path-Goal Theory of Leadership," *Journal of Contemporary Business*, Autumn 1974, p. 86; and R. J. House, "Path-Goal Theory of Leadership: Lessons, Legacy, and a Reformulated Theory," *Leadership Quarterly*, Fall 1996, pp. 323–352.

17. J. C. Wofford and L. Z. Liska, "Path-Goal Theories of Leadership: A Meta-Analysis," *Journal of Management*, Winter 1993, pp. 857–876; M. G. Evans, "R. J. House's 'A Path-Goal Theory of Leader Effectiveness,'" *Leadership Quarterly*, Fall 1996, pp. 305–309; C. A. Schriesheim and L. L. Neider, "Path-Goal Leadership Theory: The Long and Winding Road," *Leadership Quarterly*, Fall 1996, pp. 317–321; A. Somech, "The Effects of Leadership Style and Team Process on Performance and Innovation in Functionally Heterogeneous Teams," *Journal of Management* 32, no. 1 (2006), pp. 132–157; and S. Yun, S. Faraj, and H. P. Sims, "Contingent Leadership and Effectiveness of Trauma Resuscitation Teams," *Journal of Applied Psychology* 90, no. 6 (2005), pp. 1288–1296.

18. Based on "Magnotta: Breaking New Ground with Innovative Marketing Strategies," Industry Canada, http://www.ic.gc.ca/eic/site/061.nsf/eng/rd02457.html; S. Fife, "Break the Competitive Roadblock: Three Canadian Success Stories," *Canadian Business*, May 18, 2007, www.canadianbusiness.com; G. Stimmell, "Wine's Scrappy Duo," *Toronto Star*, January 24, 2007, p. D4;

"Canada's Most Award-Winning Magnotta Winery," December 8, 2008, http://thewineladies.com; and "Magnotta Winery Corporation Announces January 31, 2009 Annual Results," *Marketwire*, April 30, 2009, www.marketwire.com.

19. B. M. Bass and R. E. Riggio, *Transformational Leadership*, 2nd ed. (Mahwah, NJ: Lawrence Erlbaum Associates, Inc., 2006), p. 3.

20. F. Vogelstein, "Mighty Amazon," *Fortune*, May 26, 2003, pp. 60–74.

21. J. A. Conger and R. N. Kanungo, "Behavioral Dimensions of Charismatic Leadership," in *Charismatic Leadership*, eds. J. A. Conger and R. N. Kanungo (San Francisco: Jossey-Bass, 1988), pp. 78–97; G. Yukl and J. M. Howell, "Organizational and Contextual Influences on the Emergence and Effectiveness of Charismatic Leadership," *Leadership Quarterly*, Summer 1999, pp. 257–283; and J. M. Crant and T. S. Bateman, "Charismatic Leadership Viewed from Above: The Impact of Proactive Personality," *Journal of Organizational Behavior*, February 2000, pp. 63–75.

22. J. A. Conger and R. N. Kanungo, *Charismatic Leadership in Organizations* (Thousand Oaks, CA: Sage, 1998).

23. K. S. Groves, "Linking Leader Skills, Follower Attitudes, and Contextual Variables via an Integrated Model of Charismatic Leadership," *Journal of Management*, April 2005, pp. 255–277; J. J. Sosik, "The Role of Personal Values in the Charismatic Leadership of Corporate Managers: A Model and Preliminary Field Study," *Leadership Quarterly*, April 2005, pp. 221–244; A. H. B. deHoogh, D. N. den Hartog, P. L. Koopman, H. Thierry, P. T. van den Berg, J. G. van der Weide, and C. P. M. Wilderom, "Leader Motives, Charismatic Leadership, and Subordinates' Work Attitudes in the Profit and Voluntary Sector," *Leadership Quarterly*, February 2005, pp. 17–38; J. M. Howell and B. Shamir, "The Role of Followers in the Charismatic Leadership Process: Relationships and Their Consequences," *Academy of Management Review*, January 2005, pp. 96–112; J. Paul, D. L. Costley, J. P. Howell, P. W. Dorfman, and D. Trafimow, "The Effects of Charismatic Leadership on Followers' Self-Concept Accessibility," *Journal of Applied Social Psychology*, September 2001, pp. 1821–1844; J. A. Conger, R. N. Kanungo, and S. T. Menon, "Charismatic Leadership and Follower Effects," *Journal of Organizational Behavior*, vol. 21, 2000, pp. 747–767; R. W. Rowden, "The Relationship between Charismatic Leadership Behaviors and Organizational Commitment," *Leadership & Organization Development Journal*, January 2000, pp. 30–35; G. P. Shea and C. M. Howell, "Charismatic Leadership and Task Feedback: A Laboratory Study of Their Effects on Self-Efficacy," *Leadership Quarterly*, Fall 1999, pp. 375–396; S. A. Kirkpatrick and E. A. Locke, "Direct and Indirect Effects of Three Core Charismatic Leadership Components on Performance and Attitudes," *Journal of Applied Psychology*, February 1996, pp. 36–51; D. A. Waldman, B. M. Bass, and F. J. Yammarino, "Adding to Contingent-Reward Behavior: The Augmenting Effect of Charismatic Leadership," *Group & Organization Studies*, December 1990, pp. 381–394; and R. J. House, J. Woycke, and E. M. Fodor, "Charismatic and Noncharismatic Leaders: Differences in Behavior and Effectiveness," in *Charismatic Leadership*, eds. J. A. Conger and R. N. Kanungo (San Francisco: Jossey-Bass, 1988), pp. 103–104.

24. T. Dvir, D. Eden, B. J. Avolio, and B. Shamir, "Impact of Transformational Leadership on Follower Development and Performance: A Field Experiment," *Academy of Management*

*Journal* 45, no. 4 (2002), pp. 735–744; R. J. House, J. Woycke, and E. M. Fodor, "Charismatic and Noncharismatic Leaders: Differences in Behavior and Effectiveness," in *Charismatic Leadership in Organizations*, eds. J. A. Conger and R. N. Kanungo (Thousand Oaks, CA: Sage, 1998), pp. 103–104; D. A. Waldman, B. M. Bass, and F. J. Yammarino, "Adding to Contingent-Reward Behavior: The Augmenting Effect of Charismatic Leadership," *Group & Organization Studies*, December 1990, pp. 381–394; S. A. Kirkpatrick and E. A. Locke, "Direct and Indirect Effects of Three Core Charismatic Leadership Components on Performance and Attitudes," *Journal of Applied Psychology*, February 1996, pp. 36–51; and J. A. Conger, R. N. Kanungo, and S. T. Menon, "Charismatic Leadership and Follower Outcome Effects" (paper presented at the 58th Annual Academy of Management Meetings, San Diego, CA, August 1998).

**25.** J. M. Howell and P. J. Frost, "A Laboratory Study of Charismatic Leadership," *Organizational Behavior & Human Decision Processes* 43, no. 2 (April 1989), pp. 243–269.

**26.** "Building a Better Boss," *Maclean's*, September 30, 1996, p. 41.

**27.** "Building a Better Boss," *Maclean's*, September 30, 1996, p. 41.

**28.** B. R. Agle, N. J. Nagarajan, J. A. Sonnenfeld, and D. Srinivasan, "Does CEO Charisma Matter? An Empirical Analysis of the Relationships Among Organizational Performance, Environmental Uncertainty, and Top Management Team Perceptions of CEO Charisma," *Academy of Management Journal*, February 2006, pp. 161–174.

**29.** A. Elsner, "The Era of CEO as Superhero Ends Amid Corporate Scandals," *Globe and Mail*, July 10, 2002, www.globeandmail.com.

**30.** J. A. Conger and R. N. Kanungo, "Training Charismatic Leadership: A Risky and Critical Task," in *Charismatic Leadership*, eds. J. A. Conger and R. N. Kanungo (San Francisco: Jossey-Bass, 1988), pp. 309–323; S. Caudron, "Growing Charisma," *IndustryWeek*, May 4, 1998, pp. 54–55; and R. Birchfield, "Creating Charismatic Leaders," *Management*, June 2000, pp. 30–31.

**31.** R. J. House, "A 1976 Theory of Charismatic Leadership" in *Leadership: The Cutting Edge*, eds. J. G. Hunt and L. L. Larson (Carbondale, IL: Southern Illinois University Press, 1977); R. J. House and R. N. Aditya, "The Social Scientific Study of Leadership: Quo Vadis?" *Journal of Management* 23, no. 3 (1997), pp. 316–323; and J. G. Hunt, K. B. Boal, and G. E. Dodge, "The Effects of Visionary and Crisis-Responsive Charisma on Followers: An Experimental Examination," *Leadership Quarterly*, Fall 1999, pp. 423–448.

**32.** This definition is based on M. Sashkin, "The Visionary Leader," in *Charismatic Leadership*, eds. J. A. Conger and R. N. Kanungo (San Francisco: Jossey-Bass, 1988), pp. 124–125; B. Nanus, *Visionary Leadership* (New York: Free Press, 1992), p. 8; N. H. Snyder and M. Graves, "Leadership and Vision," *Business Horizons*, January–February 1994, p. 1; and J. R. Lucas, "Anatomy of a Vision Statement," *Management Review*, February 1998, pp. 22–26.

**33.** B. Nanus, *Visionary Leadership* (New York: Free Press, 1992), p. 8.

**34.** Based on M. Sashkin, "The Visionary Leader," in *Charismatic Leadership*, eds. J. A. Conger and R. N. Kanungo (San Francisco: Jossey-Bass, 1988), pp. 128–130; and J. R. Baum, E. A. Locke, and S. A. Kirkpatrick, "A Longitudinal Study of the Relation of Vision and Vision Communication to Venture Growth in Entrepreneurial Firms," *Journal of Applied Psychology*, February 1998, pp. 43–54.

**35.** See "Harper Named *Time*'s Top Canadian Newsmaker," *CBC News*, December 17, 2006, www.cbc.ca/canada/story/2006/12/17/time-harper.html.

**36.** J. M. Howell and B. Shamir, "The Role of Followers in the Charismatic Leadership Process: Relationships and Their Consequences," *Academy of Management Review* 30, no. 1 (2005), pp. 96–112.

**37.** L. Manfield, "Creating a Safety Culture from Top to Bottom," *Worksafe Magazine*, February 2005, pp. 8–9; "Canadian CEOs Give Themselves Top Marks for Leadership!" *Canada Newswire*, September 9, 1999.

**38.** B. J. Avolio and B. M. Bass, "Transformational Leadership, Charisma, and Beyond" (working paper, School of Management, State University of New York, Binghamton, 1985), p. 14.

**39.** R. S. Rubin, D. C. Munz, and W. H. Bommer, "Leading from Within: The Effects of Emotion Recognition and Personality on Transformational Leadership Behavior," *Academy of Management Journal*, October 2005, pp. 845–858; T. A. Judge and J. E. Bono, "Five-Factor Model of Personality and Transformational Leadership," *Journal of Applied Psychology*, October 2000, pp. 751–765; B. M. Bass and B. J. Avolio, "Developing Transformational Leadership: 1992 and Beyond," *Journal of European Industrial Training*, January 1990, p. 23; and J. J. Hater and B. M. Bass, "Supervisors' Evaluation and Subordinates' Perceptions of Transformational and Transactional Leadership," *Journal of Applied Psychology*, November 1988, pp. 695–702.

**40.** R. F. Piccolo and J. A. Colquitt, "Transformational Leadership and Job Behaviors: The Mediating Role of Core Job Characteristics," *Academy of Management Journal*, April 2006, pp. 327–340; O. Epitropaki and R. Martin, "From Ideal to Real: A Longitudinal Study of the Role of Implicit Leadership Theories on Leader-Member Exchanges and Employee Outcomes," *Journal of Applied Psychology*, July 2005, pp. 659–676; J. E. Bono and T. A. Judge, "Self-Concordance at Work: Toward Understanding the Motivational Effects of Transformational Leaders," *Academy of Management Journal*, October 2003, pp. 554–571; T. Dvir, D. Eden, B. J. Avolio, and B. Shamir, "Impact of Transformational Leadership on Follower Development and Performance: A Field Experiment," *Academy of Management Journal*, August 2002, pp. 735–744; N. Sivasubramaniam, W. D. Murry, B. J. Avolio, and D. I. Jung, "A Longitudinal Model of the Effects of Team Leadership and Group Potency on Group Performance," *Group & Organization Management*, March 2002, pp. 66–96; J. M. Howell and B. J. Avolio, "Transformational Leadership, Transactional Leadership, Locus of Control, and Support for Innovation: Key Predictors of Consolidated-Business-Unit Performance," *Journal of Applied Psychology*, December 1993, pp. 891–911; R. T. Keller, "Transformational Leadership and the Performance of Research and Development Project Groups," *Journal of Management*, September 1992, pp. 489–501; and B. M. Bass and B. J. Avolio, "Developing Transformational Leadership: 1992 and Beyond," *Journal of European Industrial Training*, January 1990, p. 23

**41.** R. Pillai, C. A. Schriesheim, and E. S. Williams, "Fairness Perceptions and Trust as Mediators of Transformational and Transactional Leadership: A Two-Sample Study," *Journal of Management* 25, 1999, pp. 897–933.

**42.** G. M. Spreitzer, K. H. Perttula, and K. Xin, "Traditionality Matters: An Examination of the Effectiveness of Transformational Leadership in the United States and Taiwan," *Journal of Organizational Behavior* 26, no. 3 (2005), pp. 205–227.

**43.** Based on "Magnotta: Breaking New Ground with Innovative Marketing Strategies," Industry Canada, http://www.ic.gc.ca/eic/site/061.nsf/eng/rd02457.html; S. Fife, "Break the Competitive Roadblock: Three Canadian Success Stories," *Canadian Business*, May 18, 2007, www.canadianbusiness.com; G. Stimmell, "Wine's Scrappy Duo," *Toronto Star*, January 24, 2007, p. D4; "Canada's Most Award-Winning Magnotta Winery," December 8, 2008, http://thewineladies.com; and "Magnotta Winery Corporation Announces January 31, 2009 Annual Results," *Marketwire*, April 30, 2009, www.marketwire.com.

**44.** See J. R. P. French Jr. and B. Raven, "The Bases of Social Power," in *Group Dynamics: Research and Theory*, eds. D. Cartwright and A. F. Zander (New York: Harper & Row, 1960), pp. 607–623; P. M. Podsakoff and C. A. Schriesheim, "Field Studies of French and Raven's Bases of Power: Critique, Reanalysis, and Suggestions for Future Research," *Psychological Bulletin*, May 1985, pp. 387–411; R. K. Shukla, "Influence of Power Bases in Organizational Decision Making: A Contingency Model," *Decision Sciences*, July 1982, pp. 450–470; D. E. Frost and A. J. Stahelski, "The Systematic Measurement of French and Raven's Bases of Social Power in Workgroups," *Journal of Applied Social Psychology*, April 1988, pp. 375–389; and T. R. Hinkin and C. A. Schriesheim, "Development and Application of New Scales to Measure the French and Raven (1959) Bases of Social Power," *Journal of Applied Psychology*, August 1989, pp. 561–567.

**45.** See the Royal Australian Navy website, www.navy.gov.au.

**46.** J. Partridge and J. Saunders, "Milton's Right-Hand Man Quits Air Canada," *Globe and Mail*, April 7, 2004, p. A1.

**47.** J. M. Kouzes and B. Z. Posner, *Credibility: How Leaders Gain and Lose It, and Why People Demand It* (San Francisco: Jossey-Bass, 1993), p. 14.

**48.** Based on L. T. Hosmer, "Trust: The Connecting Link Between Organizational Theory and Philosophical Ethics," *Academy of Management Review*, April 1995, p. 393; R. C. Mayer, J. H. Davis, and F. D. Schoorman, "An Integrative Model of Organizational Trust," *Academy of Management Review*, July 1995, p. 712; and G. M. Spreitzer and A. K. Mishra, "Giving Up Control Without Losing Control," *Group & Organization Management*, June 1999, pp. 155–187.

**49.** P. L. Schindler and C. C. Thomas, "The Structure of Interpersonal Trust in the Workplace," *Psychological Reports*, October 1993, pp. 563–573.

**50.** H. H. Tan and C. S. F. Tan, "Toward the Differentiation of Trust in Supervisor and Trust in Organization," *Genetic, Social, and General Psychology Monographs*, May 2000, pp. 241–260.

**51.** K. T. Dirks and D. L. Ferrin, "Trust in Leadership: Meta-Analytic Findings and Implications for Research and Practice," *Journal of Applied Psychology*, August 2002, pp. 611–628

**52.** This section is based on F. Bartolome, "Nobody Trusts the Boss Completely—Now What?" *Harvard Business Review*, March–April 1989, pp. 135–142; J. K. Butler Jr., "Toward Understanding and Measuring Conditions of Trust: Evolution of a Conditions of Trust Inventory," *Journal of Management*, September 1991, pp. 643–663; and K. T. Dirks and D. L. Ferrin,

"Trust in Leadership: Meta-Analytic Findings and Implications for Research and Practice," *Journal of Applied Psychology*, August 2002, pp. 611–628.

**53.** This section is based on R. B. Morgan, "Self- and Co-Worker Perceptions of Ethics and Their Relationships to Leadership and Salary," *Academy of Management Journal*, February 1993, pp. 200–214; E. P. Hollander, "Ethical Challenges in the Leader–Follower Relationship," *Business Ethics Quarterly*, January 1995, pp. 55–65; J. C. Rost, "Leadership: A Discussion About Ethics," *Business Ethics Quarterly*, January 1995, pp. 129–142; R. N. Kanungo and M. Mendonca, *Ethical Dimensions of Leadership* (Thousand Oaks, CA: Sage Publications, 1996); J. B. Ciulla, ed., *Ethics: The Heart of Leadership* (New York: Praeger Publications, 1998); J. D. Costa, *The Ethical Imperative: Why Moral Leadership Is Good Business* (Cambridge, MA: Perseus Press, 1999); and N. M. Tichy and A. McGill, eds., *The Ethical Challenge: How to Build Honest Business Leaders* (New York: John Wiley & Sons, 2003).

**54.** J. M. Burns, *Leadership* (New York: Harper & Row, 1978).

**55.** J. M. Avolio, S. Kahai, and G. E. Dodge, "The Ethics of Charismatic Leadership: Submission or Liberation?" *Academy of Management Executive*, May 1992, pp. 43–55.

**56.** L. K. Trevino, M. Brown, and L. P. Hartman, "A Qualitative Investigation of Perceived Executive Ethical Leadership: Perceptions From Inside and Outside the Executive Suite," *Human Relations*, January 2003, pp. 5–37.

**57.** C. Kleiman, "Virtual Teams Make Loyalty More Realistic," *Chicago Tribune*, January 23, 2001, p. B1.

**58.** B. J. Alge, C. Wiethoff, and H. J. Klein, "When Does the Medium Matter? Knowledge-Building Experiences and Opportunities in Decision-Making Teams," *Organizational Behavior and Human Decision Processes* 91, no. 1 (2003), pp. 26–37; C. O. Grosse, "Managing Communication Within Virtual Intercultural Teams," *Business Communication Quarterly*, December 2002, pp. 22–38; M. M. Montoya-Weiss, A. P. Massey, and M. Song, "Getting It Together: Temporal Coordination and Conflict Management in Global Virtual Teams," *Academy of Management Journal*, December 2001, pp. 1251–1262; M. L. Maznevski and K. M. Chudoba, "Bridging Space Over Time: Global Virtual-Team Dynamics and Effectiveness," *Organization Science* 11 (2000), pp. 473–492; W. F. Cascio, "Managing a Virtual Workplace," *Academy of Management Executive*, August 2000, pp. 81–90; A. M. Townsend, S. M. DeMarie, and A. R. Hendrickson, "'Virtual Teams' Technology and the Workplace of the Future," *Academy of Management Executive*, August 1998, pp. 17–29.

**59.** W. F. Cascio, "Managing a Virtual Workplace," *Academy of Management Executive*, August 2000, pp. 88–89.

**60.** N. Desmond, "The CEO Dashboard," *Business* 2.0, August 2002, p. 34.

**61.** S. Caminiti, "What Team Leaders Need to Know," *Fortune*, February 20, 1995, p. 93.

**62.** S. Caminiti, "What Team Leaders Need to Know," *Fortune*, February 20, 1995, p. 100.

**63.** N. Steckler and N. Fondas, "Building Team Leader Effectiveness: A Diagnostic Tool," *Organizational Dynamics*, Winter 1995, p. 20.

**64.** R. S. Wellins, W. C. Byham, and G. R. Dixon, *Inside Teams* (San Francisco: Jossey-Bass, 1994), p. 318.

**65.** N. Steckler and N. Fondas, "Building Team Leader Effectiveness: A Diagnostic Tool," *Organizational Dynamics*, Winter 1995, p. 21

**66.** Ray Williams, "Women Don't Have a Whole Lot to Celebrate on Equality Front," *Financial Post*, March 19, 2012, http://business.financialpost.com/2012/03/19/women-dont-have-a-whole-lot-to-celebrate-in-equality-picture.

**67.** Statistics Canada, *Survey on Financing of Small and Medium Enterprises*, 2009 (Ottawa: Statistics Canada, 2009); Industry Canada, *Key Small Business Statistics* (Ottawa: Industry Canada, 2009).

**68.** Canadian Imperial Bank of Commerce, "Women Entrepreneurs: Leading the Change," 2005, www.cibc.com/ca/small-business/article-tools/women-entrepreneurs.html.

**69.** United Nations, Statistics and Indicators on Women and Men, Table 5f: Women Legislators and Managers, http://mdgs.un.org/unsd/demographic/products/indwm/default.htm.

**70.** G. N. Powell, D. A. Butterfield, and J. D. Parent, "Gender and Managerial Stereotypes: Have the Times Changed?" *Journal of Management* 28, no. 2 (2002), pp. 177–193.

**71.** A. H. Eagly and B. T. Johnson, "Gender and Leadership Style: A Meta-Analysis," *Psychological Bulletin*, September 1990, pp. 233–256; A. H. Eagly and S. J. Karau, "Gender and the Emergence of Leaders: A Meta-Analysis," *Journal of Personality and Social Psychology*, May 1991, pp. 685–710; J. B. Rosener, "Ways Women Lead," *Harvard Business Review*, November–December 1990, pp. 119–125; A. H. Eagly, M. G. Makhijani, and B. G. Klonsky, "Gender and the Evaluation of Leaders: A Meta-Analysis," *Psychological Bulletin*, January 1992, pp. 3–22; A. H. Eagly, S. J. Karau, and B. T. Johnson, "Gender and Leadership Style Among School Principals: A Meta-Analysis," *Educational Administration Quarterly*, February 1992, pp. 76–102; L. R. Offermann and C. Beil, "Achievement Styles of Women Leaders and Their Peers," *Psychology of Women Quarterly*, March 1992, pp. 37–56; R. L. Kent and S. E. Moss, "Effects of Size and Gender Role on Leader Emergence," *Academy of Management Journal*, October 1994, pp. 1335–1346; C. Lee, "The Feminization of Management," *Training*, November 1994, pp. 25–31; H. Collingwood, "Women as Managers: Not Just Different: Better," *Working Woman*, November 1995, p. 14; J. B. Rosener, *America's Competitive Secret: Women Managers* (New York: Oxford University Press, 1995); and J. Cliff, N. Langton, and H. Aldrich, "Walking the Talk? Gendered Rhetoric vs. Action in Small Firms," *Organizational Studies* 26, no. 1 (2005), pp. 63–91.

**72.** See F. J. Yammarino, A. J. Dubinsky, L. B. Comer, and M. A. Jolson, "Women and Transformational and Contingent Reward Leadership: A Multiple-Levels-of-Analysis Perspective," *Academy of Management Journal*, February 1997, pp. 205–222; M. Gardiner and M. Tiggemann, "Gender Differences in Leadership Style, Job Stress and Mental Health in Male- and Female-Dominated Industries," *Journal of Occupational and Organizational Psychology*, September 1999, pp. 301–315; C. L. Ridgeway, "Gender, Status, and Leadership," *Journal of Social Issues*, Winter 2001, pp. 637–655; W. H. Decker and D. M. Rotondo, "Relationships Among Gender, Type of Humor, and Perceived Leader Effectiveness," *Journal of Managerial Issues*, Winter 2001, pp. 450–465; J. M. Norvilitis and H. M. Reid, "Evidence for an Association Between Gender-Role Identity and a Measure of Executive Function," *Psychological Reports*, February 2002, pp. 35–45; N. Z. Selter, "Gender Dif-

ferences in Leadership: Current Social Issues and Future Organizational Implications," *Journal of Leadership Studies*, Spring 2002, pp. 88–99; J. Becker, R. A. Ayman, and K. Korabik, "Discrepancies in Self/Subordinates' Perceptions of Leadership Behavior: Leader's Gender, Organizational Context, and Leader's Self-Monitoring," *Group & Organization Management*, June 2002, pp. 226–244; A. H. Eagly and S. J. Karau, "Role Congruity Theory of Prejudice Toward Female Leaders," *Psychological Review*, July 2002, pp. 573–598; and K. M. Bartol, D. C. Martin, and J. A. Kromkowski, "Leadership and the Glass Ceiling: Gender and Ethnic Influences on Leader Behaviors at Middle and Executive Managerial Levels," *Journal of Leadership & Organizational Studies*, Winter 2003, pp. 8–19.

**73.** M. Gardiner and M. Tiggemann, "Gender Differences in Leadership Style, Job Stress and Mental Health in Male- and Female-Dominated Industries," *Journal of Occupational and Organizational Psychology*, September 1999, pp. 301–315.

**74.** "Women 'Take Care,' Men 'Take Charge:' Stereotyping of U.S. Business Leaders Exposed," *Catalyst* (New York, 2005).

**75.** C. Hymowitz, "Too Many Women Fall for Stereotypes of Selves, Study Says," *Wall Street Journal*, October 24, 2005, p. B1; B. Kantrowitz, "When Women Lead," *Newsweek*, October 24, 2005, pp. 46–61; and "Why Can't Women Be Leaders Too?" *Gallup Management Journal*, gmj.gallup.com, October 13, 2005.

**76.** J. M. Norvilitis and H. M. Reid, "Evidence for an Association Between Gender-Role Identity and a Measure of Executive Function," *Psychological Reports*, February 2002, pp. 35–45; W. H. Decker and D. M. Rotondo, "Relationships Among Gender, Type of Humor, and Perceived Leader Effectiveness," *Journal of Managerial Issues*, Winter 2001, pp. 450–465; H. Aguinis and S. K. R. Adams, "Social-Role Versus Structural Models of Gender and Influence Use in Organizations: A Strong Inference Approach," *Group & Organization Management*, December 1998, pp. 414–446; A. H. Eagly, S. J. Karau, and M. G. Makhijani, "Gender and the Effectiveness of Leaders: A Meta-Analysis," *Psychological Bulletin* 117 (1995), pp. 125–145.

**77.** A. H. Eagly, M. C. Johannesen-Schmidt, and M. L. van Engen, "Transformational, Transactional, and Laissez-Faire Leadership Styles: A Meta-Analysis Comparing Women and Men," *Psychological Bulletin* 129, no. 4 (July 2003), pp. 569–591; K. M. Bartol, D. C. Martin, and J. A. Kromkowski, "Leadership and the Glass Ceiling: Gender and Ethnic Influences on Leader Behaviors at Middle and Executive Managerial Levels," *Journal of Leadership & Organizational Studies*, Winter 2003, pp. 8–19; and R. Sharpe, "As Leaders, Women Rule," *BusinessWeek*, November 20, 2000, pp. 74–84.

**78.** R.Sharpe, "As Leaders Women Rule," *Business Week*, November 20, 2000, p. 75.

**79.** K. M. Bartol, D. C. Martin, and J. A. Kromkowski, "Leadership and the Glass Ceiling: Gender and Ethnic Influences on Leader Behaviors at Middle and Executive Managerial Levels," *Journal of Leadership & Organizational Studies*, Winter 2003, pp. 8–19.

**80.** Jacqueline Nelson, "How to Be Your Best Friend's Boss," *Canadian Business*, March 5, 2012.

**81.** L. M. Fisher, "Ricardo Semler Won't Take Control," *Strategy+Business*, Winter 2005, pp. 78–88; R. Semler, *The Seven-Day Weekend: Changing the Way Work Works* (New York: Penguin Group, 2004); A. J. Vogl, "The Anti-CEO," *Across the Board*, May–June 2004, pp. 30–36; G. Colvin, "The

Anti-Control Freak," *Fortune*, November 26, 2001, p. 22; and R. Semler, "Managing without Managers," *Harvard Business Review*, September–October 1989, pp. 76–84.

**82.** Laura Quinn and Jessica Baltes, "Leadership and the Triple Bottom Line" (white paper for the Centre for Creative Leadership, 2007), http://www.ccl.org/leadership/pdf/research/triple BottomLine.pdf.

**83.** See C. Cattaneo, "The Oil Patch Crusader," *Financial Post Magazine*, November 1, 2011, http://business.financialpost. com/2011/11/01/the-oil-patch-crusader/; and investor information from Enbridge's website, http://www.enbridge.com/Investor Relations.aspx.

## CHAPTER 9

**1.** Chris Atchison, "The Gen Y Whisperer," *Profit*, June 1, 2011, http://www.profitguide.com/article/28252—the-gen-y-whisperer.

**2.** "Profit 200—2012 Rankings: #16, Yellow House Events Inc.," *Profit*, http://www.profitguide.com/microsite/profit200/2012/16-Yellow-House-Events.

**3.** G. P. Latham and C. C. Pinder, "Work Motivation Theory and Research at the Dawn of the Twenty-First Century," *Annual Review of Psychology* 56, no. 1 (2005), pp. 485–516; and C. C. Pinder, *Work Motivation in Organizational Behavior* (Upper Saddle River, NJ: Prentice Hall, 1998), p. 11. See also E. A. Locke and G. P. Latham, "What Should We Do About Motivation Theory? Six Recommendations For the Twenty-First Century," *Academy of Management Review* 29, no. 3 (July 1, 2004), pp. 388–403.

**4.** See, for example, T. R. Mitchell, "Matching Motivational Strategies With Organizational Contexts," in *Research in Organizational Behavior*, vol. 19, eds. B. M. Staw and L. L. Cummings (Greenwich, CT: JAI Press, 1997), pp. 60–62; and R. Katerberg and G. J. Blau, "An Examination of Level and Direction of Effort and Job Performance," *Academy of Management Journal*, June 1983, pp. 249–257.

**5.** Graham Lowe, *21st Century Job Quality: Achieving What Canadians Want* (Ottawa, ON: Canadian Policy Research Networks, Research Report Wl37, September 2007), http://www.cprn.org/doc.cfm?doc=1745&l=en.

**6.** See "Job Satisfaction Wanes, but SHRM Survey Shows Majority of U.S. Employees Satisfied," *PR Newswire-US Newswire*, October 3, 2012, http://www.prnewswire.com/news-releases/job-satisfaction-wanes-but-shrm-survey-shows-majority-of-us-employees-satisfied-172521231.html; and Society for Human Resource Management (SHRM), *2012 Job Satisfaction and Engagement Research Report* (SHRM, October 3, 2012), http://www.shrm.org/Research/SurveyFindings/Articles/Pages/2012EmployeeJobSatisfaction.aspx.

**7.** G. Shaw, "Canada Lags World on Job Quality," *Vancouver Sun*, September 18, 2004, p. F5.

**8.** Chris Atchison, "The Gen Y Whisperer," *Profit*, June 1, 2011, http://www.profitguide.com/article/28252—the-gen-y-whisperer.

**9.** A. Maslow, *Motivation and Personality* (New York: McGraw-Hill, 1954); A. Maslow, D. C. Stephens, and G. Heil, *Maslow on Management* (New York: John Wiley & Sons, 1998); M. L. Ambrose and C. T. Kulik, "Old Friends, New Faces: Motivation Research in the 1990s," *Journal of Management* 25, no. 3 (1999), pp. 231–292; and "Dialogue," *Academy of Management Review*, October 2000, pp. 696–701.

**10.** G. P. Latham and C. C. Pinder, "Work Motivation Theory and Research at the Dawn of the Twenty-First Century," *Annual Review of Psychology* 56, no. 1 (2005), pp. 485–516.

**11.** See, for example, D. T. Hall and K. E. Nongaim, "An Examination of Maslow's Need Hierarchy in an Organizational Setting," *Organizational Behavior and Human Performance*, February 1968, pp. 12–35; E. E. Lawler III and J. L. Suttle, "A Causal Correlational Test of the Need Hierarchy Concept," *Organizational Behavior and Human Performance*, April 1972, pp. 265–287; R. M. Creech, "Employee Motivation," *Management Quarterly*, Summer 1995, pp. 33–39; J. Rowan, "Maslow Amended," *Journal of Humanistic Psychology*, Winter 1998, pp. 81–92; J. Rowan, "Ascent and Descent in Maslow's Theory," *Journal of Humanistic Psychology*, Summer 1999, pp. 125–133; and M. L. Ambrose and C. T. Kulik, "Old Friends, New Faces: Motivation Research in the 1990s," *Journal of Management* 25, no. 3 (1999), pp. 231–292.

**12.** D. McGregor, *The Human Side of Enterprise* (New York: McGraw-Hill, 1960). For an updated analysis of theories X and Y, see R. J. Summers and S. F. Conshaw, "A Study of McGregor's Theory X, Theory Y and the Influence of Theory X, Theory Y Assumptions on Causal Attributions for Instances of Worker Poor Performance," in *Organizational Behavior*, ASAC 1988 Conference Proceedings, vol. 9, part 5, ed. S. L. McShaneed (Halifax, NS: ASAC, 1988), pp. 115–123.

**13.** K. W. Thomas, *Intrinsic Motivation at Work* (San Francisco: Berrett-Koehler, 2000); and K. W. Thomas, "Intrinsic Motivation and How It Works," *Training*, October 2000, pp. 130–135.

**14.** F. Herzberg, B. Mausner, and B. Snyderman, *The Motivation to Work* (New York: John Wiley, 1959); F. Herzberg, *The Managerial Choice: To Be Effective or to Be Human*, rev. ed. (Salt Lake City: Olympus, 1982); R. M. Creech, "Employee Motivation," *Management Quarterly*, Summer 1995, pp. 33–39; and M. L. Ambrose and C. T. Kulik, "Old Friends, New Faces: Motivation Research in the 1990s," *Journal of Management* 25, no. 3 (1999), pp. 231–292.

**15.** G. Bellett, "Firm's Secret to Success Lies in Treating Workers Right," *Vancouver Sun*, March 21, 2001, pp. D7, D11; V. Galt, "Getting Fit on the Job," *Globe and Mail*, November 6, 2002, p. C1.

**16.** C. Lochhead, "Healthy Workplace Programs at Pazmac Enterprises Ltd.," Canadian Labour and Business Centre, March 2002.

**17.** D. C. McClelland, *The Achieving Society* (New York: Van Nostrand Reinhold, 1961); J. W. Atkinson and J. O. Raynor, *Motivation and Achievement* (Washington, DC: Winston, 1974); D. C. McClelland, *Power: The Inner Experience* (New York: Irvington, 1975); and M. J. Stahl, *Managerial and Technical Motivation: Assessing Needs for Achievement, Power, and Affiliation* (New York: Praeger, 1986).

**18.** D. C. McClelland, *The Achieving Society* (New York: Van Nostrand Reinhold, 1961).

**19.** D. C. McClelland, *Power: The Inner Experience* (New York: Irvington, 1975); D. C. McClelland and D. H. Burnham, "Power Is the Great Motivator," *Harvard Business Review*, March–April 1976, pp. 100–110.

**20.** D. Miron and D. C. McClelland, "The Impact of Achievement Motivation Training on Small Businesses," *California Management Review*, Summer 1979, pp. 13–28.

**21.** "McClelland: An Advocate of Power," *International Management*, July 1975, pp. 27–29.

**22.** R. A. Clay, "Green Is Good for You," *Monitor on Psychology*, April 2001, pp. 40–42.

**23.** M. L. Ambrose and C. T. Kulik, "Old Friends, New Faces: Motivation Research in the 1990s," *Journal of Management* 25, no. 3 (1999), pp. 231–292.

**24.** P. R. Lawrence and N. Nohria, *Driven: How Human Nature Shapes Our Choices* (San Francisco: Jossey-Bass, 2002).

**25.** S. McShane and S. Steen, *Canadian Organizational Behaviour*, 7th ed. (Toronto, ON: McGraw-Hill, 2009), p. 113.

**26.** B. F. Skinner, *Science and Human Behavior* (New York: Free Press, 1953); and B. F. Skinner, *Beyond Freedom and Dignity* (New York: Knopf, 1972).

**27.** The same data, for example, can be interpreted in either goal-setting or reinforcement terms, as shown in E. A. Locke, "Latham vs. Komaki: A Tale of Two Paradigms," *Journal of Applied Psychology*, February 1980, pp. 16–23. Also, see M. L. Ambrose and C. T. Kulik, "Old Friends, New Faces: Motivation Research in the 1990s," *Journal of Management* 25, no. 3 (1999), pp. 231–292.

**28.** J. S. Adams, "Inequity in Social Exchanges," in *Advances in Experimental Social Psychology*, vol. 2, ed. L. Berkowitz (New York: Academic Press, 1965), pp. 267–300; and M. L. Ambrose and C. T. Kulik, "Old Friends, New Faces: Motivation Research in the 1990s," *Journal of Management* 25, no. 3 (1999), pp. 231–292.

**29.** See, for example, P. S. Goodman and A. Friedman, "An Examination of Adams' Theory of Inequity," *Administrative Science Quarterly*, September 1971, pp. 271–288; E. Walster, G. W. Walster, and W. G. Scott, *Equity: Theory and Research* (Boston: Allyn & Bacon, 1978); and J. Greenberg, "Cognitive Reevaluation of Outcomes in Response to Underpayment Inequity," *Academy of Management Journal*, March 1989, pp. 174–184.

**30.** See, for example, M. R. Carrell, "A Longitudinal Field Assessment of Employee Perceptions of Equitable Treatment," *Organizational Behavior and Human Performance*, February 1978, pp. 108–118; R. G. Lord and J. A. Hohenfeld, "Longitudinal Field Assessment of Equity Effects on the Performance of Major League Baseball Players," *Journal of Applied Psychology*, February 1979, pp. 19–26; and J. E. Dittrich and M. R. Carrell, "Organizational Equity Perceptions, Employee Job Satisfaction, and Departmental Absence and Turnover Rates," *Organizational Behavior and Human Performance*, August 1979, pp. 29–40.

**31.** P. S. Goodman, "An Examination of Referents Used in the Evaluation of Pay," *Organizational Behavior and Human Performance*, October 1974, pp. 170–195; S. Ronen, "Equity Perception in Multiple Comparisons: A Field Study," *Human Relations*, April 1986, pp. 333–346; R. W. Scholl, E. A. Cooper, and J. F. McKenna, "Referent Selection in Determining Equity Perception: Differential Effects on Behavioral and Attitudinal Outcomes," *Personnel Psychology*, Spring 1987, pp. 113–127; and C. T. Kulik and M. L. Ambrose, "Personal and Situational Determinants of Referent Choice," *Academy of Management Review*, April 1992, pp. 212–237.

**32.** A. Wahl, J. Castaldo, Z. Olijnyk, E. Pooley, and A. Jezovit, "The Best Workplaces in Canada 2007," *Canadian Business*, April 23, 2007, pp. 39–61. http://resources.greatplacetowork.com/article/pdf/the_best_workplaces_in_canada_2007.pdf.

**33.** See, for example, R. C. Dailey and D. J. Kirk, "Distributive and Procedural Justice as Antecedents of Job Dissatisfaction and Intent to Turnover," *Human Relations*, March 1992, pp. 305–316; D. B. McFarlin and P. D. Sweeney, "Distributive and Procedural Justice as Predictors of Satisfaction with Personal and Organizational Outcomes," *Academy of Management Journal*, August 1992, pp. 626–637; M. A. Konovsky, "Understanding Procedural Justice and Its Impact on Business Organizations," *Journal of Management* 26, no. 3, 2000, pp. 489–511; J. A. Colquitt, "Does the Justice of One Interact with the Justice of Many? Reactions to Procedural Justice in Teams," *Journal of Applied Psychology*, August 2004, pp. 633–646; J. Brockner, "Why It's So Hard to Be Fair," *Harvard Business Review*, March 2006, pp. 122–129; and B. M. Wiesenfeld, W. B. Swann, Jr., J. Brockner, and C. A. Bartel, "Is More Fairness Always Preferred? Self-Esteem Moderates Reactions to Procedural Justice," *Academy of Management Journal*, October 2007, pp. 1235–1253

**34.** V. H. Vroom, *Work and Motivation* (New York: John Wiley, 1964).

**35.** See, for example, H. G. Heneman III and D. P. Schwab, "Evaluation of Research on Expectancy Theory Prediction of Employee Performance," *Psychological Bulletin*, July 1972, pp. 1–9; and L. Reinharth and M. Wahba, "Expectancy Theory as a Predictor of Work Motivation, Effort Expenditure, and Job Performance," *Academy of Management Journal*, September 1975, pp. 502–537.

**36.** See, for example, V. H. Vroom, "Organizational Choice: A Study of Pre- and Post-decision Processes," *Organizational Behavior and Human Performance*, April 1966, pp. 212–225; L. W. Porter and E. E. Lawler III, *Managerial Attitudes and Performance* (Homewood, IL: Richard D. Irwin, 1968); W. Van Eerde and H. Thierry, "Vroom's Expectancy Models and Work-Related Criteria: A Meta-Analysis," *Journal of Applied Psychology*, October 1996, pp. 575–586; and M. L. Ambrose and C. T. Kulik, "Old Friends, New Faces: Motivation Research in the 1990s," *Journal of Management* 25, no. 3 (1999), pp. 231–292.

**37.** See, for example, M. Siegall, "The Simplistic Five: An Integrative Framework for Teaching Motivation," *Organizational Behavior Teaching Review* 12, no. 4 (1987–1988), pp. 141–143.

**38.** S. Butcher, "Relentless Rise in Pleasure Seekers," *Financial Times*, July 6, 2003; "Tesco Pilots Student Benefits," *Employee Benefits*, November 7, 2003, p. P12; and Tesco PLC, *Corporate Responsibility Report 2009*, pp. 40–45, http://www.investis.com/plc/storage/tesco_cr_09.pdf.

**39.** J. R. Billings and D. L. Sharpe, "Factors Influencing Flextime Usage Among Employed Married Women," *Consumer Interests Annual*, vol. 45 (Ames, IA: American Council on Consumer Interests, 1999), pp. 89–94; and I. Harpaz, "The Importance of Work Goals: An International Perspective," *Journal of International Business Studies*, First Quarter 1990, pp. 75–93.

**40.** N. Ramachandran, "New Paths at Work," *US News & World Report*, March 20, 2006, p. 47; S. Armour, "Generation Y: They've Arrived at Work with a New Attitude," *USA Today*, November 6, 2005, pp. B1+; R. Kanfer and P. L. Ackerman, "Aging, Adult Development, and Work Motivation," *Academy of Management Review*, July 2004, pp. 440–458; and R. Bernard, D. Cosgrave, and J. Welsh, *Chips and Pop: Decoding the Nexus Generation* (Toronto: Malcolm Lester Books, 1998).

**41.** N. J. Adler, *International Dimensions of Organizational Behavior*, 4th ed. (Cincinnati: South-Western College Publishing, 2002), p. 174.

**42.** G. Hofstede, "Motivation, Leadership and Organization: Do American Theories Apply Abroad?" *Organizational Dynamics*, Summer 1980, p. 55.

**43.** J. K. Giacobbe-Miller, D. J. Miller, and V. I. Victorov, "A Comparison of Russian and U.S. Pay Allocation Decisions, Distributive Justice Judgments and Productivity Under Different Payment Conditions," *Personnel Psychology*, Spring 1998, pp. 137–163.

**44.** S. L. Mueller and L. D. Clarke, "Political–Economic Context and Sensitivity to Equity: Differences Between the United States and the Transition Economies of Central and Eastern Europe," *Academy of Management Journal*, June 1998, pp. 319–329.

**45.** I. Harpaz, "The Importance of Work Goals: An International Perspective," *Journal of International Business Studies*, First Quarter 1990, pp. 75–93.

**46.** G. E. Popp, H. J. Davis, and T. T. Herbert, "An International Study of Intrinsic Motivation Composition," *Management International Review*, January 1986, pp. 28–35.

**47.** R. W. Brislin, B. MacNab, R. Worthley, F. Kabigting Jr., and B. Zukis, "Evolving Perceptions of Japanese Workplace Motivation: An Employee-Manager Comparison," *International Journal of Cross-Cultural Management*, April 2005, pp. 87–104.

**48.** P. Falcone, "Motivating Staff Without Money," *HR Magazine*, August 2002, pp. 105–108.

**49.** P. Falcone, "Motivating Staff Without Money," *HR Magazine*, August 2002, pp. 105–108.

**50.** See, for example, M. Alpert, "The Care and Feeding of Engineers," *Fortune*, September 21, 1992, pp. 86–95; G. Poole, "How to Manage Your Nerds," *Forbes ASAP*, December 1994, pp. 132–136; and T. J. Allen and R. Katz, "Managing Technical Professionals and Organizations: Improving and Sustaining the Performance of Organizations, Project Teams, and Individual Contributors," *Sloan Management Review*, Summer 2002, pp. S4–S5.

**51.** "One CEO's Perspective on the Power of Recognition," *Workforce Management*, February 27, 2004, www.workforce.com; and R. Fournier, "Teamwork Is the Key to Remote Development—Inspiring Trust and Maintaining Motivation Are Critical for a Distributive Development Team," *InfoWorld*, March 5, 2001, p. 48.

**52.** R. J. Bohner Jr. and E. R. Salasko, "Beware the Legal Risks of Hiring Temps," *Workforce*, October 2002, pp. 50–57.

**53.** J. P. Broschak and A. Davis-Blake, "Mixing Standard Work and Nonstandard Deals: The Consequences of Heterogeneity in Employment Arrangements," *Academy of Management Journal*, April 2006, pp. 371–393; M. L. Kraimer, S. J. Wayne, R. C. Liden, and R. T. Sparrowe, "The Role of Job Security in Understanding the Relationship Between Employees' Perceptions of Temporary Workers and Employees' Performance," *Journal of Applied Psychology*, March 2005, pp. 389–398; and C. E. Connelly and D. G. Gallagher, "Emerging Trends in Contingent Work Research," *Journal of Management*, November 2004, pp. 959–983.

**54.** D. W. Krueger, "Money, Success, and Success Phobia," in *The Last Taboo: Money as a Symbol and Reality in Psychotherapy and Psychoanalysis*, ed. D. W. Krueger (New York: Brunner/Mazel, 1986), pp. 3–16.

**55.** T. R. Mitchell and A. E. Mickel, "The Meaning of Money: An Individual-Difference Perspective," *Academy of Management*, July 1999, pp. 568–578.

**56.** This paragraph is based on Graham Lowe, *21st Century Job Quality: Achieving What Canadians Want*, Research Report W|37, Work and Learning (Ottawa, ON: Canadian Policy Research Networks, September 2007).

**57.** D. Grigg and J. Newman, "Labour Researchers Define Job Satisfaction," *Vancouver Sun*, February 16, 2002, p. E2.

**58.** This paragraph is based on T. R. Mitchell and A. E. Mickel, "The Meaning of Money: An Individual-Difference Perspective," *Academy of Management*, July 1999, pp. 568–578. The reader may want to refer to the myriad references cited in the article.

**59.** F. Luthans and A. D. Stajkovic, "Provide Recognition for Performance Improvement," in *Principles of Organizational Behavior*, ed. E. A. Locke (Oxford, UK: Blackwell, 2000), pp. 166–180.

**60.** "Secrets of Their Success (and Failure)," *Report on Business*, January 2006, pp. 54–55.

**61.** S. L. Rynes, B. Gerhart, and L. Parks, "Personnel Psychology: Performance Evaluation and Pay for Performance," *Annual Review of Psychology* 56, no. 1 (2005), p. 572; and A. M. Dickinson, "Are We Motivated by Money? Some Results from the Laboratory," *Performance Improvement* 44, no. 3 (March 2005), pp. 18–24.

**62.** R. K. Abbott, "Performance-Based Flex: A Tool for Managing Total Compensation Costs," *Compensation and Benefits Review*, March–April 1993, pp. 18–21; J. R. Schuster and P. K. Zingheim, "The New Variable Pay: Key Design Issues," *Compensation and Benefits Review*, March–April 1993, pp. 27–34; C. R. Williams and L. P. Livingstone, "Another Look at the Relationship Between Performance and Voluntary Turnover," *Academy of Management Journal*, April 1994, pp. 269–298; and A. M. Dickinson and K. L. Gillette, "A Comparison of the Effects of Two Individual Monetary Incentive Systems on Productivity: Piece Rate Pay Versus Base Pay Plus Incentives," *Journal of Organizational Behavior Management*, Spring 1994, pp. 3–82.

**63.** Canadian Newswire (CNW), "Calgary Salary Increases Reach New Heights, According to Hewitt," news release, www.newswire.ca/en/releases/archive/September2007/06/c5734.html; G. Teel, "City Leads Nation in Salary Increases," *Calgary Herald*, September 7, 2007; Hewitt Associates, "Hewitt Study Shows Pay-for-Performance Plans Replacing Holiday Bonuses," news release, December 6, 2005; and P. Brieger, "Variable Pay Packages Gain Favour: Signing Bonuses, Profit Sharing Taking Place of Salary Hikes," *Financial Post* (*National Post*), September 13, 2002, p. FP5.

**64.** E. Beauchesne, "Pay Bonuses Improve Productivity, Study Shows," *Vancouver Sun*, September 13, 2002, p. D5; and The Conference Board of Canada, "Variable Pay Offers a Bonus for Unionized Workplaces," news release, September 12, 2002.

**65.** "Hope for Higher Pay: The Squeeze on Incomes Is Gradually Easing Up," *Maclean's*, November 25, 1996, pp. 100–101.

**66.** Hewitt Associates, LLC, "Hewitt Study Shows Base Pay Increases Flat for 2006 with Variable Pay Plans Picking Up the Slack," August 31, 2005.

**67.** E. Beauchesne, "Pay Bonuses Improve Productivity, Study Shows," *Vancouver Sun*, September 13, 2002, p. D5; and "More Than 20 Percent of Japanese Firms Use Pay Systems Based on Performance," *Manpower Argus*, May 1998, p. 7.

**68.** M. Tanikawa, "Fujitsu Decides to Backtrack on Performance-Based Pay," *New York Times*, March 22, 2001, p. W1.

**69.** G. D. Jenkins Jr., N. Gupta, A. Mitra, and J. D. Shaw, "Are Financial Incentives Related to Performance? A Meta-Analytic Review of Empirical Research," *Journal of Applied Psychology*, October 1998, pp. 777–787.

**70.** T. Coupé, V. Smeets, and F. Warzynski, "Incentives, Sorting and Productivity Along the Career: Evidence from a Sample of Top Economists," *Journal of Law Economics & Organization* 22, no. 1 (April 2006), pp. 137–167.

**71.** A. Kauhanen and H. Piekkola, "What Makes Performance-Related Pay Schemes Work? Finnish Evidence," *Journal of Management and Governance* 10, no. 2 (2006), pp. 149–177.

**72.** E. Beauchesne, "Pay Bonuses Improve Productivity, Study Shows," *Vancouver Sun*, September 13, 2002, p. D5.

**73.** P. A. Siegel and D. C. Hambrick, "Pay Disparities Within Top Management Groups: Evidence of Harmful Effects on Performance of High-Technology Firms," *Organization Science* 16, no. 3 (May–June 2005), pp. 259–276; S. Kerr, "Practical, Cost-Neutral Alternatives That You May Know, but Don't Practice," *Organizational Dynamics* 28, no. 1 (1999), pp. 61–70; and E. E. Lawler, *Strategic Pay* (San Francisco: Jossey Bass, 1990); and J. Pfeffer, *The Human Equation: Building Profits by Putting People First* (Boston: Harvard Business School Press, 1998).

**74.** T. Reason, "Why Bonus Plans Fail," *CFO*, January 2003, p. 53; and J. D. Day, P. Y. Mang, A. Richter, and J. Roberts, "Has Pay for Performance Had Its Day?" *McKinsey Quarterly*, no. 4 (November 2002).

**75.** V. Sanderson, "Sweetening Their Slice: More Hardware and Lumberyard Dealers Are Investing in Profit-Sharing Programs as a Way to Promote Employee Loyalty," *Hardware Merchandising*, May–June 2003, p. 66.

**76.** W. J. Duncan, "Stock Ownership and Work Motivation," *Organizational Dynamics*, Summer 2001, pp. 1–11.

**77.** P. Brandes, R. Dharwadkar, and G. V. Lemesis, "Effective Employee Stock Option Design: Reconciling Stakeholder, Strategic, and Motivational Factors," *Academy of Management Executive*, February 2003, pp. 77–95; J. Blasi, D. Kruse, and A. Bernstein, *In the Company of Owners: The Truth About Stock Options* (New York: Basic Books, 2003).

**78.** "Health Club Membership, Flextime Are Most Desired Perks," *Business West*, September 1999, p. 75.

**79.** ACT Conferencing, "Utilize Collaboration Tools to Make Virtual Meetings More Productive," *ACT Conferencing's Corporate Communication Blog*, August 28, 2012, http://blog.actconferencing.com/default.aspx?Tag=unified%20communications%20and%20collaboration.

**80.** D. Penner, "Survey: Top Pay Trumps Work-Life Balance," *The Gazette* (Montreal), March 10, 2007, p. G2.

**81.** "What Employees Want," *CMA Management* 75, no. 7 (October 2001), p. 8.

**82.** Information in this paragraph is based on D. Grigg and J. Newman, "Labour Researchers Define Job Satisfaction," *Vancouver Sun*, February 16, 2002, p. E2.

**83.** Jacqueline Nelson, "A 21st-century Factory Town," *Canadian Business*, April 16, 2012.

**84.** K. Clark, "Perking Up the Office," *U.S. News & World Report*, November 22, 1999, p. 73: L. Brenner, "Perks That Work," *BusinessWeek Frontier*, October 11, 1999, pp. F22–F40.

**85.** Jackie Pitera, "Aligned Incentives and Engaged Employees Improve Triple Bottom Line Performance," *Environmental Leader*, August 4, 2011, http://www.environmentalleader.com/2011/08/04/aligned-incentives-and-engaged-employees-improve-triple-bottom-line-performance/.

**86.** Jackie Pitera, "Aligned Incentives and Engaged Employees Improve Triple Bottom Line Performance," *Environmental Leader*, August 4, 2011, http://www.environmentalleader.com/2011/08/04/aligned-incentives-and-engaged-employees-improve-triple-bottom-line-performance/.

**87.** Canadian International Development Agency (CIDA), Microfinance: The Government of Canada Supports Microfinance in Developing Countries," CIDA website, http://www.acdi-cida.gc.ca/acdi-cida/ACDI-CIDA.nsf/eng/RAC-1110131744-PG5.

**88.** Based on J. Marquez, "Best Buy Offers Choice in Its Long-term Incentive Program to Keep the Best and Brightest," *Workforce Management*, April 24, 2006, pp. 42–43; M. Boyle, "Best Buy's Giant Gamble," *Fortune*, April 3, 2006, pp. 68–75; J. S. Lublin, "A Few Share the Wealth," *Wall Street Journal*, December 12, 2005, pp. B1+; J. Thotta, "Reworking Work," *Time*, July 25, 2005, pp. 50–55; and M. V. Copeland, "Best Buy's Selling Machine," *Business* 2.0, July 2004, pp. 92–102.

## CHAPTER 10

**1.** See Industry Canada, "Great Little Box Company: A Team Approach to Success," http://www.ic.gc.ca/eic/site/061.nsf/eng/rd02456.html; Terrence Belford and Kira Vermond, "Great Little Company Aims to Contain Great Little Products," *National Post*, December 15, 1999; Ashley Ford, "Great People Make Great Boxes," *Province* (Vancouver), December 22, 1999; Great Little Box Company, Various company reports, press releases, and information. http://www.greatlittlebox.com; Philip Quinn, "Employees Are Face of Box Company," *Financial Post* (*National Post*), January 17, 2005; and "The Great Little Box Company," Best Practices, The Workplace Council, August 8, 2005, http://www.workplacecouncil.com/glbc.html.

**2.** B. W. Tuckman and M. C. Jensen, "Stages of Small-Group Development Revisited," *Group and Organizational Studies*, December 1977, pp. 419–427; and M. F. Maples, "Group Development: Extending Tuckman's Theory," *Journal for Specialists in Group Work*, Fall 1988, pp. 17–23.

**3.** L. N. Jewell and H. J. Reitz, *Group Effectiveness in Organizations* (Glenview, IL: Scott, Foresman, 1981); and M. Kaeter, "Re-potting Mature Work Teams," *Training*, April 1994, pp. 54–56.

**4.** See, for example, J. E. Salk and M. Y. Brannien, "National Culture, Networks, and Individual Influence in a Multinational Management Team," *Academy of Management Journal*, April 2000, p. 191; B. L. Kirkman, C. B. Gibson, and D. L. Shapiro, "Enhancing the Implementation and Effectiveness of Work Teams in Global Affiliates," *Organizational Dynamics*, Summer 2001, pp. 12–30; and B. L. Kirkman and D. L. Shapiro, "The Impact of Cultural Values on Employee Resistance to Teams: Towards a Model of Globalized Self-Managing Work Team Effectiveness," *Academy of Management Review*, July 1997, pp. 730–757.

**5.** S. Stern, "Teams That Work," *Management Today*, June 2001, p. 48.

**6.** G. Prince, "Recognizing Genuine Teamwork," *Supervisory Management*, April 1989, pp. 25–36; R. F. Bales, *SYMOLOG*

*Case Study Kit* (New York: Free Press, 1980); and K. D. Benne and P. Sheats, "Functional Roles of Group Members," *Journal of Social Issues* 4, no. 2 (1948), pp. 41–49.

**7.** A. R. Jassawalla and H.C. Sashittal, "Strategies of Effective New Product Team Leaders," *California Management Review* 42, no.2 (Winter 2000), pp. 34–51.

**8.** R. M. Yandrick, "A Team Effort," *HR Magazine*, June 2001, pp. 136–141.

**9.** R. M. Yandrick, "A Team Effort," *HR Magazine*, June 2001, pp. 136–141.

**10.** M. A. Marks, C. S. Burke, M. J. Sabella, and S. J. Zaccaro, "The Impact of Cross-Training on Team Effectiveness," *Journal of Applied Psychology*, February 2002, pp. 3–14; and M. A. Marks, S. J. Zaccaro, and J. E. Mathieu, "Performance Implications of Leader Briefings and Team Interaction for Team Adaptation to Novel Environments," *Journal of Applied Psychology*, December 2000, p. 971.

**11.** C. Garvey, "Steer Teams with the Right Pay: Team-Based Pay Is a Success When It Fits Corporate Goals and Culture, and Rewards the Right Behavior," *HR Magazine*, May 2002, pp. 71–77.

**12.** G. R. Jones and G. M. George, "The Experience and Evolution of Trust: Implications for Cooperation and Teamwork," *Academy of Management Review*, July 1998, pp. 531–546; A. R. Jassawalla and H. C. Sashittal, "Building Collaborative Cross-Functional New Product Teams," *Academy of Management Executive*, August 1999, pp. 50–63; R. Forrester and A. B. Drexler, "A Model for Team-Based Organization Performance," *Academy of Management Executive*, August 1999, pp. 36–49; V. U. Druskat and S. B. Wolff, "The Link Between Emotions and Team Effectiveness: How Teams Engage Members and Build Effective Task Processes," *Academy of Management Proceedings*, CD-ROM, 1999; M. Mattson, T. Mumford, and G. S. Sintay, "Taking Teams to Task: A Normative Model for Designing or Recalibrating Work Teams," *Academy of Management Proceedings*, CD-ROM, 1999; J. D. Shaw, M. K. Duffy, and E. M. Stark, "Interdependence and Preference for Group Work: Main and Congruence Effects on the Satisfaction and Performance of Group Members," *Journal of Management* 26, no. 2 (2000), pp. 259–279; G. L. Stewart and M. R. Barrick, "Team Structure and Performance: Assessing the Mediating Role of Intrateam Process and the Moderating Role of Task Type," *Academy of Management Journal*, April 2000, pp. 135–148; J. E. Mathieu, T. S. Heffner, G. F. Goodwin, E. Salas, and J. A. Cannon-Bowers, "The Influence of Shared Mental Models on Team Process and Performance," *Journal of Applied Psychology*, April 2000, pp. 273–283; J. M. Phillips and E. A. Douthitt, "The Role of Justice in Team Member Satisfaction With the Leader and Attachment to the Team," *Journal of Applied Psychology*, April 2001, pp. 316–325; J. A. Colquitt, R. A. Noe, and C. L. Jackson, "Justice in Teams: Antecedents and Consequences of Procedural Justice Climate," *Personnel Psychology* 55 (2002), pp. 83–100; M. A. Marks, M. J. Sabella, C. S. Burke, and S. J. Zaccaro, "The Impact of Cross-Training on Team Effectiveness," *Journal of Applied Psychology*, February 2002, pp. 3–13; and S. W. Lester, B. W. Meglino, and M. A. Korsgaard, "The Antecedents and Consequences of Group Potency: A Longitudinal Investigation of Newly Formed Work Groups," *Academy of Management Journal*, April 2002, pp. 352–368.

**13.** D. R. Ilgen, J. R. Hollenbeck, M. Johnson, and D. Jundt, "Teams in Organizations: From Input-Process-Output Models to IMOI Models," *Annual Review of Psychology* 56, no. 1 (2005), pp. 517–543.

**14.** C. R. Evans and K. L. Dion, "Group Cohesion and Performance: A Meta-Analysis," *Small Group Research*, May 1991, pp. 175–186; B. Mullen and C. Copper, "The Relation Between Group Cohesiveness and Performance: An Integration," *Psychological Bulletin*, March 1994, pp. 210–227; P. M. Podsakoff, S. B. MacKenzie, and M. Ahearne, "Moderating Effects of Goal Acceptance on the Relationship Between Group Cohesiveness and Productivity," *Journal of Applied Psychology*, December 1997, pp. 974–983.

**15.** See, for example, L. Berkowitz, "Group Standards, Cohesiveness, and Productivity," *Human Relations*, November 1954, pp. 509–519; and B. Mullen and C. Copper, "The Relation Between Group Cohesiveness and Performance: An Integration," *Psychological Bulletin*, March 1994, pp. 210–227.

**16.** S. E. Seashore, *Group Cohesiveness in the Industrial Work Group* (Ann Arbor: University of Michigan, Survey Research Center, 1954).

**17.** This *Tips for Managers* is based on R. Kreitner and A. Kinicki, *Organizational Behavior*, 6th ed. (New York: McGraw Hill/Irwin, 2004), p. 460. Reprinted by permission of McGraw-Hill Education.

**18.** Paragraph based on R. Kreitner and A. Kinicki, *Organizational Behavior*, 6th ed. (New York: Irwin, 2004), pp. 459–461.

**19.** This section is adapted from S. P. Robbins, *Managing Organizational Conflict: A Nontraditional Approach* (Upper Saddle River, NJ: Prentice Hall, 1974), pp. 11–14. Also, see D. Wagner-Johnson, "Managing Work Team Conflict: Assessment and Preventative Strategies," Center for the Study of Work Teams, University of North Texas, 1999; and M. Kennedy, "Managing Conflict in Work Teams," Center for the Study of Work Teams, University of North Texas, 1998.

**20.** See K. A. Jehn, "A Multimethod Examination of the Benefits and Detriments of Intragroup Conflict," *Administrative Science Quarterly*, June 1995, pp. 256–282; K. A. Jehn, "A Qualitative Analysis of Conflict Type and Dimensions in Organizational Groups," *Administrative Science Quarterly*, September 1997, pp. 530–557; K. A. Jehn, "Affective and Cognitive Conflict in Work Groups: Increasing Performance Through Value-Based Intragroup Conflict," in *Using Conflict in Organizations*, eds. C. K. W. DeDreu and E. Van deVliert (London: Sage, 1997), pp. 87–100; K. A. Jehn and E. A. Mannix, "The Dynamic Nature of Conflict: A Longitudinal Study of Intragroup Conflict and Group Performance," *Academy of Management Journal*, April 2001, pp. 238–251; and C. K. W. DeDreu and A. E. M. Van Vianen, "Managing Relationship Conflict and the Effectiveness of Organizational Teams," *Journal of Organizational Behavior*, May 2001, pp. 309–328.

**21.** C. K. W. DeDreu, "When Too Little or Too Much Hurts: Evidence for a Curvilinear Relationship Between Task Conflict and Innovation in Teams," *Journal of Management*, February 2006, pp. 83–107.

**22.** K. W. Thomas, "Conflict and Negotiation Processes in Organizations," in *Handbook of Industrial and Organizational Psychology*, vol. 3, 2nd ed., eds. M. D. Dunnette and L. M. Hough, pp. 651–717 (Palo Alto, CA: Consulting Psychologists Press, 1992).

**23.** See D. R. Comer, "A Model of Social Loafing in Real Work Groups," *Human Relations*, June 1995.

**24.** S. G. Harkins and K. Szymanski, "Social Loafing and Group Evaluation," *Journal of Personality and Social Psychology*, December 1989, pp. 934–941.

**25.** B. L. Kirkman, C. B. Gibson, and D. L. Shapiro, "Exporting Teams: Enhancing the Implementation and Effectiveness of Work Teams in Global Affiliates," *Organizational Dynamics*, Summer 2001, pp. 12–29; J. W. Bing and C. M. Bing, "Helping Global Teams Compete," *Training & Development*, March 2001, pp. 70–71; P. Christopher Earley and E. Mosakowski, "Creating Hybrid Team Cultures: An Empirical Test of Transnational Team Functioning," *Academy of Management Journal*, February 2000, pp. 26–49; J. Tata, "The Cultural Context of Teams: An Integrative Model of National Culture, Work Team Characteristics, and Team Effectiveness," *Academy of Management Proceedings* (CD-ROM), 1999; D. I. Jung, K. B. Baik, and J. J. Sosik, "A Longitudinal Investigation of Group Characteristics and Work Group Performance: A Cross-Cultural Comparison," *Academy of Management Proceedings* (CD-ROM), 1999; and C. B. Gibson, "They Do What They Believe They Can? Group-Efficacy Beliefs and Group Performance Across Tasks and Cultures," *Academy of Management Proceedings* (CD-ROM), 1996.

**26.** R. Bond and P. B. Smith, "Culture and Conformity: A Meta-Analysis of Studies Using Asch's [1952, 1956] Line Judgment Task," *Psychological Bulletin*, January 1996, pp. 111–137.

**27.** I. L. Janis, *Groupthink*, 2nd ed. (New York: Houghton Mifflin Company, 1982), p. 175.

**28.** See P. C. Earley, "East Meets West Meets Mideast: Further Explorations of Collectivistic and Individualistic Work Groups," *Academy of Management Journal*, April 1993, pp. 319–348; and P. C. Earley, "Social Loafing and Collectivism: A Comparison of the United States and the People's Republic of China," *Administrative Science Quarterly*, December 1989, pp. 565–581.

**29.** See P. C. Earley, "Social Loafing and Collectivism: A Comparison of the United States and the People's Republic of China," *Administrative Science Quarterly*, December 1989, pp. 565–581; and P. C. Earley, "East Meets West Meets Mideast: Further Explorations of Collectivistic and Individualistic Work Groups," *Academy of Management Journal*, April 1993, pp. 319–348.

**30.** N. J. Adler, *International Dimensions of Organizational Behavior*, 4th ed. (Cincinnati, OH: South-Western College Publishing, 2002), p. 142.

**31.** K. B. Dahlin, L. R. Weingart, and P. J. Hinds, "Team Diversity and Information Use," *Academy of Management Journal*, December 2005, pp. 1107–1123.

**32.** N. J. Adler, *International Dimensions of Organizational Behavior*, 4th ed. (Cincinnati, OH: South-Western College Publishing, 2002), p. 142.

**33.** S. Paul, I. M. Samarah, P. Seetharaman, and P. P. Mykytyn, "An Empirical Investigation of Collaborative Conflict Management Style in Group Support System-Based Global Virtual Teams," *Journal of Management Information Systems*, Winter 2005, pp. 185–222.

**34.** S. Chang and P. Tharenou, "Competencies Needed for Managing a Multicultural Workgroup," *Asia Pacific Journal of Human Resources* 42, no. 1 (2004), pp. 57–74; and N. Adler, *International Dimensions of Organizational Behavior* (Boston, MA: Kent Publishing Co., 1986), p. 153.

**35.** C. E. Nicholls, H. W. Lane, and M. Brehm Brechu, "Taking Self-Managed Teams to Mexico," *Academy of Management Executive*, August 1999, pp. 15–27.

**36.** D. Brown, "Innovative HR Ineffective in Manufacturing Firms," *Canadian HR Reporter*, April 7, 2003, pp. 1–2.

**37.** A. B. Drexler and R. Forrester, "Teamwork—Not Necessarily the Answer," *HR Magazine*, January 1998, pp. 55–58.

**38.** R. Forrester and A. B. Drexler, "A Model for Team-Based Organization Performance," *Academy of Management Executive*, August 1999, p. 47. See also S. A. Mohrman, with S. G. Cohen and A. M. Mohrman Jr., *Designing Team-Based Organizations* (San Francisco: Jossey-Bass, 1995); and J. H. Shonk, *Team-Based Organizations* (Homewood, IL: Business One Irwin, 1992).

**39.** Adapted from D. A. Whetten and K. S. Cameron, *Developing Management Skills*, 3rd ed. (New York: HarperCollins, 1995), pp. 534–535.

**40.** Based on P. L. Hunsaker, *Training in Management Skills* (Upper Saddle River, NJ: Prentice Hall, 2001), Chapter 12.

**41.** Based on L. Copeland, "Making the Most of Cultural Differences at the Workplace," *Personnel*, June 1988, pp. 52–60; C. R. Bantz, "Cultural Diversity and Group Cross-Cultural Team Research," *Journal of Applied Communication Research*, February 1993, pp. 1–19; L. Strach and L. Wicander, "Fitting In: Issues of Tokenism and Conformity for Minority Women," *SAM Advanced Management Journal*, Summer 1993, pp. 22–25; M. L. Maznevski, "Understanding Our Differences: Performance in Decision-Making Groups With Diverse Members," *Human Relations*, May 1994, pp. 531–552; F. Rice, "How to Make Diversity Pay," *Fortune*, August 8, 1994, pp. 78–86; J. Jusko, "Diversity Enhances Decision Making," *IndustryWeek*, April 2, 2001, p. 9; and K. Lovelace, D. L. Shapiro, and L. R. Weingart, "Maximizing Cross-Functional New Product Teams' Innovativeness and Constraint Adherence: A Conflict Communications Perspective," *Academy of Management Journal*, August 2002, pp. 779–793.

# CHAPTER 11

**1.** "Curling as a Business Model: The Off-Ice Success of the Canadian Curling Association," *Canadian Business Journal*, March 12, 2012, http://www.cbj.ca/business_in_action/mar_12/canadian_curling_association.html.

**2.** See the Canadian Curling Association website, www.curling.ca; "Curling as a Business Model: The Off-Ice Success of the Canadian Curling Association," *Canadian Business Journal*, March 12, 2012, http://www.cbj.ca/business_in_action/mar_12/canadian_curling_association.html.

**3.** J. Kluger and B. Liston, "A Columbia Culprit?" *Time*, February 24, 2003, p. 13.

**4.** K. A. Merchant, "The Control Function of Management," *Sloan Management Review*, Summer 1982, pp. 43–55.

**5.** E. Flamholtz, "Organizational Control Systems as a Managerial Tool," *California Management Review*, Winter 1979, p. 55.

**6.** "Top 1000: Ranking Canada's Top 1000 Public Companies by Profit," *Globe and Mail: Report on Business Magazine*, June 28, 2012, http://www.theglobeandmail.com/report-on-business/rob-magazine/top-1000/2012-rankings-of-canadas-top-1000-public-companies-by-profit/article4371923.

**7.** Aon Hewitt, "Best Employers in Canada," https://ceplb03. hewitt.com/bestemployers/canada/pages/currentlist2011.htm.

**8.** J. McElgunn, "Profit 200 Overview: Who are Canada's Fastest-Growing Companies?" *Profit*, June 1, 2012, http://www. profitguide.com/microsite/profit200/2012.

**9.** P. Magnusson, "Your Jitters Are Their Lifeblood," *Business- Week*, April 14, 2003, p. 41; S. Williams, "Company Crisis: CEO Under Fire," *Hispanic Business*, March 2003, pp. 54–56; T. Purdum, "Preparing for the Worst," *IndustryWeek*, January 2003, pp. 53–55; and S. Leibs, "Lesson from 9/11: It's Not About Data," *CFO*, September 2002, pp. 31–32.

**10.** S. Kerr, "On the Folly of Rewarding A, While Hoping for B," *Academy of Management Journal*, December 1975, pp. 769–783.

**11.** Y. F. Jarrar and M. Zairi, "Future Trends in Benchmarking for Competitive Advantage: A Global Survey," *Total Quality Management*, December 2001, pp. 906–912.

**12.** M. Simpson and D. Kondouli, "A Practical Approach to Benchmarking in Three Service Industries," *Total Quality Man- agement*, July 2000, pp. S623–S630.

**13.** K. N. Dervitsiotis, "Benchmarking and Paradigm Shifts," *Total Quality Management*, July 2000, pp. S641–S646.

**14.** See "Entrepreneur: BouClair," Roynat Capital Business Pro- files, *National Post*, www.canada.com/nationalpost/entrepreneur/ bouclair.html.

**15.** T. Leahy, "Extracting Diamonds in the Rough," *Business Finance*, August 2000, pp. 33–37.

**16.** "Recognizing Commitment to Diversity," *Canadian HR Reporter*, November 3, 2003, p. 12.

**17.** B. Bruzina, B. Jessop, R. Plourde, B. Whitlock, and L. Rubin, "Ameren Embraces Benchmarking as a Core Business Strategy," *Power Engineering*, November 2002, pp. 121–124; and T. Leahy, "Extracting Diamonds in the Rough," *Business Finance*, August 2000, pp. 33–37.

**18.** H. Koontz and R. W. Bradspies, "Managing through Feedfor- ward Control," *Business Horizons*, June 1972, pp. 25–36.

**19.** "An Open Letter to McDonald's Customers," *Wall Street Journal*, August 22, 2001, p. A5.

**20.** W. H. Newman, *Constructive Control: Design and Use of Control Systems* (Upper Saddle River, NJ: Prentice Hall, 1975), p. 33.

**21.** R. Ilies and T. A. Judge, "Goal Regulation across Time: The Effects of Feedback and Affect," *Journal of Applied Psychology* 90, no. 3 (May 2005), pp. 453–467.

**22.** John Carver and Miriam Carver, "Carver's Policy Gover- nance® Model in Nonprofit Organizations," *PolicyGovernance. com*, http://www.carvergovernance.com/pg-np.htm.

**23.** W. G. Ouchi, "A Conceptual Framework for the Design of Organizational Control Mechanisms," *Management Science*, Au- gust 1979, pp. 833–838; and W. G. Ouchi, "Markets, Bureaucra- cies, and Clans," *Administrative Science Quarterly*, March 1980, pp. 129–141.

**24.** Based on P. Fitzpatrick, "Wacky WestJet's Winning Ways: Passengers Respond to Stunts That Include Races to Determine Who Leaves the Airplane First," *National Post*, October 16, 2000, p. C1.

**25.** L. Smircich, "Concepts of Culture and Organizational Analy- sis," *Administrative Science Quarterly*, September 1983, p. 339;

D. R. Denison, "What Is the Difference between Organizational Culture and Organizational Climate? A Native's Point of View on a Decade of Paradigm Wars" (paper presented at Academy of Management Annual Meeting, Atlanta, Georgia, 1993); and M. J. Hatch, "The Dynamics of Organizational Culture," *Academy of Management Review*, October 1993, pp. 657–693.

**26.** K. Shadur and M. A. Kienzle, "The Relationship Between Organizational Climate and Employee Perceptions of Involve- ment," *Group & Organization Management*, December 1999, pp. 479–503; and A. M. Sapienza, "Believing Is Seeing: How Culture Influences the Decisions Top Managers Make," in *Gain- ing Control of the Corporate Culture*, eds. R. H. Kilmann, M. J. Saxton, and R. Serpa (San Francisco: Jossey-Bass, 1985), p. 68.

**27.** C. A. O'Reilly III, J. Chatman, and D. F. Caldwell, "People and Organizational Culture: A Profile Comparison Approach to Assessing Person–Organization Fit," *Academy of Management Journal*, September 1991, pp. 487–516; and J. A. Chatman and K. A. Jehn, "Assessing the Relationship Between Industry Char- acteristics and Organizational Culture: How Different Can You Be?" *Academy of Management Journal*, June 1994, pp. 522–553.

**28.** See, for example, D. R. Denison, *Corporate Culture and Organizational Effectiveness* (New York: Wiley, 1990); G. G. Gordon and N. DiTomaso, "Predicting Corporate Performance from Organizational Culture," *Journal of Management Studies*, November 1992, pp. 793–798; J. P. Kotter and J. L. Heskett, *Corporate Culture and Performance* (New York: Free Press, 1992), pp. 15–27; J. C. Collins and J. I. Porras, *Built to Last* (New York: HarperBusiness, 1994); J. C. Collins and J. I. Porras, "Building Your Company's Vision," *Harvard Business Review*, September–October 1996, pp. 65–77; R. Goffee and G. Jones, "What Holds the Modern Company Together?" *Harvard Busi- ness Review*, November–December 1996, pp. 133–148; and J. B. Sorensen, "The Strength of Corporate Culture and the Reliability of Firm Performance," *Administrative Science Quarterly* 47, no. 1 (2002), pp. 70–91.

**29.** J. B. Sorensen, "The Strength of Corporate Culture and the Reliability of Firm Performance," *Administrative Science Quar- terly* 47, no. 1 (2002), pp. 70–91.

**30.** G. Probst and S. Raisch, "Organizational Crisis: The Logic of Failure," *Academy of Management Executive* 19, no. 1 (February 2005), pp. 90–105.

**31.** J. Forman, "When Stories Create an Organization's Future," *Strategy & Business*, Second Quarter 1999, pp. 6–9; D. M. Boje, "The Storytelling Organization: A Study of Story Performance in an Office-Supply Firm," *Administrative Science Quarterly*, March 1991, pp. 106–126; C. H. Deutsch, "The Parables of Cor- porate Culture," *New York Times*, October 13, 1991, p. F25; and T. Terez, "The Business of Storytelling," *Workforce*, May 2002, pp. 22–24.

**32.** A. M. Pettigrew, "On Studying Organizational Cultures," *Administrative Science Quarterly*, December 1979, p. 576.

**33.** A. M. Pettigrew, "On Studying Organizational Cultures," *Administrative Science Quarterly*, December 1979, p. 576.

**34.** F. Hansen, "The Value-Based Management Commitment," *Business Finance*, September 2001, pp. 2–5.

**35.** M. Acharya and T. Yew, "A New Kind of Top 10," *Toronto Star*, June 30, 2002, p. C01.

**36.** M. Acharya and T. Yew, "A New Kind of Top 10," *Toronto Star*, June 30, 2002, p. C01.

**37.** K. Lehn and A. K. Makhija, "EVA and MVA as Performance Measures and Signals for Strategic Change," *Strategy & Leadership*, May–June 1996, pp. 34–38.

**38.** S. Taub, "MVPs of MVA: Which Companies Created the Most Wealth for Shareholders Last Year? *CFO*, July 1, 2003, www.cfo.com/article.cfm/3009758/c_2984284/?f=archives.

**39.** Debra Black, "Rogers Data on Clients Found in Lot," *Toronto Star*, April 8, 2007, www.thestar.com/News/article/200727.

**40.** J. McPartlin, "Hackers Find Backers," *CFO*, January 2006, pp. 75–77; J. Swartz, "Data Losses Push Businesses to Encrypt Backup Tapes," *USA Today*, June 13, 2005, p. 1B; J. Goff, "New Holes for Hackers," *CFO*, May 2005, pp. 64–73; B. Grow, "Hacker Hunters," *BusinessWeek*, May 30, 2005, pp. 74–82; J. Swartz, "Crooks Slither into Net's Shady Nooks and Crannies," *USA Today*, October 21, 2004, pp. 1B+; J. Swartz, "Spam Can Hurt in More Ways Than One," *USA Today*, July 7, 2004, p. 3B; and T. Reason, "Stopping the Flow," *CFO*, September 2003, pp. 97–99.

**41.** D. Whelan, "Google Me Not," *Forbes*, August 16, 2004, pp. 102–104.

**42.** J. Levitz and J. Hechinger, "Laptops Prove Weakest Link in Data Security," *Wall Street Journal*, March 24, 2006, pp. B1+.

**43.** J. Markoff, "Study Says Chips in ID Tags Are Vulnerable to Viruses," *New York Times*, March 15, 2006, www.nytimes.com/2006/03/15/technology/15tag.html.

**44.** J. Yaukey and C. L. Romero, "Arizona Firm Pays Big for Workers' Digital Downloads," *Springfield News-Leader*, May 6, 2002, p. 6B.

**45.** R. S. Kaplan and D. P. Norton, "How to Implement a New Strategy without Disrupting Your Organization," *Harvard Business Review*, March 2006, pp. 100–109; L. Bassi and D. McMurrer, "Developing Measurement Systems for Managing in the Knowledge Era," *Organizational Dynamics*, May 2005, pp. 185–196; G. M. J. de Koning, "Making the Balanced Scorecard Work (Part 2), *Gallup Business Journal*, http://businessjournal.gallup.com/content/12571/making-balanced-scorecard-work-part.aspx; G. M. J. de Koning, "Making the Balanced Scorecard Work (Part 1), *Gallup Business Journal*, http://businessjournal.gallup.com/content/12208/making-balanced-scorecard-work-part.aspx; K. Graham, "Balanced Scorecard," *New Zealand Management*, March 2003, pp. 32–34; K. Ellis, "A Ticket to Ride: Balanced Scorecard," *Training*, April 2001, p. 50; T. Leahy, "Tailoring the Balanced Scorecard," *Business Finance*, August 2000, pp. 53–56; and R. S. Kaplan and D. P. Norton, "Using the Balanced Scorecard as a Strategic Management System," *Harvard Business Review* 74, no. 1 (January–February 1996), pp. 75–85.

**46.** T. Leahy, "Tailoring the Balanced Scorecard," *Business Finance*, August 2000, pp. 53–56.

**47.** "Hospital Reports," Ontario Hospital Association (OHA), http://www.oha.com/KnowledgeCentre/Library/HospitalReports/Pages/HospitalReports.aspx; and T. Leahy, "Tailoring the Balanced Scorecard," *Business Finance*, August 2000, pp. 53–56.

**48.** "A Revolution Where Everyone Wins: Worldwide Movement to Improve Corporate-Governance Standards," *BusinessWeek*, May 19, 2003, p. 72.

**49.** J. S. McClenahen, "Executives Expect More Board Input," *IndustryWeek*, October 2002, p. 12.

**50.** D. Salierno, "Boards Face Increased Responsibility," *Internal Auditor*, June 2003, pp. 14–15.

**51.** R. Corbett, "Sport Canada Introduces Governance Principles for Sport Organizations," Sport Law & Strategy Group, November 8, 2011, http://www.sportlaw.ca/2011/11/sport-canada-to-introduce-governance-principles-for-sport-organizations/.

**52.** N. Shirouzu and J. Bigness, "7-Eleven Operators Resist System to Monitor Managers," *Wall Street Journal*, June 16, 1997, p. B1.

**53.** E. O'Connor, "Pulling the Plug on Cyberslackers," *StarPhoenix*, May 24, 2003, p. F22.

**54.** E. O'Connor, "Pulling the Plug on Cyberslackers," *StarPhoenix*, May 24, 2003, p. F22.

**55.** Kathryn Leger, "'Stealing' Time at Work on Net," *Gazette* (Montreal), April 4, 2008, www2.canada.com/montrealgazette/news/business/story.html?id=32125d78-a479-497a-ae19-4f461ea18060.

**56.** D. Hawkins, "Lawsuits Spur Rise in Employee Monitoring," *U.S. News & World Report*, August 13, 2001, p. 53; L. Guernsey, "You've Got Inappropriate Mail," *New York Times*, April 5, 2000, p. C11; and R. Karaim, "Setting E-Privacy Rules," *Cnnfn Online*, December 15, 1999.

**57.** E. Bott, "Are You Safe? Privacy Special Report," *PC Computing*, March 2000, pp. 87–88.

**58.** E. O'Connor, "Pulling the Plug on Cyberslackers," *StarPhoenix*, May 24, 2003, p. F22.

**59.** A. Tomlinson, "Heavy-Handed Net Policies Push Privacy Boundaries," *Canadian HR Reporter*, December 2, 2002, pp. 1–2.

**60.** C. Sorensen, "Canada Ranks High in Employee Theft: Global Survey Findings," *National Post*, May 28, 2004, p. FP9.

**61.** A. Perry, "Back-to-School Brings Pilfering: Some Employees Raid Office for Kids," *Toronto Star*, August 30, 2003, p. B01.

**62.** Joshua Bamfield, *Global Retail Theft Barometer 2007: Monitoring the Costs of Shrinkage and Crime on the Global Retail Industry* (Nottingham, UK: Centre for Retail Research, 2007), http://www.globalretailtheftbarometer.com/pdf/Global-Retail-Theft-Barometer-2007.pdf; "Detering Employee Theft," Watchdog Loss Prevention for Businesses, March 22, 2012, http://watchdogloss.com/blog/detering-employee-theft/; and C. Powell, "Pro Thieves: They're Shopping More Often," *Canadian Grocer*, May 2, 2011, http://www.canadiangrocer.com/top-stories/grocery-theft-gone-in-30-seconds-6162.

**63.** J. Greenberg, "The STEAL Motive: Managing the Social Determinants of Employee Theft," in *Antisocial Behavior in Organizations*, eds. R. Giacalone and J. Greenberg (Newbury Park, CA: Sage, 1997), pp. 85–108.

**64.** "Crime Spree," *BusinessWeek*, September 9, 2002, p. 8; B. P. Niehoff and R. J. Paul, "Causes of Employee Theft and Strategies That HR Managers Can Use for Prevention," *Human Resource Management*, Spring 2000, pp. 51–64; and G. Winter, "Taking at the Office Reaches New Heights: Employee Larceny Is Bigger and Bolder," *New York Times*, July 12, 2000, p. C11.

**65.** This section is based on J. Greenberg, *Behavior in Organizations: Understanding and Managing the Human Side of Work*, 8th ed. (Upper Saddle River, NJ: Prentice Hall, 2003), pp. 329–330.

**66.** A. H. Bell and D. M. Smith, "Why Some Employees Bite the Hand That Feeds Them," *Workforce*, May 16, 2000.

**67.** A. H. Bell and D. M. Smith, "Protecting the Company Against Theft and Fraud," *Workforce*, May 16, 2000; J. D. Hansen, "To Catch a Thief," *Journal of Accountancy*, March

2000, pp. 43–46; and J. Greenberg, "The Cognitive Geometry of Employee Theft," in *Dysfunctional Behavior in Organizations: Nonviolent and Deviant Behavior*, eds. S. B. Bacharach, A. O'Leary-Kelly, J. M. Collins, and R. W. Griffin (Stamford, CT: JAI Press, 1998), pp. 147–193.

**68.** Information from company website, www.enterprise.com; and A. Taylor, "Driving Customer Satisfaction," *Harvard Business Review*, July 2002, pp. 24–25.

**69.** S. D. Pugh, J. Dietz, J. W. Wiley, and S. M. Brooks, "Driving Service Effectiveness through Employee-Customer Linkages," *Academy of Management Executive*, November 2002, pp. 73–84.

**70.** T. S. Bateman and J. M. Crant, "The Proactive Component of Organizational Behavior: A Measure and Correlates," *Journal of Organizational Behavior*, March 1993, p. 112; and J. M. Crant, "Proactive Behavior in Organizations," *Journal of Management* 26, no. 3 (2000), pp. 435–462.

**71.** Based on P. L. Hunsaker, *Training in Management Skills* (Upper Saddle River, NJ: Prentice Hall, 2001), pp. 60–61.

**72.** See "100 Years Siemens in Canada," http://www.siemens.com/entry/ca/en/; and Jared Mitchell, "Green Giant: Interview with Peter Loescher, president and CEO of Siemens AG," *Canadian Business*, November 16, 2011, http://www.canadian-business.com/article/57428—green-giant.

**73.** "Siemens Wind Energy Facility to Create 300 Jobs in Tillsonburg, Ontario," *The Green Pages*, December 2, 2010, http://thegreenpages.ca/ca/ 2010/12/02/siemens_wind_energy_facility_t/.

**74.** Siemens Canada, "Siemens Canada Limited Signs MOU with Ontario Government," Press Release, May 20, 2011, http://www.siemens.ca/web/portal/en/press/Pages/MOU-signed-with-Ontario-Government.aspx.

**75.** Jared Mitchell, "Green Giant: Interview with Peter Loescher, president and CEO of Siemens AG," *Canadian Business*, November 16, 2011, http://www.canadianbusiness.com/article/57428—green-giant.

**76.** City of Vancouver, *Greenest City 2020 Action Plan* (Vancouver, BC: City of Vancouver, 2012), http://vancouver.ca/files/cov/Greenest-city-action-plan.pdf.

**77.** M. Swift, "A Look Inside Facebook's 'Bootcamp' for New Employees," *Toronto Star*, April 18, 2012, http://www.thestar.com/business/article/1163373—a-look-inside-facebook-s-boot-camp-for-new-employees.

**78.** Jessica Guynn, "The Grunts Are Geeks at Facebook Bootcamp," *Los Angeles Times*, August 1, 2010, http://articles.latimes.com/2010/aug/01/business/la-fi-facebook-bootcamp-20100801.

**79.** M. Swift, "A Look Inside Facebook's 'Bootcamp' for New Employees," *Toronto Star*, April 18, 2012, http://www.thestar.com/business/article/1163373—a-look-inside-facebook-s-boot-camp-for-new-employees.

**80.** Facebook, "Hackathon," https://www.facebook.com/hackathon.

## CHAPTER 12

**1.** Based on "BP's Fiona MacLeod: A Change Agent Sees Change Addiction," *Knowledge Wharton*, July 8, 2009, ://knowledge.wharton.upenn.edu/article.cfm?articleid=2280; and information from the BP company website, .bp.com.

**2.** "BP's Fiona MacLeod: A Change Agent Sees Change Addiction," *Knowledge Wharton*, July 8, 2009, http://knowledge.wharton.upenn.edu/article.cfm?articleid=2280.

**3.** "BP's Fiona MacLeod: A Change Agent Sees Change Addiction," *Knowledge Wharton*, July 8, 2009, http://knowledge.wharton.upenn.edu/article.cfm?articleid=2280.

**4.** "BP's Fiona MacLeod: A Change Agent Sees Change Addiction," *Knowledge Wharton*, July 8, 2009, http://knowledge.wharton.upenn.edu/article.cfm?articleid=2280.

**5.** "BP's Fiona MacLeod: A Change Agent Sees Change Addiction," *Knowledge Wharton*, July 8, 2009, http://knowledge.wharton.upenn.edu/article.cfm?articleid=2280.

**6.** "BP's Fiona MacLeod: A Change Agent Sees Change Addiction," *Knowledge Wharton*, July 8, 2009, http://knowledge.wharton.upenn.edu/article.cfm?articleid=2280.

**7.** C. R. Leana and B. Barry, "Stability and Change as Simultaneous Experiences in Organizational Life," *Academy of Management Review*, October 2000, pp. 753–759.

**8.** J. Gallaugher, *Information Systems: A Manager's Guide to Harnessing Technology*, v. 1.0 (Flat World Knowledge, 2010), http://catalog.flatworldknowledge.com/catalog/editions/p61083.

**9.** "Oil Giant BP Reaches 'Turning Point,'" *BBC News*, October 25, 2011, http://www.bbc.co.uk/news/business-15441607.

**10.** Based on R. D. Hof, "Back to the Future at Yahoo!" *BusinessWeek*, July 02, 2007, p. 34.

**11.** M. Arrington, "Panama Not Enough to Battle Google: Yahoo Acquires RightMedia," *TechCrunch*, April 29, 2007, www.techcrunch.com/2007/04/29/panama-not-enough-to-battle-google-yahoo-acquires-rightmedia/.

**12.** R.D. Young, "Yahoo! Discusses Their SEO Strategy," *Search Engine Journal*, August 2, 2011, http://www.searchenginejournal.com/ yahoo-discusses-their-seo-strategy/31455/; and Yahoo!, *Yahoo!® Annual Report, 2011*, http://yhoo.client.shareholder.com/annuals.cfm.

**13.** The idea for these metaphors came from J. E. Dutton, S. J. Ashford, R. M. O'Neill, and K. A. Lawrence, "Moves That Matter: Issue Selling and Organizational Change," *Academy of Management Journal*, August 2001, pp. 716–736; B. H. Kemelgor, S. D. Johnson, and S. Srinivasan, "Forces Driving Organizational Change: A Business School Perspective," *Journal of Education for Business*, January–February 2000, pp. 133–137; G. Colvin, "When It Comes to Turbulence, CEOs Could Learn a Lot from Sailors," *Fortune*, March 29, 1999, pp. 194–196; and P. B. Vaill, *Managing as a Performing Art: New Ideas for a World of Chaotic Change* (San Francisco: Jossey-Bass, 1989).

**14.** K. Lewin, *Field Theory in Social Science* (New York: Harper & Row, 1951).

**15.** S. McShane and S. Steen, *Canadian Organizational Behaviour,* 7th ed. (Toronto, ON: McGraw-Hill, 2009), pp. 354–355.

**16.** For contrasting views on episodic and continuous change, see K. E. Weick and R. E. Quinn, "Organizational Change and Development," in *Annual Review of Psychology*, vol. 50, ed. J. T. Spence, J. M. Darley, and D. J. Foss (Palo Alto, CA: Annual Reviews, 1999), pp. 361–386.

**17.** G. Hamel, "Take It Higher," *Fortune*, February 5, 2001, pp. 169–170.

**18.** BP, "BP Releases Report on Causes of Gulf of Mexico Tragedy," Press Release, September 8, 2010, http://www.bp.com/genericarticle.do?categoryId=2012968&contentId=7064893.

**19.** BP, "BP Releases Report on Causes of Gulf of Mexico Tragedy," Press Release, September 8, 2010, http://www.bp.com/genericarticle.do?categoryId=2012968&contentId=7064893.

**20.** D. E. Lane, R. L. Stephenson, "Fisheries Co-management: Organization, Process, and Decision Support, *Journal of Northwest Atlantic Fishery Science* 23 (1998), pp. 251–265, http://journal.nafo.int/J23/lane.pdf.

**21.** See, for example, T. C. Head and P. F. Sorensen, "Cultural Values and Organizational Development: A Seven-Country Study," *Leadership & Organization Development Journal*, March 1993, pp. 3–7; A. H. Church, W. W. Burke, and D. F. Van Eynde, "Values, Motives, and Interventions of Organization Development Practitioners," *Group & Organization Management*, March 1994, pp. 5–50; W. L. French and C. H. Bell Jr., *Organization Development: Behavioral Science Interventions for Organization Improvement*, 6th ed. (Upper Saddle River, NJ: Prentice Hall, 1998); N. A. Worren, K. Ruddle, and K. Moore, "From Organizational Development to Change Management," *Journal of Applied Behavioral Science*, September 1999, pp. 273–286; G. Farias, "Organizational Development and Change Management," *Journal of Applied Behavioral Science*, September 2000, pp. 376–379; W. Nicolay, "Response to Farias and Johnson's Commentary," *Journal of Applied Behavioral Science*, September 2000, pp. 380–381; and S. Hicks, "What Is Organization Development?" *Training & Development*, August 2000, p. 65.

**22.** T. White, "Supporting Change: How Communicators at Scotiabank Turned Ideas into Action," *Communication World*, April 2002, pp. 22–24.

**23.** S. McShane and S. Steen, *Canadian Organizational Behaviour,* 7th ed. (Toronto, ON: McGraw-Hill, 2009), p. 359.

**24.** P. A. McLagan, "Change Leadership Today," *Training & Development*, November 2002, p. 29.

**25.** H. L. Sirkin, P. Keenan, and A. Jackson, "The Hard Side of Change Management," *Harvard Business Review* 83, no. 10 (October 1, 2005), pp. 108–118.

**26.** W. Pietersen, "The Mark Twain Dilemma: The Theory and Practice for Change Leadership," *Journal of Business Strategy*, September–October 2002, pp. 32–37; C. Hymowitz, "To Maintain Success, Managers Must Learn How to Direct Change," *Wall Street Journal*, August 13, 2002, p. B1; and J. E. Dutton, S. J. Ashford, R. M. O'Neill, and K. A. Lawrence, "Moves That Matter: Issue Selling and Organizational Change," *Academy of Management Journal*, August 2001, pp. 716–736.

**27.** P. A. McLagan, "The Change-Capable Organization," *Training & Development*, January 2003, pp. 50–58.

**28.** M. Young and J. E. Post, "Managing to Communicate, Communicating to Manage: How Leading Companies Communicate With Employees," *Organizational Dynamics*, Summer 1993, pp. 31–43.

**29.** M. Javidan, P. W. Dorfman, M. S. deLuque, and R. J. House, "In the Eye of the Beholder: Cross-Cultural Lessons in Leadership from Project GLOBE," *Academy of Management Perspective*, February 2006, pp. 67–90; and E. Fagenson-Eland, E. A. Ensher, and W. W. Burke, "Organization Development and Change Interventions: A Seven-Nation Comparison," *Journal of Applied Behavioral Science*, December 2004, pp. 432–464.

**30.** E. Fagenson-Eland, E. A. Ensher, and W. W. Burke, "Organization Development and Change Interventions: A Seven-Nation Comparison," *Journal of Applied Behavioral Science*, December 2004, p. 461.

**31.** See, for example, B. M. Staw, "Counterforces to Change," in *Change in Organizations*, eds. P. S. Goodman and Associates (San Francisco: Jossey-Bass, 1982), pp. 87–121; A. A. Armenakis and A. G. Bedeian, "Organizational Change: A Review of Theory and Research in the 1990s," *Journal of Management* 25, no. 3 (1999), pp. 293–315; C. R. Wanberg and J. T. Banas, "Predictors and Outcomes of Openness to Changes in a Reorganizing Workplace," *Journal of Applied Psychology*, February 2000, pp. 132–142; S. K. Piderit, "Rethinking Resistance and Recognizing Ambivalence: A Multidimensional View of Attitudes Toward an Organizational Change," *Academy of Management Review*, October 2000, pp. 783–794; R. Kegan and L. L. Lahey, "The Real Reason People Won't Change," *Harvard Business Review*, November 2001, pp. 85–92; M. A. Korsgaard, H. J. Sapienza, and D. M. Schweiger, "Beaten Before Begun: The Role of Procedural Justice in Planning Change," *Journal of Management* 28, no. 4 (2002), pp. 497–516; and C. E. Cunningham, "Readiness for Organizational Change: A Longitudinal Study of Workplace, Psychological and Behavioral Correlates," *Journal of Occupational and Organizational Psychology*, December 2002, pp. 377–392.

**32.** J. P. Kotter and L. A. Schlesinger, "Choosing Strategies for Change," *Harvard Business Review*, March–April 1979, pp. 107–109; P. Strebel, "Why Do Employees Resist Change?" *Harvard Business Review*, May–June 1996, pp. 86–92; J. Mariotti, "Troubled by Resistance to Change," *IndustryWeek*, October 7, 1996, p. 30; and A. Reichers, J. P. Wanous, and J. T. Austin, "Understanding and Managing Cynicism About Organizational Change," *Academy of Management Executive*, February 1997, pp. 48–57

**33.** S. McShane and S. Steen, *Canadian Organizational Behaviour,* 7th ed. (Toronto, ON: McGraw-Hill, 2009), p. 357.

**34.** S. McShane and S. Steen, *Canadian Organizational Behaviour,* 7th ed. (Toronto, ON: McGraw-Hill, 2009), p. 358.

**35.** J. P. Kotter and L. A. Schlesinger, "Choosing Strategies for Change," *Harvard Business Review*, March–April 1979, pp. 106–111; K. Matejka and R. Julian, "Resistance to Change Is Natural," *Supervisory Management*, October 1993, p. 10; C. O'Connor, "Resistance: The Repercussions of Change," *Leadership & Organization Development Journal*, October 1993, pp. 30–36; J. Landau, "Organizational Change and Barriers to Innovation: A Case Study in the Italian Public Sector," *Human Relations*, December 1993, pp. 1411–1429; A. Sagie and M. Koslowsky, "Organizational Attitudes and Behaviors as a Function of Participation in Strategic and Tactical Change Decisions: An Application of Path-Goal Theory," *Journal of Organizational Behavior*, January 1994, pp. 37–47; V. D. Miller, J. R. Johnson, and J. Grau, "Antecedents to Willingness to Participate in a Planned Organizational Change," *Journal of Applied Communication Research*, February 1994, pp. 59–80; P. Pritchett and R. Pound, *The Employee Handbook for Organizational Change* (Dallas: Pritchett Publishing, 1994); R. Maurer, *Beyond the Wall of Resistance: Unconventional Strategies That Build Support for Change* (Austin, TX: Bard Books, 1996); D. Harrison, "Assess and Remove Barriers to Change," *HRfocus*, July 1999, pp. 9–10; L. K. Lewis, "Disseminating Information and Soliciting Input During Planned Organizational Change," *Management Communication Quarterly*, August 1999, pp. 43–75; J. P. Wanous, A. E. Reichers, and J. T. Austin, "Cynicism About Organizational Change," *Group & Organization Management*, June 2000, pp. 132–153; K. W. Mossholder, R. P. Settoon, and A. A. Armenakis,

"Emotion During Organizational Transformations," *Group & Organization Management*, September 2000, pp. 220–243; and S. K. Piderit, "Rethinking Resistance and Recognizing Ambivalence: A Multidimensional View of Attitudes Toward an Organizational Change," *Academy of Management Review*, October 2000, pp. 783–794.

**36.** T. M. Egan and C. M. Lancaster, "Comparing Appreciative Inquiry to Action Research: OD Practitioner Perspectives," *Organizational Development Journal* 23, no. 2 (Summer 2005): pp. 29–49.

**37.** S. McShane and S. Steen, *Canadian Organizational Behaviour*, 7th ed. (Toronto, ON: McGraw-Hill, 2009), pp. 364–365.

**38.** S. McShane and S. Steen, *Canadian Organizational Behaviour*, 7th ed. (Toronto, ON: McGraw-Hill, 2009), pp. 365–367.

**39.** "Team Values the Canadian Tire Way," *Appreciative Inquiry Commons*, http://appreciativeinquiry.case.edu/practice/ppCT.cfm.

**40.** C. Krauss, "BP Chief Says Industry Must Change to Guard Against Spills," *New York Times*, March 8, 2011, http://www.nytimes.com/2011/03/09/business/energy-environment/09bp.html.

**41.** C. Krauss, "BP Chief Says Industry Must Change to Guard Against Spills," *New York Times*, March 8, 2011, http://www.nytimes.com/2011/03/09/business/energy-environment/09bp.html.

**42.** C. Hymowitz, "How Leader at 3M Got His Employees to Back Big Changes," *Wall Street Journal*, April 23, 2002, p. B1; and J. Useem, "Jim McNerney Thinks He Can Turn 3M from a Good Company into a Great One—With a Little Help from His Former Employer: General Electric," *Fortune*, August 12, 2002, pp. 127–132.

**43.** See T. H. Fitzgerald, "Can Change in Organizational Culture Really Be Managed?" *Organizational Dynamics*, Autumn 1988, pp. 5–15; B. Dumaine, "Creating a New Company Culture," *Fortune*, January 15, 1990, pp. 127–131; P. F. Drucker, "Don't Change Corporate Culture—Use It!" *Wall Street Journal*, March 28, 1991, p. A14; J. Martin, *Cultures in Organizations: Three Perspectives* (New York: Oxford University Press, 1992); D. C. Pheysey, *Organizational Cultures: Types and Transformations* (London: Routledge, 1993); C. G. Smith and R. P. Vecchio, "Organizational Culture and Strategic Management: Issues in the Strategic Management of Change," *Journal of Managerial Issues*, Spring 1993, pp. 53–70; P. Bate, *Strategies for Cultural Change* (Boston: Butterworth-Heinemann, 1994); and P. Anthony, *Managing Culture* (Philadelphia: Open University Press, 1994).

**44.** M. L. Wald and J. Schwartz, "Shuttle Inquiry Uncovers Flaws in Communication," *New York Times*, August 4, 2003, http://www.nytimes.com/2003/08/04/us/shuttle-inquiry-uncovers-flaws-in-communication.html.

**45.** M. L. Wald and J. Schwartz, "Shuttle Inquiry Uncovers Flaws in Communication," *New York Times*, August 4, 2003, http://www.nytimes.com/2003/08/04/us/shuttle-inquiry-uncovers-flaws-in-communication.html.

**46.** See, for example, R. H. Kilmann, M. J. Saxton, and R. Serpa, eds., *Gaining Control of the Corporate Culture* (San Francisco: Jossey-Bass, 1985); and D. C. Hambrick and S. Finkelstein, "Managerial Discretion: A Bridge Between Polar Views of Organizational Outcomes," in *Research in Organizational Behavior*, vol. 9, eds. B. M. Staw and L. L. Cummings (Greenwich, CT: JAI Press, 1987), p. 384.

**47.** M. A. Cavanaugh, W. R. Boswell, M. V. Roehling, and J. W. Boudreau, "An Empirical Examination of Self-Reported Work Stress Among U.S. Managers," *Journal of Applied Psychology*, February 2000, pp. 65–74; M. A. Verespej, "Stressed Out," *IndustryWeek*, February 21, 2000, pp. 30–34; J. Laabs, "Time-Starved Workers Rebel," *Workforce*, October 2000, pp. 26–28; and C. Daniels, "The Last Taboo," *Fortune*, October 28, 2002, pp. 137–144.

**48.** Elaine Lowe, *Social Innovations: Conversations on Work and Well-Being*, (Ottawa, ON: Vanier Institute of the Family, October 2005), p. 5, http://www.vanierinstitute.ca/modules/news/newsitem.php?ItemId=309.

**49.** Ipsos-Reid/sanofi-aventis Canada, *The sanofi-aventis Healthcare Survey, 2011* (Laval, PQ: sanofi-aventis Canada, 2011), p. 18, http://www.sanofi.ca/l/ca/en/layout.jsp?scat=C3588838-0978-4F25-9A92-6F37FA912C05.

**50.** Adapted from R. S. Schuler, "Definition and Conceptualization of Stress in Organizations," *Organizational Behavior and Human Performance*, April 1980, p. 189. For an updated review of definitions, see R. L. Kahn and P. Byosiere, "Stress in Organizations," in *Handbook of Industrial and Organizational Psychology*, vol. 3, 2nd ed., eds. M. D. Dunnette and L. J. Hough (Palo Alto, CA: Consulting Psychologists Press, 1992), pp. 573–580.

**51.** B. L. de Mente, "Karoshi: Death from Overwork," Asia Pacific Management Forum, www.apmforum.com, May 2002.

**52.** S. E. Jackson, "Participation in Decision Making as a Strategy for Reducing Job-Related Strain," *Journal of Applied Psychology*, February 1983, pp. 3–19; C. D. Fisher, "Boredom at Work: A Neglected Concept," *Human Relations*, March 1993, pp. 395–417; C. A. Heaney, B. A. Israel, S. J. Schurman, E. A. Baker, J. S. House, and M. Hugentobler, "Industrial Relations, Worksite Stress Reduction and Employee Well-Being: A Participatory Action Research Investigation," *Journal of Organizational Behavior*, September 1993, pp. 495–510; P. Froiland, "What Cures Job Stress?" *Training*, December 1993, pp. 32–36; C. L. Cooper and S. Cartwright, "Healthy Mind, Healthy Organization—A Proactive Approach to Occupational Stress," *Human Relations*, April 1994, pp. 455–471; A. A. Brott, "New Approaches to Job Stress," *Nation's Business*, May 1994, pp. 81–82; and C. Daniels, "The Last Taboo," *Fortune*, October 28, 2002, pp. 137–144.

**53.** See R. S. Schuler, "Time Management: A Stress Management Technique," *Personnel Journal*, December 1979, pp. 851–855; and M. E. Haynes, *Practical Time Management: How to Make the Most of Your Most Perishable Resource* (Tulsa, OK: Penn Well Books, 1985).

**54.** "Employee Wellness," *Canadian HR Reporter*, February 23, 2004, pp. 9–12.

**55.** Adapted from P. B. Vaill, *Managing as a Performing Art: New Ideas for a World of Chaotic Change* (San Francisco: Jossey-Bass, 1989), pp. 8–9.

**56.** Based on K. Lewin, *Field Theory in Social Science* (New York: Harper & Row, 1951); and S. McShane and S. Steen, *Canadian Organizational Behaviour*, 7th ed. (Toronto, ON: McGraw-Hill, 2009).

**57.** L. Friedman, "Ladder of Sustainability: Moving Sustainable Business Practices," *Leadership Excellence*, http://www.enterprisedevelop.com/pdf/Ladder_Sustainability.pdf.

**58.** M. Shin, "Westport's Time to Shine," *Corporate Knights* 24 (2008), http://www.corporateknights.ca/article/westports-time-shine.

**59.** Information from Nike Grind website, http://www.nikere-useashoe.com/using-nike-grind.

**60.** L. Friedman, "Ladder of Sustainability: Moving Sustainable Business Practices," *Leadership Excellence*, http://www.enterprisedevelop.com/pdf/Ladder_Sustainability.pdf.

**61.** Algonquin College, "Sustainability: Explore the Sustainable Algonquin Centre for Construction Excellence," *Algonquin College website*, http://www2.algonquincollege.com/acce/home/sustainability.

**62.** Based on information from the ShareGreen website, http://www.sharegreen.ca/about.

**63.** Information from press kit on company's website, www.1800gotjunk.com; A. Wahl, "Canada's Best Workplaces: Overview," *Canadian Business*, April 26, 2007; "Fastest-Growing Franchises 2006 Rankings," *Entrepreneur*, April 29, 2006, http://www.entrepreneur.com/franchises/rankings/fastestgrow-ing-115162/2006,-4.html; J. Hainsworth, The Associated Press, "Canadian Company Finds Treasures in People's Trash," *Springfield News-Leader*, April 24, 2006, p. 5B; J. Martin, "Cash from Trash," *Fortune*, November 2003, pp. 52–56; and M. Carbonaro, "1-800-GOT-JUNK? Quickly Opens Second Area Site," *CNY Business Journal*, August 10, 2007.

**64.** Jeff Beer, "Q&A: Brian Scudamore, founder/CEO, 1-800-Got-Junk?" May 7, 2012, http://www.canadianbusiness.com/article/81127—q-a-brian-scudamore-founder-ceo-1-800-got-junk.

**65.** Based on M. Warner, "Under the Knife," *Business* 2.0, January 1, 2004, http://money.cnn.com/magazines/business2/business2_archive/2004/01/01/359617/index.htm.

# Glossary

## A

**accommodative approach** Managers make choices that try to balance the interests of shareholders with those of other stakeholders.

**accountability** The need to report and justify work to a manager's superiors.

**active listening** Listening for full meaning without making premature judgments or interpretations.

**adjourning** The final stage of team development for temporary teams, in which members are concerned with wrapping up activities rather than task performance.

**analytic style** A decision-making style characterized by a high tolerance for ambiguity and a rational way of thinking.

**Association of Southeast Asian Nations (ASEAN)** A trading alliance of 10 Southeast Asian countries.

**authority** The rights inherent in a managerial position to tell people what to do and to expect them to do it.

**autocratic style** A leadership style where the leader tends to centralize authority, dictate work methods, make unilateral decisions, and limit employee participation.

## B

**balanced scorecard** A performance measurement tool that looks at four areas that contribute to an organization's performance: financial, customer, internal business process, and learning and growth assets.

**basic corrective action** Corrective action that looks at how and why performance deviated and then proceeds to correct the source of deviation.

**behavioural style** A decision-making style characterized by a low tolerance for ambiguity and an intuitive way of thinking.

**behavioural theories** Leadership theories that identify behaviours that differentiate effective leaders from ineffective leaders.

**behaviourally anchored rating scales (BARS)** A performance appraisal method in which the evaluator rates an employee on examples of actual job behaviours.

**benchmark** The standard of excellence against which to measure and compare.

**benchmarking** The search for the best practices among competitors or noncompetitors that lead to their superior performance.

**body language** Gestures, facial expressions, and other body movements that convey meaning.

**born globals** International companies that choose to go global from inception.

**boundaryless organization** An organization that is not defined by a chain of command, places no limits on spans of control, and replaces departments with empowered teams.

**bounded rationality** Limitations on a person's ability to interpret, process, and act on information.

**Brazil, Russia, India, China and South Africa (BRICS)** An association of leading emerging economies aiming to create mechanisms for consultation and cooperation.

**bureaucratic control** An approach to control that emphasizes organizational authority and relies on administrative rules, regulations, procedures, and policies.

**business model** A strategic design for how a company intends to profit from its strategies, work processes, and work activities.

## C

**capabilities** An organization's skills and abilities that enable it to do the work activities needed in its business.

**centralization** The degree to which decision making is concentrated at a single point in the organization.

**certainty** A condition in which a decision maker can make accurate decisions because the outcome of every alternative is known.

**chain of command** The continuous line of authority that extends from the top of the organization to the lowest level and clarifies who reports to whom.

**change agent** Someone who acts as a catalyst and assumes the responsibility for managing the change process.

**channel** The medium a message travels along.

**charismatic leader** An enthusiastic, self-confident leader whose personality and actions influence people to behave in certain ways.

**civil servants** People who work in a local, provincial, or federal government department.

**clan control** An approach to control in which employee behaviour is regulated by the shared values, norms, traditions, rituals, beliefs, and other aspects of the organization's culture.

**classical view** The view that management's only social responsibility is to maximize profits.

**code of ethics** A formal statement of an organization's primary values and the ethical rules it expects its employees to follow.

**coercive power** The power a leader has through his or her ability to punish or control.

**communication** The transfer and understanding of meaning.

**communication networks** The variety of patterns of vertical and horizontal flows of organizational communication.

**communication process** The seven elements involved in transferring meaning from one person to another.

**competitive advantage** What sets an organization apart; its distinct edge.

**compressed workweek** A workweek in which employees work longer hours per day but fewer days per week.

**conceptual skills** The mental ability to analyze and generate ideas about abstract and complex situations.

**conceptual style** A decision-making style characterized by a high tolerance for ambiguity and an intuitive way of thinking.

**concurrent control** A type of control that takes place while an activity is in progress.

**conflict** Perceived differences that result in some form of interference or opposition.

**control** The process of monitoring activities to ensure that they are being accomplished as planned, and correcting any significant deviations.

**control process** A three-step process that includes measuring actual performance, comparing actual performance against a standard, and taking managerial action to correct deviations or inadequate standards.

**controlling** A management function that involves monitoring actual performance, comparing actual performance to a standard, and taking corrective action when necessary.

**core competencies** An organization's major value-creating skills, capabilities, and resources that determine its competitive weapons.

**corporate governance** The system used to govern a corporation so that the interests of corporate owners are protected.

**corporate social responsibility** A business's obligation, beyond that required by law and economics, to do the right things and act in ways that are good for society.

**corporate strategy** An organizational strategy that evaluates what businesses a company is in, should be in, or wants to be in, and what it wants to do with those businesses.

**cost leadership strategy** A business strategy in which the organization sets out to be the lowest-cost producer in its industry.

**credibility** The degree to which someone is perceived as honest, competent, and able to inspire.

**critical incidents** A performance appraisal method in which the evaluator focuses on the critical or key behaviours that separate effective from ineffective job performance.

**cross-functional teams** Work teams made up of individuals who are experts in various functional specialties.

**Crown corporations** Commercial companies owned by the government but independently managed.

**customer departmentalization** Grouping jobs on the basis of customers who have common needs or problems.

**D**

**data** Raw, unanalyzed facts.

**decentralization** The degree to which lower-level employees provide input or actually make decisions.

**decision** A choice from two or more alternatives.

**decision criteria** Criteria that define what is relevant in making a decision.

**decision-making process** A set of eight steps that includes identifying a problem, selecting an alternative, and evaluating the decision's effectiveness.

**decisional roles** Management roles that involve making significant choices that affect the organization.

**decoding** A receiver's translation of a sender's message.

**defensive approach** Managers relying only on legally established rules to take the minimal position toward corporate social responsibility.

**delegation** The assignment of authority to another person to carry out specific duties, allowing the employee to make some of the decisions.

**democratic style** A leadership style where the leader tends to involve employees in decision making, delegate authority, encourage participation in deciding work methods and goals, and use feedback as an opportunity for coaching employees.

**departmentalization** The basis on which jobs are grouped together.

**diagonal communication** Communication that cuts across both work areas and organizational levels.

**differentiation strategy** A business strategy in which a company seeks to offer unique products that are widely valued by customers.

**directional plans** Plans that are flexible and that set out general guidelines.

**directive style** A decision-making style characterized by a low tolerance for ambiguity and a rational way of thinking.

**discipline** Actions taken by a manager to enforce an organization's standards and regulations.

**distributive justice** Perceived fairness of the amount and allocation of rewards among individuals.

**divisional structure** An organizational structure that consists of separate business units or divisions.

**downward communication** Communication that flows downward from managers to employees.

**drive to acquire** The drive to seek, take control of, and retain objects and personal experiences.

**drive to bond** The drive to form social relationships with others.

**drive to defend** The drive to protect ourselves both physically and socially.

**drive to learn** The drive to satisfy our curiosity and understand ourselves and the world around us.

**dysfunctional conflicts** Conflicts that are destructive and prevent a group from achieving its goals.

**E**

**economic value added (EVA)** A financial tool that measures corporate and divisional performance, calculated by taking after-tax operating profit minus the total annual cost of capital.

**effectiveness** Completing activities so that organizational goals are achieved; referred to as "doing the right things."

**efficiency** Getting the most output from the least amount of inputs; referred to as "doing things right."

**employee counselling** A process designed to help employees overcome performance-related problems.

**employee empowerment** Giving more authority to employees to make decisions.

**employee recognition programs** Reward programs that provide managers with opportunities to give employees personal attention and express interest, approval, and appreciation for a job well done.

**employee theft** Any unauthorized taking of company property by employees for their personal use.

**encoding** Converting a message into symbols.

**environmental complexity** The number of components in an organization's environment and the extent of the organization's knowledge about those components.

**environmental uncertainty** The degree of change and the degree of complexity in an organization's environment.

**equity theory** The theory that an employee compares his or her job's input–outcome ratio with that of relevant others and then responds to correct any inequity.

**escalation of commitment** An increased commitment to a previous decision despite evidence that the decision might have been wrong.

**esteem needs** A person's need for internal esteem factors such as self-respect, autonomy, and achievement, and external esteem factors such as status, recognition, and attention.

**ethics** Rules and principles that define right and wrong behaviour.

**European Union (EU)** A union of 27 European countries that forms an economic and political entity.

**expectancy theory** The theory that an individual tends to act in a certain way based on the expectation that the act will be followed by a given outcome and on the attractiveness of that outcome to the individual.

**expert power** The influence a leader has based on his or her expertise, special skills, or knowledge.

**exporting** An approach to going global that involves making products at home and selling them abroad.

**external environment** Outside forces and institutions that can potentially affect the organization's performance.

**extrinsic motivation** Motivation that comes from outside the person and includes such things as pay, bonuses, and other tangible rewards.

## F

**family-friendly benefits** Benefits that accommodate employees' needs for work–life balance.

**feedback control** A type of control that takes place after a work activity is done.

**feedforward control** A type of control that focuses on preventing anticipated problems, since it takes place before the actual activity.

**filtering** The deliberate manipulation of information to make it appear more favourable to the receiver.

**flexible work hours (flextime)** A scheduling option in which employees are required to work a specific number of hours per week but are free to vary those hours within certain limits.

**focus strategy** A business strategy in which a company pursues a cost or differentiation advantage in a narrow industry segment.

**foreign subsidiary** An approach to going global that involves a direct investment in a foreign country by setting up a separate and independent production facility or office.

**formal communication** Communication that follows the official chain of command or is part of the communication required to do one's job.

**formalization** The degree to which jobs within the organization are standardized and the extent to which employee behaviour is guided by rules and procedures.

**forming** The first stage of team development in which people join the group and then define the team's purpose, structure, and leadership.

**four-drive theory** The theory that behaviour is influenced by our innate drives to acquire, bond, learn, and defend.

**franchising** An approach to going global in which a service organization gives a person or group the right to sell a product, using specific business methods and practices that are standardized.

**functional conflicts** Conflicts that support the goals of the work group and improve its performance.

**functional departmentalization** Grouping jobs by functions performed.

**functional strategy** A strategy used by a functional department to support the business strategy of the organization.

**functional structure** An organizational structure that groups similar or related occupational specialties together.

## G

**general environment** Broad external conditions that may affect the organization.

**geographical departmentalization** Grouping jobs on the basis of territory or geography.

**global company** An international company that centralizes management and other decisions in the home country.

**global sourcing** Purchasing materials or labour from around the world, wherever they are cheapest.

**goals (objectives)** Desired outcomes for individuals, groups, or entire organizations.

**grapevine** The informal organizational communication network.

**graphic rating scales** A performance appraisal method in which the evaluator rates an employee on a set of performance factors.

**group cohesiveness** The degree to which group members are attracted to each other and share the group's goals.

**groupthink** The withholding by group members of different views in order to appear to be in agreement.

**growth strategy** A corporate strategy used when an organization wants to grow and does so by expanding the number of products offered or markets served, either through its current business(es) or through new business(es).

## H

**heuristics** Rules of thumb that managers use to simplify decision making.

**hierarchy of needs theory** Maslow's theory proposing a hierarchy of five human needs: physiological, safety, social, esteem, and self-actualization; as each need becomes satisfied, the next need becomes dominant.

**human relations view of conflict** The view that conflict is a natural and inevitable outcome in any group and has the potential to be a positive force in contributing to a group's performance.

**human resource management process** Activities necessary for staffing the organization and sustaining high employee performance.

**human resource planning** The process by which managers ensure that they have the right number and kinds of people in the right places at the right times, who are capable of effectively and efficiently performing assigned tasks.

**human skills** The ability to work well with other people both individually and in a group.

**hygiene factors** Factors that eliminate job dissatisfaction, but do not motivate.

## I

**immediate corrective action** Corrective action that corrects problems at once to get performance back on track.

**importing** An approach to going global that involves acquiring products made abroad and selling them at home.

**informal communication** Communication that is not defined by the organization's structural hierarchy.

**information** Processed and analyzed data.

**information overload** A situation in which information exceeds a person's processing capacity.

**informational roles** Management roles that involve receiving, collecting, and disseminating information.

**integrative social contracts theory** A view of ethics proposing that ethical decisions be based on existing ethical norms in industries and communities in order to determine what constitutes right and wrong.

**interactionist view of conflict** The view that some conflict is absolutely necessary for a group to perform effectively.

**interpersonal communication** Communication between two or more people.

**interpersonal roles** Management roles that involve working with people or performing duties that are ceremonial and symbolic in nature.

**intrinsic motivation** Motivation that comes from the person's internal desire to do something, due to such things as interest, challenge, and personal satisfaction.

**intuitive decision making** Making decisions on the basis of experience, feelings, and accumulated judgment.

## J

**jargon** Specialized terminology or technical language that members of a group use to communicate among themselves.

**job analysis** An assessment that defines jobs and the behaviours necessary to perform them.

**job description** A written statement of what a jobholder does, how the job is done, and why the job is done.

**job design** The process of looking at a job to determine what set of tasks is is required, how they are done, and in what order.

**job sharing** The practice of having two or more people split a full-time job.

**job specification** A statement of the minimum qualifications that a person must possess to perform a given job successfully.

**joint venture** An approach to going global in which the partners agree to form a separate, independent organization for some business purpose; it is a type of strategic alliance.

## L

**labour union** An organization that represents employees and seeks to protect their interests through collective bargaining.

**laissez-faire style** A leadership style where the leader tends to give the group complete freedom to make decisions and complete the work in whatever way it sees fit.

**lateral communication** Communication that takes place among employees on the same organizational level.

**leader** Someone who can influence others and provide vision and strategy to the organization.

**leadership** The process of influencing individuals or groups toward the achievement of goals.

**leading** A management function that involves motivating subordinates, directing the work of individuals or teams, selecting the most effective communication channels, and resolving employee behaviour issues.

**legitimate power** The power a leader has as a result of his or her position in the organization.

**licensing** An approach to going global in which a manufacturer gives another organization the right to use its brand name, technology, or product specifications.

**line managers** Managers responsible for the essential activities of the organization, including production and sales.

**long-term plans** Plans with a time frame beyond three years.

**lower-level managers** Managers at the lowest level of the organization who manage the work of nonmanagerial employees directly or indirectly involved with the production or creation of the organization's products.

## M

**maintenance roles** Roles performed by group members to maintain good relations within the group.

**management** Coordinating work activities so that they are completed efficiently and effectively with and through other people.

**management by objectives (MBO)** An approach to goal setting in which specific measurable goals are jointly set by employees and their managers, progress toward accomplishing those goals is periodically reviewed, and rewards are allocated on the basis of this progress.

**management by walking around** A term used to describe a manager who is out in the work area and interacting directly with employees.

**management functions** Planning, organizing, leading, and controlling.

**management information system (MIS)** A system used to provide management with needed information on a regular basis.

**management roles** Specific categories of managerial behaviour.

**manager** Someone who works with and through other people by coordinating their work activities in order to accomplish organizational goals.

**market control** An approach to control that emphasizes the use of external market mechanisms such as price competition and relative market share to establish the standards used in the control system.

**market economy** An economic system in which resources are primarily owned and controlled by the private sector.

**market value added (MVA)** A financial tool that measures the stock market's estimate of the value of a firm's past and expected capital investment projects.

**mass production** The production of items in large batches.

**matrix structure** An organizational structure that assigns specialists from different functional departments to work on one or more projects.

**mechanistic organization** An organizational design that is rigid and tightly controlled.

**message** A purpose to be conveyed.

**middle-level managers** Managers between the first-line level and the top level of the organization who manage the work of first-line managers.

**motivation** An individual's willingness to exert high levels of effort to reach organizational goals, conditioned by the degree to which that effort satisfies some individual need.

**motivation-hygiene theory** Herzberg's theory that intrinsic factors are related to job satisfaction and motivation, whereas extrinsic factors are related to job dissatisfaction.

**motivators** Factors that increase job satisfaction and motivation.

**multidomestic corporation** An international company that decentralizes management and other decisions to the local country.

**multinational corporation (MNC)** A broad term referring to any and all types of international companies that maintain operations in multiple countries.

**multiperson comparisons** A performance appraisal method by which one individual's performance is compared with that of others.

## N

**national culture** The values and attitudes shared by individuals from a specific country that shape their behaviour and beliefs about what is important.

**need** An internal state that makes certain outcomes appear attractive.

**need for achievement (nAch)** The drive to excel, to achieve in relation to a set of standards, and to strive to succeed.

**need for affiliation (nAff)** The desire for friendly and close interpersonal relationships.

**need for power (nPow)** The need to make others behave in a way that they would not have behaved otherwise.

**network organization** A small core organization that outsources major business functions.

**noise** Disturbances that interfere with the transmission, receipt, or feedback of a message.

**nongovernmental organization (NGO)** A nongovernmental organization that emphasizes humanitarian issues, development, and sustainability.

**nonprofit sector** The part of the economy run by organizations that operate for purposes other than making a profit (that is, providing charity or services).

**nonprogrammed decisions** Decisions that are unique and nonrecurring, and require custom-made solutions.

**nonverbal communication** Communication transmitted without words.

**norming** The third stage of team development, which is characterized by close relationships and cohesiveness.

**North American Free Trade Agreement (NAFTA)** An agreement among the Canadian, American, and Mexican governments in which barriers to free trade are reduced.

## O

**obstructionist approach** The avoidance of corporate social responsibility; managers engage in unethical and illegal behaviour that they try to hide from organizational stakeholders and society.

**omnipotent view of management** The view that managers are directly responsible for an organization's success or failure.

**operational plans** Plans that specify the details of how the overall goals are to be achieved.

**opportunities** Positive trends in external environmental factors.

**organic organization** An organizational design that is highly adaptive and flexible.

**organization** A deliberate arrangement of people who act together to accomplish some specific purpose.

**organizational change** Any alteration of people, structure, or technology in an organization.

**organizational communication** All the patterns, networks, and systems of communication within an organization.

**organizational culture** A system of shared values, norms, and beliefs held by organization members that determines, in large degree, how employees act.

**organizational design** The process of developing or changing an organization's structure.

**organizational development (OD)** Techniques or programs meant to change people and the nature and quality of interpersonal work relationships.

**organizational effectiveness** A measure of how appropriate organizational goals are and how well an organization is achieving those goals.

**organizational performance** The accumulated end results of all the organization's work activities.

**organizational structure** How job tasks are formally divided, grouped, and coordinated within an organization.

**organizing** A management function that involves determining what tasks are to be done, who is to do them, how the tasks are to be grouped, who reports to whom, and where decisions are to be made.

**orientation** The introduction of a new employee to his or her job and to the organization.

## P

**path-goal theory** A leadership theory that says the leader's job is to assist his or her followers in attaining their goals and to provide the necessary direction and/or support to ensure that their goals are compatible with the overall objectives of the group or organization.

**pay-for-performance programs** Variable compensation plans that pay employees on the basis of some performance measure.

**performance** The end result of an activity.

**performance management system** A process of establishing performance standards and evaluating performance in order to arrive at objective human resource decisions and to provide documentation in support of those decisions.

**performing** The fourth stage of team development, in which the team structure is fully functional and accepted by team members.

**PESTEL analysis** A way for a company to align its strategy with the external environment by analyzing six contextual factors that shape the external environment: political, economic, socio-cultural, technological, environmental, and legal.

**physiological needs** A person's need for food, drink, shelter, sexual satisfaction, and other physical requirements.

**planned economy** An economic system in which all economic decisions are planned by a central government.

**planning** A management function that involves defining goals, establishing a strategy for achieving those goals, and developing plans to integrate and coordinate activities.

**plans** Documents that outline how goals are going to be met and describe resource allocations, schedules, and other necessary actions to accomplish the goals.

**policy** A guideline for making a decision.

**private sector** The part of the economy run by organizations that are free from direct government control; enterprises in this sector operate to make a profit.

**privately held organizations** Companies whose shares are not available on the stock exchange but are privately held.

**proactive approach** When managers actively promote the interests of stockholders and stakeholders, using organizational resources to do so.

**problem** A discrepancy between an existing and a desired state of affairs.

**procedural justice** Perceived fairness of the process used to determine the distribution of rewards.

**procedure** A series of interrelated sequential steps that a decision maker can use to respond to a structured problem.

**process conflict** Conflict over how the work gets done.

**process departmentalization** Grouping jobs on the basis of product or customer flow.

**process production** The production of items in continuous processes.

**product departmentalization** Grouping jobs by product line.

**productivity** The overall output of goods or services produced divided by the inputs needed to generate that output.

**programmed decision** A repetitive decision that can be handled by a routine approach.

**project structure** An organizational structure in which employees continuously work on projects.

**public sector** The part of the economy directly controlled by government.

**publicly held organization** A company whose shares are available on the stock exchange for public trading by brokers/dealers.

## Q

**quality management** A philosophy of management driven by continual improvement and responding to customer needs and expectations.

## R

**range of variation** The acceptable degree of variation between actual performance and the standard.

**rational decision making** Making decisions that are consistent and value-maximizing within specified constraints.

**readiness** The extent to which people have the ability and willingness to accomplish a specific task.

**realistic job preview (RJP)** A preview of a job that includes both positive and negative information about the job and the company.

**recruitment** The process of locating, identifying, and attracting capable applicants.

**referent power** The power a leader has because of his or her desirable resources or personal traits.

**referents** Those things individuals compare themselves against in order to assess equity.

**reinforcement theory** The theory that behaviour is influenced by consequences.

**reinforcers** Consequences that, when given immediately following a behaviour, increase the probability that the behaviour will be repeated.

**related diversification** When a company grows by combining with firms in different, but related, industries.

**relationship conflict** Conflict based on interpersonal relationships.

**reliability** The ability of a selection device to measure the same thing consistently.

**renewal strategies** Corporate strategies designed to address organizational weaknesses that are leading to performance declines.

**resources** An organization's assets—financial, physical, human, intangible—that are used to develop, manufacture, and deliver products or services to customers.

**responsibility** The obligation or expectation to perform any assigned duties.

**retrenchment strategy** A short-term renewal strategy that reduces the organization's activities or operations.

**reward power** The power a leader has to give positive benefits or rewards.

**rights view of ethics** A view of ethics concerned with respecting and protecting individual liberties and privileges.

**risk** A condition in which a decision maker is able to estimate the likelihood of certain outcomes.

**role** A set of expected behaviour patterns attributed to someone who occupies a given position in a social unit.

**rule** An explicit statement that tells a decision maker what he or she can or cannot do.

## S

**safety needs** A person's need for security and protection from physical and emotional harm, as well as assurance that physical needs will continue to be met.

**satisfice** To accept solutions that are "good enough."

**selection process** The process of screening job applicants to ensure that the most appropriate candidates are hired.

**self-actualization needs** A person's need to grow and become what he or she is capable of becoming.

**service profit chain** The service sequence from employees to customers to profit.

**shareholders** Individuals or companies that own stocks in a business.

**short-term plans** Plans with a time frame of one year or less.

**simple structure** An organizational structure with low departmentalization, wide spans of control, authority centralized in a single person, and little formalization.

**single-use plan** A one-time plan specifically designed to meet the needs of a unique situation.

**Situational Leadership® (SL)** A leadership theory that focuses on the readiness of followers.

**skill-based pay** A pay system that rewards employees for the job skills and competencies they can demonstrate.

**social loafing** The tendency of individuals to expend less effort when working collectively than when working individually.

**social needs** A person's need for affection, belongingness, acceptance, and friendship.

**socio-economic view** The view that management's social responsibility goes beyond making profits to include protecting and improving society's welfare.

**span of control** The number of employees a manager can efficiently and effectively manage.

**specific environment** The part of the external environment that is directly relevant to the achievement of an organization's goals.

**specific plans** Plans that are clearly defined and leave no room for interpretation.

**stability strategy** A corporate strategy characterized by an absence of significant change in what the organization is currently doing.

**staff managers** Managers who work in the supporting activities of the organizations (such as human resources or accounting).

**stakeholders** Any constituencies in the organization's external environment that are affected by the organization's decisions and actions.

**standing plans** Ongoing plans that provide guidance for activities performed repeatedly.

**stock options** A financial incentive that gives employees the right to purchase shares of company stock at some time in the future, at a set price.

**storming** The second stage of team development, which is characterized by intragroup conflict.

**strategic alliance** An approach to going global that involves a partnership between a domestic and a foreign company in which both share resources and knowledge in developing new products or building production facilities.

**strategic management** What managers do to develop the organization's strategies.

**strategic management process** A six-step process that encompasses strategic planning, implementation, and evaluation.

**strategic plans** Plans that apply to the entire organization, establish the organization's overall goals, and seek to position the organization in terms of its environment.

**strategies** The decisions and actions that determine the long-run performance of an organization.

**strengths** Any activities the organization does well or any unique resources that it has.

**stress** The adverse reaction people have to excessive pressure placed on them from extraordinary demands, constraints, or opportunities.

**strong cultures** Organizational cultures in which the key values are deeply held and widely shared.

**structured problems** Problems that are straightforward, familiar, and easily defined.

**stuck in the middle** A situation in which an organization is unable to develop a competitive advantage through cost or differentiation.

**SWOT analysis** An analysis of the organization's strengths, weaknesses, opportunities, and threats.

**symbolic view of management** The view that managers have only a limited effect on substantive organizational outcomes because of the large number of factors outside their control.

**synergy** Combined efforts that are greater than the sum of individual efforts.

## T

**task conflict** Conflict over content and goals of the work.

**task-oriented roles** Roles performed by group members to ensure that group tasks are accomplished.

**team structure** An organizational structure in which the entire organization is made up of work groups or teams.

**technical skills** Knowledge of and expertise in a specialized field.

**telework** A job arrangement in which employees work at home and are linked to the workplace by computer and other technology.

**theory of justice view of ethics** A view of ethics in which managers impose and enforce rules fairly and impartially, and do so by following all legal rules and regulations.

**theory of needs** McClelland's theory that the needs for achievement, power, and affiliation are major motives in work.

**Theory X** The assumption that employees have little ambition, dislike work, want to avoid responsibility, and must be closely controlled to perform effectively.

**Theory Y** The assumption that employees can exercise self-direction, accept and seek out responsibility, and consider work a natural activity.

**threats** Negative trends in external environmental factors.

**top-level managers** Managers at or near the top level of the organization who are responsible for making organization-wide decisions and establishing the plans and goals that affect the entire organization.

**traditional goal setting** An approach to setting goals in which goals are set at the top of the organization and then broken into subgoals for each organizational level.

**traditional view of conflict** The view that all conflict is bad and must be avoided.

**transactional leaders** Leaders who guide or motivate their followers in the direction of established goals by clarifying role and task requirements.

**transformational leaders** Leaders who inspire followers to transcend their own self-interests for the good of the organization, and who have a profound and extraordinary effect on their followers.

**transnational corporation (TNC) or borderless organization** A type of international company in which artificial geographical barriers are eliminated.

**Trans-Pacific Partnership (TPP)** A group of nine countries that is intending to revolutionize Asian trade relations.

**trust** The belief in the integrity, character, and ability of a person.

**turnaround strategy** A renewal strategy for situations in which the organization's performance problems are more serious.

## U

**uncertainty** A condition in which a decision maker is not certain about the outcomes and cannot even make reasonable probability estimates.

**unit production** The production of items in units or small batches.

**unity of command** The management principle that states every employee should receive orders from only one superior.

**universality of management** The reality that management is needed in all types and sizes of organizations, at all organizational levels, in all organizational work areas, and in organizations in all countries around the globe.

**unrelated diversification** When a company grows by combining with firms in different and unrelated industries.

**unstructured problems** Problems that are new or unusual and for which information is ambiguous or incomplete.

**upward communication** Communication that flows upward from employees to managers.

**utilitarian view of ethics** A view of ethics maintaining that ethical decisions are made solely on the basis of their outcomes or consequences.

## V

**validity** The proven relationship that exists between the selection device and some relevant job criterion.

**variable pay** A pay system in which an individual's compensation is contingent on performance.

**verbal intonation** An emphasis given to words or phrases that conveys meaning.

**virtual organization** An organization that has elements of a traditional organization, but also relies on recent developments in information technology to get work done.

**vision and mission** The purpose of an organization.

**visionary leadership** The ability to create and articulate a realistic, credible, and attractive vision of the future that improves on the present situation.

## W

**weaknesses** Activities the organization does not do well or resources it needs but does not possess.

**work specialization** The degree to which tasks in an organization are subdivided into separate jobs; also known as division of labour.

**work team** Two or more interacting and interdependent individuals whose members work intensely on a specific, common goal using their positive synergy, individual and mutual accountability, and complementary skills.

**World Trade Organization (WTO)** A global organization of 153 member countries that deals with the rules of trade among nations.

**written essay** A performance appraisal method in which the evaluator writes out a description of an employee's strengths and weaknesses, past performance, and potential.

## NUMBERS/SYMBOLS

**360-degree feedback** A performance appraisal method that uses feedback from supervisors, employees, co-workers, and customers.

# Subject Index

## A

accommodative approach, 111–112
accountability, 130
achievement, 37, 250
achievement-oriented leader, 222
acid test, 317
action research approach, 346
active listening, 165–166
activity ratios, 316, 317
adjourning, 278
advisory teams, 277
affiliation, 250
agreeableness, 218
all-channel network, 168
alternatives, 93–94
ambiguity, 344
"Americanization," 44
analytic style, 101–102
anti-globalization positions, 44
application forms, 194
appreciative inquiry, 346, 347
ASEAN. *See* Association of Southeast Asian Nations (ASEAN)
Asia, 288
Association of Southeast Asian Nations (ASEAN), 35–36
assumptions of rationality, 96
attentive deliberation, 97
attractiveness of reward, 255
attrition, 192
audiotapes, 197
Australia, 38, 231, 258, 323
authority, 130
autocratic style, 219

## B

background investigations, 194
balanced scorecard, 320–321
bankruptcies, corporate, 224
bargaining power of buyers, 76
bargaining power of suppliers, 76
barriers to effective communication. *See* communication barriers
basic corrective action, 308
behavioural interview questions, 194
behavioural style, 102
behavioural theories, 219
behaviourally anchored rating scales (BARS), 197
Belgium, 258
benchmark, 307
benchmarking, 65, 307
benefits, 201
best practices, 307
biases
    confirmation bias, 105
    hindsight bias, 106
    overconfidence bias, 105
    selective perception bias, 105
    self-serving bias, 106
Big Five personality framework, 218
blogs, 171
body language, 161
borderless organization, 39
born globals, 40
boundaryless organization, 139, 141–143
bounded awareness, 97
bounded ethicality, 97
bounded rationality, 96–97
bounded self-interest, 97
bounded willpower, 97
Brazil, Russia, India, China, and South Africa (BRICS), 36
breadth potential, 160
BRICS. *See* Brazil, Russia, India, China, and South Africa (BRICS)
Britain, 258
budgets, 317
bureaucratic control, 312
business cases
    Best Buy, 273
    Canadian wine industry, 86
    Cisco Canada, 182
    Earth Rated PoopBags, 52–53
    Enbridge, 241
    Facebook, 333
    Levitt-Safety Limited, 153
    1–800–GOT-JUNK?, 358–359
    Ontario Realty Corporation, 297
    Prairie General Hospital, 359
    Research in Motion (RIM), 121
    Shopify, 21
    Silverbirch Hotels & Resorts, 86
    small business social media success stories, 183
    Wellington West, 211–212
business model, 66
business strategy, 76–79
    competitive strategies, 76–79
    cost leadership strategy, 77, 78
    differentiation strategy, 78
    focus strategy, 78–79
buyers, 76

## C

calm waters metaphor, 338–339
Canada, 38
    aging population, 187
    indirect control devices, 323
    individualistic culture, 288
    interesting work, desire for, 258
    labour market, 186–187
    labour market issues, 187–188
Canada Labour Code, 188, 324

Canadian dollar, 57
Canadian Human Rights Act, 188
Canadian Securities Administrators rules, 322
capabilities, 68
career, 202–203
career development, 202–203
cases. *See* business cases; video case incidents
CD-ROM, 197
Central Europe, 257
centralization, 132–133
centrally planned economies, 257
certainty, 100
chain network, 168
chain of command, 130–131
chair of the board, 5
change
    action research approach, 346
    appreciative inquiry, 346, 347
    calm waters metaphor, 338–339
    change agent, 340
    change-capable organizations, 343
    change management, 340–345, 347–351
    change process, 337–339
    common approaches to organizational change, 346
    cultural change, 347–349
    current issues, 347–351
    effective communication, 344
    employee stress, 349–351
    external forces, 336–337
    forces for change, 336–337, 338
    global organizational development, 344
    internal forces, 337
    leading change, 223–225
    making change happen successfully, 342–344
    mistakes when leading change, 343
    organizational change, 340, 346
    organizational culture, 347–349
    organizational design, 341
    organizational development (OD), 341–342
    organizational structure, 340–341
    people, 341–342
    resistance to change, 344–345
    situational factors, 348
    technology, 341
    types of change, 340–342
    white-water rapids metaphor, 339
change agent, 340
change-capable organizations, 343
change management, 340–345, 347–351
channel, 158, 159–161
charismatic leader, 223–224
charismatic-visionary leadership, 223–225
Charter of Rights and Freedoms, 188
chief executive officer, 5
chief operating officer, 5
China, 29, 36, 38, 231, 288
civil servants, 13
clan control, 312–313
classical view, 110
classroom lectures, 197
coaching, 197, 231
code of ethics, 108–109

coercive power, 226
cognitive intelligence, 218
cohesiveness. *See* group cohesiveness
collaborative work, 172
collective agreements, 188, 324
collectivism, 37, 288
communication, 156–157
    barriers to effective communication. *See* communication
      barriers
    channel, 158, 159–161
    communication networks, 168–169
    communication process, 159
    communication process model, 158
    decoding, 158, 160
    diagonal communication, 168
    direction of communication flow, 166–168
    distortions, 159–160
    with diverse individuals, 164
    downward communication, 166–167
    effective communication, 156
    encoding, 158
    feedback loop, 160
    formal communication, 166
    functions of communication, 157–158
    good communication, 157
    grapevine, 169
    informal communication, 166
    and information technology, 170–171
    interpersonal communication, 157, 158–166
    lateral communication, 168
    message, 158, 159
    noise, 159
    nonverbal communication, 161
    online communication, 229
    organizational communication, 157, 166–169
    perfect communication, 157
    receiver, 160
    sender, 159
    teams, 282
    understanding communication, 156–158
    understanding of meaning, 157
    upward communication, 167
    when undergoing change, 344
communication barriers
    active listening, 165–166
    defensiveness, 163
    emotions, 162, 166
    feedback, 164
    filtering, 162
    information overload, 162
    language, 163
    mental models, 163
    national culture, 164
    nonverbal cues, 166
    overcoming barriers, 164–166
    selective perception, 162–163
    simplification of language, 165
communication networks, 168–169
communication process, 159
communism, 257
communities, 76
company rankings, 303

compensation, 200–203
competence, 227
Competition Act, 32
Competition Bureau, 32
competitive advantage, 76–79, 186
competitive strategies, 76–79
    cost leadership strategy, 77, 78
    differentiation strategy, 78
    focus strategy, 78–79
    requirements for successful pursuit of, 78
    stuck in the middle, 79
competitors, 31–32
complementors, 76
complexity, 43
complexity capacity, 160
compressed workweek, 263
concentration, 73
conceptual skills, 10
conceptual style, 102
concurrent control, 310–311
confidentiality, 160
confirmation bias, 105
conflict, 284–286
conflict management, 231, 284–286, 288
conformity, 287
conscientiousness, 218
consistency, 227
consumer records, 318
contemporary motivation theories, 250–256
    equity theory, 253–254, 257
    expectancy theory, 255, 256
    four-drive theory, 250–251
    integration of, 256
    reinforcement theory, 252
contemporary organizational designs, 138–143
    boundaryless organization, 139, 141–143
    matrix structure, 139, 140–141
    network organization, 142–143
    project structure, 139, 140–141
    team structure, 139–140
    virtual organization, 142
contingency factors, 135–137
contingency planning, 65
contingency theories of leadership, 220–223
contingency variables, 132
contingent workers, 260
control, 302–304
    *see also* controlling
    balanced scorecard, 320–321
    bureaucratic control, 312
    clan control, 312–313
    concurrent control, 310–311
    control process, 304–310
    corporate governance, 321–322
    cross-cultural differences, 322–323
    current issues, 320–327
    customer interactions, 325–327
    employee theft, 324–325
    feedback control, 311
    feedforward control, 310
    financial controls, 316–318
    importance of, 303–304

information controls, 318–319
    introduction of control, 310–311
    management by walking around, 310–311
    market control, 312
    measures of organizational performance, 302–303
    of member behaviour, 157
    methods of control, 311–316
    organizational culture, 313–316
    performance standards, 302
    reasons for control, 303–304
    types of control, 310
    workplace concerns, 323–325
    workplace privacy, 323–324
control process, 304–310
    benchmarking, 307
    decisions, 309–310
    managerial action, 308–309
    measurement of performance, 304–305
    performance *vs.* standard, 306–307
controlling, 8
    *see also* control
    amount of control, 28–29
    decisions, 95
    information and, 318–319
    and organizational culture, 316
core competencies, 68
corporate bankruptcies, 224
corporate governance, 321–322
corporate scandals, 224
corporate social responsibility, 109–113
    accommodative approach, 111–112
    approaches to, 111–112
    classical view, 110
    comparison of views of, 111–112
    defensive approach, 111
    and economic performance, 112–113
    obstructionist approach, 111
    proactive approach, 112
    socio-economic view, 110–111
corporate strategy, 72–75
    growth strategy, 73–74
    renewal strategies, 75
    retrenchment strategy, 75
    stability strategy, 74–75
    turnaround strategy, 75
corporate wellness initiatives, 204
corrective action, 308, 323
cost, 160
cost leadership strategy, 77, 78
cost minimization, 136
counselling. *See* employee counselling
creativity, 60
credibility, 227
Criminal Code, 324
critical incidents, 197
cross-cultural differences. *See* national culture
cross-functional teams, 129, 277
Crown corporations, 13
cultural change, 347–349
culture. *See* national culture; organizational culture
culture shock, 280
curling, 301

current-competitor rivalry, 76
current ratio, 317
customer departmentalization, 129
customer interactions, 325–327
customer service, 325–326
customers, 30

## D

data, 319
debt to assets, 317
decentralization, 132–133
decision, 90
  in control process, 309–310
  nonprogrammed decisions, 99
  organizational design decisions, 134–137
  programmed decision, 98–99
  selection decision outcomes, 193
decision commitment, 104
decision criteria, 90–92
decision knowledge, source of, 104
decision makers, 95
  *see also* decision making
decision making
  analytic style, 101–102
  assumptions of rationality, 96
  behavioural style, 102
  biases and errors, 104–106
  bounded rationality, 96–97
  certainty, 100
  conceptual style, 102
  and corporate social responsibility, 109–113
  decision-making conditions, 100–101
  decision-making styles, 101–102
  decision rules, 108–109
  directive style, 101
  and ethics, 106–109
  group decision making, 102–104
  groupthink, 103–104
  individual *vs.* group decision making, 104
  intuitive decision making, 97
  manager as decision maker, 95–106
  nonprogrammed decisions, 99
  programmed decision, 98–99
  rational decision making, 95–96
  risk, 100
  structured problems, 98–99
  types of problems and decisions, 98–99
  uncertainty, 101
  unstructured problems, 99
decision-making conditions, 100–101
decision-making process, 90–94
  analysis of alternatives, 93
  decision criteria, 90–92
  development of alternatives, 93
  evaluation of decision effectiveness, 94
  implementation of alternative, 94
  problem, identification of, 90
  selection of an alternative, 93–94
  weighted criteria, 92–93, 94
decision-making styles, 101–102
decision rules, 108–109
decision structure, 104

decisional roles, 9, 10
decoding, 158, 160
decoding ease, 160
defensive approach, 111
defensiveness, 163
delegation, 130, 220
deliberate structure, 11
democratic style, 219
demographics, 33
Denmark, 257
department managers, 5
departmentalization, 127–129
  customer departmentalization, 129
  five common forms of, 128
  functional departmentalization, 127
  geographical departmentalization, 129
  process departmentalization, 129
  product departmentalization, 127–129
desire to lead, 218
diagonal communication, 168
differentiation strategy, 78
direction of communication flow, 166–168
directional plans, 64
directive leader, 222
directive style, 101
discipline, 199
dispersion of responsibility, 286
disseminator, 9
distinct purpose, 11
distortions, 159–160
distributive justice, 254
district managers, 5
disturbance handler, 9
diverse workforce, 202, 257–260
diversification, 74
division manager, 5
divisional structure, 138
downsizing, 203
downward communication, 166–167
drive, 218
drive to acquire, 251, 252
drive to bond, 251, 252
drive to defend, 251, 252
drive to learn, 251, 252
driving forces, 338
  *see also* forces for change
dual chain of command, 140
DVD, 197
dynamic environment, 42, 60
dysfunctional conflicts, 284

## E

e-learning, 197
e-recruiting, 191–192
early leadership theories, 217–219
early management theorists, 131
early motivation theories, 245–250
  hierarchy of needs theory, 246–247, 257
  motivation-hygiene theory, 248–249, 258
  Theory X, 247
  Theory Y, 247
early retirements, 192

Eastern Europe, 257
economic changes, 337
economic conditions, 32, 186–187
economic performance, 112–113
economic system, 36–37
economic value added (EVA), 317–318
effective communication, 156
effective teams, 281–286
effectiveness, 6, 7, 44, 132
efficiency, 6, 7
effort-performance linkage, 255
email, 170, 172
emotional expression, 158
emotional intelligence, 218
emotional stability, 218
emotions, 162, 166
employee assistance programs (EAPs). *See* employee
    counselling
employee attitudes, 337
employee connection, 144
employee counselling, 199, 201, 351
employee empowerment, 133, 304
employee engagement, 204–205
employee involvement, 104
employee motivation. *See* motivation
employee recognition programs, 261
employee relations, 203–205
employee services, 201
employee stress, 202, 349–351
employee theft, 324–325
employee training, 196–197
Employment Equity Act, 188
employment standards legislation, 188
encoding, 158
encoding ease, 160
entrepreneur, 9, 89
environmental complexity, 43
environmental conditions, 33–34
environmental constraints
    amount of control, 28–29
    economic conditions, 32
    environmental conditions, 33–34
    external environment, 29–34
    general environment, 32–34
    global environment, 34–38
    legal conditions, 34
    managers, effect on, 42–45
    political conditions, 32
    socio-cultural conditions, 33
    specific environment, 29–32
    technological conditions, 33
environmental factors affecting HRM, 186–189
    economic conditions, 186–187
    government legislation, 188
    labour market issues, 187–188
    organizational culture, 186
    technology, 188–189
environmental uncertainty, 42–44, 137
environmental uncertainty matrix, 43
equipment, 337
equity, 253, 264
equity theory, 253–254, 257

errors
    escalation-of-commitment error, 106
    sunk-costs error, 105
escalation of commitment, 106
esteem needs, 246
ethics, 106
    bounded ethicality, 97
    code of ethics, 108–109
    and decision making, 106–109
    decision rules, 108–109
    and employee stress, 351
    four views of ethics, 107–108
    improving ethical behaviour, 108–109
    integrative social contracts theory, 107–108
    and leadership, 228
    moral leadership, 228
    and organizational culture, 315
    questions for examination of ethics of business decision, 109
    rights view of ethics, 107
    theory of justice view of ethics, 107
    utilitarian view of ethics, 107
EU. *See* European Union (EU)
European Union (EU), 35
evaluation of results, 72
executive compensation, 201
executive vice-president, 5
expectancy, 255
expectancy theory, 255, 256
experiential exercises, 197
expert power, 226
exporting, 40–41
external analysis, 68–71
external environment, 29–34
    general environment, 32–34
    specific environment, 29–32
external forces for change, 336–337
extrinsic motivation, 247
extroversion, 218

**F**

facial expressions, 161
family-friendly benefits, 201–202
federal government, 34, 188
feedback, 158–159, 160, 164, 167
feedback control, 311
feedback loop, 160
feedforward control, 310
figurehead, 9
filtering, 162
financial controls, 316–318
financial performance, 112–113
financial ratios, 316–317
financial reporting, 322
financing
    in small and medium-sized enterprises (SMEs), 24
    in small and medium-sized organizations (SMOs), 24
Finland, 257
firing, 192
flexible work hours (flextime), 263
flexible work schedules, 263
flextime, 263
focus strategy, 78–79

follower readiness, 220
forces for change, 336–337, 338
forecasting, 65
foreign subsidiary, 42
formal communication, 166
formal planning, 58
formality, 160
formalization, 133–134
forming, 277
four-drive theory, 250–251
France, 38, 42, 231, 288
franchising, 41
free riders, 286
functional conflicts, 284
functional departmentalization, 127
functional strategies, 79
functional structure, 138
future needs, 190

## G

gender-based stereotyping, 232
gender differences, and leadership, 231–233
general environment, 32–34
   economic conditions, 32
   environmental conditions, 33–34
   legal conditions, 34
   political conditions, 32
   socio-cultural conditions, 33
   technological conditions, 33
Generally Accepted Accounting Principles (GAAP), 336
geographical departmentalization, 129
Germany, 37, 38, 231, 258, 323
gestures, 161
global business, 38–42
   borderless organization, 39
   born globals, 40
   exporting, 40–41
   foreign subsidiary, 42
   franchising, 41
   global company, 39
   global outsourcing, 40
   global sourcing, 40
   how organizations go global, 40–42
   importing, 40–41
   international new ventures (INVs), 40
   international organizations, types of, 39–40
   joint venture, 42
   licensing, 41
   multidomestic corporation, 39
   multinational corporation (MNC), 39
   and organizational design, 144
   organizational development, 344
   pros and cons of globalization, 44–45
   strategic alliance, 42
   structural issues, 144
   teams, management of, 287–288
   transnational corporation (TNC), 39
global challenge, 34
global company, 39
global environment, 34–38
   global trade, 35–36
   PESTEL, 36–38

global organizational development, 344
global outsourcing, 40
global sourcing, 40
global teams, 287–288
global trade, 35–36
globalization. *See* global business
goals (objectives), 60
   approaches to establishing goals, 61
   effective teams, 282
   identification of, 66–67
   management by objectives (MBO), 61, 62
   and motivation, 245
   steps in goal setting, 62
   traditional goal setting, 61
   well-designed goals, 61, 62
good communication, 157
government legislation, 188, 336
grapevine, 169
graphic rating scales, 197
Great Britain, 323
Greece, 38
group cohesiveness, 283–284, 288
group decision making, 102–104
groups
   *see also* teams
   conflict management, 284–286
   group decision making, 102–104
   informal groups, 276
   roles, 280
   turning into effective teams, 281–286
   understanding groups, 276–279
groupthink, 103–104
growth strategy, 73–74

## H

Hersey and Blanchard's Situational Leadership®, 220–221
Herzberg's motivation-hygiene theory, 248–249, 258
heuristics, 104–106
hierarchy of needs theory, 246–247, 257
hindsight bias, 106
Hofstede's five dimensions of national culture, 37–38
honesty, 218, 227
horizontal integration, 74
Human Capital Index, 186
human relations view of conflict, 284
human resource inventory, 189
human resource management (HRM)
   compensation and benefits, 200–203
   economic conditions, 186–187
   employee relations, 203–205
   environmental factors, 186–189
   future needs, 190
   government legislation, 188
   human resource management process, 186–189
   human resource planning, 190
   human resource requirements, 189–190
   human resources information system (HRIS), 188–189
   job analysis, 189
   job description, 190
   job design, 190
   job specification, 190
   labour market issues, 187–188

and organizational culture, 186
   orientation, 195–196
   performance management, 197–199
   recruitment, 191–192
   selection process, 192–195
   in small and medium-sized enterprises (SMEs), 24
   in small and medium-sized organizations (SMOs), 24
   staffing the organization, 190–195
   technology, 188–189
   total rewards, 200–203
   training, 196–197
   workforce reduction options, 192
human resource management process, 186–189
human resource planning, 190
human resources information system (HRIS), 188–189
human skills, 10
hygiene factors, 249

**I**

imitation, 136
immediate corrective action, 308
importing, 40–41
India, 40
individual differences, 264
individual *vs.* group decision making, 104
individualism, 37, 288
industry analysis, 77
industry rankings, 303
informal communication, 166
informal groups, 276
informal planning, 58
information, 158, 319
information controls, 318–319
information overload, 162
information technology, 169–173
   blogs, 171
   email, 170
   instant messaging, 170–171
   and organizational communication, 170–171
   organizations, effect on, 172
   social media, 172–173
   social networking websites, 171
   wikis, 171
informational roles, 9–10
innovation, 136
   in small and medium-sized enterprises (SMEs), 24
   in small and medium-sized organizations (SMOs), 24
instant messaging, 170–171
instrumental cohesiveness, 284
instrumentality, 255
integrative social contracts theory, 107–108
integrity, 218, 227
interactionist view of conflict, 284
intermediate term, 63
internal analysis, 68
internal benchmarking best-practices program, 307
internal forces for change, 337
International Financial Reporting Standards (IFRS), 336
international new ventures (INVs), 40
international organizations
   borderless organization, 39
   born globals, 40

global company, 39
   international new ventures (INVs), 40
   multidomestic corporation, 39
   multinational corporation (MNC), 39
   transnational corporation (TNC), 39
   types of, 39–40
Internet
   communication, 229
   job offerings, 171
   online leadership, 228–230
   social media, 27, 155, 172–173
   social networking, 155, 191
   social networking websites, 171
   Web-based recruiting (e-recruiting), 191–192
interpersonal communication, 157, 158–166
   barriers to effective interpersonal communication. *See*
      communication barriers
   channels, 160–161
   distortions, 159–160
interpersonal roles, 9
interpersonal warmth, 160
interviews, 194
intrinsic motivation, 247
intuition, 60, 97, 98
intuitive decision making, 97
inventory turnover, 317
involuntarily temporary employees, 260
Israel, 258, 288
Italy, 38

**J**

Japan, 38, 258, 323, 351
Japan-262, 261
jargon, 163
job analysis, 189
job description, 190
job design, 190
job-relevant knowledge, 218
job rotation, 197
job sharing, 192, 263
job specification, 190
joint venture, 42

**K**

karoshi, 351

**L**

labour market issues, 187–188
labour markets, 337
labour union, 188
laissez-faire style, 219
language, 163, 165, 315–316
lateral communication, 168
Latin America, 288
layoffs, 192, 203
leader, 9, 216
   achievement-oriented leader, 222
   charismatic leaders, 223–224
   directive leader, 222
   participative leader, 222
   supportive leader, 222
   tips for future leaders, 233
   transactional leaders, 223

leader (*continued*)
transformational leaders, 225
*vs.* manager, 216–217
leadership, 216
autocratic style, 219
behavioural theories, 219
charismatic-visionary leadership, 223–225
contingency theories of leadership, 220–223
current issues in leadership, 226–233
democratic style, 219
early leadership theories, 217–219
ethical leadership, 228
gender differences, 231–233
laissez-faire style, 219
leadership styles, 219
leading change, 223–225
moral leadership, 228
online leadership, 228–230
path-goal theory, 221–223
power, management of, 226–227
Situational Leadership® (SL), 220–221
team leadership, 230–231
trait theories, 217–219
trust, development of, 227–228
visionary leadership, 224–225
*vs.* management, 216–217
leadership styles, 219
leading, 8
decisions, 95
and organizational culture, 316
learning organization, 144
legal conditions, 34
legitimate power, 226
leverage ratios, 316, 317
liaison, 9
licensing, 41
line managers, 130
liquidity ratios, 316, 317
local governments, 34
long-term orientation, 37
long-term plans, 63
low-cost leaders, 77
lower-level managers, 5
loyalty, 227
lump-sum bonuses, 261

**M**

maintenance roles, 280
management, 6–10
effectiveness, 6, 7
efficiency, 6, 7
and environmental uncertainty, 44
functions, 7–8
omnipotent view of management, 28
quality management, 68
roles, 8–10
skills, 10
in small and medium-sized enterprises
(SMEs), 24
in small and medium-sized organizations
(SMOs), 24
study of management, 13–15

symbolic view of management, 28
universality of management, 14
*vs.* leadership, 216–217
management by objectives (MBO), 61, 62, 198–199
management by walking around, 310–311
management functions, 6–8, 7
controlling, 8
leading, 8
organizing, 8
planning, 8
*vs.* management roles, 10
management information system (MIS), 319
management roles, 8–10
management skills, 10
manager, 4–5
control, amount of, 28–29
as decision maker, 95–106
environment, effect of, 42–45
lower-level managers, 5
managerial action, and control process, 308–309
middle-level managers, 5
organizational culture, effect of, 316
top-level managers, 5
types of, 5
*vs.* leader, 216–217
managing director, 5
manuals, 197
manufacturing organizations, 12
market control, 312
market economy, 36
market value added (MVA), 318
marketing boards, 32
marketplace, 336
Maslow's hierarchy of needs theory, 246–247, 257
mass production, 136
material symbols, 315
matrix structure, 139, 140–141
McGregor's Theory X and Theory Y, 247
measurement of performance, 304–305
measures of organizational performance, 302–303
mechanistic organization, 134–135
mental models, 163
mentoring, 197
message, 158, 159
Mexico, 38
middle-level managers, 5
minimum-wage employees, 258–259
mission. *See* vision and mission
mission statement, 67
mobile HRM applications, 189
money, 260, 265
monitor, 9
moral leadership, 228
motivation, 244–245
and communication, 157
contemporary theories of motivation, 250–256
contingent workers, 260
current issues in motivation, 256–264
diverse cultures, employees from, 257–258
diverse workforce, 257–260
early theories of motivation, 245–250
effective rewards programs, 260–262

effort, 244–245
equity theory, 253–254, 257
expectancy theory, 255, 256
extrinsic motivation, 247
four-drive theory, 250–251
hierarchy of needs theory, 246–247, 257
intrinsic motivation, 247
minimum-wage employees, 258–259
motivation-hygiene theory, 248–249, 258
motivation process, 245
need-satisfying process, 245
organizational goals, 245
professionals, 259
reinforcement theory, 252
suggestions for motivating employees, 264–265
technical employees, 259
temporary workers, 260
theory of needs, 250
Theory X, 247
Theory Y, 247
work-life balance, 262–264
motivation-hygiene theory, 248–249, 258
motivators, 249
multidomestic corporation, 39
multinational corporation (MNC), 39
multiperson comparisons, 197

**N**

NAFTA. *See* North American Free Trade Agreement (NAFTA)
national culture, 37
achievement *vs.* nurturing, 37
collectivism, 37, 288
as communication barrier, 164
and control, 322–323
Hofstede's five dimensions of national culture, 37–38
individualism, 37, 288
long-term orientation, 37
motivation of employees from diverse cultures, 257–258
power distance, 37
short-term orientation, 37
and status, 288
uncertainty avoidance, 37
*vs.* organizational culture, 37
need, 245
esteem needs, 246
hierarchy of needs theory, 246–247
need for achievement (nAch), 250
need for affiliation (nAff), 250
need for power (nPow), 250
physiological needs, 246
safety needs, 246
self-actualization needs, 246
social needs, 246
theory of needs, 250
need for achievement (nAch), 250
need for affiliation (nAff), 250
need for power (nPow), 250
need-satisfying process, 245
negative feedback, 311
negotiating skills, 282–283
negotiator, 9
the Netherlands, 257, 258

network organization, 142–143
networks, 24
new entrants, 76
niche, 65–72
noise, 159
nongovernmental organizations (NGOs), 13
nonprofit sector, 13, 185
nonprogrammed decisions, 99
nonverbal communication, 161
nonverbal cues, 166
norming, 277
North American Free Trade Agreement (NAFTA), 35
North Korea, 36
Norway, 257
nurturing, 37

**O**

objectives. *See* goals (objectives)
obstructionist approach, 111
occupational health and safety, 204
Occupational Health and Safety Act, 188
office managers, 5
omnipotent view of management, 28
on-the-job training, 197
online leadership, 228–230
openness, 227
openness to experience, 218
operational plans, 63
opportunities, 69
organic organization, 134–135
organization, 11–13
boundaryless organization, 139, 141–143
change-capable organizations, 343
characteristics of organizations, 11
information technology, effect of, 172
international organizations, types of, 39–40
learning organization, 144
mechanistic organization, 134–135
network organization, 142–143
nongovernmental organizations (NGOs), 13
organic organization, 134–135
privately held organizations, 13
publicly held organization, 13
size of organizations, 12
small and medium-sized organizations (SMOs), 22–25
types of organizations, 12–13
virtual organization, 142
organization orientation, 195
organizational adjustments, 203
organizational change, 340
*see also* change
organizational communication, 157, 166–169
communication networks, 168–169
diagonal communication, 168
direction of communication flow, 166–168
downward communication, 166–167
formal communication, 166
grapevine, 169
informal communication, 166
and information technology, 170–171
lateral communication, 168
upward communication, 167

organizational culture, 186
  changing organizational culture, 347–349
  and control, 313–316
  development of, 315
  dimensions of, 314
  ethical culture, 315
  language, 315–316
  learning, 315–316
  managers, effect on, 316
  material symbols, 315
  rituals, 315
  stories, 315
  strong cultures, 314–315
  *vs.* national culture, 37
  weak cultures, 314–315
organizational design, 126
  *see also* organizational structure
  boundaryless organization, 139, 141–143
  challenges, 144
  changes in, 341
  common organizational designs, 137–145
  contemporary organizational designs, 138–143
  contingency factors, 135–137
  decisions, 134–137
  divisional structure, 138
  functional structure, 138
  global structural issues, 144
  learning organization, 144
  matrix structure, 139, 140–141
  mechanistic organization, 134–135
  network organization, 142–143
  organic organization, 134–135
  project structure, 139, 140–141
  simple structure, 138
  team structure, 139–140
  traditional organizational designs, 138
  virtual organization, 142
organizational development (OD), 341–342
organizational effectiveness, 303
organizational goals. *See* goals (objectives)
organizational performance, 302–303
organizational strategies. *See* strategies
organizational structure, 126
  centralization, 132–133
  chain of command, 130–131
  changing structure, 340–341
  decentralization, 132–133
  defining organizational structure, 126–134
  departmentalization, 127–129
  and environmental uncertainty, 137
  formalization, 133–134
  and size, 136
  span of control, 131–132
  and strategies, 136
  and technology, 136–137
  work specialization, 127
organizing, 8, 126
  *see also* organizational structure
  decisions, 95
  and organizational culture, 316
  purposes of, 126
orientation, 195–196

other, 254
overconfidence bias, 105

**P**

paralinguistics, 161
parity of Canadian dollar with US dollar, 57
participating, 220
participative leader, 222
partnerships, 24
path-goal theory, 221–223
pay-for-performance programs, 261–262
peer-to-peer network, 172
people, 11, 341–342
perfect communication, 157
performance, 302
  *see also* performance management
  corporate social responsibility and economic performance, 112–113
  corrective action, 308
  measurement of, 304–305
  organizational performance, 302–303
  and planning, 59
  *vs.* standard, 306–307
performance appraisal methods, 197–199
performance management, 197–199, 202, 229
performance management system, 197
performance-reward linkage, 255
performance-simulation tests, 194
performance standards, 302
performing, 278
Personal Information Protection and Electronic Documents Act, 324
PESTEL analysis, 71
Philippines, 40
physical examinations, 194
physiological needs, 246
piece-rate pay plans, 261
planned economy, 36
planning, 8, 58
  benchmarking, 65
  contingency planning, 65
  criticisms of, 59–60
  decisions, 95
  direction, provision of, 58
  forecasting, 65
  formal planning, 58
  goals (objectives), 58–59, 60–62
  how managers plan, 60–65
  human resource planning, 190
  informal planning, 58
  and organizational culture, 316
  overlapping and wasteful activities, reduction of, 58
  and performance, 59
  plans, 60, 63–65
  purposes of planning, 58–59
  scenario planning, 65
  tools and techniques, 64–65
  uncertainty, reduction of, 58
plans, 60
  developing plans, 63–65
  directional plans, 64
  long-term plans, 63

operational plans, 63
short-term plans, 63
single-use plan, 64
specific plans, 63–64
standing plans, 64
strategic plans, 63
types of plans, 63–64
plant manager, 5
Poland, 231
policy, 99
political conditions, 32
power, 226–227, 250
power distance, 37
power of complementors, 76
president, 5
privacy, 323–324
Privacy Act, 172
private sector, 12–13
privately held organizations, 13
pro-globalization positions, 44
proactive approach, 112
problem, 90
    structured problems, 98–99
    types of problems and decisions, 98–99
    unstructured problems, 99
problem-solving teams, 277
procedural justice, 254
procedure, 99
process conflict, 285
process departmentalization, 129
process production, 136
product departmentalization, 127–129
productivity, 302–303
professionals, 259
profit margin on sales, 317
profit-sharing, 261
profitability ratios, 316, 317
programmed decision, 98–99
project leader, 5
project structure, 139, 140–141
provincial governments, 34, 188
public-private partnerships (P3s), 341
public sector, 12, 13
publicly held organization, 13

**Q**

quality management, 68

**R**

racial harassment, 324
range of variation, 306
rational decision making, 95–96
ratios, 316–317
readiness, 220
realistic job preview (RJP), 194–195
reality of work, 14–15
receiver, 160
recognition, 265
recruitment, 191–192
reduced workweeks, 192
referent power, 226
referents, 254

refreezing, 338, 339, 346
regional manager, 5
regional trading alliances, 35–36
reinforcement theory, 252, 256
reinforcers, 252
related diversification, 74
relationship conflict, 285
reliability, 193–194
renewal strategies, 75
resistance to change, 344–345
resource allocator, 9
resources, 68
responsibility, 130
restraining forces, 338
restructuring, 203
retrenchment strategy, 75
return on investment, 317
revising the standard, 309
reward power, 226
rewards, 256, 281
rewards programs, 260–262, 264–265
rights view of ethics, 107
risk, 100
risk of conflict, 104
rituals, 315
role, 280
rule, 99
Russia, 257

**S**

SaaS technologies, 189
safety needs, 246
Sarbanes-Oxley Act, 322
satellite TV, 197
satisfice, 96
scanability, 160
scandals, 224
scenario planning, 65
selection devices, 194
selection process, 192–195
    realistic job preview (RJP), 194–195
    reliability, 193–194
    selection, 193
    selection decision outcomes, 193
    selection devices, 194
    validity, 193
selective perception, 162–163
selective perception bias, 105
self, 254
self-actualization needs, 246
self-confidence, 218
self-employment, 15
self-managed teams, 277
self-service HRM applications, 189
self-serving bias, 106
selling, 220
sender, 159
service profit chain, 326–328
service sector, 12
sexual harassment, 204, 324
shareholders, 13, 30
shift managers, 5

short-term plans, 63
simple structure, 138
simplification of language, 165
Singapore, 38, 258
single-use plan, 64
situational interview questions, 194
Situational Leadership® (SL), 220–221
size, and structure, 136
size of organizations, 12
skill-based pay, 201
Skilled Worker Program, 187
small and medium-sized enterprises (SMEs),
 12, 22–25
small and medium-sized organizations (SMOs),
 22–25
small businesses, 12
social interaction, 158
social loafing, 286, 288
social media, 27, 155, 172–173
social needs, 246
social networking, 155, 191
social networking websites, 171
socio-cultural conditions, 33
socio-economic view, 110–111
socio-emotional cohesiveness, 284
span of control, 131–132
special interest groups, 76
specific environment, 29–32
 competitors, 31–32
 customers, 30
 shareholders, 30
 stakeholders, 30
 suppliers, 30–31
specific plans, 63–64
spokesperson, 9
sport organizations, 322
stability strategy, 74–75
stable environment, 42
staff managers, 130–131
staffing the organization, 190–195
 recruitment, 191–192
 selection process, 192–195
stages of team development, 277–279
stakeholder-relationship management, 30
stakeholders, 30, 76
standard
 performance standards, 302
 revising the standard, 309
 *vs.* performance, 306–307
standing plans, 64
status, 288
stock options, 262
stockholders, 13
 *see also* shareholders
stories, 315
storming, 277
strategic alliance, 42
strategic compensation, 200–201
strategic management, 66
 *see also* strategies
 business model, 66
 process, 66–72

strategic management process, 66–72
 evaluation of results, 72
 external analysis, 68–71
 formulation of strategies, 71–72
 goals, 66–67
 identification of strategies, 66–67
 implementation of strategies, 72
 internal analysis, 68
 PESTEL analysis, 71
 SWOT analysis, 69–70
 vision and mission, 66–67
strategic plans, 63
strategies, 66
 *see also* strategic management
 business model, 66
 business strategy, 76–79
 competitive strategies, 76–79
 corporate strategy, 72–75
 cost leadership strategy, 77, 78
 differentiation strategy, 78
 focus strategy, 78–79
 as force for change, 337
 formulation of, 71–72
 functional strategies, 79
 growth strategy, 73–74
 identification of, 66–67
 implementation, 72
 niche, choosing a, 65–72
 and organizational design, 136
 and organizational structure, 136
 renewal strategies, 75
 retrenchment strategy, 75
 social media strategy, 173
 stability strategy, 74–75
 turnaround strategy, 75
 types of, 72–79
strengths, 68
stress, 202, 349–350
 causes, 350
 karoshi, 351
 reducing stress, 351
 symptoms, 350–351
strong cultures, 314–315
structured problems, 98–99
stuck in the middle, 79
subsidiaries, 13, 42
substitutes, 76
sunk-costs error, 105
supervisors, 5
suppliers, 30–31, 76
supportive leader, 222
sustainable competitive advantage, 186
Sweden, 38, 231, 257
SWOT analysis, 69–70
symbolic view of management, 28
synergy, 276
system, 254

**T**

Taiwan, 38
task conflict, 285
task-oriented roles, 280

team structure, 139–140
teams
    adjourning, 278
    advisory teams, 277
    appropriateness of, 288–289
    conflict management, 284–286
    cross-functional teams, 129, 277
    current challenges in managing teams, 287–289
    effective teams, 281–286
    forming, 277
    global teams, 287–288
    group cohesiveness, 283–284
    leadership, 230–231, 283
    norming, 277
    performing, 278
    problem-solving teams, 277
    rewards, 281
    roles of team members, 280
    selection, 280
    self-managed teams, 277
    shaping team behaviour, 280–281
    social loafing, 286
    stages of team development, 277–279
    storming, 277
    support, 283
    team players, creating, 279–281
    training, 280–281
    types of teams in organizations, 277
    understanding teams, 276–279
    virtual teams, 277
    work teams, 276
technical employees, 259
technical skills, 10
technological conditions, 33
technology
    changing technology, 341
    as force for change, 337
    and human resource management, 188–189
    and organizational structure, 136–137
technology-based training methods, 197
teleconferencing, 197
telework, 263–264
telling, 220
temporary workers, 260
Thailand, 38
theory of justice view of ethics, 107
theory of needs, 250
Theory X, 247
Theory Y, 247
threat of new entrants, 76
threat of substitutes, 76
threats, 69
360-degree feedback, 198, 199
time management program, 351
time of consumption, 160
time-space constraint, 160
times interest earned, 317
top-level managers, 5
total asset turnover, 317
total rewards, 200–203
TPP. *See* Trans-Pacific Partnership (TPP)
trade associations, 76

traditional financial control measures, 316–317
traditional goal setting, 61
traditional organizational designs, 138
traditional training methods, 197
traditional view of conflict, 284
training, 196–197, 280–281
trait theories, 217–219
Trans-Pacific Partnership (TPP), 36
transactional leaders, 223
transfers, 192
transformational leaders, 225
transnational corporation (TNC), 39
troubleshooting, 231
trust, 227–228, 229–230, 282
truthfulness, 227
turnaround strategy, 75

**U**
uncertain and unpredictable environment,
    42–44
uncertainty, 58, 101, 344
uncertainty avoidance, 37
unfreezing, 338, 346
unified commitment, 282
unionization, 187–188, 324
unit production, 136
United Kingdom, 38
United States, 29, 38, 44, 257, 258, 288, 322, 323
unity of command, 130
universality of management, 14
University of Iowa studies, 219
unrelated diversification, 74
unstable governments, 36
unstructured problems, 99
upward communication, 167
US dollar, 57
utilitarian view of ethics, 107

**V**
valence, 255
validity, 193
variable pay, 201
verbal intonation, 161
vertical integration, 73–74
video case incidents
    Ben & Jerry's Ice Cream Dream, 123
    Bulldog Interactive Fitness, 122
    Eco-Preneurs: Easywash, the World's Most Eco-friendly
        Carwash Company, 360
    Greenlite, 54
    Leading with Integrity: Quova's Marie
        Alexander, 298
    Mountain Equipment Co-op, 55
    NB Power and Protest, 361
    Tamarack Lake Electric Boat Company, 213
    Work-Life Balance: Canadian Voices and the British
        Experiment, 299
videoconferencing, 197
videotapes, 197
Vietnam, 36
virtual organization, 142
virtual teams, 277

vision and mission, 62, 66–67
visionary leadership, 224–225
voice mail, 172

## W

wage-incentive plans, 261
weak cultures, 314–315
weaknesses, 68
Web-based recruiting (e-recruiting), 191–192
weighted criteria, 92–93, 94
well-designed goals, 61, 62
wellness programs, 351
wheel network, 168
white-water rapids metaphor, 339
wikis, 171
women, and leadership, 231–233

work, reality of, 14–15
work-life balance, 201–202, 262–264
work specialization, 127
work team, 276
work unit orientation, 195
workbooks, 197
workforce, 337
workforce reduction options, 192
workplace concerns, and control, 323–325
Workplace Hazardous Materials Information System (WHMIS), 188
workplace monitoring policy, 324
workplace privacy, 323–324
World Trade Organization (WTO), 36
written essay, 197
written tests, 194

# Name/Organization Index

## A

Aariak, Eva, 231
Accentra, Inc., 97
Accenture, Ltd., 143, 259
Accor, 73
Adams, John Stacey, 253
Adaptec, 49
Adler, N., 287n
Agassiz, 306f
Agriculture and Agri-Food Canada, 87n
AHL, 125
AIG, 106
Air Canada, 11, 30, 69, 79, 84, 89, 227, 313, 319, 324
Air Canada Centre, 125
Alexander, Marie, 298
Alexander Keith, 74
Algonquin College, 357
Alley Kat, 306f
Amazon.ca, 11
Amazon.com, 223
Anderson, Brad, 273
Anderson, Dave, 225
Anderson, Ian, 51
Andrés Wines, 86
Angry Birds, 21
Anheuser-Busch InBev, 74, 306
Annaert, Rick, 212
Apple Computer (Apple), 30, 33, 60, 74, 93, 224
aQuantive, 337
Ash, Mary Kay, 225
Ask Jeeves, 336
ATCO Structures & Logistics (ATCO), 269
Athabasca Oil Sands Corporation, 27
Au Premier Spa Urbain, 157
Avis, 68
Aviva Canada, 129
Avon Products, 110
A&W (Canada), 69
Axcelis Technologies, 49

## B

Babcock, Rob, 130
Back in Motion Rehab, 254
Bagg, Geoff, 171
The Bagg Group, 171
Bakan, Joel, 44, 110
Baker, Geoff, 360
Baker, Morrie, 123
Balsillie, Jim, 121
Bank of Montreal, 132, 324
Bard on the Beach Festival, 13
Barrett, F.J., 347n

Barrick Gold Corporation, 219
BBC Worldwide, 298
BC Chamber of Commerce, 51
BC Hydro, 351
Beddoe, Clive, 313
Beer Unlimited, 306, 306f, 308–309
Belanger, Dorys, 157
Bell, A.H., 325
Bell Canada Enterprises (BCE), 35, 40, 125, 126, 137, 320
Ben & Jerry's, 123, 123n
Benimadhu, Prem, 261–262
Bennett, Chris, 142
Best Buy, 273
Best Western, 86
Bezos, Jeff, 223
BHP Billiton (BHP), 269
Birks, 32
Blanchard, Ken, 220
Blue Water Café, 134
Bly, Mark, 340
BMO Field, 125
Bobbitt, Gordon, 318
Bombardier, 39, 128f, 128n
Bond, Holly, 122
Bond, James, 122
Bond, Matthew, 122
Bono, J.E., 218n
Boone, J., 203n
Boston Market, 74
Boston Pizza, 41, 196
Bouclair, 307
Brandeis University, 246
Branson, Richard, 103, 171, 295, 295n
Brascan, 74
Brasseries Unibroue, 306f
Brayer, Jean-Paul, 42
BreconRidge, 142
Brin, Sergey, 139
British Airways, 320
British Columbia Voluntary Organizations Coalition, 24
British Petroleum (BP), 51, 335–336, 337, 340, 352
British Telecom, 299
Brookfield Asset Management, 74
Brookfield Power, 74
Brookfield Properties, 74
Brutus, Stephane, 199
Bryan, J.P., 220
Buddo, Peter, 351
Bulldog Interactive Fitness, 122
Bureau of Competition Policy (Canada), 32
Burke, Brian, 126

Burke, L.A., 98*n*
Business Development Bank of Canada, 13

## C

Cadbury Schwepps (Cadbury), 73
Calgary Chamber of Charities, 24
Calgary Chamber of Voluntary Organizations (CCVO), 185, 186, 192, 205–206
Canada Line, 28, 341
Canada Post, 12, 13
Canada Revenue Agency, 98, 139
Canadian 88 Energy, 220
Canadian Association of Petroleum Producers (CAPP), 33
Canadian Broadcasting Corporation (CBC), 122, 122*n,* 123, 123*n,* 210, 213*n,* 299*n,* 360, 360*n,* 361
*Canadian Business,* 232*n,* 358
Canadian Cancer Society, 183
Canadian Chamber of Commerce, 187
Canadian Curling Association (CCA), 301, 311, 312, 316, 320, 327–328
Canadian Federation of Independent Business (CFIB), 24
Canadian Franchise Association, 95
*Canadian HR Reporter,* 191*n*
Canadian Imperial Bank of Commerce (CIBC), 231, 318
Canadian Pacific Railway (CPR), 277
Canadian Policy Research Network, 245
Canadian Radio-television and Telecommunications Commission (CRTC), 74
Canadian Securities Administrators, 108, 322
Canadian Tire, 346
Capital City Condors, 23
Caranci, Beata, 89
Carlson Wagonlit Travel, 73
Cascades, 133
Cato Institute, 45
Cattaneo, Claudia, 51*n*
Cavanagh, Christina, 162, 170
CBC News, 54*n,* 55*n,* 361*n*
CBC Television (CBC), 13, 54, 55, 67*f*
Celestial Aerospace Company (CAP), 358
Celestica, 308
Centre for Construction Excellence, 357
Centre for Creative Leadership, 239
Centre for Research on Globalization, 45
Cerner, 156, 159
Certified General Accountants (CGAs) of Ontario, 295
Chapters, 32
Chapters Indigo, 32
Charal Winery, 215
Charles Schwab, 64
Chipotle Mexican Grill, 74
Choi, Jim Nam, 10
Christensen, Karen, 97*n*
Chubb Insurance Co. of Canada, 232*f*
Cirque du Soleil, 67*f*
Cisco Canada, 182
Cisco Systems, 142
City of Toronto, 30, 155
City of Vancouver, 323
Clinique, 127
Coach, 74
Coca-Cola, 30, 68, 79

Cogeco, 318
Cognos, 59
Cohen, Jordan, 149–150
Colangelo, Bryan, 131
Compania Chilena de Fosforos SA, 78
COMPAS, 32
Competition Bureau Canada, 32, 74, 125
Competitive Enterprise Institute, 45
Concordia, 4
Conference Board of Canada, 189, 204–205, 261
ConocoPhillips, 220
Continental Airlines, 298
Coolbrands, 41
Cooperrider, D.L., 347*n*
Copp, Lynne, 299
Corel, 75, 137
Cromack, Wille, 183
CTV, 301
Cypress Semiconductor, 230

## D

Dadd, Greg, 297
Daft, R.L., 222
Dale-Harris, Sarah, 142
Daniel, Patrick, 241
David, F., 67*n*
Davis LLP, 142
Dawson College, 4
Daylight Energy, 27
De Dreu, C.K.W., 286*n*
Debrayen, Mehrdad, 199
DeCenzo, David A., 101*n*
DeHart, John, 89
Dell, Michael, 225
Dell Canada, 129
Dell Inc., 10, 66, 225
Denghui, Ji, 38
Department of Fisheries and Oceans (DFO), 341
Deutsche Bank AG, 39
Di Zio Magnotta, Gabe, 215, 217, 223
Di Zio Magnotta, Rossana, 215, 217, 223, 226, 234
DIRTT (Doing It Right This Time), 225
Dofasco, 351
Domtar, 133, 318
Donely, Christina, 108
DoubleClick, 337
Dow Chemical, 67*f*
Drucker, Peter, 6
Drum, Brian, 169–170
Drum Associates, 169
Ducks Unlimited Canada (DUC), 67*f*
Dudley, Robert (Bob), 340, 347, 352
DuPont, 39
Duxbury, Linda, 201, 299

## E

Earth Rated PoopBags, 52–53
Easywash, 360
eBay, 33, 137
Ebbers, Bernard, 224
Ecotrust Canada, 75
Edmonton City Centre Mall, 191

Edmonton Police Service, 191
Electric Vehicle Society, 213
Electronic Arts Canada, 192, 259
EllisDon, 259
Enbridge Inc., 27, 241
Enrico, Roger, 233
Enron, 224, 315, 321
Enterprise Rent-a-Car, 325
*Entrepreneur*, 358
Epting, Lee, 49
Ericsson, 142
Ericsson Canada, 217, 351
Ernst & Young, 167, 212
Estée Lauder, 127, 129
EthicScan Canada, 109
E*TRADE, 43
Eustache, Jean-Marc, 63
Evans, Martin, 221
Evers, A., 286*n*
Exxon Mobile, 318

**F**

Facebook, 27, 53, 155, 158, 171, 172, 173, 174, 180, 183, 191,
    249, 333, 337–338
Fastow, Andrew, 321
Fayol, Henri, 131
Federal Express (FedEx), 3, 358
Federal Free Trade Commission (United States), 74
FedEx Kinko, 136
Fidelity Investments, 319
Fiedler, Fred, 220, 222
*Financial Times*, 123*n*
Finkelstein, Harley, 21
Fisher, Roger, 283
Flatt, Bruce, 74
Fletcher, Steven, 218
Foo Fighters, 21
Ford, Henry, 127
Ford Australia, 127
Ford Canada, 137
Ford Motor Company, 13, 301
Forest Stewardship Council (FSC), 75
*Fortune*, 34, 202
Forum Nokia, 49
Fraser Paper, 74
Friedman, Milton, 110
Frito-Lay, 39, 72
Frito Lay Canada, 33
Frost, Peter, 224
Fujian Sanming Dinghui Chemical Company, 38
Fujitsu, 261–262

**G**

Gallup Organization, 4
Ganong Bros., 78
G.A.P. Adventures, 67*f*
Gatorade, 72
GE Energy, 141, 162
GE Money, 141
GE Water & Process Technologies, 141
General Cable Corporation, 5
General Electric (GE), 60, 141–142, 198, 318, 347

General Motors, 11, 13, 280, 307
General Motors Centre, 125
General Motors (GM), 73
Genome Sciences Centre, 359
Georgetown University, 179
Gibbons, John, 205
Gisborne, Montgomery, 213
Global Assignment Task Force, 51
*Globalisation Guide*, 44*n*
GlobeScan, 113
GM Canada, 42
Gnanendran, Abby, 52–53
Goldberg, Gerry, 307
Goldwyn, David, 29
Google, 33, 36, 93, 139, 276, 319, 336, 337–338
Google+, 155, 172, 180
Google AdWords, 53
Government of Canada, 54, 187
Graham, Shawn, 361
Great Little Box Company Ltd. (GLBC), 275–276,
    279, 290
Great Western Brewery, 301
Greenberg, J., 325
Greenlite Lighting Corporation, 54, 54*n*
Greenpeace, 45
Grenny, Joseph, 348
Groupe Robert, 270
Grupo VIPS, 42
Guay, Marc, 33
Gulf Canada, 220, 224
Gupta, Nina, 54
Guzman, Pablo, 142

**H**

Hakan, 105
Handelman, Stephen, 225
Hansen, J.D., 325
Harary, Ronnen, 348
Haribhai's Spice Emporium, 40
Harper, Stephen, 29, 46, 225
Harvard, 250, 252
Harvard Business School, 76, 250, 342
Hasbro, 43
Health Canada, 204*n*
Heart and Stroke Foundation, 32
Hemlock Printers, 112
Henderson, Mark, 217
Henderson, R.I., 200*n*
Hersey, Paul, 220
Herzberg, Frederick, 246, 248–249, 248*f*, 258, 261
Heskett, J.L., 326*n*
Hewitt Associates, 261
Hewlett-Packard Canada, 351
Hewlett-Packard (HP), 42, 93, 171, 319
Higgins, Chris, 201
Hill & Knowlton Canada, 199
Hilton, 86
Hilton Hotels, 320
Hitachi, 42
H.J. Heinz Company, 39
Hofstede, Geert, 37, 38, 38*n*
Holland, Paul, 69

Holt Renfrew, 79
HomeSense, 318
Hotel Association of Canada (HAC), 86
House, Robert, 221–222, 224
Howell, Jane, 224
*HRMarketer.com,* 203n
Hudson's Bay Company, 11, 79
Hunsaker, P.L., 165
Husband, Tim, 182
Husky Injection Molding Systems, 127
Hydro Quebec, 361
Hyundai, 77

**I**

IBM, 37, 39, 170
iGEN Knowledge Solutions, 142
Iisaak Forest Resources, 75
IKEA, 32
Ilies, R., 218n
Imagine Canada, 23
Indigo Books & Music (Indigo), 32, 69
Industry Canada, 12
Infosys Technologies, 196
Integrated Information Systems, 320
Intel, 60, 79
International Forum on Globalization, 45
International Franchise Association, 358
International Institute for Sustainable Development, 45
International Policy Network, 45
Ipsos-Reid, 323, 349
IQ Partners, 171
Iskat, G.J., 345n
iTunes, 42, 60

**J**

JAnis, Irving, 103
JDS Uniphase, 98
Jobs, Steve, 60, 224
John Henry Bikes, 183
John Molson School of Business (Concordia University), 199
Johnson & Johnson, 67f
Jones, T.O., 326n
Jordan, Kendrick, 87n
Judge, T.A., 218n

**K**

Kaplan, R.S., 321n
Katz, Robert L., 10
KDPainc & Partners, 155
Kenner Toys, 43
KFC, 41, 72
Kidder, Rushworth, 119, 120n
Kinder Morgan Canada, 51
Kinder Morgan Energy Partners, 51
King, Martin Luther Jr., 224
Kirkpatrick, S.A., 218n
Klein, Naomi, 45
Klout, 180
Kluwer, E.S., 286n
Kmart, 273
Koteski, Allyson, 5
Kotter, John P., 216n, 342, 343n

Kouwenhoven, Richard, 112
Kouzes, James, 227
KPMG International, 228
KPMG/Ipsos-Reid, 4
Kwintessential, 50

**L**

Labatt, 74
LaCoste, 74
Lawrence, Paul, 250
Lay, Kenneth, 224
Lazaridid, Mike, 121
Leafs TV, 125
Leahy, T., 307n
Lee, Leonard, 69
Lee, Robin, 262
Lee Valley Tools, 69, 78, 262
Lego, 74
Lemon, Dani, 142
Levitt, Bruce, 153
Levitt, Heidi, 153
Levitt-Safety Limited, 153
Lewin, Kurt, 219, 338–339, 346, 356
Li, Victor, 227
Liebowitz, J., 345n
Lim, Philip, 276
LinkedIn, 155, 169, 171, 180
Linton, Roxann, 195
Liquor Control Board of Ontario (LCBO), 217, 223, 234
L.L. Bean, 142, 326
Loblaw Companies Limited (Loblaw), 74
Locke, E.A., 218n
Lockheed Martin Aeronautics Company, 281
Lorinc, John, 183
Loveman, G.W., 326n
Lowe, Graham, 265
Lunn, Gary, 54
Lütke, Tobias, 21

**M**

Maastricht University, 37
MAC Cosmetics, 129
MaCain, Michael, 57
MacDougal, Deanna, 171
MacLeod, Fiona, 335–336, 352
MacPherson Leslie and Tyerman LLP, 173
Magna International, 225, 226, 234
Magnotta Winery, 215–216, 217, 223
Major League Soccer, 125
Mansbridge, Peter, 163
Manulife Financial, 212, 224
Manulife Securities, 212
Maple Leaf Foods Inc., 57, 65, 68, 72, 73, 80
Maple Leaf Sports & Entertainment (MLSE), 125–126, 129, 130, 131, 137, 138, 146
Mark Kay Cosmetics, 225
Marriott International Inc., 86
Marsolais, Annie, 163
Martha Sturdy, 78
Maslow, Abraham, 246, 246f, 247, 257, 261
Massachusetts Institute of Technology (MIT) Sloan School of Management, 247

Matsushita, 311
Mattel, 43
Matthews, Bill, 49
McCain, Michael, 72
McCain Foods, 137
McClelland, David, 246, 250, 251
McDonald's, 3, 41, 74, 127, 134, 258, 311
McDonald's Canada, 42, 310
McGill Business School, 72
McGill University, 8, 10
McGregor, Douglas, 246, 247
McIntyre, Mark, 183
McLagan, P.A., 343n
McLeod, Richard, 182
McNerney, W. James Jr., 347
McQuiggen, Kevin, 191
McShane, S., 278n, 346n
McTavish's Kitchens, 49
Mega Bloks, 40
Mega Brands, 40–41
Meggy, Robert, 275–276, 279, 281
Menu Foods, 34, 38
Merrill Lynch, 39, 106
Metcalfe, Chris, 142
Metro, 75
Michelin, 131
Microsoft, 14, 93, 171, 277, 318, 337, 339, 348
Miller, 306
Miller, M.K., 98n
Milton, Robert, 227
Ministry of Labour (Japan), 351
Mintzberg, Henry, 8–9, 9n, 10, 72
Mitel Networks, 142
Mitsubishi, 27
Mohajer, Fatemaeh Divsaler, 69
Mohr, B.J., 347n
Molson, 79, 224, 318
Molson Coors, 173
Moore, Ellen, 232f
Morton, Brian, 360n
Moscow Ballet, 217
Moses, Todd, 97
Motel 6, 73
Motorola, 140
Mountain Equipment Co-op (MEC), 55, 55n
Murray, A., 200n
Muskoseepi Park, 277
MySpace, 169, 171, 336

**N**

Nanterme, Pierre, 143
NASA, 302, 348
Nash, L.L., 109
National Bank, 212
National Energy Board (Canada), 27
National Speleological Society, 319
Natura Cosméticos SA, 110
Nauta, A., 286n
NB Power, 361
NBA, 125
NBC Universal Studios, 141
Nelly, 163

Nestlé, 30, 39, 132
Neto, João Vendramin, 238
Network World Canada, 182
Neustar, 298
NHL, 125, 126
Nike, 142
Nilekani, Nandan, 196
Nitkin, David, 109
NL Technologies, 153
Noble, Grail, 243–244, 245–247, 249, 257, 266
Nohria, Nitin, 250
Nokia, 60
Nooyi, Indra, 233
Norbord, 74
Normandeau, Laura-Lee, 360
Nortel Networks, 75, 224
North American Soft Drinks, 72
Norton, D.P., 321n
Nova Scotia Association of Social Workers (NSASW), 151
Nova Scotia Business Inc., 277
Nurse Next Door, 89, 114

**O**

Obama, Barack, 27, 28, 29
O'Day, Pat, 228–229
Ohio State University, 277
Okanagan Spring, 306f
1-800-GOT-JUNK?, 3–4, 5, 6, 11, 16, 358–359
1-888-WOW-1Day! Painting, 3, 4
O'Neill, Daniel, 318
Ontario Hospital Association, 320
Ontario Power Authority, 78
Ontario Provincial Police, 158
Ontario Realty Corporation (ORC), 297, 297n
Oracle, 189
Orser, Barbara, 204
Oticon A/S, 141
Ottawa Business Journal, 21

**P**

Paddock Wood Brewing, 306f
Page, Larry, 139
Paine, Katie Delahaye, 155
Palmer, James, 275
Pareto, 68
Parker Brothers, 43
Parthenis, Dean, 191
Pascoe, Ricardo, 212
Patterson, Neal L., 156
Pazmac Enterprises, 249
Peddie, Richard, 125, 130, 137
Pelletier, David, 197
Pembina Institute, 51
PepsiCo Inc., 30, 39, 72–73, 233
PepsiCo International, 72
Peter Drucker Canadian Foundation, 24, 25n
Petro-Canada, 11
PetroChina, 27
Pfizer, 149–150
Phillips, John, 21
Pitney Bowes Canada, 170

Pixar, 21
Pizza Hut, 72
PK-35, 90
Playboy.com, 324
Polsky, Len, 173
Pooley, E., 203n
Porter, Michael, 76, 78n, 79
Posner, Barry, 227
Prairie General Hospital, 359
Preston, Leslie, 89
PricewaterhouseCoopers (PwC), 143
Proctor & Gamble Canada, 42
Proctor & Gamble (P&G), 68, 75, 137
*PROFIT,* 303
*Profit,* 243
Progressive Conservative Part of Manitoba, 218
Pythian, 183

**Q**

Qinghou, Zong, 100
Queen's University, 217
Quova Inc., 298

**R**

Rabie, Anton, 348
Radialpoint, 270
Radisson, 86
Ramada, 86
Raptors NBA TV, 125
RCMP, 277, 318
Recording Industry Association of America, 320
Red Roof Inns, 73
Reebok, 142
Regent, Aaron, 219
Reisman, Heather, 32
*Report on Business Magazine,* 303
Research In Motion (RIM), 93, 121, 244
Retail Council of Canada, 324
Revlon, 138, 243
Richard Ivey School of Business (University of Western Ontario), 162, 170
Ricoh Coliseum, 125
RightMedia, 337
Rio Tinto Alcan, 39, 68, 318
Robbins, Stephen P., 101n
Robin Hood Multifoods, 318
Robinson, Steve, 55
Rodgers, T.J., 230
Rogers, 125, 126, 137
Rolex, 29
Roots, 32
Rovinescu, Calin, 227
Royal Bank of Canada, 108
Royal Dutch Shell (Shell), 27, 65
Royal Ontario Museum, 13
Russell, Arlene, 190–191

**S**

Safeway, 13
Salé, Jamie, 197
Saleh, George, 339
Samsung Electronics Canada, 30

SAP, 189
Sasser, W.E. Jr., 326n
Saturn Corporation, 280
Saul, John Ralston, 44
S.C. Johnson & Son, 270
Scarlett, Steve, 249
Schau, C., 347n
Schlesinger, L.A., 326n
Schneider Corporation, 65
Schrage, Elliot, 36
Schwartz, Gerry, 32
Scotiabank, 35, 190–191, 192, 195, 342
Scudamore, Brian, 3–4, 5, 6, 10, 11, 16, 358–359
Sears, 13, 108
Sears Canada, 75
*Second Life,* 142, 171, 191–192
Seed, Paul, 186
Semco Group, 238–239
Semler, Ricardo, 238–239
Seral, John, 162
7-Eleven, 323
Seven & i Holdings, 323
Shapansky, Kerry, 68
Shapansky, Mandy, 232f
ShareGreen.ca, 357
Shaw, Lucie, 89, 95, 114
Shellenbarger, S., 203n
Shopify, 21
Siemens, 332
SilverBirch Hotels & Resorts, 86
Sim, Ken, 89
Sinopec, 27
Sirius Satellite Radio, 74
Sitel India, 40
Skinner, B.F., 252
Smed, Mogens, 225
SMED International, 225
Smith, Adam, 127
Smith, D.M., 325
Sodexho Alliance SA, 171
Sommers, David, 49
Sony Corporation, 30, 39, 60, 101, 122, 314
SPCA (Society for the Prevention of Cruelty to Animals), 13
Spin Master, 348
Spiring, Charlie, 212
Sport Canada, 322, 322n
Spratley, David, 142
Sprott School of Business (Carleton University), 201
Stanfield's, 183
Starbucks, 30, 42
StarTech, 186
Statistics Canada, 23n, 264, 288
Steen, S., 278n, 346n
Stelco, 74
Stewart, Jane, 299
Stremlaw, Greg, 301, 302, 312, 327–328
Stronach, Frank, 225
Sun Life Assurance Company of Canada, 139–140
Suzuki, David, 30
Syncrude Canada, 67f

**T**

Taco Bell, 72
Tamarack Lake Electric Boat Company, 213
Tanenbaum, Larry, 130
Tannen, Deborah, 179
Tanner, Chris, 306, 308–309
Target, 66, 77, 336
TAXI Canada, 135
Taylor, Frederick, 131
TD, 89
Team North, 78
Ted's Outfitters Shop, 217
TELUS, 129
TELUS Québec, 129
Tesco, 144
TheFranchiseMall.com, 123, 123n
Thomas, K.W., 286n
3M, 347
Tiger Electronics, 43
Tim Hortons, 73, 295, 301
*Time,* 225
Timex, 29
TJX Companies, 318
Tonka Toys, 43
Toronto Blue Jays, 280
Toronto FC, 125, 137
Toronto Maple Leafs (Maple Leafs), 125, 129, 130, 137, 138, 146
Toronto Marlies, 125, 137
Toronto Raptors (Raptors), 11, 125, 129, 130, 131, 137, 138, 146
Tossell, Ivor, 183
Tourism BC, 67f
Towers Perrin, 270
Toyota Motor Corporation, 79, 140, 217, 307
Toys "R" Us, 5
Transat A.T., 63
TransCanada, 27, 28, 29, 46
Tropicana Products, 72
Trudeau, Pierre, 225
Tuckman, Bruce, 277
Twitter, 27, 155, 173, 183, 191

**U**

UFC, 269
Unilever, 123
United Way, 11, 32
University of Alberta, 265
University of British Columbia, 4, 44, 64, 110, 224, 351
University of Iowa, 219
University of Manitoba Student's Union, 218
University of Toronto, 221
University of Utah, 248
University of Washington, 220
University of Western Ontario, 201, 224
Upper Canada Brewery, 306f
UPS, 166
Ury, William, 283
US Environmental Protection agency, 27

**V**

Vancouver City Savings Credit Union (Vancity), 78, 232f
Vancouver International Airport, 341

Vancouver Police Department (VPD), 191–192
*Vancouver Sun,* 59
Vanier Institute, 349
Varadi, Ben, 348
Verizon Communications, 171, 281
VEVO, 42
Vincor, 86
Vintners Quality Alliance (VQA), 86
Virgin Group, 103, 171, 295
Virgin Mobile, 243, 247
Vroom, Victor, 255
Vrooman, Tamara, 232f
Vrootman, Harry, 33
Vrootman Cookies, 33

**W**

Wadley, Geoffrey, 226
Wahaha, 100
Wales, Jimmy, 135
Walker, Mardi, 131
Walmart, 33, 66, 73, 75, 79, 315
Walmart Canada, 357
Walt Disney World, 31
Washbrook, Shannon, 196
Watkins, J.M., 347n
Watson Wyatt Worldwide, 4, 169, 186, 189
Weber, Max, 131
Welch, Jack, 141, 198
Wellington West, 211–212
Wellington West Financial Services, 212
Werner, M., 218n
Westcoast Energy, 35
Western Compensation and Benefits Consultants, 264
WestJet Airlines (WestJet), 30, 67f, 68, 69, 77, 78, 79, 84, 312, 313, 327
Weston Foods, 74
Westport Innovations, 357
Weyerhaeuser Canada, 112
Wharton School of Business, 222
Whirlpool, 136
Whitehead, Abigail, 202
Whitehead, Sheila, 202
Whitney, D., 347n
Whole Foods Market, 139
Wikipedia, 135
Williams, Danny, 361
Williams-Sonoma, 32
Wilson Learning Worldwide, 49
Winners, 318
Wizards of the Coast, 43
Wood Mackenzie, 28
Woodward, Joan, 136
Woolworth, 273
Work Safe BC, 66, 225
Workers' Compensation Board of BC, 66
Workopolis, 263
World Trade Organization (WTO), 35, 36, 37
WorldatWork, 187n
WorldCom, 224

**X**

Xerox, 140

Xerox Canada, 232*f*
XM Satellite Radio, 74
Xuzhou Anying, 38

## Y

Yahoo!, 156, 336, 337–338
Yale, 233
Yale School of Management, 255
Yammer, 173
Yanke Group, 307
Yellow House Events, 243–244, 245–247, 249, 250,
        257, 266
Yellow Pages, 163
YMCA, 101

Yogen Früz, 41
York, Pat, 192
York University, 204
YouTube, 171, 337
YUM! Brands Inc., 73

## Z

Zambonini, Renato, 59
Zapata, Gustavo Romero, 78
Zara, 51–52
Zellers, 66
Zip, 79
Zippo Canada, 42
Zuckerberg, Mark, 333

# List of Canadian Companies, by Province

## ALBERTA

Alley Kat, 306*f*
Athabasca Oil Sands Corporation, 27
Calgary Chamber of Charities, 24
Calgary Chamber of Voluntary Organizations (CCV), 185, 186, 192, 205–206
Canadian 88 Energy, 220
Canadian Association of Petroleum Producers (CAPP), 33
Canadian Pacific Railway (CPR), 277
Daylight Energy, 27
DIRTT (Doing it Right This Time), 225
Edmonton City Centre Mall, 191
Edmonton Police Service, 191
Enbridge Inc., 27, 241
Gulf Canada, 220, 224
MacPherson Leslie and Tyerman LLP, 173
Muskoseepi Park, 277
Pembina Institute, 51
SMED International, 225
Syncrude Canada, 67*f*
TransCanada, 27, 28, 29, 46
University of Alberta, 265
Westcoast Energy, 35
WestJet Airlines (WestJet), 30, 67*f*, 68, 69, 77, 78, 79, 84, 312, 313, 327

## BRITISH COLUMBIA

A&W (Canada), 69
Back in Motion Rehab, 254
Bard on the Beach Festival, 13
BC Chamber of Commerce, 51
BC Hydro, 351
Blue Water Café, 134
British Columbia Voluntary Organizations Coalition, 24
Canada Line, 28, 341
City of Vancouver, 323
Davis LLP, 142
Easywash, 360
Ecotrust Canada, 75
Electronic Arts Canada, 192, 259
Forest Stewardship Council (FSC), 75
Genome Sciences Centre, 359
Great Little Box Company Ltd. (GLBC), 275–276, 279, 290
GreatCanadianHotels, 86
Hemlock Printers, 112
iGEN Knowledge Solutions, 142
Iisaak Forest Resources, 75
John Henry Bikes, 183
Kinder Morgan Canada, 51
Levitt-Safety Limited, 153
Martha Sturdy, 78
Mountain Equipment Co-op (MEC), 55, 55*n*
Okanangan Spring, 306*f*

1–800-GOT-JUNK?, 3–4
1–888-WOW-1DAY! Painting, 3–4
Pazmac Enterprises, 249
ShareGreen.ca, 357
SilverBirch Hotels & Resorts, 86, 86*n*
TELUS, 129
Tourism BC, 67*f*
University of British Columbia, 4, 44, 64, 110, 224, 351
Vancouver City Savings Credit Union (Vancity), 78, 232*f*
Vancouver International Airport, 341
Vancouver Police Department (VPD), 191–192
*Vancouver Sun,* 59
Western Compensation and Benefits Consultants, 264
Westport Innovations, 357
Weyerhaeuser Canada, 112
Work Safe BC, 66
Workers' Compensation Board of BC, 66

## MANITOBA

Agassiz, 306*f*
Progressive Conservative Party of Manitoba, 218
University of Manitoba Student's Union, 218
Wellington West, 211–212
Wellington West Financial Services, 211–212

## NEW BRUNSWICK

Ganong Bros., 78
McCain Foods, 137
NB Power, 361

## NOVA SCOTIA

Alexander Keith's, 74
Bulldog Interactive Fitness, 122
Nova Scotia Association of Social Worlers (NSASW), 151
Nova Scotia Business Inc., 277
Stanfield's, 183

## ONTARIO

The Bagg Group, 171
Agriculture and Agri-Food Canada, 87*n*
Air Canada Centre, 125
Algonquin College, 357
Amazon.ca, 11
Andrés Wines, 86
Aviva Canada, 129
Barrick Gold Corporation, 219
Birks, 32
BMO Field, 125
Brascan, 74
BreconRidge, 142
Brookfield Asset Management, 74
Brookfield Power, 74

Brookfield Properties, 74
Bureau of Competition Policy (Canada), 32
Business Development Bank of Canada, 13
Canada Post, 12, 13
Canada Revenue Agency, 98, 139
Canadian Broadcasting Corporation (CBC), 122, 122n, 123, 123n, 210, 213n, 299n, 360, 360n, 361
*Canadian Business,* 232n, 358
Canadian Cancer Society, 183
Canadian Chamber of Commerce, 187
Canadian Curling Association (CCA), 301, 311, 312, 316, 320, 327–328
Canadian Federation of Independent Business (CFIB), 24
Canadian Franchise Association, 95
*Canadian HR Reporter,* 191n
Canadian Imperial Bank of Commerce (CIBC), 231, 318
Canadian Policy Research Network, 245
Canadian Radio-television and Telecommunications Commission (CRTC), 74
Canadian Securities Administrators, 108, 322
Canadian Tire, 346
Capital City Condors, 23
CBC News, 54n, 361n
CBC Television (CBC), 13, 54, 55, 67f
Celestica, 308
Centre for Construction Excellence, 357
Centre for Creative Leadership, 239
Certified General Accountants (CGAs) of Ontario, 295
Chapters, 32
Chapters Indigo, 32
Charal Winery, 215
Chubb Insurance Co. of Canada, 232f
Cisco Canada, 182
City of Toronto, 30, 155
CNC News, 55n
Cognos, 59
COMPAS, 32
Competition Bureau Canada, 32, 74, 125
Conference Board of Canada, 189, 204–205, 261
Coolbrands, 41
Corel, 75, 137
CTV, 301
Dell Canada, 129
Department of Fisheries and Oceans (DFO), 341
Dofasco, 351
Ducks Unlimited Canada (DUC), 67f
DuPont, 39
Electric Vehicle Society, 213
EllisDon, 259
EthiScan Canada, 109
Ford Canada, 137
Fraser Paper, 74
Frito Lay Canada, 33
G.A.P. Adventures, 67f
General Motors Centre, 125
GlobeScan, 113
GM Canada, 42
Government of Canada, 54, 187
Health Canada, 204n
Heart and Stroke Foundation, 32
Hill & Knowlton Canada, 199
Hilton, 86

Holt Renfrew, 79
Hotel Association of Canada (HAC), 86
Hudson's Bay Comapny, 11, 19
Husky Injection Molding Systems, 127
Imagine Canada, 23
Indigo Books & Music (Indigo), 32, 69
Industry Canada, 12
IQ Partners, 171
JDS Uniphase, 98
KPMG/Ipsos Reid, 4
Labatt, 74
Leafs TV, 125
Lee Valley Tools, 69, 78, 262
Liquor Control Board of Ontario (LCBO), 217, 223, 234
Loblaw Companies Limited (Loblaw), 74
Magna International, 225, 226, 234
Magnotta Winery, 215–216, 217, 223
Manulife Financial, 212, 224
Manulife Securities, 212
Maple Leaf Foods Inc., 57, 65, 68, 72, 73, 80
Maple Leaf Sports & Entertainment (MLSE), 125–126, 129, 130, 131, 137, 138, 146
McDonald's Canada, 42, 310
Mitel Netwroks, 142
National Bank, 212
National Energy Board (Canada), 27
Network World Canada, 182
NL Technologies, 153
Norbord, 74
Nortel Networks, 74, 224
Ontario Hospital Association, 320
Ontario Power Authoruty, 78
Ontario Provincial Police, 158
Ontario Realty Corporation (ORC), 297, 297n
*Ottawa Business Journal,* 21
Pareto, 68
Petro-Canada, 11
Pitney Bowes Canada, 170
Proctor & Gamble Canada, 42
Pythian, 183
Queen's University, 217
Radialpoint, 270
Radisson, 86
Ramada, 86
Raptors NBA TV, 125
RCMP, 277, 318
*Report on BusinessMagazine,* 303
Research In Motion (RIM), 93, 121, 244
Retail Council of Canada, 324
Richard Ivey School of Business (University or Western Ontario), 162, 170
Ricoh Coliseum, 125
Robin Hood Multifoods, 318
Rogers, 125, 126, 137
Royal Bank of Canada, 108
Royal Ontrio Museum, 13
S.C. Johnson & Son, 270
Samsung Electronics Canada, 30
Scotiabank, 35, 190–191, 192, 195, 342
Sears Canada, 75
Shopify, 21
SPCA (Society for the Prevention of Cruelty to Animals), 13

Spin Master, 13
Sport Canada, 322, 322*n*
Sprott School of Business (Carleton University), 201
StarTech, 186
Statistics Canada, 23*n*, 264, 288
Stelco, 74
Tamarack Lake Electric Boat Company, 213
TAXI Canada, 135
TD, 89
Team North, 78
Tim Hortons, 73, 295, 301
Toronto Blue Jays, 280
Toronto FC, 125, 137
Toronto Maple Leafs (Maple Leafs), 125, 129, 130, 137,
        138, 146
Toronto Marlies, 125, 137
Toronto Raptors (Raptors), 11, 125, 129, 130, 131, 137, 138, 146
University of Toronto, 221
University of Western Ontario, 201, 224
Upper Canada Brewery, 306*f*
Vanier Institute, 349
Vincor, 86
Vintners Quality Alliance (VQA), 86
Vrootman Cookies, 33
Walmart Canada, 357
Westin Foods, 74
Xerox Canada, 232*f*
Yellow House Events, 243–244, 245–247, 249, 250, 257, 266
Yogen Früz, 41
York University, 204
Zellers, 66
Zippo Canada, 42

## QUÉBEC

Air Canada, 11, 30, 69, 79, 84, 89, 227, 313, 319, 324
Au Premier Spa Urbain, 157
Bank of Montreal, 132, 324
Bell Canada Enterprises (BCE), 35, 40, 125, 126, 137, 320
Bombardier, 39, 128*f*, 128*n*
Bouclair, 307
Brasseries Unibroue, 306*f*
Cascades, 133
Centre for Research on Globalization, 45
Cirque du Soleil, 67*f*
Cogeco, 318
Concordia, 4
Dawson College, 4
Domtar, 133, 318
Earth Rated PoopBags, 52–53
Ericsson Canada, 217, 351
Greenlite Lighting Company, 54, 54*n*
Groupe Robert, 270
Hewlett-Packard Canada, 351
Hydro Quebec, 361
John Molson School of Business (Concordia University), 199
McGill Business School, 72
McGill University, 8, 10
Mega Bloks, 40
Mega Brands, 40–41
Metro, 75
Molson, 79, 224, 318
Molson Coors, 173
Rio Tinto Alcan, 39, 68, 318
Schneider Corporation, 65
TELUS Québec, 129
Transat A.T., 63
Yellow Pages, 163
Zip, 79

## SASKATCHEWAN

ATCO Structures & Logistics
        (ATCO), 269
General Cable Corporation, 5
Great Western Brewery, 301
Paddock Wood Brewing, 306*f*
Yanke Group, 307

# List of International Companies, by Country

## AUSTRALIA
BHP Billiton (BHP), 269
Ford Australia, 127

## BRAZIL
Natura Cosméticos SA, 110
Semco Group, 238–239

## CHILE
Compania Chilena de Fosforos SA, 78

## CHINA
PetroChina, 27
Sinopec, 27
Wahaha, 100
Xuzhou Anying, 38

## DENMARK
Lego, 74
Oticon A/S, 141

## ENGLAND
BBC Worldwide, 298
British Airways, 320
British Petroleum (BP), 51, 335–336, 337, 340, 352
British Telecom, 299
Cadbury Schwepps (Cadbury), 73
Ernst & Young, 167, 212
Kwintessential, 50
PricewaterhouseCoopers (PwC), 143
Unilever, 123
Virgin Group, 103, 171, 295
Virgin Mobile, 243, 247

## FINLAND
Forum Nokia, 49
Nokia, 60
PK-35, 90

## FRANCE
Accor, 73
Michelin, 131
Sodexho Alliance SA, 171

## GERMANY
Deutsche Bank AG, 39
SAP, 189
Siemens, 332

## INDIA
Infosys Technologies, 196
Sitel India, 40

## JAPAN
Fujian Sanming Dinghui Chemical Company, 38
Fujitsu, 261–262
Hitachi, 42
Hyundai, 77
Matsushita, 311
Ministry of Labour (Japan), 351
Mitsubishi, 27
Seven & i Holdings, 323
Toyota Motor Company, 79, 140, 217, 307

## NETHERLANDS
Maastricht University, 37
Royal Dutch Shell (Shell), 27, 65

## RUSSIA
Moscow Ballet, 217

## SCOTLAND
McTavish Kitchens, 49

## SOUTH AFRICA
Haribhai's Spice Emporium, 40

## SPAIN
Grupo VIPS, 42
Zara, 51–52

## SWEDEN
Ericsson, 142
IKEA, 32

## SWITZERLAND
KPMG International, 228
Nestlé, 30, 39, 132
World Trade Organization (WTO), 35, 36, 37

## UNITED STATES OF AMERICA
Accentra, Inc., 97
Accenture, Ltd., 143, 259
Adaptec, 49
AIG, 106
Amazon.com, 223
Angry Birds, 21
Anheuser-Busch InBev, 74, 306
Apple Computer (Apple), 30, 33, 60, 74, 93, 224
aQuantive, 337
Ask Jeeves, 336
Avis, 68
Avon Products, 110
Axcelis Technologies, 49
Ben & Jerry's, 123, 123n

Best Buy, 273
Best Western, 86
Boston Market, 74
Brandeis University, 246
Carlson Wagonlit Travel, 73
Celestial Aerospace Company (CAP), 358
Cerner, 156, 159
Charles Schwab, 64
Chipotle Mexican Grill, 74
Cisco Systems, 142
Clinique, 127
Coach, 74
Coca-Cola, 30, 68, 79
Competitive Enterprise Institute, 45
ConocoPhillips, 220
Continental Airlines, 298
Cypress Semiconductor, 230
Dell Inc., 10, 66, 225
DoubleClick, 108
Dow Chemical, 67f
Drum Associates, 169
eBay, 33, 137
Enron, 224, 315, 321
Enterprise Rent-a-Car, 325
*Entrepreneur,* 358
Estée Lauder, 127, 129
E*TRADE, 43
Exxon Mobil, 318
Facebook, 27, 53, 155, 158, 171, 172, 173, 174, 180, 183, 191,
 249, 333, 337–338
Federal Express (FedEx), 3, 358
Federal Free Trade Commission (United States), 74
FedEx Kinko, 136
Fidelity Investments, 319
*Financial Times,* 123n
Foo Fighters, 21
Ford Motor Company, 13, 301
*Fortune,* 34, 202
Gallup Organization, 4
Gatorade, 72
GE Energy, 141, 162
GE Money, 141
GE Water & Process Technologies, 141
General Electric (GE), 60, 141–142, 198,
 318, 347
General Motors, 11, 13, 280, 307
Georgetoen University, 179
*Globalisation Guide,* 44n
Google, 33, 36, 93, 139, 276, 319, 336, 337–338
Google+, 155, 172, 180
Google AdWords, 53
Greenpeace, 45
Harvard, 250, 252
Harvard Business School, 76, 250, 342
Hasbro, 43
Hewitt Associates, 261
Hewlett-Packard (HP), 42, 93, 171, 319
Hilton Hotels, 320
H.J. Heinz Comapany, 39
HomeSense, 318
*HRMarketer.com,* 203n
IBM, 37, 39, 170

Integrated Information Systems, 320
Intel, 60, 79
International Forum on Globalization, 45
International Franchise Association, 45
International Institute for Sustainable Development, 45
International Policy Network, 45
iTunes, 42, 60
Johnson & Johnson, 67f
KDPaine & Partners, 155
Kenner Toys, 43
KFC, 41, 72
Kinder Morgan Energy Partners, 51
Klout, 180
Kmart, 273
LaCoste, 74
LinkedIn, 155, 169, 171, 180
Lockheed Martin Aeronautics Company, 281
MAC Cosmetics, 129
Major League Soccer, 125
Marriott International Inc., 86
Mary Kay Cosmetics, 225
Massachusetts Institute of Technology (MIT) Sloan School of
 Management, 24
Mattel, 43
McDonald's, 3, 41, 74, 127, 134, 258, 311
Menu Foods, 34, 38
Merrill Lynch, 39, 106
Microsoft, 14, 93, 171, 277, 318, 337, 339, 348
Miller, 306
MySpace, 169, 171, 336
NASA, 302, 348
National Speleological Society, 319
NBA, 125
NBC Universal Studios, 141
Neustar, 298
NHL, 125, 126
Nike, 143
North American Soft Drinks, 72
Nurse Next Dorr, 89, 114
Ohio State University, 277
Oracle, 180
Parker Brothers, 43
PepsiCo Inc., 30, 39, 72–73, 233
PepsiCo International, 72
Pfizer, 149–150
Pixar, 21
Pizza Hut, 72
Playboy.com, 324
Proctor & Gamble (P&G), 68, 75, 137
*PROFIT,* 243, 303
Quova Inc., 298
Recording Industry Association of America, 320
Red Roof Inns, 73
Reebok, 142
Revlon, 138, 243
RightMedia, 243
Rolex, 29
Safeway, 13
Saturn Corporation, 280
Sears, 13, 108
*Second Life,* 142, 171, 191–192
7-Eleven, 323

Sirius Satellite Radio, 74
Sun Life Assurance Company of Canada (US), 139–140
Taco Bell, 72
Target, 66, 77, 336
Ted's Outfitters Shop, 217
TheFranchiseMall.com, 123, 123*n*
3M, 347
Tiger Electronics, 43
*Time,* 225
Timex, 29
TJX Companies, 318
Tonka Toys, 43
Towers Perrin, 270
Toys "R" Us, 5
Tropicana Products, 72
Twitter, 27, 155, 173, 183, 191
UFC, 269
United Way, 11, 32
University of Iowa, 219
University of Utah, 248
University of Washington, 220
UPS, 166
US Environmental Protection Agency, 27
Verizon Communications, 171, 281
VEVO, 42

Walmart, 33, 66, 73, 75, 79, 315
Walt Disney World, 31
Watson Wyatt Worldwide, 4, 169, 186, 189
Wharton School of Business, 222
Whirlpool, 136
Whole Foods Market, 139
Wikipedia, 135
Williams-Sonoma, 32
Wilson Learning Worldwide, 49
Winners, 318
Wizards of the Coast, 43
Wood Mackenzie, 28
Woolworth, 273
Workopolis, 263
WorldatWork, 187*n*
WorldCom, 224
Xerox, 140
XM Satellite Radio, 74
Yahoo!, 156, 336, 337–338
Yale, 233
Yale School of Management, 255
Yammer, 173
YMCA, 101
YouTube, 171, 337
YUM! Brands Inc., 73

# Photo Credits

## CHAPTER 1
Page 2, Associated Press; page 5, Associated Press; page 12, Joe Gibbons/CP.

## CHAPTER 2
Page 26, Jonathan Nafzger/Shutterstock; page 30, © ckellyphoto/Fotolia; page 33, Natika/Fotolia; page 41, Zhu Gang-Feature China/Newscom; page 45, © nebari/Fotolia; pages 54–55, TL bioraven/Shutterstock; TR CBC..

## CHAPTER 3
Page 56, Photo By Deborah Baic The Globe and Mail/The Canadian Press; page 59, Peter Battistoni/Vancouver Sun; page 69, Mark Van Manen/The Vancouver Sun; page 73, mediagram/Fotolia; page 75, oksana.perkins/Shutterstock; page 84, Pressmaster/Shutterstock.

## CHAPTER 4
Page 88, Maridav/Fotolia; page 92, Fotolia; page 100, Quentin Shih aka Shi Xiaofan; page 103, Luminis/Fotolia; Ric Ernst/The Province; pages 122–123, TL bioraven/Shutterstock; TR CBC.

## CHAPTER 5
Page 124, aihumnoi/Fotolia; page 129, Dick Hemingway; page 133, picsfive/Fotolia; page 135, Stauke/Fotolia; page 143, Associated Press.

## CHAPTER 6
Page 154, andrea michele piacquadio/Shutterstock; page 157, Yevgen Kotyukh/Fotolia; page 162, © Tetra Images/Corbis; page 163, volff/Fotolia; page 171, pressmaster/Fotolia; page 172, 1000 Words/Shutterstock.com; page 172, Shariff Che'Lah/Fotolia.

## CHAPTER 7
Page 184, FotolEdhar/Fotolia; page 192, The Vancouver Police Department; page 196, Lynsey Addario/CORBIS-NY; page 202, Bill Keay/Vancouver Sun; page 213, TL bioraven/Shutterstock; TR CBC.

## CHAPTER 8
Page 214, CP PHOTO/Toronto Globe and Mail -John Morstad; page 218, Mike Aporlus/CP/Photo Archive; page 231, Nathan Denette/CP; page 233, Associated Press.

## CHAPTER 9
Page 242, Anatoly Maslennikov/Fotolia; page 249, Inga Ivanova/Shutterstock; page 254, Marcus/Fotolia; page 258, luchshen/Fotolia; page 259, Marcio Jose Sanchez/AP Wide World Photos; page 263, MAXFX/Fotolia.

## CHAPTER 10
Page 274, Arpad Nagy-Bagoly/Fotolia; page 276, Robyn Twomey/Robyn Twomey Photography; page 283, Deklofenak/Shutterstock; pages 298–299, TL bioraven/Shutterstock; TR CBC.

## CHAPTER 11
Page 300, Associated Press; page 308, © Cultura Creative/Alamy; page 313, CP PHOTO/Adrian Wyld; page 326, Pat Wellenbach/AP Wide World Photos.

## CHAPTER 12
Page 334, Ryan McVay/Getty Images; page 339, Ron Berg Photography; page 348, Maclean's Photo/Rick Chard/CP Photo; pages 360–361, TL bioraven/Shutterstock; TR CBC.